To my parents, Ed and Ginny,

to my wife, Nasrin,

and my kids, Ryan, Roxanne, and Steven

ABOUT THE AUTHOR

Raymond G. Miltenberger received his Ph.D. in Clinical Psychology in 1985 from Western Michigan University. He is currently a Professor of Psychology at North Dakota State University, where he teaches courses in behavior modification and behavior therapy to undergraduate and graduate students. Dr. Miltenberger conducts applied behavior analysis research with his students and publishes widely in the areas of habit disorders, functional assessment and treatment of behavioral disorders, and self-protection skills training. He utilizes behavior modification in clinical work with children and individuals with mental retardation. In addition to spending time with his family, he enjoys running, golf, baseball, and travel.

BRIEF CONTENTS

CONTENTS

ONE Introduction to Behavior Modification 1

PART 1 Measurement of Behavior and Behavior Change

TWO Observing and Recording Behavior 19

Extinction 95

Punishment 111

Stimulus Control: Discrimination and Generalization 133

EIGHT Respondent Conditioning 153

PART 3 Procedures to Establish New Behavior

Shaping 173

Prompting and Transfer of Stimulus Control 193

Chaining 215

Behavioral Skills Training Procedures 237

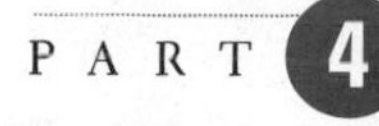

PART 4 **PROCEDURES TO INCREASE DESIRABLE BEHAVIOR AND DECREASE UNDESIRABLE BEHAVIOR**

THIRTEEN *Understanding Problem Behaviors through Functional Assessment* 257

FOURTEEN *Applying Extinction* 287

Differential Reinforcement 311

Antecedent Control Procedures 341

SEVENTEN Using Punishment: Time-Out and Response Cost 369

Positive Punishment Procedures and the Ethics of Punishment 391

NINETEEN Promoting Generalization 411

PART 5 OTHER BEHAVIOR CHANGE PROCEDURES

TWENTY Self-Management 433

TWENTY-ONE Habit Reversal Procedures 453

TWENTY-TWO The Token Economy 471

TWENTY-THREE Behavioral Contracts 493

TWENTY-FOUR Fear and Anxiety Reduction Procedures 513

TWENTY-FIVE Cognitive Behavior Modification 537

PREFACE

We are gratified that the first two editions of *Behavior Modification: Principles and Procedures* received positive reviews from students and professors. The third edition has kept the positive features of the first two editions, and has been revised to address the suggestions of reviewers and updated to reflect the latest research in behavior modification.

The goal of this third edition (as with the earlier editions) is to describe basic principles of behavior, so that the student learns how environmental events influence human behavior, and to describe behavior modification procedures, so that the student learns the strategies by which human behavior may be changed. The text is divided into 25 relatively short chapters, each of which covers a manageable amount of information (for example, one principle or procedure). This text can be used in a standard one-semester course in behavior modification, applied behavior analysis, behavior management, or behavior change.

The material in the text is discussed at an introductory level, so that it may be understood by students with no prior knowledge of the subject. This text is intended for college students at the sophomore level. It would also be valuable for individuals working in human services, education, or rehabilitation who must use behavior modification procedures to manage the behavior of the individuals in their care.

I have made a concerted effort in this text to be gender neutral. When discussing case examples, I include males and females about equally often.

Features of the Text Continued from the First Two Editions

The following features of the text are intended to help the reader learn easily.

Organization of the Text Following a general introduction to the field, Chapters 2 and 3 present information on behavior recording, graphing, and measuring change. This information will be utilized in each subsequent chapter. Next, Chapters 4–8 focus on the basic principles of operant and respondent behavior. The application of these principles forms the subject of the remaining 17 chapters. Procedures to establish new behaviors are described in Chapters 9–12, while procedures to increase desirable behaviors and decrease undesirable behaviors are considered in Chapters 13–19. Finally, Chapters 20–25 present a survey of other important behavior modification procedures.

Principles and Procedures The various procedures for changing behavior are based on fundamental principles of behavior established in experimental research over the last 60 years. In the belief that the student will better understand the procedures after first learning the fundamental principles, the principles underlying operant and respondent behavior are reviewed in Chapters 4–8, and then the application of the principles in the behavior modification procedures is described in Chapters 9–25.

Examples from Everyday Life Each chapter uses a variety of real-life examples—some relevant to college students, some chosen from the author's clinical experience—to bring the principles and procedures to life.

Examples from Research In addition, both classic studies and the most up-to-date research on behavior modification principles and procedures are integrated into the text.

Application Exercises At the end of each chapter where procedures are taught (Chapters 2, 3, and 9–25), several application exercises are provided. In each exercise, a real-life case is described and then the student is asked to apply the procedure described in the chapter. These exercises give students an opportunity to think about how the procedures are applied in real life.

Misapplication Exercises The application exercises are followed by misapplication exercises. In each one, a case example is provided, and the procedure from the chapter is applied to the case in an incorrect or inappropriate manner. The student is asked to analyze the case example and to describe what is wrong with the application of the procedure in that case. These misapplication exercises require the student to think critically about the application of the procedure.

Step-by-Step Approach In each chapter where a particular behavior modification procedure is taught, the implementation of the procedure is outlined in a step-by-step fashion, for ease of comprehension.

Summary Boxes Periodically throughout the text, information from a chapter is summarized in a box set off from the text. These boxes are intended to help the student organize the material in the chapter.

Examples for Self-Assessment In the early chapters on basic principles (Chapters 4–7) there are tables with examples of the principle discussed in the chapter. Later in the chapter (or in a subsequent chapter), the student is directed to return to a table and analyze specific aspects of the examples in the table using new information being presented.

Self-Assessment Questions At intervals throughout the text, students are presented with self-assessment questions. To answer these questions, students will need to utilize the information already presented in the chapter. These questions will help students assess their understanding of the material. In most cases, answers are presented in the text immediately following the question.

Figures Most of the chapters include figures from the research literature to illustrate important principles or procedures. Students must use information from earlier chapters on behavior recording, graphing, and measuring change to analyze the graphs.

Glossary At the end of the text is a glossary of the important behavior modification terms used in the text. Each term is followed by a succinct and precise definition.

Streamlined Organization The third edition has 25 chapters (down from 28 chapters in the first edition). Three chapters from the first edition were incorporated into other similar chapters to cover the material more efficiently with less overlap of topics.

Reorganized Sections The two sections on procedures (that follow the section on basic principles) were reorganized in the second edition to consist of "Procedures to Establish New Behaviors" and "Procedures to Increase Desirable Behaviors and Decrease Undesirable Behaviors." These reorganized sections allowed for a better sequencing of material.

Enhanced Functional Assessment Chapter Chapter 13 on functional assessment was expanded in the second edition to include more information on different functions of problem behaviors and more detail on conducting a functional analysis.

Improved Test Bank The test bank includes multiple-choice questions, fill-in-the-blank questions, true-false questions, and short-answer essay questions.

Other Features Other features that were added to the second edition continue in the third edition. Chapter summaries provide information consistent with the opening questions in each chapter. Practice tests at the end of each chapter have questions with page numbers on which the answers can be found. Answers to Applications and Misapplications were removed from the text and put into the Instructors Manual so that the Applications and Misapplications can be used by instructors in class to assess students' ability to apply the information. There is more descriptive labeling of many of the examples in the text. In Chapter 2 on recording behavior, information was added on real time recording and frequency-within-interval recording. In Chapter 4 on the principle of reinforcement, information was added on reinforcing different dimensions of behavior. In Chapter 12 on behavioral skills training procedures, information was added on enhancing generalization following training. Chapters 14 (differential reinforcement), 16 (antecedent control procedures), and 19 (promoting generalization) were rewritten to incorporate information from deleted chapters. Chapter 20 on self-management was moved to a position earlier in the text so that the information can be used by instructors who require students to conduct a self-management project. Chapter 21 on habit reversal has new information on other treatments for habit disorders. Chapter 25 on cognitive behavior modification has new information on Acceptance and Commitment Therapy and Functional Analytic Psychotherapy

NEW FEATURES IN THE THIRD EDITION

In addition to the features continued from the first two editions, a major new feature has been incorporated into the text in the third edition.

Quizzes Accompany Each Chapter At the end of each chapter are three 10-item fill-in-the-blank quizzes. The quizzes provide students with further exercises for self-assessment of their knowledge of the chapters' content. The quizzes are on perforated pages that can be easily torn out so that the instructor can have students hand the quizzes in as homework assignments or have students take the quizzes in class.

Other New Features There is a brief discussion of differential reinforcement at the beginning of the shaping chapter. There is a clearer distinction between extinction and response cost in Chapter 17. More examples for self-assessment were added in Chapter 14. Functional/nonaversisve interventions were more clearly defined in Chapter 16. The distinction between contact desensitization and in vivo desensitization was clarified in Chapter 24. More recent references were added throughout the text. A number of unneccessary figures were removed from the text. The self-management chapter was moved to section 5.

ACKNOWLEDGMENTS

I want to thank the anonymous reviewers for their constructive comments on this manuscript and the first three editions: Robert W. Allan, Lafayette College; Viviette Allen, Fayetteville State University; Cynthia Anderson, West Virginia University; Jennifer Austin, Florida State University; Charles Blose, MacMurry College; Kristine Brady, California School of Professional Psychology; James Carr, Western Michigan University; Carl Cheney, Utah State University; Paula Davis, Southern Illinois University; Richard N. Feil, Mansfield University; Deirdre Beebe Fitzgerald, Eastern Connecticut State University; Stephan Flanagan, The University of North Carolina at Chapel Hill; Roger Harnish, Rochester Institute of Technology; Robert Heffer, Texas A&M University;

Stephen W. Holborn, University of Manitoba; Dorothea Lerman, Louisiana State University; Tom Lombardo, University of Mississippi; John Malouff, Nova Southern Eastern University; Guenn Martin, Cumberland University; Kay McIntyre, University of Missouri–St. Louis; Robert W. Montgomery, Georgia State University; Charles S. Peyser, University of the South; Brady Phelps, South Dakota State University; Joseph J. Plaud, University of North Dakota; Robyn Rogers, Southwest Texas State University; Alison Thomas-Cottingham, Rider University; J. Kevin Thompson, University of Southern Florida; Bruce Thyer, University of Georgia; James T. Todd, Eastern Michigan University; Sharon Van Leer, Delaware State University; Timothy Vollmer, University of Florida; Robert W. Wildblood, Northern Virginia Community College; Kenneth N. Wildman, Ohio Northern University; Douglas Woods, University of Wisconsin–Milwaukee; and Todd Zakrajsek, Southern Oregon State College. I especially want to thank Marianne Taflinger, senior editor at Wadsworth, for her guidance and support throughout the development of the third edition.

For the Behavior Modification Student

To get the most out of this text and out of your behavior modification course, you are encouraged to consider the following recommendations.

1. Read the assigned chapters before the class meeting when the chapter is to be discussed. You will benefit more from the class if you have first read the material.

2. Answer each of the self-assessment questions in the chapter to see if you understand the material just covered.

3. Answer the practice test questions at the end of each chapter. If you can answer each question, you know that you understand the material in the chapter.

4. Complete the end-of-chapter quizzes to assess your knowledge of the chapter content (unless your professor plans to use the quizzes in class).

5. Complete the application and misapplication exercises at the end of the procedure chapters. In that way, you will understand the material in the chapter well enough to apply it or to identify how it is applied incorrectly.

6. The best way to study for a test is to test yourself. After reading and rereading the chapter and your class notes, test yourself in the following ways.

- Look at key terms in the chapter and see if you can define them without looking at the definitions in the text.
- Look at each practice test question at the end of the chapter and see if you can give the correct answer without looking up the answer in the text or in your notes.
- Come up with novel examples of each principle or procedure in the chapter.
- You may find it helpful to make flash cards with a term or question on one side and the definition of the term or the answer to the question on the other side. While studying, you look at the term (or question) on one side of the card and then read the definition (or answer) on the other. As you study, you will find that you need to turn the cards over less and less. Once you can supply the material on the back of the card without looking, you'll know that you understand the material.
- Always study in a location that is reasonably free from distractions or interruptions.
- Always begin studying for a test at least a few days in advance. Give yourself more days to study as more chapters are included on the test.

The following Web sites provide a range of valuable information about different aspects of behavior modification or applied behavior analysis.

www.envmed.rochester.edu/ wwwrap/ behavior/jaba/jabahome.htm	Journal of Applied Behavior Analysis
www.abainternational.org	The Association for Behavior Analysis
www.apa.org/divisions/div25/	APA Division 25 (Behavior Analysis)
www.aabt.org	Association for Advancement of Behavior Therapy
http://fabaworld.org	Florida Association for Behavior Analysis
www.behavior.org	Cambridge Center for Behavioral Studies
www.bfskinner.org/	B.F. Skinner Foundation
www.bacb.com/	Behavior Analysis Certification Board
www.abatraining.org	The May Institute
www.polyxo.com/aba/	Information of behavior analysis/autism
http://rsaffran.tripod.com/aba.html	Information on behavior analysis/autism

Raymond G. Miltenberger

ONE

Introduction to Behavior Modification

In this textbook you will learn about behavior modification, the principles and procedures used to understand and change human behavior. Behavior modification procedures come in many forms. Consider the following examples.

Ted and Jane were having some difficulties in their marriage because of frequent arguments. Their marriage counselor arranged a behavioral contract with them in which they agreed to do several nice things for each other every day. As a result of this contract, their positive interactions increased and their negative interactions (arguments) decreased.

- How is human behavior defined?
- What are the defining features of behavior modification?
- What are the historical roots of behavior modification?
- In what ways has behavior modification improved people's lives?

Karen pulled her hair incessantly; as a result, she created a bald spot on the top of her head. Although she was embarrassed by the bald spot, which measured 1 inch in diameter, she continued to pull her hair. Her psychologist implemented a treatment in which Karen was to engage in a competing activity with her hands (e.g., needlepoint) each time she started to pull her hair or had the urge to pull. Over time, the hair-pulling stopped and her hair grew back in.

Francisco was putting on a lot of weight and decided to do something about it. He joined a weight loss group. At each group meeting, Francisco deposited a sum of money, set a goal for daily exercise, and earned points for meeting his exercise goals each week. If he earned a specified number of points, he got his deposit back. If he did not earn enough points, he lost part of his deposit money. Francisco began to exercise regularly and lost weight as a result of his participation in the group.

The residents of Cincinnati were making thousands of unnecessary directory assistance calls per day. These calls were clogging up the phone lines and costing the company money. The company instituted a charge for each directory assistance call, and the number of calls decreased dramatically.

You will notice that each of these examples focuses on some aspect of human behavior and describes ways to change the behavior. Because behavior modification focuses on behavior and behavior change, it is appropriate to begin with a discussion of behavior.

Defining Human Behavior

Human behavior is the subject matter of behavior modification. The characteristics that define behavior are as follows.

- **Behavior** is what people do and say. Behavior involves a person's actions, so it is not a static characteristic of the person. If you say that a person is angry, you have not identified the person's behavior; you have simply labeled the behavior. If you identify what the person says or does when angry, then you have identified behavior. For example, "Jennifer screamed at her mother, ran upstairs, and slammed the door to her room." This is a description of behavior that might be labeled as anger.
- Behaviors have one or more **dimensions** that can be measured. You can measure the **frequency** of a behavior. In other words, you can count the number of times a behavior occurs (e.g., Shane bit his fingernails 12 times in the class period). You can measure the **duration** of a behavior, or the time from when an instance of the behavior starts until it stops (e.g., Rita jogged for 25 minutes). You can measure the **intensity** of a behavior, or the physical force involved in the behavior (e.g., Garth bench-pressed 220 pounds). Frequency, duration, and intensity are all physical dimensions of a behavior.
- Behaviors can be observed, described, and recorded by others or by the person engaging in the behavior. Because a behavior is an action that has physical dimensions, its occurrence can be observed. People can see the behavior (or detect it through one of the senses) when it takes place. Because it is observable, the person who sees the behavior can describe it and record its occurrence. (Chapter 2 describes methods for recording behavior.)
- Behaviors have an impact on the environment, including the physical or the social environment (other people and ourselves). Because a behavior is an action that involves movement through space and time (Johnston & Pennypacker, 1981), the occurrence of a behavior has some effect on the environment in which it takes place. Sometimes, the effect on the environment is obvious. You turn the light switch, and the light goes on (an effect on the physical environment). You raise your hand in class, and your professor calls on you (an effect on other people). You recite a phone number from the phone book, and you are more likely to remember it and to dial the correct number (an effect on yourself). Sometimes the effect of a behavior on the environment is not obvious. Sometimes it has an effect only on the person who engages in the behavior. However, all human behavior operates on the physical or social environment in some way, regardless of whether we are aware of its impact.
- Behavior is lawful; that is, its occurrence is systematically influenced by environmental events. Basic behavioral principles describe the functional relationships between our behavior and environmental events. These principles describe how our behavior is influenced by, or occurs as a function of, environmental events. (See Chapters 4–8.) These basic behavioral principles are the building blocks of behavior modification procedures. Once you understand the environmental events that cause behaviors to occur, you can change the events in the environment in order to change behavior.

Consider the graph in Figure 1-1, which shows the disruptive behavior of an autistic child in the classroom. When the child receives high levels of attention from the teacher, his disruptive behavior rarely occurs. When the child receives low levels of attention from the teacher, his disruptive behavior occurs more frequently. We conclude that the disruptive behavior is functionally related to the level of teacher attention.

■ Behaviors may be overt or covert. Most often, behavior modification procedures are used to understand and change overt behaviors. An **overt behavior** is an action that can be observed and recorded by a person other than the one engaging in the behavior. However, some behaviors are covert. **Covert behaviors,** also called private events (Skinner, 1974), are not observable to others. For example, thinking is a covert behavior; it cannot be observed and recorded by another person. Thinking can be observed only by the person engaging in the behavior. The field of behavior modification fo-

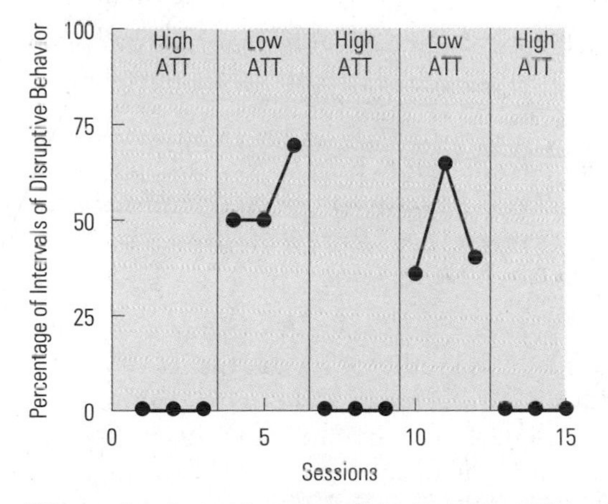

FIGURE 1-1 This graph, adapted from a study by Durand and Carr (1992), shows the influence of teacher attention on the disruptive behavior (defined as pushing away task materials; loud screaming, whining, or crying; and hitting or knocking over objects) of a young boy (Paul) in a special education classroom. The graph shows that disruptive behavior does not occur when Paul receives frequent teacher attention (High ATT). However, when Paul receives teacher attention infrequently (Low ATT), he engages in disruptive behavior about 50% of the time. This graph shows the functional relationship between the teacher's attention and Paul's disruptive behavior. (Reprinted by permission of the author.)

CHARACTERISTICS OF BEHAVIOR

Behavior is what people do and say.
Behaviors have one or more dimensions.
Behaviors can be observed, described, and recorded.
Behaviors have an impact on the environment.
Behavior is lawful.
Behaviors may be overt or covert.

cuses primarily on overt or observable behaviors, as does this textbook. However, Chapters 8, 24, and 25 discuss covert behaviors and behavior modification procedures applied to them.

Examples of Behavior

Now let's illustrate these defining characteristics of behavior with some examples. The following examples include both common behaviors and problematic behaviors for which behavior modification procedures might be used.

Martha sits at her computer and types a letter to her parents.

This is behavior because pressing the keys on the keyboard while typing is an action, has physical dimensions (frequency of pressing keys, duration of typing), is observable and measurable, has an impact on the environment (produces letters on the screen), and is lawful (occurs because of previous learning that pressing the keys produces letters on the screen).

Curtis puts a bucket under the car to catch the oil and unscrews the plug to the oil pan. He then removes the oil filter. When the oil is drained, he puts on a new oil filter, screws the plug back in, and adds four quarts of oil. Finally, he pulls out the dipstick and looks at it to check the oil level.

This is a chain of behaviors with multiple components. Each component behavior has the characteristics listed earlier. Consider the second component behavior, in which Curtis used a wrench to unscrew the plug. This is an action (turning the wrench), has physical dimensions (six turns of the wrench in 10 seconds), can be observed and recorded by Curtis or another person, has an impact on the environment (the plug is removed and oil drains into the bucket), and is lawful (Curtis engages in this behavior because it has produced this same outcome in the past). There is a functional relationship between the behavior and its outcome.

Mandy lies in her crib and cries loudly. Her mother then picks her up and feeds her.

This behavior has all five of the characteristics described earlier (an action that has physical dimensions, is observable by others, produces an effect on the environment, and is lawful). One difference is that the effect of crying is on the social environment; her mother responds to her crying by picking her up and feeding her. Each time it has occurred in the past, crying has resulted in her mother feeding her, so the crying continues to occur when Mandy is hungry. There is a functional relationship between the crying and the mother's behavior of feeding her.

Jerry's paper for his behavior modification class is a week late. Jerry gives the paper to his professor and lies, saying that it is late because he had to go home to see his sick grandmother. The professor then accepts the paper without any penalty. Jerry also missed his history test. He tells his history professor he missed the test because of his sick grandmother. The professor lets him take the test a week late.

Jerry's behavior—lying about his visit to his sick grandmother—has all five characteristics of a behavior. It is an action (something he said) that occurred twice (frequency), was observed by his professors, and resulted in an effect on his social environment (his professors let him take a test late and hand in a paper late with no penalty); it is lawful because there is a functional relationship between the behavior (lying) and the outcome (getting away with late papers or tests).

Samantha is a mentally retarded 6-year-old who attends special education classes. When the teacher is helping other students and not paying attention to Samantha, Samantha cries and bangs her head on the table or floor. Whenever Samantha bangs her head, the teacher stops what she is doing and picks Samantha up and comforts her. She tells her to calm down, assures her that everything is all right, gives her a hug, and often lets Samantha sit on her lap.

Identify each of the five characteristics of Samantha's behavior.

Samantha's head-banging is a behavior. It is an action that she repeats a number of times each day. The teacher could observe and record the number of occurrences each day. The head banging produces an effect on the social environment: The teacher provides attention each time the behavior occurs. Finally, the behavior is lawful; it continues to occur because there is a functional relationship between the head banging behavior and the outcome of teacher attention.

Defining Behavior Modification

Behavior modification is the field of psychology concerned with analyzing and modifying human behavior.

- *Analyzing* means identifying the functional relationship between the environment and a particular behavior to understand the reasons for behavior or to determine why a person behaved as he or she did.
- *Modifying* means developing and implementing procedures to help people change their behavior. It involves altering environmental events so as to influence behavior.
- Behavior modification procedures are used by professionals or paraprofessionals to help a person change socially significant behaviors, with the goal of improving some aspect of the person's life. An alternative term for behavior modification is *applied behavior analysis* (Baer, Wolf, & Risley, 1968, 1987). The following are some characteristics that define behavior modification (Gambrill, 1977; Kazdin, 1994).

Characteristics of Behavior Modification

- *Focus on behavior.* Behavior modification procedures are designed to change behavior, not a personal characteristic or trait. Therefore, behavior modification deemphasizes labeling. For example, behavior modification is not used to change autism (a label); rather, behavior modification is used to change problem behaviors exhibited by autistic children.

Behavioral excesses and behavioral deficits are targets for change with behavior modification procedures. In behavior modification, the behavior to be modified is called the **target behavior.** A **behavioral excess** is an undesirable target behavior the person wants to decrease in frequency, duration, or intensity. Smoking is an example of a behavioral excess. A **behavioral deficit** is a desirable target behavior the person wants to increase in frequency, duration, or intensity. Exercise or studying are possible examples of behavioral deficits.

- *Procedures based on behavioral principles.* Behavior modification is the application of basic principles originally derived from experimental research with laboratory animals (Skinner, 1938). The scientific study of behavior is called the **experimental analysis of behavior,** or behavior analysis (Skinner, 1953b, 1966). The scientific study of human behavior is called the experimental analysis of human behavior, or **applied behavior analysis** (Baer et al., 1968, 1987). Behavior modification procedures are based on research in applied behavior analysis that has been conducted for more than 40 years (Ullmann & Krasner, 1965; Ulrich, Stachnik, & Mabry, 1966).

- *Emphasis on current environmental events.* Behavior modification involves assessing and modifying the current environmental events that are functionally related to the behavior. Human behavior is controlled by events in the immediate environment, and the goal of behavior modification is to identify those events. Once these **controlling variables** have been identified, they are altered to modify the behavior. Successful behavior modification procedures alter the functional relationships between the behavior and the controlling variables in the environment to produce a desired change in the behavior. Sometimes labels are mistakenly identified as the causes of behavior. For example, a person might say that an autistic child engages in problem behaviors (such as screaming, hitting himself, refusal to follow instructions) because the child is autistic. In other words, the person is suggesting that autism causes the child to engage in the behavior. However, autism is simply a label that describes the pattern of behaviors the child engages in. The label cannot be the cause of the behavior because the label does not exist as a physical entity or event. The causes of the behavior must be found in the environment (including the biology of the child).

- *Precise description of behavior modification procedures* (Baer et al., 1968). Behavior modification procedures involve specific changes in environmental events that are functionally related to the behavior. For the procedures to be effective each time they are used, the specific changes in environmental events must occur each time. By describing procedures precisely, researchers and other professionals make it more likely that the procedures will be used correctly each time.

- *Treatment implemented by people in everyday life* (Kazdin, 1994). Behavior modification procedures are developed by professionals or paraprofessionals trained in behavior modification. However, behavior modification procedures often are implemented by people such as teachers, parents, job supervisors, or others to help people change their behavior. People who implement behavior modification procedures should do so only after sufficient training. Precise descriptions of procedures and professional supervision make it more likely that parents, teachers, and others will implement procedures correctly.

▪ *Measurement of behavior change.* One of the hallmarks of behavior modification is its emphasis on measuring the behavior before and after intervention to document the behavior change resulting from the behavior modification procedures. In addition, ongoing assessment of the behavior is done well beyond the point of intervention to determine whether the behavior change is maintained in the long run. If a supervisor is using behavior modification procedures to increase work productivity (to increase the number of units assembled each day), he would record the workers' behavior for a period of time before implementing the procedures. The supervisor would then implement the behavior modification procedures and continue to record the behavior. This recording would establish whether the number of units assembled increased. If the workers' behaviors changed after the supervisor's intervention, he would continue to record the behavior for a further period. Such long-term observation would reveal whether the workers continued to assemble units at the increased rate or whether further intervention was necessary.

▪ *De-emphasis on past events as causes of behavior.* As stated earlier, behavior modification places emphasis on current environmental events as the causes of behavior. However, knowledge of the past might also provide some useful information about environmental events related to the current behavior. For example, previous learning experiences have been shown to influence current behavior. Therefore, understanding these learning experiences can be valuable in analyzing current behavior and choosing behavior modification procedures. Although information on past events is useful, knowledge of current controlling variables is most relevant to developing effective behavior modification interventions because those variables, unlike past events, can still be changed.

▪ *Rejection of hypothetical underlying causes of behavior.* Although some fields of psychology, such as Freudian psychoanalytic approaches, might be interested in hypothesized underlying causes of behavior, such as an unresolved Oedipal complex, behavior modification rejects such hypothetical explanations of behavior. Skinner (1974) has called such explanations "explanatory fictions" because they can never be proven or disproven and thus are unscientific. These supposed underlying causes can never be measured or manipulated to demonstrate a functional relationship to the behavior they are intended to explain.

CHARACTERISTICS OF BEHAVIOR MODIFICATION

Focus on behavior
Based on behavioral principles
Emphasis on current environmental events
Precise description of procedures
Implemented by people in everyday life
Measurement of behavior change
De-emphasis on past events as causes of behavior
Rejection of hypothetical underlying causes of behavior

HISTORICAL ROOTS OF BEHAVIOR MODIFICATION

A number of historical events contributed to the development of behavior modification. Let's briefly consider some important figures, publications, and organizations in the field.

Major Figures

Here are some of the major figures who were instrumental in developing the scientific principles on which behavior modification is based (Figure 1-2; Michael, 1993a).

Ivan P. Pavlov (1849–1936) Pavlov conducted experiments that uncovered the basic processes of respondent conditioning (see Chapter 8). He demonstrated that a reflex (salivation in response to food) could be conditioned to a neutral stimulus. In his experiments, Pavlov presented the neutral stimulus (the sound of a metronome) at the same time that he presented food to a dog. Later, the dog salivated in response to the sound of the metronome alone. Pavlov called this a conditioned reflex (Pavlov, 1927).

Edward L. Thorndike (1874–1949) Thorndike's major contribution was the description of the **law of effect.** The law of effect says that a behavior that produces a favorable effect on the environment is more likely to be repeated in the future. In Thorndike's famous experiment, he put a cat in a cage and set food outside the cage where the cat could see it. To open the cage door, the cat had to hit a lever with its paw. Thorndike showed that the cat learned to hit the lever and open the cage door. Each time it was put into the cage, the cat hit the lever more quickly because that behavior—hitting the lever—produced a favorable effect on the environment: It allowed the cat to reach the food (Thorndike, 1911).

John B. Watson (1878–1958) In the article "Psychology as the Behaviorist Views It," published in 1913, Watson asserted that observable behavior was the proper subject matter of psychology and that all behavior was controlled by environmental events. In particular, Watson described a stimulus–response psychology in which environmental events (stimuli) elicited responses. Watson started the movement in psychology called behaviorism (Watson, 1913, 1924).

B. F. Skinner (1904–1990) Skinner expanded the field of behaviorism originally described by Watson. Skinner described the distinction between respondent conditioning (the conditioned reflexes described by Pavlov and Watson) and operant conditioning, in which the consequence of behavior controls the future occurrence of the behavior (as in Thorndike's law of effect). Skinner's research elaborated the basic principles of operant behavior (see Chapters 4–7). In addition to his laboratory research demonstrating basic behavioral principles, Skinner wrote a number of books in which he applied the principles of behavior analysis to human behavior, as we will see later. Skinner's work is the foundation of behavior modification (Skinner, 1938, 1953a).

FIGURE 1-2 Four major figures who were instrumental in developing the scientific principles on which behavior modification is based. Clockwise from top left: Ivan P. Pavlov, Edward L. Thorndike, B. F. Skinner, John B. Watson. (Photo credits: Sovfoto/East Photo; Archives of the History of American Psychology; courtesy of Dr. Julie Vargas, Department of Educational Psychology, West Virginia University; Archives of the History of American Psychology, The University of Akron.)

Early Behavior Modification Researchers

After Skinner laid out the principles of operant conditioning, researchers continued to study operant behavior in the laboratory (Catania, 1968; Honig, 1966). In addition, in the 1950s, researchers began demonstrating behavioral principles and evaluating behavior modification procedures with people. These early researchers studied the behavior of children (Azrin & Lindsley, 1956; Baer, 1960; Bijou, 1957), adults (Goldiamond, 1965; Verplanck, 1955; Wolpe, 1958), patients with mental illness (Ayllon & Azrin, 1964; Ayllon & Michael, 1959), and mentally retarded people (Ferster, 1961; Fuller, 1949; Wolf, Risley, & Mees, 1964). Since the beginning of behavior modification research with humans in the 1950s, thousands of studies have established the effectiveness of behavior modification principles and procedures.

Major Publications and Events

A number of books heavily influenced the development of the behavior modification field. In addition, scientific journals were developed to publish research in behavior analysis and behavior modification, and professional organizations were started to support research and professional activity in behavior analysis and behavior modification. These books, journals, and organizations are listed in the timeline in Figure 1-3. For a more complete description of these publications and organizations, see Cooper, Heron, and Heward (1987) and Michael (1993a).

AREAS OF APPLICATION

Behavior modification procedures have been used in many areas to help people change a vast array of problematic behaviors (Carr & Austin, 2001; Gambrill, 1977; Lutzker & Martin, 1981; Vollmer et al., 2001). This section briefly reviews these areas of application.

Developmental Disabilities

More behavior modification research has been conducted in the field of developmental disabilities than perhaps any other area (Iwata et al., 1997). People with developmental disabilities often have serious behavioral deficits, and behavior modi-

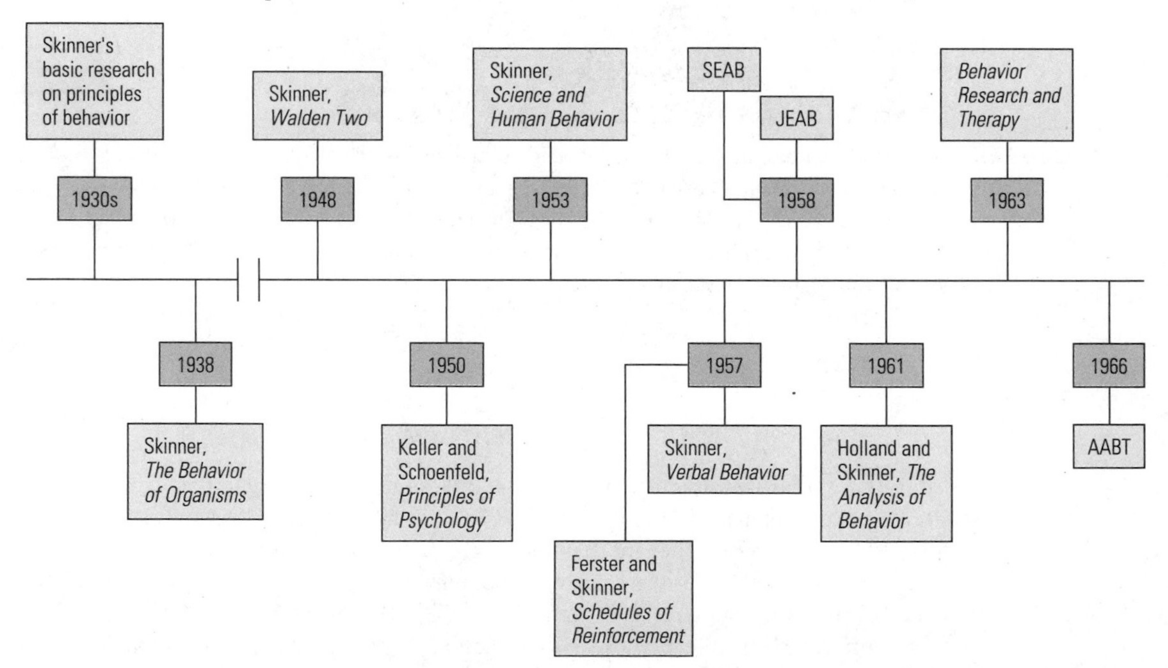

FIGURE 1-3 This timeline shows the major events in the development of behavior modification. Starting in the 1930s with Skinner's basic research on the principles of behavior, the timeline includes major books, journals, and professional organizations. SEAB = Society for the Experimental Analysis of Behavior. JEAB = *Journal of the Experimental Analysis of Behavior.* AABT = Association for Advancement of Behavior Therapy. JABA = *Journal of Applied Behavior Analysis.*

fication has been used to teach a variety of functional skills to overcome these deficits (Repp, 1983). In addition, people with developmental disabilities may exhibit serious problem behaviors such as self-injurious behaviors, aggressive behaviors, and destructive behaviors. A wealth of research in behavior modification demonstrates that these behaviors often can be controlled or eliminated with behavioral interventions (Barrett, 1986; Van Houten & Axelrod, 1993; Whitman, Scibak, & Reid, 1983). Behavior modification procedures also are used widely in staff training and staff management in the field of developmental disabilities (Reid, Parsons, & Green, 1989).

Mental Illness

Some of the earliest research in behavior modification demonstrated its effectiveness in helping people with mental illness in institutional settings (Ayllon, 1963; Ayllon & Michael, 1959). Behavior modification has been used with patients with chronic mental illness to modify such behaviors as daily living skills, social behavior, aggressive behavior, treatment compliance, psychotic behaviors, and work skills (Scotti, McMorrow, & Trawitzki, 1993). One particularly important contribution of behavior

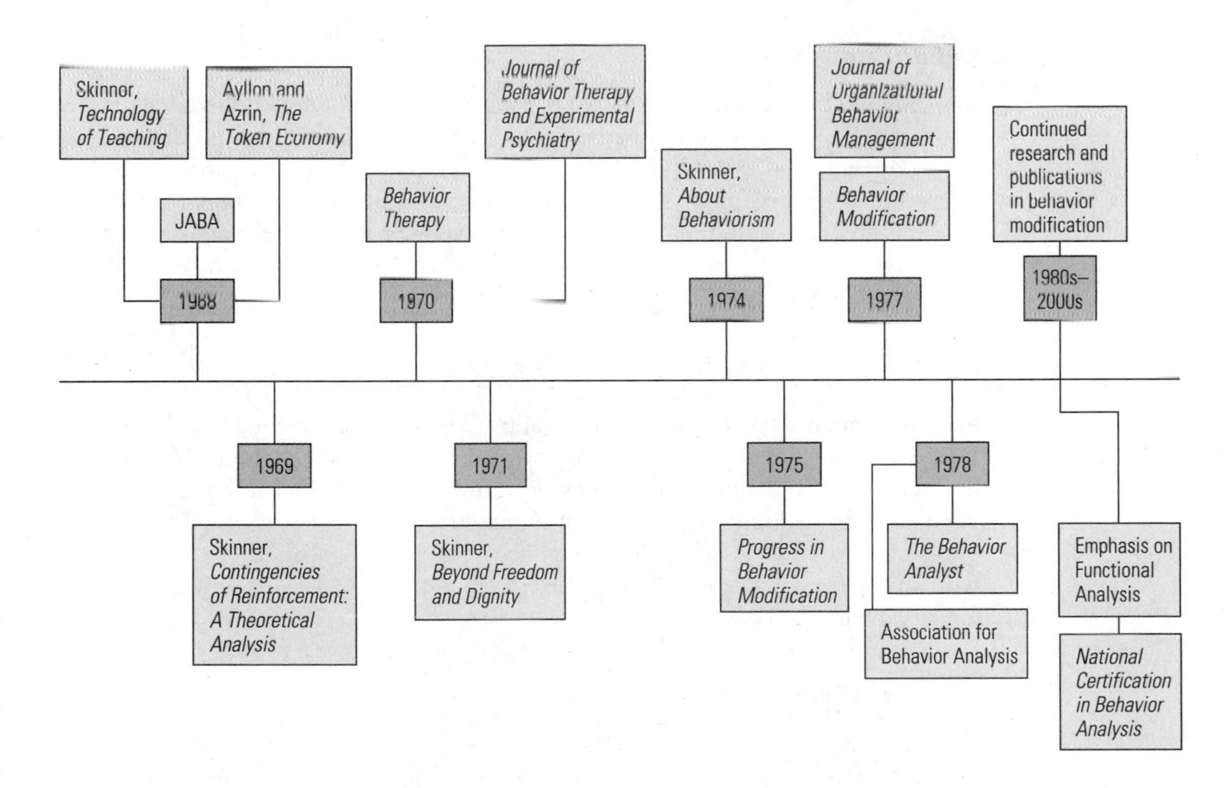

modification was the development of a motivational procedure for institutional patients called a token economy (Ayllon & Azrin, 1968). Token economies are still widely used in a variety of treatment settings (Kazdin, 1982).

Education and Special Education

Great strides have been made in the field of education because of behavior modification research (Bijou & Ruiz, 1981). Researchers have analyzed student–teacher interactions in the classroom, improved teaching methods, and developed procedures for reducing problem behaviors in the classroom (Becker & Carnine, 1981; Madsen, Becker, & Thomas, 1968; Thomas, Becker, & Armstrong, 1968). Behavior modification procedures have also been used in higher education to improve instructional techniques and increase student learning (Michael, 1991).

In special education, that is, the education of people with developmental disabilities, behavior modification has played a major role (Rusch, Rose, & Greenwood, 1988) in developing teaching methods, controlling problem behaviors in the classroom, improving social behaviors and functional skills, promoting self-management, and training teachers.

Rehabilitation

Rehabilitation is the process of helping people regain normal function after an injury or trauma, such as a head injury from an accident or brain damage from a stroke. Behavior modification is used in rehabilitation to promote compliance with rehabilitation routines such as physical therapy, to teach new skills that can replace skills lost through the injury or trauma, to decrease problem behaviors, to help manage chronic pain, and to improve memory performance (Bakke et al., 1994; Davis & Chittum, 1994; O'Neill & Gardner, 1983).

Community Psychology

Within community psychology, behavioral interventions are designed to influence the behavior of large numbers of people in ways that benefit everybody. Some targets of behavioral community interventions include reducing littering, increasing recycling, reducing energy consumption, reducing unsafe driving, reducing illegal drug use, increasing the use of seat belts, decreasing illegal parking in spaces for the disabled, and reducing speeding (Cope & Allred, 1991; Geller & Hahn, 1984; Ludwig & Geller, 1991; Van Houten & Nau, 1981).

Clinical Psychology

In clinical psychology, psychological principles and procedures are applied to help people with personal problems. Typically, clinical psychology involves individual or group therapy conducted by a psychologist. Behavior modification in clinical psychology, often called behavior therapy, has been applied to the treatment of a wide range of human problems (Hersen & Bellack, 1985; Hersen & Van Hasselt, 1987; Turner, Calhoun, & Adams, 1981). Behavior modification procedures have also been used to train clinical psychologists (Veltum & Miltenberger, 1989).

Business, Industry, and Human Services

The use of behavior modification in this field is called organizational behavior modification or organizational behavior management (Frederickson, 1982; Luthans & Kreitner, 1985; Reid et al., 1989; Stajkovic & Luthans, 1997). Behavior modification procedures have been used to improve work performance and job safety and to decrease tardiness, absenteeism, and accidents on the job. In addition, behavior modification procedures have been used to improve supervisors' performance. The use of behavior modification in business and industry has resulted in increased productivity and profits for organizations and increased job satisfaction for workers.

Self-Management

People use behavior modification procedures to manage their own behaviors. They use self-management procedures to control personal habits, health-related behaviors, professional behaviors, and personal problems (Brigham, 1989; Epstein, 1996; Watson & Tharp, 1993; Yates, 1986). Chapter 20 discusses the application of behavior modification procedures for self-management.

Child Management

There are numerous applications of behavior modification to the management of child behavior (Miller, 1975; Patterson, 1975; Schaeffer & Millman, 1981). Parents and teachers can learn to use behavior modification procedures to help children overcome bed-wetting, nail-biting, temper tantrums, noncompliance, aggressive behaviors, bad manners, stuttering, and other common problems (Watson & Gresham, 1998).

Prevention

Behavior modification procedures have been applied to preventing problems in childhood (Roberts & Peterson, 1984). Other applications of behavior modification in the area of prevention include preventing child sexual abuse, child abduction, accidents in the home, child abuse and neglect, and sexually transmitted diseases (Carroll, Miltenberger, & O'Neill, 1992; Montesinos, Frisch, Greene, & Hamilton, 1990; Poche, Yoder, & Miltenberger, 1988). Preventing problems in the community with behavior modification is one aspect of community psychology.

Sports Psychology

Behavior modification is used widely in the field of sports psychology (Martin & Hrycaiko, 1983). Behavior modification procedures have been used to improve athletic performance in a wide variety of sports during practice and in competition (Brobst & Ward, 2002; Hume & Crossman, 1992; Kendall, Hrycaiko, Martin, & Kendall, 1990; Wolko, Hrycaiko, & Martin, 1993; Zeigler, 1994). Behavior modification procedures have been shown to result in better athletic performance than do traditional coaching procedures.

Health-Related Behaviors

Behavior modification procedures are used to promote health-related behaviors by increasing healthy lifestyle behaviors (such as exercise and proper nutrition) and decreasing unhealthy behaviors (such as smoking, drinking, and overeating). Behavior modification procedures are also used to promote behaviors that have a positive influence on physical or medical problems—such as headaches, high blood pressure, and gastrointestinal disturbances (Blumenthal & McKee, 1987; Gentry, 1984)—and to increase compliance with medical regimens (Levy, 1987). Applying behavior modification to health-related behaviors is called behavioral medicine or health psychology.

Gerontology

Behavior modification procedures are applied in nursing homes and other care facilities to help manage the behavior of older adults (Hussian, 1981; Hussian & Davis, 1985). Behavior modification procedures are used to help older adults deal with their declining physical abilities, to help them adjust to nursing home environments, to promote health-related behaviors and appropriate social interactions, and to decrease problem behaviors that may arise from Alzheimer's disease, other types of dementia, or institutional demands (Carstensen & Erickson, 1986; Stock & Milan, 1993).

The Structure of This Textbook

This textbook is divided into five major sections. These sections discuss the following:

- Measurement of behavior and behavior change
- Basic principles of behavior
- Procedures to establish new behaviors
- Procedures to decrease undesirable behaviors and increase desirable behaviors
- Other behavior change procedures

The book is designed so that the information in earlier sections is applied in later sections.

Measurement of Behavior and Behavior Change

There are two chapters in this section. Chapter 2 teaches you how to observe and record behaviors that are to be modified in a behavior modification program. Chapter 3 teaches you how to construct graphs and evaluate graphed data to analyze behavior change resulting from a behavior modification program.

Basic Principles of Behavior

The five chapters in this section discuss the basic principles of behavior modification derived from scientific research in behavior analysis. The behavior modification procedures discussed in the remainder of the book are based on the basic behavioral principles reviewed in this section, which include reinforcement, extinction, punishment, stimulus control, and respondent conditioning. Once you understand these basic principles, it will be easier to understand and apply the behavior modification procedures described in later sections.

Procedures to Establish New Behaviors

One goal of behavior modification is to establish desirable new behaviors or skills. The four chapters in this section discuss behavior modification procedures used to establish new behaviors: shaping, prompting and transfer of stimulus control, chaining, and behavioral skills training procedures.

Procedures to Decrease Undesirable Behaviors and Increase Desirable Behaviors

Another goal of behavior modification procedures is to decrease the occurrence of undesirable behaviors and increase the occurrence of desirable behaviors that are not occurring frequently enough. The occurrence of undesirable behaviors is a behavioral excess. Desirable behaviors that occur too infrequently are behavioral deficits. The seven chapters in this section describe how to analyze behaviors and how to apply reinforcement, extinction, stimulus control, and punishment to decrease excess behaviors while increasing more desirable behaviors.

Other Behavior Change Procedures

The six chapters in this section describe more complex behavior modification procedures. Chapter 20 discusses self-management procedures. Chapter 21 discusses habit disorders and procedures for decreasing these excess behaviors. Chapter 22 on token economies and Chapter 23 on behavioral contracting discuss procedures that extend the reinforcement and punishment procedures described earlier. Chapter 24 applies procedures based on respondent conditioning to decrease fear and anxiety. Chapter 25 discusses behavior modification procedures to change cognitive behaviors, a type of covert behavior.

CHAPTER SUMMARY

1. Human behavior is defined as actions that have one or more physical dimensions and can be observed and recorded. Behaviors have an impact on the physical or social environment. Behavior is lawful; its occurrence is influenced by environmental events. A behavior may be overt or covert.
2. Behavior modification procedures involve analyzing and manipulating current environmental events to change behavior. A behavioral excess or behavioral deficit may be targeted for change with behavior modification procedures. Behavior modification procedures are based on behavioral principles derived from scientific research. B. F. Skinner conducted the early scientific research that laid the foundation for behavior modification. He also published a number of books demonstrating the application of behavioral principles to everyday life. Behavior modification procedures often are implemented by people in everyday life. Behavior is measured before

and after the behavior modification procedures are applied to document the effectiveness of the procedures. Behavior modification de-emphasizes past events and rejects hypothetical underlying causes of behavior.

3. The historical roots of behavior modification can be found in the work of Pavlov, Thorndike, Watson, and especially B. F. Skinner, who identified a number of basic principles of behavior and wrote about applying the principles of behavior analysis to human behavior.
4. Behavior modification procedures have been applied successfully to all aspects of human behavior, including developmental disabilities, mental illness, education and special education, rehabilitation, community psychology, clinical psychology, business, industry, and human services, self-management, child management, prevention, sports psychology, health-related behaviors, and gerontology.

Practice Test

1. What is the basic definition of human behavior? (p. 2)
2. Provide an example of a description of behavior and the label applied to that behavior. (p. 2)
3. Describe the three physical dimensions of behavior that can be observed and recorded. (p. 2)
4. Provide an example of how a behavior has an impact on the physical environment and on the social environment. (p. 2)
5. What does it mean to say that behavior is lawful? What is a functional relationship? (p. 2)
6. Describe the distinction between overt behavior and covert behavior. Provide an example of each. Which type of behavior is the focus of this book? (p. 3)
7. Identify the six characteristics of human behavior. (pp. 2–3)
8. What does it mean to say that behavior modification procedures are based on behavioral principles? (p. 6)
9. What causes human behavior? Describe how a label might be mistakenly identified as a cause of a behavior. (p. 6)
10. Why is it important to describe behavior modification procedures precisely? (p. 6)
11. Who implements behavior modification procedures? (p. 6)
12. Why is it important to measure behavior before and after behavior modification procedures are used? (p. 7)
13. Why doesn't behavior modification focus on the past as the cause of the behavior? (p. 7)
14. Identify eight defining characteristics of behavior modification. (pp. 5–7)
15. Briefly describe the contributions of Pavlov, Thorndike, Watson, and Skinner to the development of behavior modification. (p. 8)
16. Identify at least one way in which behavior modification has been applied in each of the following areas: developmental disabilities, education, community psychology, business, industry, human services, self-management, prevention, health-related behaviors, mental illness, rehabilitation, clinical psychology, child management, sports psychology, and gerontology. (pp. 10–14)

CHAPTER 1 *Quiz 1*

Name:

1. Behavior is defined as what people ________________ and ____________________.

2. Behavior has an impact on the ________________ and/or ________________ environment.

3. Behavior modification is the field of psychology concerned with the

   ________________ and ________________ of human behavior.

4. Too much of a particular behavior is called a behavioral ____________________.

5. Too little of a particular behavior is called a behavioral ____________________

6. Frequency, duration, latency, and intensity are called ________________ of behavior.

7. Match the following individuals with their contribution to behavior modification.

   a. Skinner   b. Watson   c. Pavlov   d. Thorndike

   __________ First to describe the conditioned reflex

   __________ Demonstrated the law of effect

   __________ Conducted research on basic principles of operant behavior and laid the foundation for behavior modification

8. ______________________________ started the movement in psychology called behaviorism.

9. A(n) ________________ behavior is a behavior that can be observed and recorded by another person.

10. A(n) ______________ behavior is not observable by others.

CHAPTER 1 *Quiz 2* Name:

1. ______________________ is what people say and do.

2. Four dimensions of behavior that can be measured include ______________________,

   ______________________, ______________________, and ______________________.

3. ______________________ is the field of psychology concerned with analyzing and modifying human behavior.

4. Charlie drinks too many cups of coffee each day. This behavior would be considered a

   behavioral ______________________ (deficit/excess).

5. Claire doesn't eat enough fruits and vegetables each day. This behavior would be

   considered a behavioral ______________________ (deficit/excess).

6. John Watson started the movement in psychology called ______________________.

7. Edward Thorndike's major contribution to psychology was the description of the

   ______________________.

8. ______________________ conducted laboratory research demonstrating basic behavioral principles.

9. An overt behavior is defined as ____

   ____.

10. A covert behavior is defined as ____

    ____.

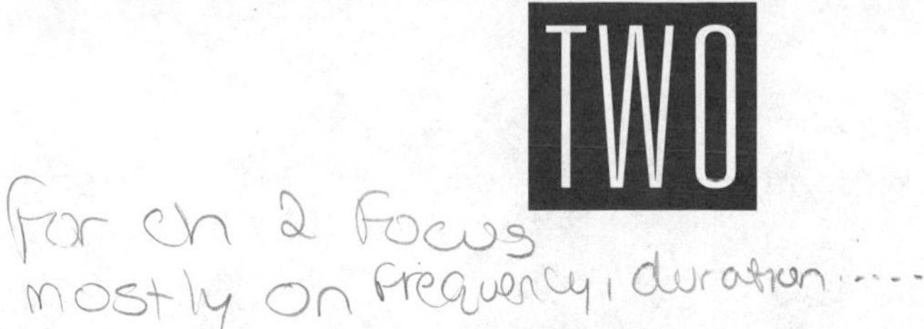

Observing and Recording Behavior

One fundamental aspect of behavior modification is measuring the behavior that is targeted for change. Measurement of the target behavior (or behaviors) in behavior modification is called **behavioral assessment** and is important for a number of reasons.

- Measuring the behavior before treatment provides information that can help you determine whether treatment is necessary.
- Behavioral assessment can provide information that helps you choose the best treatment.
- Measuring the target behavior before and after treatment allows you to determine whether the behavior changed after the treatment was implemented.

- How do you define a target behavior in a behavior modification program?
- What different methods can you use to record a target behavior?
- How does continuous recording differ from interval and time sample recording?
- What is reactivity of behavior recording, and how can you minimize it?
- What is interobserver reliability, and why is it important?

Consider the following example.

A supervisor in a manufacturing plant believed the company had a problem with workers showing up late for work. Before taking any remedial action, the supervisor recorded the arrival times of the workers for a number of days (Figure 2-1). The assessment showed that there were very few instances of tardiness. In this case, behavioral assessment demonstrated that there was not a problem and that intervention was not necessary.

If the measurement of the workers' arrival times showed that there was a problem, the supervisor would develop a behavior modification procedure to change the workers' behavior. The supervisor would continue to record arrival times as the intervention was implemented. The measurement of the workers' arrival times before, during, and after intervention would demonstrate whether the workers arrived late less frequently once intervention had been implemented.

There are two types of behavioral assessment: direct and indirect (Iwata, Vollmer, & Zarcone, 1990; Martin & Pear, 1999; O'Neill et al., 1997). **Indirect assessment** involves using interviews, questionnaires, and rating scales to obtain information on the target behavior from the person exhibiting the behavior or others (e.g., parents, teachers, or staff). With **direct assessment,** a person observes and records the target behavior as it occurs. To observe the target behavior, the observer (or a video camera, in

FIGURE 2-1 The supervisor collects data on the number of workers who arrive late.

some cases) must be in close proximity to the person exhibiting the behavior so that the target behavior can be seen (or heard). In addition, the observer must have a precise definition of the target behavior so that its occurrence can be distinguished from occurrences of other behaviors. To record the target behavior, the observer must register the occurrence of the behavior when it is observed; various methods of recording are described later in the chapter. When a school psychologist observes a socially withdrawn child on the playground and records each social interaction with another child, the psychologist is using direct assessment. When the psychologist interviews the student's teacher and asks the teacher how many times the child usually interacts with other children on the playground, the psychologist is using indirect assessment.

Direct assessment usually is more accurate than indirect assessment. This is because in direct assessment, the observer is trained specifically to observe the target behavior and record its occurrence immediately. In indirect assessment, information on the target behavior depends on people's memories. In addition, the people providing information may not have been trained to observe the target behavior and may not have noticed all the occurrences of the behavior. As a result, indirect assessment may be based on incomplete information about the target behavior. Therefore, most research and application in behavior modification relies on direct assessment.

The remainder of this chapter discusses direct assessment methods for observing and recording the target behavior in a behavior modification program. The chapter discusses the steps needed to develop a behavior recording plan. These steps include the following:

1. Defining the target behavior
2. Determining the logistics of recording
3. Choosing a recording method
4. Choosing a recording instrument

Defining the Target Behavior

The first step in developing a behavior recording plan is to define the target behavior you want to record. To define the target behavior for a particular person, you must identify exactly what the person says or does that constitutes the behavioral excess or deficit targeted for change. A behavioral definition includes active verbs describing specific behaviors that a person exhibits. A behavioral definition is objective and unambiguous. As an example of defining a target behavior, unsportsmanlike behavior for a particular baseball player may be defined as yelling obscenities, throwing the bat or batting helmet, and kicking the dirt as the player walks back to the bench after striking out.

Note that the example does not refer to any internal states such as being angry, upset, or sad. Such internal states cannot be observed and recorded by another person. The behavioral definition does not make inferences about a person's intentions. Intentions cannot be observed, and inferences about intentions often are incorrect. Finally, a label ("a bad sport") is not used to define the behavior because labels do not identify the person's actions.

Labels for behaviors are ambiguous; they can mean different things to different people. For example, to one person, unsportsmanlike behavior might mean fighting with a member of the other team, whereas another person considers it to mean cursing, throwing a bat, and kicking dirt. Specific behaviors can be observed and recorded; labels for the behavior cannot. In addition, labels can be used incorrectly as explanations of a behavior. For example, if a person is observed to repeat syllables or words when he talks, we might label him a stutterer. To then say that the person repeats syllables or words because he is a stutterer is an incorrect use of the label as a cause of the behavior. Repeating words or syllables is not caused by stuttering; it is a behavior called stuttering. The main value of labels is that they may be used as convenient shorthand when referring to a target behavior. However, the behavior must always be defined before it can be observed and recorded.

One characteristic of a good behavioral definition is that after seeing the definition, different people can observe the same behavior and agree that the behavior is occurring. When two people independently observe the same behavior and both record that the behavior occurred, this is called **interobserver reliability** (IOR; Bailey, 1977; Bailey & Burch, 2002) or interobserver agreement. IOR, which is commonly reported in behavior modification research, is discussed in more detail later in this chapter.

Table 2-1 lists behavioral definitions for common target behaviors and the labels associated with those behaviors. The behaviors that are described could be observed and agreed upon by two independent observers. The labels, on the other hand, are general names that are commonly used for these types of behaviors. Labels such as these may also be used to refer to behaviors other than those defined here. For example, in contrast to the definition given for Bobby in Table 2-1, a tantrum could be a label for the behavior of screaming, cursing at parents, slamming doors, and throwing toys on the floor. You must develop a specific behavioral definition that fits the target behavior of the person you are observing.

Researchers in behavior modification carefully define the target behaviors of people for whom they provide treatment. For example, Iwata and his colleagues (Iwata, Pace, Kalsher, Cowdery, & Cataldo, 1990) used behavior modification procedures to decrease self-injurious behavior in children with mental retardation. Their definitions

TABLE 2-1 Behavioral Definitions and Labels for Common Problems

Behavioral Definition	Label
When Bobby cries and sobs, lies on the floor and kicks the floor or walls, or pounds toys or other objects on the floor, it is defined as a tantrum.	Tantrumming
Studying for Rae involves reading pages from a textbook, underlining sentences in the text, completing math or physics workbook exercises, reading notes from class, and outlining chapters from the text.	Studying
When Pat says no to someone who asks her to do something that is not part of her job, when she asks co-workers not to smoke in her office, and when she asks co-workers to knock before entering her office, it is defined as assertiveness.	Assertiveness
Stuttering is defined for Joel as repeating a word or a word sound, prolonging the sound when saying a word, or hesitating more than 2 seconds between words in a sentence or between syllables in a word.	Stuttering
Any time Mark's finger is in his mouth and his teeth are closed together on the fingernail, cuticle, or skin around the nail, it is defined as nail-biting.	Nail-biting

for three types of self-injurious behavior were as follows: "arm biting—closure of upper and lower teeth on any portion of the skin extending from fingers to elbow; face hitting—audible contact of an open or closed hand against the face or head; and head banging—audible contact of any portion of the head against a stationary object (e.g., desk, floor, wall)" (p. 13). In another example, Rogers-Warren, Warren, and Baer (1977) used behavior modification procedures to increase sharing in preschool children. They defined sharing as occurring "when one subject passed or handed a material to a second subject, when subjects exchanged materials, or when two or more subjects simultaneously used the same material (for example, two subjects coloring on the same piece of paper)" (p. 311).

THE LOGISTICS OF RECORDING

The Observer

We have defined the target behavior to be recorded for a client, that is, a person who exhibits the target behavior and with whom the behavior modification program will be implemented. The next step is to identify who will observe and record the behavior. In a behavior modification program, the target behavior typically is observed and recorded by a person other than the one exhibiting the target behavior. The observer may be a professional such as a psychologist, or a person routinely associated with the client in the client's natural environment, such as a teacher, parent, staff person, or supervisor. The observer must have proximity to the client to observe the target behavior when it occurs. The exception would be when the target behavior is observed via videotape. He or she must be trained to identify the occurrence of the target behavior and to record the behavior immediately. He or she also must have the time to observe and record the behavior and must be willing to function as an observer. For example, a teacher may be asked to observe and record the target behavior of one of her students but may not agree to do so because the demands of teaching her students do not allow her the time to function as an observer. In most cases, it is possible to develop a behavior recording plan such that a person can observe and record the target behavior of the client without too much disruption of his or her normal routine.

In some cases, the observer is the person exhibiting the target behavior. When the client observes and records his or her own target behavior, it is called **self-monitoring.** Self-monitoring is valuable when it is not possible for another observer to record the target behavior, as when the target behavior occurs infrequently or when it occurs only when no one else is present (Stickney & Miltenberger, 1999; Stickney, Miltenberger, & Wolff, 1999). Self-monitoring may also be combined with direct observation by another observer. For example, a psychologist might directly observe and record the behavior of a person who is receiving treatment for a nervous habit such as hair-pulling. In addition, the client might be asked to self-monitor the target behavior outside the therapy sessions. If self-monitoring is used in a behavior modification program, the client must be trained to record his or her own behavior in the same way that an observer would be trained.

When and Where to Record

The observer records the target behavior in a specific period of time called the **observation period.** It is important to choose an observation period at the time when the target behavior is likely to occur. Indirect assessment information from the client or others (e.g., from an interview) may indicate the best times to schedule the observation period. For example, if staff report that a patient in a psychiatric ward is most likely to engage in disruptive behavior (defined as screaming, pacing, and cursing at other residents) around mealtimes, the observation period would be scheduled during meals. The timing of the observation periods also is determined by the availability of the observer(s) and the constraints imposed by the client's activities or preferences. Note that the client or the client's parent or guardian must give consent before you can observe and record his or her behavior. This is particularly important when observation occurs without the client's knowledge. In such cases, the client must provide consent for observations to occur, with the understanding that some observations may occur at times unknown to him or her.

Observation and recording of behavior take place in **natural settings** or in **contrived settings.** A natural setting consists of the places in which the target behavior typically occurs. Observing and recording a target behavior in the classroom is an example of a natural setting for a student. Observing a target behavior in a clinic playroom is a contrived setting because being in the clinic is not part of the child's normal daily routine. Observation in a natural setting is likely to provide a more representative sample of the target behavior. The target behavior may be influenced by the contrived setting, and observation in this setting may provide a sample that is not representative of the behavior under normal circumstances. However, there are benefits of observing in a contrived setting: It is more controlled than a natural setting, and the variables that influence the behavior are easier to manipulate.

When self-monitoring is used, the client may be able to observe and record the target behavior throughout the day and may not be constrained by a specific observation period. For example, clients who are self-monitoring the number of cigarettes they smoke each day can record each cigarette smoked regardless of when they smoke it. On the other hand, some behaviors may occur with such frequency that the client could not record continuously throughout the day; for example, a client who stutters may engage in stuttering hundreds of times throughout the day. In cases such as this, the client would be instructed to record the behavior during observation periods agreed upon in advance with the psychologist.

In behavior modification research, the people observing and recording the target behaviors usually are trained research assistants. They study the behavioral definition of the target behavior and then practice recording under the supervision of the researcher. When they can record the behavior reliably during practice sessions (after they have good IOR with the researcher), they record the target behavior during actual observation periods as part of the study. The observation periods used in behavior modification research often are brief (say, 15–30 minutes). When observations occur in natural settings, researchers usually choose observation periods that are representative of the usual occurrence of the target behavior. For example, observations may take place in a classroom, workplace, hospital, or other setting in which the target behavior usually occurs. In a study using behavior modification to improve children's behavior during trips to the dentist, Allen and Stokes (1987) recorded children's disruptive behavior (defined as head and body movements, crying, gagging, and moaning) while they were in the dentist's chair and the dentist performed dental procedures on them. In another study, Durand and Mindell (1990) taught parents how to use behavior modification procedures to decrease nighttime tantrum behavior (defined as loud screaming and hitting furniture) in their young child. In this study, the parents recorded the target behaviors for an hour before the child's bedtime because this was the time period when the tantrum behaviors occurred.

When observations occur in contrived settings (also called analogue settings), researchers often simulate events that are likely to occur in natural settings. For example, Iwata, Dorsey, Slifer, Bauman, and Richman (1982) observed and recorded the self-injurious behavior of children with mental retardation in therapy rooms in a hospital. During their observation periods, they simulated different events or activities that the children were likely to experience at home or at school. For example, the researchers observed the children as they played with toys and as teachers gave them instructions. Iwata and his colleagues found that for each child, the self-injurious behavior occurred at different rates in observation periods that simulated different events or activities.

Choosing a Recording Method

Different aspects of the target behavior may be measured using different recording methods. These methods include continuous recording, product recording, interval recording, and time sample recording. Each method is described here.

Continuous Recording

In **continuous recording,** the observer observes the client continuously throughout the observation period and records each occurrence of the behavior. To do so, the observer must be able to identify the onset and the offset (or beginning and end) of each instance of the behavior. In continuous recording, the observer can record various dimensions of the target behavior, particularly, its frequency, duration, intensity, and latency.

The **frequency** of a behavior is the number of times the behavior occurs in an observation period. You measure the frequency of a behavior by simply counting each time that it occurs. One occurrence is defined as one onset and offset of the behavior. For example, you can count the number of cigarettes someone smokes. For this target behavior, the onset may be defined as lighting the cigarette and the offset as putting it out. You will use a frequency measure when the number of times the behavior occurs is the most important information about the behavior. Frequency may be reported as **rate,** which is frequency divided by the time of the observation period.

The **duration** of a behavior is the total amount of time occupied by the behavior from start to finish. You measure the duration of a behavior by timing it from its onset to its offset. For example, you might record the number of minutes a student studies per day, the number of minutes a person exercises, or the number of seconds a patient who has had a stroke stands up without assistance during rehabilitation sessions in the hospital. You will use a duration measure when the most important aspect of the behavior is how long it lasts. Duration may be reported as percentage of time, which is duration divided by the time of the observation period (Miltenberger, Rapp, & Long, 1999).

Some researchers use a **real-time recording** method in which the exact time of each onset and offset of the target behavior is recorded (Miltenberger et al., 1999; Miltenberger, Long, Rapp, Lumley, & Elliott, 1998). With real-time recording, the researchers have a record of the frequency and duration of the target behavior as well as the exact timing of each occurrence of the behavior. Real-time recording can be carried out after videotape recording the target behavior in the observation period. The observer then plays the videotape and records the time indicated on the VCR timer at the onset and offset of each occurrence of the behavior on a data sheet developed for real-time recording (Rapp, Carr, Miltenberger, Dozier, & Kellum, 2001). Alternatively, hand-held or laptop computers with software that permits recording of the exact timing of events can be used for real-time recording (Kahng & Iwata, 1998).

The **intensity** of a behavior is the amount of force, energy, or exertion involved in it. Intensity (also called magnitude) is more difficult to measure than frequency or duration because it does not involve simply counting the number of times the behavior occurs or recording the amount of time it takes to occur. Intensity often is recorded with a measurement instrument or by using a rating scale. For example, you could use a decibel meter to measure the loudness of someone's speech. A physical therapist might measure the strength of a person's grip to judge recovery from an injury. Parents might use a rating scale from 1 to 5 to measure how intense a child's tantrum was. The parents would have to define the behavior associated with each point on the rating scale so that their ratings were reliable; their ratings would be reliable if they both observed a tantrum and recorded the same number on the rating scale. Intensity is not used as often as frequency or duration, but it is a useful measure when you are most interested in the force or magnitude of the behavior (Bailey, 1977; Bailey & Burch, 2002).

The **latency** of the behavior is the time from some stimulus event to the onset of the behavior. You measure latency by recording how long it takes the person to initiate the behavior after a particular event occurs. For example, you could record how long it takes a child to start putting toys away after being asked to do so. The shorter the latency, the sooner the child initiates the behavior after the request. Another example of latency is the time it takes a person to answer the phone after it starts ringing.

How does latency differ from duration?

Latency is the time from some stimulus event to the onset of the behavior, whereas duration is the time from the onset of the behavior to its offset. In other words, latency is how long it takes to start the behavior and duration is how long the behavior lasts.

When using continuous recording, you can choose one or more dimensions to measure. The dimension you choose depends on which aspect of the behavior is most important and which dimension is most sensitive to change in the behavior after treatment. For example, if you want to record a person's stuttering, frequency may be the most important dimension because you are interested in the number of stuttered words. You can then compare the number of stuttered words before, during, and after treatment. If treatment is successful, there should be fewer stuttered words. However, duration may also be an important dimension of stuttering if there are long speech blocks or prolongations. In this case, you would expect the duration of stuttering to decrease following treatment.

If you were recording a child's tantrum behavior (screaming, throwing toys, slamming doors), which dimension of the behavior would you measure?

The example of a child's tantrum behavior is less clear. You may be interested in the number of tantrums per day (frequency), but you may also be interested in how long each tantrum lasts (duration). Finally, you may be interested in how loud the child screams or how forcefully the child throws toys or slams doors (intensity). We hope that, after treatment, the tantrums will decrease in frequency, duration, and intensity; that is, they will occur less often, will not last as long, and will not be as loud or violent.

Unless you measure the right dimension of a behavior, you may not be able to judge the effectiveness of treatment. If you are in doubt, or if multiple dimensions of the behavior seem relevant, the best course of action is to measure more than one dimension. Go back to the example of the child's tantrums. In Figure 2-2 you can see that, from an average of more than six per day during baseline, the frequency of tantrums decreased to less than two per day during treatment. (**Baseline** is the period during which the target behavior is recorded before treatment is implemented.) It appears that treatment was effective. However, in Figure 2-3 you can see the duration of tantrums before and during treatment. Before treatment, each of the five to eight tantrums per day lasted about 1 minute each, for a total of 5–8 minutes of tantrum be-

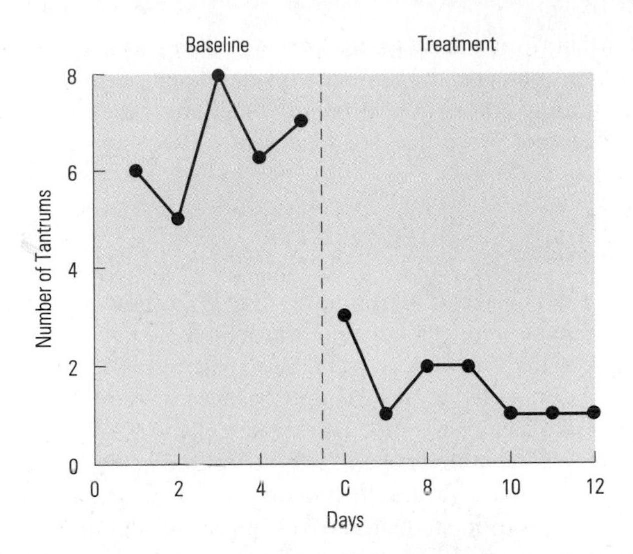

FIGURE 2-2 The frequency of tantrums during baseline and treatment phases. During the baseline phase, the target behavior is recorded, but treatment is not yet implemented. Tantrums decreased from an average of more than six per day during baseline to less than two per day during treatment.

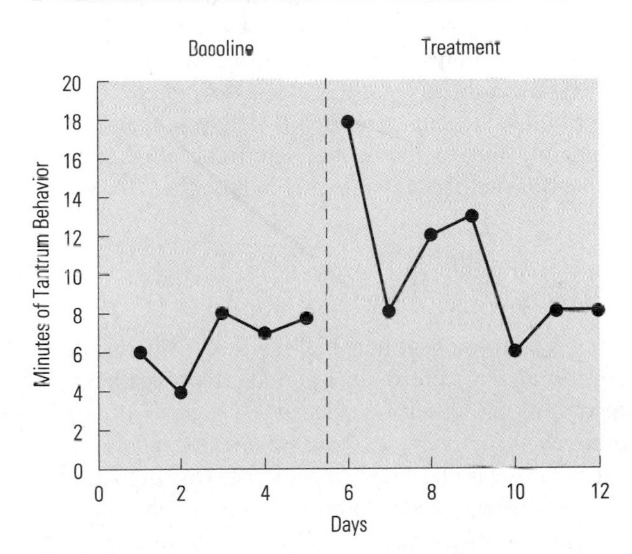

FIGURE 2-3 The duration of tantrums during baseline and treatment phases. Tantrums increased from an average duration of 1 minute each or a total of 5–8 minutes per day during baseline to about 6 minutes each or a total of 6–18 minutes per day during treatment. Therefore, the duration of tantrum behavior per day did not decrease, even though the frequency of tantrums decreased.

havior per day. During treatment, the duration of each tantrum was much longer, resulting in more minutes of tantrum behavior per day. Therefore, according to the duration measure, the tantrums got worse during treatment. This underscores the importance of measuring more than one dimension of a target behavior because more than one dimension can change following treatment.

Note also that, to demonstrate the effectiveness of treatment, you must use established research methods and an experimental design. Simply measuring the behavior before, during, and after treatment demonstrates whether the target behavior changed but does not prove that the treatment caused the behavior change. (See Chapter 3.)

Product Recording

Another aspect of a behavior that may be recorded is its product. **Product recording,** also called permanent product recording (Marholin & Steinman, 1977), is an indirect assessment method that can be used when a behavior results in a certain tangible outcome that you are interested in. For example, a supervisor could count the number of units assembled in a factory as a product measure of a worker's job performance, or a teacher could record the number of correctly completed homework problems or workbook pages as a product measure of students' academic performance (Noell et al., 2000). In their research on student behavior problems and academic performance, Marholin and Steinman (1977) looked at the math worksheets of students and recorded the number of math problems completed correctly as permanent products of the students' academic performance.

One benefit of product recording is that the observer does not have to be present when the behavior occurs. The teacher probably won't be present when students complete their homework assignments but can still measure the product of the behavior (completed homework problems). One drawback of product recording is that you cannot always determine who engaged in the behavior that led to the product you recorded. For example, the teacher cannot determine whether the students completed their own homework, whether someone else helped them, or whether someone did it for them.

Interval Recording

Another aspect of a behavior that may be recorded is whether the behavior occurred or did not occur during consecutive time periods. This is called **interval recording.** To use interval recording, the observer divides the observation period into a number of smaller time periods or intervals, observes the client throughout each consecutive interval, and then records whether the behavior occurred in that interval. There are two types of interval recording: partial interval recording and whole interval recording. With partial interval recording, you are not interested in the number of times the behavior occurs (frequency) or how long it lasts (duration). You do not have to identify the onset and offset of the behavior; rather, you simply record whether the behavior occurred during each interval of time.

Suppose that a teacher is recording whether a child disrupts the class during each 15-minute interval in the class period. The teacher sets a timer to beep every 15 minutes. When the disruptive behavior occurs, the teacher marks the corresponding interval on a data sheet. Once an interval is marked, the teacher does not have to observe the child or record the behavior until the next interval begins. Thus, one benefit of partial interval recording is that it takes less time and effort: The observer records the behavior only once during the interval, regardless of how many times the behavior occurs or how long it lasts. With whole interval recording, the occurrence of the behavior is marked in an interval only when the behavior occurs throughout the entire interval. If the behavior occurs only in part of the interval, the behavior is not scored as occurring in that interval.

When researchers use interval recording, they often choose very short intervals, such as 6 or 10 seconds (Bailey, 1977; Bailey and Burch, 2002). In this way, they make many recordings of the behavior during the observation period and obtain a more representative sample of the target behavior than they could derive from longer intervals. For example, Iwata, Pace, et al. (1990) used 10-second intervals to record the occurrence of self-injurious behavior (e.g., head-banging, slapping, and scratching) in children with mental retardation. Miltenberger, Fuqua, and McKinley (1985) used 6-second intervals to record the occurrence of motor tics (e.g., jerking movements of the head or facial muscles, rapid eye-blinking) in adults. In this study, the researchers videotaped the adults in the observation sessions and then recorded the number of intervals containing motor tics from the videotapes. Every 6 seconds, the researchers recorded the presence or absence of the tic behavior.

In some cases, frequency recording and interval recording can be combined to produce **frequency-within-interval recording**. With this method, the observer records the frequency of the target behavior but does so within consecutive intervals of time in the observation period (Bailey, 1977; Bailey & Burch, 2002). Frequency-within-interval recording shows you the frequency of the behavior and the specific intervals in which the behavior occurred.

Time Sample Recording

When using **time sample recording**, you divide the observation period into intervals of time, but you observe and record the behavior during only part of each interval. The observation periods are separated by periods without observation. For example, you might record the behavior for only 1 minute during each 15-minute interval or you might record the behavior only if it is occurring at the end of the interval. Consider an observer who is using time sample recording to record a client's poor posture (defined as slouching, bending the back forward). The observer sets a timer to beep every 10 minutes and records an instance of bad posture only if the client's posture is bad when the timer beeps at the end of the interval. Time sample recording is valuable because the person does not have to observe the behavior for the entire interval. Rather, the observer records only the behavior that occurs during a portion of the interval or at a specific time in the interval.

In interval recording or time sample recording, the level of the behavior is reported as the percentage of intervals in which the behavior occurred. To calculate the percentage of intervals, you divide the number of scored intervals by the total number of intervals during the observation period. A scored interval is an interval in which the behavior was recorded.

RECORDING METHODS

Continuous recording	Record every instance of the behavior occurring during the observation period. May record frequency, duration, intensity, or latency.
Product recording	Record the tangible outcome or permanent product of the occurrence of the behavior.
Interval recording	Record the occurrence or nonoccurrence of the behavior in consecutive intervals of time during an observation period.
Time sample recording	Record the occurrence or nonoccurrence of the behavior in discontinuous intervals of time (time samples) during an observation period.

CHOOSING A RECORDING INSTRUMENT

The final step in developing a behavior recording plan is to choose a recording instrument. The recording instrument is what the observer uses to register the occurrence of the behavior. Paper and pencil are most often used to record behavior. Put simply, the observer makes a note on the paper each time he or she observes the behavior. To record behavior most effectively, the observer uses a data sheet prepared in advance for the particular behavior. The data sheet helps organize the recording process by making it clear what the observer is to write down when the behavior occurs.

The data sheet in Figure 2-4 is used to record the frequency of a target behavior. Each time the behavior occurs on a particular day, the observer marks an *x* in one of the boxes for that day. The number of boxes with *x*s filled in for each day signifies the frequency, or the number of times that the behavior occurred on each day.

The data sheet in Figure 2-5 is used to record the duration of a target behavior. On each day, there are places to record the times the behavior started (onset) and ended (offset). By recording the onset and offset of each instance of a behavior, you end up with a recording of how long the behavior occurred (duration) as well as how often it occurred (frequency).

An example of a data sheet used for 10-second interval recording is shown in Figure 2-6 Notice that there are six boxes on each line and 15 lines of boxes. Each box represents one 10-second interval, for a total of 90 intervals in 15 minutes. To use the 10-second interval recording method, the observer listens to a tape recorder that signals the start of each interval. When the target behavior occurs, the observer puts a check mark in the corresponding interval box. If the target behavior does not occur during an interval, the observer leaves that interval box blank. Alternatively, each interval box could have one or more codes. The observer circles or puts a check mark through the code that represents the behavior observed in that interval. For example, the codes *AT* and *RP* could be used to signify the behaviors of attention and reprimand when observing a parent's behavior while interacting with a child. If the parent pays attention to the child or reprimands the child in an interval, the observer would circle *AT* or *RP*, respectively, for that interval.

Other procedures for recording behavior involve writing the behavior down each time it occurs. For example, a person who wants to count the number of cigarettes she smokes each day may keep a note card tucked into the cellophane wrapper on the cig-

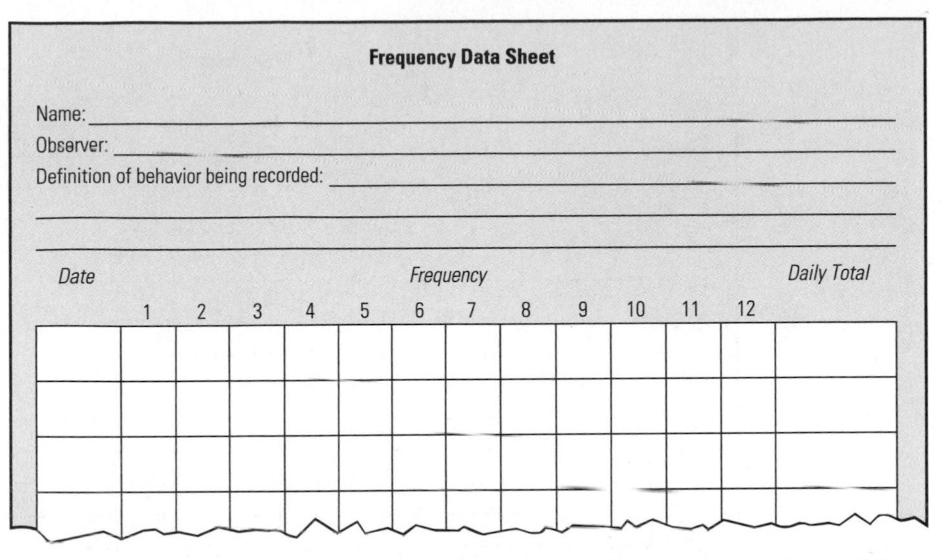

Frequency Data Sheet

Name: ______________________________

Observer: ______________________________

Definition of behavior being recorded: ______________________________

____

____

Date	*Frequency* 1	2	3	4	5	6	7	8	9	10	11	12	*Daily Total*

FIGURE 2-4 This data sheet is used to record the frequency of a behavior. You put an *x* into a box each time the behavior occurs. If more than 12 instances of the behavior occur per day, continue recording on the next line.

Duration Data Sheet

Name: ______________________________

Observer: ______________________________

Definition of behavior being recorded: ______________________________

____

____

Date	*Duration* Onset	Offset	Onset	Offset	Onset	Offset	*Daily Duration*

FIGURE 2-5 This data sheet is used to record the duration of a behavior. You record the onset and offset time for each instance of the behavior. If there are more than three instances of the behavior per day, continue recording on the next line.

Interval Data Sheet

Name: ______________________________

Observer: ______________________________

Date and time of observation: ______________________________

Definition of behavior being recorded: ______________________________

____

____

Ten-second intervals

	1	2	3	4	5	6
1						
2						
3						
4						
5						
6						
7						
8						
9						
10						
11						
12						
13						
14						
15						

Minutes of observation

FIGURE 2-6 This is an interval recording data sheet. Each box corresponds to an interval, and a check mark is placed in a box when the behavior occurs during that interval. When the behavior does not occur during an interval, the box is left blank.

arette pack. Each time she smokes a cigarette, she makes a check mark on the note card and counts the check marks at the end of each day. Likewise, a person who is recording his rude behavior might keep a small note pad in his shirt pocket; every time he makes a rude remark, he pulls out the note pad and makes a note of it.

Not all instruments for recording behavior depend on paper and pencil. Anything you can use to register each occurrence of a behavior can be considered a behavior recording instrument. The following are some common examples.

- *Using a golf stroke counter to record the frequency of a behavior.* The golf stroke counter is worn on the wrist like a wristwatch. Each time the behavior occurs, you push the button on the counter (Lindsley, 1968).
- *Using a stopwatch to record the cumulative duration of a behavior.* You start and stop the stopwatch each time the behavior starts and stops. Runners and joggers often wear watches with a stopwatch function that allows them to record the duration of their workouts.

- *Using a hand-held computer to record the frequency and duration of many behaviors at once.* You push different keys on the computer each time different behaviors occur; as long as you keep pressing the key, the duration of the behavior is recorded (Iwata, Pace, et al., 1990).
- *Transferring a coin from one pocket to another to record the frequency of a behavior.* Each time you observe the behavior, you move a coin from your right pocket to your left pocket. The number of coins in your left pocket at the end of the day equals the frequency of the behavior (assuming that you don't spend any of the coins from your left pocket).
- *Making small tears in a piece of paper each time a behavior occurs.* At the end of the observation period, the frequency of the behavior is equal to the number of tears in the paper (Epstein, 1996).
- *Using ranger beads.* Ranger beads (brought to my attention by Jason Hicks, a student in my behavior modification class, who first used them when he was an Army Ranger), consist of a strip of leather or nylon threaded through beads. They have two sections, each with nine beads. With the beads in one section, the person can record 1 through 9; with the beads in the other section, the person can count by 10s, for a maximum frequency count of 99. Whenever a target behavior occurs, the person moves a bead from one side of the strip to the other. At the end of the day or observation period, the number of beads moved to one side indicates the frequency of the target behavior. A similar recording system involves beads on a piece of leather or string worn around the wrist.
- *Using a pedometer.* The pedometer is an automatic device, worn on the belt, that records each step a person takes while walking or running.

Regardless of the instrument used, the one characteristic of all behavior recording procedures is that the person observes the behavior and records it immediately. The sooner the observer records the behavior after it occurs, the less likely the observer is to record incorrectly. A person who waits some time to record an observation may forget to record it at all.

One other aspect of a behavior recording procedure is that it must be practical. The person responsible for recording the target behavior must be able to use the recording procedure without much difficulty or disruption of ongoing activities. If a recording procedure is practical, the person is more likely to carry out the recording (or self-monitoring) successfully. A recording procedure that takes substantial time or effort is not practical. In addition, the recording procedure should not draw attention to the person who is doing the observation and recording. If this happens, the person may be less likely to carry out the recording procedure.

Reactivity

Sometimes the process of recording a behavior causes the behavior to change, even before any treatment is implemented. This is called **reactivity** (Foster, Bell-Dolan, & Burge, 1988; Hartmann & Wood, 1990; Tryon, 1998). Reactivity may occur when an observer is recording the behavior of another person or when a person engages in self-monitoring. Reactivity may be undesirable, especially for research purposes, because the behavior recorded during the observation period is not representative of the level of the behavior occurring in the absence of the observer or in the absence of self-monitoring. For example, when a disruptive child sees that someone is recording her behavior in the classroom, she may decrease her disruptive behavior while the observer is present. Usually this change in behavior is only temporary, and the behavior returns to its original level once the child becomes accustomed to the observer's presence. One way to reduce reactivity is to wait until the people who are being observed become accustomed to the observer. Another is to have the observer record the behavior without the people knowing that they are being observed. This may be accomplished with the use of one-way observation windows or with participant observers. A participant observer is a person who is normally in the setting where the target behavior occurs, such as a teacher's aide in a classroom.

Likewise, when a person starts to record his or her own behavior as part of a self-management project, the behavior often changes in the desired direction as a result of the self-monitoring (Epstein, 1996). For this reason, self-monitoring sometimes is used as a treatment to change a target behavior. For example, Ollendick (1981) and Wright and Miltenberger (1987) found that self-monitoring of motor tics led to reductions in their frequency. Ackerman and Shapiro (1984) reported that when adults with mental retardation self-monitored their work productivity, their productivity increased. Winett, Neale, and Grier (1979) showed that self-monitoring of electricity use by people in their homes resulted in decreases in electricity use. Self-monitoring and other self-control strategies are discussed in more detail in Chapter 20.

INTEROBSERVER RELIABILITY

You assess IOR to determine whether the target behavior is being recorded consistently. To evaluate IOR, two people independently observe and record the same target behavior of the same subject during the same observation period. The recordings of the two observers are then compared and a percentage of agreement between observers is calculated. When the percentage of agreement is high, it indicates that there is consistency in the scoring by the two observers. This suggests that the definition of the target behavior is clear and objective and that the observers are using the recording system correctly. When high IOR is reported in a research study, it suggests that the observers in the study recorded the target behavior consistently. IOR should be checked at least occasionally when direct observation and recording are used in nonresearch settings also. In research studies, the minimally acceptable IOR is typically 80%, although 90% or better is preferred.

IOR is calculated differently depending on the recording method used. For frequency recording, IOR (expressed as a percentage) is calculated by dividing the smaller frequency by the larger frequency. For example, if observer A records ten occurrences of aggressive behavior in an observation period and observer B records nine, the reliability equals 90%. For duration recording, IOR is calculated by dividing the smaller duration by the larger duration. For example, if observer A records

	A	A	A	A	A	D	A	A	A	A	A	D	A	A	D	A	A	A	A	A
Observer A	X	X	X		X		X	X			X		X		X	X		X		
Observer B	X	X	X		X	X	X	X			X	X	X			X		X		

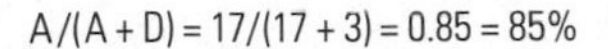

FIGURE 2-7 A comparison of interval recording by two observers. An A indicates that the observers agreed that the behavior did or did not occur in an interval. D indicates that the observers disagreed: One recorded the occurrence of the behavior in an interval, and the other did not.

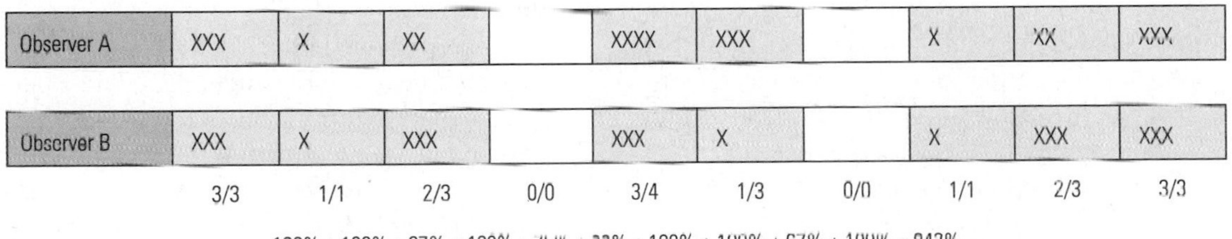

Observer A
XXX
X
XX
XXXX
XXX
X
XX
XXX
Observer B
XXX
X
XXX
XXX
X
X
XXX
XXX
3/3
1/1
2/3
0/0
3/4
1/3
0/0
1/1
2/3
3/3
100% + 100% + 67% + 100% + 75% + 33% + 100% + 100% + 67% + 100% = 842%
842% divided by 10 (the number of intervals) = 84.2%

FIGURE 2-8 Calculation of interobserver reliability for frequency-within-interval recording. A percentage of agreement is calculated for each interval, the percentages are summed, and the sum is divided by the number of intervals.

48 minutes of exercise and observer B records 50 minutes, the reliability equals 48/50, or 96%. For interval recording, you check the agreement between the two observers in each interval. You then divide the number of intervals with agreement by the total number of intervals. Agreement is defined as the case in which the two observers both recorded the target behavior as occurring or as not occurring in a particular interval. Figure 2-7 shows the interval recording data from two independent observers recording the behavior of the same client at the same time. There were 20 intervals of observation and the two observers agreed on the occurrence or nonoccurrence of the behavior 17 times. Therefore, you divide 17 by 17 + 3, which equals 0.85, or 85%. IOR for time sample recording is calculated in the same manner as for interval recording.

To calculate IOR for frequency-within-interval recording, you calculate a percentage of agreement between observers for each interval (smaller frequency divided by the larger frequency), sum the percentages for all the intervals, and divide by the number of intervals in the observation period. Figure 2-8 shows the calculation of IOR for two independent observers using frequency-within-interval recording.

Chapter Summary

1. You define a target behavior by identifying exactly what the person says or does that constitutes the behavioral excess or behavioral deficit targeted for change. The behavioral definition should include active verbs describing the behavior the person exhibits.
2. The different methods you can use to record the target behavior include continuous recording of the frequency, duration, latency, or magnitude of the behavior, product recording, interval recording, or time sample recording.
3. With continuous recording, the observer observes the client continuously throughout the observation period and records each occurrence of the behavior. With interval and time sample recording, the observation period is divided into a number of smaller time periods or intervals and the behavior is recorded as occurring or not occurring within each interval. With interval recording, the intervals are consecutive periods of time and with time sample recording, the intervals are separated by periods without observation.
4. Reactivity occurs when the process of behavior recording causes the behavior to change, even before any treatment is implemented. Reactivity can be minimized by waiting until the person being observed becomes accustomed to the observer's presence. Another way to reduce reactivity is to observe people without letting them know they are being observed.
5. Interobserver reliability is determined by having two observers independently record a person's behavior during the same observation period and then comparing the recordings of the two observers. You assess interobserver reliability to determine whether the target behavior is being recorded consistently.

Practice Test

1. Why is it important to record the behavior you are trying to change when using behavior modification? (p. 19)
2. Identify the four steps involved in a behavior recording plan. (p. 20)
3. What is a behavioral definition? How does it differ from a label for a behavior? (p. 21)
4. Provide a possible behavioral definition of politeness.
5. Why is it important to identify who will record a behavior? (pp. 22–23)
6. What is meant by the term *observation period?* (p. 23)
7. Identify and define four dimensions of a behavior that may be recorded in a continuous recording method. (pp. 25–26)
8. Provide an example of frequency recording, duration recording, intensity recording, and latency recording. (pp. 25–26)
9. What is real-time recording? Provide an example. (p. 25)
10. What is product recording? Provide an example. (p. 28)
11. What is interval recording? Provide an example. (pp. 28–29)
12. What is frequency-within-interval recording? Provide an example. (p. 29)
13. What is time sample recording? Provide an example. (p. 29)
14. Provide examples of three different recording instruments. (pp. 30–33)
15. Why is it important to record a behavior immediately after it occurs? (p. 33)
16. What is reactivity? Describe two ways to reduce reactivity during direct observation. (pp. 33–34)
17. What is interobserver reliability, and why is it assessed? (p. 34)
18. Describe how you calculate interobserver reliability for frequency recording, duration recording, and interval recording. (pp. 34–35)
19. Describe how you would calculate interobserver reliability for frequency-within-interval recording. (p. 35)

APPLICATIONS

1. When people want to change their own behavior, they can design and implement a self-management program. A self-management program involves applying behavior modification to one's own behavior. There are five steps in a self-management program:

    i. *Self-monitoring.* Define and record the target behavior you want to change.
    ii. *Graphing.* Develop a graph and plot the daily level of the target behavior on the graph.
    iii. *Goal setting.* Establish a goal for the desired change in the target behavior.
    iv. *Intervention.* Develop and implement specific behavior modification strategies to change the behavior.
    v. *Evaluation.* Continue to record the behavior and plot it on the graph to determine whether you changed your target behavior and achieved your goal.

In this exercise, take the first step to start your own self-management program. Define a target behavior you want to change and develop a behavior recording plan to measure the target behavior. As you complete this first step, consider the following questions.

    a. Did you define your target behavior in clear, objective terms?
    b. Did you determine the appropriate dimension of your target behavior to record (e.g., frequency or duration)?
    c. Did you choose a practical recording method?
    d. Will you be able to record your target behavior immediately each time that it occurs?
    e. What problems might you encounter as you record your target behavior, and how will you deal with these problems?

Good luck in starting the self-monitoring component of your self-management program. You will learn the information you need to carry out the remaining steps of your self-management program in subsequent chapters.

2. Imagine you have a friend James who is studying to be an elementary school teacher. James is doing his student teaching this semester in a second grade classroom in a public school. James mentioned to you that one of his students has trouble staying in her seat, paying attention during class, and participating in activities. This student, Sara, gets out of her seat and talks to or teases other children. When she is out of her seat, she does not pay attention to James, does not participate in activities, and disrupts the other children. James believes that if he could just get Sara to stay in her seat, he could get her to pay attention and participate. As a result, she would do better in class, and the other students would also do better. James knows you are taking a behavior modification class, so he has come to you for help.

You inform James that the first step he must take, if he is going to use behavior modification with Sara, is to develop a recording plan to measure her behavior. In this exercise, develop a plan that James could use to record Sara's out-of-seat behavior. Consider the following questions.

    a. What is the behavioral definition of out-of-seat behavior?
    b. What recording method will you have James use to record Sara's out-of-seat behavior?
    c. What instrument will you have James use to record the behavior? Will this instrument be practical for James to use as a teacher?

3. Eve plans to start a weight-lifting program. She wants to record her behavior once she starts the program so that she can measure the changes in her behavior as the program progresses. Describe how Eve could use frequency recording, duration recording, and intensity recording to measure her weight-lifting behavior.

MISAPPLICATIONS

1. Gloria is taking a behavior modification class and has to do a self-management project. The behavior she has chosen to modify is her hair-twirling. She has defined this behavior as any instance in which she reaches up to the back of her head and wraps hair around her finger. The first step in her self-management project is to develop a behavior recording plan. Because she usually does the hair-twirling in her classes, she decides to record the behavior immediately after each class period. She will keep a 3- × 5-inch note card in her purse and, as soon as she leaves the classroom, she will get the note card out of her purse and write down the number of times that she twirled her hair in the class.

   a. What is wrong with this behavior recording plan?
   b. What changes would you make to improve it?

2. Ralph is going to implement a self-management project to help him decrease the number of cigarettes he smokes per day. He will define the behavior of smoking a cigarette as any instance in which he takes a cigarette out of the pack in his pocket, lights it, and smokes any part of it. He will record the number of cigarettes he smokes each day by counting the cigarettes left in his pack at the end of the day and subtracting this number from the number of cigarettes that were in the pack at the start of the day.

   a. What is wrong with this behavior recording plan?
   b. What would you do to improve it?

3. Below are examples of behavioral definitions of target behaviors in students' self-management programs. What is wrong with each of these behavioral definitions?

   a. Losing my temper will be defined as getting mad at my husband and yelling at him, walking into the bedroom and slamming the door, or telling him to "shut up" when he says something that frustrates me.
   b. Overeating will be defined as anytime I eat more than I wanted to eat at a meal, or any time I eat so much that I feel bloated or my belt is too tight.
   c. Studying will be defined as any time I have my books open in front of me in the library or at my desk, the TV is off, and there are no other distractions.

CHAPTER 2 *Quiz 1*

Name:

1. There are two types of behavioral assessment: ______________________ assessment and ______________________ assessment.

2. The first step in developing a behavior recording plan is to define the ______________________ you want to record.

3. A(n) ______________________ includes active verbs that describe the specific behaviors a person exhibits.

4. When two people independently observe the same behavior and both record that the behavior occurred, this is called ______________________.

5. The ______________________ is the specific period of time in which the observer records the target behavior.

6. Jason recorded the number of times he used a specific curse word each day. What dimension of behavior was Jason recording? ______________________

7. Kevin recorded how many minutes he ran each day. What dimension of behavior was Kevin recording? ______________________

8. The supervisor of a radar technician recorded how long it took for the technician to identify a plane after it appeared on the radar screen. What dimension of behavior was the supervisor recording? ______________________

9. In interval recording, the occurrence of the behavior is scored in ______________________ (consecutive/nonconsecutive) intervals of time. In time sample recording, the occurrence of the behavior is scored in ______________________ (consecutive/nonconsecutive) intervals of time.

10. ______________________ is when the process of recording a behavior causes the behavior to change.

CHAPTER 2 *Quiz 2* Name:

1. ________________ (Direct/Indirect) assessment involves recording the target behavior as it occurs.

2. ________________ (Direct/Indirect) assessment involves the use of interviews or questionnaires to gather information.

3. Match the following terms to their definition.

   frequency duration latency intensity

   ______________ The number of times the behavior occurs in the observation period

   ______________ The time from some stimulus event to the onset of the behavior

   ______________ The time of the behavior from onset to offset

4. Recording the behavior in brief observation intervals each separated by longer periods of time is called ________________________ recording.

5. Recording the behavior in consecutive intervals of time is called ________________ recording.

6. When Mark started recording his nail biting, his nail biting started to decrease as a result of the recording. What is this process called? ________________________

7. Recording the exact time of each onset and offset of the target behavior is called ______________________ recording.

8. Verlin's watch beeped every 10 minutes, and he recorded whether his son was playing appropriately at the time the watch beeped. This is an example of ____________________ recording.

9. Clayton's watch beeped every 10 minutes, and he recorded whether he had picked his nose at any time during the 10 minutes since the last beep. This is an example of ____________________ recording.

10. Linda recorded the number of math problems her students completed in a 20-minute period of time. This is an example of ____________________ recording.

CHAPTER 2 *Quiz 3* Name:

1. Janice recorded the number of times that she checked her e-mail each day. This is an example of ________________ recording.
2. Janice recorded the number of minutes she spent reading her e-mail each day. This is an example of ________________ recording.
3. A respiratory therapist used an instrument to measure the force of a patient's exhale. This is an example of ________________ recording.
4. Mr. Sims recorded how long it took his swimmers to dive in once the starting gun sounded. This is an example of ________________ recording.
5. Once every 15 minutes, Ms. Snorkle observed her students and recorded whether anyone was talking at that moment. This is an example of ________________ recording.
6. Chester was conducting a study on motor tics in children with Tourette's Syndrome. He recorded whether a child engaged in a motor tic in each consecutive 10-second time period throughout the observation period. This is an example of ________________ recording.
7. Maria used a machine to count the number of apples her workers picked each day from the orchard. This is an example of ________________ recording.
8. What will likely happen to a target behavior once you start recording the behavior?

   ____

9. Lacey observed parent–child interaction in a research project and recorded the exact time of onset and offset of specific parent and child behaviors. This is an example of

   ________________ recording.
10. Which type of assessment is usually more accurate, direct assessment or indirect assessment?

    ____

THREE

Graphing Behavior and Measuring Change

As we saw in Chapter 2, people who use behavior modification define their target behavior carefully and directly observe and record the behavior. In this way, they can document whether the behavior has indeed changed when a behavior modification procedure is implemented. The primary tool used to document behavior change is the graph.

A **graph** is a visual representation of the occurrence of a behavior over time. After instances of the target behavior are recorded (on a data sheet or otherwise), the information is transferred to a graph. A graph is an efficient way to view the occurrence of the behavior because it shows the results of recording during many observation periods.

- What are the six essential components of a behavior modification graph?
- How do you graph behavioral data?
- What different dimensions of behavior can you show on a graph?
- What is a functional relationship, and how do you demonstrate a functional relationship in behavior modification?
- What different research designs can you use in behavior modification research?

Behavior analysts use graphs to identify the level of behavior before treatment and after treatment begins. In this way, they can document changes in the behavior during treatment and make decisions about the continued use of the treatment. The graph makes it easier to compare the levels of the behavior before, during, and after treatment because the levels are presented visually for comparison. In Figure 3-1, for example, it is easy to see that the frequency of the behavior is much lower during treatment (competing response) than before treatment (baseline). This particular graph is from a student's self-management project. The student's target behavior involved biting the insides of her mouth when she studied. She recorded the behavior on a data sheet each time it occurred. After 10 days of recording the behavior without any treatment (baseline), she implemented a behavior modification plan in which she used a competing response (a behavior that is incompatible with mouth-biting and interrupts each occurrence of mouth-biting) to help her control the mouth-biting behavior. After implementing this competing response procedure, she continued to record the behavior for 20 more days. She then recorded the behavior four more times, after 1, 5, 10, and 20 weeks. The long period of time after treatment has been implemented is called the follow-up period. From this graph, we can conclude that the mouth-biting behavior (as recorded by the

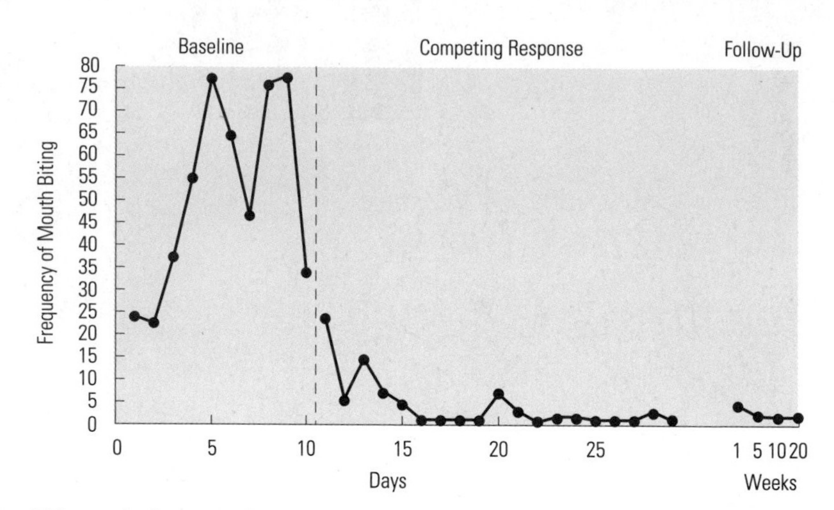

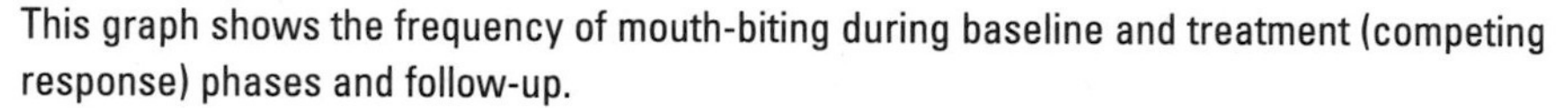

FIGURE 3-1 This graph shows the frequency of mouth-biting during baseline and treatment (competing response) phases and follow-up.

student) decreased substantially while the student implemented the treatment. We can also see that the behavior continued to occur at a low level up to 20 weeks after treatment was implemented.

Components of a Graph

In the typical behavior modification graph, time and behavior are the two variables illustrated. Each data point on a graph gives you two pieces of information: It tells you when the behavior was recorded (time) and the level of the behavior at that time. Time is indicated on the horizontal axis (also called the *x*-axis or the **abscissa**) and the level of the behavior is indicated on the vertical axis (also called the *y*-axis or the **ordinate**). In Figure 3-1, the frequency of mouth-biting is indicated on the vertical axis, and days and weeks are indicated on the horizontal axis. By looking at this graph, you can determine the frequency of mouth-biting on any particular day, before or after treatment was implemented. Because follow-up is reported, you can also see the frequency of the behavior at intervals of up to 20 weeks.

Six components are necessary for a graph to be complete.

- *The* y*-axis and the* x*-axis.* The vertical axis (*y*-axis) and the horizontal axis (*x*-axis) meet at the bottom left of the page. On most graphs, the *x*-axis is longer than the *y*-axis; it is usually one to two times as long (Figure 3-2).
- *The labels for the* y*-axis and the* x*-axis.* The *y*-axis label usually tells you the behavior and the dimension of the behavior that is recorded. The *x*-axis label usually tells you the unit of time during which the behavior is recorded. In Figure 3-3, the *y*-axis label is "Hours of Studying" and the *x*-axis label is "Days." Thus, you know that the hours of studying will be recorded each day for this particular person.

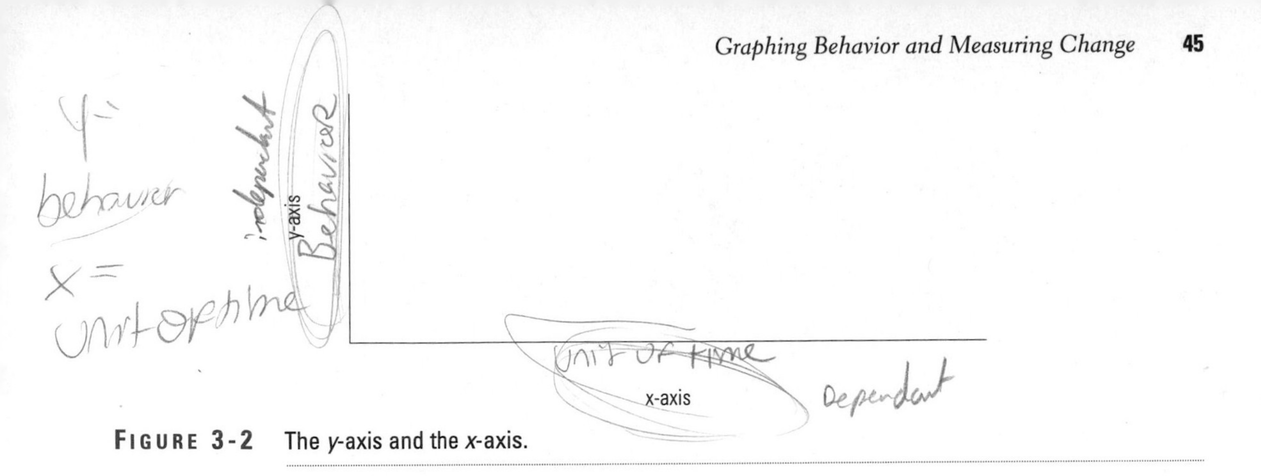

FIGURE 3-2 The *y*-axis and the *x*-axis.

FIGURE 3-3 Labels for the *y*-axis and the *x*-axis.

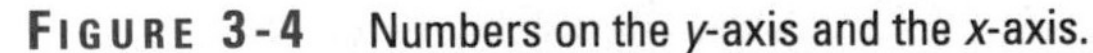

FIGURE 3-4 Numbers on the *y*-axis and the *x*-axis.

■ *The numbers on the* y*-axis and the* x*-axis.* On the *y*-axis, the numbers indicate the units of measurement of the behavior; on the *x*-axis the numbers indicate the units of measurement of time. There should be a hash-mark on the *y*-axis and the *x*-axis to correspond to each of the numbers. In Figure 3-4, the numbers on the *y*-axis indicate

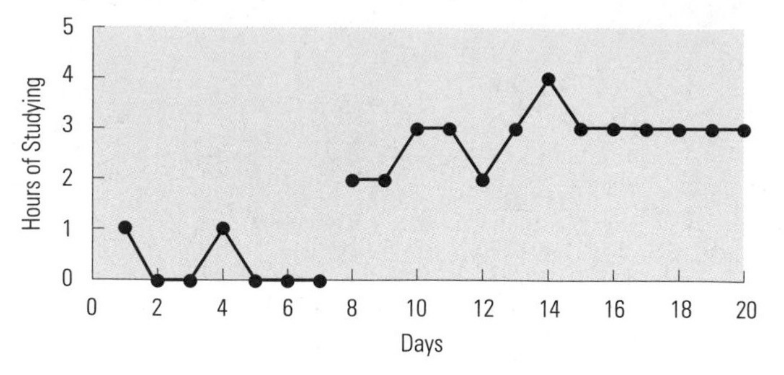

FIGURE 3-5 Data points plotted on a graph.

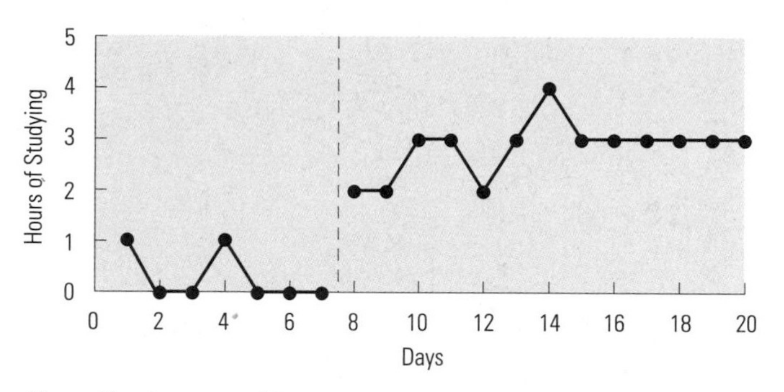

FIGURE 3-6 Phase lines on a graph.

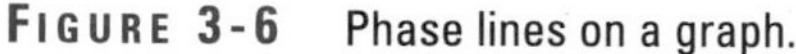

the number of hours the studying behavior occurred and the numbers on the *x*-axis indicate the days on which studying was measured.

- *Data points.* The data points must be plotted correctly to indicate the level of behavior that occurred at each particular time period. The information on the level of behavior and the time periods is taken from the data sheet or other behavior-recording instrument. Each data point is connected to the adjacent data points by a line (Figure 3-5).
- *Phase lines.* A phase line is a vertical line on a graph that indicates a change in treatment. The change can be from a no-treatment phase to a treatment phase, from a treatment phase to a no-treatment phase, or from one treatment phase to another treatment phase. A phase is a period of time in which the same treatment (or no treatment) is in effect. In Figure 3-6, the phase line separates baseline (no-treatment) and treatment phases. Data points are not connected across phase lines. This allows you to see differences in the level of the behavior in different phases more easily.
- *Phase labels.* Each phase in a graph must be labeled. The phase label appears at the top of the graph above the particular phase (Figure 3-7). Most behavior modification graphs have at least two phases that are labeled: the no-treatment phase and the treatment phase. "**Baseline**" is the label most often given to the no-treatment

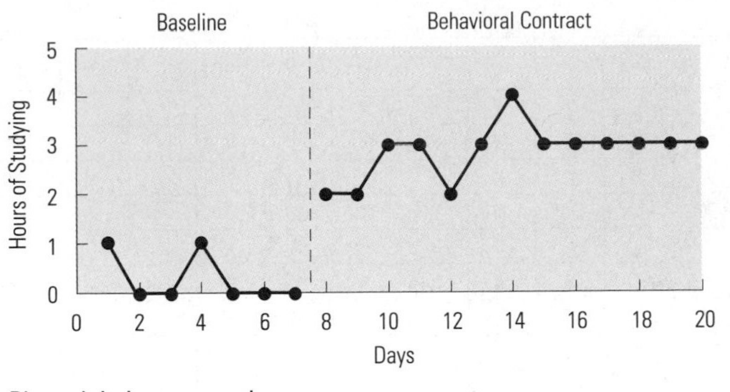

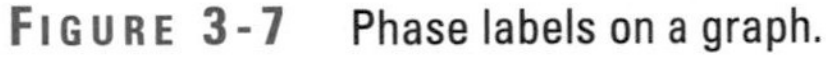
FIGURE 3-7 Phase labels on a graph.

phase. The label for the treatment phase should identify the particular treatment being used. In Figure 3-7 the two phase labels are "Baseline" and "Behavioral Contract." The behavioral contract is the particular treatment the student is using to increase studying. Some graphs have more than one treatment phase or more than one baseline phase.

GRAPHING BEHAVIORAL DATA

As you recall from Chapter 2, behavioral data are collected through direct observation and recording of the behavior on a data sheet or other instrument. Once the behavior has been recorded on the data sheet, it can be transferred to a graph. For example, Figure 3-8a is a frequency data sheet that shows 2 weeks of behavior recording, and Figure 3-8b is a graph of the behavioral data from the data sheet. Notice that days 1–14 on the data sheet correspond to the 14 days on the graph. Also notice that the frequency of the behavior listed on the data sheet for each day corresponds to the frequency recorded on the graph for that day. As you look at the graph, you can immediately determine that the frequency of the behavior is much lower during treatment than during baseline. You have to look more closely at the data sheet to be able to detect the difference between baseline and treatment. Finally, notice that all six essential components of a graph are included in this graph.

Consider a second example. A completed duration data sheet is shown in Figure 3-9a, and Figure 3-9b is a table that summarizes the daily duration of the behavior recorded on the data sheet. Notice that the duration of the behavior listed in the summary table for each of the 20 days corresponds to the duration that was recorded each day on the data sheet.

Below the data summary table (Figure 3-9b) is a graph that is only partially completed (Figure 3-9c). Using the information provided in the data summary table, complete this graph. Be sure that the completed graph includes all six components that were discussed earlier.

(a)

Days	Frequency 1	2	3	4	5	6	7	8	9	10	11	12	Daily Total
1	X	X	X	X	X	X	X	X					8
2	X	X	X	X	X	X	X	X					8
3	X	X	X	X	X	X	X						7
4	X	X	X	X	X	X	X						7
5	X	X	X	X	X	X	X	X	X				9
6*	X	X	X	X	X	X	X	X					8
7	X	X	X	X	X								5
8	X	X	X	X	X								5
9	X	X	X	X									4
10	X	X	X	X									4
11	X	X	X										3
12	X	X	X										3
13	X	X											2
14	X	X											2

*Day 6 was the last day of baseline and day 7 was the first day of treatment.

(b)

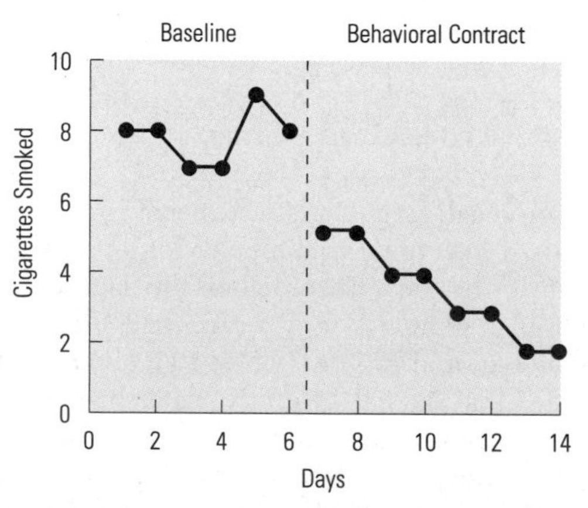

FIGURE 3-8 A completed frequency data sheet is shown in (a); the number of cigarettes smoked each day is recorded on the sheet. The graph of the behavioral data from the data sheet (b) is also shown. The treatment involved a behavioral contract in which the client agreed to smoke one fewer cigarette per day every second day. Behavioral contracts are described in Chapter 23.

To complete Figure 3-9c, you must add four components. First, you should add the data points for days 8–20 and connect them. Second, include the phase line between days 7 and 8. Data points on days 7 and 8 should not be connected across the phase line. Third, add the phase label "Behavioral Contract," to the right of the phase line. Fourth, add the label "Days" to the *x*-axis. When these four components are added, the graph includes all six essential components (Figure 3-10).

(a)

Days	Onset	Offset	Onset	Offset	Onset	Offset	Daily Duration
1							0
2	**7:00**	**7:15**					15
3							0
4							0
5	**7:10**	**7:25**					15
6							0
7*							0
8	**7:00**	**7:15**					15
9	**7:30**	**8:00**					30
10	**7:30**	**8:00**					30
11	**6:30**	**6:45**					15
12	**6:45**	**7:15**					30
13							0
14	**7:00**	**7:30**					30
15	**6:30**	**6:45**	**7:00**	**7:30**			45
16	**6:45**	**7:15**					30
17	**6:30**	**7:15**					45
18	**7:00**	**7:30**	**7:45**	**8:00**			45
19							0
20	**6:45**	**7:15**	**7:30**	**8:00**			60

*Baseline ended on day 7. On day 8, the subject implemented treatment involving a behavioral contract.

(b)

Days	1	2	3	4	5	6	7	8	9	10	11	12	13	14	15	16	17	18	19	20
Duration (minutes)	0	15	0	0	15	0	0	15	30	30	15	30	0	30	45	30	45	45	0	60

(c)

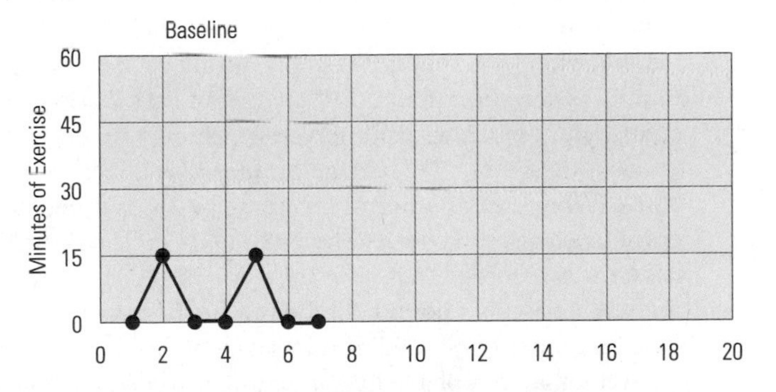

FIGURE 3-9 A completed frequency data sheet is shown in (a); the sheet records the duration of exercise each day. The completed data summary table (b) is also shown. The incomplete graph (c) is for the student to complete using the behavioral data in (b).

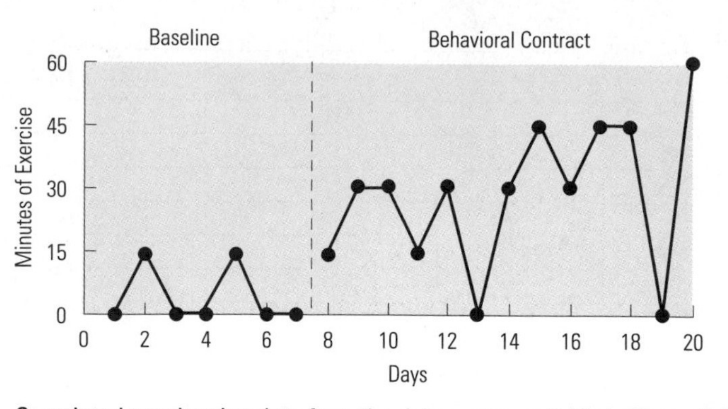

FIGURE 3-10 Completed graph using data from the data summary table in Figure 3-9b.

GRAPHING DIFFERENT DIMENSIONS OF BEHAVIOR

Figures 3-8 and 3-10 illustrate graphs of frequency data and duration data, respectively. Because other dimensions of behavior data also exist, other types of graphs are possible. Regardless of the dimension of behavior that is being graphed, however, the same six components of a graph must be present. What will change with different dimensions of behavior are the *y*-axis label and the numbering on the *y*-axis. For example, if you are recording the percentage of math problems a student completes correctly during each math class, you would label the *y*-axis "Percentage of Correct Math Problems" and number the *y*-axis from 0 to 100%. As you can see, the *y*-axis label identifies the behavior (correct math problems) and the dimension (percentage) of the behavior that is recorded.

Consider another example. A researcher is studying Tourette disorder, a neurological disorder in which certain muscles in the body twitch or jerk involuntarily. (These are called motor tics.) The researcher uses an interval recording system and records whether a motor tic occurs during each consecutive 10-second interval in 30-minute observation periods. At the end of each observation period, the researcher calculates the percentage of intervals in which a tic occurred. The researcher labels the *y*-axis of the graph "Percentage of Intervals of Tics" and numbers the *y*-axis from 0 to 100%. Whenever an interval recording system is used, the *y*-axis is labeled "Percentage of Intervals of (Behavior)." The *x*-axis label indicates the time periods in which the behavior was recorded (e.g., "Sessions" or "Days"). The *x*-axis is then numbered accordingly. A session is a period of time in which a target behavior is observed and recorded. Once treatment is started, it is implemented during the session also.

Other aspects of a behavior may be recorded and graphed, such as intensity or outcome. In each case, the *y*-axis label should clearly reflect the behavior and the dimension or aspect of the behavior that is recorded. For example, as a measure of how intense or serious a child's tantrums are, you might use the label "Tantrum Intensity Rating" and put the numbers of the rating scale on the *y*-axis. For a measure of loudness of speech, the *y*-axis label might be "Decibels of Speech," with decibel levels numbered on the *y*-axis. To graph product recording data, you would label the *y*-axis to indicate the unit of measurement and the behavior. For example, "Number of

Brakes Assembled" is a *y*-axis label that indicates the work output of a person who puts together bicycle brakes.

RESEARCH DESIGNS

When people conduct research in behavior modification, they use research designs that include more complex types of graphs. The purpose of a research design is to determine whether the treatment (independent variable) was responsible for the observed change in the target behavior (dependent variable) and to rule out the possibility that extraneous variables caused the behavior to change. In research an *independent variable* is what the researcher manipulates to produce a change in the target behavior. The target behavior is called the *dependent variable.* An extraneous variable, also called a confounding variable, is any event that the researcher did not plan that may have affected the behavior. For a person with a problem, it may be enough to know that the behavior changed for the better after using behavior modification procedures. However, a researcher also wants to demonstrate that the behavior modification procedure is what caused the behavior to change.

When a researcher shows that a behavior modification procedure causes a target behavior to change, the researcher is demonstrating a **functional relationship** between the procedure and the target behavior. In other words, the researcher demonstrates that the behavior changes as a function of the procedure. A functional relationship is established if a target behavior changes when an independent variable is manipulated (a procedure is implemented), while all other variables are held constant, and the process is replicated or repeated one or more times and the behavior changes each time. A behavior modification researcher uses a research design to demonstrate a functional relationship. A research design involves both treatment implementation and replication. If the behavior changes each time the procedure is implemented and only when the procedure is implemented, a functional relationship is demonstrated. In this case, we would say that the researcher has demonstrated experimental control over the target behavior. It is unlikely that an extraneous variable caused the behavior change if it changed only when the treatment was implemented. This section reviews research designs used in behavior modification (for further information on behavior modification research designs see Bailey, 1977; Barlow & Hersen, 1984; Hayes, Barlow, & Nelson-Gray, 1999; Poling & Grossett, 1986).

A-B Design

The simplest type of design used in behavior modification has just two phases: baseline and treatment. This is called an **A-B design,** where A = baseline and B = treatment. A-B designs are illustrated in Figures 3-1, 3-7, 3-8b, and 3-10. By means of an A-B design, we can compare baseline and treatment to determine whether the behavior changed in the expected way after treatment. However, the A-B design does not demonstrate a functional relationship because treatment is not implemented a second time. Therefore, the A-B design is not a true research design; it does not rule out the possibility that an extraneous variable was responsible for the behavior change. For example, although the mouth-biting behavior decreased when the competing response treatment was implemented in Figure 3-1, it is possible that some other event (extraneous variable) occurred at the same time as treatment was implemented. In that case, the decrease in mouth-biting may have resulted from the other event or a combination of treatment and the other event. For example, the person may have seen a TV show about controlling nervous habits and learned from that how to control her mouth-biting. Because the A-B design does not rule out other causes, it is rarely used by behavior modification researchers. It is most often used in applied, nonresearch situations, in which people are more interested in demonstrating that behavior change has occurred than in proving that the behavior modification procedure caused the behavior change. You probably would use an A-B graph in a self-management project to show whether your behavior changed after you implemented a behavior modification procedure.

A-B-A-B Reversal Design

The **A-B-A-B reversal design** is an extension of the simple A-B design (where A = baseline and B = treatment). In the A-B-A-B design, baseline and treatment phases are implemented twice. It is called a reversal design because after the first treatment phase, the researcher removes the treatment and reverses back to baseline. This second baseline is followed by replication of the treatment. Figure 3-11 illustrates an A-B-A-B design.

The A-B-A-B graph in Figure 3-11 shows the effect of a teacher's demands on the aggressive behavior of an adolescent with mental retardation named Bob. Carr and his colleagues (Carr, Newsom, & Binkoff, 1980) studied the influence of demands on Bob's aggressive behavior by alternating phases in which teachers made frequent demands with phases in which teachers made no demands. In Figure 3-11 you can see that the behavior changed three times. In the baseline phase ("Demands"), the aggressive behavior occurred frequently. When the treatment phase ("No Demands") was first implemented, the behavior decreased. When the second "Demands" phase occurred, the behavior returned to its level during the first "Demands" phase. Finally, when the "No Demands" phase was implemented a second time, the behavior decreased again. The fact that the behavior changed three times, and only when the phase changed, is evidence that the change in demands (rather than some extraneous variable) caused the behavior change. When the demands were turned on and off each time, the behavior changed accordingly. It is highly unlikely that an extraneous variable was turned on and off at exactly the same time as the demands, so it is highly unlikely that any other variable except the independent variable (change in demands) caused the behavior change.

A number of considerations must be taken into account in deciding whether to use the A-B-A-B research design. First, it may not be ethical to remove the treatment in the second baseline if the behavior is dangerous (for example, self-injurious behavior). Second, you must be fairly certain that the level of the behavior will reverse when treatment is withdrawn. If the behavior fails to change when the treatment is withdrawn, a functional relationship is not demonstrated. Another consideration is whether you can actually remove the treatment after it is implemented. For example, if the treatment is a teaching procedure and the subject learns a new behavior, you cannot take away the learning that took place. For a more detailed discussion of considerations

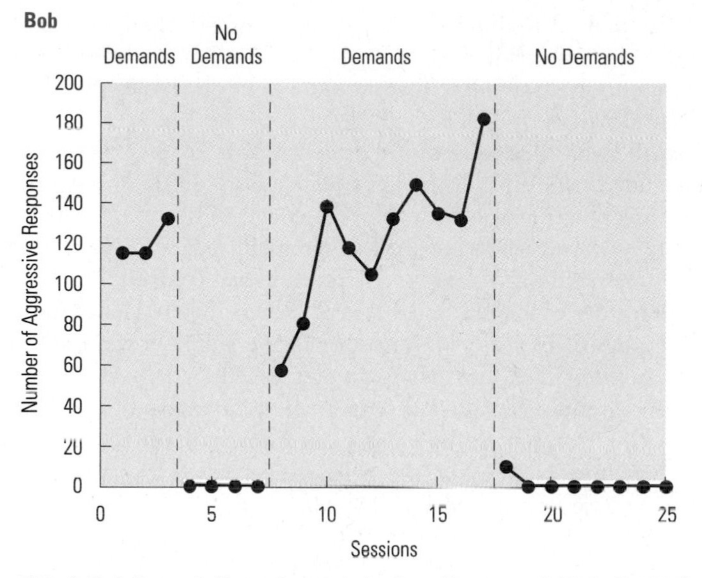

FIGURE 3-11 This A-B-A-B graph (from the study by Carr, Newsom, & Binkoff, 1980) shows the frequency of aggressive behaviors by an adolescent with mental retardation during baseline phases involving demands (A) and treatment phases involving no demands (B).

in the use of the A-B-A-B design, see Bailey (1977), Bailey and Burch (2002), and Barlow and Hersen (1984).

Multiple-Baseline Design

There are three types of multiple-baseline designs.

- In a **multiple-baseline-across-subjects design,** there is a baseline and a treatment phase for the same target behavior of two or more different subjects.
- In a **multiple-baseline-across-behaviors design,** there is a baseline and treatment phase for two or more different behaviors of the same subject.
- In a **multiple-baseline-across-settings design,** there is a baseline and treatment phase for two or more settings in which the same behavior of the same subject is measured.

Remember that the A-B-A-B design can also have two baseline phases and two treatment phases, but both baseline and treatment phases occur for the same behavior of the same subject in the same setting. With the multiple-baseline design, the different baseline and treatment phases occur for different subjects, or for different behaviors, or in different settings.

A multiple-baseline design may be used when you are interested in the same target behavior exhibited by multiple subjects, when you have targeted more than one behavior of the same subject, or when you are measuring a subject's behavior across two or more settings. A multiple-baseline design is useful when you cannot use an A-B-A-B design for the reasons listed previously. The multiple-baseline design and the appropriate time to use it are described in more detail by Bailey (1977), Bailey and Burch (2002), and Barlow and Hersen (1984).

Figure 3-12 illustrates the *multiple-baseline-across-subjects design*. This graph, from a study by DeVries, Burnette, and Redmon (1991), shows the effect of an intervention involving feedback on the percentage of time that emergency room nurses wore rubber gloves when they had contact with patients. Notice that there is a baseline and treatment phase for four different subjects (nurses). Figure 3-12 also illustrates a critical feature of the multiple-baseline design: The baselines for each subject are of different lengths. Treatment is implemented for subject 1 while subjects 2, 3, and 4 are still in baseline. Then treatment is implemented for subject 2 while subjects 3 and 4 are still in baseline. Next, treatment is implemented for subject 3 and, finally, for subject 4. When treatment is implemented at different times, we say that treatment is staggered over time. Notice that the behavior increased for each subject only after the treatment phase was started for that subject. When treatment was implemented for subject 1, the behavior increased, but the behavior did not increase at that time for subjects 2, 3, and 4, who were still in baseline and had not yet received treatment. The fact that the behavior changed for each subject only after treatment started is evidence that the treatment, rather than an extraneous variable, caused the behavior change. It is highly unlikely that an extraneous variable would happen to occur at exactly the same time that treatment started for each of the four subjects.

A *multiple-baseline-across-behaviors design* is illustrated in Figure 3-13. This graph, from a study by Franco, Christoff, Crimmins, and Kelly (1983), shows the effect of treatment (social skills training) on four different social behaviors of a shy adolescent: asking questions, acknowledging other people's comments, making eye contact, and showing affect (e.g., smiling). Notice in this graph that treatment is staggered across the four behaviors and that each of the behaviors changes only after treatment is implemented for that particular behavior. Because each of the four behaviors changed only after treatment was implemented for that behavior, the researchers demonstrated that treatment, rather than some extraneous variable, was responsible for the behavior change.

A graph used in a *multiple-baseline-across-settings design* would look like those in Figures 3-12 and 3-13. The difference is that in a multiple-baseline-across-settings graph, the same behavior of the same subject is being recorded in baseline and treatment phases in two or more different settings, and treatment is staggered across the settings.

Draw a graph of a multiple-baseline-across-settings design with hypothetical data. Be sure to include all six components of a complete graph. Assume that you have recorded the disruptive behavior of a student in two different classrooms using an interval recording system. Include baseline and treatment across two settings in the graph.

The graph in Figure 3-14, from a study by Dunlap, Kern-Dunlap, Clarke, and Robbins (1991), shows the percentage of intervals of disruptive behavior by a student during baseline and treatment (revised curriculum) in two settings, the morning and afternoon classrooms. It also shows follow-up, in which the researchers collected data

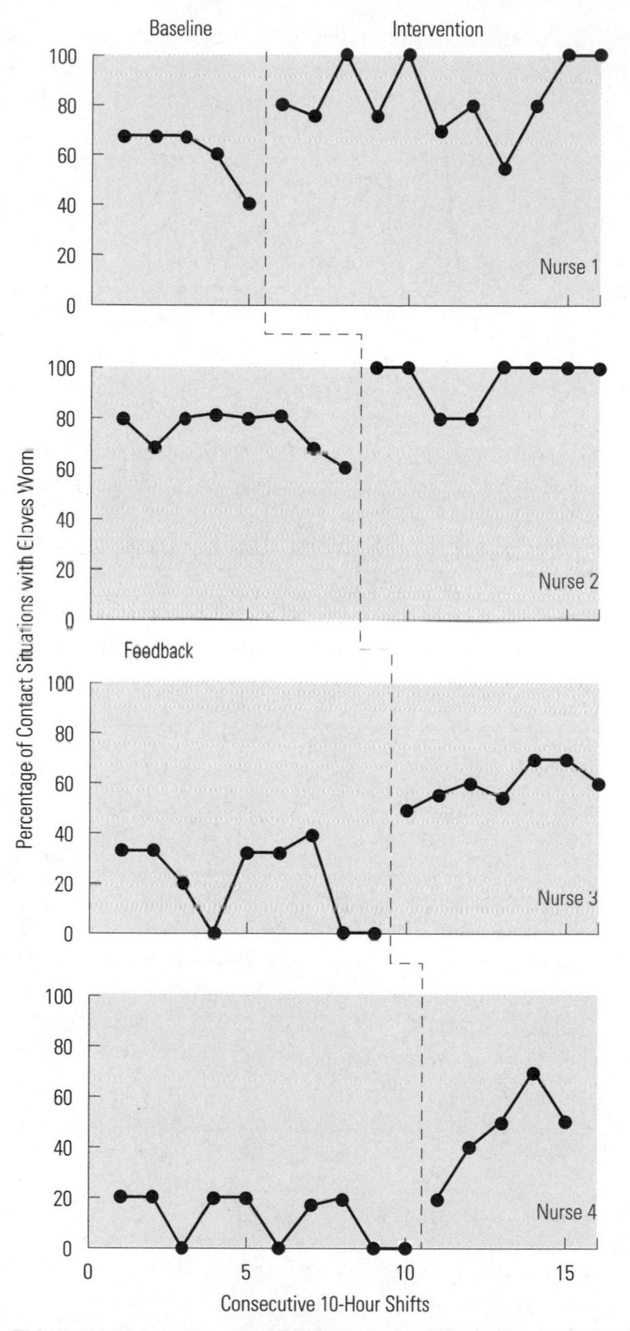

FIGURE 3-12 This multiple-baseline-across-subjects graph (from the study by DeVries, Burnette, & Redmon, 1991) shows the percentage of time that four emergency room nurses wear rubber gloves when they have contact with patients. The intervention, which involves feedback from their supervisor, is staggered over time and results in an increase in the behavior for each of the four nurses.

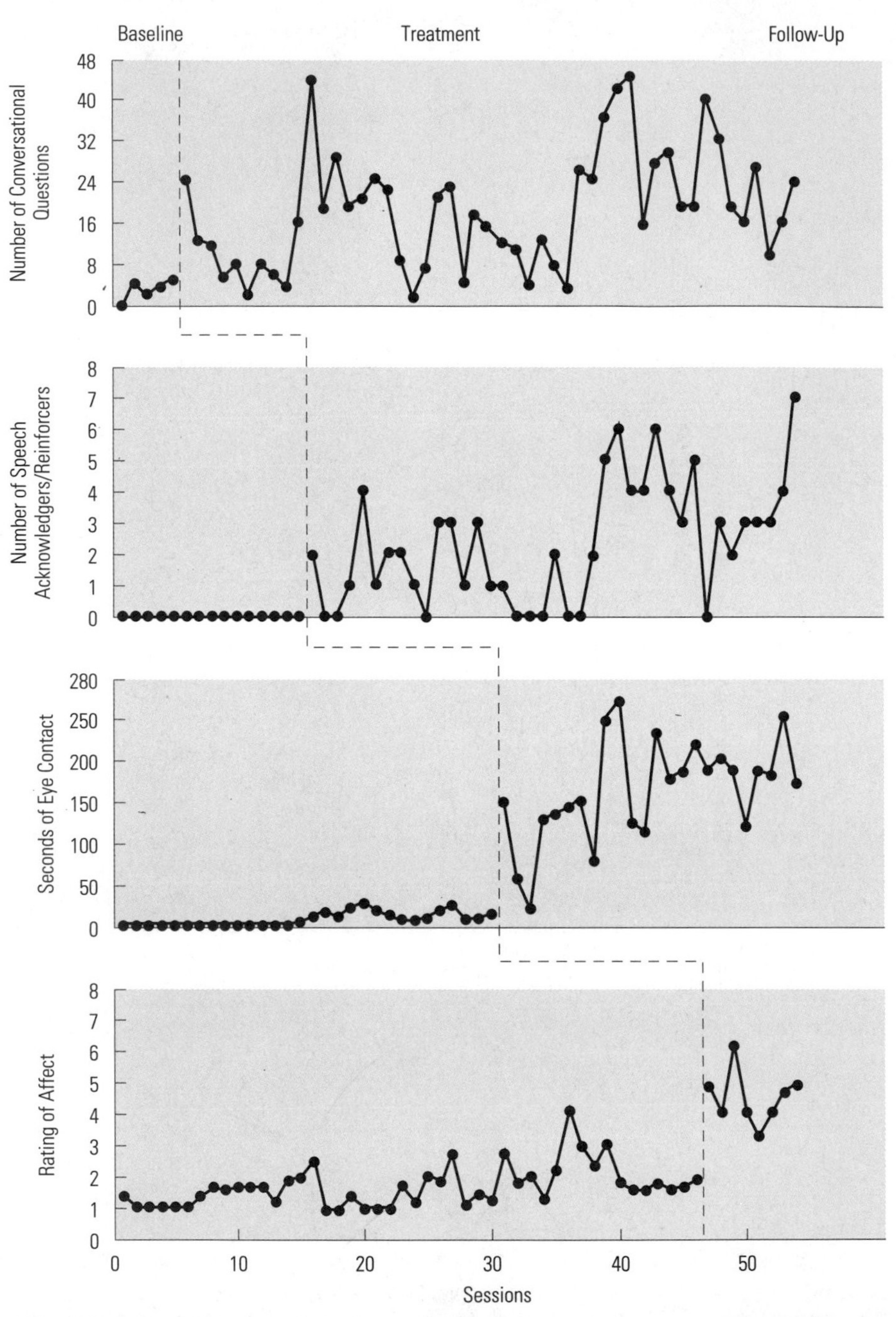

FIGURE 3-13 This multiple-baseline-across-behaviors graph (from the study by Franco, Christoff, Crimmins, & Kelly, 1983) shows four social behaviors exhibited by a shy adolescent. A social skills training intervention is applied to each of these four behaviors, and each behavior increases when the intervention is applied to it.

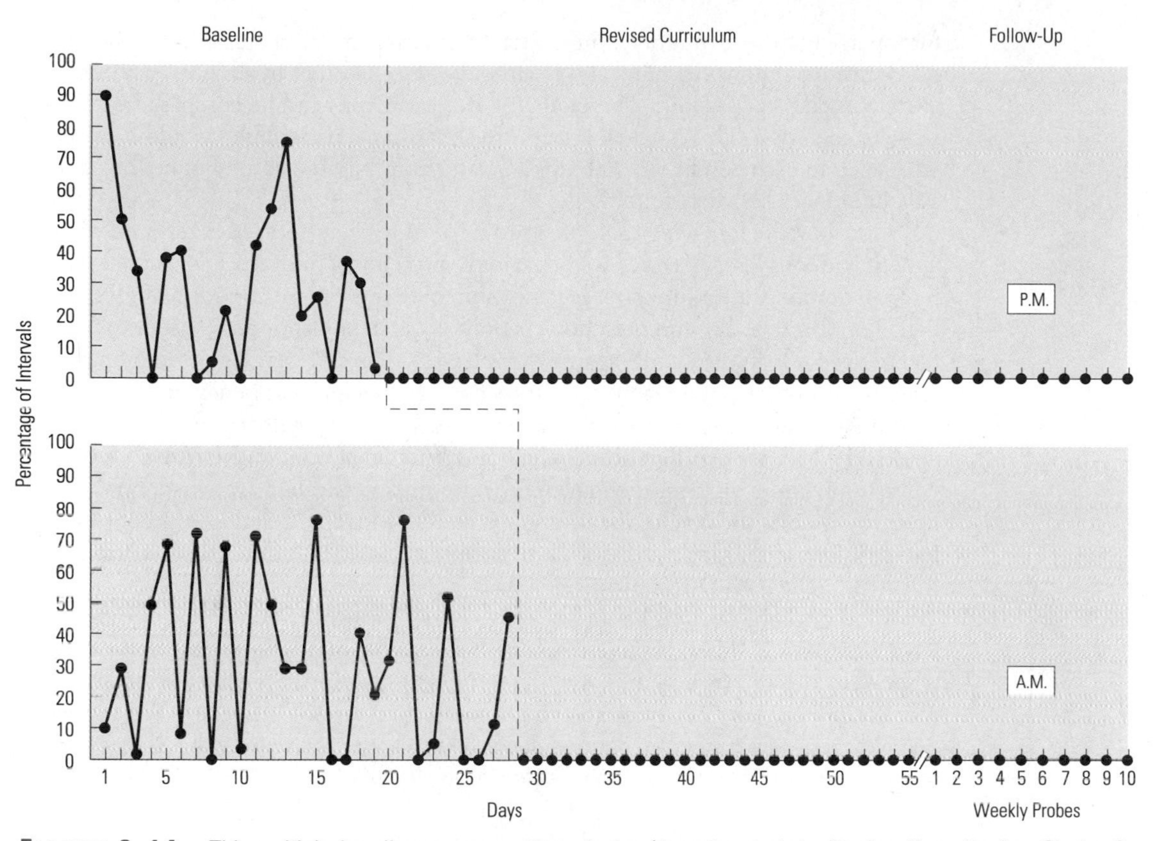

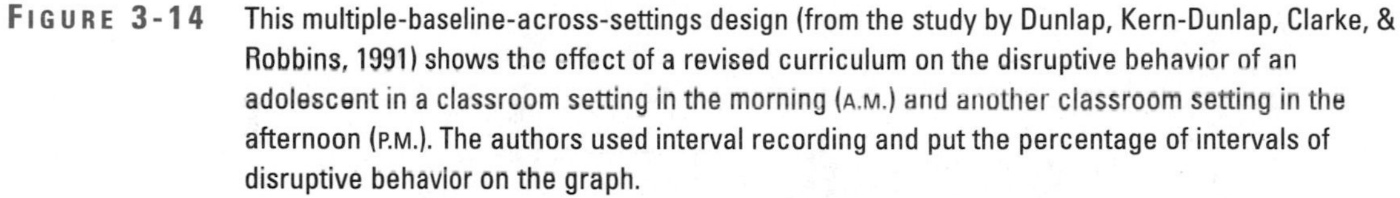
FIGURE 3-14 This multiple-baseline-across-settings design (from the study by Dunlap, Kern-Dunlap, Clarke, & Robbins, 1991) shows the effect of a revised curriculum on the disruptive behavior of an adolescent in a classroom setting in the morning (A.M.) and another classroom setting in the afternoon (P.M.). The authors used interval recording and put the percentage of intervals of disruptive behavior on the graph.

once a week for 10 weeks. Notice that treatment was implemented first in one setting and then in the other, and the student's disruptive behavior changed only after treatment was implemented in each setting. Your graph of a multiple-baseline-across-settings design would look like Figure 3-14.

Alternating-Treatments Design

The **alternating-treatments design** (ATD), also called a multielement design, differs from the research designs just reviewed in that baseline and treatment conditions (or two treatment conditions) are conducted in rapid succession and compared with each other. For example, treatment is implemented on one day, baseline the next day, treatment the next day, baseline the next day, and so on. In the A-B, A-B-A-B, or multiple-baseline designs, a treatment phase occurs after a baseline phase has been implemented for a period of time; in other words, baseline and treatment occur sequentially. In the ATD, two conditions (baseline and treatment or two different treatments) occur during alternating days or sessions. Therefore, the two conditions can be compared within the same time period. This is valuable because any extraneous variables would have a similar effect on both conditions and thus an extraneous variable could not be the cause of any differences between conditions.

Consider the following example of an ATD. A teacher wants to determine whether violent cartoons lead to aggressive behavior in preschool children. The teacher uses an ATD to demonstrate a functional relationship between violent cartoons and aggressive behavior. On one day, the preschoolers do not watch any cartoons (baseline) and the teacher records the students' aggressive behavior. The next day, the students watch a violent cartoon and the teacher again records their aggressive behavior. The teacher continues to alternate a day with no cartoons and a day with cartoons. After a few weeks, the teacher can determine whether a functional relationship exists. If there is consistently more aggressive behavior on cartoon days and less aggressive behavior on no-cartoon days, the teacher has demonstrated a functional relationship between violent cartoons and aggressive behavior in the preschoolers. An example of a graph from this hypothetical ATD is shown in Figure 3-15.

In this graph, the number of aggressive behaviors occurring per day is graphed on days when the children watched violent cartoons (odd-numbered days) and on days when they did not (even-numbered days). Notice that the aggressive behavior occurs more frequently on days when the children watched cartoons. Because the aggressive behavior is always higher on cartoon days, the researchers conclude that the aggressive behavior occurred as a function of watching violent cartoons.

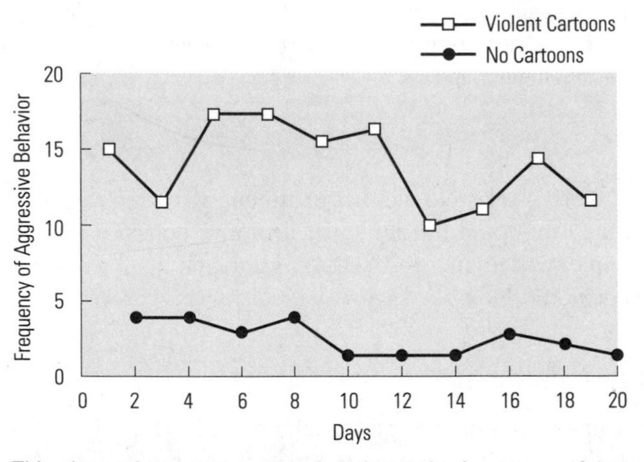

FIGURE 3-15 This alternating-treatments design shows the frequency of aggressive behavior on days when children watched violent cartoons compared to days when they did not watch cartoons. The level of the aggressive behavior is higher on days with violent cartoons than on days with no cartoons.

Changing-Criterion Design

A **changing-criterion design** typically includes a baseline and a treatment phase. What makes a changing-criterion design different from an A-B design is that within the treatment phase, sequential performance criteria are specified; that is, successive goal levels for the target behavior specify how much the target behavior should change during treatment. The effectiveness of treatment is determined by whether the subject's behavior changes to meet the changing performance criteria. In other words, does the subject's behavior change each time the goal level changes? A graph used in a changing-criterion design indicates each criterion level so that when the behavior is plotted on the graph, we can determine whether the level of the behavior matches the criterion level.

Consider the graph in Figure 3-16, from a study by Foxx and Rubinoff (1979). These researchers helped people reduce their excessive caffeine consumption through a positive reinforcement and response cost procedure. (These procedures are discussed in Chapters 15 and 17.) As you can see in the graph, they set four different criterion levels for caffeine consumption, each lower than the previous level. When subjects consumed less caffeine than the criterion level, they earned money. If they drank more, they lost money. This graph shows that treatment was successful: This subject's

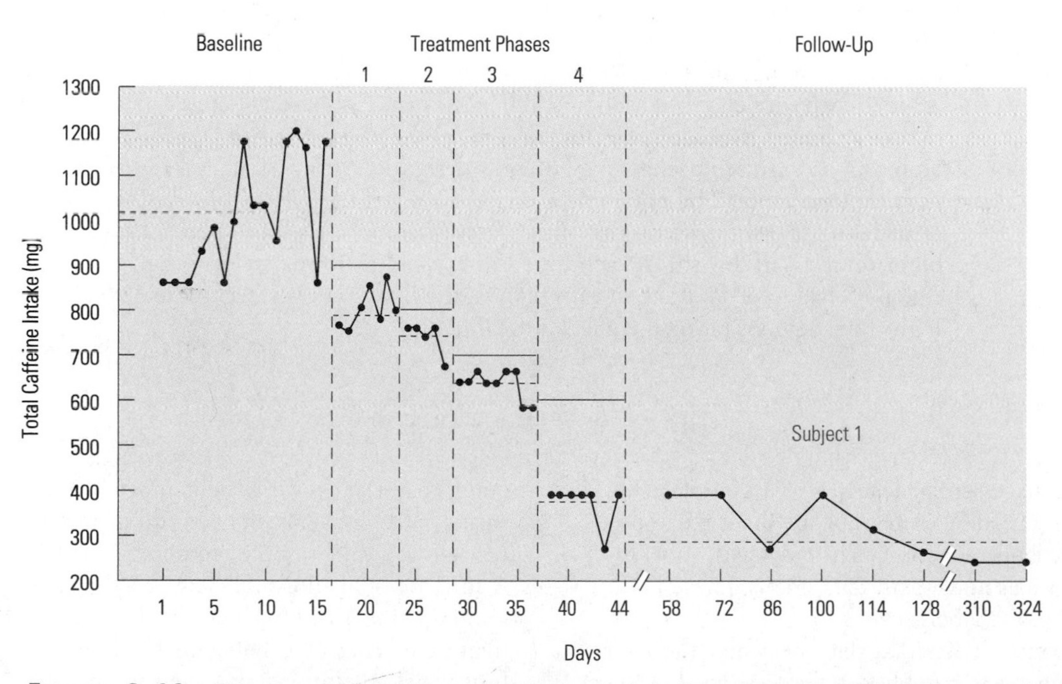

FIGURE 3-16 This changing-criterion graph is from a study by Foxx and Rubinoff (1979). They found that caffeine consumption decreased to a level below the criterion each time the criterion was lowered. The solid horizontal bars in treatment phases 1–4 are the criterion lines. The dashed lines show the mean level of the behavior in each phase.

Summary of Research Designs

A-B	One baseline and one treatment phase. Not a true research design.
A-B-A-B	Two (or more) baseline phases and two (or more) treatment phases for the same behavior of one subject. Also called a reversal design.
Multiple-baseline-across-behaviors	Baseline and treatment phases for two or more different behaviors of one subject. Treatment is staggered across behaviors.
Multiple-baseline-across-subjects	Baseline and treatment phases for the same behavior of two or more subjects. Treatment is staggered across subjects.
Multiple-baseline-across-settings	Baseline and treatment phases for the same behavior of the same subject in two or more settings. Treatment is staggered across settings.
Alternating-treatment design	Baseline and treatment sessions are alternated rapidly. Baseline and treatment sessions may occur on alternating days or may occur in different sessions on the same day.
Changing-criterion design	A baseline phase and treatment phase for one subject. In the treatment phase, there are progressive performance criteria or increasing goal levels of the behavior.

caffeine consumption level was always below each of the criterion levels. Because the subject's behavior changed each time the performance criterion changed, it is unlikely that an extraneous variable was responsible for the change in behavior. DeLuca and Holborn (1992) used a changing-criterion design in a study designed to help obese boys exercise more. The boys rode exercise bikes and received points for the amount of pedaling that they did on the bikes. They later exchanged the points for toys and other rewards. In this study, each time the exercise performance criterion was raised (the boys had to pedal more to earn points), the boys' exercise level increased accordingly, thus demonstrating the effect of treatment.

Chapter Summary

1. The six essential features of a complete behavior modification graph are the *y*-axis and *x*-axis, labels for the *y*-axis and *x*-axis, units for the *y*-axis and *x*-axis, data points, phase lines, and phase labels.
2. To graph behavioral data, you plot the data points on the graph to reflect the level of the behavior on the vertical axis (*y*-axis) and the unit of time on the horizontal axis (*x*-axis).
3. The different dimensions of behavior you can show on a graph include the frequency, duration, intensity, and latency of the behavior. A graph may also show the percentage of intervals of the behavior derived from interval recording or time sample recording.
4. A functional relationship between the treatment and the target behavior exists when the treatment causes the behavior to change. A functional relationship or experimental control is demonstrated when a target behavior changes after the implementation of treatment and the treatment procedure is repeated or replicated one or more times and the behavior changes each time.

5. The different research designs you can use in behavior modification research include the following:

The A-B design shows baseline and treatment for the behavior of one subject.

The A-B-A-B design shows two baseline and treatment phases repeated for the behavior of one subject.

A multiple-baseline design presents baseline and treatment phases for one of the following options: multiple behaviors of one subject, one behavior of multiple subjects, or one behavior of one subject across multiple settings. In each type of multiple-baseline design, treatment is staggered across behaviors, subjects, or settings.

The alternating-treatments design presents data from two experimental conditions that are rapidly alternated (baseline and treatment or two treatments).

Finally, in the changing-criterion design, a baseline phase is followed by a treatment phase in which sequential performance criteria are specified.

All research designs, except the A-B design, control for the influence of extraneous variables, so that the effectiveness of a treatment can be evaluated.

PRACTICE TEST

1. Why are graphs used in behavior modification to evaluate behavior change? (p. 43)
2. What two variables are illustrated in a behavior modification graph? (p. 44)
3. What is the *y*-axis? What is the *x*-axis? (p. 44)
4. What is labeled on the *y*-axis? On the *x*-axis? (p. 44)
5. What is a phase? (p. 46)
6. Why are data points not connected across phase lines? (p. 46)
7. Draw a hypothetical graph that illustrates the six essential components of a behavior modification graph. Label all six components on this hypothetical graph. (p. 47)
8. What will you label the *y*-axis of a graph based on interval recording? (p. 50)
9. What is an A-B design? What do *A* and *B* refer to? (p. 51)
10. What is an A-B-A-B reversal design? Draw a hypothetical A-B-A-B graph. Be sure all six components are included. (pp. 52–53)
11. What is a multiple-baseline design? Identify three types of multiple-baseline designs. Draw a hypothetical graph of a multiple-baseline-across-subjects design. Be sure to include all six essential components. (pp. 53–55)
12. What is an extraneous variable? How does an A-B-A-B design help you rule out extraneous variables as the cause of the behavior change? (pp. 51–52)
13. What does it mean to say that treatment is staggered in a multiple-baseline design? (p. 54)
14. What is an alternating-treatments design (ATD)? Draw a hypothetical graph of an ATD. Be sure to include all six essential components. (pp. 57–58)
15. How do you judge the effectiveness of treatment in an ATD? (p. 58)
16. Describe the changing-criterion design. Draw a hypothetical graph of a changing-criterion design. Include all six components. (p. 59)
17. How do you determine that treatment is effective in a changing-criterion design? (p. 59)
18. What is a functional relationship? How do you determine that a functional relationship exists between a target behavior and a treatment procedure? (p. 51)

APPLICATIONS

1. In the application exercise in Chapter 2, you developed a self-monitoring plan as the first step in your self-management program. Once you start to record your own target behavior, the next step is to develop a graph and plot your behavior on the graph each day. Some people prefer to use a computer to generate a graph, but all that is really necessary is a sheet of graph paper, a ruler, and a pencil. Using a sheet of graph paper, prepare the graph that you will use to plot the target behavior from your self-management project. As you develop your graph, be sure to observe the following rules.

   a. Label the *y*-axis and *x*-axis appropriately.
   b. Put the appropriate numbers on the *y*-axis and the *x*-axis.
   c. Ensure that the time period on the *x*-axis covers at least 3 or 4 months so that you can record the behavior for an extended period of time.
   d. Plot the behavior on your graph every day as you record the behavior.
   e. Continue the baseline period for at least a couple weeks so that any reactivity of the self-monitoring stabilizes.

2. The data summary table in Figure 3-17 shows the monthly total kilowatts of electricity used by a fraternity house. In the two baseline phases, no intervention was in place. In the two intervention phases, the fraternity president gave daily reminders to the fraternity brothers at breakfast to turn out lights and turn off appliances. Develop a graph from the data summary table to show the effects of daily reminders on the kilowatts of electricity used each month.

3. Winifred worked with two autistic children who engaged in self-injurious behavior (SIB) involving head-slapping. She recorded the frequency of the SIB during baseline for both children, Kale and Bud, and then implemented a treatment involving reinforcement of alternative behavior (see Chapter 15) and continued to collect data for a period of time. The frequency of SIB for Kale was 25, 22, 19, 19, 22, 22, and 23 in baseline and 12, 10, 5, 6, 5, 2, 1, 1, 1, 1, 0, 0, 1, 1, 0, 0, 0, and 0 during treatment. The frequency of SIB for Bud was 12, 12, 15, 14, 13, 12, 12, 13, 10, 12, 14, and 17 in baseline and 5, 3, 4, 2, 0, 2, 0, 0, 0, 2, 0, 0, and 0 during treatment. Draw the graph of the SIB data for Kale and Bud. What kind of research design did Winifred use when she provided treatment for the SIB?

	Baseline				Intervention				
Months	1	2	3	4	5	6	7	8	9
Kilowatts (rounded to nearest 100)	4100	3900	4100	4200	3100	3000	2900	3000	2900

	Baseline			Intervention			
Months	10	11	12	13	14	15	16
Kilowatts (rounded to nearest 100)	3800	3900	3800	2900	2900	2800	2900

FIGURE 3-17 Data summary table showing kilowatts of electricity used per month across two baseline and two intervention phases.

MISAPPLICATIONS

1. The Acme Widget Company was near bankruptcy. Ace Consultants were called in to help. They collected baseline data on employee productivity for 4 weeks and determined that the employees were assembling widgets only half as fast as they were able to. They implemented an incentive system, and employee productivity doubled. After 8 weeks of doubled productivity, the Acme Company was making a profit again. Ace Consultants decided to take away the incentive system and return to baseline for 4 weeks and then reimplement the incentive system (A-B-A-B research design) so that they could determine whether the incentive system caused the increase in productivity or whether some extraneous variable was responsible.

a. What is wrong with the use of an A-B-A-B research design in this case?
b. What would you do if you worked for Ace Consultants?

2. Alice was starting a self-management project to increase the amount of running she did each week. She planned to record her behavior for 2 or 3 weeks as a baseline before she implemented an intervention. She decided that she would keep a log of the distance that she ran every day and plot her running distance on a graph each week. She kept the log on her desk and wrote down the duration of her run immediately after she ran. She put her graph on the door to her room and at the end of each week, on Sunday night, she plotted the number of miles she had run for the last 7 days. What was Alice doing wrong?

3. Dr. Pete was investigating an intervention for improving social skills in socially anxious college students. He identified three important types of social behavior that he wanted to increase in his subjects: initiating conversations, answering questions, and smiling. He decided to use a multiple-baseline-across-behaviors design in his experiment. He would record all three behaviors in each subject in a baseline before intervention. He would then implement the intervention for all three behaviors at one time and continue to record the behaviors to see whether they increased after the intervention was implemented.

a. What mistake did Dr. Pete make in his multiple-baseline design?
b. What should he do differently?

CHAPTER 3 *Quiz 1*

Name:

1. A(n) ____________ is a visual representation of the occurrence of behavior over time.

2. In a graph, the __________ axis shows the level of behavior.

3. In a graph, the __________ axis shows the units of time.

4. In an A-B design, A = ____________ and B = ________________.

5. An A-B design does not demonstrate a functional relationship between the treatment (independent variable) and behavior (dependent variable) because ____.

6. In a research project, you conduct a baseline period for a week. Following the baseline you implement treatment for a week. After the treatment phase you return to the baseline phase and after a week in the second baseline, you conduct one more week of treatment.

   What research design is illustrated in this description? ________________________

7. In a multiple-baseline-across-________________ research design, one treatment is implemented for the same behavior of one subject in two or more different settings.

8. In a(n) ____________________ research design, there is a baseline phase and a treatment phase, and in the treatment phase, there are different criterion levels for the behavior.

9. In a multiple-baseline-across-________________ research design, one treatment is implemented for the same target behavior of two or more subjects.

10. In a multiple-baseline-across-________________ research design, one treatment is implemented for two or more behaviors of the same subject.

CHAPTER 3 *Quiz 2*

Name:

1. In a graph, what is represented on the *y* (vertical) axis?______________________________
2. In a graph, what is represented on the *x* (horizontal) axis? ____________________________
3. What two phases are represented in an A-B design? ______________________________

   and ______________________________.
4. When a researcher shows that a behavior modification procedure causes a target behavior to

   change, the researcher is demonstrating a(n) ______________________________ between the procedure and the target behavior.
5. A research design in which a baseline phase is followed by a treatment phase and then

   both baseline and treatment phases are repeated is called a(n) ______________________ design.
6. In a multiple-baseline-across-subjects design, when treatment is implemented at different points

   in time for the different subjects, we say that treatment is ______________________ over time.
7. In a(n) ______________________________ research design, baseline and treatment conditions (or two treatment conditions) are conducted in rapid succession and compared with each other.
8. In a multiple-baseline-across-behaviors research design, the same treatment is implemented

   for two or more ______________________________ of the same subject.
9. In a multiple-baseline-across-______________________ research design, one treatment is implemented for one behavior of one subject in two or more settings.
10. The ______________________ design is not a true research design because there is no replication.

CHAPTER 3 *Quiz 3* Name:

1. A graph is a visual representation of the occurrence of _______________ over time.

2. You are recording the number of cans of soda you drink each day. On your graph, the *x* (horizontal) axis is labeled _________________________and the *y* (vertical) axis is labeled _______________________________.

3. After recording the number of cans of soda you drink each day for 2 weeks, you implement a treatment for 2 weeks to decrease the number of cans you drink each day.

   What kind of design is illustrated in this example? __________________________

4. A behavior modification researcher uses a research design to demonstrate a(n) _______________________ between a treatment procedure and a target behavior.

5. An A-B design __________ (is/is not) a true research design.

6. In a(n) ________________________ research design, a baseline phase occurs and then treatment is implemented for a period of time. After treatment, the baseline phase occurs again for a period of time and then treatment is implemented again.

7. If it would be unsafe to remove treatment once it produces a change in behavior, then you should not use a(n) ________________________ research design.

8. You are recording a child's behavior of saying *please* and *thank you*. After a week of baseline, you use reinforcement to increase the behavior of saying *please*. After 2 weeks of baseline you then use reinforcement to increase the behavior of saying *thank you*. What research design is illustrated in this example? ________________________

9. You are recording a child's behavior of saying *please* and *thank you* in day care and at home. After a week of baseline, you use reinforcement to increase the behavior of saying *please* and *thank you* at day care. After 2 weeks of baseline you then use reinforcement to increase the behavior of saying *please* and *thank you* at home. What research design is illustrated in this example?

   ____

10. You are recording the behavior of saying *please* and *thank you* for three different children at school. After a week of baseline for Sally, you use reinforcement to increase the behavior. After 2 weeks of baseline for Pete, you use reinforcement to increase the behavior. After 3 weeks of baseline for Pat you use reinforcement to increase the behavior. What research design is illustrated in this example? ____________________

FOUR

Reinforcement

This chapter focuses on the basic behavioral principle of reinforcement. Scientific research has established a number of basic principles that explain the behavior of people and other animals. Reinforcement is one of the first basic principles that was systematically investigated by behavioral scientists, and it is a component of many applications of behavior modification described in this text. **Reinforcement** is the process in which a behavior is strengthened by the immediate **consequence** that reliably follows its occurrence. When a behavior is strengthened, it is more likely to occur again in the future.

- What is the principle of reinforcement?
- How is positive reinforcement different from negative reinforcement?
- How are unconditioned reinforcers different from conditioned reinforcers?
- What factors influence the effectiveness of reinforcement?
- What are intermittent schedules of reinforcement, and how do they affect the rate of behavior?

Perhaps the earliest demonstration of reinforcement was reported by Thorndike in 1911. Thorndike placed a hungry cat in a cage and put food outside of the cage where the cat could see it. Thorndike rigged the cage so that a door would open if the cat hit a lever with its paw. The cat was clawing and biting the bars of the cage, reaching its paws through the openings between the bars, and trying to squeeze through the opening. Eventually, the cat accidentally hit the lever, the door opened, and the cat got out of the cage and ate the food. Each time Thorndike put the hungry cat inside the cage it took less time for the cat to hit the lever that opened the door. Eventually the cat hit the lever with its paw as soon as Thorndike put it in the cage (Thorndike, 1911). Thorndike called this phenomenon the law of effect.

In this example, when the hungry cat was put back in the cage (Figure 4-1), the cat was more likely to hit the lever because this behavior had resulted in an immediate conse-

Reinforcement
Response
Consequence
Outcome: Behavior is more likely to occur in the future.

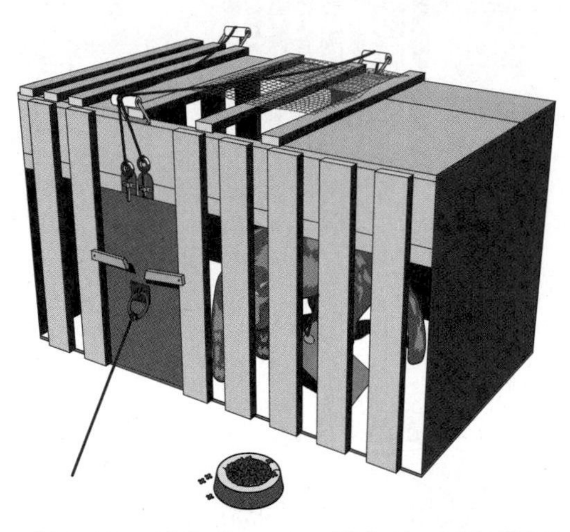

FIGURE 4-1 A hungry cat is in the cage with food outside. When the cat hits the lever, the cage door opens and the cat eats the food. As a result, the cat is more likely to hit the lever when it is put into the cage.

Response → Consequence

The cat hits the lever with a paw and immediately the door opens and food is available.

Outcome: The cat is more likely to hit the lever when it is put in the cage in the future.

quence: escaping the cage and getting food. Getting to the food was the consequence that reinforced (strengthened) the cat's behavior of hitting the lever with a paw.

Starting in the 1930s, B. F. Skinner conducted numerous studies on the principle of reinforcement in laboratory animals such as rats and pigeons (Skinner, 1938, 1956). For example, in experiments with rats, Skinner placed the animal in an experimental chamber and delivered a pellet of food each time the rat pressed a lever located on one of the walls of the chamber. At first the rat explored the box by moving around, sniffing, climbing up on its hind legs, and so on. When it happened to press the lever with one of its paws, the device automatically delivered a pellet of food to an opening in the wall. Each time the hungry rat pressed the lever, it received a pellet of food. Thus, the rat was more likely to press the lever each time it was placed in the chamber. This one behavior, pressing the lever, was strengthened because when it occurred, it was immediately followed by food. The behavior of pressing the lever increased in frequency relative to all the other behaviors the rat had exhibited when put in the chamber.

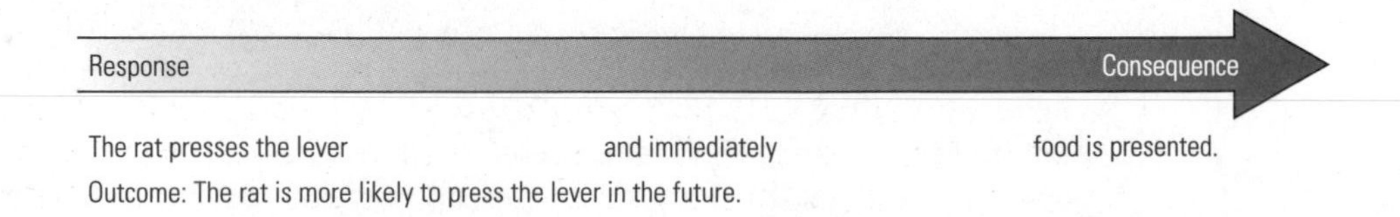
Response
Consequence
The rat presses the lever
and immediately
food is presented.
Outcome: The rat is more likely to press the lever in the future.

DEFINING REINFORCEMENT

The examples of Thorndike's cat and Skinner's rat illustrate very clearly the principle of reinforcement. When a behavior results in a favorable outcome (one that contributes to the well-being or survival of the animal), that behavior is more likely to be repeated in the future in similar circumstances. Although the principle of reinforcement was first systematically illustrated in laboratory animals, reinforcement is a natural process that influences human behavior also. In Science and Human Behavior (1953a), Skinner discussed the role of reinforcement in determining a wide variety of human behaviors. As stated by Sulzer-Azaroff and Mayer (1991), reinforcement may occur naturally, as a result of our day-to-day interactions with our social and physical environment, or may be planned as part of a behavior modification program used to change a person's behavior. Table 4-1 provides examples of reinforcement.

As you can see from each of the examples in Table 4-1, reinforcement is defined as follows:

1. The occurrence of a particular behavior
2. is followed by an immediate consequence
3. that results in the strengthening of the behavior. (The person is more likely to engage in the behavior again in the future.)

A behavior that is strengthened through the process of reinforcement is called an operant behavior. An **operant behavior** acts on the environment to produce a consequence and in turn is controlled by, or occurs again in the future as a result of, its immediate consequence. The consequence that strengthens an operant behavior is called a **reinforcer**.

In the first example in Table 4-1, the child cried at night when her parents put her to bed. The child's crying was an operant behavior. The reinforcer for her crying was the parents' attention. Because crying at night resulted in this immediate consequence (reinforcer), the child's crying was strengthened: She was more likely to cry at night in the future.

For each of the other examples in Table 4-1, identify the operant behavior and the reinforcer. The answers are available in Appendix A at the end of the chapter.

Identify four operant behaviors from your own life, and identify the reinforcers for these operant behaviors.

The graph in Figure 4-2 presents hypothetical data showing the effect of reinforcement on behavior. Notice that the frequency of the behavior is low during baseline and higher during the reinforcement phase. As illustrated in Figure 4-2, when the occurrence of a behavior is reinforced, it increases in frequency over time. Other dimensions of a behavior (duration, intensity) may also increase as a function of reinforcement.

The graph in Figure 4-3 shows the effect of reinforcement on the duration of a behavior. This graph, from a study by Liberman, Teigen, Patterson, and Baker (1973), shows the duration of rational (nondelusional) talk by patients with schizophrenia who were being treated in an institution. Liberman and colleagues measured the duration of rational talk during conversations with nurses. Liberman wanted to reinforce rational talk so that it would increase and, thus, the schizophrenic patients would appear more normal. In this study, rational talk was reinforced by the nurses with attention

TABLE 4-1 **EXAMPLES FOR SELF-ASSESSMENT (REINFORCEMENT)**

1. A child cries at night after being put to bed and her parents come to her room to comfort her and calm her down. As a result, the child now cries more often at bedtime.
2. A woman waiting for a bus opens up her umbrella when it rains. The umbrella keeps the rain from hitting her. Now she always opens up her umbrella when it rains.
3. When a chef cooks well-done steaks, it creates smoke. He turns on the exhaust fan, and the smoke is sucked out of the kitchen. He is now more likely to turn on the fan when he cooks well-done steaks.
4. A college student is answering study guide questions for her behavior modification class. When she can't figure out an answer to a question, she asks her friend who already took the class. Her friend tells her the correct answer. As a result, she is more likely to ask her friend for answers to questions she doesn't know.
5. A teacher smiles at Johnny and praises him when he stays in his seat and pays attention in the classroom. As a result, Johnny is more likely to sit in his seat and pay attention (that is, to look at his teacher when she teaches).
6. When Patricia is watching TV and the picture gets fuzzy, she puts a piece of tin foil on the antenna and the picture becomes clearer. Now she is more likely to put tin foil on the antenna when the picture is fuzzy.
7. Instead of paying workers by the hour, a bicycle manufacturing company begins paying piece rate, in which workers on the assembly line earn a certain amount of money for each bicycle they assemble. As a result, the workers assemble more bicycles each day and earn more money.
8. A 2-year-old child has a tantrum (crying and screaming) in the grocery store when he demands candy and his mother says no. His mother eventually buys him the candy and he stops his tantrum. As a result, the mother is more likely to give him candy when he demands it and has a tantrum. In addition, the child is more likely to have a tantrum in the store because it results in candy from his mother.

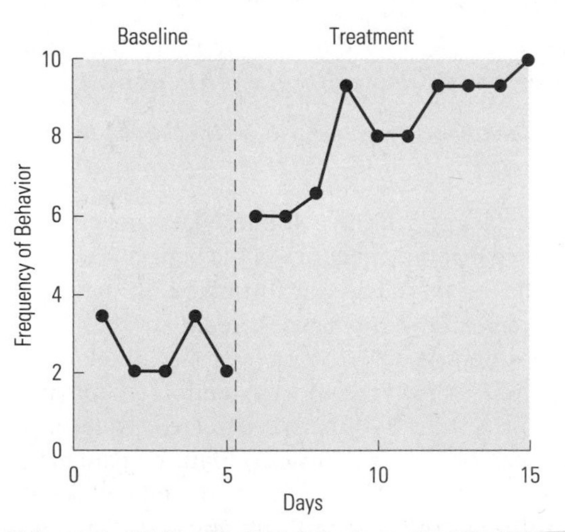

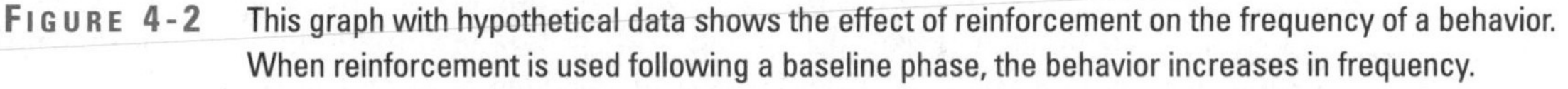
FIGURE 4-2 This graph with hypothetical data shows the effect of reinforcement on the frequency of a behavior. When reinforcement is used following a baseline phase, the behavior increases in frequency.

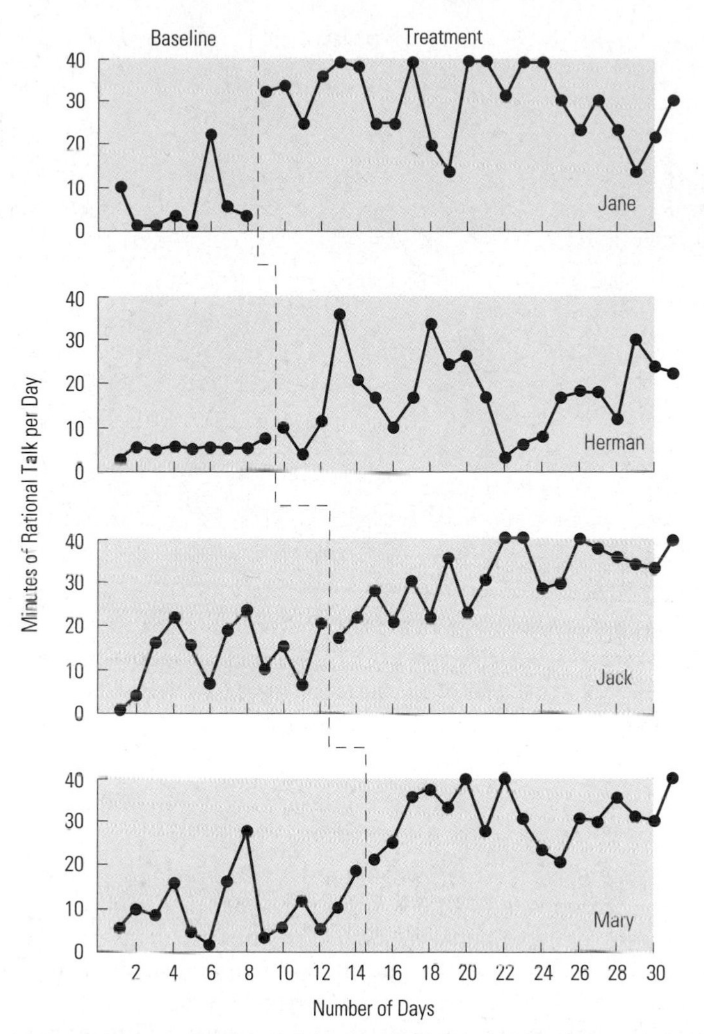

FIGURE 4-3 This graph of a multiple-baseline-across-subjects design from a study by Liberman et al. (1973) shows the effect of reinforcement on the duration of rational talk by four schizophrenic patients. Note that the duration of rational talk increased for all four subjects when reinforcement was used (treatment).

and one-on-one chats during snack time. At the same time, delusional talk was not reinforced (the nurses withheld the social attention). Figure 4-3 shows that rational talk increased in duration during the treatment phase, when social reinforcement was used.

What type of research design is illustrated in the graph in Figure 4-3?

This is a multiple-baseline-across-subjects design. There is a baseline and treatment (reinforcement) phase for each of four patients. The implementation of the reinforcement procedure is staggered over time for the four patients.

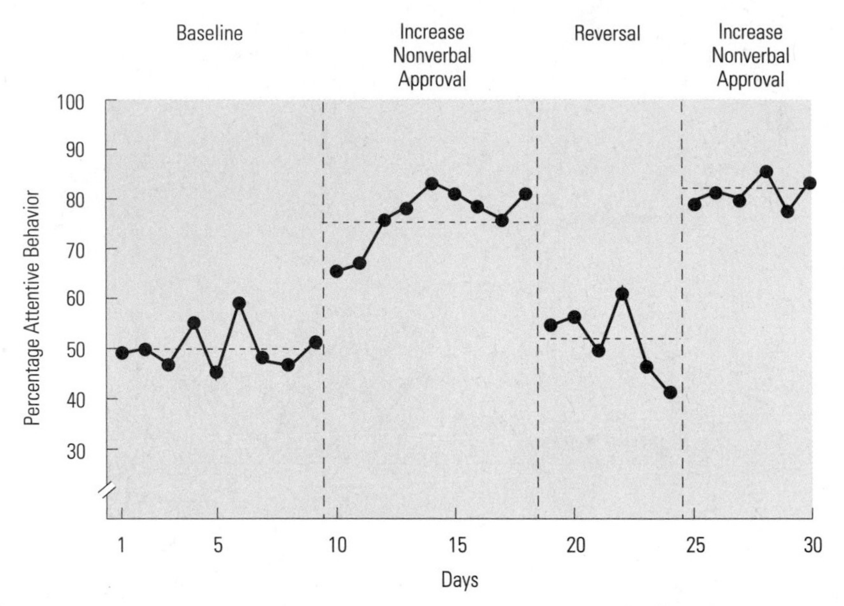

FIGURE 4-4 This graph from an A-B-A-B reversal design by Kazdin and Klock (1973) shows the effect of increased nonverbal attention from a teacher (smiling) on the amount of time that students paid attention in class. The attention from the teacher was a reinforcer that increased the students' behavior of paying attention.

The graph in Figure 4-4 is from a study by Kazdin and Klock (1973). These researchers used nonverbal approval by the teacher (e.g., smiles, pats on the back) as a reinforcer for attentive behavior in a classroom of students with moderate mental retardation. The graph illustrates the effect of reinforcement. When the students' attentive behavior was followed by teacher approval, it occurred more often in the classroom. This showed that the teacher's approval was a reinforcer here, as defined by its effects on the students' behavior.

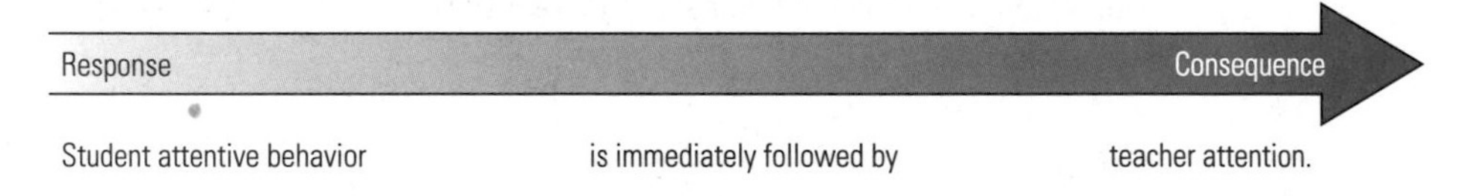

Student attentive behavior is immediately followed by teacher attention.

Outcome: Student attentive behavior is strengthened. Students are more attentive in the future.

What type of research design is illustrated in Figure 4-4?

This is an example of an A-B-A-B reversal design. It shows the percentage of intervals of attentive behavior of the students in a classroom. After a baseline period, reinforcement is implemented. The reinforcement is then discontinued (the second baseline or reversal phase) and finally implemented again.

Now that you understand the basic definition of reinforcement, it is important to understand the distinction between positive reinforcement and negative reinforcement.

Positive and Negative Reinforcement

It is extremely important to remember that both positive reinforcement and negative reinforcement are processes that strengthen a behavior; that is, they both increase the probability that the behavior will occur in the future. Positive and negative reinforcement are distinguished only by the nature of the consequence that follows the behavior. **Positive reinforcement** is defined as follows.

1. The occurrence of a behavior
2. is followed by the addition of a stimulus or an increase in the intensity of a stimulus,
3. which results in the strengthening of the behavior.

Negative reinforcement, by contrast, is defined as follows.

1. The occurrence of a behavior
2. is followed by the removal of a stimulus or a decrease in the intensity of a stimulus,
3. which results in the strengthening of the behavior.

A **stimulus** is an object or event that can be detected by one of the senses and thus has the potential to influence the person. The object or event may be a feature of the physical environment or the social environment (the behavior of the person or of others).

In positive reinforcement, the stimulus that is presented or that appears after the behavior is called a **positive reinforcer.** In negative reinforcement, the stimulus that is removed or avoided after the behavior is called an **aversive stimulus.** The essential difference, therefore, is that in positive reinforcement, a response produces a stimulus (a positive reinforcer), whereas in negative reinforcement a response removes or prevents the occurrence of a stimulus (an aversive stimulus). In both cases, the behavior is more likely to occur in the future.

Consider example 8 in Table 4-1. Mom's behavior of buying her child candy results in termination of the child's tantrum (an aversive stimulus is removed). As a result, mom is more likely to buy her child candy when he tantrums in a store. This is an example of negative reinforcement. On the other hand, when the child tantrums, he gets candy (a positive reinforcer is presented). As a result, he is more likely to tantrum in the store. This is an example of positive reinforcement.

Some people confuse negative reinforcement and punishment (see Chapter 6). They are not the same. Negative reinforcement (like positive reinforcement) increases or strengthens a behavior. Punishment, on the other hand, decreases or weakens a behavior. The confusion comes from the use of the word negative in negative reinforcement. In this context, the word negative does not mean bad or unpleasant but simply refers to the removal (subtraction) of the stimulus after the behavior.

Numerous examples of positive and negative reinforcement abound in our everyday lives. Of the eight examples in Table 4-1, four illustrate positive reinforcement and four illustrate negative reinforcement.

Read each example in Table 4-1. Which ones are examples of positive reinforcement? Which are negative reinforcement? Explain your selections. The answers may be found in Appendix B at the end of the chapter.

The important thing to remember about positive reinforcement and negative reinforcement is that both have the same impact on the behavior: They strengthen it. Reinforcement is always defined by the effect it has on the behavior (Skinner, 1958). This is called a functional definition. Consider the following example: A child completes an academic task independently and his teacher walks up to his desk, says "Good job," and pats him on the back.

Is this an example of positive reinforcement?

In this case, we cannot tell because not enough information is presented. This situation would be an example of positive reinforcement only if, as a result of the praise and pat on the back, the child was more likely to complete academic tasks independently in the future. Remember, this is the functional definition of reinforcement: The consequence of a behavior increases the probability that the behavior will occur again in the future. For most children, praise and teacher attention are reinforcers that would strengthen the behavior of completing academic tasks. However, for some children (autistic children, for example), teacher attention may not be a reinforcer. Therefore, praise and a pat on the back would not strengthen the behavior (Durand, Crimmins, Caufield, & Taylor, 1989). Durand and his colleagues illustrated that to determine whether a particular consequence will be a reinforcer for a particular person, you have to try it out and measure its effect on the behavior. Working with children who had severe developmental disorders, they compared two consequences for their academic performance. Sometimes the children received praise for correct performance, and sometimes correct performance resulted in a brief break from the academic task. Durand and colleagues found that praise increased correct performance for some children but not for others and that the brief break (removal of the academic demand) increased correct performance for some children but not for others. Durand emphasized the importance of identifying reinforcers by measuring their effects on the behavior.

Whenever you have to analyze a situation and determine whether it illustrates positive or negative reinforcement, ask yourself three questions:

1. What is the behavior?
2. What happened immediately after the behavior? (Was a stimulus added or removed?)
3. What happened to the behavior in the future? (Was the behavior strengthened? Was it more likely to occur?)

If you can answer each of these three questions, you can identify an example as positive reinforcement, negative reinforcement, or neither one.

Identify two or three examples of how negative reinforcement operates to influence behaviors in your own life.

One type of positive reinforcement involves the opportunity to engage in a high-probability behavior (a preferred behavior) as a consequence for a low-probability behavior (a less-preferred behavior), to increase the low-probability behavior (Mitchell & Stoffelmayr, 1973). This is called the **Premack principle** (Premack, 1959). For example, the Premack principle operates when parents require their fourth grade son to complete his homework before he can go outside to play with his friends. The opportunity to play (a high-probability behavior) following the completion of the homework (low-probability behavior) reinforces the behavior of doing homework; that is, it makes it more likely that the son will complete his homework.

Escape and Avoidance Behaviors

When defining negative reinforcement, a distinction is made between escape and avoidance. In **escape behavior**, the occurrence of the behavior results in the termination of an aversive stimulus that was already present when the behavior occurred. In other words, the person escapes from the aversive stimulus by engaging in a particular behavior, and that behavior is strengthened. In **avoidance behavior**, the occurrence of the behavior prevents the presentation of an aversive stimulus. In other words, the person avoids the aversive stimulus by engaging in a particular behavior, and that behavior is strengthened.

In an avoidance situation, a warning stimulus often signals the occurrence of an aversive stimulus, and the person engages in an avoidance behavior when this warning stimulus is present. Both escape and avoidance are types of negative reinforcement; therefore, both result in an increase in the rate of the behavior that terminated or avoided the aversive stimulus.

The distinction between escape and avoidance is shown in the following situation. A laboratory rat is placed in an experimental chamber that has two sides separated by a barrier; the rat can jump over the barrier to get from one side to the other. On the floor of the chamber is an electric grid that can be used to deliver a shock to one side or the other. Whenever the shock is presented on the right side of the chamber, the rat jumps to the left side and thus escapes from the shock. Jumping to the left side of the chamber is escape behavior because the rat escapes from an aversive stimulus (the shock). When the shock is applied to the left side, the rat jumps to the right side. The rat learns this escape behavior rather quickly and jumps to the other side of the chamber as soon as the shock is applied.

In the avoidance situation, a tone is presented just before the shock is applied. (Rats have better hearing than vision.)

What does the rat learn to do when the tone is presented?

After a number of instances in which the tone is presented just before the shock, the rat starts to jump to the other side of the chamber as soon as it hears the tone. The tone is the warning stimulus; the rat avoids the shock by jumping to the other side as soon as the warning stimulus is presented.

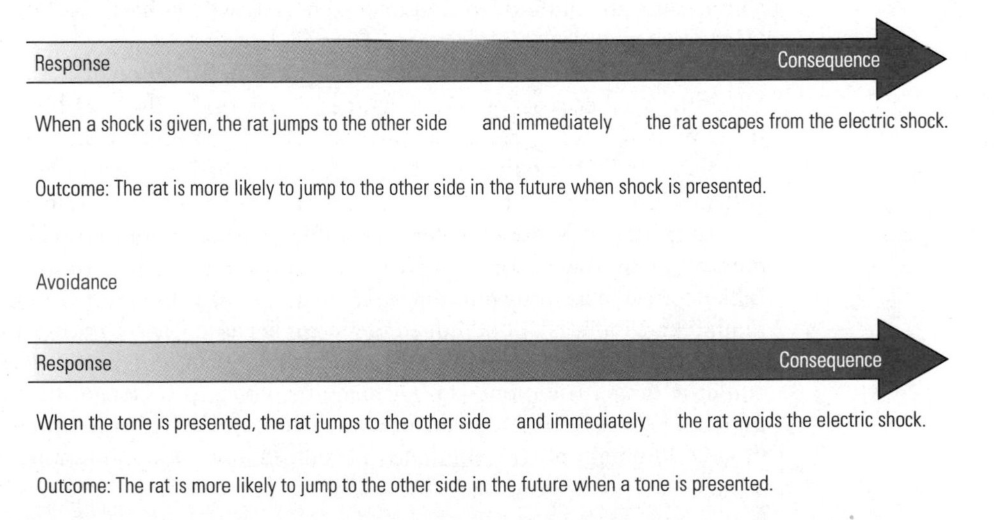
Escape
Response
Consequence
When a shock is given, the rat jumps to the other side
and immediately
the rat escapes from the electric shock.
Outcome: The rat is more likely to jump to the other side in the future when shock is presented.
Avoidance
Response
Consequence
When the tone is presented, the rat jumps to the other side
and immediately
the rat avoids the electric shock.
Outcome: The rat is more likely to jump to the other side in the future when a tone is presented.

Everyday Examples of Escape and Avoidance Behaviors

Escape	A person steps barefoot on the hot asphalt and immediately steps onto the grass. Stepping onto the grass results in escape from the heat of the hot asphalt.
Avoidance	A person puts on shoes the next time she walks on hot asphalt. Wearing shoes results in avoidance of the heat from the hot asphalt.
Escape	You start your car and the radio blasts on because someone left the volume all the way up. You turn down the volume to escape the ear-piercing noise.
Avoidance	You turn down the volume on the car radio before you start the car. In this case you avoid the noise from the radio.
Escape	You sit down in a movie theater near a large group of kids. They are very loud during the movie, and so you move to a seat far away from them to escape the noise.
Avoidance	You walk into a movie theater and take a seat far away from a group of kids. In this way you avoid the noise they make.

Conditioned and Unconditioned Reinforcers

Reinforcement is a natural process that affects the behavior of humans and other animals. Through the process of evolution, we have inherited certain biological characteristics that contribute to our survival. One characteristic we have inherited is the ability to learn new behaviors through reinforcement. In particular, certain stimuli are naturally reinforcing because the ability of our behaviors to be reinforced by these stimuli has survival value (Cooper, Heron, & Heward, 1987). For example, food, water, and sexual stimulation are natural positive reinforcers because they contribute to survival of the individual and the species. Escape from painful stimulation or extreme levels of stimulation (cold, heat, or other discomforting or aversive stimulation) is naturally negatively reinforcing because escape from or avoidance of these stimuli also contributes to survival. These natural reinforcers are called **unconditioned reinforcers** because they function as reinforcers the first time they are presented to most human beings; no prior experience with these stimuli is needed for them to function as reinforcers. Unconditioned reinforcers sometimes are called primary reinforcers. These stimuli are unconditioned reinforcers because they have biological importance (Cooper et al., 1987).

Another class of reinforcers is the **conditioned reinforcers.** A conditioned reinforcer (also called a secondary reinforcer) is a stimulus that was once neutral (a neutral stimulus does not currently function as a reinforcer; that is, it does not influence the behavior that it follows) but became established as a reinforcer by being paired with an unconditioned reinforcer or an already established conditioned reinforcer. For example, a parent's attention is a conditioned reinforcer for most children because attention is paired with the delivery of food, warmth, and other reinforcers many times in the course of a young child's life. Money is perhaps the most common conditioned reinforcer. Money is a conditioned reinforcer because it can buy (is paired with) a wide variety of unconditioned and conditioned reinforcers throughout a person's life. If you could no longer use money to buy anything, it would no longer be a conditioned reinforcer. People would not work or engage in any behavior to get money if it could not be used to obtain other reinforcers. This illustrates one important point about conditioned reinforcers: They continue to be reinforcers only if they are at least occasionally paired with other reinforcers.

Nearly any stimulus may become a conditioned reinforcer if it is paired with an existing reinforcer. For example, when trainers teach dolphins to perform tricks at aquatic parks, they use a hand-held clicker to reinforce the dolphin's behavior. Early in the training process, the trainer uses a fish as a reinforcer and pairs the sound of the clicker with the delivery of the fish to eat. Eventually the clicking sound itself becomes a conditioned reinforcer. After that, the trainer occasionally pairs the sound with the unconditioned reinforcer (the fish) so that the clicking sound continues to be a conditioned reinforcer (Pryor, 1985). To modify human behavior, a neutral stimulus such as a plastic poker chip or a small square piece of colored cardboard can be used as a conditioned reinforcer (or **token**) in a token reinforcement program. In a token reinforcement program, the token is presented to the person following a desirable behavior and later the person exchanges the token for other reinforcers (called **backup reinforcers**). Because the tokens are paired with (exchanged for) the backup reinforcers, the tokens themselves become reinforcers for the desirable behavior. (See Kazdin, 1982, for a review of research on token reinforcement programs.) Chapter 22 explains token reinforcement programs in more detail.

When a conditioned reinforcer is paired with a wide variety of other reinforcers, it is called a **generalized conditioned reinforcer**. Money is a generalized conditioned reinforcer because it is paired with (exchanged for) an almost unlimited variety of reinforcers. As a result, money is a powerful reinforcer that is less likely to diminish in value (to become satiated) when it is accumulated. In other words, satiation (losing value as a reinforcer) is less likely to occur for generalized reinforcers such as money. Tokens used in a token economy are another example of a generalized conditioned reinforcer because they are exchanged for various other backup reinforcers. As a result, people can accumulate tokens without rapid satiation. Praise is also a generalized conditioned reinforcer because praise is paired with numerous other reinforcers across a person's lifetime.

Factors Influencing the Effectiveness of Reinforcement

The effectiveness of reinforcement is influenced by a number of factors. These include the immediacy and consistency of the consequence, establishing operations, the magnitude of the reinforcer, and individual differences.

Immediacy

The time between the occurrence of a behavior and the reinforcing consequence is important. For a consequence to be most effective as a reinforcer, it should occur immediately after the behavior occurs (after the **response**). The longer the delay between the response and the consequence, the less effective the consequence will be because the contiguity or connection between the two is weakened. If the time between the response and the consequence becomes too long and there is no contiguity, the consequence will not have an effect on the behavior. For example, if you wanted to teach your dog to sit on command and you gave the dog a treat 5 minutes after it performed the behavior, the treat would not function as a reinforcer for sitting. In this case, the delay would be too long. Rather, the treat would function as a reinforcer for whatever behavior the dog engaged in immediately before receiving the treat (probably begging, which is the behavior usually reinforced with treats). On the other hand, if you gave the dog a treat immediately after it sat, the treat would reinforce sitting behavior, and the dog would be more likely to sit in the future when given the corresponding command.

Consider the importance of immediate reinforcement on social behavior. When you talk to someone, you receive immediate social responses from the listener, such as smiles, head nods, eye contact, and laughter, that reinforce the things you say. These social reinforcers strengthen your appropriate social behavior. You learn what is appropriate to say and what is not appropriate, according to the immediate response of the listener. For example, if you tell a joke and people laugh, you are more likely to repeat the joke in the future. If you don't get immediate laughs, you will probably not tell the joke in the future.

Contingency

If a response is consistently followed by an immediate consequence, that consequence is more likely to reinforce the response. When the response produces the consequence and the consequence does not occur unless the response occurs first, we say that a **contingency** exists between the response and the consequence. When a contingency exists, the consequence is more likely to reinforce the response. Consider the example of turning the key in your ignition to start your car. This is an example of contingency: Every time you turn the key, the car starts. The behavior of turning the key is reinforced by the engine starting. If the engine started only sometimes when you turned the key, and if it started sometimes when you did not turn the key, the behavior of turning the key in this particular car would not be strengthened very much. A person is more likely to repeat a behavior when it results in a consistent reinforcing consequence. In other words, a behavior is strengthened when a reinforcer is contingent on the behavior (when the reinforcer occurs only if the behavior occurs).

Establishing Operations

Some events can make a particular consequence more reinforcing at some times than at other times. For example, food is a more powerful reinforcer for a person who hasn't eaten recently than for a person who just finished a large meal. Likewise, water is a more potent reinforcer for someone who has not had a drink all day than for someone who just finished a large glass of water. Water or other beverages are more reinforcing for a person who just ate a large amount of salty popcorn than for a person who did not. (That is why some bars give you free salty popcorn.) In these examples, going without food (food deprivation) and eating salty popcorn are events that make food and liquids more reinforcing. These events that change the value of a stimulus as a reinforcer are called **establishing operations** (Michael, 1982, 1993b). To say it another way, these are operations that establish the effectiveness of a reinforcer at a particular time or in a particular situation and make the behavior that results in that reinforcer more likely to occur.

Deprivation is a type of establishing operation that increases the effectiveness of most unconditioned reinforcers and some conditioned reinforcers. A particular reinforcer (such as food or water) is more powerful if a person has gone without it for some time. For example, attention may be a more powerful reinforcer for a child who has gone without attention for a period of time. Similarly, although money is almost always a reinforcer, it may be a more powerful reinforcer for someone who has gone without money (or enough money) for a period of time. In addition, any circumstances in which a person needs more money (e.g., unexpected doctor bills) make money a stronger reinforcer.

Satiation, on the other hand, makes a stimulus less potent as a reinforcer. Satiation occurs when a person has recently consumed a large amount of a particular reinforcer (such as food or water) or has had substantial exposure to a reinforcing stimulus. For example, your favorite music may be less reinforcing if you have listened to it for the past 5 hours.

Instructions or rules may also function as an establishing operation and influence the reinforcing value of a stimulus (Schlinger, 1993). For example, pennies are not very potent reinforcers for most people. However, if you were told that there was a copper shortage and that pennies were now worth 50 cents apiece, the reinforcing value of pennies would increase and you would be more likely to engage in behavior that resulted in obtaining more pennies. Consider another example. Suppose that you have just bought a new table for your computer and printer. When you read the assembly instructions and discover that you need a screwdriver to assemble it, this increases the value of a screwdriver as a reinforcer at that time. As a result, you are more likely to go look for a screwdriver. Searching for a screwdriver is strengthened by finding it and successfully assembling the table.

Establishing operations also influence the effectiveness of negative reinforcement. When an event increases the aversiveness of a stimulus, escape from or removal of the stimulus becomes more reinforcing. For example, a headache may be an establishing operation that makes loud music more aversive; therefore, turning off the loud music is more reinforcing when you have a headache. (You are more likely to turn off loud music when you have a headache.) Consider another example. Sunshine probably is not aversive for most people, but when a person has a bad sunburn, escape from the heat of the sun is more reinforcing. Therefore, the bad sunburn is an establishing operation that makes going swimming or sitting in the shade more reinforcing because these behaviors terminate the heat of the sun (aversive stimulus). Some medications increase your sensitivity to the sun. Therefore, taking such medications is an establishing operation that makes escape from direct sunlight more reinforcing. As a result, the behavior of wearing a hat or sunglasses or staying indoors is strengthened. For a more complete discussion of establishing operations, see Michael (1982, 1993b).

Individual Differences

The likelihood of a consequence being a reinforcer varies from person to person, so it is important to determine that a particular consequence is a reinforcer for a particular person. It is important not to assume that a particular stimulus will be a reinforcer for a person just because it appears to be a reinforcer for most people. For example, praise may be meaningless to some people, even though it is a reinforcer for most. M & Ms may be reinforcers for most children, but they won't be for the child who is allergic to chocolate and gets sick when she eats it. Chapter 15 discusses various ways to identify what consequences function as reinforcers for people.

FACTORS INFLUENCING THE EFFECTIVENESS OF REINFORCEMENT	
Immediacy	A stimulus is more effective as a reinforcer when it is delivered immediately after the behavior.
Contingency	A stimulus is more effective as a reinforcer when it is delivered contingent on the behavior.
Establishing operations	Deprivation and other events make a stimulus more effective as a reinforcer at a particular time.
Individual differences	Reinforcers vary from person to person.
Magnitude	Generally, a more intense stimulus is a more effective reinforcer.

Magnitude

The other characteristic of a stimulus that is related to its power as a reinforcer is its amount or magnitude. Given the appropriate establishing operation, generally, the effectiveness of a stimulus as a reinforcer is greater if the amount or magnitude of a stimulus is greater. This is true for both positive and negative reinforcement. A larger positive reinforcer strengthens the behavior that produces it to a greater extent than a smaller amount or magnitude of the same reinforcer does. For example, a person would work longer and harder for a large amount of money than for a small amount. Likewise, a more intense aversive stimulus strengthens the behavior that terminates it more than a lower magnitude or intensity of the same stimulus would. For example, a person would work harder or engage in more behavior to decrease or eliminate an extremely painful stimulus than a mildly painful stimulus. You would work a lot harder to escape from a burning building than you would to get out of the hot sun.

SCHEDULES OF REINFORCEMENT

The **schedule of reinforcement** for a particular behavior specifies whether every response is followed by a reinforcer or whether only some responses are followed by a reinforcer. A **continuous reinforcement schedule** (CRF schedule) is one in which each occurrence of a response is reinforced. In an **intermittent reinforcement schedule,** by contrast, each occurrence of the response is not reinforced. Rather, responses are occasionally or intermittently reinforced. Consider the following example. Maria was recently hired by a company that makes furniture, and her job involves screwing knobs on cabinet doors. The first day on the job, the supervisor showed Maria how to properly screw on the knobs. The supervisor then watched Maria do the job for the first few minutes and praised her each time she correctly screwed a knob on a cabinet door. This is a continuous reinforcement schedule because every response (screwing on a knob correctly) was followed by the reinforcing consequence (praise from the supervisor). After Maria's first few minutes on the job, the supervisor left and came back occasionally during the day, watched Maria do her job, and praised her when she screwed on a knob correctly. This is an intermittent reinforcement schedule because Maria's behavior of putting knobs on cabinet doors was not reinforced every time that it occurred.

In this example, you can see that a continuous reinforcement schedule was used initially when Maria was first learning the behavior. After Maria had learned the behavior (as determined by the fact that she performed it correctly each time), the supervisor shifted to an intermittent reinforcement schedule. This illustrates the two different uses of continuous and intermittent reinforcement schedules. A CRF schedule is used when a person is learning a behavior or engaging in the behavior for the first time. This is called **acquisition:** The person is acquiring a new behavior. Once the person has acquired or learned the behavior, an intermittent reinforcement schedule is used so that the person continues to engage in the behavior. This is called **maintenance:** The behavior is maintained over time with the use of intermittent reinforcement. A supervisor could not stand by Maria and praise her for every correct behavior every day that she works. Not only is this impossible, but it is also unnecessary. Intermittent reinforcement is more effective than a CRF schedule for maintaining a behavior.

Describe how a vending machine illustrates a CRF schedule and a slot machine illustrates an intermittent reinforcement schedule.

The behavior of putting money in a vending machine and pushing the selection button is reinforced every time it occurs because the machine gives you the item that you paid for. The behavior of putting money in a slot machine and pulling the handle is reinforced on an intermittent schedule because the slot machine pays off only occasionally (Figure 4-5).

Ferster and Skinner (1957) studied various types of intermittent reinforcement schedules. In their experiments, pigeons in experimental chambers pecked round disks (or keys) mounted on the wall of the chamber in front of them. The key could be illuminated, and the apparatus automatically recorded each key peck. As reinforcers for key-pecking behavior, small amounts of food were delivered through an opening in the wall below the key. Ferster and Skinner described four basic types of schedules: fixed ratio, variable ratio,

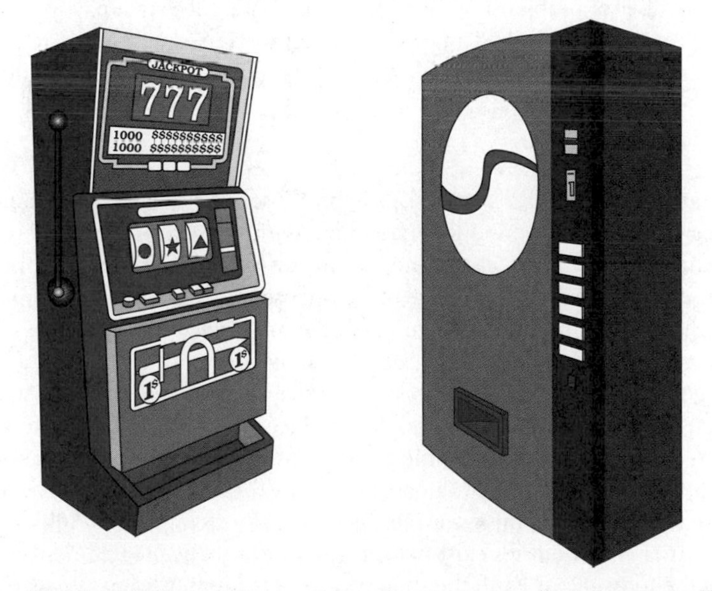

FIGURE 4-5 The slot machine works on an intermittent schedule of reinforcement. You do not hit the jackpot and get money from the machine every time you put money in the machine. The vending machine works on a continuous schedule of reinforcement. Every time you put money in the machine, you get an item from the machine.

fixed interval, and variable interval. Although these reinforcement schedules originally were studied with laboratory animals, they are also applied to human behavior.

Fixed Ratio

In fixed ratio and variable ratio schedules of reinforcement, the delivery of the reinforcer is based on the number of responses that occur. In a **fixed ratio (FR)** schedule, a specific or fixed number of responses must occur before the reinforcer is delivered. In other words, a reinforcer is delivered after a certain number of responses. For example, in a fixed ratio 5 (FR 5) schedule, the reinforcer follows every fifth response. In an FR schedule, the number of responses needed before the reinforcer is delivered does not change. Ferster and Skinner found that pigeons would engage in high rates of responding on FR schedules; there was often a brief pause in responding after the delivery of the reinforcer. Ferster and Skinner investigated FR schedules ranging from FR 2 up to FR 400, in which 400 responses had to occur before the reinforcer was delivered. Typically, the rate of responding is higher when more responses are needed for reinforcement in an FR schedule.

FR schedules of reinforcement sometimes are used in academic or work settings to maintain appropriate behavior. Consider the example of Paul, a 26-year-old adult with severe mental retardation who works in a factory packaging parts for shipment. As the parts come by on a conveyor belt, Paul picks them up and puts them into boxes. Paul's supervisor delivers a token (conditioned reinforcer) after every 20 parts that Paul packages. This is an example of an FR 20. At lunch and after work, Paul exchanges his tokens for backup reinforcers (e.g., snacks or pop). An FR schedule could be used in a school setting by giving students reinforcers (such as stars, stickers, or good marks) for correctly completing a fixed number of problems or other academic tasks. Piece-rate pay in a factory, in which workers get paid a specified amount of money for a fixed number of responses (for example, $5 for every 12 parts assembled), is also an example of an FR schedule.

Variable Ratio

In a **variable ratio** (VR) schedule, as in an FR schedule, delivery of a reinforcer is based on the number of responses that occur, but in this case the number of responses needed for reinforcement varies each time, around an average number. In other words, a reinforcer is delivered after an average of X responses. For example, in a variable ratio 10 (VR 10) schedule, the reinforcer is provided after an average of 10 responses. The number of responses needed for each reinforcer may range from just 2 or 3 up to 20 or 25, but the average number of responses equals 10. Ferster and Skinner evaluated VR schedules with pigeons and found that such schedules produced high, steady rates of responding; in contrast to FR schedules, there is little pausing after the delivery of the reinforcer. In their research, Ferster and Skinner evaluated various VR schedules, including some that needed a large number of responses for reinforcement (for example, VR 360).

Some VR schedules exist naturally; others may be created deliberately. Consider again the example of Paul, the mentally retarded man who packages parts in a factory.

Describe how a VR 20 schedule of reinforcement would be implemented with Paul.

The supervisor could reinforce his work performance on a VR 20 schedule by delivering a token after an average of 20 parts that Paul packages. Sometimes the number of responses needed would be less than 20 and sometimes more than 20. The number of responses needed for any particular token delivery would not be predictable to Paul, in contrast to the FR 20 schedule, where the token is provided after every 20 responses (packaged parts). Another common example of a VR schedule is the slot machine found in casinos. The response of putting a coin in the machine and pulling the handle is reinforced on a VR schedule. The gambler never knows how many responses are needed for a jackpot (the reinforcer). However, the more responses the gambler makes, the more likely a jackpot is (because a VR schedule is based on number of responses, not on time or some other factor). Therefore, the VR schedule in a slot machine produces high, steady rates of responding. Of course, the casino makes sure that the variable ratio is such that gamblers put more money in the machine than the machine pays out as reinforcers. One other example of a VR schedule can be found in the salesperson who must make calls (in person or on the phone) to sell products. The number of calls that must occur before a sale (the reinforcer) occurs is variable. The more calls the salesperson makes, the more likely it is that a sale will result. However, which call will result in a sale is unpredictable.

In the FR and VR schedules, the delivery of the reinforcer is based on the number of responses that occur. As a result, in both FR and VR schedules, more frequent responding results in more frequent reinforcement. That is why ratio schedules are the intermittent schedules used most often in behavior modification procedures.

Fixed Interval

With interval schedules (fixed interval, variable interval), a response is reinforced only after an interval of time has passed. It does not matter how many responses occur; as soon as the specified interval of time has elapsed, the first response that occurs is reinforced. In a **fixed interval (FI) schedule**, the interval of time is fixed, or stays the same each time. For example, in a fixed interval 20 seconds (FI 20 second) schedule of reinforcement, the first response that occurs after 20 seconds has elapsed results in the reinforcer. Responses that occur before the 20 seconds are not reinforced; they have no effect on the subsequent delivery of the reinforcer. (They don't make it come any sooner.) Once the 20 seconds has elapsed, the reinforcer is available, and the first response that occurs is reinforced. Then, 20 seconds later, the reinforcer is available again, and the first response that occurs produces the reinforcer. Consider again the example of Paul, who packages parts in a factory.

Describe how an FI 30 minute schedule of reinforcement would be implemented with Paul.

An FI 30 minute schedule would be in effect if the supervisor came by once every 30 minutes and gave Paul a token for the first response (packaging a part) that occurred. The number of parts that Paul packaged throughout the 30 minutes would be irrelevant. The supervisor would provide the token (reinforcer) for the first part that she saw Paul package after the 30-minute interval. This is very different from an FR or VR schedule, in which Paul gets a token for the number of parts he packages. In an FI schedule, only one response is needed for reinforcement, but it must occur after the interval.

What Ferster and Skinner found is that FI schedules of reinforcement produced a certain pattern of responding: The pigeon made an increasing number of responses near the end of the interval, up until the reinforcer was delivered. After that, there was a pause in responding; as the end of the interval approached, the pigeon again started responding more quickly until the reinforcer was delivered. We might expect to see the same pattern of behavior with Paul in the factory. After he receives the token from the supervisor and the supervisor walks away (to observe other workers), Paul may slow down or stop working for a while and then start working again as the end of the 30 minutes approaches. Because he receives a token for packaging a part only after the 30-minute interval has ended, his behavior of packaging parts naturally starts to occur more frequently as the end of the interval approaches. Because he never receives a token for packaging parts during the 30-minute interval, his behavior naturally starts to occur less frequently in the early part of the interval. This pattern of behavior (a higher rate of responding near the end of the interval) is characteristic of FI schedules of reinforcement. For this reason, FI schedules rarely are used in teaching or training programs. Instead, FR or VR schedules are more commonly used because they produce higher and more steady rates of responding. With an FR or VR schedule, Paul learned to package more parts to receive more tokens. With an FI schedule, Paul learned to package parts in a limited period around the end of each 30-minute interval.

Variable Interval

In a **variable interval (VI) schedule** of reinforcement, as in an FI schedule, the reinforcer is delivered for the first response that occurs after an interval of time has elapsed. The difference is that in a VI schedule, each time interval is a different length. The interval varies around an average time. For example, in a variable interval 20 second (VI 20 second) schedule, sometimes the interval is more than 20 seconds and other times it is less than 20 seconds. The interval length is not predictable each time, but the average length is 20 seconds. Ferster and Skinner investigated various VI schedules of reinforcement. They found that the pattern of responding on a VI schedule was different from that on an FI schedule. On the VI schedule, the pigeon's behavior (pecking the key) occurred at a steady rate, whereas on the FI schedule the frequency decreased in the early part of the interval and increased near the end of the interval. Because the length of the interval—and thus the availability of the reinforcer—was unpredictable in a VI schedule, this off-and-on pattern of responding did not develop.

Once again, consider the case of Paul packaging parts in a factory.

Describe how the supervisor would implement a VI 30 minute schedule with Paul. Describe how Paul's behavior would be different on a VI 30 minute schedule from his behavior on an FI 30 minute schedule.

Using a VI 30 minute schedule, the supervisor would come around at unpredictable intervals of time (for example, after 5 minutes, 22 minutes, 45 minutes, 36 minutes) and give Paul a token for the first part that she saw Paul package. The various intervals of time would average 30 minutes. The reinforcer (token) would be given for the first response after the interval. On a VI 30 minute schedule, Paul probably would package parts more steadily throughout the day. The slowing down and speeding up of his work rate observed on the FI 30 minute schedule would not occur because the length of the intervals is unpredictable.

SCHEDULES OF REINFORCEMENT

Fixed Ratio	Reinforcer delivered after a certain number of responses. Produces high rate of behavior, with a pause after reinforcement.
Variable ratio	Reinforcer delivered after an average of X responses. Produces a high and steady rate of behavior, with no pause after reinforcement.
Fixed interval	Reinforcer delivered for the first response that occurs after a fixed interval of time. Produces a low rate of behavior, with an on-and-off pattern. The response rate increases near the end of the interval.
Variable interval	Reinforcer delivered for the first response that occurs after a variable interval of time. Produces a steady, low to moderate rate of behavior, with no on-and-off pattern.

REINFORCING DIFFERENT DIMENSIONS OF BEHAVIOR

Although reinforcement often is used to increase the rate of a behavior, reinforcement may also influence other dimensions of a behavior such as duration, intensity, or latency. If a reinforcer is contingent on a particular duration of a behavior, that duration of the behavior is more likely to occur. For example, if a child is allowed to go outside and play after school only after she completes a half hour of homework, she will be more likely to work on her homework for 30 minutes. Likewise, if the reinforcer is contingent on a particular intensity of a behavior, the behavior is more likely to occur with that intensity. For example, if a door gets stuck in cold weather and you must push harder to open it, then pushing harder is reinforced and you are more likely to push harder (increased intensity) to open the door. Likewise, if a reinforcer is contingent on decreasing the latency of a response, then decreased latency (increased speed) is strengthened. For example, if a child receives a reinforcer for complying with a parent's instruction immediately after the instruction is given, then an immediate response (short latency) is strengthened and the child is more likely to respond immediately when the parent makes a request.

CONCURRENT SCHEDULES OF REINFORCEMENT

In most situations, it is possible for a person to engage in more than one behavior. For each of the possible behaviors a person could engage in at a particular time, there is a specific schedule of reinforcement. All of the schedules of reinforcement that are in effect for a person's behaviors at one time are called **concurrent schedules of reinforcement.** In other words, a number of different behaviors or response options are concurrently available for the person. Concurrent schedules of reinforcement (and punishment) for the different response options at a particular time influence the effectiveness of reinforcement for a particular behavior at that time. The person typically will engage in one of the response options depending on the schedule of reinforcement, the magnitude of reinforcement, the immediacy of reinforcement, and the **response effort** for the various response options (Neef, Mace, & Shade, 1993; Neef, Mace, Shea, & Shade, 1992; Neef, Shade, & Miller, 1994). For example, if Rayford had the opportunity to do yard work for his friend for $10.00 per hour or to help his cousin at the hardware store for $8.00 an hour, he probably would help his friend because the magnitude of reinforcement is greater. If both jobs paid $10.00 per hour but one job was much easier, Rayford probably would choose the easier job. However, if he had the opportunity to spend the afternoon water-skiing with his girlfriend, he might choose that over either job because it involved a more powerful reinforcer than the amount of money from either job.

Research into concurrent schedules of reinforcement has shown that people most often engage in the behavior that results in more frequent reinforcement, a greater magnitude of reinforcement, more immediate reinforcement, or less response effort (Friman & Poling, 1995; Neef et al., 1992, 1993, 1994). Information about concurrent schedules is important in applying behavior modification because a schedule of reinforcement for an undesirable behavior may exist concurrently with a schedule of reinforcement for a desirable behavior. When using reinforcement to increase the desirable behavior, you must also consider (and in some cases modify) the schedule of reinforcement for the undesirable behavior (Mace & Roberts, 1993).

Chapter Summary

1. Reinforcement is a basic principle of behavior. Reinforcement is defined to occur when the occurrence of a behavior is followed by an immediate consequence that results in a strengthening of the behavior or an increase in the probability of the behavior in the future. Reinforcement is the process responsible for the occurrence of operant behavior.
2. Positive and negative reinforcement both strengthen behavior. They differ only in whether the consequence following the behavior is the addition of a stimulus (positive reinforcer) or the removal of a stimulus (aversive stimulus).
3. Unconditioned reinforcers are stimuli that are naturally reinforcing because they have survival value or biological importance. Conditioned reinforcers are originally neutral stimuli that have been established as reinforcers because they were paired with unconditioned reinforcers or other conditioned reinforcers.
4. A number of factors influence the effectiveness of reinforcement. A reinforcer should be delivered immediately to be most effective. A reinforcer is most effective when it is contingent on the behavior, that is, when it is delivered only if the behavior occurs. Reinforcers are effective when there is a state of deprivation or some other establishing operation in effect. Generally, a reinforcer is more effective the larger its amount or magnitude.
5. Reinforcement may be scheduled to occur every time the behavior occurs (continuous reinforcement, CRF) or it may occur intermittently. CRF schedules are used for acquisition, that is, learning a new behavior. Intermittent schedules are used to maintain the occurrence of a behavior once it has been learned. There are four basic intermittent reinforcement schedules. In ratio schedules, a number of responses must occur for the reinforcer to be delivered. In an FR schedule, the number of responses is fixed, or constant; in a VR schedule, the number of responses required for reinforcement varies around an average number. In interval schedules, an interval of time must pass before a response is reinforced. In an FI schedule, the interval is fixed; in a VI schedule, the interval varies around an average time. Ratio schedules produce the highest rate of responding, although there is often a pause after reinforcement in FR schedules. Interval schedules produce lower rates of responding than do ratio schedules. The VI schedule produces a steady rate, whereas the FI schedule produces an off-and-on pattern of responding in which most responses occur as the end of the interval approaches.

PRACTICE TEST

1. What is the definition of reinforcement? (p. 71)
2. What was the reinforcer for Thorndike's cat? What behavior resulted in the reinforcer? What effect did reinforcement have on the cat's behavior? (pp. 69–70)
3. What does it mean to say that a behavior is strengthened? (p. 69)
4. What is an operant behavior? What operant behavior of the rat was reinforced in Skinner's experiments? (pp. 70–71)
5. Draw a graph that shows the effect of reinforcement on the duration of cooperative play in a child.
6. Provide a definition of positive reinforcement. (p. 75)
7. Provide a definition of negative reinforcement. (p. 75)
8. Provide a novel example (not from the chapter) of positive reinforcement.
9. Provide a novel example of negative reinforcement.
10. In what way are positive and negative reinforcement alike? How are they different? (p. 75)
11. How is negative reinforcement different from punishment? (p. 75)
12. What is an aversive stimulus? Provide an example. (p. 75)
13. What is an unconditioned reinforcer? Provide examples of unconditioned positive reinforcers and unconditioned negative reinforcers. (p. 78)
14. What is a conditioned reinforcer? Provide examples. How did the stimulus in each example become a conditioned reinforcer? (p. 78)
15. Identify the five factors that influence the effectiveness of reinforcement. (p. 82)
16. What is meant by contiguity between a response and a reinforcer? How does contiguity influence the effectiveness of reinforcement? (p. 79)
17. What is a reinforcement contingency? How does a contingency influence the effectiveness of reinforcement? (p. 80)
18. What is an establishing operation? Provide some examples. (pp. 80–81)
19. How can you determine whether a particular stimulus is a reinforcer for a particular person? (p. 76)
20. Distinguish between intermittent and continuous schedules of reinforcement. (p. 82)
21. A CRF schedule is used for acquisition and an intermittent schedule is used for maintenance. Describe what this means. (p. 83)
22. What is a fixed ratio schedule? A variable ratio schedule? Describe an example that illustrates each schedule. (pp. 84–85)
23. What is a fixed interval schedule? A variable interval schedule? Describe the pattern of responding you would expect with a fixed interval schedule. (pp. 85–86)
24. Are interval or ratio schedules more likely to be used in teaching or training programs? Why? (pp. 85–86)
25. What are concurrent schedules of reinforcement? Provide an example. (pp. 87–88)
26. Identify each of the following as an example of positive reinforcement or negative reinforcement.
    a. Althea interrupts her parents and they scold her each time she interrupts. Althea continues to interrupt her parents.
    b. Dick curses at his teacher whenever she asks him to do his math problems. The teacher always sends him to sit at the back of the room by himself for 15 minutes when he curses at her. He continues to curse at her when she tells him to do his math problems.
    c. Maxine has a bad rash. Whenever she scratches it, the itching goes away for a while. Maxine continues to scratch her rash when it itches.
    d. Jorge handed in his homework on time and his teacher smiled at him. As a result, he continues to hand in his homework on time.

e. Wiley drives his pickup truck fast down a dirt road and spins out of control in the mud. As a result, he is more likely to drive his pickup truck fast down the dirt road.

f. Marcia's mother yells at her when she doesn't clean her room on Saturday. As a result, Marcia is more likely to stay at a friend's house on Saturday so as to avoid being yelled at by her mother.

APPENDIX A

Operant Behaviors and Reinforcers from Each Example in Table 4-1

Operant Behavior	*Reinforcer*
1. Child's crying	Parents' attention
2. Opening the umbrella	Keeps rain from falling on her
3. Turning on the fan	Removes smoke from the kitchen
4. Asking her friend for the answer to a study question	Friend provides correct answer
5. Johnny sits in his seat	Teacher smiles and praises him
6. Patricia puts foil on the antenna	TV picture becomes clearer
7. Employees assemble bicycles	They earn money
8. Child's tantrum	Receiving candy
Mother gives child candy	Tantrum stops

APPENDIX B

Examples of Positive Reinforcement and Negative Reinforcement from Table 4-1

1. Positive reinforcement. The parents' attention is a positive reinforcer for the child's crying. (The cessation of crying is also negatively reinforcing for the parents' behavior of providing attention to their child when she cries.)
2. Negative reinforcement. Opening the umbrella prevents the rain from hitting the woman's head (removes an aversive stimulus).
3. Negative reinforcement. Turning on the exhaust fan removes the smoke.
4. Positive reinforcement. Her friend provides the correct answer to the question when the student asks her for the correct answer.
5. Positive reinforcement. The teacher's smile and praise are a positive reinforcer for Johnny's sitting and paying attention.
6. Negative reinforcement. Putting the tin foil on the antenna removes the fuzzy picture. (Alternatively, it could be regarded as positive reinforcement. Putting tin foil on the antenna produces a clear picture on the TV.)
7. Positive reinforcement. Money is a positive reinforcer for assembling bicycles.
8. Negative reinforcement for the mother's behavior. The termination of the child's tantrum reinforces the mother's behavior of giving the child candy. Positive reinforcement for the child's behavior. Getting candy from his mother reinforces the child's tantrum behavior.

CHAPTER 4 *Quiz 1* Name:

1. A(n) ________________ behavior is strengthened through the process of reinforcement.
2. When a person has recently had a large amount of a reinforcer, will the reinforcer be more or less potent? ________________
3. ______________ reinforcement is defined as the occurrence of a behavior followed by the addition of a stimulus, and the behavior is more likely to occur in the future.
4. ______________ reinforcement is defined as the occurrence of a behavior followed by the removal of a stimulus, and the behavior is more likely to occur in the future.
5. What are three of the five factors that influence the effectiveness of reinforcement?

   ____________________, ____________________, ____________________
6. A(n) ________________ reinforcer became established as a reinforcer by being paired with other reinforcers.
7. All of the schedules of reinforcement that are in effect for a person's behaviors at one time are called ________________________________.

Identify the following schedules of reinforcement:

8. ______________ The reinforcer is delivered after every response.
9. ______________ The reinforcer is delivered after an average of *x* responses.
10. ______________ The reinforcer is delivered for the first response after *x* amount of time.

CHAPTER 4 *Quiz 2*

Name:

1. A consequence that strengthens operant behavior is a(n) ____________________.

2. When a person has not had a particular reinforcer for a long time, will the reinforcer be more or less potent? ________________

3. When Todd gets mosquito bites on his body he puts medication on the bites and the medication relieves the itching. As a result, Todd is more likely to put medication on his mosquito bites. This an example of ________________ (positive/negative) reinforcement.

4. When Frida knocks her little brother down, she gets scolded by her parents. As a result, she is more likely to knock her little brother down. This is an example of ______________ (positive/negative) reinforcement.

5. Escape and avoidance behavior are two types of behaviors that are maintained by ____________________ (positive/negative) reinforcement.

6. A continuous reinforcement schedule is used for ________________ (acquisition/maintenance) of behavior.

7. The stimulus that is removed following the behavior in negative reinforcement is called a(n) ____________________ stimulus.

8. Positive reinforcement and negative reinforcement both ______________ behavior.

Identify the following schedules of reinforcement:

9. ____________________ A reinforcer is delivered after *x* responses.

10. ____________________ A reinforcer is delivered for the first response after an average of *x* amount of time.

CHAPTER 4 *Quiz 3*

Name:

1. An operant behavior is strengthened through the process of ______________________.
2. What is the schedule of reinforcement in which the reinforcer is delivered after every

   response? ________________________
3. What is the schedule of reinforcement in which the reinforcer *is not* delivered after

   every response? ________________________
4. Deprivation makes a reinforcer ______________ (more/less) potent.
5. Satiation makes a reinforcer ______________ (more/less) potent.
6. In what way are positive reinforcement and negative reinforcement alike?

   ____
7. In negative reinforcement, a(n) ________________________ is removed following the behavior.
8. In positive reinforcement a(n) ________________________ is delivered following the behavior.
9. Shae checks her e-mail periodically throughout the day. E-mail messages come at unpredictable intervals so Shae never knows when she will have an e-mail. Shae's behavior of checking her

   e-mail is reinforced on what schedule of reinforcement? ________________________
10. Rob is a telemarketer, and makes phone calls in an attempt to sell a product. Rob never knows when someone will agree to buy the product, but he must make an average of 13 calls to make a sale. Rob's behavior of making calls is reinforced on what schedule of reinforcement?

    ____

Extinction

As we saw in Chapter 4, reinforcement is responsible for the acquisition and maintenance of operant behavior. This chapter discusses extinction, a process that weakens operant behavior. Consider the two examples that follow.

- What is the principle of extinction?
- What happens during an extinction burst?
- How is extinction different after positive reinforcement and negative reinforcement?
- What is a common misconception about extinction?
- What factors influence extinction?

Every Monday, Wednesday, and Friday, Rae walks to her behavior modification class at 8 A.M. Right before class each day, she stops at the coffee machine, puts 50 cents in the machine, pushes the button, and gets her coffee for class. One day, she walks up to the machine, puts her money in, and pushes the button, and nothing happens. She pushes the button again, and nothing happens. She pushes the button harder and harder and then slams the button a few times, but she still does not get her coffee. Finally, she gives up and walks to class without her coffee. She doesn't try the machine again for a week, but then she tries it again, and the same thing happens. From then on, she never tries the machine again and, instead, gets her coffee at the convenience store on the way to school.

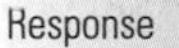

Rae puts money in coffee machine. — No coffee comes out of coffee machine.

Outcome: Rae is less likely to put money in the coffee machine in the future.

Each evening when Greg gets home from work, he goes into his apartment building through the emergency exit in back because that door is close to his apartment and he doesn't have to walk all the way around to the front door. The apartment manager doesn't want people to use this door except in emergencies, so she installs a new lock on the door. That day, when Greg gets home from work, he turns the doorknob but the door doesn't open. He turns the knob again, but nothing happens. He starts turning the knob harder and pulling harder on the door, but still nothing happens. Eventually he stops and walks to the front door. Greg tries the door again the next couple of days when he gets home from work, but still it will not open. Finally, he quits trying to go in through the emergency door.

Response → Consequence

Greg turns the handle on the emergency exit door. → The door does not open.

Outcome: In the future, Greg is less likely to try to open the emergency exit door.

DEFINING EXTINCTION

The basic behavioral principle that is illustrated in these examples is **extinction.** In each example, a behavior that had been reinforced for a period of time was no longer reinforced and, therefore, the behavior stopped occurring. Rae's behavior of putting money in the coffee machine and pushing the button was reinforced by getting coffee. Greg's behavior of turning the doorknob and opening the emergency door was reinforced by entering his apartment building at a point closer to his apartment. These behaviors were reinforced on a continuous schedule. Once the reinforcement stopped, Rae and Greg both engaged in the behavior less and less and ultimately stopped engaging in the behavior.

Extinction is a basic principle of behavior. The behavioral definition of extinction is as follows: Extinction occurs when

1. A behavior that has been previously reinforced
2. no longer results in the reinforcing consequences
3. and, therefore, the behavior stops occurring in the future.

As long as a behavior is reinforced, at least intermittently, it will continue to occur. If a behavior is no longer followed by a reinforcing consequence, however, the person will stop engaging in the behavior. When a behavior stops occurring because it is no longer reinforced, we say that the behavior has undergone extinction or that the behavior has been extinguished.

Skinner (1938) and Ferster and Skinner (1957) demonstrated the principle of extinction with laboratory animals. When the pigeon in the experimental chamber no longer received food as a reinforcer for pecking the key, the pigeon's key-pecking behavior stopped. When the laboratory rat no longer received food pellets for pressing the lever, the lever-pressing behavior decreased and eventually stopped.

Of course, numerous research studies have also demonstrated the principle of extinction with human behavior (Chapter 7 of Kazdin, 1994; Lerman & Iwata, 1996b). In one of the earliest studies reporting the use of extinction to decrease a problem behavior, Williams (1959) illustrated the effectiveness of extinction in decreasing the nighttime tantrums of a young child. Because Williams had determined that the child's tantrum behavior was being reinforced by the parents' attention, the extinction procedure called for the parents to refrain from providing attention when the child engaged in tantrum behaviors at night.

Response → Consequence

Child tantrums at bedtime. → Parent does not pay attention to the child.

Outcome: In the future, child is less likely to engage in tantrum behavior at bedtime.

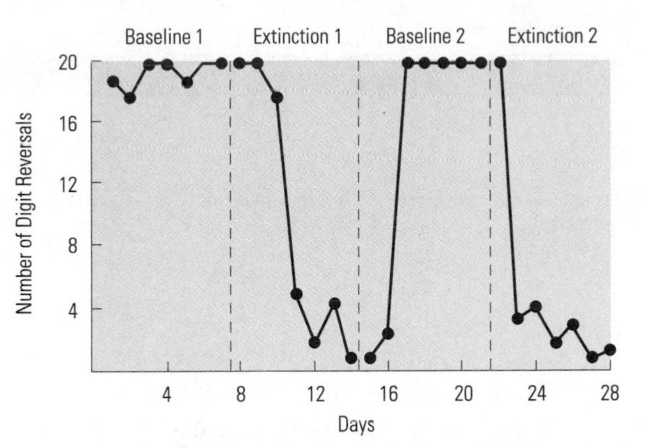

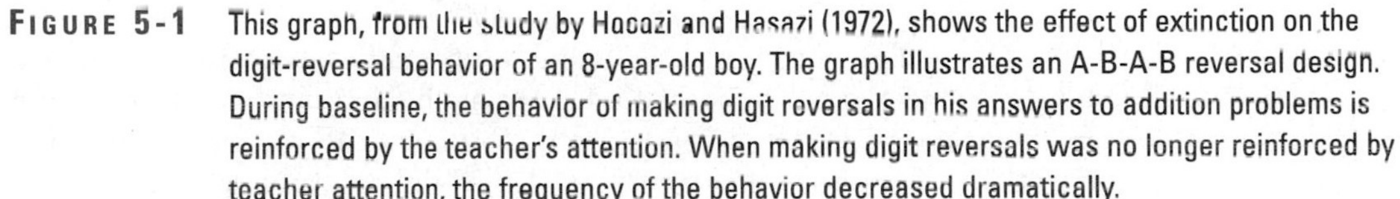
FIGURE 5-1 This graph, from the study by Hasazi and Hasazi (1972), shows the effect of extinction on the digit-reversal behavior of an 8-year-old boy. The graph illustrates an A-B-A-B reversal design. During baseline, the behavior of making digit reversals in his answers to addition problems is reinforced by the teacher's attention. When making digit reversals was no longer reinforced by teacher attention, the frequency of the behavior decreased dramatically.

Numerous studies have demonstrated the effectiveness of extinction for decreasing problem behaviors in children and adults (Ayllon & Michael, 1959; Ducharme & Van Houten, 1994; Holz, Azrin, & Ayllon 1963; Lerman & Iwata, 1995; Mazaleski, Iwata, Vollmer, Zarcone, & Smith, 1993; Neisworth & Moore, 1972; Rincover, 1978; Wright, Brown, & Andrews, 1978). In each of these studies, the reinforcer for a problem was eliminated or withheld, and the behavior decreased. Consider the study by Hasazi and Hasazi (1972), who used extinction to reduce arithmetic errors made by an 8 year-old boy. Whenever the boy did addition problems with two-digit answers, he reversed the digits (for example, he wrote 21 instead of 12 as the answer to 7 + 5). The researchers determined that the attention (extra help) provided by the teacher for incorrect answers was reinforcing the child's behavior of reversing the digits. The extinction procedure required the teacher to refrain from providing attention for incorrect answers. The teacher also praised the child for correct answers. (This is differential reinforcement; see Chapter 15.) The child's digit-reversal behavior decreased dramatically when extinction was implemented (Figure 5-1). This study is particularly interesting because many professionals would have considered the digit reversal to be a sign of a learning disability, whereas the authors demonstrated that the digit reversal actually was an operant behavior reinforced by the teacher's attention.

In another example, Lovaas and Simmons (1969) used extinction to reduce the self-injurious behavior of a mentally retarded child. Lovaas and Simmons believed the child's head-hitting behavior was being reinforced by social consequences (attention) from adults. Extinction therefore involved removing adult attention whenever the child hit himself. The results showed that the frequency of head-hitting decreased from more than 2500 hits in a 1-hour session to zero per session. It took ten sessions of extinction for the frequency of the behavior to decrease to zero.

Response → Consequence

The child hits his head. | He receives no attention from adults.

Outcome: The child is less likely to hit himself in the head because the behavior is no longer reinforced by adult attention.

EXTINCTION BURST

One characteristic of the extinction process is that once the behavior is no longer reinforced, it often increases briefly in frequency, duration, or intensity before it decreases and ultimately stops (Lerman & Iwata, 1995). In the first example, when Rae did not get her coffee, she pushed the button on the coffee machine repeatedly (increase in frequency) and then pushed it harder and harder (increase in intensity) before finally giving up. When Greg found the back door to his apartment building would not open, he turned the handle and pulled the doorknob a number of times (increase in frequency) and he pulled harder on the doorknob (increase in intensity) before finally giving. up. Increase in frequency, duration, or intensity of the unreinforced behavior during the extinction process is called an **extinction burst.** Consider two other examples.

When Mark pushes the on button on the remote control for his TV set and it does not turn on the TV (because the batteries are dead), he pushes it longer (increased duration) and harder (increased intensity) before he finally gives up. His behavior of pushing the on button was not reinforced by the TV turning on; therefore, he quit trying, but not until he tried pushing it longer and harder (extinction burst).

Each night, 4-year-old Amanda cried at bedtime for 10–15 minutes, and her parents came to her room and talked to her until she fell asleep. By doing so, her parents were accidentally reinforcing her crying. After talking to her pediatrician, the parents decided not to go into her room or talk to her when she cried at bedtime. The first night, she cried for 25 minutes before falling asleep. By the end of the week, she quit crying at all at bedtime. When they stopped going to her room after she cried, the parents were using extinction. The increase in crying duration the first night is an extinction burst. Figure 5-2 shows the graph of Amanda's crying duration before and after her parents used extinction. Once the parents implemented extinction, the behavior increased briefly but then decreased and eventually stopped altogether.

One other characteristic of an extinction burst is that novel behaviors (behaviors that do not typically occur in a particular situation) may occur for a brief period when a behavior is no longer reinforced (Bijou, 1958; Lalli, Zanolli, & Wohn, 1994). For example, when Amanda's parents no longer reinforced her crying at night, she cried longer and louder (increased duration and intensity), but she also screamed and hit her pillow (novel behaviors). In the first example, Rae not only pushed the button on the coffee machine repeatedly when the coffee didn't come out but also pushed the coin return button and shook the machine (novel behaviors; Figure 5-3).

Sometimes, the novel behaviors during extinction bursts may include emotional responses (Chance, 1988). For example, Rae may act in an angry fashion and curse at the coffee machine or kick it. Azrin, Hutchinson, and Hake (1966) reported that ag-

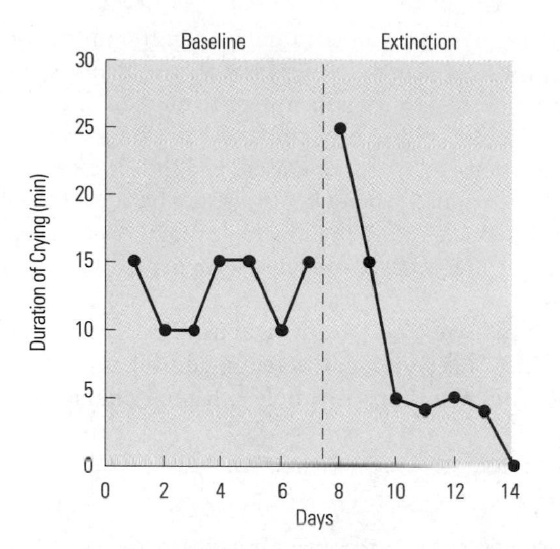

FIGURE 5-2 The graph shows hypothetical data on the duration of crying during baseline and extinction. On the first day of extinction, an extinction burst occurred. The behavior increased in duration. On subsequent days, it decreased and eventually stopped.

FIGURE 5-3 When Rae does not get her coffee from the vending machine, she pushes the buttons repeatedly and shakes the machine. This is an example of an extinction burst.

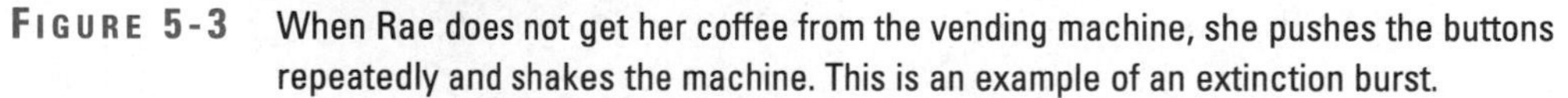

gressive behavior often is seen when extinction is used. It is not uncommon for young children to exhibit emotional responses when their behavior is no longer reinforced. The child whose request for candy is denied may scream and cry. The parent may then unwittingly reinforce this screaming and crying by giving the child some candy. As you may recall from the previous chapter, the parent's behavior of giving candy to the child is negatively reinforced by the termination of the child's screaming and crying.

The extinction burst, which involves an increase in the unreinforced behavior or the occurrence of novel (and sometimes emotional) behaviors for a brief period of time, is a natural reaction to the termination of reinforcement. The increased frequency, duration, or intensity of the unreinforced behavior—or the novel behaviors that occur during extinction—may be reinforced, and thus the extinction burst serves a valuable purpose. For example, when Greg tugs very hard on the doorknob, it may open for him if it is only stuck, rather than locked. When Amanda screams and cries louder, her parents may come into the room and give her the attention she wasn't getting for simply crying.

The extinction burst is not necessarily a conscious process, however. Amanda probably is not thinking, "I'll cry louder, scream, and hit my pillow to get my parents' attention." The extinction burst is simply a natural characteristic of an extinction situation.

Extinction Burst

When a behavior is no longer reinforced, the consequences may be as follows.

- The behavior may briefly increase in frequency, duration, or intensity.
- Novel behaviors may occur.
- Emotional responses or aggressive behavior may occur.

Spontaneous Recovery

One other characteristic of extinction is that the behavior may occur again even after it has not occurred for some time. This is called **spontaneous recovery.** Spontaneous recovery is the natural tendency for the behavior to occur again in situations that are similar to those in which it occurred before extinction (Chance, 1988; Zeiler, 1971). If extinction is still in place when spontaneous recovery occurs—that is, if there is no reinforcement—the behavior will not continue for very long. Once in a while, Amanda may cry at night long after extinction but, if she gets no attention for the crying, it will not occur very often or for very long. However, if spontaneous recovery occurs and the behavior is now reinforced, the effect of extinction will be lost. For example, Greg may still try occasionally to open the back door to his apartment building. If the door happens to open one day, his behavior of using that door will be reinforced, and he will be more likely to try to use that door again. Finding the door open occasionally would be an example of intermittent reinforcement, which would increase behavioral persistence or resistance to extinction in the future.

Procedural Variations of Extinction

As we saw in Chapter 4, there are two procedural variations or types of reinforcement: positive reinforcement and negative reinforcement. A behavior may undergo extinction regardless of whether it is maintained by positive or negative reinforcement. The outcome of extinction is the same: The behavior decreases and stops occurring. Procedurally, however, extinction is slightly different in the two cases. If a behavior is positively reinforced, a consequence is applied or added after the behavior. Therefore, extinction of a positively reinforced behavior involves withholding the consequence that was previously delivered after the behavior. To put it another way, when the behavior no longer results in the delivery of the reinforcing consequence, the behavior no longer occurs.

If a behavior is negatively reinforced, the behavior results in the removal or avoidance of an aversive stimulus. Extinction of a negatively reinforced behavior therefore involves eliminating the escape or avoidance that was reinforcing the behavior. When the behavior no longer results in escape from or avoidance of an aversive stimulus, the behavior eventually stops. For example, suppose that you wear earplugs in your job at the factory to decrease the loud noise of the equipment. Wearing earplugs is negatively reinforced by escape from the loud noise. If the earplugs wore out and they no longer decreased the noise, you would stop wearing them. The behavior of wearing earplugs would be extinguished because wearing them no longer produced escape from the noise. This may be a difficult concept to grasp. Consider the following examples.

Procedural Variations of Extinction

The positive reinforcer is no longer delivered after the behavior.
The aversive stimulus is no longer removed after the behavior.

Shandra has an 11 P.M. curfew. If she comes in later than 11 P.M., her parents scold her, lecture her, and ground her for a week. Because the parents go to bed at 10 P.M., they do not know what time their daughter comes home. They ask her the next morning and, if she came home after 11 P.M., she lies and tells them she was home earlier. Lying is negatively reinforced by the avoidance of aversive consequences from her parents. Extinction of lying would occur if lying no longer helped her to avoid aversive consequences. Thus, if a parent were awake in bed and knew when Shandra came home, she would not avoid aversive consequences by lying. As a result, she would quit lying when she got home late.

Reinforcement

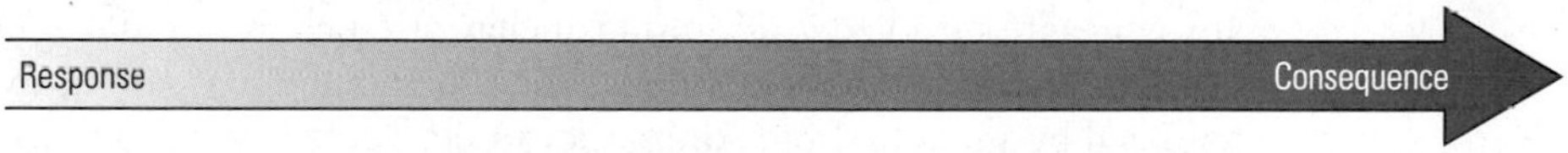

Response → Consequence

Shandra lies to her parents when she comes home after curfew. → Shandra avoids getting scolded and grounded.

Outcome: Shandra is more likely to lie about coming home late in the future.

Extinction

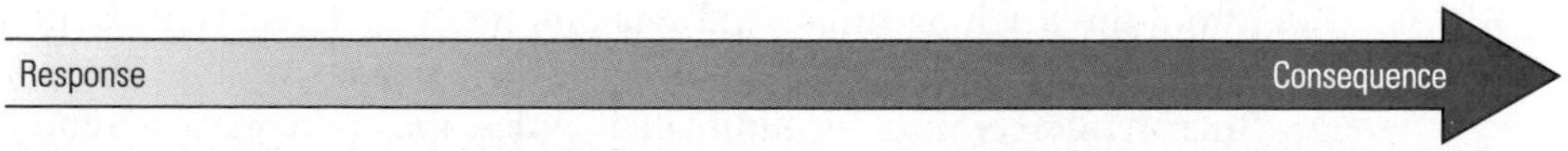

Response → Consequence

Shandra lies to her parents when she comes home after curfew. → The parents scold her and ground her. She does not avoid aversive consequences.

Outcome: Shandra is less likely to lie about coming home late in the future.

Consider another example. Joe is a college student who works part time as a custodian. He hates to clean the bathrooms. Whenever the supervisor asks Joe to do so, Joe makes up excuses, and the supervisor lets him out of the job and asks someone else to do it. Joe's behavior of making up excuses helps him avoid cleaning bathrooms. Making up excuses therefore is negatively reinforced.

How would the supervisor use extinction to stop Joe from making excuses?

Every time Joe makes up excuses, the supervisor tells him to clean the bathroom anyway. Therefore, when Joe cannot avoid cleaning bathrooms by making up excuses, he will quit making up excuses.

Reinforcement

Response → Consequence

Joe makes excuses when asked to clean the bathroom. | Joe avoids cleaning the bathroom.

Outcome: Joe is more likely to make excuses when asked to clean the bathroom in the future.

Extinction

Response → Consequence

Joe makes excuses when asked to clean the bathroom. | The supervisor does not let him avoid cleaning the bathroom.

Outcome: Joe is less likely to make excuses when asked to clean the bathroom in the future.

Research by Brian Iwata and his colleagues (Iwata, Pace, Cowdery, & Miltenberger, 1994) has demonstrated that extinction is procedurally different when a behavior has been maintained by positive reinforcement and by negative reinforcement. Iwata and his colleagues studied self-injurious behavior (such as self-hitting) exhibited by children who were mentally retarded. When they found that self-injury was positively reinforced by attention from adults, they implemented extinction by removing the adult attention after the behavior. For some children, however, self-injury was negatively reinforced: The self-injurious behavior resulted in escape from academic tasks. In other words, a teacher quit making demands on a child (removed the academic demand) once the child started to engage in self-injurious behavior. In these cases of negative reinforcement, extinction required the teacher not to remove the academic demand after the self-injury. Therefore, the self-injurious behavior no longer resulted in escape from the teaching situation. Iwata and his colleagues clearly demonstrated that if extinction is to occur, the reinforcer for the behavior must be identified and that particular reinforcer must be eliminated. Unless the appropriate reinforcer is identified and eliminated, the process does not function as extinction.

Edward Carr and his colleagues (Carr, Newsom, & Binkoff, 1980) studied the behavior disorders of children with mental retardation. They showed that aggressive behavior in two children occurred only in demand situations and functioned as escape behavior. In other words, the aggressive behavior was negatively reinforced by the termination of demands.

How would extinction be used with the aggressive behavior of these two children?

Carr and his colleagues demonstrated that when the child could not escape from the demand situation by engaging in aggressive behavior, the aggressive behavior decreased dramatically. Because escape was reinforcing the aggressive behavior, preventing escape functioned as extinction.

A Common Misconception about Extinction

Although extinction is procedurally different depending on the type of reinforcement for the behavior, the outcome is always the same: The behavior stops. A common misconception is that using extinction simply means ignoring the behavior. This is inaccurate in most cases. Extinction means removing the reinforcer for a behavior. Ignoring the problem behavior functions as extinction only if attention is the reinforcer. For example, a person's shoplifting is reinforced by getting merchandise from a store. If the salespeople in the store ignore the shoplifting behavior, this will not cause that behavior to stop. Again, suppose that a child runs from the table whenever he is told to eat his vegetables, and the outcome is that he does not eat his vegetables. If the parents ignore this behavior, it will not stop. Running from the table is reinforced by escape from eating the vegetables. Ignoring the behavior does not take away this reinforcer and therefore does not function as extinction.

Take each example of reinforcement in Table 4-1 (p. 72) and turn it into an example of extinction. Answers are provided at the end of this chapter in Appendix A.

Factors Influencing Extinction

Two important factors influence the extinction process: the reinforcement schedule before extinction and the occurrence of reinforcement after extinction. The reinforcement schedule partly determines whether extinction results in a rapid decrease in the behavior or a more gradual decrease (Bijou, 1958; Kazdin & Polster, 1973; Lerman, Iwata, Shore, & Kahng, 1996; Neisworth, Hunt, Gallop, & Madle, 1985). Recall from Chapter 4 that in continuous reinforcement, every occurrence of a behavior is followed by a reinforcer; in intermittent reinforcement, not every occurrence of a behavior results in a reinforcer, but instead the behavior is only occasionally reinforced. When a behavior is continuously reinforced, it decreases rapidly once the reinforcement is terminated. On the other hand, when a behavior is intermittently reinforced, it often decreases more gradually once the reinforcement is terminated. This occurs because the change from reinforcement to extinction is more discriminable (there is a larger contrast) when a behavior is reinforced every time than when only some occurrences of the behavior result in reinforcement.

For example, if you put money into a vending machine and push the button, you always get the item you want. This is a case of continuous reinforcement, and the decrease in behavior during extinction would be fairly rapid. You would not continue to

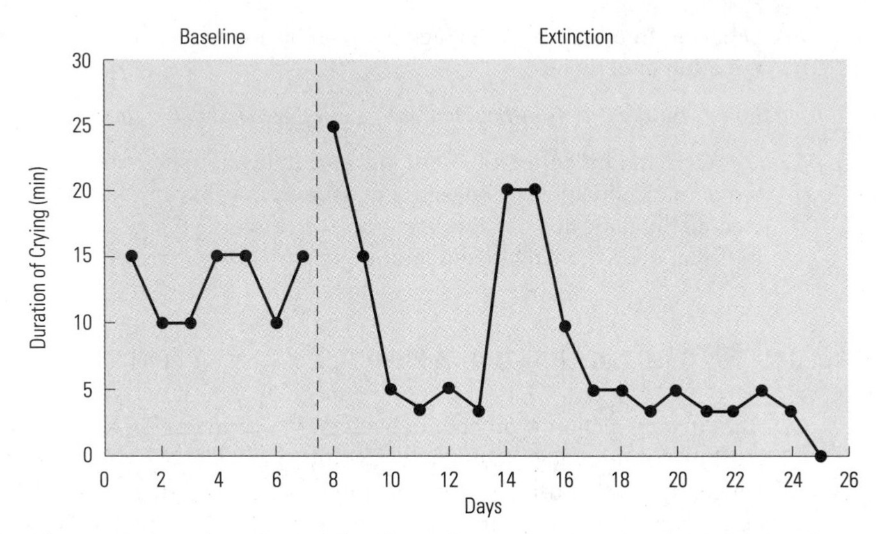

FIGURE 5-4 The graph shows hypothetical data illustrating the duration of crying during baseline and extinction if the behavior was accidentally reinforced on day 13. After day 13, the duration of the behavior increased, and extinction was prolonged.

put money into a vending machine if you no longer got the item you paid for; the lack of reinforcement would be immediately apparent. Contrast this with what happens when you put money into a slot machine or a video gambling machine. This is a case of intermittent reinforcement: Putting money into the slot machine is only occasionally reinforced by hitting the jackpot and winning money from the machine. If the machine was broken and never again produced a jackpot (no reinforcement), you might put many more coins into the machine before finally giving up. It takes longer for the gambling behavior to stop because it is harder to determine that there is no longer reinforcement for the behavior.

Intermittent reinforcement before extinction produces **resistance to extinction**; in other words, the behavior persists once extinction is implemented. Continuous reinforcement before extinction produces much less resistance to extinction and behavioral persistence. Because of resistance to extinction, the reinforcement schedule before extinction has implications for the successful use of extinction in a behavior modification program. (See Chapter 14.)

A second factor that influences extinction is the occurrence of reinforcement after extinction. If reinforcement occurs in the course of extinction, it takes longer for the behavior to decrease. This is because reinforcement of the behavior, once extinction has been started, amounts to intermittent reinforcement, which makes the behavior more resistant to extinction. In addition, if the behavior is reinforced during an episode of spontaneous recovery, the behavior may then increase to its level before extinction. Consider the case of Amanda again. We see in Figure 5-2 that her crying at night decreased to zero by day 14, 7 days after extinction was started. What if, on day 13, the babysitter came into her room and talked to her when she cried that night? This would reinforce the crying behavior, and crying would occur for many more days

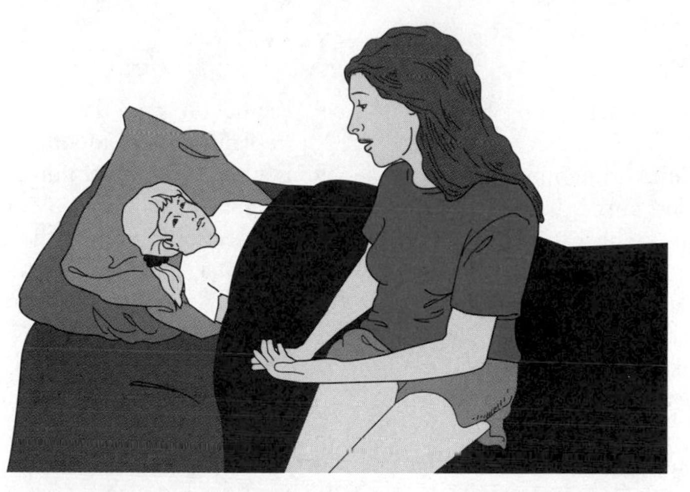

FIGURE 5-5 When Amanda cries at night, the babysitter comes into Amanda's room and talks to her. By doing so, the babysitter accidentally reinforces the crying. As a result, it will take longer for the behavior to decrease and stop when the parents use extinction.

(Figure 5-4). The babysitter's action (Figure 5-5) would amount to intermittent reinforcement and would produce resistance to extinction.

In the case of extinction of the child's bedtime tantrum reported by Williams (1959), the tantrums had almost stopped after the parents had used extinction for a few days. However, when an aunt paid attention to the child's tantrums one night, they increased in intensity. Only when the parents again used extinction consistently did the tantrums finally stop.

CHAPTER SUMMARY

1. Extinction is a basic behavioral principle. It occurs when a previously reinforced behavior is no longer reinforced and, as a result, the behavior decreases and stops occurring.
2. Extinction often is characterized by an extinction burst, in which the unreinforced behavior temporarily increases in frequency, intensity, or duration or novel behaviors are exhibited temporarily.
3. Procedurally, extinction is different for behaviors that are positively reinforced than for those that are negatively reinforced. In each case, however, the particular reinforcer for the behavior is terminated, and the outcome is the elimination of the behavior. With extinction of a positively reinforced behavior, the positive reinforcer is no longer delivered after the behavior. With extinction of a negatively reinforced behavior, the aversive stimulus is no longer removed after the behavior.
4. A common misconception about extinction is that extinction means ignoring the behavior. Ignoring the behavior functions as extinction only if attention was the reinforcer for the behavior.
5. The behavior decreases more rapidly during extinction if the behavior was reinforced on a continuous schedule before extinction and if the behavior is never reinforced during the extinction process.

PRACTICE TEST

1. What is the behavioral definition of extinction? (p. 96)
2. Provide an example of extinction. (p. 95)
3. What is an extinction burst? (p. 98)
4. Provide an example of an extinction burst. (pp. 98–100)
5. Draw a graph of extinction. Be sure to show the extinction burst. (p. 99)
6. What is negative reinforcement? Explain the extinction of a negatively reinforced behavior. (pp. 100–102)
7. Provide an example of extinction of a negatively reinforced behavior. (pp. 101–102)
8. Extinction is not the same thing as ignoring. Explain this statement. (p. 103)
9. Explain how the reinforcement schedule for a behavior (continuous or intermittent) influences extinction of the behavior. (p. 104)
10. What happens to a behavior when it is accidentally reinforced during the extinction process? (pp. 104–105)
11. Draw a graph of extinction that shows what happens when a behavior is accidentally reinforced. (p. 104)
12. What is spontaneous recovery during extinction? (p. 100)

APPENDIX A

Applying Extinction with Each Example of Reinforcement from Table 4-1

1. If the parents quit coming to the child's room when she cried at night, the child would quit crying in the future.
2. If the umbrella did not open correctly each time the woman tried to open it and, as a result, it did not keep the rain from hitting her, she would quit using the umbrella in the future.
3. If the exhaust fan did not respond to the cook's attempts to turn it on, or if it did not effectively draw the smoke out of the room, he would eventually stop trying to turn on the exhaust fan.
4. If the student's roommate no longer gave her the answers to the questions, she would quit asking her roommate for the answers.
5. If the teacher ignored Johnny when he looked at her in class, he would be less likely to look at her in the future.
6. If the picture on Patricia's TV no longer became clearer when she put the tin foil on the antenna, she would quit putting the tin foil on the antenna.
7. If the workers no longer earned money for assembling bicycles (because the company was bankrupt), they would stop assembling bicycles for the company.
8. If the child did not stop crying when his mother gave him candy in the store, the mother would be less likely to give him candy when he cried because giving him candy was not reinforced by the termination of his crying. If the mother did not give candy to her child when he cried in the store, the child would be less likely to cry in the store.

CHAPTER 5 *Quiz 1* Name:

1. During extinction, a previously reinforced behavior is no longer followed by a reinforcer, and the behavior ______________________________ in the future.
2. During an extinction burst, the behavior may temporarily increase in ______________, ______________, or ______________.
3. During extinction of a positively reinforced behavior, the ______________ is no longer delivered following the behavior.
4. During extinction of a negatively reinforced behavior, the ______________ is no longer removed following the behavior.
5. During ______________________ a previously extinguished behavior occurs again in the future.
6. Besides a temporary increase in the behavior, what are two other things that might happen during an extinction burst? ______________________________ and ______________________________
7. When does extinction involve ignoring the behavior? ______________________________
8. The behavior will decrease ______________ (more/less) quickly during extinction following intermittent reinforcement than continuous reinforcement.

A child cries in the store and the parent gives the child candy. As a result, the child is more likely to cry in the store.

9. What is the reinforcer for crying in this case? ______________________________
10. How would the parent use extinction for crying in this case? ______________________________

CHAPTER 5 *Quiz 2* Name:

1. During extinction, a previously reinforced behavior ______________________________, and the behavior stops occurring in the future.

2. The temporary increase in a behavior during extinction is called a(n) ____________________.

3. During extinction of a ______________________ (positively/negatively) reinforced behavior, a reinforcer is no longer delivered following the behavior.

4. During extinction of a ______________________ (positively/negatively) reinforced behavior, an aversive stimulus is no longer removed following the behavior.

5. During spontaneous recovery, what happens to a behavior that had stopped occurring as a result of extinction? ____

6. During an extinction burst, the behavior might temporarily increase. In addition, __________________ behaviors or ______________________ behaviors might occur.

7. Two factors that influence extinction are the schedule of reinforcement before extinction and ____________________________________ after extinction.

8. The behavior will decrease __________________ (more/less) quickly during extinction following continuous reinforcement than intermittent reinforcement.

A child cries when mom is brushing the child's teeth, and mom stops brushing. As a result, the child is more likely to cry when she gets her teeth brushed.

9. Does this example illustrate positive or negative reinforcement for crying? ________________

10. How would mom use extinction for crying in this case? ______________________________

CHAPTER 5 *Quiz 3* Name:

1. During extinction, what happens following the occurrence of the behavior?

   ____

2. During an extinction burst, a behavior ______________ in frequency, duration, or intensity.

3. During extinction of a positively reinforced behavior, the positive reinforcer is ______________ following the behavior.

4. During extinction of a negatively reinforced behavior, the aversive stimulus is

   ______________ following the behavior.

5. When a behavior occurs again in the future after it had stopped occurring following

   extinction, the process is called ______________.

6. What are two types of behaviors that might occur during an extinction burst?

   ______________ and ______________

7. Two factors that influence extinction are the ______________ before extinction and the occurrence of reinforcement after extinction.

8. What type of reinforcement schedule before extinction results in the most rapid decrease in

   the behavior during extinction? ______________

Ms. Jones pushes the button on her garage door opener each time she drives in the driveway, and the door opens.

9. Is this an example of positive or negative reinforcement?______________

10. Describe extinction of the behavior of pushing the button on the garage door opener.

    ____

Punishment

In Chapters 4 and 5, we discussed the basic principles of reinforcement and extinction. Positive and negative reinforcement are processes that strengthen operant behavior, and extinction is a process that weakens operant behavior. This chapter focuses on punishment, another process that weakens operant behavior. Consider the following examples.

- What is the principle of punishment?
- What is a common misconception about the definition of punishment in behavior modification?
- How does positive punishment differ from negative punishment?
- How are unconditioned punishers different from conditioned punishers?
- What factors influence the effectiveness of punishment?
- What are the problems with punishment?

Kathy, a college senior, moved into a new apartment near campus. On her way to class, she passed a fenced-in yard with a big friendly-looking dog. One day, when the dog was near the fence, Kathy reached over to pet the dog. At once, the dog growled, bared its teeth, and bit her hand. After this, she never again tried to pet the dog.

On Mother's Day, Otis decided to get up early and make breakfast for his mom. He put the cast iron skillet on the stove and turned the burner on high. Then he mixed a couple of eggs in a bowl with some milk to make scrambled eggs. After about 5 minutes, he poured the eggs from the bowl into the skillet. Immediately, the eggs started to burn and smoke rose from the skillet. Otis grabbed the handle of the skillet to move it off of the burner. As soon as he touched the handle, pain shot through his hand; he screamed and dropped the skillet. After that episode, Otis never grabbed the handle of a hot cast iron skillet again. He always used a hot pad to avoid burning himself.

Defining Punishment

These two examples illustrate the behavioral principle of punishment. In each example, a person engaged in a behavior and there was an immediate consequence that made it less likely that the person would repeat the behavior in similar situations in the future. Kathy reached over the fence to pet the dog, and the dog immediately bit her. As a result, Kathy is less likely to reach over the fence to pet that dog or other unfamiliar dogs.

Otis grabbed the hot handle of a cast iron skillet, which resulted immediately in painful stimulation as he burned his hand. As a result, Otis is much less likely to grab the handle of a cast iron skillet on a hot stove (at least not without a hot pad).

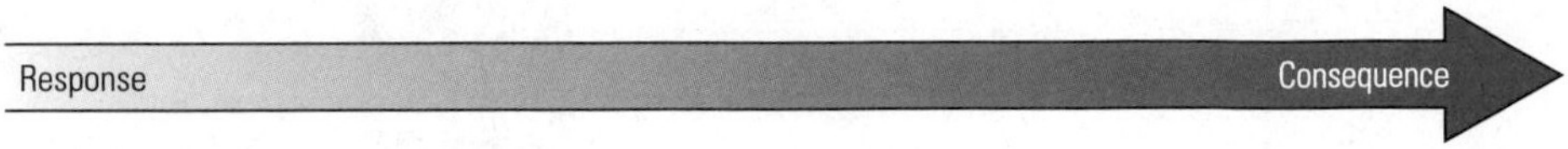

Response → Consequence

Kathy reaches over the fence and immediately the dog bites her.

Outcome: Kathy is less likely to reach over the fence in the future.

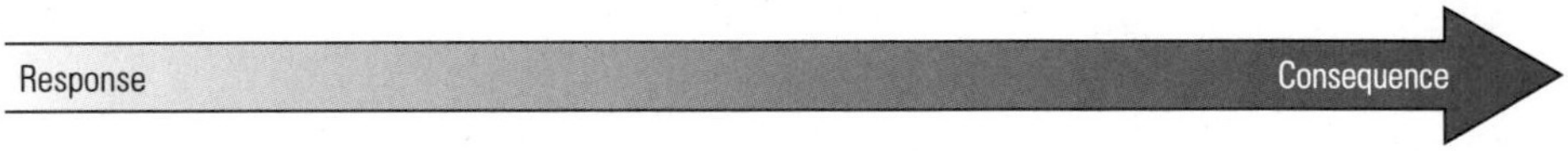

Response → Consequence

Otis touches a hot skillet and immediately he burns his hand (a painful stimulus).

Outcome: Otis is less likely to grab a hot cast iron skillet in the future.

As you can see from these examples, there are three parts to the definition of ***punishment.***

1. A particular behavior occurs.
2. A consequence immediately follows the behavior.
3. As a result, the behavior is less likely to occur again in the future. (The behavior is weakened.)

Identify some recent examples of punishment in your life.

A ***punisher*** (also called an aversive stimulus) is a consequence that makes a particular behavior less likely to occur in the future. For Kathy, the dog bite was a punisher for her behavior of reaching over the fence. For Otis, the painful stimulus (burning his hand) was the punisher for grabbing the handle of the cast iron skillet. A punisher is defined by its effect on the behavior it follows. A stimulus event is a punisher when it decreases the frequency of the behavior it follows.

Consider the case of an aggressive and disruptive 5-year-old. Juan teases and hits his sisters until they cry. His mother scolds him and spanks him each time he teases or hits his sisters. Although Juan stops teasing and hitting his sisters at the moment that his mom scolds and spanks him, he continues to engage in these aggressive and disruptive behaviors with his sisters day after day.

Is the scolding and spanking by his mother a punisher for Juan's aggressive and disruptive behavior? Why or why not?

No, the scolding and spanking do not function as punishers. They have not resulted in a decrease in Juan's problem behavior over time.

This example actually illustrates positive reinforcement. Juan's behavior (teasing and hitting) results in the presentation of a consequence (scolding and spanking by his mother and crying by his sisters), and the outcome is that Juan continues to engage in the behavior day after day. These are the three parts of the definition of positive reinforcement.

Response		Consequence
Juan's teasing and hitting	is immediately followed by	his sisters' crying scolding and spanking from his mother.

Outcome: Juan continues to hit and tease his sisters in the future.

This raises an important point about the definition of punishment. You cannot define punishment by whether the consequence appears unfavorable or aversive. You can conclude that a particular consequence is punishing only if the behavior decreases in the future. In Juan's case, scolding and spanking appear to be unfavorable consequences, but he continues to hit and tease his sisters. If the scolding and spanking functioned as a punisher, Juan would quit hitting and teasing his sisters over time. When we define punishment (or reinforcement) according to whether the behavior decreases (or increases) in the future as a result of the consequences, we are adopting a functional definition. See Table 6-1 for examples of punishment.

TABLE 6-1

EXAMPLES FOR SELF-ASSESSMENT (PUNISHMENT)

1. Ed was riding his bike down the street and looking down at the ground as he pedaled. All of a sudden he ran into the back of a parked car, flew off the bike, and hit the roof of the car with his face. In the process, he knocked his front teeth loose. In the future, Ed was much less likely to look down at the ground when he rode his bike.
2. When Alma was in the day care program, she sometimes hit the other kids if they played with her toys. Alma's teacher made her quit playing and sit in a chair in another room for 2 minutes each time she hit someone. As a result, Alma quit hitting the other children.
3. Carlton made money in the summer by mowing his neighbor's lawn each week. One week, Carlton ran over the garden hose with the lawn mower and ruined the hose. His neighbor made Carlton pay for the hose. Since then, whenever Carlton mows the lawn, he never runs over a hose or any other objects laying in the grass.
4. Sarah was driving down the interstate on her way to see a friend who lived a few hours away. Feeling a little bored, she picked up the newspaper on the seat next to her and began to read it. As she was reading, her car gradually veered to the right without her noticing. Suddenly, the car was sliding on gravel and side-swiped a speed limit sign. As a result, Sarah no longer reads when she drives on the highway.
5. Helen goes to school in a special class for children with behavior disorders. Her teachers use poker chips as conditioned reinforcers for her academic performance. The teachers place a poker chip in a container to reinforce her correct answers. However, each time Helen gets out of her seat without permission, the teachers take one token away from her. As a result, Helen quit getting out of her seat without permission.
6. Kevin used to make jokes about his wife's cooking at parties and got a lot of laughs from his friends. At first his wife smiled at his jokes, but eventually she got upset; whenever Kevin made a joke about her cooking, she gave him an icy stare. As a result, Kevin quit joking about his wife's cooking.

One other point to consider is whether a behavior decreases or stops only temporarily when the consequence is administered, or whether the behavior decreases in the future. Juan stopped hitting his sisters at the time that he received a spanking from his mother, but he did not stop hitting his sisters in the future. Some parents continue to scold or spank their children because it puts an immediate stop to the problem behavior, even though their scolding and spanking do not make the child's problem behavior less likely to occur in the future. The parents believe they are using punishment. However, if the behavior continues to occur in the future, the scolding and spanking do not function as punishers and may actually function as reinforcers.

What reinforces the parents' behavior of scolding and spanking the child?

Because the child temporarily stops the problem behavior after the scolding or spanking, the parents' behavior of scolding or spanking is negatively reinforced, so the parents continue to scold or spank the child in the future when he misbehaves.

A Common Misconception about Punishment

In behavior modification, *punishment* is a technical term with a specific meaning. Whenever behavior analysts speak of punishment, they are referring to a process in which the consequence of a behavior results in a future decrease in the occurrence of that behavior. This is quite different from what most people think of as punishment. In general usage, *punishment* can mean many different things, most of them unpleasant.

Many people define punishment as something meted out to a person who has committed a crime or other inappropriate behavior. In this context, punishment involves not only the hope that the behavior will cease, but also elements of retribution or retaliation; part of the intent is to hurt the person who has committed the crime. Seen as something that a wrongdoer deserves, punishment has moral or ethical connotations. Authority figures such as governments, police, churches, or parents impose punishment to inhibit inappropriate behavior—that is, to keep people from breaking laws or rules. Punishment may involve prison time, the electric chair, fines, the threat of going to hell, spanking, or scolding. However, the everyday meaning of punishment is very different from the technical definition of punishment used in behavior modification.

People who are unfamiliar with the technical definition of punishment may believe that the use of punishment in behavior modification is wrong or dangerous. It is unfortunate that Skinner adopted the term *punishment*, a term that has an existing meaning and many negative connotations. As a student, it is important for you to understand the technical definition of *punishment* in behavior modification and to realize that it is very different from the common view of punishment in society.

Positive and Negative Punishment

There are two basic procedural variations of punishment: positive punishment and negative punishment. The difference between positive and negative punishment is determined by the consequence of the behavior. ***Positive punishment*** is defined as follows.

1. The occurrence of a behavior
2. is followed by the presentation of an aversive stimulus
3. and, as a result, the behavior is less likely to occur in the future.

Negative punishment is defined as follows.

1. The occurrence of a behavior
2. is followed by the removal of a reinforcing stimulus
3. and, as a result, the behavior is less likely to occur in the future.

Notice that these definitions parallel the definitions of positive and negative reinforcement (Chapter 4). The critical difference is that reinforcement strengthens a behavior or makes it more likely to occur in the future, whereas punishment weakens a behavior or makes it less likely to occur in the future.

Many researchers have examined the effects of punishment on the behavior of laboratory animals. Azrin and Holz (1966) discussed the early animal research on punishment, much of which they had carried out themselves. Since then, researchers have investigated the effects of positive and negative punishment on human behavior (Axelrod & Apsche, 1983). For example, Corte, Wolf, and Locke (1971) helped institutionalized adolescents with mental retardation decrease self-injurious behavior by using punishment. One subject slapped herself in the face. Each time she did so, the researchers immediately applied a brief electric shock with a hand-held shock device. (Although the shock was painful, it did not harm the girl.) As a result of this procedure, the number of times she slapped herself in the face each hour decreased immediately from 300–400 to almost zero.

Note that this study is from 1971. Electric shock is rarely, if ever, used as a punisher today because of ethical concerns. This study is cited to illustrate the basic principle of positive punishment, not to support the use of electric shock as a punisher.

Why is this an example of positive punishment?

This is an example of positive punishment because the painful stimulus was presented each time the girl slapped her face, and the behavior decreased as a result. Sajwaj, Libet, and Agras (1974) also used positive punishment to decrease life-threatening rumination behavior in a 6-month-old infant. Rumination in infants involves repeatedly regurgitating food into the mouth and swallowing it again. It can result in dehydration, malnutrition, and even death. In this study, each time the infant engaged in rumination, the researchers squirted a small amount of lemon juice into her mouth. As a result, the rumination behavior immediately decreased, and the infant began to gain weight.

One other form of positive punishment is based on the Premack principle, which states that when a person is made to engage in a low-probability behavior contingent on a high-probability behavior, the high-probability behavior will decrease in frequency (Miltenberger & Fuqua, 1981). In other words, if, after engaging in a problem behavior, a person has to do something he or she doesn't want to do, the person will be less likely to engage in the problem behavior in the future. Luce, Delquadri, and Hall (1980) used this principle to help a developmentally delayed 6-year-old boy stop engaging in aggressive behavior. Each time the boy hit someone in the classroom, he was required to stand up and sit down on the floor ten times in a row. As you can see from Figure 6-1, this punishment procedure, called contingent exercise, resulted in an immediate decrease in the hitting behavior.

One thing you will notice in Figure 6-1 is that punishment results in an immediate decrease in the target behavior. Although extinction also decreases a behavior, it usually takes longer for the behavior to decrease, and an extinction burst often occurs before the behavior decreases. With punishment, there is no extinction burst. However, other side effects are associated with the use of punishment; these are described later.

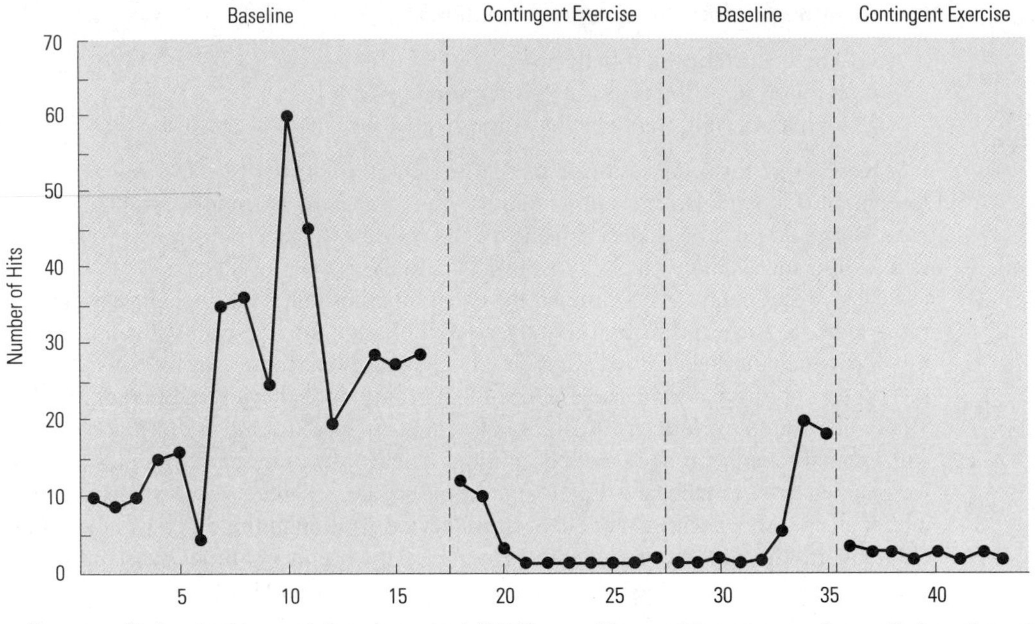

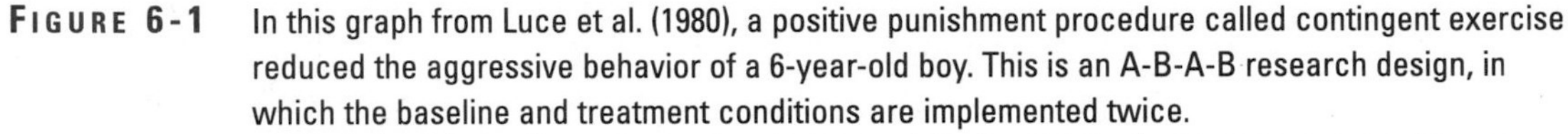
FIGURE 6-1 In this graph from Luce et al. (1980), a positive punishment procedure called contingent exercise reduced the aggressive behavior of a 6-year-old boy. This is an A-B-A-B research design, in which the baseline and treatment conditions are implemented twice.

Negative punishment has also been the subject of extensive research. Two examples of negative punishment are **time-out from positive reinforcement** and **response cost.** (See Chapter 17 for more detail.) Both involve the loss of a reinforcing stimulus or activity after the occurrence of a problem behavior. Some students may confuse negative punishment and extinction. They both weaken behavior. Extinction involves withholding the reinforcer that was maintaining the behavior. Negative punishment, by contrast, involves removing or withdrawing a positive reinforcer after the behavior; the reinforcer that is removed in negative punishment is one the individual had already acquired and is not necessarily the same reinforcer that was maintaining the behavior. For example, Johnny interrupts his parents and the behavior is reinforced by his parents' attention. (They scold him each time he interrupts.) In this case, extinction would involve withholding the parents' attention each time Johnny interrupts. Negative punishment would involve the loss of some other reinforcer—such as allowance money or the opportunity to watch TV—each time he interrupted. Both procedures would result in a decrease in the frequency of interrupting.

Clark, Rowbury, Baer, and Baer (1973) used time-out to decrease aggressive and disruptive behavior in an 8-year-old girl with Down syndrome. In time-out, the person is removed from a reinforcing situation for a brief period of time after the problem behavior occurs. Each time the girl engaged in the problem behavior in the classroom, she had to sit by herself in a small time-out room for 3 minutes. As a result of time-out, her problem behaviors decreased immediately (Figure 6-2). Through the use of time-out, the problem behavior was followed by the loss of access to attention (social reinforcement) from the teacher and other reinforcers in the classroom (Figure 6-3).

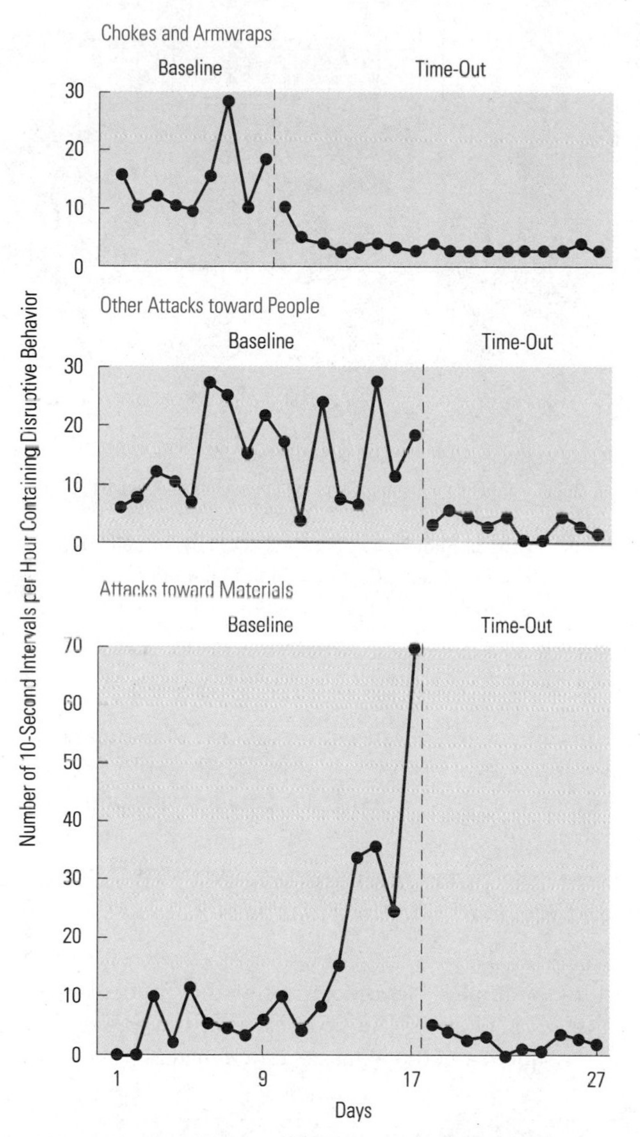

FIGURE 6-2 In this graph from Clark et al. (1973), you can see the effect of a negative punishment procedure (time-out) on the aggressive and disruptive behavior of a young girl with Down syndrome. This graph illustrates a multiple-baseline-across-behaviors design. Time-out was implemented for three different behaviors of one subject, and the use of time-out was staggered over time.

In a study by Phillips, Phillips, Fixsen, and Wolf (1971), "predelinquent" youths in a residential treatment program earned points for engaging in appropriate behavior and traded in their points for backup reinforcers such as snacks, money, and privileges. The points were conditioned reinforcers. The researchers then used a negative punishment procedure called response cost to decrease late arrivals for supper. When the youths arrived late, they lost some of the points they had earned. As a result, late arrivals decreased until the youths always showed up on time.

FIGURE 6-3 This 8-year-old child has to sit in the small time-out room by herself each time she engages in aggressive behavior in the classroom. By sitting in the time-out room, she loses access to such reinforcers as teacher attention, attention from other students, and toys. As a result, the aggressive behavior decreases.

Positive punishment and negative punishment sometimes are called other names, which are more descriptive. However, it is simpler to speak of positive punishment and negative punishment, and these terms are parallel with positive reinforcement and negative reinforcement.

Look at the examples of punishment in Table 6-1. Which are examples of positive punishment and which are negative punishment? Answers are provided at the end of the chapter in Appendix A.

In all of these examples, the process resulted in a decrease in the future occurrence of the behavior. Therefore, in each example, the presentation or removal of a stimulus as a consequence of the behavior functioned as punishment.

Other Names for Positive Punishment

- Punishment by application
- Punishment by contingent presentation of a stimulus
- Punishment by presentation of an aversive stimulus
- Response-contingent presentation of a punisher

Other Names for Negative Punishment

- Punishment by withdrawal
- Punishment by loss of reinforcers
- The penalty contingency
- Response-contingent removal of a positive reinforcer

Sources: Cooper, Heron, & Heward, 1987; Malott, Whaley, & Malott, 1993; Sundel & Sundel, 1993.

Unconditioned and Conditioned Punishers

Like reinforcement, punishment is a natural process that affects human behavior. Some events or stimuli are naturally punishing because avoiding or minimizing contact with these stimuli has survival value (Cooper et al., 1987). Painful stimuli or extreme levels of stimulation often are dangerous. Behaviors that produce painful or extreme stimulation are naturally weakened, and behaviors that result in escape or avoidance of such stimulation are naturally strengthened. For this reason, painful stimuli or extreme levels of stimulation have biological importance. Such stimuli are called **unconditioned punishers.** Through the process of evolution, we have developed the capacity for our behavior to be punished by these naturally aversive events without any prior training or experience.

For example, extreme heat or cold, extreme levels of auditory or visual stimulation, or any painful stimulus (e.g., from electric shock, a sharp object, or a forceful blow) naturally weakens the behavior that produces it. If these were not unconditioned punishers, we would be more likely to engage in dangerous behaviors that could result in injury or death. We quickly learn not to put our hands into a fire, look directly into the sun, touch sharp objects, or go barefoot in the snow or on hot asphalt because each of these behaviors results in a naturally punishing consequence.

A second type of punishing stimulus is called a **conditioned punisher.** Conditioned punishers are stimuli or events that function as punishers only after being paired with unconditioned punishers or other existing conditioned punishers. Any stimulus or event may become a conditioned punisher if it is paired with an established punisher.

The word "no" is a common conditioned punisher. Because it is often paired with many other punishing stimuli, it eventually becomes a punisher itself. For example, if a child reaches for an electrical outlet and the parent says "no," the child may be less likely to reach for the outlet in the future. When the child spells a word incorrectly in the classroom and the teacher says "no," the child will be less likely to spell that word incorrectly in the future. The word "no" is considered a **generalized conditioned punisher** because it has been paired with a variety of other unconditioned and conditioned punishers over the course of a person's life. Van Houten and his colleagues found that if firm reprimands were delivered to students in the classroom when they engaged in disruptive behavior, their disruptive behavior decreased. In this study (Van Houten, Nau, MacKenzie-Keating, Sameoto, & Colavecchia, 1982), reprimands were conditioned punishers for the students' disruptive behavior. Threats of harm often are conditioned punishers. Because threats have often been associated with painful stimulation in the past, threats may become conditioned punishers.

Stimuli that are associated with the loss of reinforcers may become conditioned punishers. A parking ticket or a speeding ticket is associated with the loss of money (paying a fine), so the ticket is a conditioned punisher for many people. In reality, whether speeding tickets or parking tickets function as conditioned punishers depends on a number of factors, including the schedule of punishment and the magnitude of the punishing stimulus. These and other factors influencing the effectiveness of punishment are discussed later in the chapter.

A warning from a parent may become a conditioned punisher if it has been paired with the loss of reinforcers such as allowance money, privileges, or preferred activities. As a result, when a child misbehaves and the parent gives the child a warning, the child may be less likely to engage in the same misbehavior in the future. A facial expression or a look of disapproval may be a conditioned punisher when it is associated with the loss of attention or approval from an important person (such as a parent or teacher). A facial expression may also be associated with an aversive event such as a scolding or a spanking and thus may function as a conditioned punisher (Doleys, Wells, Hobbs, Roberts, & Cartelli, 1976; Jones & Miller, 1974).

Once again, it is important to remember that a conditioned punisher is defined functionally. It is defined as a punisher only if it weakens the behavior that it follows. If a person exceeds the speed limit and receives a speeding ticket and the outcome is that the person is less likely to speed in the future, the ticket functioned as a punisher. However, if the person continues to speed after receiving a ticket, the ticket was not a punisher. Consider the following example.

Response		Consequence
Child belches at the dinner table	and immediately	mom gives the child an angry look.

Outcome: Child continues to belch at the dinner table in the future.

Is the mother's angry look a conditioned punisher in this situation? Why or why not?

The look was not a conditioned punisher because the child's behavior of belching at the table was not weakened; the child did not stop engaging in the behavior. Mom's look may have functioned as a positive reinforcer, or perhaps other family members laughed when the child belched and thus reinforced the belching behavior. Alternatively, belching may be naturally reinforcing because it relieves an unpleasant sensation in the stomach.

Contrasting Reinforcement and Punishment

There are important similarities and differences between positive and negative reinforcement on one hand and positive and negative punishment on the other. The defining features of each principle are that a behavior is followed by a consequence and that the consequence influences the future occurrence of the behavior. The similarities and differences between the two types of reinforcement and punishment can be summarized as follows:

	Consequence of the Behavior	
Outcome	Stimulus is presented	Stimulus is removed
Behavior is strengthened (increases in the future)	Positive reinforcement	Negative reinforcement
Behavior is weakened (decreases in the future)	Positive punishment	Negative punishment

Note that, when a stimulus is presented after a behavior (left column), the process may be positive reinforcement or positive punishment, depending on whether the behavior is strengthened (reinforcement) or weakened (punishment) in the future. When a stimulus is removed after the behavior (right column), the process may be negative reinforcement or negative punishment. It is negative reinforcement if the behavior is strengthened and negative punishment if the behavior is weakened.

One particular stimulus may be involved in reinforcement and punishment of different behaviors in the same situation, depending on whether the stimulus is presented or removed after the behavior. Consider the example of Kathy and the dog. When Kathy reached over the fence, this behavior was followed immediately by the presentation of an aversive stimulus (the dog bit her). The dog's bite served as a punisher: Kathy was less likely to reach over the fence in the future. However, when Kathy pulled her hand back quickly, she terminated the dog bite. Because pulling her hand back removed the pain of being bitten, this behavior was strengthened. This is an example of negative reinforcement. As you can see, when the dog bite was *presented* after one behavior, the behavior was weakened; when the dog bite was *removed* after another behavior, that behavior was strengthened.

Positive Punishment

Response → Consequence

Kathy reached over the fence and immediately the dog bit her.

Outcome: Kathy is less likely to reach over the fence in the future.

Negative Reinforcement

Response → Consequence

Kathy pulled her hand back and immediately she terminated the dog bite.

Outcome: Kathy is more likely to pull her hand back when presented with a similar painful stimulus.

In the example of Otis and the hot skillet, the immediate consequence of grabbing the skillet handle was a painful stimulus. The outcome was that Otis was less likely to grab a hot skillet in the future. This is positive punishment.

How was negative reinforcement involved in this example?

When Otis used a hot pad, he avoided the painful stimulus. As a result, he is more likely to use a hot pad when grabbing a hot skillet in the future (negative reinforcement). Touching the hot skillet is punished by the presentation of a painful stimulus; using the hot pad is reinforced by avoidance of the painful stimulus.

Now consider how the same stimulus may be involved in negative punishment of one behavior and positive reinforcement of another behavior. If a reinforcing stimulus is removed after a behavior, the behavior will decrease in the future (negative punishment) but, if a reinforcing stimulus is presented after a behavior, the behavior will increase in the future (positive reinforcement). You know that a stimulus is functioning as a positive reinforcer when its presentation after a behavior increases that behavior and its removal after a behavior decreases that behavior. For example, Fred's parents take his bicycle away for a week whenever they catch him riding after dark. This makes Fred less likely to ride his bike after dark (negative punishment). However, after a few days Fred pleads with his parents to let him ride his bike again and promises never to ride after dark. They give in and give him his bike back. As a result, he is more likely to plead with his parents in the future when his bike is taken away (positive reinforcement).

Negative Punishment

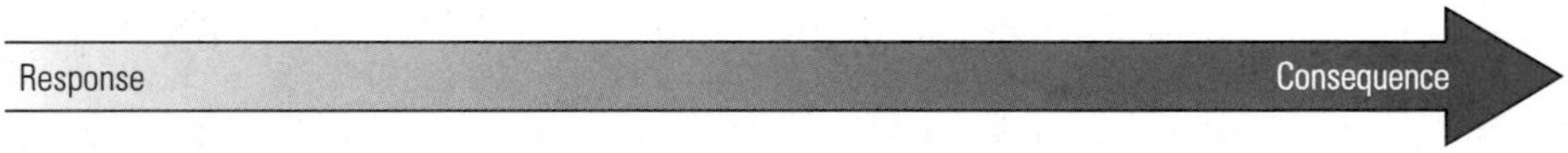

Response → Consequence

Fred rides his bike after dark and then bike is removed for 1 week.

Outcome: Fred is less likely to ride his bike after dark.

Positive Punishment

Response → Consequence

Fred pleads with his parents and then bike is presented to Fred.

Outcome: Fred is more likely to plead with his parents when his bike is taken away.

FACTORS INFLUENCING THE EFFECTIVENESS OF PUNISHMENT

The factors that influence the effectiveness of punishment are similar to those that influence reinforcement. They include immediacy, contingency, establishing operations, individual differences, and magnitude.

Immediacy

When a punishing stimulus follows a behavior immediately, or when the loss of a reinforcer occurs immediately after the behavior, the behavior is more likely to be weakened. In other words, for punishment to be most effective, the consequence must follow the behavior immediately. As the delay between the behavior and the consequence increases, the effectiveness of the consequence as a punisher decreases.

To illustrate this point, consider what would happen if a punishing stimulus occurred some time after the behavior occurred. A student makes a sarcastic comment in class and the teacher immediately gives her an angry look. As a result, the student is less likely to make a sarcastic comment in class. If the teacher had given the student an angry look 30 minutes after the student made the sarcastic comment, the look would not function as a punisher for the behavior of making sarcastic comments. Instead, the teacher's angry look probably would have functioned as a punisher for whatever behavior the student had engaged in immediately before the look.

Contingency

For punishment to be most effective, the punishing stimulus should occur every time the behavior occurs. We would say that the punishing consequence is contingent on the behavior when the punisher follows the behavior each time the behavior occurs and the punisher does not occur when the behavior does not occur. A punisher is most likely to weaken a behavior when it is contingent on the behavior. This means that punishment is less effective when it is applied inconsistently—that is, when the punisher follows only some occurrences of the behavior or when the punisher is presented in the absence of the behavior. If a reinforcement schedule continues to be in effect for the behavior, and punishment is applied inconsistently, some occurrences of the behavior may be followed by a punisher and some occurrences of the behavior may be followed by a reinforcer. In this case, the behavior is being influenced by an intermittent schedule of reinforcement at the same time that it is resulting in an intermittent punishment schedule. When a concurrent schedule of reinforcement is competing with punishment, the effects of punishment are likely to be diminished.

If a hungry rat presses a bar in an experimental chamber and receives food pellets, the rat will continue to press the bar. However, if punishment is implemented and the rat receives an electric shock each time it presses the bar, the bar-pressing behavior will stop. Now suppose that the rat continues to receive food for pressing the bar and receives a shock only occasionally when it presses the bar. In this case, the punishing stimulus would not be very effective because it is applied inconsistently or intermittently. The effect of the punishing stimulus in this case depends on the magnitude of the stimulus (how strong the shock is), how often it follows the behavior, and the magnitude of the establishing operation for food (how hungry the rat is).

Establishing Operations

Just as establishing operations may influence the effectiveness of reinforcers, they also influence the effectiveness of punishers. An establishing operation is an event or a condition that makes a consequence more effective as a punisher (or a reinforcer). In the case of negative punishment, satiation makes the loss of some reinforcers (such as food) less punishing, and deprivation makes the loss of some reinforcers more effective as a punisher. For example, telling a child who misbehaves at the dinner table that dessert will be taken away as a result will not be an effective punisher if the child has had two or three helpings of the dessert already. Losing allowance money for misbehavior may not be a punisher if the child has recently received money from other sources. However, losing allowance money may function as a punisher if the child has no other money and plans to buy a toy with the allowance money.

In the case of positive punishment, any event or condition that enhances the aversiveness of a stimulus event makes that event a more effective punisher, whereas events that minimize the aversiveness of a stimulus event make it less effective as a punisher. For example, some drugs (e.g., morphine) minimize the effectiveness of a painful stimulus as a punisher. Other drugs (e.g., alcohol) may reduce the effectiveness of social stimuli (e.g., peer disapproval) as punishers. Instructions or rules may enhance the effectiveness of certain stimuli as punishers. For example, a carpenter tells his apprentice that when the electric saw produces smoke, it may damage the saw or break the blade. As a result of this instruction, smoke from the electric saw is established as a punisher. The behavior that produces the smoke (for example, sawing at an angle,

FACTORS INFLUENCING THE EFFECTIVENESS OF PUNISHMENT

Immediacy	A stimulus is more effective as a punisher when presented immediately after the behavior.
Contingency	A stimulus is more effective as a punisher when presented contingent on the behavior.
Establishing operations	Some antecedent events make a stimulus more effective as a punisher at a particular time.
Individual differences and magnitude	Punishers vary from person to person. In general, a more intense aversive stimulus is a more effective punisher.

pushing too hard on the saw) is weakened. In addition, using the saw correctly avoids the smoke, and this behavior is strengthened through negative reinforcement.

Individual Differences and Magnitude of the Punisher

Another factor that influences the effectiveness of punishment is the nature of the punishing consequence. The events that function as punishers vary from person to person (Fisher et al., 1994). Some events may be established as conditioned punishers for some people and not for others because people have different experiences or conditioning histories. Likewise, whether a stimulus functions as a punisher depends on its magnitude or intensity. In general, a more intense aversive stimulus is more likely to function as a punisher. This also varies from person to person. For example, a mosquito bite is a mildly aversive stimulus for most people; thus, the behavior of wearing shorts in the woods may be punished because of mosquito bites on the legs, and wearing long pants may be negatively reinforced by the avoidance of mosquito bites. However, some people refuse to go outside at all when the mosquitoes are biting, whereas others go outside and do not seem to be bothered much by mosquito bites. This suggests that mosquito bites may be a punishing stimulus for some people but not others. The more intense pain of a bee sting, by contrast, probably is a punisher for most people. People will stop engaging in the behavior that resulted in a bee sting and will engage in other behaviors to avoid a bee sting. Because the bee sting is more intense than a mosquito bite, it is more likely to be an effective punisher.

Can you identify a stimulus event that would function as a punisher for you but not for someone else?

PROBLEMS WITH PUNISHMENT

A number of problems or issues must be considered with the use of punishment, especially positive punishment involving the use of painful or other aversive stimuli.

- Punishment may produce elicited aggression or other emotional side effects.
- The use of punishment may result in escape or avoidance behaviors by the person whose behavior is being punished.
- The use of punishment may be negatively reinforcing for the person using punishment and thus may result in the misuse or overuse of punishment.

- When punishment is used, its use is modeled, and observers or people whose behavior is punished may be more likely to use punishment themselves in the future.
- Finally, punishment is associated with a number of ethical issues and issues of acceptability. These issues are addressed in detail in Chapter 18.

Emotional Reactions to Punishment

Behavioral research with nonhuman subjects has demonstrated that aggressive behavior and other emotional responses may occur when painful stimuli are presented as punishers. For example, Azrin, Hutchinson, and Hake (1963) showed that presenting a painful stimulus (shock) results in aggressive behavior in laboratory animals. In this study, when one monkey received a shock, it immediately attacked another monkey that was present when the shock was delivered. When such aggressive behaviors or other emotional responses result in the termination of the painful or aversive stimulus, they are negatively reinforced. Thus, the tendency to engage in aggressive behavior (especially when it is directed at the source of the aversive stimulus) may have survival value.

Escape and Avoidance

Whenever an aversive stimulus is used in a punishment procedure, an opportunity for escape and avoidance behavior is created. Any behavior that functions to avoid or escape from the presentation of an aversive stimulus is strengthened through negative reinforcement. Therefore, although an aversive stimulus may be presented after a target behavior to decrease the target behavior, any behavior the person engages in to terminate or avoid that aversive stimulus is reinforced (Azrin, Hake, Holz, & Hutchinson, 1965). For example, a child might run away or hide from a parent who is about to spank the child. Sometimes people learn to lie to avoid punishment, or learn to avoid the person who delivers the punishing stimulus. When implementing a punishment procedure, you have to be careful that inappropriate escape and avoidance behaviors do not develop.

Negative Reinforcement for the Use of Punishment

Some authors argue that punishment may be too easily misused or overused because its use is negatively reinforcing to the person implementing it (Sulzer-Azaroff & Mayer, 1991).

Describe how the use of punishment may be negatively reinforcing.

When punishment is used, it results in an immediate decrease in the problem behavior. If the behavior decreased by punishment is aversive to the person using punishment, the use of punishment is negatively reinforced by the termination of the aversive behavior. As a result, the person is more likely to use punishment in the future in similar circumstances. For example, Dr. Hopkins hated it when her students talked in class while she was teaching. Whenever someone talked in class, Dr. Hopkins stopped teaching and stared at the student with her meanest look. When she did this, the student immediately stopped talking in class. As a result, Dr. Hopkins' behavior of staring at students was reinforced by the termination of the students' talking in class. Dr. Hopkins used the stare frequently, and she was known all over the university for it.

FIGURE 6-4 One of the possible problems with punishment is observational learning, as illustrated here. To punish her daughter's misbehavior, a mother uses spanking. As a result of observing her mother, the child also engages in the behavior with her doll.

Punishment and Modeling

People who observe someone making frequent use of punishment may themselves be more likely to use punishment when they are in similar situations. This is especially true with children, for whom observational learning plays a major role in the development of appropriate and inappropriate behavior (Figure 6-4).) For example, children who experience frequent spanking or observe aggressive behavior may be more likely to engage in aggressive behavior themselves (Bandura, 1969; Bandura, Ross, & Ross, 1963).

Ethical Issues

There is some debate among professionals about whether it is ethical to use punishment, especially painful or aversive stimuli, to change the behavior of others (Repp & Singh, 1990). Some argue that the use of punishment cannot be justified (Meyer & Evans, 1989). Others argue that the use of punishment may be justified if the behavior is harmful or serious enough and, therefore, the potential benefits to the individual are great (Linscheid, Iwata, Ricketts, Williams, & Griffin, 1990). Clearly, ethical issues must be considered before punishment is used as a behavior modification procedure. Surveys show that procedures involving punishment are much less acceptable in the profession than behavior modification procedures that use reinforcement or other principles (Kazdin, 1980; Miltenberger, Lennox, & Erfanian, 1989). Professionals must consider a number of issues before they decide to use behavior modification procedures based on punishment. In addition, punishment procedures are always used in conjunction with positive reinforcement procedures to strengthen the desirable behavior. (See Chapter 18 for further discussion of these issues.)

Chapter Summary

1. Punishment is a basic principle of behavior. Its definition has three basic components. The occurrence of a behavior is followed by an immediate consequence, and the behavior is less likely to occur in the future.
2. A common misconception about punishment is that it means doing harm to another person or exacting retribution on another person for that person's misbehavior. Instead, *punishment* is a label for a behavioral principle devoid of the legal or moral connotations usually associated with the word.
3. There are two procedural variations of punishment. In positive punishment, a stimulus is presented after the behavior. In negative punishment, a stimulus is removed after the behavior. In both cases, the behavior is less likely to occur in the future.
4. The two types of punishing stimuli are unconditioned punishers and conditioned punishers. An unconditioned punisher is naturally punishing. A conditioned punisher is developed by pairing a neutral stimulus with an unconditioned punisher or another conditioned punisher.
5. Factors that influence the effectiveness of punishment include immediacy, contingency, establishing operations, individual differences, and magnitude.
6. Problems associated with the use of punishment include emotional reactions to punishment, the development of escape and avoidance behaviors, negative reinforcement for the use of punishment, modeling of the use of punishment, and ethical issues.

Practice Test

1. Define *punishment.* (p. 112)
2. In ordinary usage, what does *punishment* mean? How does this contrast with the definition of *punishment* in behavior modification? (p. 114)
3. (a) Provide an example of punishment from your own life. (b) Is this an example of positive or negative punishment? Why? (c) Does this example involve an unconditioned or a conditioned punisher? Why?
4. The behavior modification definition of *punishment* is a functional definition. What do we mean by *functional definition?* (p. 113)
5. Define *positive punishment.* Provide an example. What other terms are sometimes used in place of *positive punishment?* (pp. 114–115)
6. Define *negative punishment.* Provide an example. What other terms are sometimes used in place of *negative punishment?* (pp. 115–116)
7. (a) What is an unconditioned punisher? (b) What does it mean to say that a punishing stimulus has biological importance? (c) Provide some examples of unconditioned punishers. (p. 119)
8. (a) What is a conditioned punisher? (b) How is a neutral stimulus established as a conditioned punisher? (c) Provide some examples of conditioned punishers from your own life. (pp. 119–120)
9. Describe how a painful stimulus may be involved in both positive punishment and negative reinforcement. Provide an example. (p. 121)
10. Describe how a reinforcing stimulus may be involved in both negative punishment and positive reinforcement. Provide an example. (pp. 121–122)
11. Describe how immediacy influences the effectiveness of punishment. (p. 122)
12. How does consistency or the schedule of punishment influence the effectiveness of punishment? (p. 123)
13. What is an establishing operation? Provide an example of an establishing operation that influences the effectiveness of a punishing stimulus. (p. 123)
14. How is the intensity of a stimulus related to its effectiveness as a punisher? (p. 124)

15. Describe five problems associated with the use of punishment. (pp. 124–126)
16. Identify each of the following as an example of positive punishment, negative punishment, or extinction. When analyzing each example, be sure to ask yourself three questions:

- What is the behavior?
- What happened immediately after the behavior? (Was a stimulus added or removed, or was the reinforcer for the behavior terminated?)
- What happened to the behavior in the future? (Was the behavior weakened? Is it less likely to occur?)

  a. Rachel got up early every morning and raided the cookie jar. Her mom realized what was going on and stopped putting cookies in the jar. After this, Rachel no longer raided the cookie jar.
  b. Heather tossed eggs at the school during Halloween. The principal caught her and made her wash all the windows in the school. Heather never threw eggs at the school again.
  c. Doug threw eggs at his neighbors' house during Halloween. His parents caught him and made him give his neighbors $50 to get their house cleaned. Doug never threw eggs at the neighbors' house again.
  d. Ralph acted out in class and his teacher gave him a mean look. After this, Ralph never acted out in class again.
  e. Suzie watched a lot of TV and used the remote control to turn it on and to change channels. One day the remote did not work. She tried it a few times and eventually quit using it.
  f. Bill hit his sister and his mom took his allowance away for that week. As a result, he doesn't hit his sister anymore.
  g. Amanda tried to climb the fence into an apple orchard. The fence was electrified and gave her a shock. As a result, she doesn't climb that fence anymore.

Appendix A

Examples of Positive Punishment and Negative Punishment from Table 6-1

1. *Positive punishment.* The behavior of looking down while riding resulted in the presentation of a painful stimulus when Ed hit the car.
2. *Negative punishment.* The behavior of hitting resulted in the removal of the opportunity to play with her toys and her friends.
3. *Negative punishment.* Running the lawn mower over the hose resulted in the loss of money.
4. *Positive punishment.* Reading while driving was immediately followed by the occurrence of an accident.
5. *Negative punishment.* Each time Helen got out of her seat, the consequence was the removal of a poker chip.
6. *Positive punishment.* Kevin's telling jokes about his wife's cooking resulted in the presentation of an aversive stimulus: an icy stare from his wife.

CHAPTER 6 *Quiz 1*

Name:

1. In punishment, a behavior is followed by a consequence, and, as a result, the behavior is _________________ likely to occur in the future.
2. A(n) ______________________ is a consequence that follows a behavior and makes the behavior less likely to occur in the future.
3. In positive punishment, a stimulus is _____________________________ following the behavior.
4. A child sticks her finger in an electrical socket and get shocked. As a result, the child never sticks her finger in a socket again. This is an example of _____________________ punishment.
5. Negative punishment involves _______________ (withholding/removing) a reinforcer following a behavior, and extinction involves ____________________ (withholding/removing) a reinforcer following a behavior.
6. _________________ is considered a generalized conditioned punisher.
7. A(n) _______________________ is an event or condition that makes a consequence more effective as a punisher.
8. Provide an example of a common conditioned punisher. _________________________
9. Provide an example of an unconditioned punisher. ____________________________
10. Time out from positive reinforcement and response cost are examples of ___________________ punishment.

CHAPTER 6 *Quiz 2*

Name:

1. ______________ is defined as the process in which a behavior is followed by a consequence, and, as a result, the behavior is less likely to occur in the future.

2. In negative punishment, a stimulus is ______________________ following the behavior.

3. A child holds a baseball card out the window as he is riding in a car, and the card flies away. As a result, he never holds a baseball card out the window of the car again. His is an example of

    ____________________ punishment.

4. _________________ involves withholding the reinforcer for the behavior when the behavior

    occurs, and ___________________ involves removing a reinforcer when the behavior occurs.

5. When a stimulus is paired with a punisher, it becomes a(n) __________ punisher.

6. Painful stimuli or extreme levels of stimulation are ______________ punishers.

7. People who experience or observe punishment are ______________ (more/less) likely to use punishment themselves.

8. If punishment is applied on an intermittent schedule, it is ______________ (more/less) likely to be effective.

9. The use of punishment is ______________ (positively/negatively) reinforcing to the person implementing it.

10. Identify one of the five problems associated with the use of punishment.

    ____

CHAPTER 6 *Quiz 3* Name:

1. Punishment is a process that ____________________ behavior, and reinforcement is a process that ____________________ behavior.

2. The stimulus that is applied following the behavior in positive punishment is a(n) ____________________.

3. The stimulus that is removed following the behavior in negative punishment is a(n) ____________________.

Match the following terms to the statements below.

a. Positive reinforcement b. Negative reinforcement
c. Positive punishment d. Negative punishment

4. ______________ involves the delivery of an aversive stimulus following the behavior.

5. ______________ involves the removal of an aversive stimulus following the behavior.

6. ______________ involves the delivery of a reinforcer following the behavior.

7. ______________ involves the removal of a reinforcer following the behavior.

Match the following terms to the examples below.

a. Positive reinforcement b. Negative reinforcement
c. Positive punishment d. Negative punishment

8. ______________ Alice climbed the fence to get into the apple orchard. The fence was electrified and gave her a shock. As a result, she climbs the fence frequently.

9. ______________ Billy hit his sister and his mom took away his allowance for a week. As a result, he stopped hitting his sister.

10. ______________ Francine has a bad rash that itches terribly. When she scratches it, the itch goes away. As a result, she frequently scratches her rash.

SEVEN

Stimulus Control: Discrimination and Generalization

In discussing reinforcement, extinction, and punishment, we saw the importance of consequences in the control of operant behavior. Operant behavior is strengthened when it is followed by a reinforcing consequence; it is weakened when the reinforcing consequence no longer follows the behavior (extinction). A punishing consequence also weakens the behavior. These basic principles of behavior—reinforcement, extinction, and punishment—explain why behaviors increase and continue to occur or decrease and stop occurring. Because operant behavior is controlled by its consequences, behavior analysts analyze the events that follow the behavior to understand why it is occurring, and they manipulate the consequences of the behavior to modify it.

- What is an antecedent stimulus and how is it involved in stimulus control of operant behavior?
- How is stimulus control developed through stimulus discrimination training?
- What is the three-term contingency?
- What is generalization and how does it differ from discrimination?

This chapter expands the analysis of operant behavior and discusses the importance of **antecedents**, stimulus events that precede an operant response. The antecedents of a behavior are the stimulus events, situations, or circumstances that are present when it occurs or were present before the behavior. To understand and modify operant behavior, it is important to analyze the antecedents as well as the consequences of the behavior. Therefore, this chapter focuses on antecedents, behavior, and consequences, the ABCs of operant behavior.

Why is it important to understand the antecedents of operant behavior?

When we understand the antecedents of operant behavior, we have information on the circumstances in which the behavior was reinforced and the circumstances in which the behavior was not reinforced or was punished. A behavior continues to occur in situations in which it has been reinforced in the past, and stops occurring in situations in which it has not been reinforced or has been punished in the past. As you can see, the effects of reinforcement, extinction, and punishment are situation-specific. Consider the following examples.

Examples of Stimulus Control

Whenever Jake wants some extra cash to spend, he asks his mom and she usually gives him some money. When he asks his dad, his dad usually refuses to give him any money and tells him to get a job. As a result, he usually asks his mom for money instead of his dad.

As you can see, the behavior of asking for money was reinforced in one situation (with his mom) but was not reinforced in another situation (with his dad). Therefore, the behavior continues to occur in the situation in which it was reinforced and no longer occurs in the situation in which it was not reinforced: Jake asks only his mom for money. His mom's presence is an antecedent for Jake's behavior of asking for cash. We would say that his mom's presence has stimulus control over Jake's behavior of asking for money.

Antecedent	Behavior	Consequence
Mom is present.	Jake asks for money.	Mom gives him the cash.
Dad is present.	Jake asks for money.	Dad does not give him cash.

Outcome: Jake asks his mom for money in the future and does not ask his dad for money anymore.

Consider another example. Ginny decides she will go out back and pick a few strawberries from the bushes in her backyard. When she picks a bright red strawberry, it is sweet and juicy and tastes great. When she picks one that is still slightly green, however, it is sour and hard and doesn't taste very good. As she continues to pick the strawberries and eat them, she chooses only the red ones. A red strawberry is an antecedent stimulus. The behavior of picking and eating a red strawberry is reinforced. Therefore, she is more likely to pick and eat red ones. The behavior of eating a green strawberry is not reinforced; she no longer picks green ones. Eating only red strawberries and not green ones is an example of stimulus control. We would say that the presence of red strawberries has stimulus control over Ginny's behavior of picking and eating the strawberries.

Antecedent	Behavior	Consequence
Red strawberry	Ginny picks and eats it.	Tastes great.
Green strawberry	Ginny picks and eats it.	Tastes awful.

Outcome: Ginny is likely to pick and eat red strawberries and to stop eating green ones.

Defining Stimulus Control

These two examples illustrate the principle of **stimulus control.** In each, a behavior was more likely to occur when a specific antecedent stimulus was present. For Jake, the antecedent stimulus that was present when he asked for money was his mom. For Ginny, the antecedent stimulus when she was picking and eating strawberries was the presence of red strawberries. A behavior is said to be under stimulus control when there is an increased probability that the behavior will occur in the presence of a specific antecedent stimulus or a stimulus from a specific stimulus class. (Red strawberries are a stimulus class. Any one particular red strawberry is a member of this stimulus class.)

TABLE 7-1 EXAMPLES FOR SELF-ASSESSMENT (STIMULUS CONTROL)

1. A man says "I love you" to his wife but not to any of the people where he works.

Antecedent →	Behavior →	Consequence
His wife is present.	He says "I love you."	She says the same to him.

2. When the stop light turns red, you stop; when it is green, you go.

Antecedent →	Behavior →	Consequence
Green light.	You press the accelerator.	You travel to where you are going and avoid people honking at you.
Antecedent →	Behavior →	Consequence
Red light.	You press the brake pedal.	You avoid an accident or a traffic ticket.

3. You tell off-color jokes to your friends but not to your parents or teachers.

Antecedent →	Behavior →	Consequence
Your friends are present.	You tell off-color jokes.	They laugh and tell you jokes.

4. When the phone rings, you pick it up and talk to the person who called.

Antecedent →	Behavior →	Consequence
The phone rings.	You answer the phone.	You talk to the person who called.

5. When the light on the rechargeable electric drill is on, you use the drill.

Antecedent →	Behavior →	Consequence
The light on the rechargeable drill is on.	You take the drill and use it to drill a hole.	The drill works fine.

What are some of your own behaviors that are under stimulus control?

To answer this question, ask yourself which of your behaviors occur only in specific situations or in certain circumstances (that is, when a specific antecedent stimulus is present). What you will find is that almost all of your behaviors are under stimulus control. Behaviors usually don't occur randomly; they occur in the specific situations or circumstances in which they were reinforced in the past. Table 7-1 lists examples of behaviors that are under stimulus control.

Each example in Table 7-1 shows an antecedent stimulus, a behavior, and a consequence. In each example, the behavior is more likely to occur when the antecedent stimulus is present. Why? The behavior occurs when the antecedent is present because that is the only time the behavior has been reinforced. Consider each example.

- Saying "I love you" is reinforced by the man's wife. If he said "I love you" to people at work, they would not reinforce the behavior. (They might give him strange looks or worse.) As a result, he says "I love you" only to his wife.

■ Stopping at a red light is reinforced by avoiding an accident and a traffic ticket (negative reinforcement). However, stopping at a green light would result in people honking at you and making angry gestures (positive punishment). Therefore, you stop at red lights and not at green lights.

■ Telling an off-color joke to your friends is reinforced by laughs and attention. However, telling such jokes to your parents would not be reinforced and may be punished with dirty looks or reprimands. Therefore, you tell off-color jokes only to your friends.

■ Picking up the phone when it rings is reinforced by talking to the caller; picking the phone up when it does not ring is not reinforced because no one is on the other end. As a result, you pick up the phone only when it rings (unless you are making a call).

■ When the charger light is on, using the drill is reinforced because the drill works effectively. When the light is not on, using the drill is never reinforced because the drill doesn't work. As a result, you use the drill only when the light is on.

Developing Stimulus Control: Stimulus Discrimination Training

As you can see from these examples, stimulus control develops because a behavior is reinforced only in the presence of a particular antecedent stimulus. Therefore, the behavior continues to occur in the future only when that antecedent stimulus is present. The antecedent stimulus that is present when a behavior is reinforced is known as the **discriminative stimulus (S^D)**. The process of reinforcing a behavior only when a specific antecedent stimulus (discriminative stimulus) is present is called **stimulus discrimination training.**

Two steps are involved in stimulus discrimination training.

1. When the discriminative stimulus (S^D) is present, the behavior is reinforced.
2. When any other antecedent stimuli except the S^D are present, the behavior is not reinforced. During discrimination training, any antecedent stimulus that is present when the behavior is not reinforced is called an **S-delta (S^Δ).**

As a result of discrimination training, a behavior is more likely to occur in the future when an S^D is present but is less likely to occur when an S^Δ is present. This is the definition of stimulus control. It is important to remember that the presence of an S^D does not cause a behavior to occur. Rather, it increases the likelihood of the behavior in the present because it was associated with reinforcement of the behavior in the past. Reinforcement is what causes the behavior to occur when the S^D is present.

Discrimination Training in the Laboratory

In the experiment reported by Holland and Skinner (1961), a hungry pigeon stands in a small experimental chamber. The wall in front of the pigeon features a round disk (called a key) and two lights, green and red. A pigeon has a natural tendency to peck at objects. When it pecks at the key, a small amount of food is delivered to an opening in the chamber. The food reinforces the behavior of pecking the key.

How did Holland and Skinner bring the pigeon's key-pecking behavior under the stimulus control of the red light?

They would turn on the red light (S^D) and then, whenever the pigeon pecked the key, food would be delivered (reinforcement). Sometimes they would turn on the green light (S^Δ) and, when the pigeon pecked the key, they would not deliver food (extinction). Because of the process of discrimination training, the pigeon is more likely to peck the key when the light is red and less likely to peck the key when the light is green. The red light signals that key-pecking will be reinforced; the green light signals that key-pecking will not be reinforced.

Antecedent	Behavior	Consequence
Red light (S^D)	Pigeon pecks the key.	Food is delivered.
Green light (S^Δ)	Pigeon pecks the key.	No food is given.

Outcome: Pigeon pecks the key only when the red light is on.

In similar experiments, a rat learns to press a lever in an experimental chamber when the lever-pressing response is reinforced by food. Through discrimination training, a rat learns to press the lever when a certain audible tone is presented and not to press the lever when a different tone is presented (Skinner, 1938).

Antecedent	Behavior	Consequence
High-pitched tone (S^D)	Rat presses lever.	Food is delivered.
Low-pitched tone (S^Δ)	Rat presses lever.	No food is given.

Outcome: Rat presses the lever only when the high-pitched tone is present.

Similarly, the recess bell develops stimulus control over children's behavior in elementary school. As soon as the bell rings, the students get up and go outside for recess. This behavior is reinforced by playing and having fun. If the students got up before the bell, the behavior would not be reinforced (the teacher would not let them go outside to play). The recess bell is an S^D for leaving the classroom because the only time leaving the classroom is reinforced is after the bell rings.

For each example of stimulus control in Table 7-1, identify the S^D and the S^Δ.

Answers are listed in Table 7-2.

TABLE 7-2 Discriminative Stimuli (S^Ds) and S-Deltas (S^Δs) for the Examples in Table 7-1

Example	Behavior	S^D	S^Δ
1	Saying "I love you"	Wife	Co-workers
2	Stopping	Red light	Green light
3	Telling off-color jokes	Friends	Parents, teachers
4	Picking up the phone	Phone rings	No ring
5	Using the drill	Light is on	Light is off

Developing Reading and Spelling with Discrimination Training

Reading is a behavior that is developed through the process of stimulus discrimination training. Our reading behavior is under the stimulus control of the letters and words we see on the page. If we see the letters *DOG*, we say "dog." If we said "dog" after seeing any other combination of letters, our response would be incorrect. We learn to make correct reading responses through discrimination training, typically when we are children.

Antecedent	Behavior	Consequence
DOG (S^D)	The child says "dog."	Praise from teacher or parent.
Another word (S^Δ)	The child says "dog."	No praise or teacher says "Wrong!"

Outcome: When the letters *DOG* are present, the child says "dog," but the child does not say "dog" when any other combination of letters is presented.

Note that in this example, the adult's response "Wrong!" is a conditioned punisher.

As we learn to read, we are able to discriminate the sound of each letter in the alphabet, and we learn to read thousands of words. In each case, a particular letter is associated with one sound and a particular string of letters is associated with one word. When we see a letter and make the correct sound, or see a written word and say the correct word, our behavior is reinforced by praise from teachers or parents. Thus, the letter or the written word develops stimulus control over our reading behavior.

Describe how our behavior of spelling is developed through stimulus discrimination training.

In the case of spelling, the spoken word is the S^D and our response involves writing or saying the letters that spell the word. When we write or say the letters correctly, our spelling behavior is reinforced.

Antecedent	Behavior	Consequence
The teacher says, "Spell tree" (S^D).	You spell *TREE*.	The teacher gives praise.
The teacher says, "Spell fish" (S^Δ) or any other word.	You spell *TREE*.	The teacher says "Wrong."

Outcome: You are more likely to spell *TREE* when the teacher says "tree" and not when you hear any other spoken word.

As a result of discrimination training, stimulus control develops over our spelling behavior. Each particular word we hear (and each object or event we experience) is associated with only one correct spelling that is reinforced. Incorrect spelling is not reinforced or is punished; thus, it no longer occurs.

Stimulus Discrimination Training and Punishment

Stimulus discrimination training may also occur with punishment. If a behavior is punished in the presence of one antecedent stimulus, the behavior will decrease and stop occurring in the future when that stimulus is present. The behavior may continue to occur when other antecedent stimuli are present. For example, suppose that when your soup is boiling, you put a spoonful in your mouth to taste it. You burn your mouth and, as a result, you are less likely to put a spoonful of boiling soup in your mouth in the future. However, you might still put soup in your mouth before it is boiling, without burning yourself.

Antecedent	Behavior	Consequence
Soup is boiling.	You taste a spoonful.	Painful stimulus (burnt mouth)
Soup is not boiling.	You taste a spoonful.	No painful stimulus

Outcome: You are less likely to taste soup in the future when it is boiling.

The boiling soup is a discriminative stimulus; it signals that tasting the soup will be punished. Stimulus control has developed when you no longer try to taste soup that is boiling. Consider another example. When you talk and laugh loudly in a library, the librarian will tell you to be quiet or ask you to leave. However, talking and laughing loudly is not punished in many other situations (e.g., at a party or a ball game). Therefore, the behavior of talking and laughing loudly is less likely to occur in the library but continues to occur in other situations in which the behavior is not punished.

The library is a discriminative stimulus that signals that loud talking and laughing will be punished. Your behavior is under stimulus control when you no longer laugh and talk loudly in the library.

Antecedent	Behavior	Consequence
In a library	You laugh and talk loudly.	You are reprimanded.
At a party	You laugh and talk loudly.	You are not reprimanded.

Outcome: You are less likely to laugh and talk loudly when you are in the library.

The Three-Term Contingency

According to Skinner (1969), stimulus discrimination training involves a **three-term contingency**, in which the consequence (reinforcer or punisher) is contingent on the occurrence of the behavior only in the presence of the specific antecedent stimulus called the S^D. As you can see, a three-term contingency involves a relationship between an antecedent stimulus, a behavior, and the consequence of the behavior. Behavior analysts often call this the ABCs (antecedents, behavior, consequences) of a behavior (Arndorfer & Miltenberger, 1993; Bijou, Peterson, & Ault, 1968). The notation used to describe a three-term contingency involving reinforcement is as follows:

$$S^D \rightarrow R \rightarrow S^R$$

where S^D = discriminative stimulus, R = response (an instance of the behavior), and S^R = reinforcer (or reinforcing stimulus). The notation for a three-term contingency involving punishment is as follows:

$$S^D \rightarrow R \rightarrow S^P$$

In this case, S^P = punisher (or punishing stimulus).

As you can see, an antecedent stimulus develops stimulus control over a behavior because the behavior is reinforced or punished only in the presence of that particular antecedent stimulus. The same holds true for extinction. When a behavior is no longer reinforced in a particular situation (in the presence of a particular antecedent stimulus), the behavior decreases in the future only in that particular situation.

Stimulus Control Research

Research has established the principle of stimulus control and explored its application to help people change their behavior. For example, Azrin and Powell (1968) conducted a study to help heavy smokers reduce the number of cigarettes they smoked per day. The researchers developed a cigarette case that automatically locked for a period of time (say, an hour) after the smoker took out a cigarette. At the end of that period, the cigarette case made a sound to signal that the case would open for another cigarette. The sound (auditory signal) was an S^D that signaled that trying to get a cigarette out of the case would be reinforced. Eventually, stimulus control developed because the only time the smoker could get a cigarette was when the auditory signal (S^D) was present. When the signal was not present, trying to get a cigarette would not be reinforced because the case was locked.

Schaefer (1970) demonstrated that head-banging could be developed and brought under stimulus control in rhesus monkeys. Schaefer was interested in head-banging because this form of self-injurious behavior sometimes is seen in people with mental retardation. Through a procedure called shaping (see Chapter 9), Schaefer got the monkeys to engage in head-banging and reinforced this behavior with food. Discrimination training occurred in the following way. Standing in front of the cage, Schaefer sometimes made verbal statements (S^D) to the monkey and sometimes said nothing (S^Δ). When Schaefer said, "Poor boy! Don't do that! You'll hurt yourself!" and the monkey hit its head, he delivered a food pellet. When he did not provide the verbal stimulus and the monkey hit its head, no food was provided. As a result, stimulus control developed, and the monkey hit its head only when Schaefer made the statements (when the S^D was present). The verbal statements Schaefer used were similar to those sometimes made by staff to people with mental retardation who engage in self-injurious behavior. Therefore, the study with monkeys had implications for the stimulus control of self-injurious behavior in humans. Other researchers have evaluated the stimulus control of self-injurious behavior (Pace, Iwata, Edwards, & McCosh, 1986) and other behaviors of people with mental retardation (Dixon, 1981; Halle, 1989; Halle & Holt, 1991; Kennedy, 1994; Striefel, Bryan, & Aikens, 1974). Stimulus control research has also been conducted with a variety of other populations and target behaviors (Cooper Heron, & Heward, 1987; Sulzer-Azaroff & Mayer, 1991). Chapter 16 discusses the application of stimulus control to help people change their behavior.

Generalization

In some cases, the antecedent conditions in which a behavior is strengthened (through reinforcement) or weakened (through extinction or punishment) are fairly specific; in others, the antecedent conditions are more broad or varied. When the stimulus con-

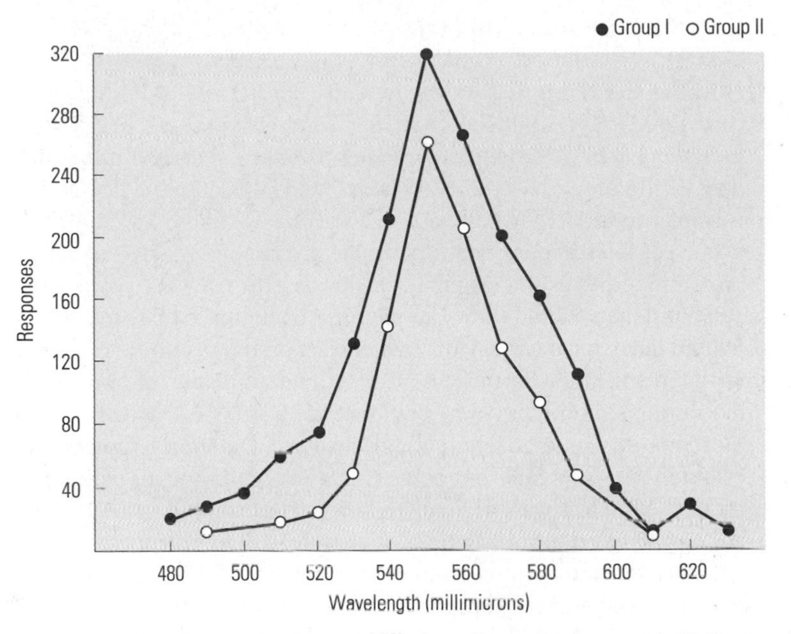

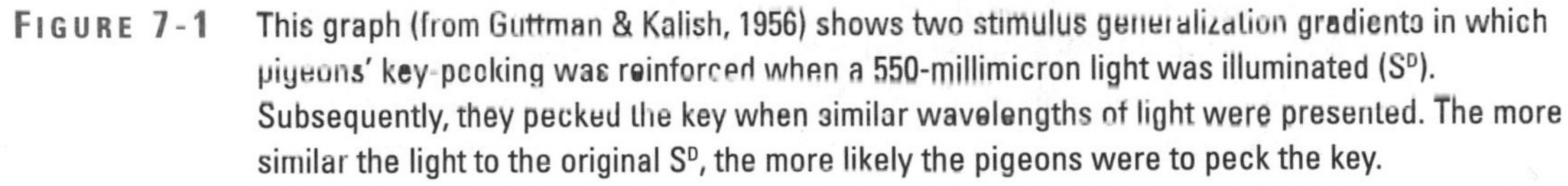

FIGURE 7-1 This graph (from Guttman & Kalish, 1956) shows two stimulus generalization gradients in which pigeons' key-pecking was reinforced when a 550-millimicron light was illuminated (S^D). Subsequently, they pecked the key when similar wavelengths of light were presented. The more similar the light to the original S^D, the more likely the pigeons were to peck the key.

trol of a behavior is more broad—that is, when the behavior occurs in a range of antecedent situations—we say that stimulus generalization has occurred.

Generalization takes place when a behavior occurs in the presence of stimuli that are similar in some ways to the S^D that was present during stimulus discrimination training (Stokes & Osnes, 1989). According to Skinner (1953a, p. 134), "Generalization is . . . a term which describes the fact that the control acquired by a stimulus is shared by other stimuli with common properties." The more similar another stimulus is to the S^D, the more likely it is that the behavior will occur in the presence of that stimulus. As stimuli are less and less similar to the S^D, the behavior is less and less likely to occur in the presence of these stimuli. This is called a generalization gradient (Skinner, 1957). Figure 7-1 presents an example of a generalization gradient from a study by Guttman and Kalish (1956). Guttman and Kalish reinforced key-pecking in pigeons when the key was illuminated with a certain wavelength of light. As a result, the light was an S^D that developed stimulus control over the behavior, and the pigeon pecked the key whenever the light was on. Th graph shows that the pigeon also pecked the key when similar wavelengths of l were presented. As the wavelength of light became less similar to the S^D, les pecking occurred. The generalization gradient shows that the behavior gen to stimuli that are similar to the S^D.

Examples of Generalization

A first grader, Erin, is learning to read with the use of flashcards. When she sees the card with *MEN* on it, she says "men" and gets praised. The *MEN* flashcard is an S^D for saying "men." At the mall with her parents one day, Erin sees the *MEN* sign on the door of the men's bathroom and says "men." Because the *MEN* sign on the bathroom is similar to the *MEN* flashcard that was the original S^D, we say that generalization has occurred; the response occurred in the presence of a different stimulus that shared the same properties as the original S^D. Now if Erin reads the word *men* anywhere that she sees the letters *MEN* (for example, in a book, on a door, in block letters, or in handwritten letters), we can say that generalization has occurred to all relevant stimuli. Stimulus generalization in this case is a desirable outcome of training. Erin has learned to discriminate all the different ways that the word *MEN* may be written.

Stimulus generalization has also occurred when a response occurs in different circumstances—in a different context, at a different time, or with different people—from those in which it was originally learned. For example, parents may teach their young child to follow their instructions or comply with their requests. When the parents make a request (S^D), the child complies with the request (R), and the parents praise the child (S^R). When the child complies with novel requests the parents make, stimulus generalization has occurred. The specific request may be new, but it shares the relevant features of the S^D present during discrimination training: It is a request or instruction made by the parent. Requests made by the parent are part of a **stimulus class:** antecedent stimuli that share similar features. Stimulus generalization has also occurred when the child complies with the request or instruction of another adult (say, a teacher), in another context, or at another time. If the child complies with the requests of other adults, the stimulus class that has acquired stimulus control over the child's compliance comprises requests made by adults (as opposed to just requests by parents).

Parents probably want to limit stimulus control so that the child does not comply with the request or instructions of all adults, including strangers. Otherwise, the child would be at risk for exploitation. The parents can prevent undesirable generalization by using stimulus discrimination training. To do so, the parents specifically reinforce compliance to requests made by parents, teachers, the babysitter, or grandparents. However, they do not reinforce compliance to requests made by any other adult. In this way, the parents are establishing a stimulus class for compliance that consists only of requests from parents, teachers, the babysitter, and grandparents.

In this case, requests from other adults represent an S^D for the child's behavior of refusing to comply. When the child refuses to comply with requests from adults other than parents, teachers, babysitter, and grandparents, the child's behavior is reinforced.

Antecedent	Behavior	Consequence
Requests from parents, teachers, babysitter, ...randparents	Compliance	Parents praise child.
... other adults	Compliance	Parents say no and prevent compliance.
...m other adults	Child refuses to comply	Parents praise child.

...: Child complies only with requests from parents, teachers, babysitter, and grandparents and does not comply with requests from other adults.

As you see, stimulus control can be very specific, or it can be more broad. If a behavior is reinforced in the presence of only one specific antecedent stimulus, stimulus control is specific; the behavior is more likely to occur only when that stimulus is present in the future. If a behavior is reinforced in the presence of a number of antecedent stimuli that share the same features (that are in the same stimulus class), stimulus control is more broad, and the behavior is more likely to occur when any one of the antecedent stimuli from that stimulus class is present in the future. Generalization is associated with broad stimulus control, or stimulus control by novel or untrained antecedent stimuli.

Consider the example of 4-year-old Millie, a girl with severe mental retardation who exhibits a self-injurious behavior. Specifically, when her mother is in the room, she gets down on her hands and knees and bangs her head on the floor. When Millie bangs her head, her mother goes to her and stops her from engaging in the behavior by holding her and talking to her (by paying attention to her).

Describe the three-term contingency (the ABCs) involved in Millie's head-banging.

The antecedent stimulus or S^D is the presence of her mother. The behavior is banging her head on the floor, and the reinforcing consequence is her mom's attention (holding her and talking to her). Head-banging is under stimulus control of her mom's presence. When her sisters are in the room but her mom is not present, Millie does not bang her head because the behavior is never reinforced by her sisters.

When Millie went to the hospital recently, she banged her head when she was with the nurse. This is an example of generalization. The presence of the nurse is a novel antecedent stimulus, but is similar to the S^D (her mom, an adult). When Millie banged her head with the nurse, the nurse held her and talked to her, just as her mother does. In this way, the nurse reinforced her behavior. While in the hospital, Millie banged her head when other adults entered her room; these adults also reinforced the behavior. However, when Millie was in the hospital playroom with another child, but no adult was present, Millie did not bang her head.

Why doesn't Millie bang her head when the only person in the room is another child?

Millie does not bang her head when only a child is present because the other children do not reinforce the behavior; they ignore Millie when she bangs her head. Therefore, a child is an S^Δ for the behavior. The behavior is under the stimulus control of the presence of an adult because only adults reinforce the behavior.

Antecedent	Behavior	Consequence
Adult in the room	Head-banging	Attention
Another child in the room (but no adult)	Head-banging	No attention

Outcome: Millie bangs her head only when an adult is present.

Identify a number of examples of stimulus generalization from your own life.

Some examples of stimulus generalization are provided in Table 7-3.

TABLE 7-3 **EXAMPLES FOR SELF-ASSESSMENT (STIMULUS GENERALIZATION)**

1. Amy is learning to identify the color red. When her teacher shows her a red block, she can say "red." Generalization has occurred when she also says "red" when the teacher shows her a red ball, a red book, or any other red object.
2. Scott stopped putting his feet on the good coffee table after his wife yelled at him for doing it. Generalization has occurred when he stops putting his feet on the coffee table even when his wife is not home.
3. Sharon's dog Bud did not beg for food from her because she never gave Bud food when he begged. However, when Sharon visited relatives for the holidays, her relatives reinforced begging behavior by giving Bud food. After the holidays, when they were back home, Bud also begged for food from Sharon and her friends. Generalization had occurred.
4. Sharon trained her dog Bud not to go into the streets around her house by using punishment. She walked Bud on a leash near the street; each time Bud stepped into the street, Sharon snapped the dog collar. Eventually, Bud no longer stepped into the streets even when not on a leash; generalization had occurred. The dog also did not walk into the streets around other people's houses; this was another instance of generalization.
5. You learn to drive your brother's car (which has a manual transmission) with your brother present. The behavior then generalizes to most other cars with a manual transmission.

In each example in Table 7-3, identify the three-term contingency used to develop stimulus control initially, and identify the stimulus class that controls the behavior after generalization has occurred.

The answers are given in Appendix A.

Look at the comic in Figure 7-2. Describe how this comic provides an example of generalization.

Initially Dagwood taught Daisy to bring in the newspaper using the following three-term contingency:

Antecedent	Behavior	Consequence
The newspaper is in the front yard.	Daisy brings the newspaper to the house.	Dagwood gives her a treat.

Outcome: In the future, Daisy brings in the newspaper when it is delivered to the front yard.

The newspaper in Dagwood's front yard is the S^D. Generalization occurred when Daisy also brought in newspapers from the neighbors' front yards. The stimulus class controlling the response was a newspaper in the front yard of any house. Dagwood wanted the stimulus class to be only the newspaper in the front yard of his house.

Describe how Dagwood would do discrimination training with Daisy to establish the correct stimulus control.

FIGURE 7-2 In this comic strip you see an example of generalization. The S^D was the paper in Dagwood's front yard, but the behavior (getting the paper) generalized to papers in the neighbor's front yards.

Dagwood should give Daisy a treat only when she brings in his paper and he should give her no treat (and maybe a punisher) when she brings in a neighbor's paper.

Antecedent	Behavior	Consequence
Paper in front of Dagwood's house (S^D)	Daisy brings in paper.	Daisy receives a treat.
Paper in front of a neighbor's house (S^{Δ})	Daisy brings in paper.	No treat; Dagwood says, "No. Bad dog!"

Outcome: Daisy brings in Dagwood's paper but does not bring in the neighbors' papers.

Behavior modification researchers and practitioners are quite interested in stimulus generalization. When they use behavior modification procedures to help people increase a behavioral deficit or decrease a behavioral excess, they want the behavior change to generalize to all relevant stimulus situations. A number of researchers have discussed strategies for promoting generalization of behavior change (Edelstein, 1989; Kendall, 1989; Stokes & Baer, 1977; Stokes & Osnes, 1989). These strategies are reviewed in Chapter 19.

CHAPTER SUMMARY

1. An antecedent stimulus is a stimulus that precedes the occurrence of the behavior. An operant behavior is under stimulus control when it is more likely to occur in the presence of a specific antecedent stimulus or a member of a specific stimulus class.
2. Stimulus control develops through a process of stimulus discrimination training, in which the behavior is reinforced in the presence of one stimulus (or stimulus class) but is not reinforced when other stimuli are present. The antecedent stimulus that is present when a behavior is reinforced is called a discriminative stimulus (S^D); an antecedent stimulus that is present when the behavior is not reinforced is called an S-delta (S^Δ). Stimulus discrimination training may occur with reinforcement, punishment, or extinction; therefore, the occurrence or nonoccurrence of a behavior may be under stimulus control. However, it is not the S^D that causes a behavior to occur or not occur. Reinforcement, extinction, and punishment are the processes responsible for the occurrence or nonoccurrence of a behavior in specific antecedent situations.
3. A three-term contingency involves a discriminative stimulus (S^D), a response that occurs in the presence of the S^D, and a reinforcing consequence that follows the response in the presence of the S^D ($S^D \rightarrow R \rightarrow S^R$).
4. When stimulus control is broad or when a behavior occurs in the presence of novel antecedent stimuli that are similar to the initial S^D, we say that generalization has occurred. Stimulus control generalizes to a class of stimuli sharing a particular feature or features.

PRACTICE TEST

1. What is an antecedent stimulus? Provide an example. (pp. 133–134)
2. What does it mean when we say that the effects of reinforcement are situation-specific? (p. 133)
3. What is stimulus control? (p. 134)
4. Provide an example of stimulus control. (p. 134)
5. What is an S^D? What is an S^Δ? (p. 136)
6. Describe stimulus discrimination training. What is the outcome of stimulus discrimination training? (p. 136)
7. Provide an example of stimulus discrimination training with reinforcement and with punishment. (pp. 136–139)
8. Does an S^D cause a behavior to occur? Explain. (p. 136)
9. What is a three-term contingency? Provide an example. (p. 139)
10. A hungry rat presses a lever and gets food only when a green light is on. What is the green light? What will happen to the rat's behavior of pressing the lever in the future? (p. 137)

11. What is stimulus generalization? (p. 141)
12. Provide an example of stimulus generalization. (p. 142)
13. What is a stimulus class? Provide an example. (p. 142)
14. Provide an example in which stimulus generalization would be desirable. Provide an example in which generalization would be undesirable. (pp. 142–143)
15. Describe how you would use stimulus discrimination training to make generalization more likely to occur or less likely to occur. (p. 143)

APPENDIX A

The Three-Term Contingency and Outcome of Generalization in Each Example from Table 7-3

1. Antecedent → Behavior → Consequence

Antecedent	Behavior	Consequence
Red block	Amy labels the color red.	Praise from the teacher
Outcome:		
Red block	Amy labels the color red.	
After generalization:		
Any red object	Amy labels the color red.	

2. Antecedent → Behavior → Consequence

Antecedent	Behavior	Consequence
Wife is present.	Scott puts feet on good coffee table.	Scott gets yelled at.
Outcome:		
Wife is present.	Scott does not put his feet on the good coffee table.	
After generalization:		
Wife is not present.	Scott does not put his feet on the good coffee table.	

3. Antecedent → Behavior → Consequence

Antecedent	Behavior	Consequence
Around the relatives	Bud begs for food.	Relatives give Bud food.
Outcome:		
Around the relatives	Bud begs for food.	
After generalization:		
Around Sharon and her friends	Bud begs for food.	

4.

Antecedent →	Behavior →	Consequence
With the leash on near Sharon's house	Bud steps into the street.	Sharon snaps the dog collar.
Outcome:		
With the leash on near Sharon's house	Bud does not step into the street.	
After generalization:		
With the leash off near Sharon's house	Bud does not step into the street.	
With the leash off near other people's houses	Bud does not step into the street.	

5.

Antecedent →	Behavior →	Consequence
In your brother's car (with manual transmission) with your brother present	You drive the car correctly.	Praise
Outcome:		
In your brother's car with your brother present	You drive the car correctly.	
After generalization:		
In another car with manual transmission, in your brother's absence	You drive the car correctly.	

CHAPTER 7 *Quiz 1*

Name:

1. An antecedent that is present when a behavior is reinforced is called a(n) ______________.

2. An antecedent stimulus that is present when a behavior is not reinforced is called a(n)

   ______________.

3. ______________ is when a behavior is more likely to occur in the presence of a specific antecedent stimulus.

4. How do you develop stimulus control? ______________

   ____

5. What are the three components of a three-term contingency? ______________,

   ______________, ______________

6. In ______________, you reinforce a behavior when the S^D is present and do not reinforce the behavior when the S^Δ is present.

Teddy screams when he asks for cookies, and he is told he can't have any. When he screams, his mom eventually gives him a cookie. However, his dad never gives him a cookie when he screams. As a result, Teddy is more likely to scream for a cookie when mom is around.

7. What is the S^D for Teddy's screaming? ______________

8. What is the S^Δ for Teddy's screaming? ______________

9. What is the reinforcer for Teddy's screaming? ______________

10. Is this an example of positive or negative reinforcement? ______________

CHAPTER 7 *Quiz 2* Name:

1. A discriminative stimulus is an antecedent that is present when a behavior is

   ______________________.

2. As a result of discrimination training, what happens in the future when an S^D is present?

   ____

3. ______________________ is developed through the process of stimulus discrimination training.

4. In discrimination training, the behavior is not reinforced when the ______________ is present.

5. ____________________ occurs when a behavior occurs in the presence of stimuli that are similar to the S^D.

Marianne steals candy in the store when a clerk is not in sight because she gets away with it. She does not steal candy when a clerk is in sight because she does not get away with it.

6. What is the S^D for stealing candy? ____________________

7. What is the S^Δ for stealing candy? ____________________

Farley says "reinforcement" when the professor provides an example of reinforcement. He does not say "reinforcement" when the professor provides an example of some other behavioral principle.

8. What is the S^D for saying "reinforcement"? ____________________

9. What is the S^Δ for saying "reinforcement"? ____________________

10. What is it called when Farley can label a novel example of reinforcement correctly?

    ____

CHAPTER 7 *Quiz 3* Name:

1. An S^{Δ} is an antecedent stimulus that is present when a behavior is ________________.

2. As a result of discrimination training, what happens in the future when an S^{Δ} is present?

   ________________________________.

3. Stimulus control develops through the process of ________________________.

4. In discrimination training, a behavior is reinforced when the ________________ is present.

5. Generalization takes place when the behavior occurs in the presence of stimuli that are

   ____________________ to the S^D.

When Patty hears thunder at school, she cries and her classmates ignore her. When Patty hears thunder at home, she cries and her parents hold her and comfort her. As a result, she cries at home but not at school when she hears thunder.

6. What is the S^{Δ} for Patty's crying when she hears thunder? ________________

7. What is the S^D for Patty's crying when she hears thunder? ________________

8. What behavioral process is illustrated in this example? ________________

9. If Patty cried when she heard thunder at her grandparents' house, we would say that

   ____________________ had occurred.

10. Provide an example of stimulus control. ____

    ____

Respondent Conditioning

Chapters 4–7 described principles of operant conditioning: reinforcement, extinction, punishment, and stimulus control. This chapter discusses a different type of conditioning: respondent conditioning. **Operant behaviors** are controlled by their consequences; **operant conditioning** involves the manipulation of consequences. In contrast, **respondent behaviors** are controlled (elicited) by antecedent stimuli, and **respondent conditioning** involves the manipulation of antecedent stimuli. Consider the following examples.

- What is respondent conditioning?
- What are conditioned emotional responses?
- How does extinction of respondent behavior occur?
- What factors influence respondent conditioning?
- How is respondent conditioning different from operant conditioning?

Examples of Respondent Conditioning

Carla worked in a factory that made children's toys. She operated a machine that molded plastic parts for the toys. Plastic pieces were fed into the machine on a conveyor belt. As each piece entered the machine, the machine made a clicking noise and then a metal punch in the machine came down to stamp the plastic. When the machine stamped the plastic, a short blast of air from one of the hydraulic hoses hit Carla in the face. It was not dangerous, but the blast of air made her blink each time the machine stamped a part. Carla found that she began to blink as soon as the machine made the clicking sound, just before it blew the air in her face. After a few days, the maintenance crew fixed the machine so that the blast of air no longer came from the hydraulic hose. Carla noticed that she continued to blink each time the machine clicked, but that the blinking went away after a few days. Carla's blinking is an example of a respondent behavior, elicited by the antecedent stimulus of a blast of air in the face. Because the clicking sound immediately preceded the blast of air each time, Carla's blinking was conditioned to occur at the clicking sound. This is an example of respondent conditioning.

Julio got out of his last class at 9:30 P.M. He took the 9:40 P.M. bus and got home at 10:00 P.M. When he got off the bus, he had to walk through a tunnel under the train tracks to get to his house. Because most of the lights in the tunnel were broken, it was usually dark as he walked through it. Since the beginning of the semester, a number of incidents in the tunnel had startled or scared him: A large rat ran right in front of him; some teenagers made threatening remarks to him; and a homeless person, who seemed to be sleeping, suddenly jumped up and started cursing at Julio as he walked by. On each occasion, Julio noticed that his heart was racing, his muscles were tensed, and he was breathing rapidly. These bodily responses continued until Julio came out of the tunnel. After these incidents, Julio noticed these same bodily responses each time he walked toward the tunnel: His heart started racing, his muscles tensed, and his breathing was more rapid. These responses did not diminish until he was out the other side. Once inside the tunnel, he usually walked quickly or ran to get out more quickly. This is an example of respondent behavior. The threatening events in the tunnel initially elicited bodily responses that we call fear responses or anxiety. Because these events happened in the tunnel, proximity to the tunnel now elicits the same bodily responses in Julio. Proximity to the tunnel is an antecedent stimulus that elicits a conditioned response we call fear or anxiety.

DEFINING RESPONDENT CONDITIONING

Certain types of stimuli typically elicit specific types of bodily responses. Infants engage in sucking responses when an object such as a nipple touches their lips. A person blinks when a puff of air is directed at the eye. The pupil of the eye constricts on exposure to bright light. Salivation occurs when food is in the mouth. A person gags or coughs when a foreign object is in the throat. These and other responses (Table 8-1) are called **unconditioned responses (UR).** These responses are elicited by antecedent stimuli even though no conditioning or learning has taken place. A UR occurs in all healthy people when an **unconditioned stimulus (US)** is presented. Humans have evolved to respond to USs because the URs have survival value (Skinner, 1953a; Watson, 1924).

TABLE 8-1 Examples of Unconditioned Responses in Humans

Unconditioned Stimulus	Unconditioned Response
Object touches infant's lips	Sucking reflex
Food in mouth	Salivation
Foreign object in throat	Gag reflex
Stimulation in the throat	Coughing
Puff of air in the eye	Eyeblink
Bright light in the eye	Pupil constriction
Painful stimulation to the body	Rapid withdrawal (of hand from a hot stove, for example) and autonomic arousal (fight or flight response)
Sudden, intense stimulation (loud noise)	Startle reflex (increased heart rate, respiration, muscle tension)
Sexual stimulation (postpuberty)	Erection or vaginal lubrication
Blow to the patella tendon	Knee jerk

Identify the ways in which each of the URs listed in Table 8-1 may have survival value.

- The natural tendency to suck allows an infant to eat when a nipple is placed in the mouth.
- Salivation contributes to chewing and digesting food.
- Gagging when a foreign object is in the throat can keep a person from choking.
- Coughing clears the throat of foreign objects.
- The natural tendency to blink when air or other matter approaches the eyes can prevent foreign objects from getting into the eyes and prevent loss of sight.
- Pupil constriction in response to bright light helps protect the eyes and thus prevent loss of sight.
- Rapid withdrawal from painful stimulation can help a person keep from getting hurt (burned, cut, and so on)
- Autonomic nervous system arousal involves bodily systems that prepare a person for action (the fight or flight response) and so may enable the person to escape from a dangerous situation or engage in protective behavior (Asterita, 1985). The bodily responses involved in autonomic arousal are listed in Table 8-2.
- The startle response includes the components of autonomic arousal that prepare the body for action in a possibly dangerous situation.
- The responses involved in sexual arousal do not have survival value for the individual, but they facilitate sexual behavior, which is necessary for survival of the human species.
- Although the knee jerk reflex may not have direct survival value itself, it is a component of a larger group of reflexes involved in postural control and muscle coordination that contribute to normal motor functioning.

A UR is a natural reflexive action of the body that occurs when a US is present. URs are common to all people. Respondent conditioning occurs when a previously neutral stimulus is paired with a US (the neutral stimulus and the US are presented together). As a result of this pairing, the neutral stimulus becomes a **conditioned**

TABLE 8-2 Bodily Responses Involved in Autonomic Nervous System Arousal

Bodily Responses Involved in Autonomic Nervous System Arousal
Increased heart rate
Increased respiration
Increased muscle tension
Increased blood flow to major muscles
Decreased blood flow to the skin
Secretion of adrenalin into the bloodstream
Increased sweating
Dry mouth
Pupil dilation
Decreased gastrointestinal activity

stimulus (CS) and elicits a **conditioned response (CR)** similar to the UR. A UR or CR is called a respondent behavior.

Respondent conditioning is also called classical conditioning (Rachlin, 1976) or Pavlovian conditioning (Chance, 1988). The Russian scientist Ivan Pavlov (1927) was the first to demonstrate the phenomenon. In his experiments, Pavlov showed that dogs salivated when meat powder was placed in their mouths. This is a demonstration that a US will elicit a UR. Pavlov then presented a neutral stimulus (the sound of a metronome) just before he put the meat powder into the dog's mouth. He presented the sound of the metronome and the meat powder together a number of times. After this, he presented the sound of the metronome by itself. He found that the dog now salivated to the sound of the metronome without the meat powder in its mouth. The sound of the metronome became a CS because it was paired a number of times with the meat powder.

Respondent Conditioning

Process US (meat powder) → UR (salivation)

US is paired with a neutral stimulus (metronome).

Outcome CS (metronome) → CR (salivation)

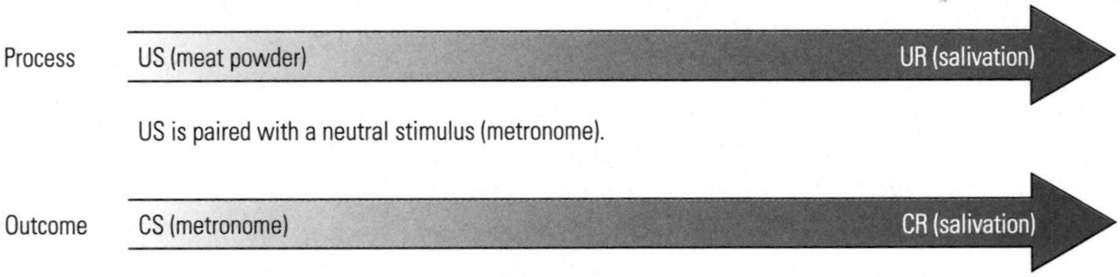

Note that the process involves pairing the US and neutral stimulus a number of times.
The outcome of the pairings is that the neutral stimulus becomes a CS and elicits a CR.

Just about any stimulus can become a CS if it is paired a number of times with a US. Consider the case of Julio. Proximity to the tunnel became a CS because it was paired with the US (startling events in the tunnel). As a result, proximity to the tunnel elicited the CR of autonomic arousal (commonly called fear or anxiety) that was previously elicited by the startling and frightening events.

Identify the US, UR, CS, and CR in the example of Carla in the toy factory.

The US is the blast of air in her face. It elicits the UR of blinking. Because the clicking sound from the machine was paired with each blast of air, the clicking sound became a CS. Now the clicking sound elicits the blinking, which has become a CR. Note that blinking is a CR when elicited by the CS but was initially a UR when elicited by the US.

Respondent Conditioning

Process Blast of air (US) → Blinking (UR)

The blast of air is paired with the clicking sound.

Outcome Clicking sound (CS) → Blinking (CR)

TIMING OF THE NEUTRAL STIMULUS AND US

The timing of the neutral stimulus (NS) and US is important if respondent conditioning is to take place. Ideally, the US should occur immediately after the onset of the NS (Pavlov, 1927). In the case of Pavlov's dogs, the metronome is sounded and, within about half a second, the meat powder is placed in the dog's mouth. This timing increases the likelihood that the metronome will become conditioned as a CS. If Pavlov put meat powder in the dog's mouth and then sounded the metronome, it is unlikely that conditioning would take place. The possible temporal relationships between the NS and US are shown in Figure 8-1 (adapted from Pierce & Epling, 1995).

In **delay conditioning,** the NS is presented and then the US is presented before the NS ends. Take the example of eyeblink conditioning. Delay conditioning occurs if a clicking sound is presented and a puff of air is presented before the clicking sound has terminated.

Trace conditioning is similar to delay conditioning in that the NS precedes the US, but in this case the NS ends before the US is presented. In the eyeblink example,

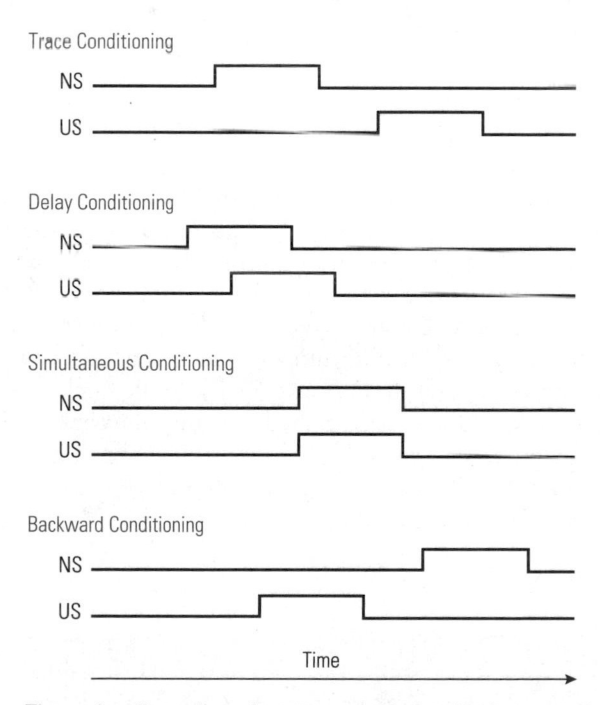

FIGURE 8-1 These time lines show the temporal relationship between the neutral stimulus (NS) and US for four types of respondent conditioning. The raised portion of each time line indicates when the stimulus (US or NS) is presented. Note that the stimulus labeled NS becomes a conditioned stimulus only after pairing with the unconditioned stimulus.

you present the clicking sound and, after the clicking sound has stopped, you present the puff of air.

In **simultaneous conditioning,** the NS and US are presented at the same time. The clicking sound and the puff of air occur simultaneously.

In **backward conditioning,** the US is presented before the NS. In our example, the puff of air is directed at the eye and then the clicking sound is presented. In those circumstances, it is unlikely that the clicking sound will elicit an eyeblink response.

Of these types of respondent conditioning, trace and delay conditioning, in which the NS is presented first, generally are most effective. Backward conditioning is least likely to be effective. Perhaps the only case in which respondent conditioning can occur without close temporal proximity of the NS and US is taste aversion. Consider the following example.

Murphy drank a glass of milk that had gone bad. Although the milk tasted normal, Murphy experienced overwhelming nausea and vomiting 15 minutes after he drank it. Since this episode, milk does not taste good to Murphy when he tries to drink it. The tainted milk was a US, and the UR was nausea and vomiting. Because the US was paired with the taste of milk, the taste of milk became a CS that elicited a CR similar to the nausea he initially experienced. Murphy might not actually get sick when drinking milk again, but the milk does not taste good and may produce a milder version of the initial nausea. This type of respondent conditioning is called taste aversion (Garcia, Kimeldorf, & Koelling, 1955).

Higher-Order Conditioning

What you have learned so far is that a neutral stimulus can become a CS when it is paired with a US. The CS then elicits a CR. This is the basic process of respondent conditioning. **Higher-order conditioning** occurs when a neutral stimulus is paired with an already-established CS and the neutral stimulus becomes a CS. Consider the example of Carla's eyeblink response. Once the clicking sound was paired with the blast of air a number of times, the clicking sound became a CS for Carla's eyeblink response. Now if another neutral stimulus is paired with the clicking sound, it can become a CS also. For example, if a light flashed each time the clicking sound was made, the light would eventually become a CS and would elicit blinking even in the absence of the clicking sound. Higher-order conditioning depends on how well established the CS is when it is paired with the neutral stimulus.

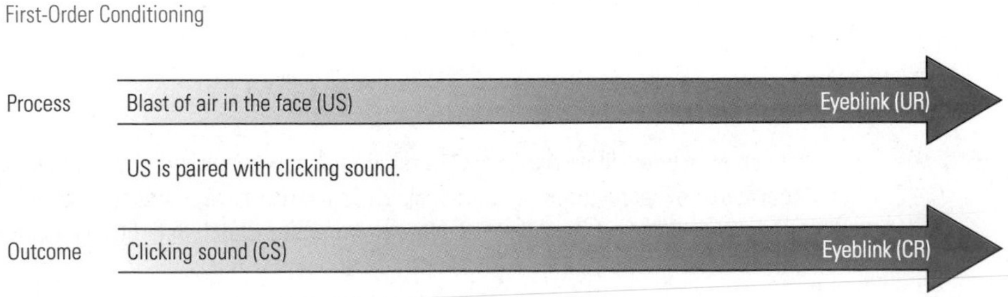

First-Order Conditioning

Process — Blast of air in the face (US) → Eyeblink (UR)

US is paired with clicking sound.

Outcome — Clicking sound (CS) → Eyeblink (CR)

Higher-Order Conditioning

Process	Clicking sound (CS) →	Eyeblink (CR)
	CS is paired with a flash of light.	
Outcome	Flash of light (CS) →	Eyeblink (CR)

CONDITIONED EMOTIONAL RESPONSES

Some types of CRs produced through respondent conditioning are called **conditioned emotional responses (CERs)**. This term was first proposed by Watson and Rayner (1920), who used respondent conditioning procedures to condition a fear response in a young child, 1-year-old Albert. Little Albert was not initially afraid of a white laboratory rat; he did not cry or try to get away. The rat was a neutral stimulus. Watson and Rayner presented the rat to Albert and immediately hit a metal bar with a hammer behind Albert's head (Figure 8-2). The loud, unexpected sound produced by the hammer on the metal was a US that elicited a startle response (UR) in Albert. The

FIGURE 8-2 Watson hits the bar to make a loud noise as Albert touches the rat. After the startling noise and the rat are paired a number of times, Albert shows a fear response when later presented with the rat.

startle response involves autonomic arousal, the same type of responses involved in fear or anxiety. After they paired the presence of the rat and the loud noise seven times in two sessions 1 week apart, the rat became a CS. The sight of the rat now elicited the CER we would call fear (e.g., crying, autonomic arousal).

Note that Watson and Rayner's experiment with Albert probably also involved operant conditioning. Initially, Albert reached for the white rat and the experimenters made the loud, startling noise. As a result of the pairing of the loud noise and the white rat, the rat became a conditioned punisher. The behavior of reaching for the rat was weakened through punishment, and the behavior of crawling away from the rat was strengthened through negative reinforcement (escape). Also note that research like this, in which a fear response is intentionally induced, would not currently be considered ethical.

The process of respondent conditioning can develop CSs for positive (desirable) CERs or negative (undesirable) CERs (Watson, 1924). The fear developed in little Albert by Watson and Rayner is an example of a negative CER; others include anger, disgust, and prejudice. In the same way, positive CERs (e.g., happiness, love) can be elicited by CSs. Initially, an emotional response is a UR elicited by a US, such as a baby's response to a mother's physical contact. The mother strokes the baby's face and the baby smiles, coos, and makes other responses indicating positive emotion. Eventually these CERs are conditioned to the sound of the mother's voice or the sight of her face. Another example would be when a young man smells the perfume usually worn by his girlfriend and it elicits a positive emotional response. Positive, affectionate interactions and physical contact with the girlfriend would be the US eliciting the positive emotional response; the perfume is the CS because it is paired with the US. Therefore, even if the girlfriend is not present, the smell of the perfume can elicit the same feelings (positive CER) that the young man experiences when he is with his girlfriend.

Identify positive CERs and negative CERs occurring in your life and the CSs that elicit these emotional responses.

Although the notion of CERs has intuitive appeal, there can be some difficulty in operationalizing or measuring the emotional responses. Some emotional responses are overt and thus easily observable; these include crying, smiling, other facial expressions, and postures indicative of autonomic arousal or calmness. Likewise, the physiological responses involved in autonomic arousal (e.g., heart rate, muscle tension, galvanic skin response), although covert, are measurable with appropriate instruments. For example, muscle tension may be measured by electromyographic (EMG) recording, in which electrodes are placed on the subject's skin. The galvanic skin response records the changes in electrodermal activity that accompany autonomic arousal because of increases in sweat gland activity. Autonomic arousal may also be detected by recording the skin temperature at the tips of the fingers. Because the blood flow is directed away from the surface of the skin during autonomic arousal, the temperature of the hands and fingers decreases.

However, other reported emotional reactions are not observable or measurable; these include feelings such as happiness or love. There is no doubt that people experience positive and negative emotions that cannot be observed directly. The difficulty is that because they cannot be observed independently, it is not clear what responses are involved in the emotions people report. Most likely, people's reports of emotional responses are a joint function of the actual CER, the situation in which it occurs, their interpretation of events, and the ways in which they have learned to label overt and covert events.

Extinction of Conditioned Responses

Extinction of a CR, called **respondent extinction,** involves the repeated presentation of the CS without presenting the US. If the CS continues to occur in the absence of the US, the CR eventually decreases in intensity and stops. If Pavlov continued to present the sound of the metronome (CS) but never paired the metronome with the delivery of meat powder (US), the dog would salivate less and less to the sound of the metronome; finally, the dog would not salivate at all when it heard the metronome.

In the case of little Albert, the white rat was a CS that elicited a fear response (CR) because the rat had been paired with a loud, startling noise (US). In this case, respondent extinction would occur if the white rat were presented to Albert numerous times without the US. Eventually, the presence of the white rat would no longer elicit a fear response.

Describe how respondent extinction occurred for Carla in the toy factory.

When the maintenance crew fixed the hydraulic hose, the blast of air no longer occurred immediately after the clicking sound the machine made when it stamped a plastic part. Because the CS (clicking sound) continued to be presented in the absence of the US (blast of air), the CR (eye-blinking) eventually stopped occurring when the CS occurred.

How would you use respondent extinction to help Julio eliminate his fear of walking through the tunnel at night?

You would have to present the CS and prevent the occurrence of the US. In other words, because proximity to the tunnel is the CS, he would have to walk through the tunnel without any frightening or startling events (US) occurring. If nothing bad ever happened in the tunnel again, the tunnel would no longer elicit the autonomic arousal (fear response). This would not be easy to accomplish because you cannot control who is in the tunnel or what happens there. One solution would be to convince the city to replace the lights in the tunnel. If the tunnel were brightly lit, startling events would be less likely to occur and threatening people would be less likely to hang around in the tunnel.

Spontaneous Recovery

After a period of respondent extinction, in which the CS is repeatedly presented in the absence of the US, the CS does not elicit the CR. However, if the CS is presented at a later time, the CR might occur again. For example, Pavlov presented the sound of the metronome repeatedly without putting meat powder in the dog's mouth. Eventually the dog quit salivating to the sound of the metronome. However, when Pavlov presented the metronome later, the dog again salivated, although to a lesser extent than before extinction. When the CS elicits the CR after extinction has taken place, **spontaneous recovery** has occurred. The magnitude of the CR usually is smaller during spontaneous recovery, and the CR should again disappear if the US is not presented with the CS during spontaneous recovery.

Discrimination and Generalization of Respondent Behavior

Discrimination in respondent conditioning is the situation in which the CR is elicited by a single CS or a narrow range of CSs. Generalization has occurred when a number of similar CSs or a broader range of CSs elicit the same CR. If a person is afraid of a specific dog or a specific breed of dog, for example, discrimination has occurred. If a person is afraid of any type of dog, generalization has occurred.

Consider how discrimination develops in respondent conditioning. When a particular stimulus (S1) is paired with the US, but similar stimuli (S2, S3, S4, etc.) are presented without the US, only S1 elicits a CR. This is discrimination training. Consider the example of Madeline, who was attacked by a German shepherd. Since the attack, every time she walks by the yard with the German shepherd, the sight of the dog (CS) elicits autonomic arousal or a fear response (CR). However, when she walks past other houses with different dogs, she does not have the fear response. The sight of the German shepherd developed into a CS because of its pairing with the attack (US). The sight of other dogs did not develop into CSs because they were never associated with attacks. Now only the sight of a German shepherd elicits the fear response (CR).

Now consider how generalization might develop. Generalization is the tendency for the CR to occur in the presence of stimuli similar to the CS that was initially paired with the US in respondent conditioning. If S1 is paired with the US but similar stimuli (S2, S3, S4, etc.) are never presented in the absence of the US, the CR is more likely to generalize to these other stimuli. If Madeline was attacked by the German shepherd but she never had encounters with friendly dogs, her fear response would be more likely to generalize to other dogs that are similar in some way to German shepherds (dogs of similar size, similar color, similar shape). In this case, there was no discrimination training because similar stimuli (other dogs) were not presented in the absence of the US.

Generalization can be enhanced if a number of similar stimuli are initially paired with the US during respondent conditioning. If Madeline was unfortunate enough to be attacked by a German shepherd, a golden retriever, a schnauzer, and a terrier, her fear probably would generalize to almost all dogs. Because a variety of similar CSs (different dogs) were all paired with the US (being attacked), generalization would be enhanced.

Factors That Influence Respondent Conditioning

The strength of respondent conditioning depends on a variety of factors (Pavlov, 1927), including the following:

- The nature of the US and CS
- The temporal relationship between the CS and US
- Contingency between the CS and US
- The number of pairings
- Previous exposure to the CS

The Nature of the US and CS

The intensity of a stimulus influences the effectiveness of the stimulus as a CS o
In general, a more intense stimulus is more effective as a US (Polenchar, Roman
Steinmetz, & Patterson, 1984). For example, a stronger puff of air in the eye is more effective than a weak puff of air as a US for an eyeblink response. Likewise, a more painful stimulus is more effective than a less painful stimulus as a US for autonomic arousal. A more intense stimulus also functions more effectively as a CS; we say that the more intense stimulus is more **salient.**

The Temporal Relationship between the CS and US

For conditioning to be most effective, the CS should precede the US. Therefore, delay conditioning and trace conditioning are most effective. It is impossible to say what time interval between the CS and the US is optimal; however, the interval should be short (e.g., less than 1 second). The exception is taste aversion. The nausea and vomiting (UR) elicited by the tainted food (US) may occur many minutes after the occurrence of the CS (the taste of the food) in taste aversion conditioning.

Contingency between the CS and US

Contingency between the CS and US means that the CS and the US are presented together on every trial. When this occurs, conditioning is much more likely than if the US is not presented after the CS in some trials or if the US occurs in some trials without the CS. When the machine clicks every time before it sends a blast of air into Carla's face, the click is much more likely to develop into a CS than if the click were followed only occasionally (e.g., one out of ten times) by the blast of air in Carla's face. Likewise, if the blast of air when the machine stamped a plastic part was only occasionally preceded by a clicking sound, the clicking sound would be unlikely to develop into a CS.

The Number of Pairings

Although one pairing between a neutral stimulus and a US often is sufficient to establish the neutral stimulus as a CS, more pairings of the CS and US produce stronger conditioning, in general. Consider a student in an experiment who receives a brief electric shock to the arm (US) after a buzzer sounds (CS); the shock is painful but, as in any behavioral experiment, not strong enough to harm the student. After one pairing, the buzzer probably will elicit autonomic arousal (CR). However, if the buzzer and the shock are paired a number of times, the autonomic arousal will be stronger and extinction will take longer to occur; in other words, when the US is not presented, the CS elicits the CR more times before the CR stops occurring. Even though more pairings produce stronger conditioning, Rescorla and Wagner (1972) demonstrated that the first pairing produces the strongest conditioning; the additional conditioning caused by each subsequent pairing steadily decreases. For example, suppose that a big black crow screeches loudly as it flies by a young child's head. As a result, he experiences a fear

ch time he sees a crow. The first pairing of the crow (CS) and the attack
lishes the crow as a CS that elicits the fear response (CR). If a crow swoops
eches at the child again, it may strengthen the child's fear response, but the in-
will not be as great as the fear response produced by the first attack. Each addi-
attack would increase the child's fear by a progressively smaller amount.

Previous Exposure to the CS

A stimulus is less likely to become a CS when paired with a US if the person has been exposed to that stimulus in the past without the US. For example, 2-year-old Grace spends a lot of time around the family dog, Knute, and nothing bad ever happens. As a result of this exposure to Knute, it is not likely that Knute will become a CS for a fear response from Grace if he accidentally knocks her down. However, imagine that Grace's friend Paula comes over and sees Knute for the first time. If Knute accidentally knocks Paula down, it is more likely that Knute will become a CS for a fear response because Paula had no previous exposure to Knute.

In the example of Knute and Paula, identify the US, CS, UR, and CR.

Getting knocked down by Knute is a US that elicits a UR of autonomic arousal (fear response) in Paula. Knute is the CS because his presence was paired with the US. As a result, Knute will elicit a fear response (CR) in Paula next time she sees him.

DISTINGUISHING BETWEEN OPERANT AND RESPONDENT CONDITIONING

From the preceding discussion, it should be clear that respondent conditioning and operant conditioning are distinct processes and that respondent and operant behaviors include different types of responses (Michael, 1993a). A respondent behavior is a UR or CR elicited by an antecedent stimulus. Respondent behaviors are bodily responses that have a biological basis. Operant behavior is controlled by its consequences. Although it may be under the stimulus control of a discriminative stimulus (S^D), an operant response is not elicited by an antecedent stimulus. An operant response is emitted by the individual in specific antecedent situations because it has been reinforced in the same or similar situations.

Respondent conditioning occurs when a neutral stimulus acquires the power to elicit a CR because the neutral stimulus has been paired with a US. Respondent conditioning simply involves pairing two stimuli: the neutral stimulus and US. The outcome of respondent conditioning is the development of a CS from a previously neutral stimulus. Operant conditioning occurs when a specific response in a particular stimulus situation is followed reliably by a reinforcing consequence. In other words, operant conditioning involves a contingency between a response and a reinforcer. The result of operant conditioning is that the behavior is more likely to occur in the future in circumstances similar to those in which the behavior was reinforced. To describe this, we say that the circumstances in which the behavior was reinforced develop stimulus control over the behavior.

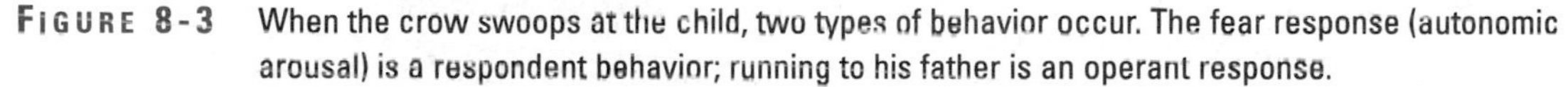

FIGURE 8-3 When the crow swoops at the child, two types of behavior occur. The fear response (autonomic arousal) is a respondent behavior; running to his father is an operant response.

Respondent extinction occurs when the CS is no longer paired with the US. As a result, the CS no longer elicits the CR. Extinction of an operant behavior occurs when the behavior no longer results in a reinforcing consequence and, as a result, the behavior stops occurring in the future.

Operant and respondent behaviors can occur together in the same situation. When the big black crow swoops down at the young child in the backyard and screeches loudly, both respondent and operant behaviors are likely to occur. The attack by the crow elicits autonomic arousal, and the child screams and runs to his father, who is sitting in the yard and reading the paper (Figure 8-3). Although autonomic arousal is a respondent behavior elicited by the crow, screaming and running to the father are operant behaviors that result in comforting and attention (positive reinforcement) and escape from the crow (negative reinforcement).

Consider the example of Carla in the toy factory. The clicking sound from the machine before the blast of air is a CS that elicits an eyeblink response (CR) because the clicking sound was paired with the blast of air. This is respondent conditioning. After a while, Carla learned to move her head to the side as soon as she heard the clicking sound. By doing so, she avoided the blast of air in the face. Moving her head to the side is an operant behavior that is reinforced by its consequence (avoiding the blast of air). The clicking sound is an S^D that develops stimulus control over the behavior of turning her head. The behavior is reinforced only when the clicking sound occurs. At any other time there is no blast of air, and turning her head would not be reinforced.

Respondent Conditioning

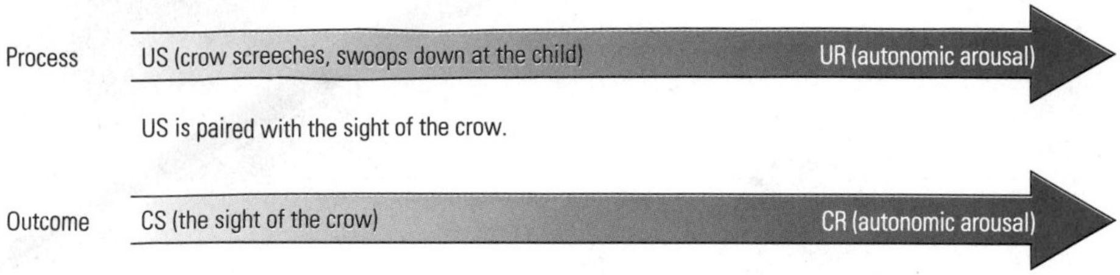

Process US (crow screeches, swoops down at the child) → UR (autonomic arousal)

US is paired with the sight of the crow.

Outcome CS (the sight of the crow) → CR (autonomic arousal)

Operant Conditioning

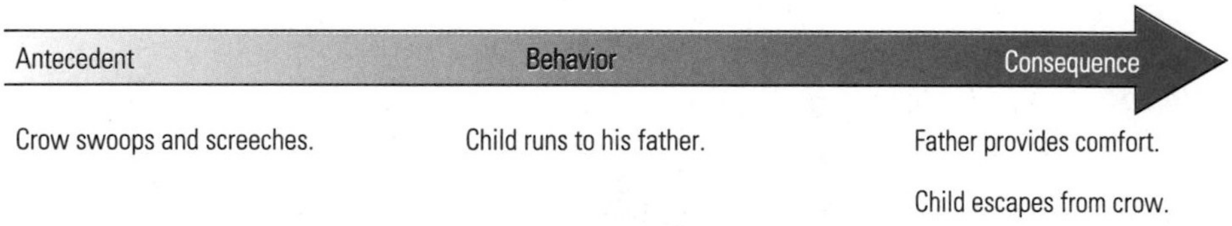

Antecedent → Behavior → Consequence

Crow swoops and screeches. Child runs to his father. Father provides comfort.

Child escapes from crow.

Outcome: Child is more likely to run to his father when he sees a crow in the backyard.

Once she has learned to turn her head every time she hears the clicking sound, respondent extinction occurs. She still hears the clicking sound, but the blast of air doesn't hit her in the face anymore. As a result, she stops blinking (CR) when the clicking sound occurs (CS).

Respondent Behavior

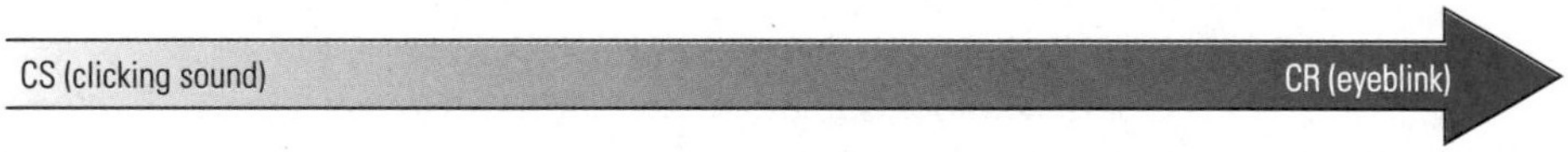

CS (clicking sound) → CR (eyeblink)

Operant Behavior

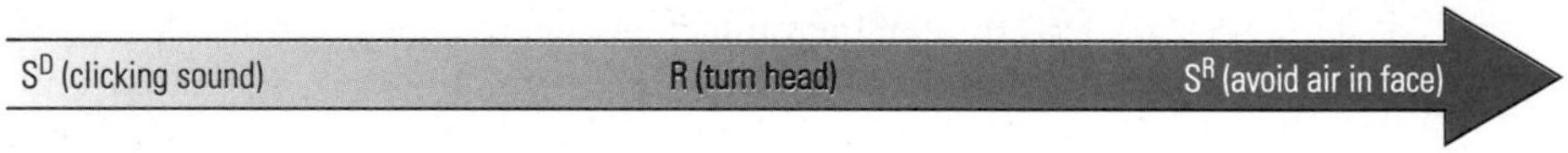

S^D (clicking sound) → R (turn head) → S^R (avoid air in face)

Identify the operant behavior and the respondent behavior in the example of Julio and the dark tunnel.

The respondent behavior is the autonomic arousal elicited by proximity to the tunnel. Proximity to the tunnel became a CS because frightening events (US) occurred in the tunnel. The operant behavior is walking quickly or running through the tunnel. This behavior is reinforced by more rapid escape from the tunnel; in other words, this is negative reinforcement. Once Julio is out of the tunnel, the autonomic arousal subsides. Therefore, the behavior is also negatively reinforced by termination of the aversive physiological state of autonomic arousal.

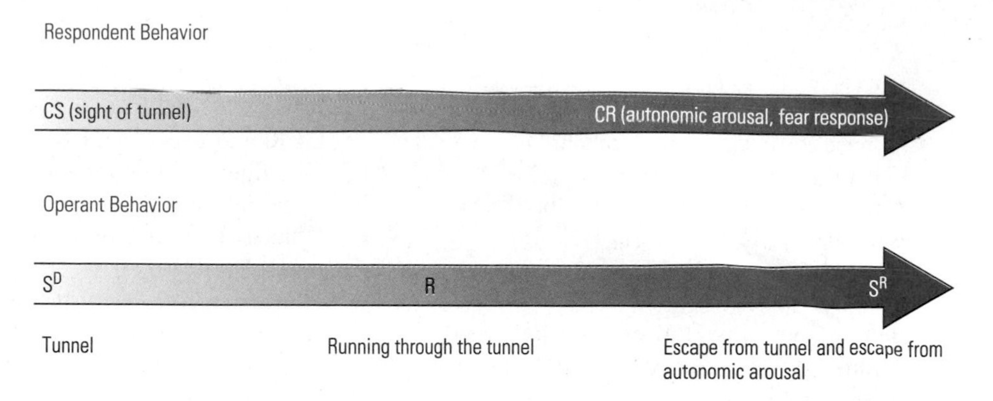

Respondent Conditioning and Behavior Modification

Most behavior modification procedures are designed to change operant behaviors because operant behaviors make up the majority of behaviors that people target for change. However, some types of respondent behaviors are also troublesome to people and thus targeted for change. Most often, the types of respondent behaviors that people want to change are CERs that interfere with normal functioning. Thus, some people experience significant discomfort as a result of anxiety (e.g., anxiety about public speaking or anxiety in sexual situations). Sometimes, the autonomic arousal elicited by the feared stimulus is so severe that the person alters his or her life to avoid it; for example, a person with fear of heights may refuse to drive over a particular bridge. Chapter 24 describes behavior modification procedures to help people alter respondent behaviors involving fear and anxiety.

Chapter Summary

1. In respondent conditioning, a previously neutral stimulus becomes a conditioned stimulus (CS) when it is paired with an unconditioned stimulus (US). The CS elicits a conditioned response (CR) similar to the unconditioned response (UR) elicited by the US. Respondent conditioning is most effective when the CS immediately precedes the US.

   Higher-order conditioning can occur when a neutral stimulus is paired with an already-established CS. Respondent behaviors involve bodily responses that have survival value.
2. One type of respondent behavior is a conditioned emotional response (CER). CERs may be negative (such as fear and anxiety) or positive (such as happiness).
3. Respondent extinction occurs when the CS is presented in the absence of the US. As a result, the CS no longer elicits a CR.
4. Factors that influence respondent conditioning include the intensity of the US or the CS, the temporal relationship between the CS and the US, the contingency between the CS and the US, the number of pairings, and the person's previous exposure to the CS.
5. Respondent conditioning occurs when an neutral stimulus is paired with a US and the neutral stimulus becomes a CS that can elicit a CR. Operant conditioning occurs when a behavior is reinforced in the presence of an S^D and the behavior is then more likely to occur in the future when the S^D is present.

PRACTICE TEST

1. Identify the terms signified by the following abbreviations: US, UR, CS, and CR. (pp. 154–156)
2. What is an unconditioned stimulus? Provide examples. (p. 154)
3. What is an unconditioned response? Provide examples. (p. 154)
4. Describe how a neutral stimulus becomes a conditioned stimulus. What is this process called? (p. 155)
5. What is the outcome of respondent conditioning? (p. 156)
6. The timing of the neutral stimulus (NS) and the US in respondent conditioning is important. There are four possible temporal relationships between the NS and US: delay conditioning, trace conditioning, simultaneous conditioning, and backward conditioning. Describe each type. (pp. 157–158)
7. Identify the most effective and least effective of these four types of conditioning. (p. 158)
8. Describe higher-order conditioning. Provide an example. (p. 158)
9. What is a CER? Provide examples of positive CERs and negative CERs. (pp. 159–160)
10. Describe respondent extinction and provide an example. (p. 161)
11. What is spontaneous recovery? Provide an example. (p. 161)
12. How does taste aversion differ from other types of respondent conditioning? (p. 158)
13. How is discrimination of respondent behavior developed? Provide an example. (p. 162)
14. How is generalization of respondent behavior developed? Provide an example. (p. 162)
15. Identify and describe the five factors that influence respondent conditioning. (pp. 162–164)
16. Describe how respondent and operant behavior may occur together in the case of a student's fear of public speaking. (p. 165)
17. How would you use respondent extinction to help a child overcome a fear of dogs? How would you use positive reinforcement in this same case?

CHAPTER 8 *Quiz 1*

Name:

1. ________________ conditioning involves manipulation of antecedent stimuli, and

   ________________ conditioning involves manipulation of consequences.

2. In respondent conditioning, what do the abbreviations US and CS stand for?

   ________________ and ________________

3. In respondent conditioning, a(n) ________________ is paired with an unconditioned stimulus (US).

4. Provide an example of an unconditioned response (identify the US and UR).

   ____

Match the following terms to the description.

a. trace conditioning
b. delay conditioning
c. simultaneous conditioning
d. backward conditioning

5. __________ The neutral stimulus (NS) occurs at exactly the same time as the US.

6. __________ The US precedes the NS.

7. What does the abbreviation CER stand for? ________________

8. Following respondent extinction, the ________________ will no longer occur when the CS is presented.

9. The professor shoots a gun (a starter's pistol that shoots blanks) in class. The loud noise elicits a startle reflex (autonomic arousal). Later, when the professor raises the gun but doesn't shoot it, you have a similar startle response. In this example, identify the following:

   US ________________ UR ________________

   CS ________________ CR ________________

10. Identify one of the five factors that influence respondent conditioning.

    ____

CHAPTER 8 *Quiz 2* Name:

1. Operant behaviors are controlled by their ____________________, and respondent behaviors are controlled (elicited) by ____________________.

2. In respondent conditioning, what do the abbreviations UR and CR stand for?

   ____________________ and ____________________

3. As a result of respondent conditioning, a conditioned stimulus (CS) elicits a(n) ____________________.

4. Identify two bodily responses involved in autonomic nervous system arousal.

   ____________________ and ____________________

Match the following terms to the description.

a. trace conditioning
b. delay conditioning
c. simultaneous conditioning
d. backward conditioning

5. __________ The neutral stimulus (NS) precedes the US.

6. __________ The NS occurs before the US and overlaps with the US.

7. Provide an example of a CER. ____________________

8. When the CS elicits a CR, later, after respondent extinction has occurred, the process is called ____________________.

9. Respondent conditioning will be strongest when the neutral stimulus ____________________ (precedes/follows) the US.

10. A child at the zoo walks by the lion cage. The lion roars and the child has a startle response (autonomic arousal). The child then runs to mommy and gets comforted and calms down. The next time the child sees the lion cage, she experiences autonomic arousal and runs to her mommy. In this example, ____________________ is the respondent behavior and ____________________ is the operant behavior.

CHAPTER 8 *Quiz 3*

Name:

1. In respondent conditioning, a neutral stimulus is paired with a(n) ________________, and the neutral stimulus becomes a(n) ________________.
2. An unconditioned response is elicited by a(n) ________________.
3. In respondent conditioning, what happens to the neutral stimulus after it is paired with a US? ________________
4. Pavlov put meat powder in a dog's mouth, and the dog salivated. In this example, salivation is a(n) ________________, and the meat powder in the mouth is a(n) ________________.

When the sound of a metronome was paired with meat powder in the dog's mouth, the dog started salivating to the sound of the metronome alone.

5. The sound of the metronome is a(n) ________________.
6. Salivation to the sound of the metronome is a(n) ________________.
7. What is this process called? ________________
8. In higher-order conditioning, a neutral stimulus is paired with a(n) ________________.
9. In respondent extinction, the ________________ is presented in the absence of the US.
10. A child at the zoo walks by the lion cage. The lion roars and the child has a startle response (autonomic arousal). The child then runs to mommy and gets comforted and calms down. The next time the child sees the lion cage, she experiences autonomic arousal and runs to her mommy. In this example, identify the following:

    US ________________ UR ________________

    CS ________________ CR ________________

NINE

Shaping

As we saw in Chapter 4, reinforcement is a procedure for increasing the frequency of a desirable behavior. To use reinforcement, the desirable behavior must already be occurring at least occasionally. If the person does not exhibit a particular target behavior at all, you need other strategies to get the behavior going. Shaping is one such strategy.

- How do you use shaping to get a novel behavior to occur?
- What are successive approximations to a target behavior?
- How are the principles of reinforcement and extinction involved in shaping?
- How might shaping be used accidentally to develop a problem behavior?
- What steps are involved in the successful use of shaping?

An Example of Shaping: Teaching a Child to Talk

Shaping happens naturally with children everywhere. A young child who has not yet learned to talk will engage in babbling; that is, the child makes word sounds that mimic the parents' language. Initially, the parents get excited and pay attention to the babbling child. The parents smile, talk to the child, imitate the word sounds, and stroke the child; this attention reinforces the babbling behavior. As a result, the child babbles more and more. Eventually the child makes sounds such as "da," "ma," or "ba" that resemble familiar words ("dada," "mama," or "ball"). Again the parents get excited and pay attention to these recognizable word sounds. As a result, the child starts to make these sounds more often. At the same time, the parents do not respond as much to the simple babbling once the child begins to make familiar word sounds. As this process continues, the child eventually puts the sounds together to make words, such as "dada" or "mama," and the parents get excited and provide more attention while paying much less attention to the fragmentary word sounds that the child made before. As a result, the child says words more often and makes word sounds (or babbles) less often. Throughout the process of developing language, over the course of many months, the parents reinforce closer and closer approximations to real words. The shaping process starts when the parents reinforce babbling. The random word sounds in babbling are approximations to actual words. Each time the child makes a sound that is a closer approximation to a word, the child gets more attention (reinforcement) from the parent, and the child gets less attention for the previous approximations.

It is also important to recognize that parents not only shape the child's language; they also bring it under proper stimulus control. The parents reinforce "ba" or "ball" when showing the child a ball. They reinforce "da" or "dada" when the child is looking or pointing at his or her dad. Through the process of shaping, the child learns to say words; through discrimination training, the child learns to say the correct words, words that are appropriate to the situation.

DEFINING SHAPING

Shaping is used to develop a target behavior that a person does not currently exhibit. Shaping is defined as the **differential reinforcement** of successive approximations of a target behavior until the person exhibits the target behavior. Differential reinforcement involves the basic principles of reinforcement and extinction. Differential reinforcement occurs when one particular behavior is reinforced and all other behaviors are not reinforced in a particular situation. As a result, the behavior that is reinforced increases and the behaviors that are not reinforced decrease through extinction. (See Chapter 15 for further detail on differential reinforcement procedures.)

When shaping is used to develop language, the **successive approximations** or shaping steps include babbling, word sounds, part words, whole words, strings of words, and sentences. To begin shaping, you identify an existing behavior that is an approximation of the target behavior. This is called the *starting behavior*, or first approximation. You reinforce this behavior and, as a result, the person starts to exhibit this behavior more often. You then stop reinforcing the behavior and, as part of the subsequent extinction burst, novel behaviors typically begin to appear. Now you start reinforcing a novel behavior that is a closer approximation to the target behavior. As a result, the person starts to exhibit the new behavior more often and exhibits the previous behavior less often. This process of differential reinforcement (reinforcement of a closer approximation and extinction of a previous approximation) continues until the person finally exhibits the target behavior.

Skinner (1938) used shaping to get laboratory rats to press the lever in an experimental chamber, which was about 1 foot by 1 foot square. The lever looked like a bar sticking out of one wall of the chamber. The rat could easily put a paw on the lever and push it. The chamber also had a small opening in the wall where food could be delivered. When the rat was first put in the chamber, it wandered around and explored.

Describe how you would use shaping to get the rat to press the lever.

First you choose the starting behavior or the first approximation. You might decide to deliver a pellet of food each time the rat steps to the side of the chamber where the lever is located. As a result, the rat spends most of its time on this side of the chamber. Now you reinforce the next approximation and put the previous approximation on extinction: You deliver a pellet of food only when the rat is facing the lever. As a result, the rat faces the lever frequently. Now, when the rat approaches or moves closer to the lever, you deliver the food pellet. Next, you deliver a pellet of food only when the rat is close to the lever and rears up on its hind legs. Once the rat engages in this behavior consistently, you put it on extinction and deliver a pellet of food only when the rat makes a movement toward the lever. Once this behavior occurs frequently, you then go to the next approximation and deliver a pellet of food only when the rat is

Successive Approximations to Lever-Pressing

1. The rat moves to the side where the lever is located.
2. The rat faces the lever.
3. The rat approaches the lever.
4. The rat rears up on its hind legs.
5. The rat makes a movement toward the lever with a paw.
6. The rat touches the lever.
7. The rat presses the lever.

touching the lever with its paw. Because this behavior is reinforced, the rat touches the lever frequently. Finally, you move to the last step and provide a pellet of food only when the rat presses the lever. Now, whenever this hungry rat is put into the experimental chamber, it will reach up and press the lever with its paw because that is the behavior that has been reinforced. Shaping allows you to begin by reinforcing a behavior that the rat engages in frequently (standing on one side of the chamber) and end up getting the rat to engage in a behavior it has never performed (pressing the lever).

Although we have outlined seven shaping steps (successive approximations), many more steps may be included when shaping the lever pressing response in the rat. For example, step 3, in which the rat approaches the lever, could be further divided into two or three steps. The important point is that each step should be a closer approximation to the target behavior than was the previous step.

Have you ever wondered how dolphins and other sea mammals at aquatic parks learn to perform complex tricks? Their trainers use shaping to get the animals to engage in these behaviors (Pryor, 1985). Using a fish to eat as an unconditioned reinforcer and a clicking sound from a hand-held clicker as a conditioned reinforcer, the dolphin trainers can shape complex behaviors by starting with natural behaviors that the dolphins engage in frequently. By reinforcing successive approximations, they can get the dolphins to engage in behaviors they have never previously exhibited (such as jumping out of the water and catching rings on their noses).

How do the trainers establish the clicking sound as a conditioned reinforcer and why do they need to use a conditioned reinforcer?

The trainers make the clicking sound each time they give the dolphin a fish to eat as a reinforcer. Because the clicking sound is paired with this unconditioned reinforcer, it becomes a conditioned reinforcer. They use the conditioned reinforcer because the trainer can make the clicking sound quickly and easily and the dolphin's behavior can be reinforced immediately without the disruption of stopping to eat the fish. When using shaping, timing is very important. You want to deliver the reinforcer at the exact instant that the correct approximation occurs; otherwise, you might accidentally reinforce a different behavior. In addition, the conditioned reinforcer is used so that the dolphins don't become satiated with fish. Fed fish as a reinforcer, the dolphins would eventually become satiated, and fish would no longer function as a reinforcer until the dolphin was hungry again. For further discussion of shaping with animals, see Pryor (1985) and Skinner (1938, 1951, 1958).

APPLICATIONS OF SHAPING

A couple of interesting examples of shaping human behavior in a medical rehabilitation setting were described by O'Neill and Gardner (1983).

Getting Mrs. F to Walk Again

One case involved Mrs. F, a 75-year-old woman who had hip replacement surgery. To walk independently again, she needed physical therapy (PT): Specifically, she had to walk between two parallel bars while supporting herself with her arms on the bars. However, Mrs. F refused to participate in the PT. Because Mrs. F was not currently exhibiting the target behavior, O'Neill and Gardner decided to use shaping. The target behavior was walking independently with her walker. For a starting behavior, they wanted Mrs. F to go to the PT room where the parallel bars were located. When Mrs. F arrived in the PT room in her wheelchair, the therapist interacted warmly with her and gave her a massage treatment (a pleasant experience for Mrs. F). As a result, going to the PT room was reinforced, and Mrs. F now went there willingly each day. After a few days, the therapist asked Mrs. F to stand up between the parallel bars for 1 second (a successive approximation to walking) before she could have her massage. Mrs. F stood up for 1 second and received her massage. The therapist increased the duration to 15 seconds the next day, and Mrs. F stood at the parallel bars for 15 seconds before receiving her massage (Figure 9-1). After

FIGURE 9-1 Mrs. F stands between the parallel bars as one of the successive approximations in the shaping process to get to the target behavior of walking with her walker.

Mrs. F was successfully standing between the parallel bars, the therapist asked her to take a few steps one day and then a few more another day until she was walking the full length of the parallel bars. Eventually, Mrs. F was walking independently with her walker and was discharged from the hospital. Because shaping involves starting with a simple behavior that the person is already engaging in and building up to the target behavior in small steps (successive approximations), the person can engage in a new target behavior or a target behavior that she previously refused to do.

Getting Mrs. S to Increase the Time between Bathroom Visits

Another case reported by O'Neill and Gardner (1983) involved Mrs. S, a 32-year-old woman with multiple sclerosis. In the hospital, she often interrupted her therapy program for bathroom visits because she had once been incontinent (lost bladder control) in public and was worried that it might happen again. She was going to the bathroom more than once per hour. In collaboration with Mrs. S, O'Neill and Gardner decided to use shaping to help her increase the time between bathroom visits. The target behavior was to wait 2 hours between trips to the bathroom. They decided that the starting behavior would be to wait 1 hour, because Mrs. S occasionally waited 1 hour between bathroom trips before the shaping program was started. Mrs. S successfully met this goal for a few days and received therapist approval and praise as a reinforcer. The next approximation was to wait 70 minutes. After Mrs. S waited successfully for 70 minutes for a few days, the duration was increased to 90, then 105, and finally 120 minutes. It took 12 days and five shaping steps for Mrs. S to reach the target behavior of waiting 120 minutes between bathroom trips (Figure 9-2). When she was discharged from the hospital, the average time between bathroom visits was 130 minutes. Months after she left the hospital, Mrs. S reported that she was maintaining her treatment gains and that her life had improved as a result.

As you can see from these examples, shaping can be used to

1. generate a novel behavior (language in a young child, lever-pressing in the laboratory rat, tricks from the dolphin)
2. reinstate a previously exhibited behavior (walking, which Mrs. F was refusing to do)
3. to change some dimension of an existing behavior (the time between urination for Mrs. S)

In each case, the target behavior is novel in that the person is not currently engaging in that particular behavior.

RESEARCH ON SHAPING

Studies by Jackson and Wallace (1974) and Howie and Woods (1982) report the use of shaping to modify a dimension of an existing behavior. Jackson and Wallace worked with a 15-year-old girl who exhibited mild mental retardation and was socially withdrawn. She spoke at a voice volume (loudness) that was barely audible. The target behavior was speaking with a normal voice volume. Jackson and Wallace used a decibel meter to measure the loudness of her speech and reinforced successive approximations (louder and louder speech) with tokens until the

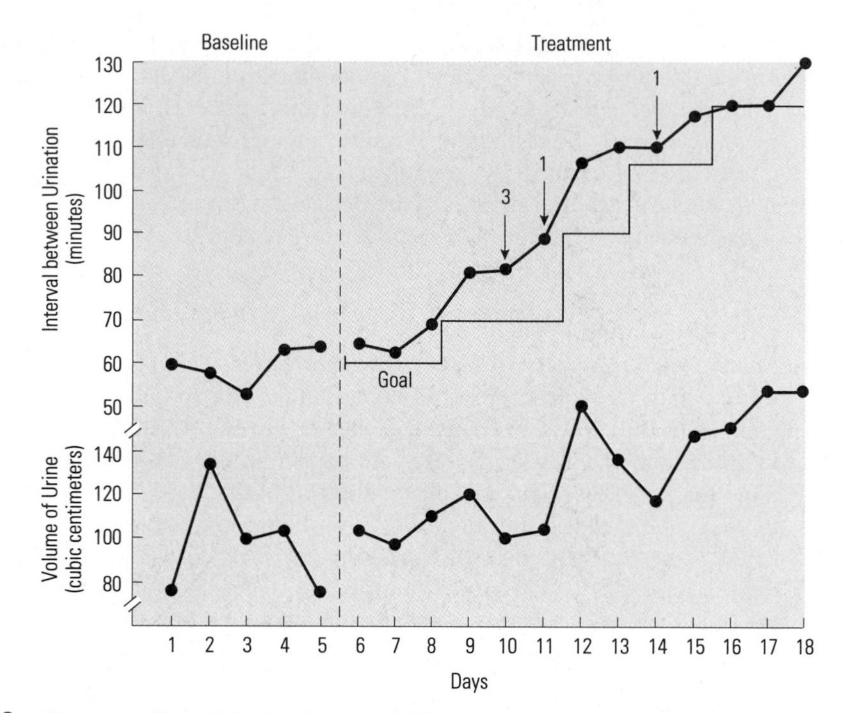

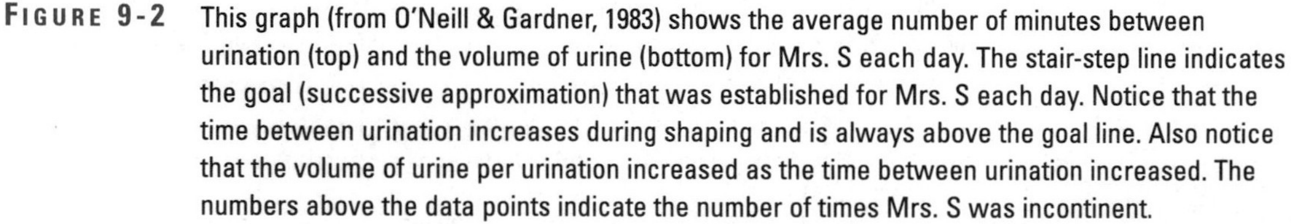
FIGURE 9-2 This graph (from O'Neill & Gardner, 1983) shows the average number of minutes between urination (top) and the volume of urine (bottom) for Mrs. S each day. The stair-step line indicates the goal (successive approximation) that was established for Mrs. S each day. Notice that the time between urination increases during shaping and is always above the goal line. Also notice that the volume of urine per urination increased as the time between urination increased. The numbers above the data points indicate the number of times Mrs. S was incontinent.

girl was speaking at a more normal voice volume. They attributed the success of the shaping program partly to the use of the decibel meter, which allowed them to detect and thus reinforce very slight increases (successive approximations) in the loudness of speech (Figure 9-3). Other researchers used a shaping procedure to increase the voice volume of two children with disabilities. Figure 9-4 shows the multiple-baseline-across-subjects graph from this study (Fleece et al., 1981); an increase in voice volume was observed for both subjects.

Howie and Woods (1982) used shaping to increase the frequency of spoken words in adults receiving treatment for stuttering. As part of their treatment, the subjects slowed down their rate of speech as they learned to speak without stuttering. After the subjects' speech was stutter-free, the authors used shaping to increase the rate of speech (syllables per minute) back to a more normal level. In their study, the shaping steps or successive approximations involved increases of five syllables spoken per minute. Using shaping, all subjects increased their rate of speech to normal levels in about 40–50 sessions.

Shaping of different topographies (new forms) of behavior has been reported in a number of studies (Horner, 1971; Isaacs, Thomas, & Goldiamond, 1960; Lovaas, Berberich, Perdoff, & Schaeffer, 1966; Wolf, Risley, & Mees, 1964). In an early

FIGURE 9-3 The psychologist uses a decibel meter in the process of shaping increased voice volume (louder speech) as a child speaks. Each shaping step involves successively louder speech, as measured by the decibel meter.

study, Wolf et al. (1964) used shaping to get a preschooler with disabilities to wear his glasses. Before the shaping procedure was used, the child refused to wear his glasses; if anyone tried to make him wear them, he threw the glasses on the ground. The researchers used food to reinforce successive approximations to the target behavior of wearing his glasses. The successive approximations included touching the glasses, picking up the glasses, putting the glasses up to his face, and finally putting the glasses on. By the end of the study, the child was wearing his glasses regularly.

Horner (1971) worked with Dennis, a 5-year-old child with mental retardation. Dennis had a condition called spina bifida, in which the spinal cord is damaged before birth and, as a result, use of the legs is limited. Dennis could crawl but had never walked. Horner conducted two shaping procedures with Dennis. In the first procedure, the target behavior was for Dennis to take ten steps while holding himself up between parallel bars with his arms. This shaping procedure included six stages. The first approximation was for Dennis to hold on to the parallel bars with both hands while sitting on a stool. Horner used drinks of root beer as the reinforcer for Dennis as he successfully completed each stage in the procedure. After Dennis could walk using the parallel bars for support, the second shaping procedure was started. The target behavior in this shaping procedure was for Dennis to take 12 steps using forearm crutches. The first approximation to the target behavior was for Dennis to hold the crutches in the correct position; the second was to stand up

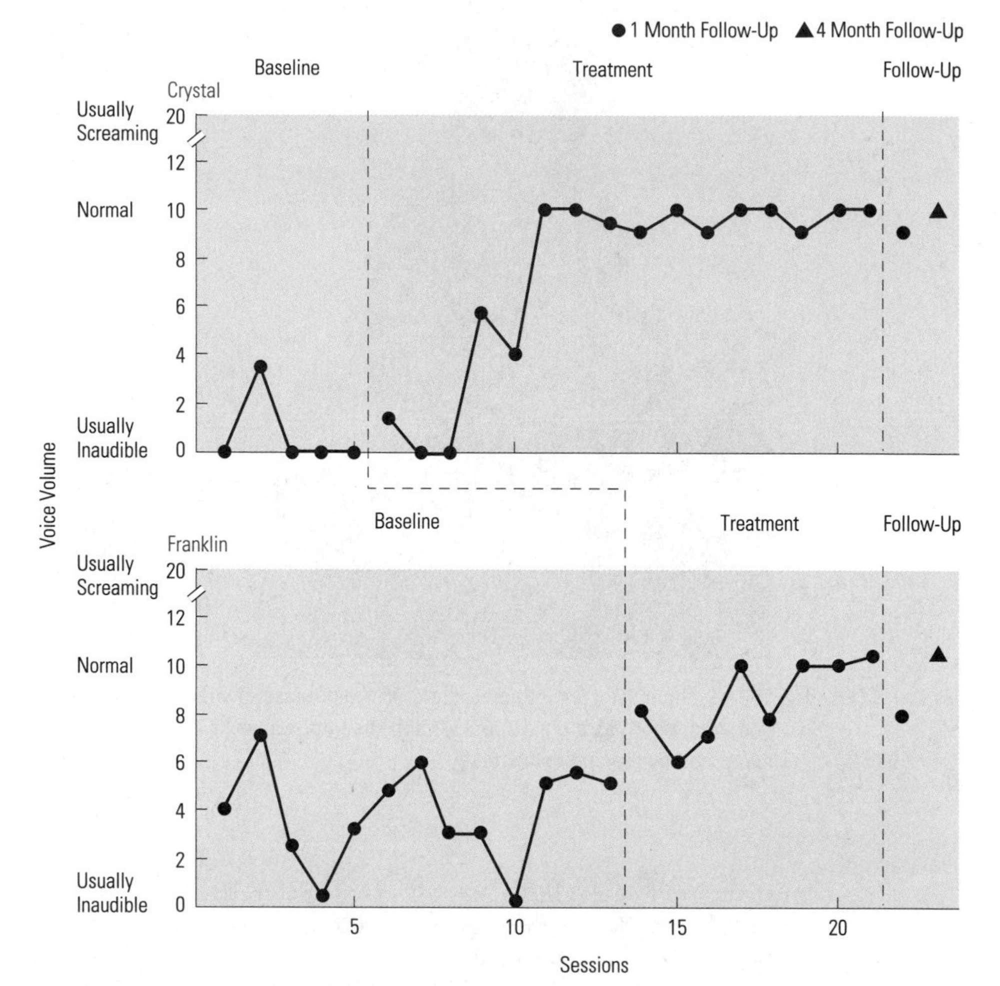

FIGURE 9-4 This graph (from Fleece et al., 1981) shows the increase in voice volume for two students once shaping treatment was implemented. For both children the voice volume increased to normal levels and stayed that way 1 and 4 months after shaping was used. This graph illustrates a multiple-baseline-across-subjects research design. Notice that the treatment (shaping) was implemented at a different time for each subject and that each subject's behavior changed only after the treatment was implemented.

using the crutches, with support from the experimenter; the third was to stand up with no support; and so on. After ten shaping steps in 120 training sessions, Dennis reached the target behavior. After he learned to use the crutches successfully, Dennis walked to and from all of his activities in the state institution where he lived. As a result of the shaping procedures conducted by Horner, Dennis learned a behavior (walking) that made him more independent and improved the quality of his life. The successive approximations involved in the two shaping procedures Horner (1971) used are listed in Table 9-1.

TABLE 9-1 Successive Approximations in the Two Shaping Procedures Used by Horner (1971)

The steps in the successive approximation sequence to establish use of parallel bars were as follows.

Step 1. Sitting on stool and gripping left parallel bar with left hand and right parallel bar with right hand.

Step 2. Step 1 plus pulling to a standing position on parallel bars and maintaining a standing position long enough to drink 1 tablespoon of root beer.

Step 3. Step 1 and step 2 plus taking one step using parallel bars for support before being reinforced.

Step 4. Same as step 3 except three steps must be taken using parallel bars for support before being reinforced.

Step 5. Same as step 3 except five steps must be taken using parallel bars for support before being reinforced.

Step 6. Same as step 3 except ten steps must be taken using parallel bars for support before being reinforced.

The steps included in the successive approximation sequence to establish use of crutches were as follows.

Step 1. Crutches secured to hands by elastic bandages. Experimenter stands behind child. Reinforcer is delivered for imitating the modeled response of placing the crutches on dots marked on floor 18 inches in front of, and 18 inches from each side of, center line bisecting starting point.

Step 2. Crutches secured to hands by elastic bandages. Experimenter stands behind child. Reinforcer is delivered contingent upon completion of step 1 and swinging his body to a crutches-supported erect position, with total assistance provided by experimenter through underarm pressure. Erect position maintained for 15 seconds before reinforcer delivery.

Step 3. Crutches secured to hands by elastic bandages. Experimenter stands behind child. Reinforcer is delivered contingent upon completion of step 1 and swinging his body to a crutches-supported erect position, with assistance provided by experimenter through pressure under the arms only to prime initial movements.

Step 4. Crutches no longer secured to hands by elastic bandages. Initial assistance is no longer provided. Reinforcement is contingent upon independently swinging his body to a crutches-supported erect position.

Step 5. Reinforcement is contingent upon completion of step 4, maintaining balance with experimenter's hand placed on child's back, and placing crutches in forward position.

Step 6. Reinforcement is contingent upon completion of step 5 plus swinging feet toward an imaginary line connecting crutch tips, maintaining balance with experimenter's hand on child's back, and placing crutches in forward position.

Step 7. Reinforcement is contingent upon completion of step 6 plus one additional cycle of placing crutches in forward position, maintaining balance with experimenter's hand on child's back, and placing crutches in forward position.

Step 8. Reinforcement is contingent upon completion of four cycles of placing crutches in forward position, and so on, with gradual fading of experimenter support during balancing.

Step 9. Reinforcement is contingent upon completion of eight cycles of placing crutches in forward position, maintaining balance without experimenter assistance, and placing crutches in forward position.

Step 10. Reinforcement is contingent upon completion of 12 cycles of placing crutches, maintaining balance, and so on, using crutches with forearm clamps (Lofstrand type) instead of crutches providing underarm support.

How to Use Shaping

As you can see from the preceding examples, many applications of shaping are reported in the research literature. It is appropriate to use shaping when your therapeutic goal is to develop a target behavior that the person is not currently exhibiting. Shaping is one of a number of procedures that can be used to achieve this goal. (See Chapters 10–12.)

The following steps ensure appropriate use of shaping (see also Cooper Heron, & Heward, 1987; Martin & Pear, 1992; Sulzer-Azaroff & Mayer, 1991; Sundel & Sundel, 1993).

1. Define the target behavior. By defining the target behavior, you can determine whether and when your shaping program is successful.
2. Determine whether shaping is the most appropriate procedure. If the person already engages in the target behavior at least occasionally, you do not need to use shaping; you can simply use differential reinforcement to increase the frequency of the target behavior. Shaping is used for the acquisition of a novel topography or a novel dimension of a behavior or to reinstate a behavior that the person does not currently exhibit. However, other, more efficient behavioral acquisition strategies (such as prompting, modeling, or instructions) may be preferable. You do not need to use shaping if you can simply tell a person how to engage in the target behavior, if you can show the person the correct behavior, or if you can physically assist the person to engage in the correct behavior. See Chapters 10–12 for a discussion of these other strategies.
3. Identify the starting behavior. The starting behavior or first approximation must be a behavior that the person already engages in, at least occasionally. In addition, the starting behavior must have some relevance to the target behavior. In every example in this chapter, the starting behavior was chosen because the behavior was already occurring and it was an approximation that could be built on to get to the target behavior.
4. Choose the shaping steps. In shaping, the person must master each step before moving to the next step. Each step must be a closer approximation to the target behavior than the previous step (successive approximation). However, the change in behavior from one step to the next must not be so large that the person's progress toward the target behavior stalls. A moderate behavior change from one step to the next is most appropriate. If the shaping steps are too small, progress will be slow and laborious. There is no easy rule for choosing the shaping steps. You must simply choose the shaping steps with the reasonable expectation that once a particular step is mastered, it will facilitate the behavior specified in the next step.
5. Choose the reinforcer to use in the shaping procedure. You must choose a consequence that will be a reinforcer for the person participating in the shaping procedure. The trainer must be able to deliver the reinforcer immediately contingent on appropriate behavior. The amount of the reinforcer should be such that the person does not satiate easily. Conditioned reinforcers (such as tokens or praise) often are useful to avoid satiation.
6. Differentially reinforce each successive approximation. Beginning with the starting behavior, reinforce each instance of the behavior until the behavior occurs reliably. Then start reinforcing the next approximation while no longer reinforcing the previous approximation. Once this approximation occurs consistently, stop

SHAPING GUIDELINES

1. Define the target behavior.
2. Determine whether shaping is the most appropriate procedure.
3. Identify the starting behavior.
4. Choose the shaping steps.
5. Choose the reinforcer.
6. Differentially reinforce successive approximations.
7. Move through the shaping steps at a proper pace.

reinforcing this behavior and begin reinforcing the next approximation. Continue with this process of differential reinforcement of successive approximations until the target behavior is occurring and being reinforced.

7. Move through the shaping steps at a proper pace. Keep in mind that each approximation is a stepping stone to the next one. Once a person masters one approximation (successfully engages in the behavior at least a few times), it is time to move to the next. Reinforcing one approximation too many times may make it difficult to move to the next step; the person may continue to engage in the previous approximation. At the same time, if the person does not master one approximation, it may be impossible or at least difficult to progress to the next step. Successful movement from one step to the next may be facilitated by telling the person what is expected or by cueing or prompting the appropriate behavior (O'Neill & Gardner, 1983; Sulzer-Azaroff & Mayer, 1991). For example, O'Neill and Gardner told Mrs. F that she had to stand using the parallel bars for 1 second before she would get her massage. They told her what they expected her to do to earn reinforcement at any particular shaping step.

SHAPING OF PROBLEM BEHAVIORS

In certain circumstances, problem behaviors may be developed unintentionally through shaping. In such cases, successive approximations of a behavior that is not beneficial to the person are reinforced.

Consider the following example. Mrs. Smith was having trouble with her 4-year-old son Tommy, who was engaging in disruptive behavior. Mrs. Smith runs a mail order business from her home. When she was busy, Tommy often interrupted her and asked or demanded that she play with him. Because Tommy was persistent, Mrs. Smith usually stopped what she was doing to play for a while. The three-term contingency was as follows.

Antecedent	Behavior	Consequence
Mom is working.	Tommy interrupts and demands that she play with him.	Mom plays with him.

Outcome: Tommy's behavior of interrupting his mom when she is working is strengthened.

Mrs. Smith asked Tommy's pediatrician what she could do about this. He suggested that when Tommy demanded that she play with him, Mrs. Smith was to say, "I'll play later, Tommy," and to continue working; she was to ignore Tommy's further attempts to interrupt her.

What is the behavioral principle involved in this plan?

The pediatrician was suggesting that Mrs. Smith use extinction and learn not to reinforce Tommy's frequent demands on her. The first time that Mrs. Smith used extinction, Tommy got upset. He ran into the other room and screamed (extinction burst). Concerned for her son, Mrs. Smith followed him, calmed him down, and then played for a few minutes. She tried extinction the next time Tommy demanded that she play with him. Again, he screamed and ran into the other room. Mrs. Smith followed him, calmed him down, and played with him again, so that he would quit screaming.

What reinforced Mrs. Smith's behavior of playing with Tommy when he screamed?

Mrs. Smith's behavior of playing with Tommy when he screamed was negatively reinforced because he stopped screaming.

Mrs. Smith began to notice that Tommy was screaming frequently to get her to play with him. She decided to use the pediatrician's advice and try to ignore this new behavior. Next time Tommy screamed, Mrs. Smith stayed at her desk and ignored the behavior. Tommy screamed for 3 minutes straight, and then Mrs. Smith heard a crash. She ran into the other room and saw that Tommy had thrown his monster truck toy against the wall (extinction burst). Tommy was still screaming and sobbing. Mrs. Smith sat Tommy down and told him not to throw his toys and that they would play later. She helped him pick up the pieces of the truck and put it back together. She talked to Tommy until he settled down.

Mrs. Smith went back to work and, a short time later, Tommy started to scream again. When Mrs. Smith did not come into the room, he threw his toys again. Mrs. Smith believed she could not ignore this behavior, and so she ran into the room and scolded Tommy. She made him sit on the couch while she lectured him on his inappropriate behavior. By the time Mrs. Smith went back to the pediatrician, 2 weeks after the previous visit, Tommy was screaming frequently and throwing his toys. His problem behavior was much worse than before. Unknown to Mrs. Smith, she had used shaping to develop a worse topography of the problem behavior.

Describe how shaping was used to develop Tommy's problem behavior of screaming and throwing his toys.

Mrs. Smith used the differential reinforcement of successive approximations. Tommy's starting behavior of interrupting and demanding was reinforced by the attention from his mom when she played with him. Then she ignored his interrupting and demanding behavior (extinction) and reinforced the behavior of running into the other room and screaming. Next she ignored running and screaming (extinction) and reinforced the behavior of screaming and throwing toys. Unwittingly, Mrs. Smith was reinforcing each new behavior problem with her attention. Most likely, many severe problem behaviors that people (especially children) exhibit are developed through a similar process of shaping.

Think of some examples of problem behaviors that may have been developed through shaping.

One possible example is the behavior of showing off; in this case, the person has to keep showing off more and more (doing more and more risky things) to continue getting people's attention (Martin & Pear, 1992). Another example is self-injurious behavior, such as head-slapping, which may have started as a mild behavior and grown more severe through shaping. Initially, when the child was upset and slapped his or her head, the parents responded with concern (attention), which reinforced the behavior. When the behavior continued, the parents tried to ignore it. However, the child slapped harder, and the parents responded again with concern. This reinforced the harder head-slapping. This process was repeated a few more times and, thus, harder and harder head-slapping was reinforced, until the behavior was causing injury. Shaping may also play a role in arguments between spouses. Over the course of many arguments, one spouse has to argue longer and harder and louder before the other spouse finally gives in; thus, the more intense arguing is reinforced. Shaping probably accounts for numerous types of problem behaviors; in each case, the people involved have no idea that they are shaping these problem behaviors by their own actions.

The duration of a young child's crying at night may be lengthened by shaping. The child's crying is reinforced by parents often as they come to the room to calm her down. Eventually, the parents may try to ignore the crying, but when it persists, they come into the room, thus reinforcing a longer duration of the behavior. After trying but failing to ignore the crying a number of times, longer and longer durations of the behavior are reinforced, until eventually the child may cry at night for an hour or more.

There is much anecdotal evidence that shaping can develop problem behaviors in people. However, there is no research documenting this conclusion because it would be unethical to intentionally shape problem behaviors in people who did not previously exhibit them. Some research studies do show that shaping can be used to create problem behaviors in laboratory animals.

For example, Schaefer (1970) used shaping with two rhesus monkeys to develop head-banging behavior, in which the monkey raised its paw and slapped itself on the head. Using food as the reinforcer, Schaefer shaped head-banging by differentially reinforcing three successive approximations. In the first approximation, Schaefer delivered a food pellet whenever the monkey raised its paw. After the monkey was consistently raising its paw, Schaefer put this behavior on extinction and started reinforcing the second approximation, raising its paw above its head. After the monkey raised its paw above its head consistently, Schaefer no longer reinforced this behavior and reinforced only the target behavior, which was to bring the paw down on top of the head. It took 12 minutes to shape head-banging in one monkey and 20 minutes to shape head-banging in the other. The target behavior looked quite similar to the self-injurious behavior sometimes exhibited by people with developmental disabilities. This study documents that such behaviors may occur as a result of shaping, at least in the rhesus monkey. It is also possible that shaping may be responsible for the development of self-injurious behavior in some developmentally disabled people.

This study and others (Rasey & Iversen, 1993) demonstrate experimentally that shaping can produce maladaptive behaviors in the laboratory. Clinical experience also suggests that shaping sometimes results in problem behavior in everyday life. For example, one mother often screamed at her son to get him to obey her. When she wanted him to do something around the house, she repeated the request five to ten times and raised her voice until she was yelling at him. It appeared that this behavior had developed through shaping.

Describe how the mother's behavior of repeating requests and yelling at her son was developed through shaping.

At first when she asked her son to do something, he obeyed right away. After a while, he ignored the first request and obeyed her only after she repeated the request. Before long, he ignored two or three requests and did what she asked only after the fourth or fifth request. Eventually, he ignored repeated requests and obeyed her only after she raised her voice and repeated the requests. Finally, she was yelling at him and repeating requests many times before he obeyed her. The son had shaped the behavior in his mother by differentially reinforcing her behavior of repeating requests more and more loudly, until she was screaming. It is important to recognize the power of shaping so that people can use shaping correctly to develop beneficial target behaviors and can avoid the accidental shaping of problem behaviors.

Chapter Summary

1. Shaping is a behavioral procedure in which successive approximations of a target behavior are differentially reinforced until the person engages in the target behavior. Shaping is used to develop a target behavior that the person does not currently exhibit.
2. Successive approximations (or shaping steps) are behaviors that are increasingly more similar to the target behavior.
3. Reinforcement and extinction are involved in shaping when successive approximations to the target behavior are reinforced and previous approximations are put on extinction.
4. Shaping may be used inadvertently to develop problem behaviors. When a mild problem behavior is put on extinction and the problem worsens during an extinction burst, the parent may then reinforce the worse behavior. If this process continues a number of times, the problem behavior may become progressively worse through a process of differential reinforcement of worse and worse instances (more intense, more frequent, or longer durations) of the behavior.
5. The following steps are involved in the successful use of shaping.
   a. Define the target behavior.
   b. Determine whether shaping is the most appropriate procedure.
   c. Identify the starting behavior.
   d. Choose the shaping steps (successive approximations).
   e. Choose the reinforcer to use in the shaping procedure.
   f. Differentially reinforce each successive approximation.
   g. Move at a proper pace through the shaping steps.

PRACTICE TEST

1. What is shaping? (p. 174)
2. When is it appropriate to use shaping? When would you not use shaping? (p. 182)
3. Which two behavioral principles are involved in shaping? Explain. (p. 174)
4. What are successive approximations? (p. 174)
5. Provide an example of the differential reinforcement of successive approximations. (pp. 174–177)
6. Provide two examples (not from the chapter) of shaping in everyday life.
7. Provide an example (not from the chapter) of how a problem behavior may be developed through shaping. (pp. 183–186)
8. The starting behavior (or first approximation) used in a shaping procedure has two basic characteristics. What are they? (p. 182)
9. Why might it be useful to use conditioned reinforcers when conducting a shaping procedure? (p. 175)
10. Describe how shaping and discrimination training are used in the development of language in young children. (pp. 173–174)
11. Shaping may be used to establish a new topography of a behavior or a new dimension of a behavior. Explain this statement. Provide an example of shaping a new dimension of a behavior. (pp. 177–179)
12. Describe how an extinction burst may play a role in shaping. Provide an example. (pp. 184–185)

APPLICATIONS

1. Imagine you live in a house with a backyard. The door to the backyard is in your family room. You let your dog Felix out into the backyard a few times a day. You decide you would like to teach Felix to bump the doorknob on the back door with his nose before you let him outside. Currently, whenever Felix wants to go outside, he walks around the family room and often walks past the back door. Describe how you will use shaping to teach Felix to bump the door knob with his nose.

   a. What is your starting behavior?
   b. What is your target behavior?
   c. What will you use as a reinforcer during shaping?
   d. What are the successive approximations?
   e. How will you use differential reinforcement with each approximation?
   f. What will you use as the natural reinforcer for the target behavior once you reach it?

2. According to a much-told story, the students in one of B. F. Skinner's classes used shaping to get Skinner to stand in the front corner of the classroom when he lectured to the class. Let's say that you wanted to play a similar trick on one of your professors. Assuming that the professor moves around the front of the classroom at least occasionally when he or she lectures and assuming that student attention in class is a reinforcer for the professor, how would you use shaping to get your professor to stand in one corner of the classroom while lecturing?

3. One other application of shaping is a game that can be educational and fun. Choose one person who will be the trainer. Choose another person whose behavior the trainer will shape. Call this person the student. The trainer should have a hand-held clicker. The clicking sound will be the reinforcer. The trainer and the student cannot say anything during the shaping game. The trainer decides on a target behavior but doesn't tell the student what it is. The game starts with the student engaging in random behaviors. The trainer tries to reinforce successive

approximations to the target behavior until the student exhibits the target behavior. The student must respond according to the principle of reinforcement; that is, the student begins to engage more often in behaviors that are greeted by the sound of the clicker. The trainer's success depends on how well he or she can choose and reinforce successive approximations immediately as they occur. This game is similar to the children's game of hot and cold, in which the child says "hotter"' as you move toward a target location and "colder" as you move away.

MISAPPLICATIONS

1. Jody asked her father to teach her how to drive. Her father had recently taken a class in behavior modification and reasoned that because driving was a novel behavior for Jody, she could be taught how to drive by a shaping procedure. What is the problem with this application of shaping?

2. Every day, Mrs. Markle gives her second graders a math worksheet to fill out. The worksheet consists of five addition or subtraction problems. Mrs. Markle noticed that Jake completes all five problems on his worksheet only once or twice a week. She wanted Jake to complete all five problems every day. She decided that she would use shaping with Jake to achieve this goal. What is the problem with this application of shaping?

3. Dr. Williams, a school psychologist, was working with an extremely socially withdrawn adolescent, Jenny. Dr. Williams decided to use shaping to help Jenny develop appropriate social skills. He identified the target behavior as making eye contact, smiling, standing up straight, talking at a normal voice volume, and nodding and paraphrasing when the other person said something. Dr. Williams was going to reinforce successive approximations of this target behavior in therapy sessions, in which he played the role of a classmate and engaged in conversations with Jenny. In each session, Dr. Williams and Jenny role-played four or five short conversations. Before each role-play, Dr. Williams reminded Jenny which behaviors she should work on. As a reinforcer for exhibiting the correct behavior in the role plays, Dr. Williams bought Jenny an ice cream cone in the school cafeteria once a week. What is the problem with this application of shaping?

CHAPTER 9 *Quiz 1* Name:

1. Shaping involves differential reinforcement of ______________________________ of a target behavior.

2. In shaping, the first behavior chosen for reinforcement is called the ____________________.

3. What two behavioral principles are involved in differential reinforcement?

   ____________________________ and ________________________________

4. What conditioned reinforcer might a trainer use when using shaping to get a dolphin to

   do tricks? ______________________________

5. In order to be able to deliver the reinforcer immediately after the desired behavior during

   shaping, it is important to use a ________________________ reinforcer.

Shaping can be used for three different outcomes:

6. To generate a ______________________ behavior.

7. To reinstate a ________________________behavior.

8. To change some ______________________ of an existing behavior.

9. You would not use shaping when ____________________________________ could be used to get the person to engage in the target behavior.

10. Mikey shares his toys only occasionally when he is playing with his friends. You want him to share more often. Is shaping an appropriate procedure to use to get him to share more?

    ____

CHAPTER 9 *Quiz 2* Name:

1. Shaping involves ________________________ of successive approximations of a target behavior.

2. The steps in a shaping procedure are called ________________________________.

3. Name three shaping steps that are reinforced when teaching a young child to talk.

   __________________, ______________________, ______________________

It is important to use a conditioned reinforcer during shaping for two reasons:

4. So the reinforcer can be delivered ____________________ after the behavior.

5. So that the reinforcer doesn't lose its effectiveness through ___________________.

Match the following uses of shaping to the examples.

a. Generating novel behavior
b. Reinstating a previously exhibited behavior
c. Changing a dimension of an existing behavior

6. ______ using shaping to get a person to walk again after an injury

7. ______ using shaping to get a person to talk louder during speech therapy sessions

8. ______ using shaping to get a young child to say "dada"

9. Shaping __________ (is/is not) an appropriate procedure to use if the target behavior is already occurring at least occasionally.

10. If the target behavior is already occurring at least occasionally, what would you do to get it to occur more often? ____

CHAPTER 9 *Quiz 3* Name:

1. ______________________ involves differential reinforcement of successive approximations of a target behavior.

2. In shaping, each ___________________________ is a behavior that is more and more like the target behavior.

3. If you were using shaping to get a rat in an experimental chamber to press a lever, pressing the lever would be called the ________________________________.

4. If you were using shaping to get a rat to press a lever in a 1-square-foot experimental chamber, what might you choose for a starting behavior? ________________________

5. In order to avoid satiation during shaping, it is important to use a _____________________ reinforcer.

Shaping is used to:

6. ____

7. ____

8. ____

You do not need to use shaping if you can get the behavior to occur by:

9. ____ or

10. ____.

TEN

Prompting and Transfer of Stimulus Control

You have already learned about shaping, a procedure for establishing desirable behavior. This chapter discusses prompting and transfer of stimulus control, which are used to develop appropriate stimulus control over a particular behavior (Billingsley & Romer, 1983).

An Example of Prompting and Fading: Teaching Little Leaguers to Hit the Ball

- What is prompting, and why is it used?
- What is fading, and why is it used?
- How do response prompts differ from stimulus prompts?
- What are the different types of response prompts?
- What does it mean to transfer stimulus control, and how do you do it?

Coach McCall was teaching first graders how to hit a baseball thrown by a pitcher. Previously, the players had only hit the baseball off of a tee. Luke was a good baseball player and a fast learner. Coach McCall told Luke to stand in the batter's box, to hold the bat back, to start his swing a little before the ball got to the plate, to swing level, and to watch the ball all the way to the bat. The assistant coach, Dave, threw some pitches to Luke while coach McCall stood nearby. Coach McCall praised Luke each time he hit the ball and continued to give Luke instructions when he needed to improve his performance. As Luke hit the balls successfully, the coach no longer gave instructions but continued to praise him for each hit.

Next up was Tom. He listened to the same instructions that Luke heard but could not hit the ball. To help him, coach McCall provided more assistance. He pointed to where Tom should stand and gestured how the ball would come in over the plate and where Tom should swing the bat. With this extra help, Tom started to hit the ball and coach McCall praised him each time. Eventually, Tom hit the ball without any extra help or instructions.

Matt watched and listened to coach McCall but still could not hit the ball. To help Matt, coach McCall decided to show him exactly how to hit the ball. Dave threw some pitches to coach McCall, who described the important aspects of his own behavior as he hit them. After Matt listened to the instructions and watched the coach hit the ball, he was able to hit the ball himself. Once Matt started to hit the ball, coach

McCall didn't need to give him any further help (instructions or modeling), but he still praised Matt each time Matt hit the ball correctly.

Finally there was Trevor. Trevor watched and listened to everything coach McCall was saying and doing, but he just couldn't connect. Because Trevor needed the most help, coach McCall stood behind him as he batted. He put his hands over Trevor's hands on the bat and helped Trevor swing the bat and connect with the ball (Figure 10-1). After doing this a few times, coach McCall backed off a little: He got Trevor positioned and started the swing with him, but then let Trevor finish the swing himself. The coach then backed off a little more: He got Trevor positioned and told him when to swing but let Trevor swing the bat himself. After a few minutes, Trevor was hitting the ball independently, and all that the coach had to do was provide praise each time.

Up to this point, Dave had been throwing easy pitches for the players to hit. The pitches were slow and thrown right over the plate. Once they could all hit the easy ones, Dave started to throw pitches that were progressively more difficult to hit. First he threw them faster. Then he threw the pitches in more difficult positions. He gradually increased the difficulty of the pitches over the next four or five practices, and the players continued to hit the ball successfully.

This example illustrates the behavior modification procedures called prompting and fading. All of the things that coach McCall did to help the players hit the ball are **prompts.** With Luke, coach McCall provided a **verbal prompt:** He told Luke how to hit the ball correctly. With Tom, he gave a verbal and **gestural prompt:** He gave in-

FIGURE 10-1 The coach is using physical prompts, hand-over-hand guidance, to help Trevor hit the baseball. Later he will fade the physical prompts and gradually eliminate the assistance until Trevor hits the ball without any assistance.

structions and motioned to Tom how to swing the bat. Coach McCall provided a verbal prompt and **modeling prompt** for Matt: He told Matt how to hit the ball and showed him the desirable behavior. Finally, for Trevor, coach McCall provided a verbal and **physical prompt.** With the physical prompt, he physically guided Trevor through the correct behavior until Trevor could do it himself.

What Is Prompting?

As you can see, prompts are used to increase the likelihood that a person will engage in the correct behavior at the correct time. They are used during discrimination training to help the person engage in the correct behavior in the presence of the discriminative stimulus (S^D). "Prompts are stimuli given before or during the performance of a behavior: They help behavior occur so that the teacher can provide reinforcement" (Cooper, Heron, & Heward, 1987, p. 312).

In this example, the S^D is the ball approaching the batter. The correct response is swinging the bat to connect with the ball, and the reinforcer is hitting the ball and getting praise from the coach.

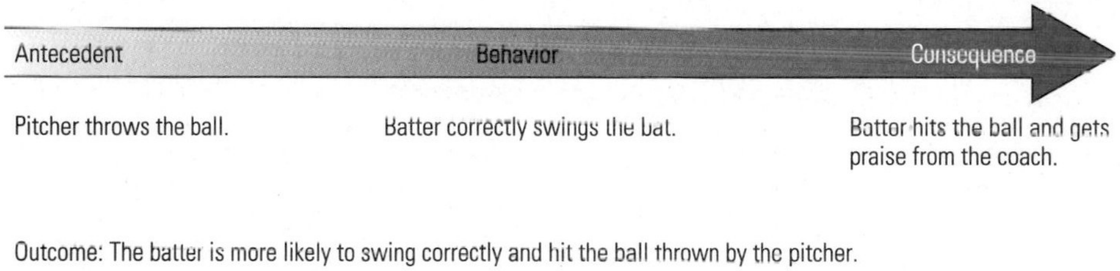

Antecedent	Behavior	Consequence
Pitcher throws the ball.	Batter correctly swings the bat.	Batter hits the ball and gets praise from the coach.

Outcome: The batter is more likely to swing correctly and hit the ball thrown by the pitcher.

However, if the correct behavior is not occurring (if the player is not correctly swinging the bat to hit the ball), the behavior cannot be reinforced. The function of prompts is to produce an instance of the correct behavior so that it can be reinforced. This is what teaching is all about: The teacher provides supplemental stimuli (prompts) along with the S^D so that the student will exhibit the correct behavior. The teacher then reinforces the correct behavior so that it will eventually occur whenever the S^D is present (Skinner, 1968).

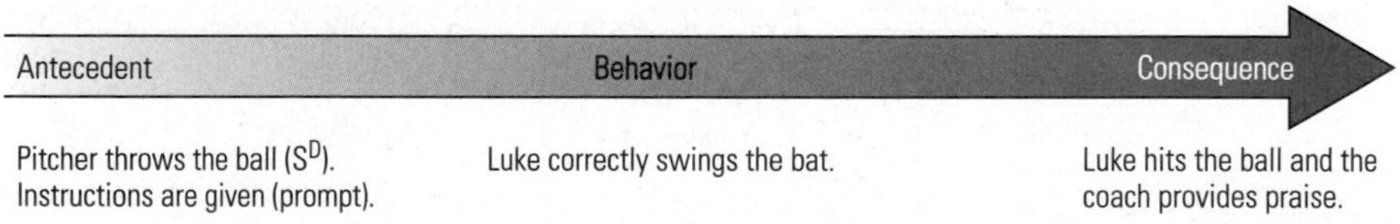

Antecedent	Behavior	Consequence
Pitcher throws the ball (S^D). Instructions are given (prompt).	Luke correctly swings the bat.	Luke hits the ball and the coach provides praise.

The use of prompts makes teaching or training more efficient. Coach McCall could have simply waited for his players to hit the ball without any prompts and praised them when they did so. But this trial-and-error process would have been very slow; some players might never have made a correct response. When coach McCall used prompts, he increased the chances that his players would make a correct response. For different players, he used different prompts (instructions, gestures, modeling, and physical assistance) to get the correct response in the presence of the S^D (the ball thrown by the pitcher).

WHAT IS FADING?

Once the players were hitting the ball correctly, coach McCall faded his prompts. **Fading** is one way to transfer stimulus control from the prompts to the S^D. He gradually removed the prompts until the behavior was occurring in the presence of the S^D without any supplemental stimuli. In other words, he stopped giving instruction and he no longer had to model the behavior or provide physical assistance to help the players hit the ball. Once the prompts were removed, the behavior was under the stimulus control of the S^D. When coach McCall was using a physical prompt with Trevor, Trevor's correct behavior was under the stimulus control of the physical prompt. In other words, he could hit the ball only because the coach was helping him. But Trevor cannot have the coach physically assisting him when he is batting in a game; he has to hit the ball on his own. Therefore, teaching is not complete until prompts are completely faded (help is removed) and the behavior is under the stimulus control of the natural S^D.

Antecedent	Behavior	Consequence
Pitcher throws the ball (S^D). No more prompts.	Trevor swings the bat correctly.	Trevor hits the ball and the coach praises him.

Outcome: Trevor hits the ball when it is pitched to him in the future.

Consider another example of prompting and fading. Natasha, a recent immigrant, is learning English in an adult education class. The class is learning to read simple words. The teacher holds up a flashcard with the letters *CAR*. When Natasha does not respond, the teacher says "car," and Natasha repeats the word "car." The teacher holds up the flashcard again and, when Natasha says "car," the teacher says "Good!" The teacher then repeats this process with each of the ten flashcards.

Antecedent	Behavior	Consequence
Flashcard is shown with the letters *CAR* (S^D). Teacher says "car" (prompt).	Natasha says "car."	Teacher praises Natasha.

What type of prompt is the teacher using?

When the teacher says the word on the flashcard, this is a verbal prompt. In this case, the verbal prompt is also a modeling prompt. The written word on the flashcard is the S^D; saying the word (reading) is the correct response for Natasha. The verbal prompt helps Natasha make the correct response in the presence of the S^D. But Natasha must be able to make the correct response when she sees the written words

FIGURE 10-2 The teacher shows the students a flashcard with a word on it (S^D). If the students cannot make the correct response (read the word), she provides a verbal prompt (says the word). Eventually she will fade the prompt, and the students will read the word presented on the flashcard without any assistance.

without the prompt. To accomplish this, the teacher begins to fade the verbal prompts. The second time through the set of flashcards, she shows Natasha a flashcard and, if she does not respond, she says part of the word as a prompt and Natasha says the whole word. The teacher shows her the flashcard again and she then reads the word without the prompt. The teacher provides praise for each correct response. The next time through the flashcards, if Natasha cannot read a word, the teacher makes the sound of the first letter in the word as a verbal prompt and Natasha says the whole word. The teacher then shows her the flashcard again, and she reads the word without a prompt. Eventually, Natasha will read the words on the flashcards without any prompts. At this point, her reading behavior is under the stimulus control of the written words, not the verbal prompts (Figure 10-2).

Engaging in the correct behavior without prompts is the goal of prompting and fading. Ultimately, the S^D must have stimulus control over the behavior. Prompting and fading help establish appropriate stimulus control. Prompting gets the correct behavior to occur; fading transfers stimulus control to the natural S^D.

Antecedent	Behavior	Consequence
CAR (S^D) No prompt	Natasha says "car."	Teacher praises Natasha.

Outcome: Whenever Natasha sees the letters *CAR*, she says "car."

In this example, the teacher faded the prompts in three steps. First, she presented the flashcard and said the whole word. The second time, she said the first part of the word. The third time, she presented the flashcard and pronounced the first letter of the word. Finally, she presented the flashcard and said nothing. Each step was a gradual elimination of the prompt. By gradually eliminating the prompt, the teacher transferred stimulus control from the prompt to the S^D (written word). In fading, transfer of stimulus control happens because the S^D is always present when the correct response is emitted and reinforced, whereas the prompt is removed over time. As you can see, the prompting and fading facilitated stimulus discrimination training: They made it possible for the correct reading response to occur in the presence of the S^D (word on the flashcard) and be reinforced.

TYPES OF PROMPTS

As we have seen, a prompt is an antecedent stimulus or event used to evoke the appropriate behavior in a particular situation. Various types of prompts are used in behavior modification; the two major categories are **response prompts** and **stimulus prompts** (Alberto & Troutman, 1986; Cooper et al., 1987).

Response Prompts

A response prompt is the behavior of another person that evokes the desired response in the presence of the S^D. Verbal prompts, gestural prompts, modeling prompts, and physical prompts are all response prompts.

Verbal Prompts When the verbal behavior of another person results in the correct response in presence of the S^D, this is a verbal prompt. It is a verbal prompt when you say something that helps the person engage in the correct behavior. When Natasha was learning to read, the teacher showed her the flashcard with the word *CAR* and said "car" (a verbal prompt). By saying "car," she prompted Natasha to make the correct response. When coach McCall told Luke how to hit the ball, he was providing a verbal prompt (instruction). The verbal prompt led to the desired behavior (swinging the bat correctly) in the presence of the S^D (the ball thrown by the pitcher). Any verbal statement from another person may act as a verbal prompt if it makes the correct behavior more likely to occur at the right time. Verbal prompts may include instructions, rules, hints, reminders, questions, or any other verbal assistance.

Gestural Prompts Any physical movement or gesture of another person that leads to the correct behavior in the presence of the S^D is considered a gestural prompt. However, if the person demonstrates or models the entire behavior, it is considered a modeling prompt (described next). It was a gestural prompt when coach McCall pointed to the place that Tom should stand in the batter's box. When coach McCall showed him the motion of the ball and where to swing the bat, he was using gestural prompts that helped Tom hit the ball. Consider another example. A special education teacher shows a student two cards, *EXIT* and *ENTER*, and asks the student to point to the word *EXIT*. Because the student does not know the word *EXIT* (has never made the correct discrimination), the teacher provides a prompt to get the student to point to the *EXIT* card: The teacher turns to look at the *EXIT* card. If this gesture makes it more likely that the student will point to the *EXIT* card, it is considered a gestural prompt.

Modeling Prompts Any demonstration of the correct behavior by another person that makes it more likely that the correct behavior will occur at the right time is a modeling prompt. (Such a demonstration also is called modeling.) A person observes the model and imitates the modeled behavior (makes the correct response) in the presence of the S^D. When coach McCall hit the ball to show Matt how to do so, he was modeling the correct behavior (providing a modeling prompt). Matt imitated the coach's behavior and hit the ball successfully himself. For a modeling prompt to be successful, the person must be able to imitate the model's behavior (Baer, Peterson, & Sherman, 1967). Because imitation is a type of behavior that most people learn early in life, most people benefit from observing models (Bandura, 1969).

Physical Prompts With a physical prompt, another person physically helps the person to engage in the correct behavior at the right time. Coach McCall held the bat with Trevor and physically helped him to swing the bat and hit the ball. The person using a physical prompt is executing all or part of the behavior with the learner. A physical prompt often involves hand-over-hand guidance, in which the trainer guides the person's hands through the behavior. For example, an art teacher may guide a student's hand when teaching how to mold clay. The pitching coach moves the pitcher's fingers into the correct position on the baseball when teaching how to grip the ball to throw a certain type of pitch. In teaching toothbrushing to a student with disabilities, the trainer puts a hand over the student's hand on the toothbrush and moves it in a brushing motion. In each of these examples, when the person could not correctly execute the behavior with the help of verbal, gestural, or modeling prompts, a physical prompt was used to guide the person through the behavior. According to Sulzer-Azaroff and Mayer (1991), physical prompts are appropriate when telling or showing the person the behavior is ineffective (when verbal, gestural, and modeling prompts do not evoke the behavior). Unless the person resists, most behaviors can be prompted physically. (Language is an exception; you cannot physically prompt a person to say something.) Physical prompting is also known as **physical guidance.**

All four types of response prompts involve the behavior of one person, who tries to influence the behavior of another person (by issuing instructions, modeling, and so on). Therefore, response prompts are intrusive; they involve one person exerting control over another. In a teaching situation, this is necessary and acceptable. However, you should always use the least intrusive type of response prompt and resort to more intrusive prompts only when they are necessary to get the person to engage in the appropriate behavior. As you can see in Table 10-1, verbal prompts are least intrusive and physical prompts are most intrusive.

TABLE 10-1 Ranking of Response Prompts by Level of Intrusiveness

Type of Response Prompt	Level of Intrusiveness
Verbal	Least (weakest)
Gestural	Moderately low
Modeling	Moderately high
Physical	Most (strongest)

TYPES OF PROMPTS

Response prompts: The behavior of another person evokes the correct response.

- Verbal prompts
- Gestural prompts
- Modeling prompts
- Physical prompts

Stimulus prompts: A change in some aspect of the S^D or S^Δ or the addition or removal of another stimulus makes a correct response more likely.

- Within-stimulus prompts
- Extrastimulus prompts

Stimulus Prompts

A stimulus prompt involves some change in a stimulus, or the addition or removal of a stimulus, to make a correct response more likely. A stimulus prompt might involve a change in the S^D or the S-delta (S^Δ) that makes the S^D more salient (more noticeable or conspicuous) and the S^Δ less salient so that the person is more likely to respond to the S^D (to make the correct discrimination). Likewise, other stimuli might be used in conjunction with the S^D or S^Δ to make the S^D more salient, thereby making a correct discrimination more likely. Changing the S^D is called a **within-stimulus prompt.** Adding another stimulus or cue to the S^D is called an **extrastimulus prompt** (Schreibman, 1975).

Within-Stimulus Prompts You can change the salience of an S^D (or S^Δ) in a number of ways. You can change the position of the S^D or you can change some dimension of the S^D (or S^Δ), such as size, shape, color, or intensity (Terrace, 1963a, 1963b). Coach McCall used a stimulus prompt (in addition to response prompts) when he taught his players to hit a baseball. The S^D is a baseball approaching the batter at normal speed. The response is to swing the bat correctly and the reinforcing consequence is hitting the ball and getting praise from the coach.

How did coach McCall change the S^D to make it easier for the kids to hit the ball?

Coach McCall used a stimulus prompt when he had Dave throw easy pitches to the kids at first. The easy pitch is a stimulus prompt: It is a change in the intensity of the S^D that makes it more likely that the kids could make the correct response and hit the ball. The teacher who wanted the student to point to the *EXIT* sign would be using a stimulus prompt if the *EXIT* sign were positioned closer to the student than the *ENTER* sign (location) or if the *EXIT* sign were bigger than the *ENTER* sign (size). Changing the size or location would make it more likely that the student would point to the correct sign. The silver stripe down one strand of the speaker wire in a stereo system is a stimulus prompt. This stripe makes it more likely that you will put the two strands of the wire into the correct connections on the stereo and the speakers. In each of these examples, the S^D is changed in some way to make it more likely that a correct response will occur (within-stimulus prompt).

Extrastimulus Prompts Sometimes stimulus prompts involve adding a stimulus to help a person make a correct discrimination (extrastimulus prompt). The plastic cover that a parent puts over an electric outlet prevents the child from putting an object in the outlet. Wacker and Berg (1983) used picture prompts to help adolescents with mental retardation complete complex vocational tasks correctly. The tasks involved assembling or packaging items. The picture prompts helped the adolescents package or assemble the correct part at the correct time. Alberto and Troutman (1986) recount an interesting use of a stimulus prompt by a teacher who wanted to teach a group of young children to identify their right hands. The teacher put an X on the back of each child's right hand to help the children make the correct discrimination. Over time the X wore off and the children continued to make the correct discrimination. The gradual elimination of the X amounted to fading of the stimulus prompt and transfer of stimulus control to the natural S^D (the right hand). When a student is learning multiplication facts using flash cards, the problem on the flashcard (for example, 8×2) is the S^D, and the answer on the opposite side of the card is the stimulus prompt. It is an added stimulus that helps the student make the correct response in the presence of the S^D.

Transfer of Stimulus Control

Once the correct response has occurred, the prompts must be eliminated, so as to transfer stimulus control to the natural S^D (Billingsley & Romer, 1983). Training is not complete until Trevor can hit the baseball without any assistance, until Natasha can read the words on the flashcards without a verbal prompt, and until the young children can identify their right hands without the X. As these examples suggest, the end result of **transfer of stimulus control** is that the correct behavior occurs at the right time without any assistance (prompts).

There are a number of ways to transfer stimulus control: prompt fading, prompt delay, and stimulus fading. The goal of each method is to move from the artificial stimulus control of the prompts to the natural stimulus control of the relevant S^D.

Prompt Fading

Prompt fading is the most commonly used method of transferring stimulus control. With prompt fading, a response prompt is removed gradually across learning trials until the prompt is no longer provided (Martin & Pear, 1992). When coach McCall provided fewer and fewer instructions to Luke as he hit the ball, the coach was fading a verbal prompt. When the coach provided less and less physical guidance to Trevor as he started to hit the ball successfully, the coach was fading a physical prompt.

How did the teacher fade verbal prompts when teaching Natasha to read words on flashcards?

Initially, the teacher said the word as a verbal prompt, then she said part of the word, then the first letter of the word, and eventually she didn't say anything as she presented the S^D. Gradually saying less of the word over time was fading the verbal prompt. In each of these examples, one type of prompt was faded; this is known as fading within prompt. A study by Berkowitz, Sherry, and Davis (1971) illustrated the

TRANSFER OF STIMULUS CONTROL

- Prompt fading: The response prompt is eliminated gradually.
- Prompt delay: After the S^D is presented, the prompt is delayed to provide the opportunity for an unprompted response to occur.
- Stimulus fading: The stimulus prompt is eliminated gradually.

use of physical prompting and fading within prompt to teach boys with profound mental retardation to eat with a spoon. Initially, the researchers held the child's hand with the spoon and physically prompted the entire behavior of scooping food with the spoon and putting it in the mouth. They then faded the physical prompt in seven steps until the child was using the spoon without any assistance. Each fading step involved less and less physical assistance as the physical prompt was eliminated gradually.

Sometimes you can eliminate a prompt in just one step. You might need to tell a person only one time how to execute a behavior before the person does the correct behavior without another verbal prompt. Likewise, you might have to model the behavior only once before the behavior occurs without further prompting. It is also possible that, after only one physical prompt, the person might engage in the correct behavior.

Another type of prompt fading involves fading across different types of prompts or fading across prompts. Consider the following example. Lucy, a woman with severe mental retardation, works in the stockroom of the shoe department at a major discount store. Her job is to take the paper stuffing out of shoes so that the shoes can be displayed on the store shelves. She sits at a large table covered with shoes. (Another worker puts the shoes on the table.) After she pulls the paper out of a pair of shoes, another worker moves the shoes to the store shelves. The job coach has to teach Lucy how to do the job correctly. The three-term contingency is as follows:

Antecedent	Behavior	Consequence
Paper stuffing in the shoe (S^D)	Lucy pulls the stuffing out.	The job coach praises Lucy.

Because Lucy cannot execute the correct behavior, the job coach uses prompts to get the behavior to occur and then fades the prompts. One method is **least-to-most** prompting and fading. The job coach provides the least intrusive prompt first and uses more intrusive prompts only as necessary to get the correct behavior to occur. If Lucy does not pull the paper out of the shoes on her own, the job coach first says, "Lucy, pull the paper out of the shoe." This is the least intrusive verbal prompt. If Lucy does not respond in 5 seconds, the job coach repeats the verbal prompt and points at the paper in the shoe (provides a gestural prompt). If Lucy does not respond in 5 seconds, the job coach models the correct behavior as she provides the verbal prompt. If Lucy still does not respond, the job coach uses physical guidance as she provides the verbal prompt. She takes Lucy's hand and helps her pull out the paper and then praises Lucy. On the next trial, the job coach goes through the same sequence until Lucy responds

PROMPT FADING

Fading within prompt
Fading across prompts
- Least-to-most prompting
- Most-to-least prompting

correctly. Over trials, Lucy will make the correct response before the physical prompt is needed, then before the modeling prompt, and then before the gestural prompt, until eventually she needs no prompt at all to pull the paper out of the shoe. The prompts were faded as Lucy needed less and less assistance. Least-to-most prompting is used when the trainer believes the learner may not need a physical prompt to engage in the correct behavior and wants to provide the opportunity for the learner to perform the task with the least assistance necessary.

Another method of fading across prompts is **most-to-least** prompting and fading. With this method, the most intrusive prompt is used first and is then faded to less intrusive prompts. Most-to-least prompting is used when the trainer believes the learner will need a physical prompt to engage in the correct behavior. Using most-to-least prompting, the job coach would start by providing a physical prompt together with a verbal prompt. She would then start to fade the physical prompt as Lucy successfully executed the behavior. Once she faded the physical prompt, she would provide a verbal and gestural prompt. Then, as Lucy continued to be successful, she would fade the gestural prompt and provide only the verbal prompt. Finally, she would fade the verbal prompt as Lucy correctly took the paper out of the shoe with no assistance. Whether fading within prompt or across prompts, the ultimate goal is to transfer stimulus control to the natural S^D so that the prompts are no longer used.

Prompt Delay

Another method to transfer stimulus control from a response prompt to the natural S^D is **prompt delay.** In this procedure, you present the S^D, wait a certain number of seconds, and then, if the correct response is not made, you provide the prompt. The time delay between the presentation of the S^D and the prompt may be constant or progressive (Handen & Zane, 1987; Snell & Gast, 1981).

Cuvo and Klatt (1992) taught adolescents with disabilities to read common words that they would encounter in everyday life (e.g., *MEN, WOMEN, STOP, ENTER*). They used a constant prompt delay procedure: They presented a word on a flashcard (S^D) and, if the student did not respond in 4 seconds, they said the word for the student (verbal prompt). The objective was for the student to read the word within the 4 seconds before the prompt was provided. Eventually, all students read the words within the 4 seconds and the prompts were no longer used. Stimulus control was transferred from the verbal prompt to the written word.

Matson, Sevin, Fridley, and Love (1990) used a progressive or graduated prompt delay procedure to teach autistic children to make appropriate social responses (to say "Please," "Thank you," and "You're welcome"). To teach a child to say "Thank you," a toy was given to the child (S^D) and, if the child said "Thank you," the experimenter delivered an edible reinforcer and praise.

Antecedent	Behavior	Consequence
Child is given a toy (S^D).	Child says "Thank you."	Child receives edible reinforcer and praise.

Outcome: Child is more likely to say "Thank you" when receiving a toy from another person.

However, because the autistic children did not say "Thank you," the trainer delivered a verbal prompt (he said "Thank you") 2 seconds after giving the toy to the child, and the child imitated the verbal prompt. These children had already demonstrated the ability to imitate verbal prompts, so Matson knew that a verbal prompt would evoke the correct behavior. After the child said "Thank you" when the prompt delay was 2 seconds, it was gradually increased by 2-second intervals until the prompt delay was 10 seconds. Eventually, as the prompt delay increased from 2 to 10 seconds, the child started to say "Thank you" before the prompt was given. Once this occurred consistently, the prompt was no longer given because stimulus control had transferred to the natural S^D (Figure 10-3).

Whether the prompt delay is constant or graduated,the first trial always begins with a 0 second delay between the S^D and the prompt. In subsequent trials the prompt delay is inserted to allow the person to make the correct response before the prompt is given. If the person cannot make the correct response, the prompt is provided to evoke the response in the presence of the S^D. Eventually, after the correct response is prompted and reinforced in a number of trials, the response will occur after the S^D is presented but before the prompt is delivered. Once this happens consistently, stimulus control has been transferred from the prompt to the S^D.

Stimulus Fading

Whenever stimulus prompts are used to get a correct response to occur, some aspect of the S^D or the stimulus situation is changed to help the person make the correct discrimination. Eventually the stimulus prompts must be removed through a process of **stimulus fading** to transfer stimulus control to the natural S^D. If the stimulus prompt involved adding a stimulus to get the correct response to occur (extrastimulus prompt), stimulus fading would involve gradually removing that additional stimulus as the response began occurring reliably in the presence of the S^D. Once this additional stimulus is completely removed and the response continues to occur in the presence of the S^D, stimulus control has been transferred to the S^D. When students are using flashcards to learn multiplication facts, the answer on the other side of the flashcard is a stimulus prompt. The students are using stimulus fading when they look at the answers to the problems less and less as they go through the flashcards. Once they get all the problems correct and no longer look at the answers, stimulus control has transferred from the written answers (stimulus prompt) to the problems (the S^D). When a young child has an X on the back of her right hand, this

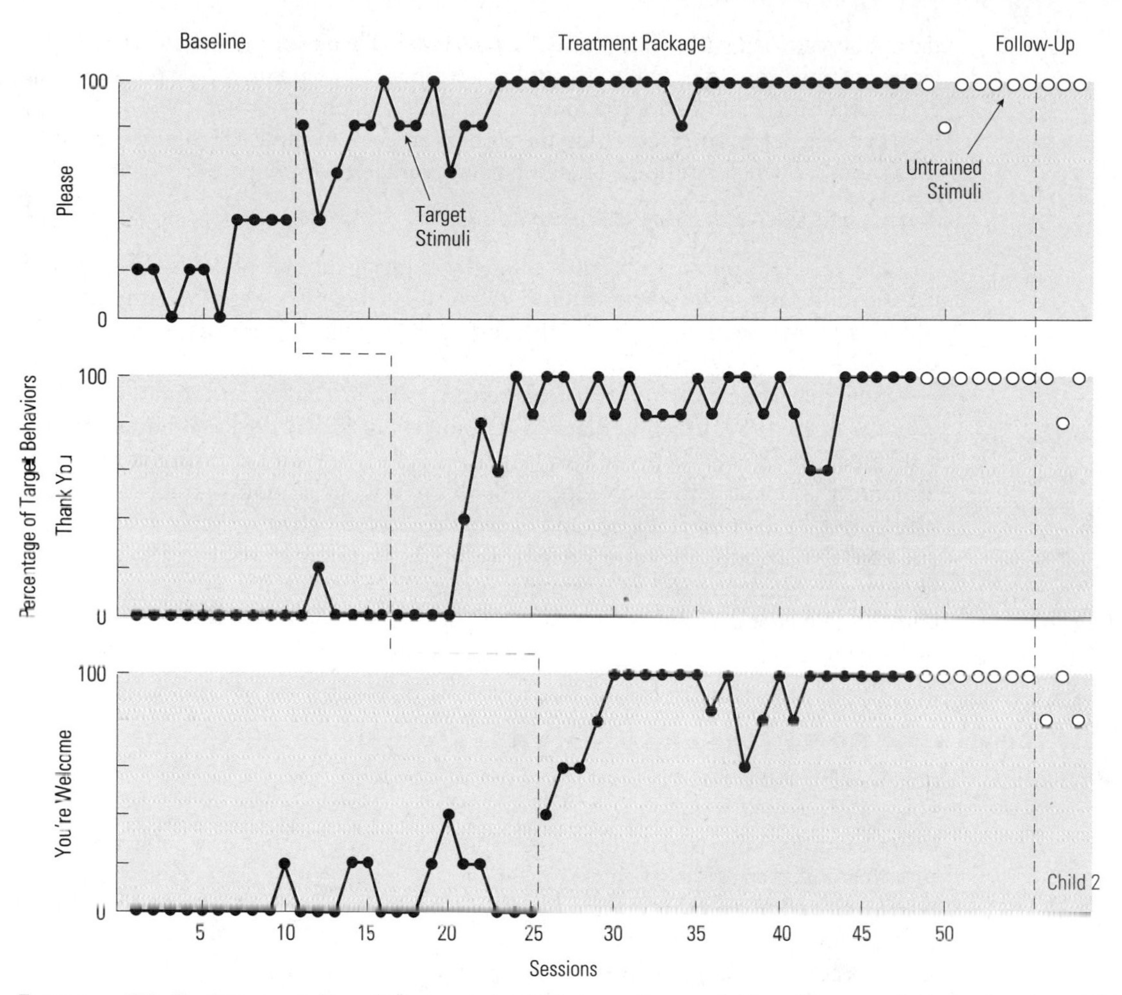

FIGURE 10-3 This graph (from Matson, et al., 1990) shows the acquisition of three social behaviors in a child with autism after the use of a graduated prompt delay procedure. This graph illustrates a multiple-baseline-across-behaviors research design.

stimulus prompt helps her identify her right hand. As the X wears off over the course of a few days, stimulus fading occurs. When the child identifies her right hand without the X, stimulus control has been transferred from the prompt to the natural S^D.

Stimulus fading is also used when the stimulus prompt involves a change in some aspect of the S^D itself (within-stimulus prompt). In this case, stimulus fading would involve gradually changing the S^D from its altered form to its natural form. Coach McCall used a stimulus prompt when he had Dave throw easy pitches for the players to hit. In this case, stimulus fading involved gradually increasing the speed of the pitches until they were being thrown at normal speed. Gradually increasing the speed while the kids continued to hit the ball successfully corresponded to fading the stimulus prompt and transferring stimulus control to the natural S^D (a pitch of normal speed).

The teacher who was teaching the student to point to the *EXIT* sign used a stimulus prompt by making the *EXIT* sign bigger than the *ENTER* sign.

How would the teacher use stimulus fading?

The teacher would use stimulus fading by reducing the size of the *EXIT* sign gradually until it was the same size as the *ENTER* sign. Once they were the same size, the stimulus prompt would be gone and stimulus control would be transferred from the size of the word (prompt) to the word itself (S^D).

Note that some authors distinguish between stimulus fading and stimulus shaping (Cooper et al., 1987; Etzel, LeBlanc, Schilmoeller, & Stella, 1981). Although there is a technical difference between the two procedures, they are very similar (Deitz & Malone, 1985) and both involve the gradual removal of a stimulus prompt to transfer stimulus control. For this reason, and to avoid confusion between shaping (Chapter 9) and stimulus shaping, the term *stimulus fading* is used here to refer to all procedures involving gradual removal of a stimulus prompt. (To study the distinction between stimulus fading and stimulus shaping, see Cooper et al., 1987; Etzel & LeBlanc, 1979; or Etzel et al., 1981.)

How to Use Prompting and Transfer of Stimulus Control

When your objective is to develop appropriate stimulus control over a behavior (to ensure that a new or existing behavior occurs in the correct circumstances at the correct time), you will use prompting and transfer of stimulus control. Before deciding to use such procedures, it is important to determine whether you are addressing a problem of stimulus control or a problem of noncompliance (a "can't do" problem or a "won't do" problem). If the person has not learned the behavior or has not learned to do the behavior in the correct situation ("can't do"), the appropriate procedure is prompting and transfer of stimulus control. However, if the person has exhibited the correct behavior in the correct situation in the past but now refuses to do it ("won't do"), the problem is noncompliance, and prompting and transfer of stimulus control would not be the most appropriate procedure. See Chapters 13–19 for procedures to treat noncompliance and other behavior problems. The following guidelines should be observed in prompting and transferring stimulus control (see also Alberto & Troutman, 1986; Martin & Pear, 1992; Rusch, Rose, & Greenwood, 1988; Sulzer-Azaroff & Mayer, 1991).

1. *Choose the most appropriate prompting strategy.* A variety of response prompts and stimulus prompts are available. You need to choose the one that best fits the learner and the learning task. If a novel behavior is being taught, response prompts are most appropriate because they can be used to generate a new behavior in the appropriate situation. For learners with limited abilities (e.g., people with de-

velopmental disabilities or young children), stronger or more intrusive prompts such as physical prompts are most appropriate. Less intrusive or weaker prompts (such as verbal prompts) should be used if the learner is capable of benefiting from them. If unsure of the level of prompt that is needed, you may use graduated prompt strategies, such as the least-to-most strategy (also called the system of least prompts), in which less intrusive prompts are tried first and more intrusive prompts are used as needed. Stimulus prompts are most appropriate when you want to help a person make a correct discrimination. Because stimulus prompts highlight the S^D (make it more salient), they increase the likelihood that the learner will respond when the S^D is present.

2. *Get the learner's attention.* Before you present the instructional stimuli (the S^D or the prompts), be sure that the learner is paying attention. Reduce or eliminate distractions and competing stimuli and, if necessary, prompt and reinforce the learner's attention before beginning an instructional trial. For example, to get Matt's attention before he provides a modeling prompt, coach McCall might say, "Matt, watch how I swing the bat."

3. *Present the S^D. The learning trial always starts with the presentation of the S^D.* This is the stimulus that should evoke the correct response in the learner once training is completed. If the learner makes the correct response in the presence of the S^D, prompts are not necessary.

4. *Prompt the correct response.* If the S^D does not evoke the correct response, the prompt should be provided. When using a stimulus prompt, you will change the stimulus situation in some way when presenting the S^D or you will change some aspect of the S^D. When using a response prompt, you will present the S^D and then immediately deliver the appropriate prompt.

5. *Reinforce the correct behavior.* When the learner engages in the correct behavior (whether prompted or unprompted) in the presence of the S^D, immediately provide a reinforcer. Because the goal is for the learner to engage in the correct behavior without prompts when the S^D is present, you should increase the magnitude of reinforcement for unprompted responses. For example, praise should be more enthusiastic or a larger amount of a reinforcer should be given.

6. *Transfer stimulus control.* As soon as possible, prompts should be eliminated to transfer stimulus control from the prompt to the natural S^D. If response prompts are being used, fading or prompt delay procedures can be used to transfer stimulus control. If stimulus prompts are being used, transfer stimulus control by means of stimulus fading procedures. When fading response prompts or stimulus prompts, the fading steps should be small (that is, the process should be gradual) so that the person continues to engage in the correct behavior as the prompts are faded. If a fading step is too big, the correct behavior may be lost (errors may occur). If this happens, you should back up to a previous fading step and provide more of the prompt or a stronger (more intrusive) prompt. When using a prompt delay procedure, you can enhance transfer of stimulus control by providing more reinforcement for responses that occur during the delay before the prompt is given.

7. *Continue to reinforce unprompted responses.* If the correct behavior is occurring in the presence of the S^D after prompts have been eliminated, continue to reinforce the behavior. As the learner continues to engage in the correct behavior, switch

Guidelines for Prompting and Transferring Stimulus Control

1. Choose the most appropriate prompting strategy.
2. Get the learner's attention.
3. Present the S^D.
4. Prompt the correct response.
5. Reinforce the correct behavior.
6. Transfer stimulus control by fading or prompt delay.
7. Continue to reinforce unprompted responses.

from a continuous reinforcement schedule to an intermittent reinforcement schedule. This will help maintain the correct behavior over time. The goal is for the behavior to eventually come under the control of natural contingencies of reinforcement. For example, once Luke learns to hit the baseball, getting a hit is a natural reinforcer.

Chapter Summary

1. A prompt is the behavior of another person or a stimulus delivered after the presentation of the S^D. Prompts are used to increase the likelihood that a correct behavior will occur in the correct situation (in the presence of the S^D).
2. Fading is the gradual elimination of a prompt. Fading is used to get the behavior to occur in the presence of the S^D without any prompts.
3. Response prompts occur when the learner's behavior is evoked by the behavior of another person. Stimulus prompts involve a change in some aspect of the S^D or some other stimulus change that makes a correct discrimination more likely.
4. Response prompts include verbal prompts, gestural prompts, physical prompts, and modeling.
5. Transfer of stimulus control is the elimination of the prompt to get the behavior under the stimulus control of the relevant S^D. Transfer of stimulus control procedures involve fading and prompt delay. In fading, a response prompt or a stimulus prompt is eliminated gradually until the response occurs in the presence of the S^D without any prompt. In a prompt delay procedure, a period of time elapses between the presentation of the S^D and the delivery of the response prompt.

Practice Test

1. What is a prompt? When is a prompt used in behavior modification? (p. 195)
2. What is a response prompt? Identify and describe four types of response prompts. (pp. 198–199)
3. Provide examples of the four types of response prompts. (pp. 198–199)
4. What is a stimulus prompt? Describe two types of stimulus prompts. (pp. 200–201)
5. Provide examples of the two types of stimulus prompts. (pp. 200–201)
6. What is least-to-most prompting? What is another term for it? Provide an example. (p. 202)
7. What is most-to-least prompting? Provide an example. (p. 203)
8. Flashing lights on a billboard that make it more likely you will read the billboard are a kind of prompt. What kind?

9. What is transfer of stimulus control? Why is it important? (p. 201)
10. Describe fading of response prompts. Provide an example. (pp. 201–203)
11. Describe fading with least-to-most prompting and fading with most-to-least prompting. (pp. 202–203)
12. Describe fading of stimulus prompts. Provide an example of within-stimulus prompt fading and extrastimulus prompt fading. (p. 204)
13. Describe the prompt delay procedure. Provide an example of the constant prompt delay procedure and an example of the progressive prompt delay procedure. (pp. 203–204)
14. Suppose you are conducting a learning trial with an autistic student. How would you use a verbal and physical response prompt to get the student to pay attention to you?
15. Describe how you could use stimulus prompts and fading to learn definitions for the behavior modification procedures described in this chapter. (p. 204)

Applications

1. Describe how you would use prompting and fading to teach your 6-month-old puppy to come to you at the command "Come." Assume that you have a 20-foot leash and a pocket full of bite-size dog treats to use during training.

2. You are interested in playing golf, but your putting is so bad that you are too embarrassed to play with any of your friends. You decide that you will use stimulus prompting and fading to improve your putting. Let's suppose that you have access to a putting green. Describe three different ways you could do stimulus prompting and fading to improve your putting. Be creative and assume that you can manipulate the putter, the green, the golf ball, or the hole in any way you want.

3. Your 14-year-old niece, Edie, has been bugging you to teach her how to drive your car. You finally give in and take her to an empty mall parking lot for her first lesson. Describe how you will use most-to-least prompting and fading to teach her how to drive.

Misapplications

1. Little Gloria was just starting to babble and make some recognizable word sounds. Her parents were thrilled. Her father, who had taken a behavior modification class, decided that he would use prompting and fading to get Gloria to say "mama" and "dada." What is wrong with this application of prompting and fading? What would be a more appropriate behavioral procedure to use with Gloria?

2. Every day, it is Roger's job to set the table for supper. Although Roger had set the table every day for weeks, he recently became interested in the TV game show *Jeopardy*, which airs at the time that he is supposed to set the table. Now Roger watches *Jeopardy* when he should be setting the table. His father reminds Roger each day, but he ignores the request and continues to watch TV. His father has decided he will use prompting and fading to get Roger to set the table. What is wrong with this application of prompting and fading? What would be a better procedure to use with Roger?

3. Michelle is an autistic youngster. She types with physical prompts from her teacher, who holds Michelle's hand as she types. Michelle has been typing words and sentences to communicate on the keyboard for more than a year and her teacher continues to provide the physical prompts as she types. If the teacher does not have her hand over Michelle's hand, Michelle will not type any words. So her teacher continues to provide the physical prompts, and Michelle continues to communicate on the keyboard. What is wrong with this application of prompting and transfer of stimulus control?

CHAPTER 10 *Quiz 1*

Name:

1. Telling a dance student how to do a dance step is what type of prompt?

   ____

2. Showing a dance student how to do the dance step you want her to perform is what type of prompt? ________________

3. What are two types of stimulus prompts? ________________________ and ________________________

4. ________________ is the gradual removal of a prompt.

5. Verbal, gestural, modeling, and physical prompts are what types of prompts?

   ____

6. Prompt fading transfers stimulus control from the prompt to the ____________.

7. In the prompt delay procedure, you present the S^D, ________________________, and then present the prompt.

8. Stimulus prompts are removed through the process of ________________________, to transfer stimulus control from the stimulus prompt to the S^D.

9. When a billboard has a flashing light that gets you to look at the billboard, the flashing light is an example of a(n) ________________ prompt.

10. What is fading? ____

CHAPTER 10 *Quiz 2* Name:

1. ____________________ are stimuli given before a behavior to get the behavior to occur.

2. ____________________ prompts involve the behavior of another person.

3. ____________________ prompts involve the change in a stimulus or the addition or removal of a stimulus.

4. What are four types of response prompts? ________________, ________________, ____________________, and ____________________

5. Which response prompt is most intrusive? ________________________

6. Which response prompt is least intrusive? ________________________

7. Extrastimulus prompts and within-stimulus prompts are what types of prompts?

   ____

8. Prompt fading, stimulus fading, and prompt delay are three ways to

   ____________________________________.

9. What is fading? ____

10. In prompt delay, what do you do after presenting the S^D?

    ____

CHAPTER 10 *Quiz 3*

Name:

1. A prompt comes ________________ (before/after) the S^D.

2. A coach is providing a(n) ________________ prompt when he motions to a batter where to stand or how to hold the bat.

3. A coach is providing a(n) ________________ prompt when he holds the bat in the player's hands and swings it with the player to show him how to swing the bat.

4. With prompt fading, a prompt is ________________ eliminated.

5. With prompt fading, stimulus control is transferred from the ____________ to the S^D.

6. Presenting the S^D and waiting 4 seconds before presenting the prompt is called

   ________________.

7. What are three ways to transfer stimulus control? ________________,

   ________________, ________________

8. ________________ come after the S^D and are used the get the correct behavior to occur in the presence of the S^D.

9. The system of least prompts is also called ________________.

10. What are the four types of response prompts? ________________,

    ________________, ________________, ________________

Chaining

As we have seen, prompts are used to evoke a behavior, and transfer of stimulus control is used to eliminate the prompts and get the behavior to occur in the presence of the relevant discriminative stimulus (S^D). Most often, these procedures are used to develop simple discriminations, in which one response occurs in the presence of one S^D. For example, a baseball player swings the bat to hit a baseball. A student reads a word correctly. You plug the speaker wire into the right outlet. You say "Thank you" when someone gives you something. Each of these examples involves one behavior occurring in the correct situation. However, many situations call for complex behaviors that have multiple component responses. A complex behavior consisting of many component behaviors that occur together in a sequence is called a **behavioral chain.**

- What is a stimulus–response chain?
- Why is it important to conduct a task analysis of a stimulus–response chain?
- How do you use forward chaining and backward chaining to teach a chain of behaviors?
- What is total task presentation, and how does it differ from the chaining procedures?
- What are three other strategies for teaching behavioral chains?

Examples of Behavioral Chains

When you want a piece of chewing gum, you have to engage in a sequence of responses. You (1) reach into your pocket, (2) pull out the pack of gum, (3) pull a single stick out of the pack, (4) unwrap the piece of gum, and (5) put the gum into your mouth. Getting a piece of gum involves at least five behaviors, which must occur together in the correct sequence. You can engage in a particular behavior in the sequence only if the previous behavior in the sequence has been completed. You can't put the gum in your mouth unless you have unwrapped it. (Actually, you could, but why would you want to?) You can't unwrap the gum unless you have pulled a piece out of the pack. You can't pull a piece of gum out of the pack unless you have gotten the pack of gum out of your pocket.

Consider another example. Bobby works for an industrial laundry company. Her job is to fold towels and put them into boxes so they can be shipped to the customers (e.g., hotels, health clubs, hospitals). As they come out of the dryer, another worker brings the towels over to Bobby in a big bin. Bobby's job consists of the following behavioral chain. She (1) grabs a towel from the bin, (2) lays it out flat on the table, (3) grabs one end and folds it in half, (4) grabs one end of the half-folded towel and folds it in half again, (5) grabs one end of the quarter-folded towel and folds it in half again, (6) picks up the folded towel, and (7) puts it into the box. When the box is full, another worker loads the box of towels on a truck. Bobby's job of folding towels consists of a seven-step behavioral chain. Each behavior in the chain can be completed only after the previous behaviors in the chain have been completed in sequence. Each component behavior in the chain depends on the occurrence of the previous behavior.

This chapter describes how to analyze the components of a behavioral chain and how to use various methods to teach a person to engage in a chain of behaviors.

Analyzing Stimulus–Response Chains

Each behavioral chain consists of a number of individual stimulus–response components that occur together in a sequence. For this reason, a behavioral chain is often called a **stimulus–response chain.** Each behavior or response in the chain produces a stimulus change that acts as an S^D for the next response in the chain. The first response produces an S^D for the second response in the sequence. The second response produces an S^D for the third response in the sequence, and so on until all the responses in the chain occur in order. Of course, the whole stimulus–response chain is under stimulus control, so the first response in the chain occurs when a particular S^D is presented. The gum in your pocket is an S^D for the first response in the chain: reaching in your pocket and grabbing the pack of gum. A bin full of towels near Bobby is an S^D for Bobby's first response: grabbing a towel from the bin. Of course, a behavioral chain continues only if the last response in the chain results in a reinforcing consequence. Chewing the gum is a reinforcer for the behavioral chain of putting the gum in your mouth. The folded towel in the box is a conditioned reinforcer for the behavioral chain of folding the towel. The folded towel is a conditioned reinforcer because it is associated with other reinforcers, such as getting paid and being praised by the boss.

The sequence of stimulus and response components involved in the behavioral chain of getting a piece of gum is as follows:

1. S^D1 (pack of gum in your pocket) → R1 (reach into your pocket)
2. S^D2 (your hand in your pocket) → R2 (pull out the pack of gum)
3. S^D3 (pack of gum in your hand) → R3 (pull out one stick of gum)
4. S^D4 (one stick of gum in your hand) → R4 (unwrap stick of gum)
5. S^D5 (unwrapped stick of gum in your hand) → R5 (put the gum in your mouth) → reinforcer (chewing the gum)

As you can see, each response creates the stimulus situation that is the S^D for the next response. Therefore, the next response in the chain depends on the occurrence of the previous response.

A five-component stimulus–response chain can be illustrated in the following way:

S^D1 → R1
S^D2 → R2
S^D3 → R3
S^D4 → R4
S^D5 → R5 → reinforcer

Analyze the seven stimulus–response components involved in Bobby's job of folding a towel and putting it into the box.

1. S^D1 (a bin full of towels) → R1 (grab a towel from the bin)
2. S^D2 (towel in hand) → R2 (lay towel flat on the table)
3. S^D3 (towel flat on the table) → R3 (fold towel in half)
4. S^D4 (half-folded towel on table) → R4 (fold towel in half again)
5. S^D5 (quarter-folded towel on table) → R5 (fold towel in half again)
6. S^D6 (folded towel on table) → R6 (pick up folded towel)
7. S^D7 (folded towel in hand) → R7 (place towel in box) → reinforcer (folded towel in box)

Once another worker brings a bin of towels over to Bobby, the full bin is the first S^D that has stimulus control over the first response in the stimulus–response chain. Each subsequent response in the chain occurs because the previous response created the S^D that has stimulus control over that response.

Before we proceed, let's look more closely at the beginning of the stimulus–response chain. We can make the outcome of the chain more reinforcing by means of an establishing operation. In our first example, the establishing operation makes the gum more reinforcing at a certain time, and this increases the likelihood that you will start the behavioral chain by reaching into your pocket and grabbing the pack of gum. The establishing operation might be having a bad taste in your mouth from onions, having an old piece of gum in your mouth, having just smoked a cigarette, or any circumstance that would make fresh breath reinforcing at the time (such as talking to your girlfriend or boyfriend). In this situation, you might say that you want gum, but that statement does not help us understand why gum might be more reinforcing at a particular time. It is better to look for stimulus events that may function as establishing operations.

TASK ANALYSIS

The process of analyzing a behavioral chain by breaking it down into its individual stimulus–response components is called a **task analysis.** Any time your goal is to teach a complex task involving two or more component responses (a behavioral chain) to a person, the first step is to identify all the behaviors that are necessary to perform the task and write them down in order. Next, you identify the S^D associated with each behavior in the task. Because teaching the task to the person involves discrimination training with each stimulus–response component of the behavioral chain, you must have a detailed task analysis that gives you an accurate understanding of each stimulus–response component.

A task analysis to identify the right sequence of behaviors in a chain may be conducted in various ways (Cooper, Heron, & Heward, 1987; Rusch, Rose, & Greenwood, 1988). One way is to observe a person engage in the task and record each of the stimulus–response components. For example, Horner and Keilitz (1975) conducted a study in which they taught adolescents with mental retardation to brush their teeth. The authors developed a task analysis of toothbrushing by observing staff members brush their teeth.

Another method is to ask a person who performs the task well (an expert) to explain all the components in the task. Finally, you can develop a task analysis by performing the task yourself and recording the sequence of responses in the task. Bellamy, Horner, and Inman (1979) suggest that the advantage of performing the task yourself when developing a task analysis is that it provides the best information about each response involved in the task and the stimulus associated with each response. In other words, you can get the most information on a task from your own experience with the task.

DIFFERENT WAYS TO CONDUCT A TASK ANALYSIS

- Observe a competent person engage in the task.
- Ask an expert (a person who performs the task well).
- Perform the task yourself and record each of the component responses.

Once you have developed your initial task analysis, you might have to revise it after you start training. You might find that you can break some behaviors down into component behaviors or that you can combine two or more behaviors into a single behavior. Whether you revise your task analysis depends on how well your training is progressing. If the learner is having difficulty with a certain behavior in the chain, it might help to break the behavior down into two or more component behaviors. However, if the learner can master larger units of behavior, two or more component behaviors can be combined into one. Consider the following example.

You want to teach a child with profound mental retardation to eat with a spoon. You have established the following task analysis.

1. S^D1 (bowl of food and spoon on the table) → R1 (pick up the spoon)
2. S^D2 (spoon in hand) → R2 (put spoon into food in the bowl)
3. S^D3 (spoon in the food) → R3 (scoop food onto the spoon)
4. S^D4 (food on the spoon) → R4 (lift spoonful of food from the bowl)
5. S^D5 (holding spoonful of food) → R5 (put the food into the mouth) → reinforcer (eat the food)

There are five steps or components to this task analysis. Each step consists of a stimulus (S^D) and response. This task analysis might be ideal for some children learning how to eat with a spoon. However, for people who can more easily master larger steps, you might want to combine some steps. The task analysis with some combined steps might look as follows.

1. S^D1 (bowl of food and spoon on table) → R1 (pick up spoon and put it into the food in the bowl)
2. S^D2 (spoon in the food) → R2 (scoop food onto the spoon)
3. S^D3 (food on the spoon) → R3 (lift the spoonful of food and put it into the mouth) → reinforcer (eat the food)

As you can see, the only difference between this three-step task analysis and the five-step task analysis is that the five-step task analysis breaks the behavior down into smaller units. Each step is still characterized by a stimulus (S^D) and a response, but the size of the response is different. For some learners, the five-step task analysis might be more appropriate; for others, the three-step task analysis might be more appropriate. There is no right or wrong number of steps in a task analysis. The only way to determine whether you have the correct number of steps is to determine how well the task analysis works for a particular learner.

In a number of studies, researchers have developed task analyses of complex tasks and then trained subjects to engage in the tasks. For example, Cuvo, Leaf, and Borakove (1978) developed a task analysis for each of six janitorial skills, which they then taught to people with mental retardation. There were 13–56 steps in the task analyses of the six skills. Alavosius and Sulzer-Azeroff (1986) taught staff in a treatment facility how to safely lift and transfer residents with physical disabilities out of their wheelchairs. They developed an 18-step task analysis of the lift and transfer task. Other complex skills that have been subjected to task analysis include menstrual care skills (Richman, Reiss, Bauman, & Bailey, 1984), apartment upkeep skills (Williams & Cuvo, 1986), pedestrian skills for walking safely through traffic (Page, Iwata, & Neef, 1976), leisure skills (Schleien, Wehman, & Kiernan, 1981), and the skills college students need to write instructional manuals for community volunteers (Fawcett & Fletcher, 1977). Figure 11-1 shows a task analysis data sheet that might be used to record the learner's progress on a complex task. Note that the data sheet lists all of the S^Ds and responses in the task. The number on the right corresponding to each task step is circled when the learner masters that step (can complete the step without prompts).

	S^D	Response	Successive Trials																		
1	Parts in bin	Pick up bearing and place on table	1	1	1	1	1	1	1	1	1	1	1	1	1	1	1	1	1	1	1
2	Bearing on table	Place hex nut in one bearing corner	2	2	2	2	2	2	2	2	2	2	2	2	2	2	2	2	2	2	2
3	Nut in one corner	Place hex nut in second corner	3	3	3	3	3	3	3	3	3	3	3	3	3	3	3	3	3	3	3
4	Nuts in two corners	Place hex nut in third corner	4	4	4	4	4	4	4	4	4	4	4	4	4	4	4	4	4	4	4
5	Nuts in three corners	Place cam base in bearing	5	5	5	5	5	5	5	5	5	5	5	5	5	5	5	5	5	5	5
6	Cam in bearing	Place roller in bearing	6	6	6	6	6	6	6	6	6	6	6	6	6	6	6	6	6	6	6
7	Roller in bearing	Place red spring in bearing	7	7	7	7	7	7	7	7	7	7	7	7	7	7	7	7	7	7	7
8	Red spring placed	Rotate bearing and cam 180	8	8	8	8	8	8	8	8	8	8	8	8	8	8	8	8	8	8	8
9	Bearing rotated	Place roller in bearing	9	9	9	9	9	9	9	9	9	9	9	9	9	9	9	9	9	9	9
10	Roller in bearing	Place green spring in bearing	10	10	10	10	10	10	10	10	10	10	10	10	10	10	10	10	10	10	10
11	Green spring placed	Wipe bearing with cloth	11	11	11	11	11	11	11	11	11	11	11	11	11	11	11	11	11	11	11
12	Bearing cleaned	Place bearing in bag	12	12	12	12	12	12	12	12	12	12	12	12	12	12	12	12	12	12	12
13	Bearing in bag	Place bag in box	13	13	13	13	13	13	13	13	13	13	13	13	13	13	13	13	13	13	13
14			14	14	14	14	14	14	14	14	14	14	14	14	14	14	14	14	14	14	14
15			15	15	15	15	15	15	15	15	15	15	15	15	15	15	15	15	15	15	15
16			16	16	16	16	16	16	16	16	16	16	16	16	16	16	16	16	16	16	16
17			17	17	17	17	17	17	17	17	17	17	17	17	17	17	17	17	17	17	17
18			18	18	18	18	18	18	18	18	18	18	18	18	18	18	18	18	18	18	18
19			19	19	19	19	19	19	19	19	19	19	19	19	19	19	19	19	19	19	19
20			20	20	20	20	20	20	20	20	20	20	20	20	20	20	20	20	20	20	20
21			21	21	21	21	21	21	21	21	21	21	21	21	21	21	21	21	21	21	21
22			22	22	22	22	22	22	22	22	22	22	22	22	22	22	22	22	22	22	22
23			23	23	23	23	23	23	23	23	23	23	23	23	23	23	23	23	23	23	23
24			24	24	24	24	24	24	24	24	24	24	24	24	24	24	24	24	24	24	24
25			25	25	25	25	25	25	25	25	25	25	25	25	25	25	25	25	25	25	25

FIGURE 11-1 This task analysis data sheet (adapted from Bellamy et al., 1979) has two columns to list the S^D and response for each component in the chain. Researchers use this data sheet to record progress when using a chaining procedure to train a person in a complex task.

Once the task analysis of a complex skill has been developed, the next step is to choose a strategy for teaching the skill. Strategies for teaching complex tasks (behavioral chains) are called chaining procedures. **Chaining procedures** involve the systematic application of prompting and fading strategies to each stimulus–response component in the chain. Three different chaining procedures are described next: backward chaining, forward chaining, and total task presentation.

BACKWARD CHAINING

Backward chaining is an intensive training procedure typically used with learners with very limited abilities. With backward chaining, you use prompting and fading to teach the last behavior in the chain first. By starting with the last behavior in the chain, the learner completes the chain on every learning trial. Once the last behavior is mastered (once the learner exhibits the behavior on presentation of the S^D, without any prompts), you teach the next to last behavior. Once this behavior is mastered and the learner engages in the last two behaviors in the chain without any prompts, the next behavior up the chain is taught. This continues until the learner can exhibit the whole chain of behaviors when presented with the first S^D, without any prompts. As an example, consider the use of backward chaining to teach Jerry, a young man with severe mental retardation, how to throw a dart at a dart board. The task analysis (adapted from Schleien et al., 1981) includes the following components.

1. S^D1 (staff member says, "Jerry, let's play darts") → R1 (Jerry walks over to the dart board)
2. S^D2 (standing near a line on the floor 8 feet from the dart board) → R2 (Jerry walks up to the line and stands facing the dart board with his toes touching the line)
3. S^D3 (standing at the line with a dart on an adjacent table) → R3 (Jerry grasps dart between thumb and first finger, with the point facing the board)
4. S^D4 (standing at the line and holding dart between thumb and first finger) → R4 (Jerry bends his elbow, so that the forearm is at a 90-degree angle)
5. S^D5 (standing at the line with dart in hand and elbow bent) → R5 (Jerry thrusts forearm and hand toward the board and releases dart when arm is extended) → reinforcer (dart hits the board)

To start the backward chaining procedure, you present the last S^D (S^D5), prompt the correct response, and provide a reinforcer.

$$S^D5 + \text{prompt} \rightarrow R5 \rightarrow \text{reinforcer}$$

In this example, you take Jerry over to the dart board, prompt him to put his toes up to the line, put the dart in his hand, and bend his elbow until his forearm is at a 90-degree angle. This position is the S^D for the last step in the chain (S^D5). Now you physically prompt the correct response. You hold Jerry's hand in your hand, thrust his hand forward, and release the dart when his arm is extended. As the dart hits the dart board, you praise Jerry. (Praise is a reinforcer for Jerry.) You continue to physically prompt this response across learning trials and, as Jerry starts to make the response himself, you begin to fade the prompt. You give him less and less help, until he is throwing the dart himself as soon as you put the dart in his hand and bend his elbow. Gestural prompts or modeling prompts may be used instead of physical prompts, if these prompts have stimulus control over Jerry's behavior. You always use the least intrusive prompt necessary to get the behavior to occur. Once Jerry has mastered the fifth component in the chain (once he throws the dart independently as soon as you put it in his hand and bend his elbow), you back up the chain and teach the fourth component.

To teach the fourth step in the chain, you arrange S^D4, prompt the correct response (R4), and provide praise as a reinforcer. You arrange S^D4 by putting the dart in Jerry's hand as he is standing at the line. Once the dart is in his hand, you physically prompt him to bend his elbow (R4). Once his elbow is bent (S^D5), Jerry will throw the dart (R5) because he has already learned to throw the dart when he is holding the dart in his hand with his elbow bent. In other words, throwing the dart (R5) is already under stimulus control of S^D5.

S^D4 + prompt → R4 → praise
S^D5 → R5 → reinforcer

You fade your prompt by giving Jerry less assistance to bend his elbow until he bends his elbow independently (without any prompts) as soon as S^D4 is presented. Now he has mastered the fourth and fifth components of the chain and it is time to teach him the third component.

To teach the third component in the chain, you present S^D3, prompt the correct response (R3), and provide praise. You present S^D3 by having Jerry stand with his toes touching the line. Then you physically prompt him to pick up the dart between his thumb and first finger (R3). Once the dart is in his hand (S^D4), Jerry will bend his elbow (R4) and throw the dart (R5) because he has already learned these behaviors. (They are already under stimulus control of S^D4.)

S^D3 + prompt → R3 → praise
S^D4 → R4
S^D5 → R5 → reinforcer

You fade your physical prompt and, as Jerry gets less assistance, he starts to pick up the dart on his own. Once Jerry picks up the dart without any prompts as soon as he is brought to the line, he has mastered this step. (R3 is under stimulus control of S^D3.) Now it is time to teach him the second step in the chain.

To teach the second step, you present S^D2, prompt the correct response (R2), and provide praise. You present S^D2 by bringing Jerry to the side of the room where the dart board is located and then physically prompt him to step up to the line (R2). Once Jerry is standing at the line (S^D3), he will pick up a dart (R3), bend his elbow (R4), and throw the dart at the dart board (R5). He has already learned the last three behaviors, so he will execute them as soon as the relevant S^D is presented.

S^D2 + prompt → R2 → praise
S^D3 → R3
S^D4 → R4
S^D5 → R5 → reinforcer

As you fade your prompts, Jerry will walk up to the line without assistance when he is presented with S^D2. Now it is time to teach the first step in the chain.

To teach the first step, you present S^D1 (you say, "Jerry, let's play darts"), prompt response R1 (walking to the side of the room where the dart board is located), and provide praise. Once Jerry walks over to the side of the room where the dart board is located, he will then walk up to the line, pick up a dart, bend his elbow, and throw the dart, because these four behaviors are under the stimulus control of S^D2 (being near the dart board), and S^D2 is the outcome of R1, the behavior you are prompting.

S^D1 + prompt → R1 → praise
S^D2 → R2
S^D3 → R3
S^D4 → R4
S^D5 → R5 → reinforcer

Once you fade the prompts, Jerry will walk over to the dart board independently as soon as you say, "Jerry, let's play darts" (S^D1). Now the whole chain of behaviors is under the stimulus control of S^D1. As soon as you say "Jerry, let's play darts," he will be able to walk over to the dart board, step up to the line, pick up a dart, bend his elbow, and throw the dart.

In backward chaining with Jerry, each trial ended with the dart hitting the board. Because you praised him each time the dart hit the dart board, the dart hitting the board is now a conditioned reinforcer for throwing the dart. Also, because you praised him each time he engaged in the behavior at each training step, each S^D generated by the behavior is also a conditioned reinforcer. For example, because you praised Jerry when he walked up to the line, standing at the line was associated with praise and therefore was established as a conditioned reinforcer. Because you praised him for picking up the dart, holding the dart in his hand is now a conditioned reinforcer. As you can see, using reinforcers at each step in the backward chaining process is important because it makes the outcome of each step a conditioned reinforcer as well as an S^D for the next response.

After Jerry is playing darts independently, you can start to praise him intermittently to help maintain the behavior. Also, you can start to praise him when he gets more points on the dart board in order to reinforce accuracy. Eventually, playing darts more successfully and playing with friends should become naturally reinforcing, and staff should not have to provide praise any longer. This is the ultimate goal of training a leisure skill.

Forward Chaining

Forward chaining is similar to backward chaining in that you teach one component of the chain at a time and then chain the components together and you use prompting and fading to teach the behavior associated with the S^D at each step in the chain. The difference between forward chaining and backward chaining is the point at which you begin training. As you just learned, with backward chaining you teach the last component first, then you teach the next to last component, and so on; that is, you move from the end of the chain to the front. In forward chaining, you teach the first component, then the second component, and so on; that is, you move from the front of the chain to the end.

To use forward chaining, you present the first S^D, prompt the correct response, and provide a reinforcer after the response.

S^D1 + prompt → R1 → reinforcer

You then fade your prompts until the person is engaging in the first response without any prompts when the first S^D is presented.

To train the second component, you present the first S^D and the learner makes the first response. Because the first response creates the second S^D, you then prompt the second response and provide a reinforcer after it occurs.

$$S^D1 \rightarrow R1$$
$$S^D2 + \text{prompt} \rightarrow R2 \rightarrow \text{reinforcer}$$

You fade the prompts until the learner is making the second response without any prompts. Now, every time you present the first S^D, the learner makes the first two responses in the chain.

When you are ready to train the third response in the chain, you present the first S^D and the learner makes the first two responses. The second response creates the third S^D, so as soon as it occurs you prompt the third response and provide a reinforcer after the response.

$$S^D1 \rightarrow R1$$
$$S^D2 \rightarrow R2$$
$$S^D3 + \text{prompt} \rightarrow R3 \rightarrow \text{reinforcer}$$

Once again, you fade the prompts until the third response occurs when the third S^D is present, without any prompts. Now, every time you present the first S^D, the learner makes the first three responses because these three responses have been chained together through training.

This process of teaching new components continues until you have taught the last component in the chain and all the steps in the task analysis have been chained together in the proper order.

Describe how you would use forward chaining to teach the three-step task analysis of eating with a spoon presented earlier in this chapter.

You start by putting a bowl of food (applesauce) and a spoon on the table in front of the learner. This is the first S^D. Now prompt the first response. Take the learner's hand, pick up the spoon, put it in the applesauce, and provide a reinforcer (praise and, occasionally, a small bite of food). As you feel the learner start to engage in the behavior with you, fade the prompt until the learner can do the behavior without any assistance.

Now add step two. Start by presenting the first S^D. As soon as the learner engages in the first response and the spoon is in the bowl (the second S^D), physically prompt the second response—scooping food on the spoon—and provide a reinforcer after the response. Fade the prompt until the learner can scoop food on the spoon without any assistance.

Finally, add step three. Again, start by presenting the first S^D. As soon as the learner makes the first two responses and food is scooped onto the spoon (the third S^D), prompt the learner to raise the spoon and put the food into his or her mouth (third response). The taste of food will be a natural reinforcer for the third response. Fade your prompts. Now the learner will make all three responses and eat applesauce with a spoon without any assistance.

Because you provide a reinforcer after each response in the chain during training, the outcome of each response (the S^D for the next response) becomes a conditioned reinforcer. This is especially important with forward chaining because you do not get to the natural reinforcer at the end of the chain until you train the last component. As with backward chaining, once the learner exhibits all the behaviors in the chain, you eventually switch from a continuous reinforcement schedule to an intermittent

Similarities between Forward Chaining and Backward Chaining

- Both are used to teach a chain of behaviors.
- To use both procedures, you first have to conduct a task analysis that breaks the chain down into stimulus–response components.
- Both teach one behavior (one component of the chain) at a time and chain the behaviors together.
- Both procedures use prompting and fading to teach each component.

Differences between Forward Chaining and Backward Chaining

- Forward chaining teaches the first component first, whereas backward chaining teaches the last component first.
- With backward chaining, because you teach the last component first, the learner completes the chain in every learning trial and receives the natural reinforcer in every learning trial. In forward chaining, the learner does not complete the chain in every learning trial; artificial reinforcers are used until the last component of the chain is taught. The natural reinforcer occurs after the last behavior of the chain.

reinforcement schedule to maintain the behavior. The ultimate goal is to have the behavior maintained by natural reinforcers.

Total Task Presentation

Both forward and backward chaining procedures break a chain of behaviors down into individual stimulus–response components, teach one component at a time, and chain the components together. In **total task presentation,** by contrast, the complex chain of behaviors is taught as a single unit. As the name of the procedure implies, the total task is completed in each learning trial.

In total task presentation procedures, you use prompting to get the learner to engage in the entire chain of behaviors from start to finish. You use whatever type of prompting strategy is necessary to get the learner to engage in the entire task. In many cases, physical prompts are used to guide the learner through the chain of behaviors. Once the learner successfully completes the task with prompts, you fade the prompts over learning trials until the learner engages in the task without any assistance. Of course, you provide a reinforcer every time the learner completes the task, with or without prompts.

One type of physical prompting and fading often used with the total task presentation procedure is called **graduated guidance** (Demchak, 1990; Foxx & Azrin, 1972; Sulzer-Azaroff & Mayer, 1991). With graduated guidance, you use hand-over-hand guidance to lead the learner through the task. Over trials, you gradually provide less and less assistance and shadow the learner's hand as the learner completes the task. Shadowing means keeping your hand close to the learner's hand as the learner engages in the behavior. This allows you to initiate physical guidance immediately if the learner fails to execute one of the component behaviors in the chain. Shadowing prevents errors and should be done a number of times as the learner exhibits the behavioral chain without assistance. As an example, consider the use of total task presentation with graduated guidance to teach a child, Alex, to eat with a spoon. Earlier in this chapter, forward chaining was illustrated with this same behavior.

To use total task presentation with graduated guidance, you begin by presenting the first S^D. You put the bowl of applesauce and the spoon on the table in front of Alex. Next, you use graduated guidance and physically guide Alex through the entire chain of behaviors. You stand behind Alex, take his hand in yours, put his fingers around the handle of the spoon, lift his hand with the spoon, put the spoon in the applesauce, guide his hand to scoop applesauce onto the spoon, and help him lift his hand with the spoonful of food and put it into his mouth. You physically guide this chain of behaviors from start to finish. The reinforcer in each learning trial is the food that Alex eats from the spoon. It is the natural outcome of the behavior.

After a few trials in which you guide Alex's hand as he takes a bite of food, he will start to make some of the behavioral movements himself. As you feel him start to engage in the behavior, you release his hand and shadow his movements. If he engages in the correct movements, you continue to shadow his hand. If he fails to make the correct movement at some point, you start the physical guidance again. But if you feel him make the correct movement again, you shadow his hand once again.

For example, as you guide Alex's hand to pick up the spoon from the table, you feel him start to put the spoon into the applesauce. You quit guiding his hand and begin shadowing his hand. Once he has the spoon in the bowl, if he fails to scoop food onto the spoon, you initiate physical guidance again. Once the food is on the spoon, if he starts to lift it from the bowl, you stop physically guiding his hand and start shadowing again. As this process continues, you begin to shadow more and physically guide less. Eventually, you no longer have to physically guide the behavior at all. You fade the physical guidance to shadowing, and you fade the shadowing until you are providing no assistance as Alex takes a bite of food.

To provide graduated guidance correctly, you have to follow Alex's movements very carefully and respond with more or less guidance as necessary. If you provide physical guidance too long and do not fade it to shadowing, Alex may become dependent on the physical prompting and may not learn to engage in the behaviors himself. In other words, if you are going to do it for him, he will not learn to do it for himself. The goal of any prompting procedure is to fade the prompts once they are no longer

When to Use Total Task Presentation

- Because the total task presentation procedure requires you to guide the learner through the entire chain of behaviors, it is appropriate for teaching a task that is not too long or too complex. If the task is too long or difficult, forward or backward chaining procedures may be better because they focus on one component at a time and chain the components together after they are mastered individually.
- The learner's ability level must be considered. Backward or forward chaining may be more appropriate for learners with very limited abilities.
- Finally, the teacher's ability level must be considered. Although training is also needed to use forward chaining and backward chaining successfully, the total task presentation procedure may be the most difficult to implement. This is because it often involves the use of graduated guidance, a procedure in which the teacher must alternately guide or shadow the learner with precise timing through the entire chain of behaviors. Done incorrectly, graduated guidance may amount to forcing the learner through the behavior without actually teaching the learner to engage in the behavior independently.

Similarities between Forward and Backward Chaining and Total Task Presentation

- They are all used to teach complex tasks or chains of behavior.
- A task analysis must be completed before training with all three procedures.
- Prompting and fading are used in all three procedures.

Difference between Forward and Backward Chaining and Total Task Presentation

- In total task presentation, the learner is prompted through the entire task in each learning trial. In the two chaining procedures, the trainer teaches one component of the chain at a time and then chains the components together.

needed. On the other hand, you want to fade the physical guidance to shadowing only as you feel the learner make correct movements. And you want to initiate the physical guidance again immediately when the learner stops making the correct behavioral movements. It is important to praise the learner when you stop physically guiding and begin shadowing. In this way, you will be providing a reinforcer when the learner engages in the behavior without prompts and thus you differentially reinforce independent movements as opposed to prompted movements. This strengthens the correct behavior and allows you to fade the physical prompts more quickly.

In some cases, prompting strategies other than graduated guidance may be used in total task presentation. For example, Horner and Keilitz (1975) used the total task presentation method to teach toothbrushing to children and adolescents with mental retardation. They developed a 15-step task analysis of toothbrushing and used three types of prompts to teach the behaviors in the task analysis: physical guidance plus verbal instruction, demonstration plus verbal instruction, and verbal instruction alone. In every learning trial, the researchers prompted every step in the task analysis. They used the more intrusive prompts only as needed and faded the prompts until they were providing no help. Figure 11-2 shows the graph for the eight subjects in the Horner and Keilitz study.

Other Strategies for Teaching Behavioral Chains

Teaching complex tasks by forward chaining, backward chaining, or total task presentation entails substantial trainer time in performing the prompting and fading procedures with the learner. Other strategies to teach complex tasks take less trainer time and involvement. These strategies—written task analysis, picture prompts, and self-instructions—involve the independent use of prompts to guide appropriate completion of the chain of behaviors.

Written Task Analysis

For people who have the ability to read, **written task analysis** can be used to guide appropriate performance of a chain of behaviors. In this strategy, the trainer presents the learner with a list of the component behaviors in their proper sequence, and the

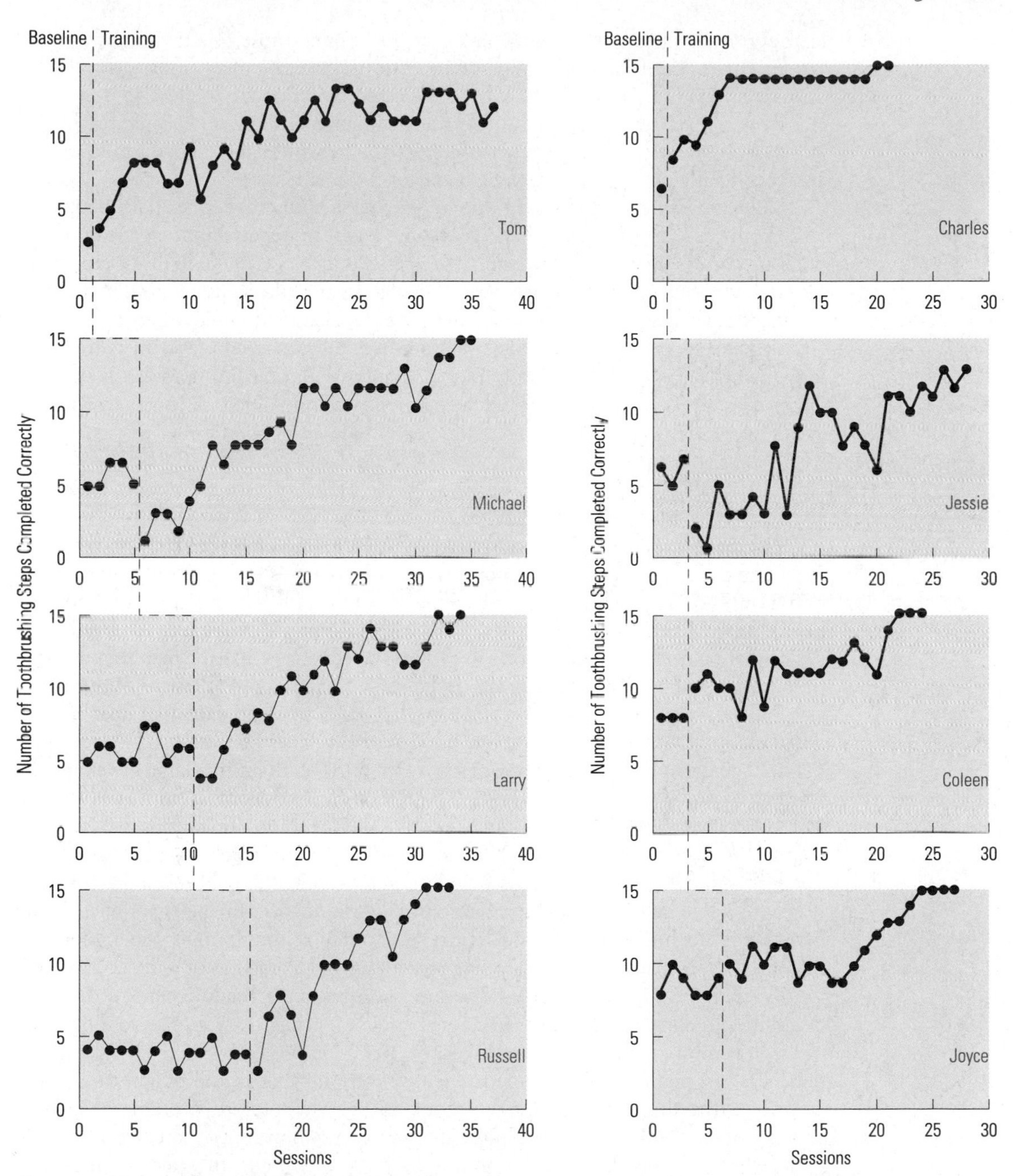

FIGURE 11-2 This graph (from Horner & Keilitz, 1978) shows the number of toothbrushing steps completed correctly by eight children and adolescents with mental retardation. Total task presentation was used to teach this task. This graph shows a multiple-baseline-across-subjects research design. The implementation of treatment was staggered over time for each subject; the number of toothbrushing steps completed correctly for each subject increased only after the treatment was implemented.

learner uses this list to perform the task correctly. For example, when you buy a stereo system, the assembly instructions guide you through the task of assembling it. The list of instructions is a written task analysis. A written task analysis is effective only if the learner can read the instructions, understand the instructions, and execute the behavior listed in the instructions. To be most effective, the written task analysis must clearly and specifically list every component behavior in the chain.

Cuvo and his colleagues used written task analyses (also called textual prompts) to teach young adults with mild mental disabilities and learning disabilities to clean household appliances such as a stove and refrigerator (Cuvo, Davis, O'Reilly, Mooney, & Crowley, 1992). They gave the learners a detailed list of all the steps involved in the tasks (a written task analysis). The learners used the detailed list to guide their behavior of cleaning the appliances. When they were finished, they received praise for correct performance or corrective feedback (further instructions) on how to improve if they made errors. The researchers found that all the learners performed the tasks correctly with the use of the written task analyses and reinforcement for correct performance.

Picture Prompts

Another strategy used to guide appropriate performance of a chain of behaviors is the use of picture prompts. With **picture prompts,** you take pictures of the outcome of each behavior or of someone engaging in each behavior in the task. The pictures are then used to prompt the learner to engage in the behaviors in the proper sequence. To be effective, the learner has to look at the pictures in the proper sequence and each picture must have stimulus control over the behavior that is depicted. Consider the following example.

Saul, a worker with mental retardation, has a job in a company that does promotional mailings. Saul's job is to put brochures into envelopes for mailing. The company mails 20 different brochures, and Saul has to put 3 to 6 of them in a large envelope, depending on the job for that day. The job trainer has pictures of all 20 brochures. At the beginning of each work day, the trainer gets the pictures of the brochures that Saul has to put in envelopes for that day. The trainer tacks the pictures onto a board at Saul's work station; Saul looks at the pictures to help him put the correct brochures in the envelope (Figure 11-3). The picture prompts have stimulus control over the behavior of choosing the correct brochures. After the job trainer sets up the picture prompts, the trainer does not have to spend any further time using prompting and fading to teach the task to Saul.

Wacker and his colleagues used picture prompts to teach adolescents with severe disabilities to complete complex vocational and daily living tasks such as folding laundry or assembling industrial parts (Wacker, Berg, Berrie, & Swatta, 1985). The researchers put pictures of each step in the tasks into notebooks and taught the adolescents to turn the pages of the notebook to see the picture prompts. All three adolescents in the study learned to use the picture prompts in the notebooks to guide their behavior. Once they learned to use the picture prompts, they did not need any further prompting to complete the tasks.

Self-Instructions

Learners can also be guided through a complex task by means of self-generated verbal prompts (also called **self-instructions**). In this procedure, you teach the learners how to give themselves verbal prompts or instructions to engage in the correct sequence of be-

FIGURE 11-3 Saul is completing a work task with the assistance of picture prompts on the bulletin board in front of him. Each picture acts as a prompt for completion of each component of the work task.

haviors in the chain. To use this procedure, the learners must be able to remember the self-instructions, say them at the appropriate time, and correctly follow the self-instructions. (The self-instructions must have stimulus control over the behavior.) The learner first learns to recite the self-instructions out loud as a prompt for the correct behavior. After the learner has mastered the self-instructions, he or she may then begin to recite the self-instructions covertly. You might think that a person capable of learning the self-instructions could also learn the behaviors in the chain, so that the self-instructions would not be necessary. Although this may be true for many people, some learners who have difficulty completing a complex task may benefit from self-instructions. In addition, because self-instructions can be recited quickly and remembered easily in many cases, they are useful for prompting behavior in a variety of situations.

Consider the following everyday examples of self-instructions. Each time you go to your locker and recite the combination on the lock as you open it, you are using self-instructions. When you recite the seven digits of a phone number as you dial the numbers, you are using self-instructions. When you talk yourself through the steps in a recipe ("I need to add 2 cups of flour, 1 cup of oats, 1 cup of raisins, and a teaspoon of baking powder"), you are using self-instructions to prompt each behavior in a behavioral chain.

A number of studies have demonstrated that learners can use self-instructions to guide themselves through complex vocational or educational tasks. For example, Salend, Ellis, and Reynolds (1989) taught adults with severe mental retardation to recite self-instructions to prompt the correct sequence of behaviors in a vocational task (packaging plastic combs). They said four simple self-instructions; "Comb up, comb down, comb in bag, comb in box." As they said each self-instruction, they completed the task associated with that instruction. The use of the self-instructions led to correct performance of the task. Whitman, Spence, and Maxwell (1987) taught adults with mental retardation to use self-instructions to prompt the behavior of correctly sorting letters into boxes. Albion and Salzburg (1982) taught students with mental disabilities to use self-instructions to complete math problems correctly. In each case, the self-instructions prompted the correct behaviors in the chain to occur in the correct sequence.

CHAINING PROCEDURES

- *Backward chaining:* Teach the last behavior in the chain first, and then teach each previous behavior in the chain.
- *Forward chaining:* Teach the first behavior in the chain first, and then teach each subsequent behavior in the chain.
- *Total task presentation:* Prompt the whole stimulus–response chain in each learning trial.
- *Written task analysis:* Use written descriptions of each step in the task analysis as prompts.
- *Picture prompts:* Use pictures of each step in the task analysis as prompts.
- *Self-instructions:* Give yourself verbal prompts to engage in each component behavior in a behavioral chain.

Although written task analyses, picture prompts, and self-instructions are prompting strategies that are often used to teach a chain of behaviors, they may also be used with single responses as well. The procedures are described in this chapter to illustrate their use with chains of behaviors.

How to Use Chaining Procedures

If your goal is to teach a person a complex task, you may use one of the procedures described in this chapter. All of the procedures described here are considered chaining procedures because they are used to teach a chain of behaviors. Thus, in the present context, chaining procedure is an inclusive term that refers to backward and forward chaining, total task presentation, written task analysis, picture prompts, and self-instructions. The following steps are important for the effective use of chaining procedures (see also Cooper et al., 1987; Martin & Pear, 1992; Sulzer-Azaroff & Mayer, 1991).

1. Determine whether a chaining procedure is appropriate. Does the problem call for behavioral acquisition, or is it related to noncompliance? If the person is not completing a complex task because he or she is not capable, a chaining procedure is appropriate. On the other hand, if the person is capable of completing the task but is refusing to engage in it, procedures for treating noncompliance are warranted.
2. Develop a task analysis. The task analysis breaks down the chain of behaviors into individual stimulus–response components.
3. Get a baseline assessment of the learner's ability. Cooper et al. (1987) describe two methods for assessing the mastery level of the learner. In the single-opportunity method, you present the learner with the opportunity to complete the task and record which components the learner completes without assistance in the correct sequence. In other words, you present the first S^D and assess the learner's responses. The first error by the learner in single-opportunity assessment will typically result in errors on all subsequent steps in the task analysis. In the multiple-opportunity method, you assess the learner's ability to complete each individual component in the chain. You present the first S^D and wait for the learner to respond. If the learner does not respond correctly, you present the second S^D and assess the learner's response. If there is no correct response, you present the third S^D, and so on until the learner has had the opportunity to respond to every S^D in the chain.
4. Choose the chaining method you will use. For learners with the most limited abilities, forward or backward chaining methods are most appropriate. If the task is

less complex or if the learner is more capable, total task presentation may be more appropriate. Other procedures such as written task analysis, picture prompts, or self-instructions may be appropriate, depending on the capabilities of the learner or the complexity of the task.

5. Implement the chaining procedure. Whichever procedure you use, the ultimate goal is to get the learner to engage in the correct sequence of behaviors without any assistance. Therefore, the appropriate use of prompting and fading is important in all the chaining procedures. Continue to collect data on the learner's performance as you implement the chaining procedure.

6. Continue reinforcement after the task has been learned. If you continue to provide reinforcement, at least intermittently, after the learner is able to complete the task without assistance, the learner will maintain the behavior over time.

CHAPTER SUMMARY

1. A behavioral chain, also called a stimulus–response chain, is a behavior composed of two or more stimulus–response components.
2. A task analysis identifies the stimulus and response in each component of the chain. It is important to conduct a task analysis so that all components of the chain (S^Ds and responses) are identified clearly.
3. Chaining procedures are used to teach a person to engage in a behavioral chain. These procedures involve prompting and fading to teach each component of the chain. In backward chaining, the last stimulus–response component is taught first. The next to last component is taught next, and so on until the whole chain is learned. In forward chaining, the first stimulus–response component is taught first. The second component is taught second, and so on until the whole chain is learned.
4. In total task presentation, the entire chain of behaviors is prompted in every learning trial. Often, graduated guidance is used with total task presentation.
5. In the written task analysis procedure, the learner uses textual prompts for each component in the chain. In the picture prompt procedure, the learner uses pictures to prompt each component in the behavioral chain. With self-instructions, the learner recites self-instructions (verbal prompts) to prompt each component in the chain.

PRACTICE TEST

1. What is a stimulus–response chain? Provide two examples of stimulus–response chains that are not in the chapter. (p. 216)
2. Identify each stimulus and response component in your two examples.
3. What is a task analysis? Why is it important to conduct a task analysis? (p. 217)
4. Provide a task analysis of the behavior of pouring water from a pitcher into a glass. Assume the pitcher of water and the glass are already on the table.
5. Describe backward chaining. (pp. 220–222)
6. Describe the use of backward chaining to teach the task identified in Question 4.
7. Describe forward chaining. (pp. 222–223)
8. Describe how you would use forward chaining to teach the task identified in Question 4.
9. How are backward chaining and forward chaining similar and how are they different? (p. 224)
10. Describe the total task presentation procedure. (pp. 224–225)

11. Describe graduated guidance. (p. 224)
12. Describe how you would use the total task presentation procedure to teach the task described in Question 4.
13. How does the total task presentation procedure differ from backward and forward chaining? How are they similar? (p. 226)
14. Describe how you would use a written task analysis to get a person to engage in a complex task. What is another name for a written task analysis? (pp. 226–228)
15. Describe the use of picture prompts. (p. 228)
16. Describe the use of self-instructions. What is another name for self-instructions? (pp. 228–229)
17. When is it appropriate to use a chaining procedure and when is it not appropriate? (p. 230)
18. Briefly describe the guidelines for using a chaining procedure to teach a complex task. (pp. 230–231)

APPLICATIONS

1. You have been hired by an agency that provides rehabilitation services for people who have sustained brain damage from head injuries. These people often have to learn basic skills all over again. One skill that you have to teach is bed-making. Your first step is to develop a task analysis of bed-making. Provide the task analysis for bed-making. Be sure to include all the stimulus–response components.

2. Once you have developed the task analysis for the complex task of bed-making, you must choose a chaining procedure and implement the procedure. You decide to use forward chaining. Describe the use of forward chaining to teach the bed-making task.

3. One of the people with brain damage has a serious memory impairment. A day after he learns the task, he cannot remember the bed-making behaviors. You decide that you will use either picture prompts or textual prompts (written task analysis) to help him make his bed each day. Describe how you would use picture prompts and how you would use textual prompts with this person.

MISAPPLICATIONS

1. Your niece has just been enrolled in a preschool program by her parents. Before she starts, you want to teach her to recite the alphabet. Because reciting the alphabet is a chain of behaviors, you decide that you will use graduated guidance to teach her. What is wrong with the use of graduated guidance in this situation? What would be a better procedure for teaching her to recite the alphabet?

2. Toby, a young man with severe retardation, recently started a job in which he assembles parts for bicycle brakes. The task has seven steps. Staff members used picture prompts to help Toby learn the task and they used tokens to reinforce the behavior. At the end of every month, Toby gets a paycheck based on the number of parts he assembles. Once Toby learned the job, staff removed the picture prompts and quit using the tokens. Now they just let Toby do his work and expect that his monthly paycheck will maintain the behavior. What is the problem with this strategy? What would be a better strategy?

3. Waylon, a college student, is home for the summer and just started a job at a retail store in the mall. He works the evening shift and has to close the store and lock up for the evening. There is a list of 20 steps involved in closing and locking up. The manager decides he will use forward chaining to teach the task to Waylon. What is the problem with this strategy? What would be a better strategy?

CHAPTER 11 *Quiz 1*

Name:

1. A complex behavior consisting of many component behaviors that occur together in sequence is called a(n) ______________________.
2. Another name for a behavioral chain is a(n) ______________________.
3. In a behavioral chain, each response creates the ______________________ for the next response in the chain.
4. The process of breaking a behavioral chain down into its individual stimulus-response components is called a(n) ______________________.
5. In backward chaining, you teach the ______________________ stimulus–response component in the chain first.
6. In forward chaining, you teach the ______________________ stimulus–response component in the chain first.
7. What two procedures are used to teach each stimulus–response component in forward and backward chaining procedures? ______________________ and ______________________
8. In the ______________________ procedure, you prompt the learner to engage in the entire chain of behavior from start to finish in each trial.
9. The ______________________ procedure involves hand-over-hand guidance and shadowing to get the learner to engage in the correct behavior.
10. In the ______________________ procedure, pictures of each step in the task analysis are used to guide the learner's behavior.

CHAPTER 11 *Quiz 2*

Name:

1. A behavioral chain is a complex behavior consisting of a number of ________________ and ________________ components occurring in sequence.

2. Another name for a stimulus–response chain is a ________________________.

3. In a behavioral chain, each ________________ creates the S^D for the next response.

4. During forward or backward chaining, praise is given following each response in a behavioral chain. As a result, the outcome of each response becomes a(n) ________________________.

5. Three ways to conduct a task analysis are:

   ____

   ____

   ____

6. In the ____________________ chaining procedure, you complete the last step in the chain on each learning trial.

7. In graduated guidance, you use physical guidance; once the learner starts to engage in the correct behavior, you begin ________________ the learner's hand.

8. The ________________________________ procedure involves giving the learner a list of the steps involved in the chain of behaviors to help the learner engage in the chain of behaviors.

9. Charlie's job is to stuff envelopes with four different colored brochures in the correct order for an advertising company. You teach Charlie to recite the steps involved in his job ("Red, yellow, blue, and green"), and Charlie is able to do the job correctly. What procedure have you used in this example to get Charlie to correctly engage in a chain of behaviors? ______________________________

10. Charlie's job is to stuff envelopes with four different colored brochures in the correct order for an advertising company. You put four pictures up on the wall in front of Charlie showing Charlie stuffing each brochure in the correct order. As a result, Charlie is able to do the job correctly. What procedure have you used in this example to get Charlie to correctly engage in a chain of behaviors? ______________________________

CHAPTER 11 *Quiz 3* Name:

1. A task analysis breaks the behavioral chain down into its individual ____________________

   and ____________________ components.

2. In the ____________________ chaining procedure, you teach the last stimulus–response component of the chain first.

3. In the ____________________ chaining procedure, you teach the first stimulus–response component of the chain first.

4. Graduated guidance is typically used to prompt the correct response when using

   ____________________ to teach a chain of behaviors.

5. In the ____________________ procedure, the learner completes the entire chain of behaviors in each learning trial.

Pete's job is to put handles on gizmos in a factory. He sits in front of a conveyor belt with a box of handles on a table beside him. Each time a gizmo comes to him on the conveyor belt, Pete picks up a handle from the box on the table, puts the handle on the metal rod on the gizmo, and twists the handle once to tighten it. Based on this description, complete the following task analysis.

6. The first S^D = Gizmo on conveyor belt in front of Pete with box of handles on the table,

   and the first response = ____________________.

7. The second S^D = ____________________, and the second response =

   ____________________.

8. The third S^D = ____________________, and the third response =

   ____________________.

9. Based on the task analysis in question 6, which S^D would you present first to start backward

   chaining? ____________________

10. Based on the task analysis in question 6, which S^D would you present first to start forward

    chaining? ____________________

Behavioral Skills Training Procedures

You have learned about prompting and fading procedures that may be used to teach a person to engage in the correct behavior at the right time (to establish stimulus control over the behavior). You have also learned about chaining procedures, in which prompting and fading are used to teach a person a complex task. In this chapter, you will learn other procedures for teaching skills. Four **behavioral skills training (BST) procedures**—modeling, instructions, rehearsal, and feedback—generally are used together in training sessions to help a person acquire useful skills (such as social skills or job-related skills). BST procedures are typically used to teach skills that can be simulated in a role-play context.

- What are the four components of a behavioral skills training procedure?
- When is the appropriate time to use behavioral skills training procedures?
- How do you use behavioral skills training procedures in groups?
- How is the concept of the three-term contingency related to behavioral skills training procedures?

Examples of BST Procedures

Teaching Marcia to Say "No" to the Professors

Marcia is a secretary at a university. She believes that faculty members in her department make unreasonable demands on her, but she has not been able to refuse these unreasonable requests (such as working through her lunch hour and running personal errands). She is seeing a psychologist, Dr. Mills, who is using BST procedures to help her develop assertiveness skills. In the psychologist's office, they role-play the difficult situations that Marcia faces at work. Dr. Mills uses the role-plays to assess Marcia's assertiveness skills and to teach her how to act more assertively. First, Dr. Mills creates a situation at work in which Marcia role-plays herself and he role-plays a co-worker. In that role, he makes an unreasonable request, such as "Marcia, I have a meeting this afternoon. I need you to go pick up my dry cleaning in your lunch hour." He then assesses what she says and how she says it (her verbal and nonverbal behavior) in response to this request. Next Dr. Mills provides instructions and modeling; that is, he describes how to respond more assertively in this situation and demonstrates the assertive behavior for Marcia in another role-play. This time Marcia role-plays the co-worker making the unreasonable request, and Dr. Mills plays Marcia responding assertively. In the role-play, Dr. Mills says, "I'm sorry, but I can't do your personal errands for you." After observing Dr. Mills model this assertive behavior, Marcia gets an opportunity to practice it (rehearsal): They switch roles again, and Marcia makes the same assertive response in the role-play. Dr. Mills then gives her feedback on her performance. He praises her for the aspects of the behavior that she performed well and he gives her suggestions on how to improve. After getting the feedback, Marcia practices the behavior again in another role-play. Again Dr. Mills praises her for her performance and makes any necessary suggestions for improvement. Once Marcia has learned this assertive behavior well, they will role-play other situations that arise at work. Marcia will learn a variety of assertiveness skills through this process of instructions, modeling, rehearsal, and feedback.

Teaching Children to Protect Themselves from Abduction

Consider another example. Cheryl Poche used modeling, instructions, rehearsal, and feedback to teach abduction prevention skills to preschool children (Poche, Brouwer, & Swearingen, 1981). She taught the children how to respond to adults who tried to lure the children into leaving with them. Poche set up realistic role-plays in which an adult walked up to the child on the playground and asked the child to leave with him. The adult would say something like, "Hi, I have a toy in my car I think you'd like. Come with me, and I'll get it for you." The skills that the children learned were to say, "No, I have to ask my teacher," and to run back into the school. First, Poche used the role-plays to assess the children's skills before training. Next, she implemented the BST procedure. The child watched as two adult trainers acted out a scene in which one trainer, playing the suspect, walked up and asked the other trainer, playing the child, to leave with him. The trainer playing the child then modeled the correct response to this lure. After watching the model, the child practiced the abduction prevention skill in another role-play. A trainer approached the child and presented the abduction lure. In response the child said, "No, I have to ask my teacher," and ran back to the school (Figure 12-1). The trainer praised the child for correct performance and, if the re-

FIGURE 12-1 After receiving the abduction solicitation from the adult, the child says, "No, I have to ask my teacher," and runs back to the school. The trainer praises the child for exhibiting the skill correctly.

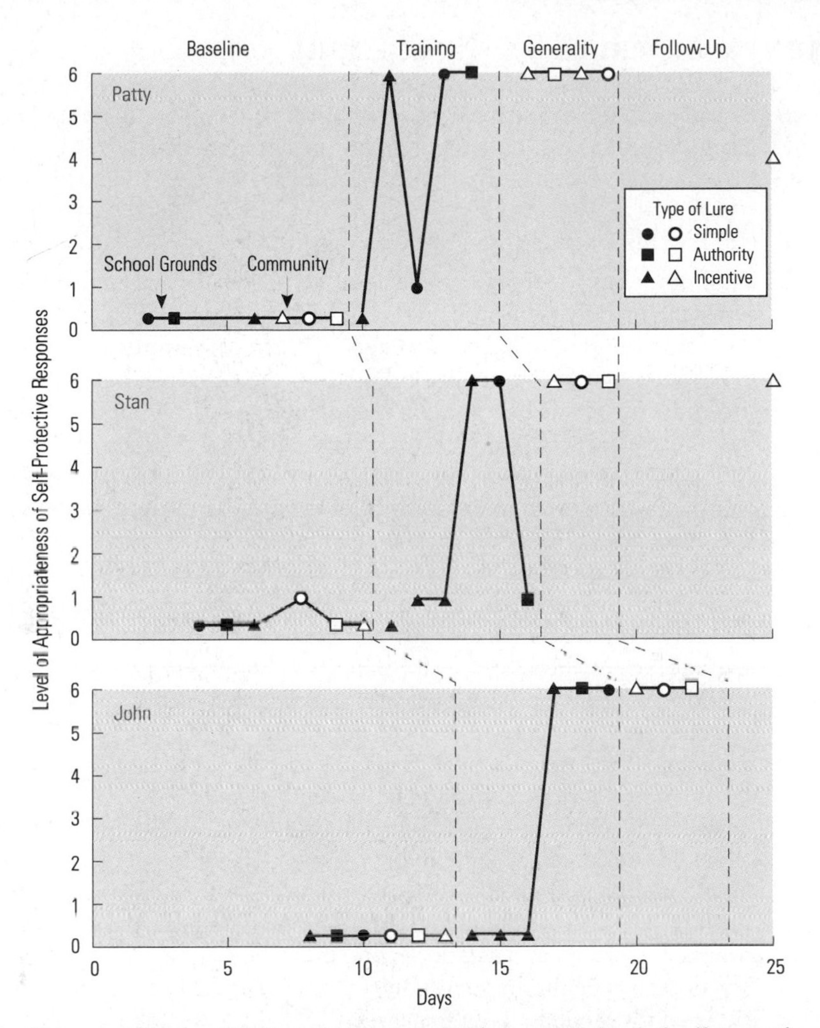

FIGURE 12-2 This graph on page 211 (from Poche et al., 1981) shows the level of self-protection skills before and after a behavioral skills training procedure was implemented with three preschool children. The self-protection skills were rated on a scale from 0 to 6. A score of 6 means that the child said, "No, I have to ask my teacher," and ran back to school when an abduction lure was presented. A score of 0 means that the child agreed to leave with the adult who presented the abduction lure. Sometimes the child was assessed on the playground and sometimes in the community. Three types of lures were used: With a simple lure, the adult simply asked the child to leave with him; with an authority lure, the adult said that the child's teacher said it was okay for the child to leave with him; with the incentive lure, the adult offered the child something like a toy if the child would leave with him. This graph shows a multiple-baseline-across subjects design in which three children received training at different times.

sponse was only partly correct, the trainer provided instructions and further modeling. The child rehearsed the behavior again in role-plays until the behavior was correct. Then the child received training with different types of abduction lures until the child could make the correct response in a variety of situations. The results of this study are illustrated in Figure 12-2.

Components of the BST Procedure

As you can see from these examples, four procedures are commonly used together to teach skills. Let's examine these procedures in more detail.

Modeling

With **modeling,** the correct behavior is demonstrated for the learner. The learner observes the model's behavior and then imitates the model. For modeling to be effective, the learner must have an imitative repertoire; in other words, the learner has to be able to pay attention to the model and perform the behavior that the model just demonstrated. Most people have imitative repertoires because imitating the behavior of others has already been reinforced in a variety of situations (Baer, Peterson, & Sherman, 1967). Reinforcement for imitation typically starts very early in a child's life. Over the course of early development, a child's behavior of imitating models (provided by parents, teachers, siblings, and peers) is reinforced many times in the presence of a wide variety of behaviors modeled by a variety of people. As a result, a model's behavior becomes an S^D for imitation, and imitation becomes a generalized response class, which means that imitation is likely to occur in the future, when a behavior is modeled for the learner (Baer & Sherman, 1964; Bijou, 1976; Steinman, 1970).

Modeling may be live or it may be symbolic. In live modeling, another person demonstrates the appropriate behavior in the appropriate situation. With symbolic modeling, the correct behavior is demonstrated on videotape, audiotape, or possibly in a cartoon or a movie. For example, in another study by Poche, grade school children viewed a videotape in which abduction prevention skills were demonstrated by child actors (Poche, Yoder, & Miltenberger, 1988). The videotape showed an adult approach a child and present an abduction lure. The child then engaged in the correct behavior in response to the abduction lure. The model's behavior in the videotape was the same as the behavior of the live model in Poche's earlier study. In this study, however, a whole class of children viewed the videotaped model at one time. The videotape also included instructions about the correct behavior. After the children viewed the videotape, they rehearsed the correct behavior and received praise or further instruction if they needed it. Another group of children viewed the videotape but did not rehearse the behavior. The researchers found that the children who received the modeling, instructions, rehearsal, and feedback learned the abduction prevention skills better than the children who got instructions and modeling from the videotape without the chance for rehearsal and feedback.

A number of factors influence the effectiveness of modeling (Bandura, 1977).

- When the model exhibits the correct behavior, it should result in a successful outcome (a reinforcer) for the model.
- The model should resemble the people observing the model or should have high status. For example, the models in Poche's videotape were children of the same age as those watching the tape. Often, teachers model correct behavior for children. Because teachers have high status, the children are likely to learn from the model. In television commercials, typically, sports stars and other celebrities (people of very high status) are shown using the product. The hope is that people will imitate the model and buy the product.

■ The complexity of the model's behavior should be appropriate to the developmental level or ability level of the learner. If the model's behavior is too complex, the learner may not be able to learn from it. However, if the model's behavior is too simple, the learner may not pay attention.

■ The learner has to pay attention to the model to learn the behavior being modeled. Often, the teacher will draw the learner's attention to important aspects of the model's behavior. When modeling assertiveness skills, Dr. Mills focused Marcia's attention by saying, "Now watch how I make eye contact and use a firm tone of voice." In Poche's videotape the narrator told the children what behaviors to look for each time a model was about to be presented.

■ The modeled behavior must occur in the proper context (in response to the relevant S^D). The behavior should be modeled in the real situation or in the context of a role-play of the real situation. For example, the children saw the abduction skills modeled in response to abduction lures from an adult, that is, in the situation in which they would be needed. Marcia watched Dr. Mills model assertive behavior in the context of role-plays of difficult interactions Marcia faced at work.

■ The modeled behavior should be repeated as often as necessary for the learner to imitate it correctly.

■ To enhance generalization, the behavior should be modeled in a variety of ways and in a variety of situations.

■ The learner should have an opportunity to rehearse (imitate) the behavior as soon as possible after observing the model. Correct imitation of the modeled behavior should be reinforced immediately.

Instructions

Instructions describe the appropriate behavior for the learner. To be most effective, instructions should be specific. They should describe exactly the behaviors that are expected from the learner. For a chain of behaviors, the instructions should specify each component in the chain in proper sequence. Instructions should also specify the appropriate circumstances in which the learner is expected to engage in the behavior. For example, when teaching abduction prevention skills to young children, the teacher might give this instruction: "Whenever any adult asks you to leave with him or when an adult asks you to go somewhere with him, you should say, 'No, I have to ask my teacher,' and run back into the school. You should run in and tell me right away and I'll be very proud of you." This instruction specifies the antecedent situation and the correct behavior. It also specifies the consequence (teacher approval). The following factors may influence the effectiveness of instructions.

■ The instructions should be presented at a level that the learner can understand. If they are too complex, the learner may not grasp the behavior. If they are too simple, the learner may be indignant or offended.

■ The instructions should be delivered by someone who has credibility with the learner (such as a parent, teacher, employer, or psychologist).

■ The learner should have the opportunity to rehearse the behavior as soon as possible after receiving the instructions.

■ Instructions should be paired with modeling whenever observing the behavior will enhance the potential for learning the behavior.

- The instructions should be given only when the learner is paying attention.
- The learner should repeat the instructions so that the teacher can be certain the learner heard the instructions correctly. Repeating the instructions during training also increases the likelihood that the learner will be able to repeat the instructions later to self-prompt the appropriate behavior.

Rehearsal

Rehearsal is the opportunity for the learner to practice the behavior after receiving instructions or watching a model demonstrate the behavior. Rehearsal is an important part of the BST procedure because (a) the teacher cannot be sure that the learner has learned the behavior until the teacher sees the learner engage in the correct behavior, (b) it provides an opportunity to reinforce the behavior, and (c) it provides an opportunity to assess and correct errors that may be present in the performance of the behavior. The following factors may influence the effectiveness of rehearsal as part of the BST procedure.

- The behavior should be rehearsed in the proper context, either in the situation to which it is appropriate or in a role-play that simulates that situation. Rehearsing the behavior in the proper context facilitates generalization when skills training is complete.
- Rehearsals should be programmed for success. Learners should practice easy behaviors first so that they are successful. After success with easy behaviors, the learners can practice more difficult or complex behaviors. In this way, engaging in the rehearsal is reinforcing, and the learners continue to participate.
- Rehearsal of the correct behavior should always be followed immediately by reinforcement.
- Rehearsals that are partly correct or are incorrect should be followed by corrective feedback.
- The behavior should be rehearsed until it is demonstrated correctly at least a few times.

Feedback

Following the learner's rehearsal of the behavior, the trainer should provide immediate feedback. Feedback involves praise or other reinforcers for correct performance. When necessary, it may also involve correction of errors or further instruction in how to improve performance. Feedback often amounts to differential reinforcement of some aspects of the behavior with correction of other aspects. In BST procedures, feedback is specifically defined as the delivery of praise for correct performance and further instruction after incorrect performance. A number of factors may influence the effectiveness of feedback.

- Feedback should be given immediately after the behavior.
- Feedback should always involve praise (or other reinforcers) for some aspect of the behavior. If the behavior was not correct, the trainer should praise the learner at least for trying. The point is to make the rehearsal a reinforcing experience for the learner.
- Praise should be descriptive. Describe what the learner said and did that was good (correct). Focus on all aspects of the behavior, verbal and nonverbal (that is, what the learner said and did and how the learner said and did it).

- When providing corrective feedback, do not be negative. Do not describe the learner's performance as bad or wrong. Rather, provide instructions that identify what the learner could do better or how the learner could improve the performance.
- Always praise some aspect of the performance before providing corrective feedback.
- Provide corrective feedback on one aspect of the performance at a time. If the learner did a number of things incorrectly, focus first on one of them so that the learner does not feel overwhelmed or discouraged. Build the correct performance in steps so that the learner is more and more successful in each subsequent rehearsal.

Enhancing Generalization after BST

The goal of BST procedures is for the learner to acquire new skills and to use these skills in the appropriate circumstances outside the training sessions. Several strategies can be used to promote generalization of the skills to the appropriate circumstances after BST.

First, training should involve a variety of role-plays that simulate the actual situations the learner is likely to encounter in real life. The closer the training scenarios are to the real-life situations, the more likely the skills are to generalize to the real situations (Miltenberger, Roberts, et al., 1999).

Second, incorporate real-life situations into training. The learner may rehearse the skills in role-plays with real peers or in real situations (e.g., at school, on the playground). For example, Olsen-Woods, Miltenberger, and Forman (1998) taught abduction prevention skills to children and conducted some role-plays out on the playground of their school as a real-life situation in which an abduction attempt may take place.

Third, provide assignments for the learner to practice the skill being learned outside the BST session, in a real-life situation. After practicing the skill outside the training session, the learner can discuss the experience in the next BST session and receive feedback on his or her performance. In some cases, practice of the skills outside of a session can be supervised by a parent or teacher who can provide immediate feedback.

Fourth, the trainer can arrange for reinforcement of the skills in situations outside the training sessions. For example, the trainer might talk to a teacher or parent and have him or her provide reinforcement when the learner exhibits the correct skill at home or school.

BST and the Three-Term Contingency

By combining modeling, instructions, rehearsal, and feedback, the BST procedure uses all three aspects of the three-term contingency. A three-term contingency—involving antecedents, the behavior, and consequences of the behavior—should be used in any teaching situation. The modeling and instructions are antecedent strategies used to evoke the correct behavior. Because most people have successfully followed instructions or imitated models in the past, instructions and modeling are effective discriminative stimuli for the correct behavior. Rehearsal involves executing the behavior that was modeled or described in the instructions. When the behavior is rehearsed correctly, feedback involves a reinforcing consequence that strengthens the correct behavior. When the behavior is partly incorrect, corrective feedback is provided in the form of instructions to improve performance. Corrective feedback functions as an antecedent that evokes the correct behavior in the next rehearsal so that it can be reinforced.

Antecedent	Behavior	Consequence
Role-play context, modeling, and instructions	Rehearsal of the skill	Feedback (praise for correct performance)

Outcome: Client is more likely to engage in the correct skill in the role-play context.

The best way to teach a skill is to provide instructions or modeling and to require that the person rehearse the skill so that it can be reinforced. Although instructions or modeling alone can evoke the correct behavior in the right situation, the behavior is not likely to continue to occur unless it is subsequently reinforced. For example, suppose your friend told you to drive in the left lane past the mall because cars that are about to turn into the mall slow the traffic in the right lane. This is an instruction. You follow the instruction, and your behavior is reinforced by avoiding slower traffic. As a result, you are more likely to drive in the left lane past the mall. However, if you followed your friend's instruction and drove in the left lane but the traffic was not faster in that lane, your behavior would not be reinforced. Therefore, even though the instruction evoked (prompted) the correct behavior initially, the behavior would not continue to occur because it was not reinforced after it occurred. When teaching a skill, we could evoke the correct behavior simply by modeling it or by providing instructions for the learner. However, to be sure that the behavior has been learned, we also have the learner rehearse it in the simulated training situation so that we can reinforce the behavior. It is much more likely that the learner will execute the behavior in the real situation if the learner has already executed the behavior successfully in training.

BST in Groups

Sometimes BST procedures are used with groups of people who all need to learn similar skills. For example, parent training might be implemented with a group of parents who are all having difficulty with their children; assertiveness training might be conducted with a group of people who have assertive skills deficits. Group BST is most effective with small groups in which all members have a chance to participate (Himle & Miltenberger, in press). In group BST, the modeling and instructions are presented for the entire group. Each group member then rehearses the skill in a role-play and receives feedback from the trainer and from other members of the group. In group training, as with individual BST, each person rehearses the skill until it is performed correctly in a variety of simulated situations.

Group BST has a number of advantages. First, it can be more efficient than individual BST because instructions and modeling are presented to the whole group. Second, each group member learns by watching other group members rehearse the skills and receive feedback on their performance. Third, group members learn by evaluating the performance of other group members and providing feedback. Fourth, with a variety of group members participating in role-plays, generalization may be enhanced. Finally, the magnitude of reinforcement for successful rehearsal is increased when praise comes from other group members as well as the trainer.

A disadvantage of group BST is that each person does not have the trainer's undivided attention. One other possible problem is that some members may not participate actively or may dominate and limit the participation of other members. The trainer can prevent this problem by taking an active role and promoting participation by all members.

Applications of BST Procedures

Numerous studies have demonstrated that BST procedures are effective in teaching a variety of skills (Rosenthal & Steffek, 1991).

These procedures have been used extensively with children. We have already discussed the studies by Poche and her colleagues. Other researchers have also used BST procedures to teach abduction prevention and sexual abuse prevention skills to children (Carroll-Rowan & Miltenberger, 1994; Miltenberger & Thiesse-Duffy, 1988; Miltenberger, Thiesse-Duffy, Suda, Kozak, & Bruellman, 1990; Olsen-Woods et al., 1998; Wurtele, Marrs, & Miller-Perrin, 1987; Wurtele, Saslawsky, Miller, Marrs, & Britcher, 1986). In each of these studies, the children learned the correct responses to dangerous situations through modeling and instructions, rehearsed the self-protection skills in role-plays of dangerous situations, and received feedback on their performance. These researchers found that the use of instructions and modeling without rehearsal and feedback was less effective for teaching children self-protection skills. The children learned much more when they had an opportunity to rehearse the skills and receive feedback on their performance after the instructions and modeling. Abduction prevention and sexual abuse prevention skills have also been taught to adults with mental retardation using the same BST approach (Haseltine & Miltenberger, 1990; Lumley, Miltenberger, Long, Rapp, & Roberts, 1998; Miltenberger, Roberts et al., 1999).

In other research, BST procedures have been used to teach fire emergency skills to children. Jones and Kazdin (1980) taught young children to make emergency phone calls to the fire department. Jones, Kazdin, and Haney (1981) taught children the skills they needed to respond to home fires. They identified nine different home fire emergencies and the correct fire safety responses for each situation. In training, they simulated a fire in a bedroom and used instructions, modeling, rehearsal, and feedback to teach the child the correct responses. The trainer told the child the correct behaviors and showed the child what to do. When the child executed the behavior correctly, the trainer provided praise and other reinforcers. If a child performed any part of the behavior incorrectly, the trainer gave feedback about what the child could do better and the child tried again until he or she did it right (Figure 12-3). Whenever any part of the performance was incorrect, the researchers always praised the child for any portion of the fire safety behavior that the child got right before providing the correction. Their results are summarized in Figure 12-4.

BST procedures have also been used extensively with people who have social skills deficits. For example, Elder, Edelstein, and Narick (1979) taught aggressive adolescents to improve their social skills in an effort to reduce their aggressive behavior. Matson and Stephens (1978) taught patients with chronic psychiatric disorders to

FIGURE 12-3 The child is rehearsing a fire safety skill after viewing a model and receiving instructions from the trainer. After the rehearsal, the trainer will provide feedback.

increase appropriate social behaviors, which resulted in a decrease in arguing and fighting. Starke (1987) used BST procedures to improve the social skills of physically disabled young adults. Warzak and Page (1990) taught sexually active adolescent girls how to refuse unwanted sexual advances from adolescent boys. In each study, the subjects learned the social skills through instructions and modeling, rehearsal of the skills in role-played situations, and feedback (reinforcement and correction) on their performance. Starke found that the BST procedure was more effective than a discussion group for increasing social skills. This finding suggested that rehearsal and feedback were important components of the skills training procedure. In other words, it is not enough to be told what skills are important and to see the skills demonstrated. The best way to learn skills is to also have the opportunity for rehearsal and feedback so that the skills can be reinforced in simulated or real situations.

Finally, researchers have demonstrated that BST procedures are effective in teaching skills to adults. Forehand and his colleagues used these procedures to teach child management skills to parents of noncompliant children (Forehand et al., 1979). The parents learned skills needed to reward their children, make requests appropriately, and use time-out when their children were noncompliant. When the parents learned these skills, their children's behavior improved. Miltenberger and Fuqua (1985b) used instructions, modeling, rehearsal, and feedback to teach college students how to conduct clinical interviews. The students learned to ask the right kinds of questions when conducting an interview with research assistants who were simulating clients with behavior problems. Dancer and his colleagues taught behavioral observation and description skills to married couples who were going to manage group homes for delinquent youths (Dancer et al., 1978). The couples needed these skills to work effectively with the youths, who exhibited a variety of behavior problems.

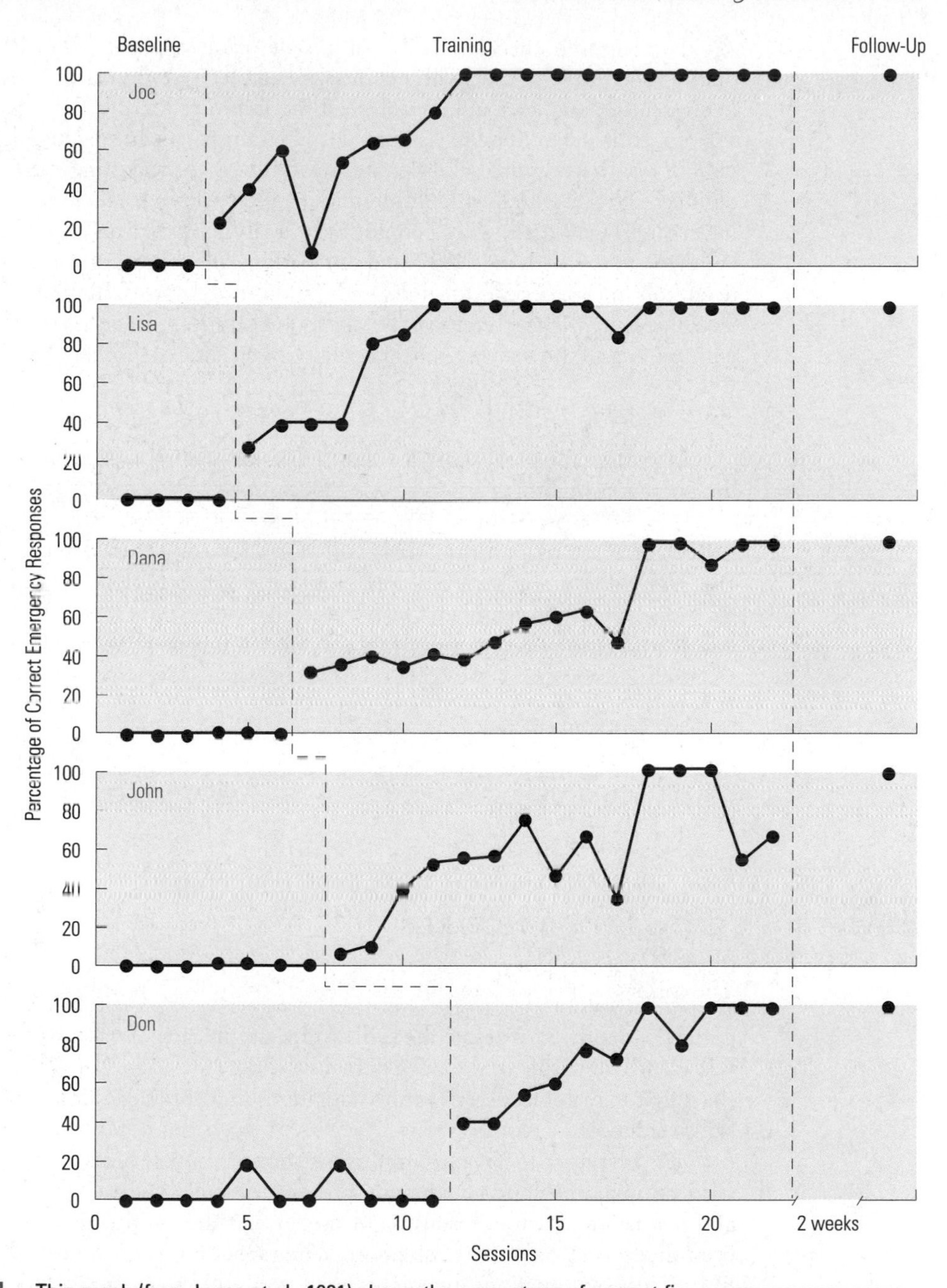

FIGURE 12-4 This graph (from Jones et al., 1981) shows the percentage of correct fire emergency responses from five children before and after behavioral skills training was implemented with each child. All of the children learned the skills as a result of training. This graph is from a multiple-baseline-across-subjects design. The performance of each child improved only after that child received training.

The research cited here is just a sample of the applications of BST procedures. Such procedures are used with people who can learn from instructions and modeling in simulated situations and do not need the intensive training provided in the chaining procedures described in Chapter 11. Chaining procedures generally are used with people who have limited abilities and need intensive prompting. BST procedures, by contrast, often are used with children and adults with normal abilities. However, they have also been used with people with disabilities. For example, Hall, Sheldon-Wildgen, and Sherman (1980) used instructions, modeling, rehearsal, and feedback to teach job interview skills to adults with mild or moderate disabilities. After describing and modeling the important verbal and nonverbal skills in an interview, Hall and her colleagues had the learners rehearse the skills in simulated interviews.

What do you think Hall did after the rehearsals in the simulated interviews?

After the rehearsal, Hall provided praise for appropriate behaviors and described the behaviors that the learners needed to improve.

Using BST procedures, Bakken, Miltenberger, and Schauss (1993) taught parents with mental retardation important skills for interacting with their children. The parents learned to praise their children and pay attention to them in appropriate ways to facilitate normal development. An interesting finding from this study was that the parents learned the skills when instructions, modeling, rehearsal, and feedback were used in training sessions, but the skills did not generalize to everyday situations in the home. When Bakken implemented training in the home, the parents started to exhibit the skills there also. This finding underscores the importance of assessing the generalization of skills to the natural settings where the skills are needed and providing further training if generalization does not occur. (For further discussion of generalization, see Chapter 19.)

How to Use BST Procedures

The following steps will ensure the effective use of BST procedures.

1. Identify and define the skills you want to teach. A good behavioral definition will clearly describe all the behaviors involved in the skills. You should define all the skills that may be needed in various situations and conduct a task analysis of complex skills (behavioral chains).

2. Identify all relevant stimulus situations (S^Ds) in which the skills must be used. For example, in teaching abduction prevention skills, you have to identify all possible abduction lures that a person might use so that the child can learn to respond successfully to every abduction situation. When teaching assertiveness, you have to identify all possible situations in which a person might act unassertively so that the person can learn to respond assertively in every situation.

3. Assess the learner's skills in the stimulus situations to establish a baseline. To assess the learner's skills, you must present each stimulus situation (either the real situation or a simulation) and record the learner's response to that situation.

4. Begin training with the easiest skill or the easiest stimulus situation. In those circumstances, the learner is more likely to be successful in training and is more likely

to continue cooperating with the BST procedure. If you start with more difficult skills or situations, the learner may not be successful initially and may become discouraged.

5. Begin a training session by modeling the behavior and describing its important aspects. Be sure to model the behavior in the proper context (in response to the relevant S^D). You can create the proper context by simulating it in a role-play. The simulation should be as real as possible for the learner. Sometimes training sessions are conducted in the real environment; for example, Poche and her colleagues (1981) modeled abduction prevention skills out on the playground, where a child might actually be approached by a potential abductor.

6. After the learner hears the instructions and sees the model, provide the opportunity for rehearsal. Simulate the proper context for the behavior and have the learner practice the behavior. Sometimes the simulation or role-play may occur in the natural situation. Poche and her colleagues (1981) had children rehearse abduction prevention skills on the playground.

7. Immediately after the rehearsal, provide feedback. Always provide descriptive praise for some aspect of the performance. Then provide instructions for improvement as needed.

8. Repeat the rehearsal and feedback process until the learner has executed the behavior correctly a couple of times.

9. After success with one training situation, move to another situation and continue the process of modeling, instructions, rehearsal, and feedback until the learner has mastered each skill in each situation. While adding new situations, continue to have learners practice training situations they have mastered to ensure maintenance.

10. Once the learner has mastered all the skills in all simulated situations during training sessions, program for generalization to the natural situations where the skills are needed. If the training situations are as similar as possible to the natural situations, or if training occurs in the natural situation (e.g., Poche et al., 1981), generalization is more likely to occur. Another way to enhance generalization is to have the learner practice the skills in progressively more difficult situations. For example, after training social skills, you give the learner instructions to use the social skills in real situations with real people in the learner's life. Start with easy assignments and, as the learner is successful, work up to harder ones. The key point is to maintain success so that the learner's efforts are reinforced. Other ways to promote generalization are reviewed in Chapter 19.

Chapter Summary

1. Behavioral skills training (BST) procedures consist of four components: modeling, instructions, rehearsal, and feedback. These training components have been used together to teach a variety of important skills to people with disabilities and to a wide range of other adults and children. First, the trainer provides live or symbolic modeling so that the learner sees how to execute the behavior. The trainer also provides instructions in which the important aspects of the behavior are described for the learner. The learner then gets the opportunity to rehearse the behavior in a simulated situation similar to the natural situation in which the behavior is needed. After the rehearsal, the trainer provides feedback consisting of reinforcement for correct aspects of the behavior and instructions on how to improve the behavior. Further

rehearsals are conducted, and feedback is provided, until the learner displays the correct behavior in a variety of relevant contexts.
2. The appropriate time to use BST procedures is when the learner can benefit from modeling and instructions and does not need more intensive training procedures (such as chaining procedures) to learn the skills.
3. You conduct BST in small groups by providing modeling and instruction for the whole group and then having each member of the group individually rehearse the skills in role-plays and receive feedback. Feedback may come from the trainer as well as from other group members.
4. BST procedures involve a three-term contingency for the skill being learned. Modeling and instructions are antecedents to get the correct behavior to occur, the correct behavior occurs in a rehearsal, and feedback is provided as a reinforcing consequence for the behavior in the rehearsal. Feedback may also involve further instructions that act as an antecedent for the behavior in the next rehearsal.

PRACTICE TEST

1. What four procedures are components of the BST procedure? Describe each component procedure. (pp. 240–243)
2. Describe the use of the BST procedure. (pp. 248–249)
3. Provide two examples (not from the chapter) of skills that could be taught through the BST procedure.
4. For both of these examples, describe how you would use the BST procedure.
5. Why is the use of instructions or modeling alone usually not effective in the long run? (pp. 243–244)
6. Describe the factors that enhance the effectiveness of modeling. What factors reduce the effectiveness of modeling? (pp. 240–241)
7. Describe the factors that influence the effectiveness of instructions. (pp. 241–242)
8. When using rehearsal, why should you start with easy behaviors or situations? What might happen if you practiced the most difficult situations first? (p. 242)
9. Describe the factors that influence the effectiveness of rehearsal. (p. 242)
10. Describe the two types of feedback you can provide after a behavioral rehearsal. (p. 242)
11. When providing feedback after a behavioral rehearsal, why should you always provide praise first? What should you do if the behavior was not correct in the rehearsal? (p. 242)
12. Describe the factors that influence the effectiveness of feedback. (pp. 242–243)
13. Describe how the three-term contingency is involved in the BST procedure. (pp. 243–244)
14. Describe the guidelines for the effective use of the BST procedure. (pp. 248–249)
15. How is the BST procedure different from the chaining procedures described in Chapter 11? How are they similar?
16. In what circumstances would a chaining procedure be most appropriate? In what circumstances would the BST procedure be most appropriate? (p. 248)

APPLICATIONS

1. You are a school counselor and you have been asked to teach a group of eighth graders the skills they will need to resist peer pressure to start smoking. Describe how you will use BST procedures to teach these kids these important skills. Assume that you will work with groups of 20–25 kids in each classroom.

a. Define the skills you will teach.
b. Identify the situations in which the kids will need these skills.
c. Create the role-plays you will use in training.
d. Describe how you will model the behavior and what instructions you will give.

e. Describe the types of rehearsal and feedback you will use.
f. Describe what you will do to increase the chances for generalization of the skills the kids will learn.

2. Your young daughter is in first grade and she wants to walk to school with her friends every day. You have decided that she must learn some personal safety skills before you will allow her to walk to school without adult supervision. You want to teach her how to respond to an adult who offers her a ride to or from school. You do not want her to accept a ride from anybody without your permission. Describe the BST procedure you will use to teach her the skills she will need to respond safely to such a situation. Address each of the points raised in Application 1. Also, describe how you will assess her skills after training to be sure that the skills have generalized to the natural situation.

3. You are teaching a class of ten parents who are having trouble with their children. All the parents have a child who engages in attention-seeking behavior such as whining, crying, or interrupting. One of the things you want to teach the parents is how to differentially reinforce their child's appropriate behavior, such as playing or doing a chore. Describe how you will use the BST procedure to teach the parents how to reinforce their child's good behavior.

MISAPPLICATIONS

1. The principal of an elementary school has decided it is time to teach the students about drugs and what how to resist someone who offers them drugs or tries to talk them into trying or selling drugs. The principal gets a film that talks about the dangers of drugs and tells kids never to take drugs or sell drugs. The film repeats the message that kids should just say no and walk away from a person with drugs. The film shows a few kids saying no and walking away. The principal shows the film in each classroom and asks the kids whether they have any questions. What is the problem with the principal's plan for teaching the students to say no to drugs? How would you improve on this plan?

2. After supper each day, workers at a group home for mentally retarded adolescents are supposed to conduct training programs in toothbrushing, grooming, housekeeping, and other skills. The supervisor goes home at 5 p.m., and the staff members often sit around and talk after supper instead of training the residents. Whenever the supervisor drops by, staff members get up and do their jobs, but they stop working again when he leaves. The supervisor decides to do BST with the staff. He conducts a few training sessions in which he uses modeling, instruction, rehearsal, and feedback to teach staff members the skills they need to work with the residents. He believes that as a result of the training, the staff will use these skills when he is not present. What is wrong with this use of the BST procedure? What would be a more appropriate procedure?

3. In a new campaign, major sports stars in TV commercials tell kids to stay in school, study hard, and get good grades. The commercials target inner-city high school and junior high kids. The sports stars tell kids why they should study and how it will improve their lives in the future. The commercial shows some kids studying and older kids telling them how smart they are for studying. It shows kids refusing to go out at night with other kids because they have to study. After the kids model this behavior, the sports star praises them and says how smart it is to study and stay in school. Finally, the commercial shows kids graduating and getting good jobs. Again the sports star comes on screen and points out the good things that studying and staying in school can get you. What is good about this strategy to get kids to study? What is missing? How could you improve this strategy?

CHAPTER 12 *Quiz 1* Name:

1. The four procedures involved in the behavioral skills training procedure are

   ____________, ____________, ____________

   and ____________.

2. The ____________ component of BST involves telling the learner how to engage in the correct behavior.

3. The ____________ component of BST involves showing the learner how to engage in the correct behavior.

4. The ____________ component of BST involves giving the learner the opportunity to practice the correct behavior.

5. The ____________ component of BST involves giving the learner praise or correction for his or her performance of the target behavior.

6. When a model engages in the correct behavior, it should result in ____________.

7. For modeling to be most effective, the model should have ____________

   to the learner, or high ____________.

8. The learner should have the opportunity to ____________ the behavior as soon as possible after observing the model.

9. In BST, instructions should be delivered by someone who has ____________ with the learner.

10. In BST, feedback should be given ____________ after the behavior is performed.

CHAPTER 12 *Quiz 2* Name:

1. ________________________ is a training procedure that includes the use of instructions, modeling, rehearsal, and feedback.

In teaching abduction preventions skills to children, which components of the behavioral skills training procedure are illustrated in the following examples?

2. ________________ Telling the child to say "no," run away, and tell an adult when someone asks the child to leave.

3. ________________ Showing the child the correct behavior to be performed when someone asks the child to leave.

4. ________________ Having the child practice saying "no," running away, and telling in a role play of an abduction lure.

5. ________________ Praising the child for her correct performance in a role play of an abduction situation.

6. In ____________ modeling, a person demonstrates the appropriate behavior, while

   in ____________ modeling, the appropriate behavior is shown via videotape, audiotape, cartoon, or movie.

7. During BST, the behavior is modeled in a variety of ways and in a variety of situations in order

   to enhance ______________________.

8. Following instructions and modeling, the learner should have the opportunity to

   ________________ the behavior.

9. In BST, feedback involves both ___________________________ and

   ___________________________.

10. To promote generalization of the behavior during BST, the role plays should

    ________________ the actual situations the learner is likely to encounter in real life.

CHAPTER 12 *Quiz 3* Name:

1. In BST, instructions involve ______________________________.

2. In BST, modeling involves ______________________________.

3. In BST, rehearsal involves ______________________________.

4. In BST, feedback involves ______________________________.

Which BST components are illustrated in the following examples?

5. ____________________ In the process of teaching a first grade class what to do if they ever find a gun, the trainer has the class watch as he walks up to the gun on a shelf, doesn't touch it, runs out of the room, and tells the teacher about the gun.

6. ____________________ After showing the first grade class the correct behavior, the trainer places a gun on a shelf and then has each student practice the skills of not touching the gun, running out of the room, and telling a teacher.

7. As a result of a history of reinforcement for imitating models, what is likely to happen when a child views a model's behavior during a BST procedure?

   ____

8. During modeling, the model's behavior should occur in the proper

   ____________________.

9. In BST, praise for correct behavior and correction of incorrect behavior are two forms

   of ____________________ .

10. What are two ways to enhance generalization after BST?

    ____

    ____

THIRTEEN

Understanding Problem Behaviors through Functional Assessment

In Chapters 9–12, procedures for establishing desirable behaviors were described. In this section of the text, behavioral procedures for understanding problem behaviors and increasing or decreasing existing behaviors are described. When using behavior modification procedures to help a person increase a desirable behavior or decrease or eliminate an undesirable behavior (a problem behavior), the first step is to understand why the person engages in the behavior. To do so, you must conduct an assessment of the three-term contingency to determine the antecedent events that evoke the behavior and the reinforcing consequences that maintain it. Identifying these variables before treating a problem behavior is called **functional assessment.**

- What is a functional assessment of a problem behavior?
- What are the three ways to conduct a functional assessment?
- How do you use indirect methods to conduct a functional assessment?
- How do you use direct observation methods to conduct a functional assessment?
- What is a functional analysis of a problem behavior? How do you carry out a functional analysis?

Examples of Functional Assessment

Jacob

Jacob, a 2-year-old boy, lived with his mother and his 4-year-old sister. His mother ran a day care business out of her house and took care of 10–15 other young children. Jacob engaged in problem behaviors involving throwing objects, banging his head on the ground, and whining. His mother was concerned about Jacob's problems and agreed to participate in a behavior modification experiment, conducted by a psychology graduate student named Rich, to try to decrease Jacob's problem behaviors (Arndorfer, Miltenberger, Woster, Rortvedt, & Gaffaney, 1994). The first step Rich took was to conduct a functional assessment to determine why Jacob was engaging in these behaviors.

First, Rich interviewed Jacob's mother and asked her questions about the problem behaviors, the setting and the day care routines, the antecedent circumstances, the consequences when Jacob engaged in the problem behaviors, other behaviors that Jacob engaged in, and previous treatments that she had tried with Jacob. After the interview, Rich observed Jacob in the day care setting and recorded information on the antecedents, behavior, and consequences each time Jacob engaged in the problem behaviors. He observed Jacob for a few days until he could determine which antecedents and consequences were reliably associated with the behavior.

On the basis of the information from the interview and the observations, Rich developed a hypothesis about the function of the problem behaviors. He determined that Jacob was more likely to engage in the problem behaviors when other children in day care took his toys or tried to play with his toys. Furthermore, when Jacob engaged in the head-banging, whining, or toy-throwing, the children were likely to stop playing with his toys and give the toys back to him. Rich hypothesized that the reinforcer for the problem behaviors was that the other children gave Jacob his toys back.

To determine whether this hypothesis was correct, Rich conducted a brief experiment. On some days, he instructed the other children in day care not to touch Jacob's toys; on other days, he instructed the children to play with Jacob's toys but to give the toys back to him immediately if he engaged in the problem behaviors. Rich found that Jacob was much more likely to engage in the problem behaviors on days when the other children played with his toys. On days when the other children did not touch his toys, Jacob rarely engaged in the problem behaviors. The brief experiment had confirmed that other children playing with Jacob's toys was an antecedent for the problem behaviors. Furthermore, it confirmed that the reinforcer for the problem behaviors was that the other children gave the toys back.

Antecedent	Behavior	Consequence
Other kids play with Jacob's toys.	Jacob bangs his head, whines, and throws toys.	The kids return Jacob's toys to him.

Outcome: Jacob is more likely to engage in head-banging, whining, and toy-throwing when other children play with his toys.

Treatment for Jacob involved teaching him to ask the other children to give his toys back when they took his toys. Asking for the toys is a behavior that is functionally equivalent to the problem behaviors. In other words, asking for the toys produced the same outcome as the problem behavior: The children gave the toys back to him. When Jacob exhibited aggressive behavior, he did not get his toys back.

Antecedent	Behavior	Consequence
Other kids play with Jacob's toys.	Jacob asks for his toys back.	The kids return Jacob's toys to him.

Outcome: Jacob is more likely to ask for his toys back when other children play with them.

The treatment helped Jacob replace the undesirable behavior (head-banging, whining, toy-throwing) with a desirable behavior (asking for the toys). This treatment strategy, using differential reinforcement to increase a desirable behavior and to decrease an undesirable behavior, is described in Chapter 15. The functional assessment Rich conducted with Jacob helped him choose an effective treatment for Jacob's problem behaviors. Conducting a functional assessment is always the first step in using behavior modification procedures to decrease problem behaviors.

Anna

Anna, a 3-year-old girl, lived with her mother and younger sister. Anna engaged in problem behaviors at home involving hitting, kicking, and screaming (Arndorfer et al., 1994). To understand the function of these behaviors, Rich again conducted a functional assessment. He interviewed Anna's mother and then conducted direct observations of the three-term contingency related to the problem behaviors. On the basis of the results of the interview and the observations, Rich hypothesized that Anna's problem behaviors were reinforced by her mother's attention. Anna was most likely to engage in the problem behavior when her mother was not paying attention to her (e.g., when her mother was working around the house). Furthermore, the most common consequence of the problem behavior was that Anna's mother immediately stopped what she was doing and paid attention to Anna. Rich conducted a brief experiment to confirm this hypothesis.

What do you think Rich did in his brief experiment?

Rich had Anna's mother manipulate her level of attention to Anna to determine whether her attention reinforced Anna's problem behaviors. In the first condition, she played with Anna and paid attention to her. If Anna engaged in a problem behavior, her mother ignored it. In the second experimental condition, she paid little attention to Anna and focused on a task instead. If Anna exhibited a problem behavior, her mother immediately stopped what she was doing and paid attention to Anna for a brief period of time. Rich found that Anna exhibited a much higher frequency of the problem behaviors in the second condition. This confirmed the hypothesis that the reinforcer for Anna's problem behavior was her mother's attention.

Antecedent	Behavior	Consequence
Anna's mother is not paying attention to her.	Anna hits, kicks, and screams.	Anna's mother pays attention to her.

Outcome: Anna is more likely to hit, kick, and scream when her mother is not paying attention to her.

Rich implemented a treatment similar to the one he used with Jacob. He taught Anna how to ask for her mother's attention when her mother was not paying attention to her. He taught her mother to differentially reinforce Anna's behavior of asking for attention. In other words, when Anna asked for attention, her mother immediately paid attention to her for a brief period of time. However, when Anna engaged in the problem behavior, her mother used extinction and did not provide any attention.

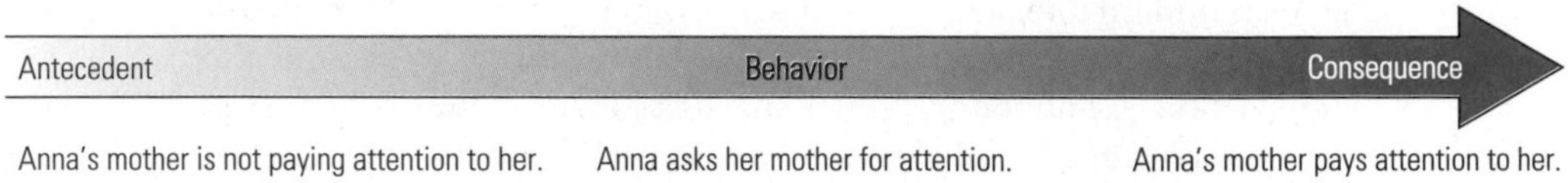

Antecedent	Behavior	Consequence
Anna's mother is not paying attention to her.	Anna asks her mother for attention.	Anna's mother pays attention to her.

Outcome: Anna is more likely to ask for her mother's attention when her mother is not paying attention to her at the time.

When Anna engaged in a problem behavior, her mother's only reaction was to take Anna's little sister into the other room with her so that the little sister would not get hurt (because Anna's problem behavior involved hitting and kicking). Rich found that the use of differential reinforcement resulted in a decrease in the problem behavior and an increase in the desirable behavior of asking her mother for attention. Once again, the particular treatment chosen for Anna was based on information from the functional assessment conducted as the first step in the treatment process.

Note that sometimes, when a child learns to ask for attention as an alternative to the problem behavior, the child may then ask for attention so often that this behavior itself becomes a problem. Carr and his colleagues have described procedures to solve this problem. With each successive request for attention, the parents wait longer and longer before responding. Eventually, the child asks less often (Carr et al., 1994).

DEFINING FUNCTIONAL ASSESSMENT

One basic principle of behavior analysis is that behavior is lawful. Regardless of whether the behavior is desirable or undesirable, its occurrence is controlled by environmental variables; in other words, it is a function of environmental variables. Respondent behavior is controlled by antecedent stimuli, and operant behavior is controlled by antecedents and consequences that make up three-term contingencies of reinforcement and punishment. Functional assessment is the process of gathering information about the antecedents and consequences that are functionally related to the occurrence of a problem behavior. It provides information that helps you determine why a problem behavior is occurring (Drasgow, Yell, Bradley, & Shiner, 1999; Ellis & Magee, 1999; Horner & Carr, 1997; Iwata, Vollmer, & Zarcone, 1990; Iwata, Vollmer, Zarcone, & Rodgers, 1993; Larson & Maag, 1999; Lennox & Miltenberger, 1989; Neef, 1994).

In addition to information on the reinforcing consequences (functions) of target behaviors, a functional assessment also provides detailed information about antecedent stimuli, including the time and place of the behavior, people present when the behavior occurs, and any environmental events immediately preceding the behavior; and the frequency (or other dimensions) of the target behavior. This information on the three-term contingency will help you to identify the antecedents that have stimulus control over the behavior and the reinforcing consequences that maintain the behavior.

Functional assessment also provides other types of information that are important for developing appropriate treatments for problem behaviors, including the existence of alternative behaviors that may be functionally equivalent to the problem behavior,

TABLE 13-1 Categories of Information from a Functional Assessment

- *Problem behaviors:* an objective description of the behaviors that make up the problem.
- *Antecedents:* an objective description of environmental events preceding the problem behavior, including aspects of the physical environment and the behavior of other people.
- *Consequences:* an objective description of environmental events that follow the problem behavior, including aspects of the physical environment and the behavior of other people.
- *Alternative behaviors:* information on desirable behaviors in the person's repertoire that may be reinforced to compete with the problem behavior.
- *Motivational variables:* information on environmental events that may function as establishing operations to influence the effectiveness of reinforcers and punishers for the problem behaviors and alternative behaviors.
- *Potential reinforcers:* information on environmental events—including physical stimuli and the behavior of other people—that may function as reinforcers and be used in a treatment program.
- *Previous interventions:* information on the interventions that have been used in the past and their effects on the problem behavior.

motivational variables (establishing operations that influence the effectiveness of stimuli as reinforcers and punishers), stimuli that may function as reinforcers for the person, and the history of previous treatments and their outcomes (Table 13-1).

FUNCTIONS OF PROBLEM BEHAVIORS

A primary purpose of a functional assessment is to identify the function of the problem behavior. There are four broad classes of reinforcing consequences or functions of problem behaviors (Iwata et al., 1993; Miltenberger, 1998, 1999).

Social Positive Reinforcement

One type of reinforcing consequence involves positive reinforcement mediated by another person. When a positively reinforcing consequence is delivered by another person after the target behavior, it is called social positive reinforcement. Social positive reinforcement may involve attention, access to activities, or tangibles provided by another person. For example, Anna received attention from her mother as a reinforcer for her problem behavior and Jacob received his toys back from the other kids (tangibles) as a reinforcer for his problem behavior.

Social Negative Reinforcement

In some cases, target behaviors are maintained by negative reinforcement that is mediated by another person. When another person terminates an aversive interaction, task, or activity after the occurrence of a target behavior, the behavior is said to be maintained by social negative reinforcement. For example, a child who complains to his parent when asked to do a chore may get out of doing the chore as a result of complaining. Likewise, a student who bangs her head when instructed to do an academic task may escape from the task as a result. In each case, being allowed to escape from the chore or task reinforces the problem behavior. Asking a friend not to smoke in your car is negatively reinforced by escape or avoidance of the smell of the smoke when the person puts out the cigarette or doesn't light it in the first place.

Automatic Positive Reinforcement

In some cases, the reinforcing consequence of a target behavior is not mediated by another person but occurs as an automatic consequence of the behavior itself. When the behavior produces a reinforcing consequence automatically, the behavior is said to be maintained by automatic positive reinforcement. For example, some behaviors produce sensory stimulation that reinforces the behavior. An autistic child who spins objects, rocks in his seat, or flaps his fingers in front of his face may do so because the behaviors produce reinforcing sensory stimulation. In this case, the reinforcing consequence for the behavior is not mediated by another person. Going to the kitchen to get a drink is automatically positively reinforced by getting the drink, and asking someone else to get you a drink is socially positively reinforced by getting the drink from the other person.

Automatic Negative Reinforcement

Automatic negative reinforcement occurs when the target behavior automatically reduces or eliminates an aversive stimulus as a consequence of the behavior. With automatic negative reinforcement, escape from the aversive stimulus is not mediated by the actions of another person. Closing the window to block a cold draft involves automatic negative reinforcement. Asking someone to close the window to get rid of the draft involves social negative reinforcement. An example of a problem behavior that may be maintained by automatic negative reinforcement is binge eating. In some cases, binge eating has been found to be maintained by the reduction in unpleasant emotional responses that were present before binge eating (Stickney & Miltenberger, 1999; Stickney, Miltenberger, & Wolff, 1999). In other words, when the person experiences strong unpleasant emotions, binge eating temporarily decreases the unpleasant emotions, thus negatively reinforcing binge eating.

FUNCTIONAL ASSESSMENT METHODS

The various methods used to conduct functional assessments fall into three categories: indirect assessment methods, in which information is gathered through interviews and questionnaires; direct observation methods, in which an observer records the antecedents, behavior, and consequences as they occur; and experimental methods (also called functional analysis), in which antecedents and consequences are manipulated to observe their effect on the problem behavior (Iwata, Vollmer, & Zarcone, 1990; Lennox & Miltenberger, 1989). Let's consider each of these approaches in turn.

FUNCTIONAL ASSESSMENT METHODS

- Indirect methods
- Direct observation methods
- Experimental methods (functional analysis)

Indirect Methods

With indirect functional assessment methods, behavioral interviews or questionnaires are used to gather information from the person exhibiting the problem behavior (the client) or from others who know this person well (e.g., family members, teachers, or staff). Indirect assessment methods are also known as informant assessment methods because an informant (the client or others) is providing information in response to assessment questions (Lennox & Miltenberger, 1989). The advantage of indirect functional assessment methods is that they are easy to conduct and do not take much time. In addition, a number of interview formats and questionnaires are available for use in conducting a functional assessment (Bailey & Pyles, 1989; Durand & Crimmins, 1988; Iwata, Wong, Riordan, Dorsey, & Lau, 1982; Lewis, Scott, & Sugai, 1994; Miltenberger & Fuqua, 1985b; O'Neill, Horner, Albin, Storey, & Sprague, 1990; O'Neill et al., 1997). The disadvantage of indirect methods is that the informants must rely on their memory of the events. Thus, information from interviews and questionnaires may be incorrect as a result of forgetting or bias.

Because of their convenience, indirect functional assessment methods are used commonly. In fact, the interview is the most common assessment method used by psychologists (Elliott, Miltenberger, Bundgaard, & Lumley, 1996; Swan & MacDonald, 1978). A good behavioral interview is structured to generate information from the informant that is clear and objective. Information about the problem behavior, antecedents, and consequences should describe environmental events (including the behavior of other people) without inferences or interpretation. For example, consider two different answers to the interview question, "When does your child engage in the tantrum behavior?" (Assume that tantrum behavior has already been described by the parent.) If the parent says, "Johnny has a tantrum when I tell him to turn off the TV and come to the dinner table," the parent is providing objective information about environmental events that immediately precede the problem. If the parent says, "Johnny has a tantrum when he doesn't get to do what he wants," the parent is interpreting the situation. This second answer does not provide objective information about the antecedents of the problem. It does not describe specific environmental events.

The goal of a behavioral interview is to generate information on the problem behaviors, antecedents, consequences, and other variables that will permit you to form a hypothesis about the controlling variables for the problem. At the same time, an effective interview teaches the client or informant about functional assessment: that behaviors and events must be identified and specified, that inferences should be minimized, and that it is important to focus on antecedents and consequences in understanding and changing behavior. The following is a list of questions an interviewer might ask to generate information about the antecedents and consequences of a child's problem behavior.

Antecedents

- When does the problem behavior usually occur?
- Where does the problem behavior usually occur?
- Who is present when the problem behavior occurs?
- What activities or events precede the occurrence of the problem behavior?
- What do other people say or do immediately before the problem behavior occurs?
- Does the child engage in any other behaviors before the problem behavior?
- When, where, with whom, and in what circumstances is the problem behavior least likely to occur?

Consequences

- What happens after the problem behavior occurs?
- What do you do when the problem behavior occurs?
- What do other people do when the problem behavior occurs?
- What changes after the problem behavior occurs?
- What does the child get after the problem behavior?
- What does the child get out of or avoid after the problem behavior?

As you can see, each of these questions asks about the events that immediately precede and follow the child's problem behavior. The interviewer asks these questions in the hope that the parent will provide objective information. If the parent does not provide specific information about environmental events in response to one or more questions, the interviewer will ask for clarification until the parent provides information that shows a clear pattern of events that precede and follow the problem behavior. Once the interviewer can discern a reliable pattern of antecedents and consequences, the interviewer can develop a hypothesis about the antecedents that have stimulus control over the problem behavior and the reinforcer that maintains it.

Various authors have developed lists of questions to generate thorough functional assessment information in a behavioral interview. Table 13-2 shows the categories of assessment information and sample interview questions from the Functional Analysis Interview Format developed for use with staff, teachers, and others who work with people with mental retardation (O'Neill et al., 1990; 1997). These questions can be answered in an interview or questionnaire format (Ellingson, Miltenberger, Stricker, Galensky, & Garlinghouse, 2000; Galensky, Miltenberger, Stricker, & Garlinghouse, 2001). In an interview format, the interviewer would ask the informant each question and record the answer. In a questionnaire format, the informant would read each question and write down the answer. If the questions are used in a questionnaire format, the professional would review the answers and then follow up with an interview to clarify any answers that did not provide complete or objective information.

Because indirect functional assessment methods have the disadvantage of relying on informants' memories of events, researchers suggest using multiple functional as-

TABLE 13-2 Categories of Assessment Information and Sample Questions from the Functional Analysis Interview Format

A. Describe the behaviors.
- What are the behaviors of concern?
- For each behavior, define how it is performed, how often it occurs, and how long it lasts.

B. Define potential ecological events that may affect the behaviors.
- What medications is the person taking, and how do you think these may affect the behaviors?
- How many other people are in the setting (work/school/home)? Do you believe that the density of people or interactions with other people affect the targeted behaviors?
- What is the staffing pattern? To what extent do you believe the number of staff, training of staff, and quality of social contact with staff affect the targeted behaviors?

C. Define events and situations that predict occurrences of the behaviors (antecedents).
- When, where, and with whom are behaviors most likely? Least likely?
- What activity is most likely to produce the behaviors? Least likely?

D. Identify the function of the undesirable behaviors. What consequences maintain the behaviors?
- What does the person get and what does the person avoid as a consequence of the behaviors?

E. Define the efficiency of the undesirable behaviors.
- What amount of physical effort is involved in the behaviors?
- Does engaging in the behaviors result in a payoff every time?

F. Define the primary methods the person uses to communicate.
- What general expressive communication strategies does the person use?

G. Identify potential reinforcers.
- In general, what factors (events/activities/objects/people) appear to be reinforcing or enjoyable for the person?

H. What functional alternative behaviors does the person know?
- What socially appropriate behaviors or skills does the person perform that may be ways of achieving the same function(s) as the behaviors of concern?

I. Provide a history of undesirable behaviors and the programs that have been attempted.
- Identify the treatment programs and how effective they have been.

Source: Adapted from O'Neill et al., 1990.

sessment methods to produce the most accurate information on antecedents, consequences, and the other variables listed in Table 13-1 (Arndorfer & Miltenberger, 1993; Arndorfer et al., 1994; Ellingson et al., 2000). Arndorfer and his colleagues suggest that a behavioral interview combined with direct observation of the antecedents and consequences provides useful information that enables you to formulate accurate hypotheses about the function of the problem behavior.

Direct Observation Methods

When conducting a functional assessment using direct observation methods, a person observes and records the antecedents and consequences each time the problem behavior occurs. The person conducting the direct observation assessment (the observer) may be the person exhibiting the problem behavior or it may be another person associated with the client, such as a parent, teacher, staff person, nurse, or psychologist.

The antecedents and consequences are observed and recorded in the natural environment where the problem behavior typically takes place. An exception would be when observations occur while a person is in a treatment setting (e.g., a hospital or clinic). Direct observation assessment also is called **ABC observation.** The goal of ABC observations is to record the immediate antecedents and consequences typically associated with the problem behavior under normal conditions (Anderson & Long, 2002; Bijou, Peterson, & Ault, 1968; Lalli, Browder, Mace, & Brown, 1993; Repp & Karsh, 1994; Vollmer, Borrero, Wright, Van Camp, & Lalli, 2001).

Advantages and disadvantages are associated with ABC observation as a method of conducting a functional assessment of a problem behavior. The main advantage of ABC observations over indirect methods is that an observer is recording the antecedents and consequences as they occur rather than reporting the antecedents and consequences from memory. The assessment information is likely to be more accurate when it comes from direct observation. A disadvantage is that ABC observations take more time and effort than interview or questionnaire methods. In addition, even though ABC observations produce objective information about the antecedents and consequences that are reliably associated with the problem behavior, ABC observations do not demonstrate a functional relationship but rather a correlation of the antecedents and consequences with the problem behavior. To demonstrate that a functional relationship exists, experimental methods must be used; these are described in the next section. However, even though the ABC observations demonstrate only a correlation of the antecedents and consequences with the problem behavior, the information allows you to develop a hypothesis about the antecedents that evoke the behavior and the reinforcer that maintains the behavior. A strong hypothesis about the controlling antecedents and consequences often is sufficient to develop effective treatment strategies. Your hypothesis about the controlling variables is strengthened when the information from indirect assessments is consistent with information from the ABC direct observation assessment.

To conduct ABC observations, the observer should be present in the client's natural environment when the problem behavior is most likely to occur. For example, if a student has problem behaviors in one class but not in others, the observer should be present in that particular class to observe and record the ABCs. Therefore, to make ABC observations most efficient, it is helpful to know in advance when the problem behavior is most likely. Information from an interview may indicate when the problem behavior is most likely to occur. In addition, Touchette and his colleagues described a method to assess the time of day that the problem occurs most often (Touchette, MacDonald, & Langer, 1985) by using a **scatter plot.** To create a scatter plot, someone in the client's natural environment records once each half-hour whether the problem behavior occurred during the preceding half-hour. As you recall from Chapter 2, scatter plot recording is an interval recording method. After recording on the scatter plot for several days, you may be able to see the time of day that the problem behavior most often occurs. You can then conduct ABC observations at those times. If the scatter plot shows that the problem behavior usually occurs at certain times of the day, you can then conduct ABC observations at those times. If the scatter plot does not reveal a pattern in the time of occurrence of the problem behavior (e.g., Kahng et al., 1998), then ABC observations would need to be scheduled for longer periods or more time periods in an attempt to observe the behavior. A scatter plot is shown in Figure 13-1.

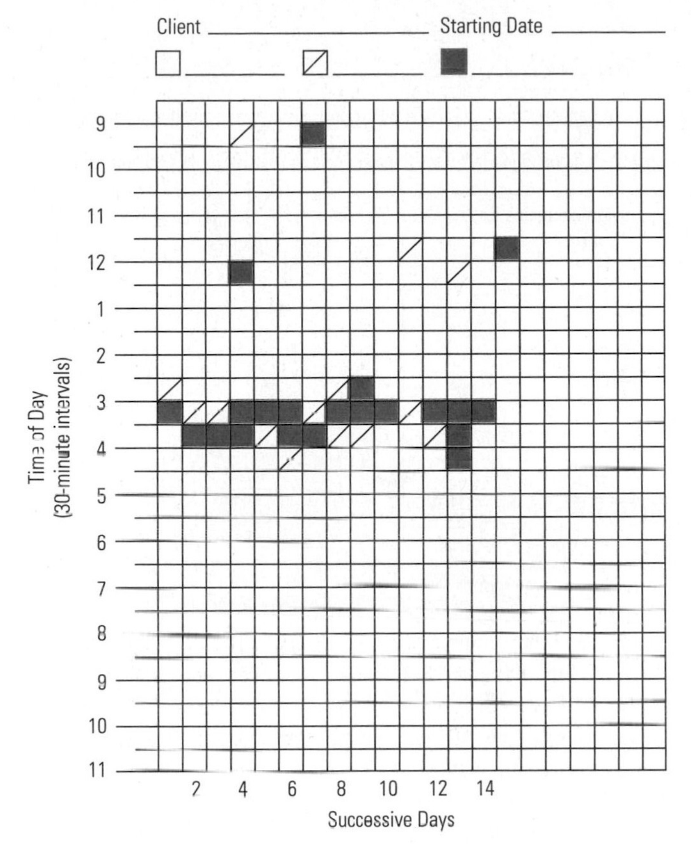

FIGURE 13-1 This is a scatter plot recording sheet (from Touchette et al., 1985) for documenting the time of day that the problem behavior occurs. Each square on the grid represents a half-hour period in a particular day. To complete the scatter plot, an observer records each half-hour whether the problem occurred within the preceding half-hour. If the behavior occurred once in the half-hour time period, the observer puts a horizontal slash through the box. If the behavior occurred two or more times, the observer darkens the box. The observer leaves the box blank if the behavior did not occur in a particular half-hour. After recording on the scatter plot grid for a week or two, you will be able to determine the time that the behavior occurs most frequently. In this completed scatter plot, notice that the behavior is occurring most frequently in the afternoon around 3 p.m. With this information, the behavior analyst would conduct ABC observations around 3 p.m. to record the antecedents and consequences of the behavior.

The observer conducting the ABC assessment must be trained to observe and record the antecedents and consequences correctly each time the problem behavior occurs. This means that the observer must be able to discriminate each instance of the problem behavior so that he or she can record the events that immediately preceded and followed the behavior. The observer must be trained to describe antecedent and consequent events objectively, in terms of the specific behavior of other people and changes in physical stimuli in the environment. The observer must record antecedents and consequences immediately as they occur to reduce reliance on memory.

OBSERVATION RECORD

1. Describe the behavior(s) ______

2. Describe what happened just *before* the behavior occurred (what you did, what they did, etc.).

3. Describe what happened just *after* the behavior occurred (what you did, what they did, etc.).

Date, time	What happened just *before* the behavior?	Behavior: What was done or said? Be specific.	What happened just *after* the behavior?

FIGURE 13-2 This ABC observation data sheet includes columns to record the antecedents, the behavior, and the consequence of the behavior. Each time the problem behavior occurs, the observer immediately writes down a description of the antecedent events, the behavior, and the consequent events. With this ABC observation method, the observer must be able to take the time to describe the events as they occur.

ABC observations can be conducted in three ways. In the *descriptive method*, the observer writes a brief description of the behavior and of each antecedent and consequent event each time that the behavior occurs. The observer typically uses a three-column data sheet similar to the one shown in Figure 13-2. This method is open-ended and results in descriptions of all events that were contiguous to the behavior. Because it is open-ended and the observer describes all antecedent and consequence events that were observed, this ABC assessment method may be conducted before indirect methods are used, before any hypotheses are developed about the function of the behavior.

The *checklist method* for conducting ABC observations involves a checklist with columns for possible antecedents, behaviors, and consequences. The checklist typically is developed after the problem behaviors and potential antecedents and consequences are identified in an interview (or other indirect assessment method) or through observation. To conduct an ABC observation using the checklist, the observer records the particular problem behavior each time it occurs, along with its antecedents and consequences, by putting a check mark in each of the relevant columns. Figure 13-3 shows an example of an ABC observation checklist.

A third way to conduct ABC observations is to record the antecedents, behaviors, and consequences using an *interval* (or *real time*) *recording method.* Recall that in interval recording, you divide an observation period into brief time intervals and mark a data sheet at the end of each interval to record whether the behavior occurred in that interval and in real time recording, you record the exact time of each occurrence of the behavior. You can also identify and define specific events that may serve as an-

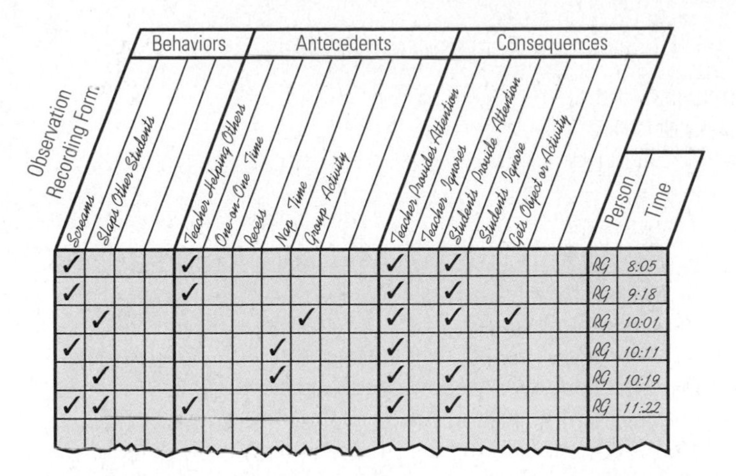

FIGURE 13-3 This ABC observation checklist includes a column for the time the behavior occurred and columns for specific antecedents, behaviors, and consequences. Each time the behavior occurs, the observer records the time and puts check marks in the columns indicating which behavior occurred, which antecedent event occurred before the behavior, and which consequence followed the behavior. The observer can record the ABCs quickly, without much disruption of ongoing activities. The target behaviors, antecedents, and consequences are written at the top of the columns in each section before recording. In this completed ABC observation checklist, the antecedent, behavior, and consequence categories have been entered and some observations have been recorded.

tecedents and consequences and record these events, as well as the behavior with interval or real time recording. You identify the specific events to record from an interview or other indirect assessment methods or through direct observation.

Rortvedt and Miltenberger (1994) conducted ABC observations using interval recording to identify the function of noncompliant behavior in two young children. Noncompliance was defined as refusing to complete a task requested by the parent. The researchers first conducted an interview with the parents to assess the function of the noncompliance. The parents of both children reported that they responded to their child's noncompliance with attention. They said that when the child refused to carry out a requested activity, they repeated the request, scolded the child, made threats of punishment, or pleaded with the child. On the basis of this information, the researchers hypothesized that attention from the parent was reinforcing noncompliance. The researchers conducted ABC observations of the parent and child in the home. They asked the parent to make a number of requests and then recorded the occurrence of child noncompliance and parental attention after noncompliance using 10-second interval recording. Their observations indicated that the children were noncompliant with 50–80% of the requests made by their parents. Furthermore, each time the child refused to follow a request, the parent responded with attention. The results of the ABC observations were consistent with the information from the interview and provided strong support for the hypothesis that attention was reinforcing the noncompliance. Successful treatment involved positive reinforcement for compliance and a procedure called time-out (Chapter 17), in which parental attention was eliminated after noncompliance. This treatment was chosen on the basis of the functional assessment results.

Direct Observation Assessment Methods

- Descriptive method
- Checklist method
- Interval or real time method

Together, indirect and direct functional assessment methods are categorized as descriptive assessments because the antecedents and consequences are described, either from memory or from direct observation of the events (Arndorfer et al., 1994; Iwata, Vollmer, & Zarcone, 1990; Mace & Lalli, 1991; Sasso et al., 1992). Descriptive functional assessments allow you to develop hypotheses about the antecedent and consequent variables controlling the problem behavior, but they do not prove that the variables are functionally related to the behavior. To demonstrate a functional relationship, the antecedents or consequences must be manipulated to show their influence on the problem behavior.

Experimental Methods (Functional Analysis)

Experimental methods of conducting a functional assessment manipulate antecedent or consequent variables to demonstrate their influence on the problem behavior. Experimental methods are also called **experimental analysis** or **functional analysis.** These terms reflect the fact that these methods experimentally demonstrate a functional relationship between the antecedents and consequences and the problem behavior.

Some researchers have manipulated both antecedents and consequences to evaluate the possible functions of a problem behavior. For example, Iwata, Dorsey, Slifer, Bauman, and Richman (1982) conducted experiments to evaluate the function of self-injurious behavior (SIB) exhibited by people with mental retardation. In the experimental conditions, Iwata arranged an establishing operation as an antecedent and a possible reinforcing consequence for the SIB. For example, to evaluate attention as a possible reinforcing consequence for SIB, Iwata arranged a condition in which the child did not receive any attention from the adult who was present, and then when SIB occurred, the adult provided attention in the form of social disapproval. Iwata et al. evaluated four conditions within an alternating-treatments design (Figure 13-4) and showed that some of the children's SIB was maintained by attention, others by escape, and others by automatic reinforcement.

Other researchers have conducted functional analyses in which antecedents were manipulated to determine their influence on the problem behavior. The function of the problem behavior was then inferred from the resulting behavior changes associated with the antecedent manipulations. For example, Carr and Durand (1985) conducted conditions involving decreased attention and increased task difficulty for children with behavior disorders in the classroom. When problem behaviors were highest in the decreased attention condition, the authors inferred that the behavior was maintained by attention. When the problem behavior was highest in the increased task difficulty condition, the authors inferred that the behaviors were maintained by escape from the task. Carr and Durand showed that some children's problem behaviors were highest in the decreased attention condition and others were highest in the increased task difficulty condition.

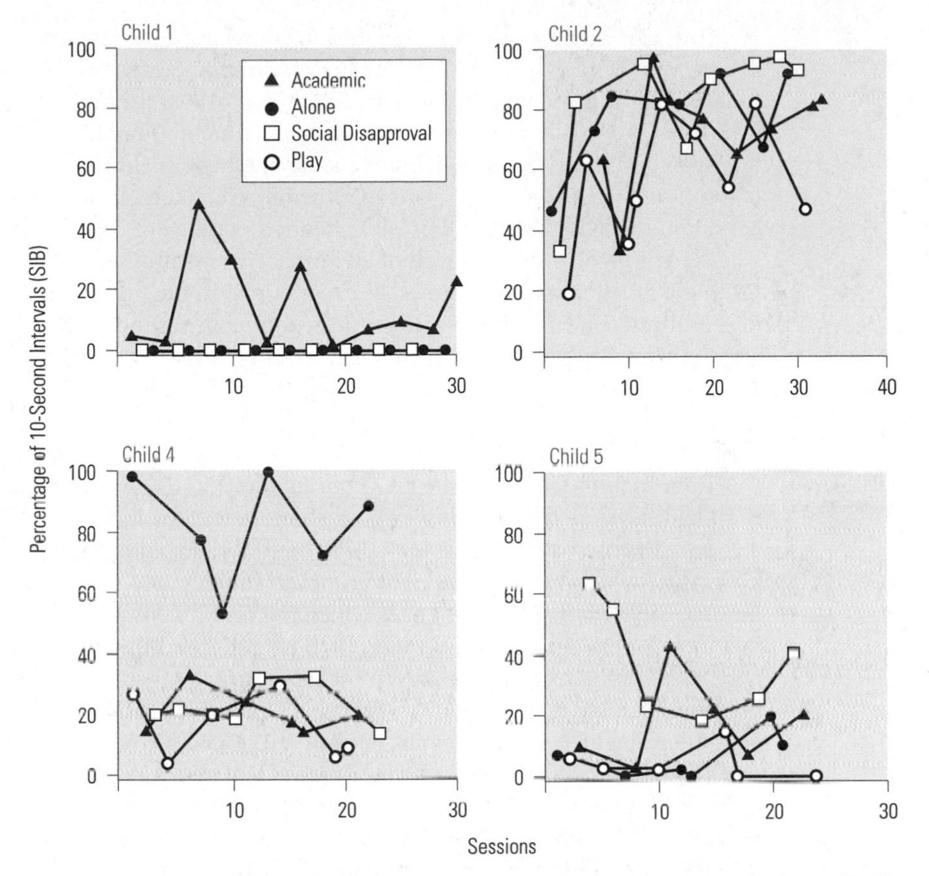

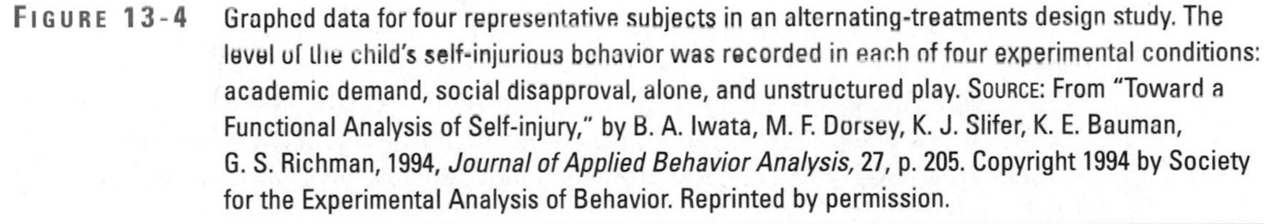
FIGURE 13-4 Graphed data for four representative subjects in an alternating-treatments design study. The level of the child's self-injurious behavior was recorded in each of four experimental conditions: academic demand, social disapproval, alone, and unstructured play. SOURCE: From "Toward a Functional Analysis of Self-injury," by B. A. Iwata, M. F. Dorsey, K. J. Slifer, K. E. Bauman, G. S. Richman, 1994, *Journal of Applied Behavior Analysis,* 27, p. 205. Copyright 1994 by Society for the Experimental Analysis of Behavior. Reprinted by permission.

Sometimes functional analyses are designed to evaluate a range of possible functions for the problem behavior (Iwata et al., 1982). In such cases, the behavior analyst may not have a hypothesis about the reinforcing consequence maintaining the problem behavior and is exploring all possibilities in the functional analysis. For example, if you did not have clear hypotheses about the function of a problem behavior, you might conduct four different conditions evaluating whether attention, tangible reinforcers, escape, or sensory stimulation was the reinforcing consequence for a problem behavior (Iwata et al., 1982; Ellingson, Miltenberger, Stricker, Garlinghouse, et al., 2000; Rapp et al., 1999). Functional analyses evaluating a range of possible reinforcing consequences can identify a particular function of a problem behavior while ruling out other functions.

In some cases, a functional analysis may involve fewer experimental conditions because the behavior analyst is basing the conditions on a specific hypothesis about the function of the problem behavior (Arndorfer et al., 1994). In such cases, the goal of the functional analysis is not to evaluate all possible functions but to confirm or disconfirm the hypothesis. For example, if you believed the target behavior was reinforced by attention, you might evaluate two experimental conditions in a functional analysis: a condition involving no attention with attention contingent on the target behavior and a condition involving high levels of attention with no attention after the target behavior. If the target behavior occurred at a higher rate in the first condition and at a lower rate in the second condition, the results would confirm the hypothesis that attention was the reinforcing consequence for the target behavior.

How did Rich conduct a functional analysis of Jacob's problem behavior in the example presented earlier?

Rich manipulated the way the other children in day care interacted with Jacob. Rich had developed a hypothesis that the antecedent for Jacob's head-banging, whining, and toy-throwing was that the other children touched or played with Jacob's toys. To analyze whether this antecedent event was functionally related to the problem behaviors, Rich arranged conditions in which this antecedent was present and conditions in which it was absent. Furthermore, Rich hypothesized that the reinforcer maintaining Jacob's problem behaviors was the act of returning toys to him. To analyze whether this consequence was functionally related to the problem behaviors, Rich arranged a condition in which the consequence was present and a condition in which it was absent. The results showed that when the antecedent and consequence were present, the problem behaviors occurred at a higher rate. When the antecedent and consequence were absent, Jacob engaged in very little head-banging, whining, and toy-throwing (Figure 13-5). Thus, Rich demonstrated a functional relationship between these particular antecedent and consequent events and the problem behaviors for Jacob. The results supported the hypothesis that Rich had based on the results of the interview and ABC observation assessments. The treatment Rich implemented was successful because it was based on the results of the functional assessment. In other words, when Rich understood why Jacob was engaging in the problem behaviors, he could develop an appropriate treatment.

In a similar manner, Rich conducted a functional analysis of Anna's hitting, kicking, and screaming. He had developed the hypothesis that the problem behaviors were most likely to happen when Anna's mother was not paying attention to her and that the reinforcer was her mother's attention after she exhibited the behaviors. Rich manipulated these antecedent and consequent events and found that his hypothesis was supported. Furthermore, because the treatment based on the results of the functional assessment was effective, it further supported those results. The results of the functional analysis of Anna's problem behaviors are shown in Figure 13-5.

Functional Analysis Research

There is substantial research on the use of functional analysis to identify the variables controlling problem behaviors in children and people with developmental disabilities (Arndorfer & Miltenberger, 1993; Lane, Umbreit, & Beebe-Frankenberger, 1999;

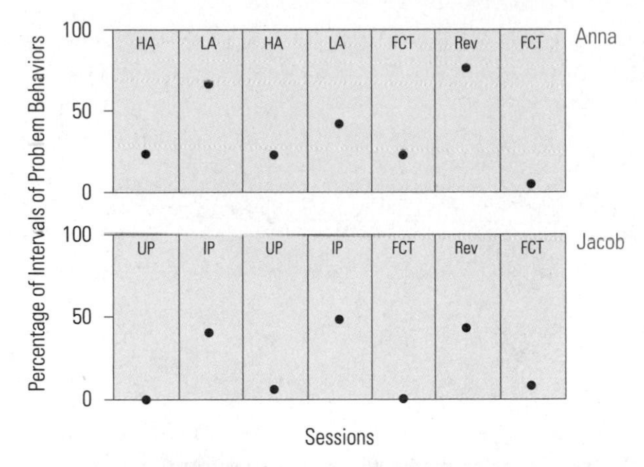

FIGURE 13-5 This graph (from Arndorfer et al., 1994) shows the data from the functional analysis conducted with Anna and Jacob. For Anna, the problem behavior increased in the low-attention (LA) condition and decreased in the high-attention (HA) condition. This demonstrates that her mother's attention was reinforcing the problem behavior. Functional communication training (FCT) was the treatment procedure (Chapter 15). Each time treatment was implemented, the behavior decreased. For Jacob, UP is the uninterrupted-play condition and IP is the interrupted-play condition. His problem behavior was more frequent when other children interrupted his play and returned his toys to him after he exhibited a problem behavior. This confirmed the hypothesis that the return of his toys was the reinforcer for Jacob's problem behaviors. When FCT was implemented, the problem behavior decreased to low levels. For Anna and Jacob, Rev refers to reversal, a condition in which functional communication was not used. After the reversal, FCT was implemented again.

Mace, Lalli, Lalli, & Shea, 1993; Repp & Horner, 1999; Sprague & Horner, 1995). Carr and his colleagues conducted a functional analysis of aggressive behavior in two boys with mental retardation (Carr, Newsom, & Binkoff, 1980). The researchers hypothesized that the antecedents to aggressive behavior were academic demands and that escape from demands was the reinforcer for the problem behaviors. To test this hypothesis, they arranged two experimental conditions: In the first condition, academic demands were presented to the two children; in the second condition, no demands were placed on the children. Carr found that the aggressive behavior occurred at a high rate when demands were made but that the problem behavior decreased substantially when no demands were made on the children. Because the children engaged in aggressive behavior in high-demand conditions, it suggested that escape from demands was the reinforcer for the aggressive behavior. Other research by Carr and Durand (1985) and Durand and Carr (1987, 1991, 1992) has shown that the problem behaviors of students with autism and mental retardation may be reinforced by teacher attention or by escape from the academic demands in the classroom. In each of these studies, the researchers manipulated antecedent variables of teacher attention or task difficulty to show a functional relationship between these variables and the problem behaviors and implemented effective treatments based on the function of the problem behavior for each child. Figure 13-6 shows the functional analysis data from Durand and Carr (1987).

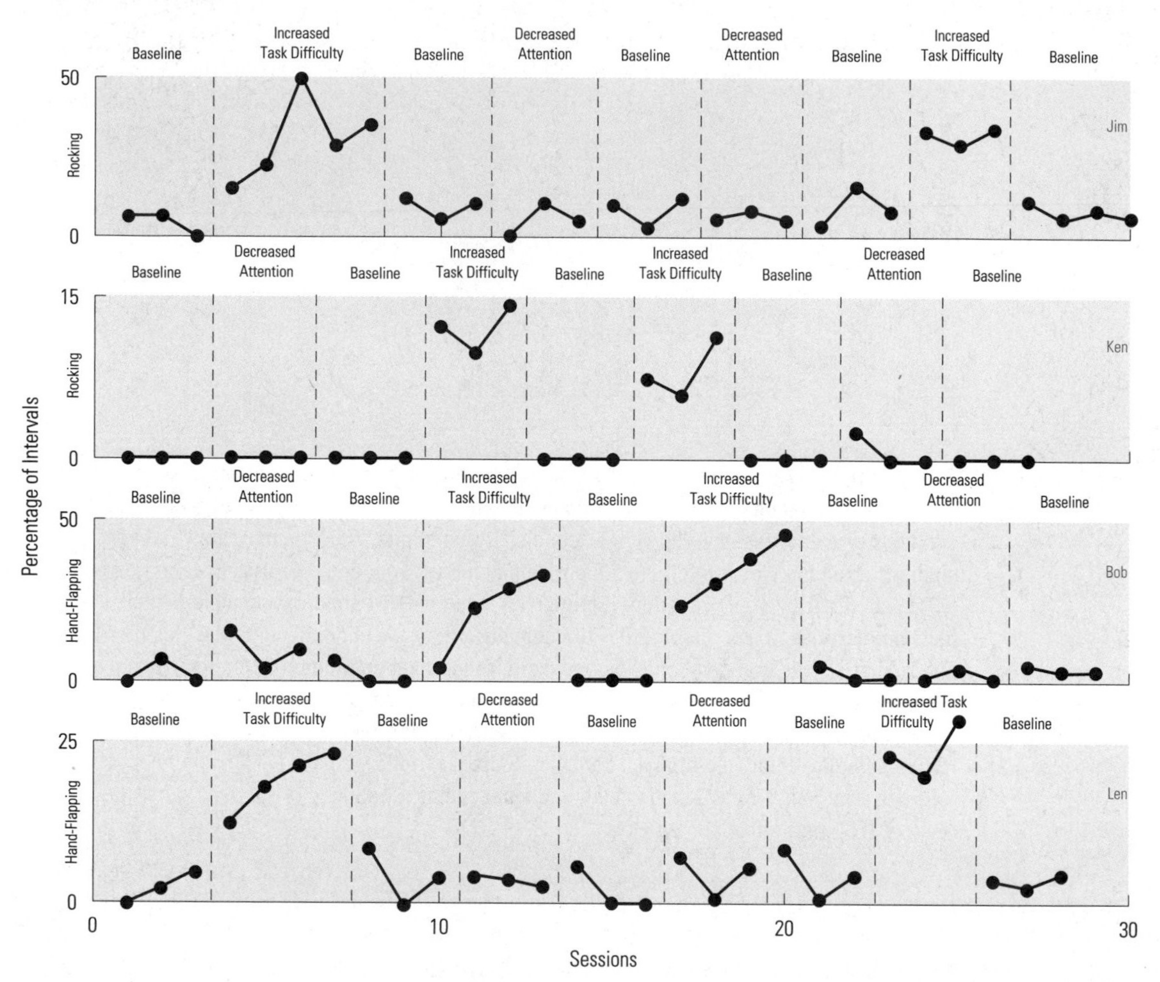

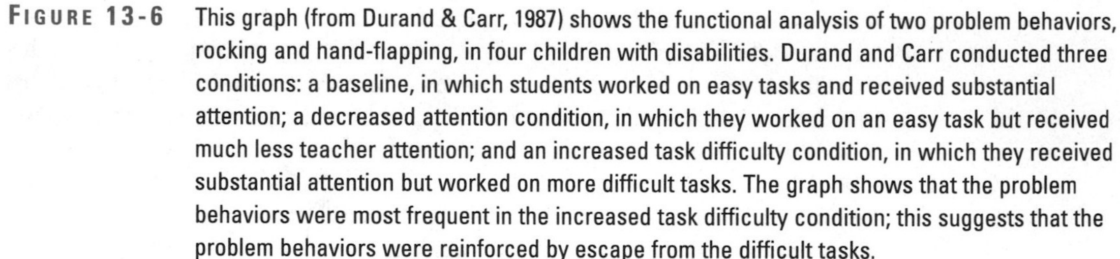

FIGURE 13-6 This graph (from Durand & Carr, 1987) shows the functional analysis of two problem behaviors, rocking and hand-flapping, in four children with disabilities. Durand and Carr conducted three conditions: a baseline, in which students worked on easy tasks and received substantial attention; a decreased attention condition, in which they worked on an easy task but received much less teacher attention; and an increased task difficulty condition, in which they received substantial attention but worked on more difficult tasks. The graph shows that the problem behaviors were most frequent in the increased task difficulty condition; this suggests that the problem behaviors were reinforced by escape from the difficult tasks.

Research by Iwata and his colleagues has illustrated the use of functional analysis methods for identifying the controlling variables for SIB. Iwata et al. (1982) worked with children and adolescents with developmental disabilities admitted to a hospital for the treatment of severe SIB. The researchers arranged different experimental conditions to determine whether the reinforcer for the SIB was attention from adults, escape from demands, or the sensory stimulation produced by the behavior itself. In the attention condition, an adult worked on a task (ignored the child) and paid attention to the child only after the occurrence of SIB. The attention from the adult involved statements of concern and prompts to stop the behavior and to engage in toy play or other activities. This condition was designed to simulate the common adult response to SIB. In the escape condition, an adult made typical educational demands on the child and, after SIB, the adult terminated the demands for a brief period. This condition was designed to simulate the situation that often occurs in the classroom when a child engages in SIB. Finally, in the alone condition, the child was put into a room alone without any toys or stimulating activities for a brief period.

Iwata compared the levels of SIB in the three experimental conditions. If the rate of SIB was high in the attention condition and low in the other conditions, it would demonstrate that attention was maintaining the SIB. If the level of SIB was high only in the demand condition, it would demonstrate that SIB was maintained by escape from demands. If the rate of SIB was high in the alone condition, it would demonstrate that the SIB was maintained by the sensory consequences produced by the behavior. Because the child was alone without any adult interaction or stimulating activities, SIB in this condition could not be reinforced by attention or escape and was presumed to be self-stimulating. Iwata called this automatic reinforcement because the behavior produces a reinforcing consequence automatically, without any response from other people in the environment.

Iwata and colleagues demonstrated that the SIB of different children had different functions. For some children, the SIB was reinforced by attention, for others by escape, and for some by sensory stimulation (automatic reinforcement). This demonstration that SIB was maintained by different types of reinforcers with different children was very important. In later research, Iwata and his colleagues carried out functional analyses of SIB exhibited by many other people with disabilities and demonstrated effective treatments for the SIB in these people (Iwata, Pace et al., 1990; Iwata, Pace, Cowdery, & Miltenberger, 1994; Lerman & Iwata, 1993; Pace, Iwata, Cowdery, Andree, & McIntyre, 1993; Smith, Iwata, Vollmer, & Zarcone, 1993; Vollmer, Iwata, Zarcone, Smith, & Mazaleski, 1993; Zarcone, Iwata, Hughes, & Vollmer, 1993). Iwata's findings, in conjunction with the findings from Carr and Durand and others, suggest that you must conduct a functional assessment of problem behaviors to understand their functions and to choose the most effective treatments.

There are advantages and disadvantages in using experimental methods (functional analysis) for the functional assessment of problem behaviors. The primary advantage is that a functional analysis demonstrates a functional relationship between the controlling variables and the problem behavior. The functional analysis provides the standard of scientific evidence that a particular type of antecedent evokes the behavior and a particular type of reinforcing consequence maintains the behavior. Descriptive methods provide less certainty, although they do allow us to formulate hypotheses about the controlling variables. The major disadvantage of conducting a functional analysis is the time, effort, and professional expertise needed to manipulate the antecedents and consequences and measure the resulting change in the behavior. A functional analysis is actually a brief experiment, and people must be trained to carry out such an experiment. Most published research on the functional assessment and treatment of problem behaviors relies on functional analysis methods, whereas practitioners using behavior modification procedures most often rely on descriptive functional assessment methods (Arndorfer & Miltenberger, 1993).

Conducting a Functional Assessment

You should always conduct some form of functional assessment before you develop treatment for a problem behavior. To develop the most appropriate treatment, you should understand the environmental events (antecedents and consequences) that control the behavior. Information on antecedents and consequences is important because treatment will involve manipulating antecedents or consequences to produce a change in the behavior (Chapters 14–16). You will need to know the antecedents that evoke the problem behavior to use antecedent control procedures, and you will need to know what the reinforcing consequence for the behavior is to use extinction and differential reinforcement procedures effectively.

Your functional assessment of a problem behavior should start with an interview with the client or other informants who know the client well and have specific knowledge of the problem behaviors. The outcome of the interview should be a clear definition of the problem behaviors and the development of hypotheses about the antecedents that evoke the behaviors and the reinforcing consequences that maintain them. This chapter focuses on this core information about controlling variables, but the interview can also yield valuable information on alternative behaviors, setting events or ecological variables, other reinforcing stimuli, and previous treatments (Table 13-2).

Once you have developed a hypothesis about the controlling variables based on information from the interview, the next step in the functional assessment is to conduct direct observations of the ABCs in the natural context. ABC observations may be conducted by the client, a professional consultant, or people in the client's environment who are trained by the consultant to conduct the observations. For example, a school psychologist might observe a child with a problem behavior in the classroom, or the psychologist might train the teacher or teacher's aide to conduct the ABC observations. It is important to take steps to reduce reactivity of the observations so that the information on the ABCs reflects the typical level of the behavior and the typical antecedents and consequences. Reactivity can be reduced through unobtrusive observation, by participant observation, or by allowing a period of time for the people in the natural setting to become accustomed to the observer.

If the information from the ABC observations is consistent with the information from the interview, the initial hypothesis about antecedents and consequences is strengthened. With a firm hypothesis from multiple sources of assessment information, you can consider the functional assessment complete and develop the most appropriate treatment. However, if the information from the ABC observations is not consistent with the interview information, another interview and further observations are needed to clarify the inconsistencies. If further descriptive assessments produce consistent information that allows you to develop firm hypotheses about the controlling antecedents and consequences, you can consider the functional assessment complete. If the information from interviews and ABC observations is still not consistent after further assessment, a functional analysis is necessary. A functional analysis is also warranted if the information from the descriptive assessments is consistent but does not lead to a firm hypothesis. Consider the following example.

Clyde, a young man with Down syndrome, started a job as part of a three-person work crew that cleaned hotel rooms, with a job coach providing training and supervision. When Clyde was asked to dust the dresser or the desk in a room, he dropped to the floor, sat with his head down, and refused to work. The job coach tried to talk Clyde into getting up and doing his job. She repeated the request, explained why Clyde needed to work, and offered rewards, but Clyde continued to sit on the floor. After a week in which the problem happened on a daily basis, the job coach called a consultant for assistance. On the basis of information from an interview with the job coach and from ABC observations, the consultant found that Clyde engaged in the problem behavior every time he was asked to work and that the job coach consistently tried to talk him into working each time he refused.

On the basis of this information, what are two possible hypotheses about the reinforcer for the problem behavior?

One possibility is that attention from the job coach reinforced Clyde's behavior. A second possibility is that escape from the dusting task reinforced Clyde's problem behavior. The only way to determine which outcome reinforced the problem behavior is to conduct a functional analysis in which these two possible reinforcers are manipulated.

How would you conduct a functional analysis of Clyde's behavior to identify the reinforcer that is maintaining the behavior?

The two variables you want to manipulate are escape and attention as consequences of the behavior. To manipulate these two variables, you arrange two conditions: attention but no escape and escape but no attention. To arrange the first condition, you tell the job coach to ask Clyde to dust and, when he drops to the floor, to provide verbal prompts and physical guidance to prompt him to get up and dust the table. In this condition, he is not escaping from the task (because the job coach is using hand-over-hand guidance to get him to dust) but he is continuing to receive attention contingent on refusing to work. In the second condition, you tell the job coach to ask Clyde to dust and, when he drops to the floor, to provide no reaction. In this condition, Clyde is escaping from the task but is not receiving attention. The job coach arranges the two conditions on alternating days to see which condition produces the highest rate of the problem behavior. If Clyde refuses to work more frequently in the first condition, it suggests that the problem behavior is reinforced by attention. If the rate of the behavior is higher in the second condition, escape is determined to be the reinforcer for the problem. If the rate of the problem behavior is high in both conditions, it suggests that the behavior is reinforced by both attention and escape.

The results of this functional analysis showed that Clyde refused to work most in the second condition and thus suggested that escape was the reinforcer for his refusal to work. On the basis of these results, treatment was developed to address the escape function of the behavior. Staff provided reinforcers for working (snacks and brief breaks) and removed the reinforcer for refusing to work by manually guiding him through the task each time he refused. (See Chapters 14, 15, and 18 for details on these procedures.)

As you can see from this example, a functional analysis does not have to be complex or difficult to implement. The essential features of a functional analysis are to have a reliable method of data collection to record the behavior in the different experimental conditions, to manipulate the antecedent or consequence while holding other variables constant, and to repeat the experimental conditions using a reversal design (or other experimental design) to demonstrate experimental control over the behavior.

CHAPTER SUMMARY

1. Conducting a functional assessment of a problem behavior is the first step in developing a treatment for the problem. The functional assessment helps you identify the antecedents that evoke the behavior and the reinforcing consequence that maintains the behavior.
2. A functional assessment may be conducted in three ways: indirect assessment, direct observation assessment, and experimental or functional analysis.
3. In an indirect assessment, you gather information on the antecedents and consequences of the target behavior from informants (people who know the client well and are familiar with the problem behavior) using behavioral interviews or questionnaires.
4. In a direct observation assessment (ABC recording), you observe and record the antecedents, behavior, and consequences as they occur in the natural context. ABC recording can be done using a descriptive method, a checklist method, or an interval method.
5. Experimental methods for conducting a functional assessment involve the manipulation of antecedents or consequences to determine their influence on the behavior. Experimental methods, also known as functional analysis or experimental analysis, allow you to establish a functional relationship between the antecedents and consequences and the problem behavior.

PRACTICE TEST

1. What is a functional assessment of a problem behavior? Why is it important to conduct a functional assessment? (p. 257)
2. Identify and describe the four possible functions of problem behaviors. (pp. 261–262)
3. Identify and describe the three major methods for conducting a functional assessment of a problem behavior. (pp. 262–272)
4. Identify and describe two ways to conduct an indirect assessment. (pp. 263–265)
5. Identify a number of questions you could ask in an interview to determine the antecedents and consequences of a problem behavior. (p. 264)
6. Identify and describe three ways to conduct ABC direct observation assessments. (pp. 268–269)
7. What are descriptive functional assessment methods? (p. 270)
8. Descriptive assessment methods do not demonstrate a functional relationship between the antecedents and consequences and the problem behavior. Explain that statement. (p. 270)
9. What is the outcome of descriptive functional assessment methods? (p. 270)
10. Describe how a functional analysis demonstrates a functional relationship between the antecedents and consequences and the problem behavior. (p. 270)
11. What is the difference between a functional assessment and a functional analysis? (p. 270)
12. What is the first step in conducting a functional assessment? (p. 276)

13. At what point would you consider your functional assessment of a problem behavior complete? Provide an example. (p. 276)
14. Under what circumstances do you need to conduct a functional analysis of a problem behavior? Provide an example. (p. 276)
15. Describe the three essential features of a functional analysis. (p. 278)
16. Iwata and his colleagues found three types of reinforcers for self-injurious behavior in children and adolescents with developmental disabilities. What were they? (p. 275)
17. Describe the three experimental conditions in the functional analysis of self-injurious behavior conducted by Iwata and his colleagues. (pp. 274–275)

APPLICATIONS

1. If the goal of your self-management project is to decrease an undesirable behavior, describe how you will conduct a functional assessment of that behavior. Describe each of the functional assessment methods you will use to identify the controlling variables for your target behavior.

2. Luther, an 80-year-old man, was recently admitted to a nursing home because he had Alzheimer's disease and his wife could no longer take care of him at home. Luther had spent his life as a farmer. This was the first time he had ever lived anywhere in which his freedom of movement was restricted. Luther could not leave the nursing home by himself and had to learn to adapt to the daily routine in the nursing home. Although the Alzheimer's disease had impaired Luther's memory, he was still physically fit, and he enjoyed walking around the building and talking to the staff and other residents. Shortly after he moved into the nursing home, Luther started to exhibit a problem behavior: He walked outside alone. He was not allowed to go outside alone for safety reasons, but he walked out the door a number of times each day. When the weather was cold, he walked outside without a coat. The staff had to bring him back inside each time. The nursing home has a main door near the nurse's station, another door near the business office, and three fire doors at the sides and back of the building. The building has four wings that form a square with a totally enclosed courtyard in the center of the building. Two doors open to the courtyard. Four hallways, one down every wing of the building, come together to form a square. Assume that you are a behavioral consultant who has been called by the nursing home staff to help them deal with Luther's problem behavior. The staff does not know whether the problem is caused by the Alzheimer's disease, which causes Luther to become confused so that he doesn't know where he is or where he is going, or whether it is the result of some contingencies of reinforcement operating in the nursing home. Your first step in developing a treatment strategy is to conduct a functional assessment to determine why the problem is occurring. You have scheduled a group interview with some of the staff who work regularly with Luther. Provide a list of the questions you will ask the staff to assess the antecedent events, the problem behavior, and the consequences of the problem.

3. Interview questions from Application 2 and their answers are provided here.

Problem behavior:

Q: What exactly does Luther do when he walks outside?

A: He just walks up to the door, opens it, and starts to go outside.

Q: Does he say or do anything as he is walking out the door?

A: He sometimes mumbles to himself about going to see his wife or going to see somebody. Or he says he has to go outside without giving a reason. Sometimes he says nothing and just walks outside. He usually looks at the nurse who is at the nursing station as he walks out the door.

Q: What does he do once he is outside?

A: He's not outside for more than a few seconds because a staff person goes after him and brings him back in. Usually, he gets outside and just stands a few feet from the door. Often, he turns and looks back in the building. Sometimes, the nurse sees him going for the door and stops him before he even gets outside.

Antecedents:

Q: What is Luther usually doing right before he walks out the door?

A: Usually, he is walking around the hallways or hanging around by the door.

Q: Is he usually by himself or with somebody when he walks out the door?

A: He likes to talk to people when he's walking around the halls, but he is most often alone when he goes for the door.

Q: What door is he most likely to go out?

A: He's tried them all, but most of the time he goes out by the main nurse's station.

Q: Does he ever walk out the door to the courtyard?

A: No, hardly ever.

Q: What time of day is he most likely to walk out?

A: Usually when the staff are the most busy: when they are providing care routines with the other residents, before meals when they are helping other residents, and at shift changes.

Q: Is there someone at the nurse's station when he walks out?

A: Almost always. We have someone at the nurse's station almost all the time.

Q: Even at busy times?

A: Yes. Usually the nurse is charting or doing paperwork at the nurse's station at that time.

Consequences:

Q: What happens as soon as Luther walks out the door?

A: A staff person runs out after him and brings him back. Usually it is the nurse or nursing assistant at the nurse's station who sees him leave.

Q: What happens then?

A: The nurse or nursing assistant walks back with Luther and tells him why he can't go outside by himself. The staff person usually takes him to the break room and sits down with him for a few minutes with a cookie or cup of coffee. The staff tries to get him interested in something other than leaving. It usually takes 5 minutes or more each time he tries to go outside.

Q: What would happen if Luther went out the door to the courtyard?

A: He has done that only once or twice. When he went out in the courtyard, staff left him alone because it is enclosed and he couldn't wander away or harm himself. He doesn't go out that door anymore.

On the basis of this information, what is your initial hypothesis about the function of Luther's problem behavior? Describe the ABC observation procedure you will develop in conjunction with the nursing home staff. Describe the data sheet you will use and the instructions you will give to the staff to carry out the direct observation procedure.

4. The ABC observation procedure for Luther is described here, along with the information derived from the ABC observation.

Because Luther almost always goes out the door by the nurse's station, the data sheet will be kept at the nurse's station. Having already gathered information on probable antecedents and consequences, the consultant will have staff record ABCs using a checklist. The checklist will itemize the probable antecedents and consequences; the staff will put a check mark in the column that corresponds to the relevant events. The staff will also record the time of the behavior. The data sheet will have a column for the time of the behavior, a column where the staff member who observes the behavior puts his or her initials, and columns for each of the antecedents and consequences, as follows.

Antecedents:

- Luther is alone or no one is talking to him.
- Luther is walking the hallways.
- Luther looks at the nurse at the nurse's station as he goes for the door or goes out the door.

Consequences:

- Staff run after Luther and walk him back.
- Staff talk to Luther as they walk with him.
- Staff spend time with Luther after he is back in the building.
- Luther gets coffee or cookies.

Staff will record these events immediately each time the problem behavior occurs for 1 week.

The results of the ABC observations were as follows. The problem behavior happened an average of five times per day. Luther was alone or no one was talking to him 100% of the times that the problem occurred. He was walking the hallways or hanging around the door 100% of the time and he looked at the nurse in the nurse's station 90% of the time before he walked out the door. When Luther walked out the door, 100% of the time a staff person ran after him and talked to him as he or she brought him back. A staff person spent a few minutes with him every time but one, and he got coffee and cookies 50% of the time.

Does this information support your initial hypothesis developed from the interview? Explain. On the basis of the information from the interview and ABC observations, describe the functional analysis procedure you will use to confirm your hypothesis about the function of the problem. Describe the two functional analysis conditions you will have the nurses conduct with Luther. Describe the type of results you expect from the functional analysis procedure.

MISAPPLICATIONS

1. Hanna, a first grade student, was exhibiting disruptive behaviors in the classroom. She was out of her seat frequently; she talked, teased other students, and got into the supply cabinet. To decrease this behavior, the teacher came up with the following plan. He decided to ignore Hanna's disruptive behavior and to praise Hanna whenever she was in her seat paying attention and not exhibiting disruptive behavior. He believed that the use of differential reinforcement (extinction of the disruptive behavior and reinforcement of appropriate behavior) would decrease the disruptive behavior while increasing the appropriate behavior. What is wrong with this plan?

2. After talking to the school psychologist, Hanna's teacher learned that before you decide on a treatment for a problem behavior, you must conduct a functional assessment of the problem to identify the environmental variables that are causing the behavior. The school psychologist wanted the teacher to collect information on the antecedents and consequences of the problem behavior by conducting ABC observations in the classroom. The psychologist gave the teacher a data sheet with three columns: one for antecedents, one for the problem behavior, and one for the consequences. The psychologist asked the teacher to keep the data sheet on his desk and, each time Hanna exhibited a problem behavior, to get the data sheet and write down a description of the antecedents, a description of the behavior, and a description of the consequences. The psychologist told the teacher that they could get a good understanding of why the problem behavior was occurring if the teacher would do this ABC recording each day for a week. What is wrong with the functional assessment method used in this situation?

3. The director of a residential program for people with severe mental retardation asked the staff to do behavioral observations of two residents who were having behavioral difficulties and to develop hypotheses about why their behavior problems were occurring. One resident, Robyn, engaged in aggressive behavior in which she screamed at and slapped staff when they asked that she engage in some training activities. The other resident, Melvin, engaged in disruptive behavior in which he knocked items off the table and grabbed recreational items (e.g., games, magazines, and needlework) from other residents.

The staff hypothesized that Robyn was frustrated with the daily expectations that staff had for her and the demands that they placed on her. They hypothesized that she was communicating her feelings of displeasure with staff. For Melvin, staff hypothesized that he was bored and jealous of other residents who were engaging in recreational activities. They hypothesized that his disruptive behavior was a demonstration of his boredom and jealousy. What is wrong with this approach to functional assessment to identify the variables responsible for Robyn's and Melvin's problem behaviors? How could the staff improve their functional assessment?

CHAPTER 13 *Quiz 1* Name:

1. You conduct a(n) ____________________ to identify the antecedents and consequences of a problem behavior.
2. What are the four broad classes of functions (or reinforcing consequences) of problem behaviors? ____________________, ____________________, ____________________, and ____________________
3. Indirect assessment, direct observation, and functional analysis are three ____________________ methods.
4. Another name for experimental analysis is ____________________.
5. What are two ways you can conduct an indirect functional assessment? ____________________ and ____________________
6. Which functional assessment method involves asking others for information? ____________________
7. In which functional assessment method might you use a scatter plot? ____________________
8. Which functional assessment method demonstrates a functional relationship between the antecedents/consequences and the problem behavior? ____________________
9. What are three direct observation methods for conducting a functional assessment? ____________________, ____________________, ____________________
10. In a functional analysis, you manipulate ____________________ and/or ____________________ to determine their effect on the behavior.

CHAPTER 13 *Quiz 2* Name:

1. A functional assessment is conducted to identify the ____________________ and ____________________ of a problem behavior.
2. When a behavior produces a reinforcing consequence automatically (the reinforcing consequence is not delivered by a person), the behavior is said to be maintained by ____________________ reinforcement.
3. When another person terminates an aversive interaction, task, or activity after the occurrence of the behavior, the behavior is said to be maintained by ____________________ reinforcement.
4. Identify the three methods for conducting a functional assessment. ______________, ______________, ______________
5. If you record the problem behavior and possible antecedents and consequences of the behavior in consecutive intervals of time, what functional assessment method are you using? ____________________
6. If you have a checklist of possible antecedents and consequences of a problem behavior, and you check off each antecedent and consequence as the problem occurs, what functional assessment method are you using? ____________________
7. If you ask the parents of an autistic child to describe the events that occur before and after self-injurious behavior, what functional assessment method are you using? ______________
8. The descriptive method, checklist method, and interval or real time recording are three ways to conduct ____________________.
9. A person has a rash that itches. If he scratches the rash to relieve the itching, the scratching is maintained by ____________________ reinforcement.
10. If a person tells outrageous stories because his friends give him substantial attention when he tells the stories, telling outrageous stories is maintained by ______________ reinforcement.

CHAPTER 13 *Quiz 3* Name:

1. ______________________ is the process of gathering information on the antecedents and consequences that are functionally related to the occurrence of the problem behavior.

2. When a behavior automatically reduces or eliminates an aversive stimulus, we say that the behavior is maintained by ______________________________ reinforcement.

3. When a positively reinforcing consequence is delivered by another person after the behavior, the behavior is said to be maintained by ______________________ reinforcement.

4. Which functional assessment method involves the use of interviews or questionnaires?

   ____

5. Which functional assessment method involves observation of the antecedents and consequences as the problem behavior occurs? ___________________________

6. Which functional assessment method can be conducted descriptively or with a checklist?

   ____

7. Which functional assessment method involves manipulation of possible antecedents and/or consequences of the problem behavior? ______________________________

8. If Nancy has a headache, the pain is lessened if she closes the blinds and makes the room darker. The behavior of closing the blinds when she has a headache is maintained by

   ________________________ reinforcement.

9. If Nancy has a headache, the pain is lessened if she closes the blinds and makes the room darker. The behavior of asking her boyfriend to close the blinds when she has a headache is maintained by ______________________ reinforcement.

10. What two functional assessment methods do not demonstrate a functional relationship between the antecedents/consequences and the problem behavior? ______________________ and

    ____

FOURTEEN

Applying Extinction

After you have conducted a functional assessment of a problem behavior, you will implement one or more treatment procedures to alter the antecedents and/or consequences of the problem behavior. This chapter describes the use of extinction to eliminate a problem behavior. As you recall from Chapter 5, extinction is a basic principle of behavior in which eliminating the reinforcing consequence for a behavior results in a decrease in the frequency of the behavior. To use extinction, you must first identify the reinforcer that maintains the problem behavior and then eliminate it. A behavior that is no longer reinforced will decrease in frequency and stop. Consider the following example.

- Why is it important to conduct a functional assessment before using an extinction procedure?
- What five questions must you address before using an extinction procedure?
- How does the schedule of reinforcement for a behavior influence extinction?
- Why is it important to reinforce alternative behaviors when using extinction?
- How can you promote generalization and maintenance after the use of extinction?

The Case of Willy

Willy, a 54-year-old man with mild mental retardation, recently moved into a group home because his parents were no longer able to take care of him. He had lived his entire life with his mother and father before coming to the group home. In the group home, Willy exhibited a problem behavior: He argued when he was asked by a staff person to do a training activity such as cooking, cleaning, laundry, or another independent living skill. The functional assessment interview and ABC observations produced the following information on the behavior problem, antecedents, and consequences. The antecedent situation was that a female staff person asked Willy to perform a daily living task. Willy did not exhibit the problem behavior when a male staff person asked him to perform a task. The problem behavior was that Willy verbally refused to do the task and made statements such as, "That's women's work" or, "A woman ought to do that" or, "That ain't man's work." This behavior continued for up to 15 minutes, but usually he completed the task eventually. The consequence of Willy's behavior was that the female staff member argued with Willy, told him that he was making sexist comments, and tried to convince him that men have to do these tasks also. The female staff member often became visibly upset at Willy's sexist remarks and usually argued with him until he started to perform the task.

The assessment information led to the hypothesis that the antecedent event was that a female staff member made a request for Willy to complete a task and that the staff person's attention (arguing, explaining, emotional reactions) after the problem behavior was the reinforcing consequence. Negative reinforcement (escape) did not appear to play a role because Willy eventually completed the requested task.

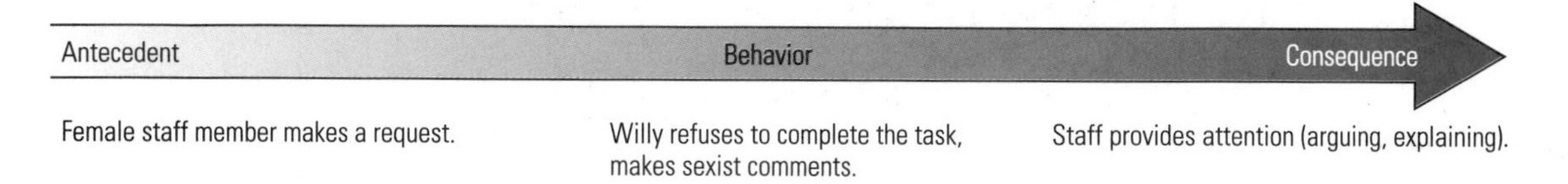
Antecedent
Behavior
Consequence
Female staff member makes a request.
Willy refuses to complete the task, makes sexist comments.
Staff provides attention (arguing, explaining).

Outcome: Willy is more likely to refuse to do tasks and to make sexist remarks when female staff members make a request.

The staff wanted to decrease the frequency of Willy's sexist comments and refusal to complete tasks. The functional assessment results suggested that to decrease the problem behavior, female staff members would have to eliminate their attention after the behavior. The group home manager held a meeting with the staff to teach them how to use extinction with Willy.

First, she told the staff about the finding of the functional assessment: that female staff members' attention appeared to be reinforcing the problem behavior. She then told them that they would have to eliminate the reinforcer for the problem behavior for the behavior to decrease. She gave the staff the following instructions. "Whenever you make a request for Willy to complete a task and he refuses or makes sexist comments, do not repeat the request and do not respond to Willy in any way. Do not argue with him. Do not try to talk him into doing the task. Do not try to explain to him that his sexist remarks are unacceptable. Do not show Willy any kind of emotional reaction. Do not make a face that looks disappointed or upset. Simply walk away and engage in another activity when Willy engages in the problem behavior."

After providing these instructions for the use of extinction, the group home manager modeled the use of extinction for her staff. She had another staff person role-play Willy refusing a request and making sexist comments and, in response, she simply walked away and made no response to Willy's problem behavior. Next, she role-played Willy and had each of the staff rehearse the use of the extinction procedure in response to Willy's problem behavior. After each of the staff had demonstrated the use of extinction in the role-plays with different variations of Willy's problem behavior, she instructed the staff to use the procedure with Willy whenever he engaged in the problem behavior in response to a request. She warned the staff that they all had to use the extinction procedure consistently and that they had to ignore Willy's sexist remarks no matter how upsetting they were. She emphasized that if just one person continued to respond to Willy's problem behavior with attention, Willy would continue to engage in the problem and the extinction procedure would not be successful. She also warned the staff members that Willy might escalate in his behavior when they started using extinction. His refusals might become louder or longer, and he might make more upsetting comments. The staff should be ready for this extinction burst and continue to ignore this behavior.

In conjunction with this extinction procedure, the group home manager instructed staff members to praise Willy as soon as he started to engage in the task that they requested. She told the staff that they must reinforce Willy's cooperative behavior with their attention so that this behavior would increase as his problem behavior decreased. Because Willy would no longer receive staff attention for refusing and making sexist comments, it was important for Willy to receive staff attention for the desirable behavior.

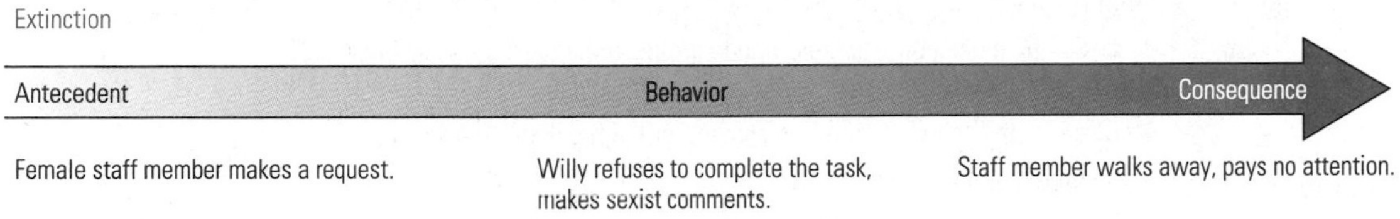

Extinction

Antecedent	Behavior	Consequence
Female staff member makes a request.	Willy refuses to complete the task, makes sexist comments.	Staff member walks away, pays no attention.

Outcome: Willy is less likely to refuse requests and make sexist comments in the future.

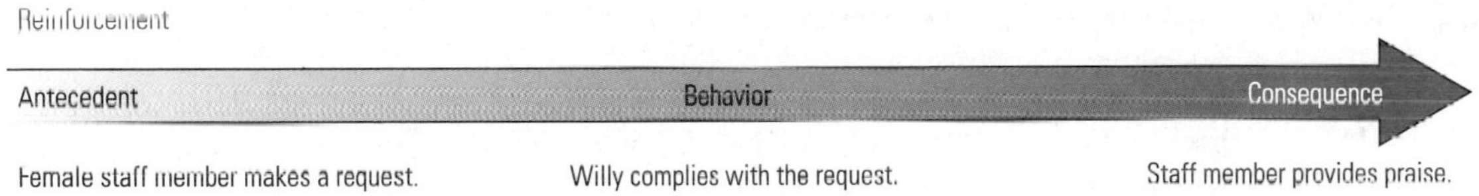

Reinforcement

Antecedent	Behavior	Consequence
Female staff member makes a request.	Willy complies with the request.	Staff member provides praise.

Outcome: Willy is more likely to comply with staff requests in the future.

To promote generalization of the behavior change, the group home manager emphasized that all staff must use the extinction procedure (and the reinforcement procedure) at all times and in all situations with Willy. This meant that all new staff and substitute staff must be trained to use the procedure. Furthermore, she had a meeting with Willy's parents and asked for their help when Willy visited them on the weekend. Because she did not want the behavior reinforced on the weekends, she asked Willy's parents to do one of two things. They could refrain from asking Willy to do any tasks when he was home, or they could use the extinction procedure in the same way that the staff were using it. By not asking Willy to do any tasks, they would be using a stimulus control procedure in which they removed the antecedent for the behavior problem so that the behavior problem would not occur. Willy couldn't refuse to do a task if he was never asked to do one. Because Willy's mother had always done everything for him in the past anyway, she was most comfortable with this option.

Staff members collected data on the percentage of times that Willy refused to complete tasks and found that his refusals decreased over time once the extinction procedure was implemented. He continued to refuse once in a while, but staff did not reinforce the behavior and the refusals did not last very long. Most often, Willy completed the tasks that staff had requested as soon as they asked him.

This example illustrates the steps involved in using extinction to decrease a problem behavior (Table 14-1).

14-1 Steps in Using Extinction

1. Collect data to assess treatment effects.
2. Identify the reinforcer for the problem behavior through functional assessment.
3. Eliminate the reinforcer after each instance of the problem behavior
   - Have you identified the reinforcer?
   - Can you eliminate the reinforcer?
   - Is extinction safe to use?
   - Can an extinction burst (escalation of the problem behavior) be tolerated?
   - Can consistency be maintained?
4. Consider the schedule of reinforcement for the problem behavior.
5. Reinforce alternative behaviors.
6. Promote generalization and maintenance.

USING EXTINCTION TO DECREASE A PROBLEM BEHAVIOR

Extinction is one of the first approaches that should be considered for treating a problem behavior. As long as a problem behavior continues, there must be a reinforcing consequence contingent on the behavior that is maintaining it. Therefore, to decrease the behavior, an important step is to identify the reinforcing consequence and eliminate it (whenever possible). When the problem behavior is no longer reinforced, it will extinguish. Let's examine the steps involved in using extinction procedures effectively (Ducharme & Van Houten, 1994).

Collecting Data to Assess Treatment Effects

As you recall from Chapters 2 and 3, observation and recording of the target behavior are important components of a behavior modification program. You must record the problem behavior before and after the use of the extinction procedure to determine whether the behavior decreased when extinction was implemented. You will need a behavioral definition of the problem behavior to be decreased, a reliable data collection method, a baseline assessment to determine the level of the problem behavior before the use of extinction, data collection in all relevant settings after treatment to determine whether the behavior decreased and whether generalization occurred, and continued data collection over time to assess the maintenance of behavior change. If you are conducting research to experimentally evaluate the effects of the extinction procedure, an acceptable research design (Chapter 3) and assessment of observer reliability also are needed. The basic point to remember is that if you are going to use an extinction procedure (or any other behavior modification procedure), you must collect data on the problem behavior to document the change in behavior after the use of the procedure. If your recording of the problem behavior shows that the behavior did not change after treatment, you can reassess the problem or the implementation of the extinction procedure and make whatever changes are necessary to decrease the problem behavior.

Identifying the Reinforcer for the Problem Behavior through Functional Assessment

In functional assessment, you identify the antecedents and consequences of the problem behavior (Chapter 13). This is a critical step in using extinction procedures effectively. You must identify the specific reinforcer for the problem behavior so that you can eliminate it in an extinction procedure. You cannot assume that a particular reinforcer is maintaining a problem behavior. The same problem behavior exhibited by different people may be maintained by different reinforcers. For example, one child's aggressive behavior might be reinforced by the parents' attention, whereas another child's aggressive behavior might be reinforced by getting toys from siblings. Sometimes, the same behavior exhibited by a particular person in different situations might be maintained by different reinforcers (e.g., Romaniuk et al., 2002). For example, a young child cries when she has trouble tying her shoes, and the crying is reinforced when the parents help her tie the shoes. This same child might cry when the parents make a request (e.g., to brush her teeth), and the crying is reinforced when the parents allow her to escape from the task that was requested. A behavior may serve different functions in different contexts (Day, Horner, & O'Neill, 1994; Haring & Kennedy, 1990).

The success of an extinction procedure depends on whether the particular reinforcer maintaining the problem behavior has been identified. A variety of stimulus events may function as reinforcers for problem behaviors. Problem behaviors may be maintained by positive reinforcement when the behavior results in the presentation of a stimulus event or negative reinforcement when the behavior results in escape from some stimulus event. The reinforcing consequence may involve the behavior of another person or a change in a physical (nonsocial) stimulus. Table 14-2 describes a variety of problem behaviors and the stimulus events reinforcing those behaviors.

For each problem behavior in Table 14-2, identify whether the example illustrates social positive reinforcement, social negative reinforcement, automatic positive reinforcement, or automatic negative reinforcement. (Answers appear in Appendix A.)

Eliminating the Reinforcer after Each Instance of the Problem Behavior

Extinction, by definition, involves eliminating the reinforcer after each instance of the problem behavior. Although this may seem straightforward, a number of considerations must be addressed for the successful use of extinction.

Have You Identified the Reinforcer? Obviously, you cannot eliminate the reinforcer for the problem behavior until you have identified it by means of a functional assessment. Failure to eliminate the particular stimulus event that functions as the reinforcer for the problem behavior is failure to implement the extinction procedure correctly (Mazaleski, Iwata, Vollmer, Zarcone, & Smith, 1993).

The extinction procedure may be different depending on the reinforcer that is maintaining the problem behavior. For example, when Iwata and his colleagues worked with three children with developmental disabilities who engaged in self-injurious behavior (SIB)—head-banging—they found that the reinforcer for the SIB

TABLE 14-2 EXAMPLES FOR SELF-ASSESSMENT (PROBLEM BEHAVIORS AND REINFORCERS)

Problem Behavior	Reinforcing Consequence
1. A child complains of being sick when told to do chores.	A parent does the household tasks for the child. +
2. A person with mental retardation runs into the street and refuses to leave the street.	A staff member offers a can of soda if the person leaves the street. +
3. A spouse has a temper outburst during a disagreement.	The other spouse stops arguing and agrees to the spouse's demand. −
4. A child with autism flicks his fingers in front of his eyes.	This behavior produces visual stimulation. +
5. A person runs away from a dog while walking down the street.	The person gets away from the dog, and the fear reaction diminishes. −
6. A child refuses to comply with a parent's request to do a task.	The child avoids the task and continues to watch television. +
7. A child refuses to comply with a parent's request to do a task.	The parent repeats the request, pleads with the child, and scolds the child. +
8. A hospital patient calls the nurses' station several times a day.	A nurse comes to the room each time to check on the patient but finds no problem. +
9. A patient with a brain injury strips naked each time the nurse enters the room for the morning routine.	The nurse reacts with surprise and indignation and orders the patient to get dressed. +
10. A factory worker on an assembly line sabotages the line so that it stops.	The factory worker sits down and has a cigarette and a cup of coffee each time the line is down. − +

was different for each child (Iwata, Pace, Cowdery, & Miltenberger, 1994). For one child, SIB was reinforced by attention from adults. For another child, SIB was reinforced by escape from educational demands. For the third child, SIB was reinforced automatically by the sensory consequences of the behavior itself. Iwata demonstrated that the extinction procedure was different for each child because the reinforcer for the SIB was different for each child.

How did Iwata implement extinction for the SIB that was reinforced by attention from adults?

Because the SIB was maintained by attention, extinction involved eliminating the attention after each instance of SIB. This particular child, Millie, was an 8-year-old who banged her head on flat surfaces such as a wall or the floor. When she banged her head, the adult who was present did not respond in any way, no matter how long the head-banging continued (Figure 14-1). (It is important to note that precautions were taken so that the child could not hurt herself.) However, the adult did provide atten-

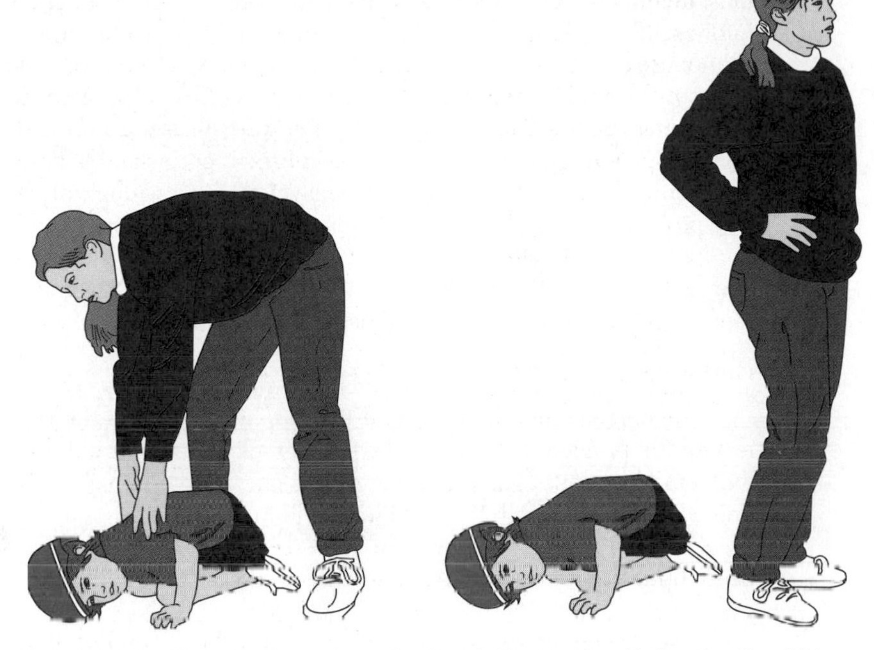

FIGURE 14-1 The child's head-banging is reinforced by the adult's attention. Notice that the child wears a helmet for safety. The adult removes the reinforcer for head-banging by not paying attention to the behavior. Because the behavior is no longer reinforced, it will stop.

tion when Millie did not bang her head. This procedure, in which a reinforcer is delivered for the absence of the problem behavior, is described in Chapter 15.

How did Iwata implement extinction for the SIB that was reinforced by escape from educational demands?

Because the SIB was reinforced by escape from educational demands, extinction involved eliminating escape after the SIB. This particular child, Jack, was a 12-year-old boy. He engaged in the SIB in teaching situations when the teacher asked him to perform learning tasks such as object identification or simple motor tasks. When the SIB occurred, the teacher used physical guidance so that Jack could not escape from the task. Regardless of how long he engaged in the SIB, the teacher continued to present the educational demands and used physical guidance to prevent escape. The teacher also provided praise when the child complied with the educational tasks.

Donnie, the third child in Iwata's study, was a 7-year-old boy who engaged in SIB that was automatically reinforced. Because there was no social reinforcement for the head-banging, it was presumed to be reinforced by the sensory consequences generated by the behavior. Iwata and his colleagues used sensory extinction: They put a padded helmet on Donnie so that the sensory consequences of the head-banging would be altered. If the head-banging no longer produced the same sensory reinforcement, the behavior would extinguish. The results showed that the SIB decreased when Donnie wore the padded helmet.

This study (Iwata et al., 1994) convincingly illustrates that to use extinction, you must identify the reinforcer for the particular problem behavior and eliminate that reinforcer. If you do not identify the reinforcer for a particular problem behavior, you cannot use extinction. For example, imagine a parent whose 3-year-old child gets cookies from the cookie jar frequently throughout the day. The parent wants the child to stop taking cookies from the cookie jar. Because of a limited understanding of extinction, the parent ignores the behavior each time it occurs and believes that not providing attention will decrease the child's behavior. What is wrong with the parent's action? The problem is that taking cookies from the cookie jar is reinforced by eating cookies, not by the parent's attention. Therefore, eliminating the attention after the behavior does not eliminate the reinforcer for the behavior. The behavior continues to be reinforced and, therefore, continues to occur (Martin & Pear, 1992).

How would the parent implement extinction in this case?

The parent would implement extinction by eliminating the reinforcer (the cookies) for the problem behavior. If the parent took the cookies out of the cookie jar, the problem behavior of going into the cookie jar would no longer be reinforced by getting cookies. As a result, the child would quit going into the cookie jar.

For each problem behavior in Table 14-2, describe how you would implement extinction. (Answers are in Appendix B.)

Can You Eliminate the Reinforcer? After you have conducted a functional assessment to identify the reinforcer for the problem behavior, you must determine whether the change agent (parent, teacher, staff member, nurse, client) can control the reinforcer. If the change agent has no control over the reinforcer, extinction cannot be implemented. For example, in the case of Willy's noncompliance and sexist comments, the reinforcer for Willy's problem behavior was attention from the staff. This reinforcer is under the control of the change agents, the staff members. They can withhold their attention after the problem behavior, and they can provide their attention after Willy's cooperative behavior. Therefore, they can successfully implement the extinction procedure.

For some problem behaviors, however, the change agents do not have control over the reinforcer. If a grade school boy threatens to hurt other children to get their lunch money, the reinforcer for this behavior is the receipt of the money (and perhaps other reactions of the victims). The teacher does not have control over this reinforcer because the problem behavior happens when the teacher or another adult is not present. Therefore, the teacher cannot use extinction. The teacher could instruct the class not to give away their lunch money when they are threatened, but it is likely that the problem behavior will still be reinforced at least occasionally by children who continue to give away their money when they are threatened. Consider another example.

A teenager plays her stereo so loudly that it disturbs the rest of the family. The reinforcer for this behavior is the loud music. (Assume you have ruled out the parents' attention as the reinforcer.) Unless the parents have installed an electronic device on the stereo that does not permit the volume to be turned up beyond a certain level, the parents do not have control over this reinforcer. The teenager's behavior of turning the knob on the stereo is immediately reinforced each time by an increase in the loudness of the music. The parents might ask her to turn it down or implement a punishment procedure to decrease the behavior, but they cannot use extinction because the loudness of the music (the reinforcer) is not under their control.

When considering the use of extinction to decrease a problem behavior, you must determine that the change agent can control the reinforcer maintaining the problem behavior. Extinction can be implemented only if the change agent can prevent the reinforcing consequence each time the problem behavior occurs.

Is Extinction Safe to Use? Before deciding to use extinction, it is important to determine whether extinction could result in harm to the person exhibiting the problem behavior or to other people in the immediate environment. Consider the following examples.

Rupert is a young man with severe mental retardation who works in a sheltered workshop during the day. He sits at a table with three other people and assembles parts for a local factory. Rupert engages in a problem behavior in which he attacks the people at his table. He grabs people by the hair and hits their heads on the table. When this happens, staff members immediately intervene and separate Rupert from the other person. The functional assessment identified staff attention as the reinforcer maintaining this problem behavior. Extinction would require the staff to provide no attention after each instance of the problem. However, it would be extremely harmful to the person being attacked if the staff did not intervene immediately. In this case, therefore, extinction is not a safe procedure and cannot be used.

Now consider the case of 4-year-old Annie, who runs out in the street when she is playing in the front yard. The babysitter, who is usually sitting in the front yard reading a book or magazine, yells for Annie to get out of the street. When Annie refuses, the babysitter runs out into the street to get her. The reinforcer for this behavior is the babysitter's attention. However, extinction cannot be used in this case because it is not safe to ignore a child when she runs into the street. Other procedures, such as differential reinforcement or antecedent control, should be used instead. (See Chapters 15–18.)

Bucky is an 18-year-old man with mental retardation in a residential training program. The staff are trying to teach him some basic self-care skills, such as shaving and toothbrushing. The problem is that Bucky engages in aggressive behavior (hair pulling, scratching, and pinching) when a staff member attempts to teach him these skills. When Bucky grabs the staff member's hair or scratches or pinches the staff member, the session is terminated. As a result, Bucky's aggressive behavior is negatively reinforced by escape from the training session. Extinction in this case would involve continuing the training session when Bucky engaged in aggressive behavior so that the problem behavior did not result in escape. However, it is dangerous for staff members to continue the session when Bucky is aggressive toward them, so it is difficult to use extinction. In this case, a procedure such as response blocking or brief restraint might facilitate the use of extinction (see Chapter 18).

As you now see, even if you have identified the reinforcer for the problem behavior and the change agent has control over the reinforcer, you cannot use extinction until you are certain that it is safe to eliminate the reinforcer.

Can an Extinction Burst (Escalation of the Problem Behavior) Be Tolerated? As you know from Chapter 5, the use of extinction often is accompanied by an extinction burst, in which the behavior increases in frequency, duration, or intensity or novel behaviors or emotional responses occur (Goh & Iwata, 1994; Lerman, Iwata, & Wallace, 1999; Vollmer et al., 1998). Before you decide to use extinction, you must anticipate the extinction burst and be certain that the change agents can tolerate the escalation in the behavior. Consider the case of a 5-year-old girl with bedtime tantrums. When taken to bed, she screams and cries. After her parents leave the room, she calls for them. When she exhibits these behaviors, the parents go into her room to calm her down and talk to her until she is asleep. Their attention is reinforcing the problem behavior. The parents could use extinction to decrease and eliminate the problem behavior, but they must realize that as soon as they no longer respond to the tantrums, the child is likely to exhibit an extinction burst in which the problem behavior escalates; she will engage in tantrum behavior that is more intense and lasts longer. If the parents are not prepared for this outcome, the use of extinction may fail. The first time the parents ignore the tantrums at bedtime and the problem behavior escalates, they might become concerned or frustrated and go into the child's room, thereby reinforcing the tantrum behavior. This is likely to make the problem even worse because the parents will reinforce the problem behavior at its higher level. As you learned in Chapter 9, serious problem behaviors often are shaped in this way.

When using an extinction procedure, you must inform the change agent of the escalation that is likely to occur during an extinction burst. Furthermore, you must instruct the change agent to persist in withholding the reinforcer as the problem behavior escalates. If escalation of the behavior is likely to harm the person with the problem behavior or other people, you must devise a plan to eliminate or minimize the harm. Iwata put a helmet on the young girl who engaged in head-banging so that she would not cause harm to herself during the extinction procedure (Iwata et al., 1994). Carr had teachers wear protective clothing to protect them from the aggressive behavior of two boys during an extinction procedure (Carr, Newsom, & Binkoff, 1980). You might instruct parents to remove breakable objects from the room when using extinction for their child's disruptive behavior or tantrums to prevent damage to objects or harm to the child.

If you predict that the change agent will be unable to persist in withholding the reinforcer during an extinction burst, or if you cannot prevent harm during an extinction burst, an extinction procedure should not be used. Other procedures for decreasing the occurrence of a problem behavior must be implemented instead. (See Chapters 15–18.)

Can Consistency Be Maintained? For extinction to be implemented correctly, the reinforcer must never follow the problem behavior. This means that all people involved in the treatment must be consistent and eliminate the reinforcing consequence each time the problem behavior occurs. If the problem behavior is reinforced even occasionally, the procedure amounts to intermittent reinforcement for the behavior rather than extinction. Lack of consistency is a common reason for the failure of extinction procedures (Vollmer, Roane, Ringdahl, & Marcus, 1999). For example, if parents are implementing extinction consistently for their child's bedtime tantrums, but the grandparents occasionally reinforce the problem when they visit, the tantrums will not be eliminated. Likewise, if most of the staff members implement extinction for Willy's refusals and sexist comments, but one or more of them continues to pay attention to the behavior, the behavior will not be eliminated.

To ensure consistency in implementing an extinction procedure, all change agents must be trained to use the procedure correctly. The change agents must receive clear instructions to be consistent and a rationale explaining why consistency is important. Furthermore, the best results are achieved if the extinction procedure is modeled for the change agents and they have the opportunity to rehearse the procedure and receive feedback. In some cases, it is beneficial to have contingencies of reinforcement for the change agents' correct use of the extinction procedure (or any other

FIVE QUESTIONS YOU MUST ADDRESS BEFORE USING EXTINCTION

- Have you identified the reinforcer?
- Can you eliminate the reinforcer?
- Is extinction safe to use?
- Can an extinction burst be tolerated?
- Can consistency be maintained?

behavior modification procedure). For example, if a large number of staff members in a treatment setting are responsible for implementing the procedure, it is beneficial to have a supervisor monitor their performance, at least occasionally, and provide feedback (reinforcement and correction) on their use of the procedure.

In summary, to use extinction procedures properly you must identify the particular reinforcer for the problem behavior in question, determine that the change agents control the reinforcer, determine that it is safe to use extinction, determine that an extinction burst (escalation in the problem behavior) can be tolerated, and determine that the change agents can implement the extinction procedure consistently. These issues must be considered before using an extinction procedure to decrease a problem behavior.

TAKING ACCOUNT OF THE SCHEDULE OF REINFORCEMENT BEFORE EXTINCTION

The schedule of reinforcement in effect for the problem behavior before the use of extinction affects the rate at which the behavior decreases during extinction (Ferster & Skinner, 1957; Skinner, 1953a). When the problem behavior is reinforced on a continuous schedule, extinction often is more rapid. When the problem behavior is maintained by an intermittent reinforcement schedule, the problem behavior is likely to decrease more gradually during extinction (Chapter 5). It is important to determine whether the reinforcement schedule for the problem behavior is continuous or intermittent so that you can anticipate the rate of decrease in the problem behavior once extinction is implemented.

Kazdin and Polster (1973) demonstrated how the effects of extinction may differ after continuous and intermittent reinforcement. The authors used tokens to reinforce social interactions by two men with mild mental retardation during daily breaks at work in a sheltered workshop. The subjects did not engage in much social interaction before token reinforcement was implemented. However, the rate of social interaction increased greatly for both subjects when they received a token for each person they talked to during the breaks. When the authors quit providing token reinforcement for social interactions (extinction), the interactions decreased to zero for both subjects. After this extinction period, the authors once again reinforced social interactions with tokens. However, one subject continued to receive a token each time he talked to a person (continuous reinforcement) and the other subject received tokens on an intermittent schedule. Sometimes he received tokens for interacting with people and sometimes he did not. After this reinforcement phase, the authors implemented extinction a second time. During this extinction phase, the subject who had received continuous reinforcement for social interactions stopped interacting, whereas the subject whose behavior

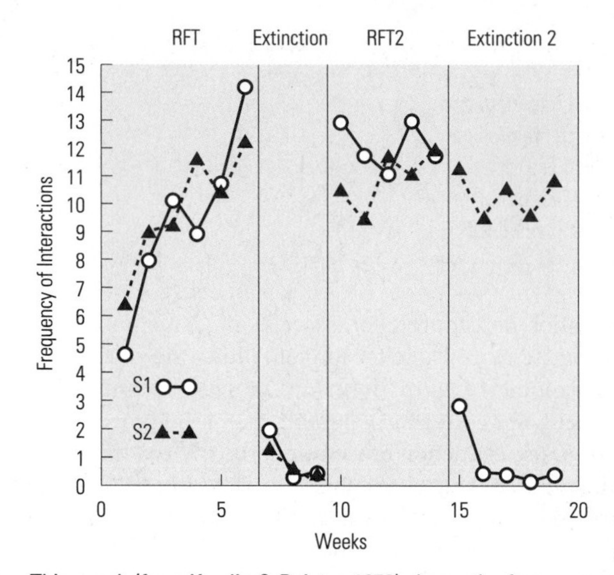

FIGURE 14-2 This graph (from Kazdin & Polster, 1973) shows the frequency of social interactions for two men with mild mental retardation. When social interactions were reinforced with tokens in the first phase (RFT), they occurred at a high level. When the authors withdrew the token reinforcement in the second phase (Extinction), the social interactions decreased to zero. The authors implemented token reinforcement again in the third phase (RFT2), and the social interactions increased again. In this phase, S1 received continuous reinforcement and S2 received intermittent reinforcement for social interactions. In the final phase (Extinction), extinction was implemented again. The behavior decreased for the subject who had received continuous reinforcement in the previous phase but not for the subject whose behavior had been intermittently reinforced. Intermittent reinforcement before extinction made the behavior resistant to extinction.

had been intermittently reinforced continued to interact (Figure 14-2). This demonstrated that the behavior was resistant to extinction after intermittent reinforcement.

The results of the studies by Kazdin and Polster (1973) and Higbee, Carr, and Patel (2002) suggest that when a problem behavior is reinforced on an intermittent schedule, it might be beneficial to implement a continuous schedule of reinforcement for a brief period of time just before using extinction. This means that you would intentionally reinforce the problem behavior each time it occurs for a brief period of time before eliminating the reinforcer in the extinction procedure. The effects of extinction would then be more rapid (Neisworth, Hunt, Gallop, & Madle, 1985).

Reinforcing Alternative Behaviors

An extinction procedure should be used in conjunction with a reinforcement procedure. The extinction procedure decreases the frequency of the problem behavior, and the reinforcement procedure increases an alternative behavior to replace the problem behavior. Because a problem behavior serves a particular function for the person (results in a particular consequence), the reinforcement procedure will increase a desirable behavior that serves the same function or results in the same consequence. When an alternative behavior produces the same reinforcing consequence as the problem behavior had done, it is less likely that the problem behavior will occur again after extinction (spontaneous recovery).

Recall the case of Anna, whose disruptive behaviors were reinforced by her mother's attention (Arndorfer, Miltenberger, Woster, Rortvedt, & Gaffaney, 1994). Arndorfer used extinction for the disruptive behavior and reinforcement for a desirable alternative behavior. When Anna engaged in disruptive behavior, her mother did not respond with attention. However, when Anna said to her mother, "Play with me, please," her mother did respond with attention and spent some time with her. The alternative behavior—asking her mother to play—increased and replaced the problem behavior, which decreased through extinction. If Anna did not have a desirable alternative behavior that resulted in her mother's attention, she would be more likely to continue to engage in the problem behavior.

Differential reinforcement procedures are described in Chapter 15. The main point to remember is that you should use a reinforcement procedure in conjunction with extinction or any other procedure that decreases a problem behavior. A major focus of behavior modification is to develop desirable behaviors that are functional in a person's life and improve the person's life in meaningful ways (Goldiamond, 1974). It is often necessary to use extinction or other procedures to help a person decrease an undesirable behavior that impairs his or her quality of life, but the focus should be on increasing desirable behaviors.

Promoting Generalization and Maintenance

Once you have identified and eliminated the reinforcer maintaining a problem behavior and have implemented a reinforcement procedure to increase a desirable alternative behavior, you should then promote the generalization and maintenance of the behavior change. Generalization of the behavior change after the use of extinction means that the problem behavior will stop (and the alternative behavior will occur) in all relevant circumstances. Maintenance means that the behavior change will last over time. To promote generalization, extinction must be implemented consistently by all change agents and must be implemented in all circumstances in which behavior change is expected. To promote maintenance of the behavior change, it is important to implement the extinction procedure after the initial suppression of the behavior whenever the problem behavior occurs again. In addition, the consistent reinforcement of an alternative behavior that is functionally equivalent to the problem behavior promotes generalization and maintenance.

In the case of Willy, all staff used extinction in all circumstances. They no longer reinforced any instances of his refusals or sexist comments, no matter when or where the behavior occurred. Furthermore, they reinforced compliance as a functionally equivalent alternative behavior to replace the problem behavior. Finally, they planned to use the extinction procedure in the future if the problem behavior occurred again.

Research Evaluating the Use of Extinction

Many studies have demonstrated the effectiveness of extinction procedures for decreasing a variety of socially significant problem behaviors. The effectiveness of extinction procedures has been demonstrated for problem behaviors maintained by positive reinforcement and negative reinforcement and for those maintained by social reinforcers and nonsocial reinforcers (Iwata et al., 1994). The following summary includes only a few of the many studies evaluating extinction.

Rekers and Lovaas (1974) used extinction to decrease inappropriate gender role behavior in a 5-year-old boy. Craig engaged in a number of exaggerated feminine mannerisms and played mostly with feminine toys. As a result, Craig was stigmatized and not accepted by his peers. His parents wanted Craig to engage in more appropriate gender role behavior, such as playing with masculine toys and using more masculine mannerisms. The researchers used extinction and reinforcement of alternative behavior to reduce Craig's feminine behavior and increase his masculine behavior. Craig and his mother participated in treatment sessions in an experimental room filled with masculine and feminine toys. His mother had a receiver in her ear (a bug-in-ear device) to receive instructions from the experimenter during the sessions. When Craig played with a feminine toy, she used extinction. Because her attention was a reinforcer for Craig, she did not look at him or talk to him as long as he was touching a feminine toy. In addition, when he picked up a masculine toy, she provided attention as a reinforcer for this behavior. The researchers cued her over the bug-in-ear device when to provide attention and when to ignore Craig's behavior. The results showed that the feminine behavior decreased and the masculine behavior increased.

Pinkston, Reese, LeBlanc, and Baer (1973) and France and Hudson (1990) also used extinction to decrease problem behaviors that were maintained by positive reinforcement. Pinkston and her colleagues demonstrated that teacher attention reinforced aggressive behavior in a young boy and that when the teacher withdrew attention after the aggressive behavior, the behavior decreased. France and Hudson (1990) worked with families with young children (less than 3 years old) who had problems with night waking and disruptive behaviors. The researchers instructed the parents to use extinction for night wakings and disruptive behaviors. Whenever the child woke at night and engaged in disruptive behavior, the parents did not enter the room. They provided no attention after the problem behavior. They were instructed to enter the room only if they perceived danger or illness and to enter in silence with a minimum of light to check on the child. After the use of this extinction procedure, the night wakings and disruptive behavior decreased to zero for all of the children involved in the study.

A number of researchers have used extinction with problem behaviors maintained by negative reinforcement (Carr et al., 1980; Iwata, Pace, Kalsher, Cowdery, & Cataldo, 1990; Iwata et al., 1994; Steege et al., 1990; Zarcone, Iwata, Hughes, & Vollmer, 1993). As described previously, the researchers prevented escape by continuing demands after the problem behaviors (aggressive and self-injurious behavior). When aggression or self-injury no longer resulted in escape from demands, the behaviors decreased for all subjects.

Sensory extinction (Rincover, 1978) is a procedural variation of extinction that is used for automatic positive reinforcement; when the reinforcer for the behavior is nonsocial and involves the sensory stimulation produced by the behavior itself (Lovaas, Newsom, & Hickman, 1987). The sensory extinction procedure involves changing or eliminating the sensory stimulation that reinforces the behavior. When the behavior no longer produces the reinforcing sensory stimulation, the behavior extinguishes (Rapp, Miltenberger, Galensky, Ellingson, et al., 1999). Rincover and his colleagues used sensory extinction to decrease problem behaviors exhibited by children with autism and developmental disabilities. The problem behaviors involved repetitive behaviors that did not serve any useful social function. For example, one subject, Reggie, spun a plate or another object on a hard table surface. The researchers hypothesized that the sound of the spinning plate on the hard table was the sensory reinforcer for the behavior. Another subject, Karen, picked lint or thread from her own or other people's clothes, threw it in the air, and vigorously flapped her hands as she watched it float to the ground. The researchers hypothesized that because Karen watched the lint or thread intently as it floated to the ground and because her hand flapping caused it to be suspended in the air longer, this behavior was maintained by the visual stimulation.

How would you use sensory extinction with Reggie's behavior of spinning plates on the table?

The sensory extinction procedure changes or removes the sensory stimulation that reinforces the behavior. In Reggie's case, the auditory stimulation arising from the sound of the spinning plate is the sensory reinforcer. To use extinction, the researchers changed the sound produced by the behavior. They carpeted the table top so that when Reggie spun the plate, it did not make the same sound as it had on the hard surface. When the behavior no longer produced the reinforcing auditory consequence, it extinguished (Figures 14-3 and 14-4).

For Karen, the sensory extinction procedure involved removing the visual stimulation produced by the behavior. The researchers implemented the sensory extinction procedure by turning off the overhead light each time Karen picked lint or thread and threw it up in the air. Although there was sufficient light from the windows to see in the classroom, Karen could not see the lint or thread float down to the floor without the overhead lights on. This sensory extinction procedure decreased Karen's problem behavior to zero.

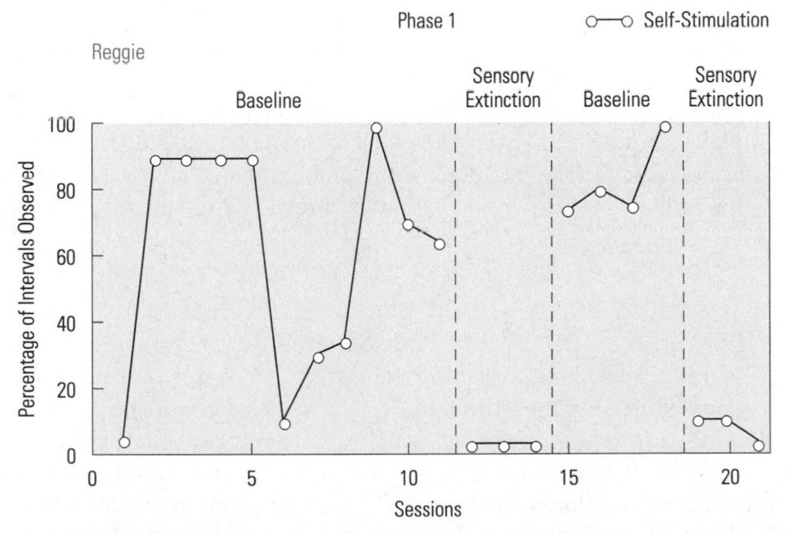

FIGURE 14-3 This graph (from Rincover, Cook, Peoples, & Packard, 1979) shows the level of Reggie's self-stimulatory behavior (plate spinning) during baseline and sensory extinction phases. During sensory extinction, the table top was carpeted so that the plate spinning did not produce the same auditory stimulation as it did during baseline. When the auditory stimulation was eliminated, the behavior decreased to zero.

FIGURE 14-4 The sound of the plate spinning on the hard surface reinforced the child's behavior of spinning the plate. After the desktop was carpeted, the plate no longer made a sound when the child tried to spin it. As a result the plate-spinning behavior stopped.

To increase desirable behaviors that could replace the problem behaviors in these children, the researchers provided toys that produced the same sensory stimulation as did the problem behaviors. Reggie was given a music box to play with and Karen was given a bubble-blowing kit. Because Reggie's plate spinning no longer produced reinforcing auditory stimulation, the behavior decreased. However, playing with the music box produced auditory stimulation to take the place of the stimulation produced by the plate spinning. For Karen, the visual stimulation produced by the bubbles replaced the visual stimulation generated by the problem behavior. As a result, Karen played with the bubbles instead of picking lint or thread and flapping her hands.

CHAPTER SUMMARY

1. Extinction is a procedure in which the reinforcer maintaining a problem behavior is eliminated to decrease the behavior. To use extinction you must first conduct a functional assessment to identify the consequence that is reinforcing the problem behavior.
2. Five questions must be addressed before using an extinction procedure:
   - Have you identified the reinforcer for the problem behavior?
   - Can you eliminate the reinforcer following the problem behavior?
   - Is extinction safe to use?
   - Can an extinction burst be tolerated?
   - Can consistency be maintained in the use of extinction?

3. The schedule of reinforcement for the problem behavior before extinction should be considered because extinction proceeds more rapidly when the behavior is reinforced on a continuous schedule than when it is reinforced on an intermittent schedule before extinction.
4. When using an extinction procedure, you should always reinforce alternative behaviors to replace the problem behavior. If alternative behaviors are occurring in place of the problem behavior, the problem behavior is less likely to occur again in the future.
5. As with any behavior modification procedure, you should program for generalization and maintenance of the behavior change produced with the extinction procedure. To promote generalization, extinction should be implemented consistently by all change agents. It should be used consistently over time whenever and wherever the problem behavior occurs. Finally, alternative behaviors should be reinforced to take the place of the problem behavior when extinction is used.

PRACTICE TEST

1. Define extinction. Provide an example that is not from this chapter. (p. 287)
2. Mr. Robinson, a second grade teacher, has a student who engages in disruptive behavior in the classroom. He ignores her each time she engages in the disruptive behavior. Is this an example of extinction? Explain. (pp. 291–294)
3. Mr. Robinson also praises the student each time she sits at her desk without engaging in disruptive behavior. Is this an example of reinforcement? Explain. (pp. 291–294)
4. Why must you conduct a functional assessment before using extinction to decrease a problem behavior? (p. 291)
5. Why is it important to collect data on the problem behavior when implementing an extinction procedure? (p. 290)
6. Draw a graph with hypothetical data illustrating the results of an extinction procedure for a problem behavior.
7. Before using an extinction procedure you must ask whether the reinforcer can be eliminated. Explain the importance of this question and its implications for the use of extinction. (p. 294)
8. Before using an extinction procedure, you must ask whether extinction is safe to use. When would it be unsafe to use extinction? What can you do to make the use of extinction safer? (p. 295)
9. What is an extinction burst? How will the predicted extinction burst influence your decision about whether to implement extinction in a particular case? (pp. 295–296)
10. What happens if the change agents cannot maintain consistency in using the extinction procedure? (pp. 296–297)
11. Why is it important to use a reinforcement procedure in conjunction with extinction? Provide an example that is not from this chapter. (pp. 298–299)
12. How is the schedule of reinforcement before extinction related to the effectiveness of extinction? (pp. 297–298)
13. What is sensory reinforcement? What is another name for sensory reinforcement? Provide an example of a behavior maintained by sensory reinforcement. (pp. 300–301)
14. What is sensory extinction? Provide an example of sensory extinction. (pp. 300–301)
15. Describe how you would promote the generalization and maintenance of the behavior change produced through an extinction procedure. (p. 299)

Applications

1. Describe how you might use extinction in your self-management project. If the use of an extinction procedure is not appropriate for your particular project, describe why not.

2. There are ten examples of problem behaviors and their reinforcers in Table 14-2. For each example, identify whether the behavior is maintained by positive or negative reinforcement and whether the reinforcer is socially mediated. Explain your answers.

3. Describe how you would use extinction for each example in Table 14-2.

4. Mr. Shoney had inadvertently shaped intense and long-lasting tantrums in his young son, Harvey. Mr. Shoney was divorced and working out of his home. When Harvey engaged in tantrum behavior, Mr. Shoney tried to ignore it and continue working, but about half of the time he eventually gave Harvey what he wanted. Often, Harvey engaged in the tantrum behavior for 20 to 30 minutes before his dad stopped working and gave him what he wanted. Harvey's tantrums consisted of whining, crying, and pleading for what he wanted (e.g., ice cream, playing a game, going to the park). Describe how Mr. Shoney should implement extinction to eliminate Harvey's tantrum behavior.

Misapplications

1. The Wilsons asked their family doctor for advice about their 4-year-old daughter, Jenny, who was exhibiting tantrums whenever she went to the store with her parents. The doctor asked a number of questions and determined that Jenny's tantrum behavior in the store was reinforced by getting candy or other items that she saw in the store. Typically, Jenny would see an item and ask for it. When her parent said no, Jenny began to scream and cry until eventually the parent got the item for her. The doctor instructed the parents to use extinction to get Jenny to stop her tantrum behavior. He said that the next time Jenny engaged in tantrum behavior in the store, the parent should ignore it. He instructed the parent not to buy the item that Jenny wanted but to keep on shopping as if nothing was wrong. What is the problem with this advice?

2. Joan complained of stomach pain and asked her mother not to make her go to school. She was in fourth grade and had complained of stomach pain and stayed home from school a few other times. Her mother thought that the stomach pain did not really exist and that Joan complained about it because she got to stay home from school. Joan's mother decided to use extinction. She figured that if staying home from school was reinforcing Joan's complaints about stomach pain, sending her to school would eliminate that reinforcer. As a result, Joan should quit complaining about stomach pain. What is wrong with this use of extinction?

3. Tim, an 18-year-old man with mental retardation, had recently moved into a group home with seven other residents. The other residents were older adults with mental retardation. Tim teased the other residents frequently. He poked people who didn't want to be touched. He got the remote control and changed channels when people were watching a program on the TV. He took leisure and recreational materials from people who were using them. Tim's behavior annoyed the other residents. They usually got upset with him, complained, cried, scolded him, or yelled at him, but Tim appeared to find their reactions humorous. The clients' reactions appeared to be reinforcing Tim's teasing. Aware that the behavior was getting out of hand, the staff decided to use extinction to decrease the problem behavior. Whenever Tim engaged in any of his teasing behaviors, staff members ignored him. They looked away or casually left the room. Whenever Tim in-

teracted in a positive way with another resident, staff praised Tim in an attempt to reinforce this desirable behavior so that it would replace the teasing. What is wrong with this plan?

4. Tim went to school each day in a van that picked him up from the group home. Almost every morning, Tim refused to get on the van. Staff members talked to him and eventually convinced him to get on the van, but it took at least a few minutes each time. The staff analyzed the situation and decided that they were reinforcing Tim's behavior of refusing to get on the van with their attention as they talked him into getting on each morning. They decided to use an extinction procedure in which they would ask Tim one time to get on the van and then they would not provide any further attention if he refused to get on. If Tim did get on the van when he was asked, staff members would provide substantial attention and praise. With the consent of the school, the van driver agreed to wait as long as it took until Tim finally agreed to get on the van. The only exception would be on the one day a week when there were special events at school and they could not wait. On those days, they would have to talk Tim into getting on the van sooner. What is good about this plan? What is wrong with it?

APPENDIX A

Reinforcement Illustrated by Each Example in Table 14-2

1. Social positive reinforcement
2. Social positive reinforcement
3. Social negative reinforcement
4. Automatic positive reinforcement
5. Automatic negative reinforcement
6. Social negative reinforcement (avoids the task); social positive reinforcement (gets to keep watching TV)
7. Social positive reinforcement
8. Social positive reinforcement
9. Social positive reinforcement
10. Automatic negative reinforcement (the worker stops working); automatic positive reinforcement (the worker has a cigarette/cup of coffee)

APPENDIX B

Extinction Implementation for Each Example in Table 14-2

1. When the child complains of being sick, she has to do the chore anyway.
2. When the person runs into the street, the staff member no longer offers a can of pop to leave the street.
3. When the spouse has a temper outburst, the other spouse does not stop arguing.
4. Dim the light so the finger flicking no longer produces visual stimulation.
5. You could not easily implement extinction in this case. It would involve not letting the person escape the dog by running away and not letting the fear response diminish when he runs away.
6. When the child refuses to do the task, the parent turns off the TV and makes the child do the task.
7. When the child refuses to do the task, the parent ignores the child's behavior.
8. When the patient calls the nurse's station, the nurse no longer comes to the room.
9. When the patient strips, the nurse no longer gives any reaction.
10. When the worker sabotages the line, he must continue working (at another task perhaps) and cannot sit down for a cup of coffee and a cigarette.

CHAPTER 14 *Quiz 1* Name:

1. To use extinction, you must first identify the ____________________ that maintains the problem and then eliminate it.

2. A behavior problem is reinforced by ____________________ when the behavior results in the presentation of a stimulus.

3. A behavior problem is reinforced by ____________________ when the behavior results in escape from some stimulus.

4. In order to identify the reinforcer maintaining a problem behavior, you must conduct a

   ____________________.

5. If a child's problem behavior was reinforced by ____________________, then extinction would involve ignoring the behavior when it occurred.

6. If a child's problem behavior was reinforced by ____________________, then extinction would involve not letting the child out of the task when the problem behavior occurred.

7. Claire had tantrums involving screaming and crying. When her parents started using extinction for the tantrum behavior, Claire screamed louder and longer for a while before the behavior

   decreased. This is an example of a(n) ____________________.

8. The decrease in the problem behavior will be more rapid following ____________________ (continuous/intermittent) reinforcement.

9. The decrease in the problem behavior will be more gradual following ____________________ (continuous/intermittent) reinforcement.

10. An extinction procedure should be used in conjunction with a(n) ____________________ procedure.

CHAPTER 14 *Quiz 2* Name:

1. With extinction, once the reinforcer for the problem behavior no longer follows the behavior, the behavior will ______________________________.

2. A child cries when asked to tie her shoes, and her parents tie her shoes for her. In this case, how would the parents use extinction for crying?

   ____

3. A child cries every time she wants cookies, and her babysitter gives her cookies. In this case, how would the babysitter use extinction for crying?

   ____

4. If you cannot eliminate the reinforcer for a problem behavior, then you should not try to use __________________________ to decrease the problem.

5. What is likely to happen during an extinction burst?

   ____

6. For extinction to be used correctly, the reinforcer should _______________________ follow the problem behavior.

7. If the problem behavior is even occasionally reinforced, the procedure amounts to __________________________ for the behavior rather than extinction.

What are two conditions under which you would decide not to use extinction?

8. ____

9. ____

10. When an alternative behavior produces the same reinforcing consequence as the problem behavior had before the use of extinction, it is ____________________ (less/more) likely that the problem behavior will occur again after extinction.

CHAPTER 14 *Quiz 3* Name:

1. ________________ is a basic principle of behavior in which eliminating the reinforcer for the behavior results in a decrease in the frequency of the behavior.

A child spins a plate on the table, and the plate spinning is reinforced by the sound the plate makes while spinning.

2. This is an example of ____________________________ reinforcement.
3. How would you implement extinction in this case? ____

Researchers have found that self-injurious behavior such as head banging may be reinforced by attention, escape, or sensory stimulation.

4. How would you implement extinction if head banging were reinforced by adult attention?
____
5. How would you implement extinction if the head banging were reinforced by escape from academic tasks? ____
6. How would you implement extinction if the head banging were reinforced by sensory stimulation? ____
7. The temporary increase in frequency, duration, or intensity of the behavior as extinction is implemented is called a(n) ______________________________________.
8. If extinction is used following continuous reinforcement, then the decrease in the problem behavior will be more ________________ (rapid/gradual).
9. If extinction is used following intermittent reinforcement, then the decrease in the problem behavior will be more ________________ (rapid/gradual).
10. ______________________ of behavior change after the use of extinction means that the problem behavior will stop in all relevant circumstances.

Differential Reinforcement

Chapter 14 described the use of extinction to decrease undesirable behaviors. This chapter describes differential reinforcement procedures, which involve applying reinforcement (Chapter 4) and extinction (Chapter 5) to increase the occurrence of a desirable target behavior or to decrease the occurrence of undesirable behaviors. There are three types of differential reinforcement procedures: differential reinforcement of alternative behavior, differential reinforcement of other behavior, and differential reinforcement of low rates of responding.

- How do you use differential reinforcement of alternative behavior (DRA) to increase the rate of a desirable behavior?
- How do you use differential reinforcement of other behavior (DRO) and differential reinforcement of low rates of responding (DRL) to decrease an undesirable behavior?
- When should you use DRA, DRO, and DRL procedures?
- How are the principles of reinforcement and extinction involved in differential reinforcement procedures?
- How is negative reinforcement used in DRA and DRO procedures?

Differential Reinforcement of Alternative Behavior

Differential reinforcement of alternative behavior (DRA) is a behavioral procedure used to increase the frequency of a desirable behavior and to decrease the frequency of undesirable behaviors. The desirable behavior is reinforced each time it occurs. This results in an increase in the future probability of the desirable behavior. At the same time, any undesirable behaviors that may interfere with the desirable behavior are not reinforced. This results in a decrease in the future probability of the undesirable behaviors. Thus, DRA involves combining reinforcement for a desirable behavior and extinction of undesirable behaviors. Consider the following example.

Getting Mrs. Williams to Be Positive

Mrs. Williams had been in the nursing home for about a year, but to the nurses it seemed like forever. Whenever Mrs. Williams saw a nurse, she immediately started to complain about the food, her room, the other patients, the noise, or her arthritis. The nurses always listened politely and tried to comfort Mrs. Williams when she complained. It seemed that over the year, her complaining was getting worse, to the point that she rarely said anything positive anymore. When she first came to the nursing home, Mrs. Williams said many nice things, she complimented people, and she rarely complained. The nurses wished they could get Mrs. Williams to act like that again, so they consulted with a behavioral psychologist to see whether there was anything they could do.

The psychologist told the nurses that they could help Mrs. Williams change her behavior by changing the way they interacted with her. The nurses were instructed to do three things. First, whenever they saw Mrs. Williams, they were to say something positive to her immediately. Second, whenever Mrs. Williams said anything positive herself, the nurse was to stop what she was doing, smile at Mrs. Williams, and actively listen to her and pay attention to what she was saying. The nurse was to keep listening and paying attention to her as long as she continued to say positive things. (Of course, the nurse could start working again and continue to pay attention to Mrs. Williams while she was working.) Third, whenever Mrs. Williams started to complain, the nurse was to excuse herself and either leave the room or become too busy to listen at that time. As soon as Mrs. Williams stopped complaining and said anything positive, the nurse was again to stop working and pay attention to her.

All the nurses consistently applied this program and, in a matter of weeks, Mrs. Williams was saying many more positive things to the nurses and complaining very little. She seemed happier, and the nurses enjoyed working with her again.

The behavioral procedure the nurses used to get Mrs. Williams to say more positive things and to complain less is DRA. After listening to the nurses describe the problem and observing Mrs. Williams for a period of time, the psychologist hypothesized that Mrs. Williams was complaining frequently because the nurses were unintentionally reinforcing her complaining behavior. When Mrs. Williams complained, they listened attentively, said comforting things to her, and spent more time with her.

Antecedent	Response	Consequence
A nurse is present.	Mrs. Williams complains.	A nurse provides attention.

Outcome: Mrs. Williams is more likely to complain each time a nurse is present.

The psychologist decided that the nurses should increase their attention when Mrs. Williams said positive things to reinforce this behavior. In addition, the nurses should make sure Mrs. Williams did not get their attention when she complained. As you can see, the nurses used reinforcement and extinction, the two principles involved in DRA.

Reinforcement

Antecedent	Response	Consequence
A nurse is present.	Mrs. Williams says positive things.	Nurses provide attention.

Outcome: In the future, Mrs. Williams is more likely to say positive things when a nurse is present.

Extinction

Antecedent	Response	Consequence
A nurse is present.	Mrs. Williams complains.	Nurses do not provide attention.

Outcome: In the future, Mrs. Williams is less likely to complain to nurses.

In the example, when Mrs. Williams said more positive things, it was not only because this behavior was reinforced by the nurses but also because complaining was decreased through extinction. If the nurses did not use extinction for the complaining, it would still occur and there would be less opportunity for positive talk to increase. DRA is an effective way to increase a desirable behavior because, by decreasing an interfering behavior through extinction, it creates an opportunity for the desirable behavior to occur and be reinforced.

When to Use DRA

Before implementing DRA, you have to decide whether it is the right procedure in a particular situation. To determine whether DRA is appropriate, you must answer three questions.

- Do you want to increase the rate of a desirable behavior?
- Is the behavior already occurring at least occasionally?
- Do you have access to a reinforcer that you can deliver after the occurrence of the behavior?

DRA is a procedure for strengthening a desirable behavior. However, the desirable behavior must be occurring at least occasionally if you are to reinforce it. If the behavior is not occurring at all, DRA by itself is not an appropriate procedure. However, if procedures such as shaping (Chapter 9) or prompting (Chapter 10) are used initially to evoke the behavior, DRA may then be used to strengthen and maintain the behavior. Finally, you must be able to identify a reinforcer that you can use each time the behavior occurs. If you cannot identify a reinforcer or if you have no control over the reinforcer, you cannot use DRA.

How to Use DRA

Several steps are involved in using DRA effectively. These steps are described here.

Define the Desirable Behavior You must clearly identify and define the desirable behavior that you plan to increase with DRA. A clear behavioral definition of the desirable behavior, as described in Chapter 2, helps ensure that you are reinforcing the correct behavior and allows you to record the behavior to determine whether treatment is successful.

Define the Undesirable Behaviors You must also clearly define the undesirable behaviors you plan to decrease with DRA. A clear behavioral definition of the undesirable behaviors helps ensure that you are not using reinforcement when the undesirable behavior occurs and also allows you to record the undesirable behaviors to determine whether they decrease after DRA.

Identify the Reinforcer The DRA procedure involves reinforcing a desirable behavior and withholding reinforcement for undesirable behaviors. Therefore, you must identify the reinforcer you will use in the DRA procedure. Because reinforcers may be different for different people, it is important to determine a reinforcer specific to the person you are working with.

One possibility is to use the reinforcer that is currently maintaining the undesirable behavior; you already know that this reinforcer is effective (Durand, Crimmins, Caufield, & Taylor, 1989). In the example of Mrs. Williams, attention from the nurses was reinforcing the undesirable behavior of complaining. Therefore, the nurses decided to use their attention to reinforce positive talk instead. Durand and his colleagues found that different reinforcers were maintaining the problem behaviors of children with disabilities in the classroom (Durand et al., 1989). Once Durand identified the reinforcer for the problem behaviors in each student, he used these same reinforcers to increase more appropriate alternative behaviors. This resulted in a decrease in the problem behavior; the appropriate alternative behaviors began to occur more regularly instead.

Another way to identify a reinforcer is to observe the person and note which activities or interests he or she pursues: What does the person enjoy doing? For example, a counselor in a program for juvenile delinquents wanted to provide reinforcers for appropriate behaviors (e.g., completing homework). Observing that Luke frequently played video games and seemed to enjoy himself when he played, the counselor chose the opportunity to play video games as a reinforcer for completing homework for Luke. The counselor was using the Premack principle (Premack, 1959): He used the opportunity to engage in a high-frequency or preferred behavior (playing video games) as a reinforcer for a low-frequency behavior (completing homework).

Another way to identify reinforcers for specific people is to ask them questions: What do they like? What do they enjoy doing? How do they spend their free time? What would they buy if they had money? What do they find rewarding? Most people

How to Identify Reinforcers

- Observe the client and identify the reinforcer for the problem behavior.
- Observe the client and identify high-rate behaviors.
- Ask the client, parents, or teachers.
- Use reinforcer questionnaires.
- Present potential reinforcers and measure approach behaviors.
- Present potential reinforcers contingent on an operant response and measure response rate or duration.

can tell you at least a few things that would be useful as reinforcers. Parents or teachers who know the people well can also provide information. Some researchers have developed questionnaires to help them identify reinforcers for the people they treat (Cautela, 1977).

Another option is to try out a variety of different stimuli and see which ones function as reinforcers. The researcher could present each of the potential reinforcers to the person and record which ones he or she approaches. Likewise, the researchers could present two or more potential reinforcers and see which ones the person chooses (Fisher et al., 1992, 1994; Green et al., 1988; Pace, Ivancic, Edwards, Iwata, & Page, 1985). For example, when a toy is presented, does the child reach for it, touch it, or try to play with it? When a snack is presented, does the child reach for it or try to eat it? These approach responses would indicate that the toy or food was a reinforcer for this child (Fisher et al., 1992).

Another technique is to make each potential reinforcer contingent on an operant response (Bowman, Piazza, Fisher, Hagopian, & Kogan, 1997; Green, Reid, Canipe, & Gardner, 1991; Wacker, Berg, Wiggins, Muldoon, & Cavenaugh, 1985). If the frequency or duration of the response increases when a stimulus is contingent on the response, you have demonstrated that the stimulus is a reinforcer. For example, Wacker had students press a switch to activate different electric games or instruments (including a tape recorder playing music, a fan, and a train). They recorded the duration of switch activation as an indication of which stimuli were reinforcers for the students. If a student pressed the switch that turned on the music for much longer than other switches, the researcher could conclude that music was a reinforcer for the student.

Reinforce the Desirable Behavior Immediately and Consistently As you recall from Chapter 4, it is important to reinforce a behavior immediately after it occurs if you want it to increase. Correspondingly, a delay in reinforcement of the desirable behavior will make DRA less effective. In addition, you should reinforce the desirable behavior every time it occurs. A behavior that is reinforced on a continuous reinforcement schedule, at least initially, is more likely to increase to the desirable level and to replace the undesirable behaviors that are not being reinforced (Vollmer, Roane, Ringdahl, & Marcus, 1999).

Eliminate Reinforcement for the Undesirable Behaviors If DRA is to be effective, you must identify and eliminate the reinforcement for undesirable behaviors. If the reinforcer for undesirable behaviors cannot be eliminated completely, it must at least be minimized so that the contrast between the reinforcement of the desirable and undesirable behaviors is maximized. The desirable and undesirable behaviors are concurrent operants. You know from Chapter 4 that when two behaviors are maintained by concurrent schedules of reinforcement, the behavior that results in greater reinforcement will increase relative to the other behavior.

For example, the nurses may not be able to eliminate all attention to Mrs. Williams when she complains. They may have to respond to some complaints to determine whether they are legitimate. However, their attention to complaints will be minimal, whereas their attention to her positive talk will be enthusiastic and extended in duration. In this way, the attention for positive talk is much greater than that for complaining. In other words, there is much more reinforcement for talking about positive things than there is for complaining.

Use Intermittent Reinforcement to Maintain the Target Behavior Continuous reinforcement for the desirable behavior is used in the early stages of DRA. However, once the desirable behavior is occurring consistently and the undesirable behaviors occur rarely, if at all, you should start to thin the schedule of reinforcement and reinforce the desirable behavior intermittently. Intermittent reinforcement maintains the desirable behavior over time by making it more resistant to extinction.

Program for Generalization In DRA, it is important not only to program for maintenance with an intermittent schedule of reinforcement but also to program for generalization. Generalization means that the target behavior should occur outside the training situation in all relevant stimulus situations. If the target behavior does not occur in all relevant situations, the DRA procedure has not been entirely effective. To program for generalization, the target behavior should be differentially reinforced in as many relevant situations as possible, by as many relevant people as possible.

USING DRA

1. Define the desirable behavior.
2. Define the undesirable behaviors.
3. Identify the reinforcer.
4. Reinforce the desirable behavior immediately and consistently.
5. Eliminate reinforcement for undesirable behaviors.
6. Use intermittent reinforcement to maintain the target behavior.
7. Program for generalization.

Using Differential Negative Reinforcement of Alternative Behaviors

The following example involves differential negative reinforcement of alternative behaviors (DNRA).

Jason is an 8-year-old autistic boy in third grade. Autistic children often prefer to be alone and engage in solitary behavior. Sometimes autistic children engage in aggressive, destructive, or self-injurious behavior when demands are placed on them. When the teacher asked Jason to do his school work (e.g., complete problems in his workbook), he often slammed his fists on his desk and rocked back and forth violently in his seat. At this, the teacher usually let Jason take a break and sit in a chair by himself at the back of the room until he calmed down. Because this behavior occurred four or five times every day, Jason was not getting much school work done. Not knowing what to do about Jason's behavior, the teacher consulted the school psychologist.

To understand the problem, the school psychologist asked the teacher several questions and observed Jason in the classroom. It became clear that the undesirable behavior (hitting his desk and rocking in his seat) was negatively reinforced.

Describe how Jason's problem behavior was being negatively reinforced.

Antecedent	Response	Consequence
Teacher asks Jason to do his work.	Jason slams the desk and rocks back and forth.	Jason escapes from his school work and sits by himself.

Outcome: Jason is more likely to engage in problem behavior when his teacher asks him to do his school work.

Each time Jason engaged in this behavior, he escaped from the demands of doing his school work. The immediate consequence of the undesirable behavior was getting out of work. The psychologist also learned that Jason exhibited the desirable behavior (completing school work) at least sometimes during the day. Therefore, the psychologist decided to use differential reinforcement to increase the desirable behavior of completing school work and decrease the undesirable behavior of slamming his desk and rocking in his seat.

First, the psychologist developed behavioral definitions for the desirable and undesirable behavior. The psychologist then asked the teacher to start recording every day the number of problems Jason completed from his workbook (desirable behavior) and the number of times he had an outburst (the undesirable behavior, defined as hitting his desk and rocking in his seat). The next step was to identify the reinforcer for Jason's desirable behavior. Because escape from school work was the reinforcer for the outbursts, the psychologist decided to use it also as a reinforcer for doing school work. Although it may seem unusual to use escape from school work as a reinforcer for doing school work, the psychologist knew that it was effective as a reinforcer for Jason.

Once the desirable and undesirable behaviors had been defined and the reinforcer had been identified, the teacher was ready to start implementing differential reinforcement. The first step was to provide the reinforcer every time Jason completed a workbook problem. This meant letting him get up and sit in the chair in the back of the room by himself for a few minutes.

Initially, the teacher asked Jason to complete only easy workbook problems, so that it was more likely he would be successful and the behavior would be reinforced. At the same time, whenever Jason had an outburst, the teacher used extinction.

Describe how the teacher would use extinction with Jason's outbursts.

Because escape from his school work was reinforcing his outbursts, she did not let him escape: He could not get out of his seat and sit in the back of the room when he had an outburst. Instead, he had to stay in his seat and, when he calmed down, he still had to do the workbook problem. In this way, doing his workbook problems resulted in reinforcement and having outbursts did not result in reinforcement.

Once Jason was completing workbook problems consistently and not engaging in the undesirable behavior, the final steps in using differential reinforcement were to switch to an intermittent reinforcement schedule and to program for generalization. Initially, Jason got to sit in the back of the room after every workbook problem he completed. After he was completing problems consistently (both easy ones and hard ones) and was no longer having outbursts, the teacher started to provide the reinforcer after every two problems he completed. Eventually Jason completed three problems before getting the reinforcer, then four problems, then five. The teacher was satisfied to let Jason sit by himself after every five problems he completed. This did not prevent him from getting his work done and it was not too disruptive to the class; it was certainly less disruptive than having four or five outbursts every day. In an attempt to program for generalization, other teachers used the differential reinforcement procedure in a variety of classrooms.

When differential reinforcement is used successfully, the desirable behavior should increase and the undesirable behavior should decrease. In this case, Jason's outbursts decreased in frequency and his rate of completing school work increased with the use of differential reinforcement.

DNRA has been used in a variety of studies to decrease problem behaviors that are maintained by negative reinforcement and increase appropriate behaviors to replace the problem behaviors (Marcus & Vollmer, 1995; Roberts, Mace, & Daggett, 1995; Steege et al., 1990). Warzak, Kewman, Stefans, and Johnson (1987) provided treatment for Adam, a 10-year-old boy who reported that he was unable to read after hospitalization for a serious respiratory infection. Before the hospitalization, Adam had no trouble reading. Adam now reported that the letters were blurry and moved around on the page when he tried to read. However, he had no difficulty playing video games and engaging in other activities requiring fine visual discriminations.

Warzak implemented treatment consisting of therapeutic reading exercises that lasted from 45 minutes to 2 hours each day. The exercises "were designed to be exceedingly tedious and boring" (p. 173). Adam was asked to read words presented on the page as part of the exercises in each treatment session. When he read the words correctly, the remainder of the therapeutic exercise was canceled for that day. Correct reading was negatively reinforced by escape from the tedious exercises. If he failed to read words correctly, the therapeutic exercises continued. (This amounted to extinction of incorrect reading.) Warzak implemented this DNRA procedure in a multiple-baseline design across different print sizes. The results show that correct reading increased to 100% for all print sizes after the use of DNRA. The results were maintained for at least 3 months after treatment.

Variations of DRA

There are a couple of variations of DRA in which different types of alternative behavior are reinforced to replace the problem behavior. One variation is **differential reinforcement of an incompatible behavior (DRI)**, in which the alternative behavior is physically incompatible with the problem behavior and, therefore, the two behaviors cannot occur at the same time. For example, if the problem behavior is head-slapping, in which individuals slap themselves on the side of the head with their hands, any alternative behavior involving the use of the hands would be an incompatible behavior.

Playing with toys or completing tasks that involve the manipulation of materials with their hands would be examples of incompatible behaviors that could be reinforced to replace the head-slapping in a DRI procedure.

In a second variation of DRA, the alternative behavior that is reinforced to replace the problem behavior is a communication response. This is referred to as **differential reinforcement of communication (DRC)** or functional communication training (Carr, McConnachie, Levin, & Kemp, 1993). In this procedure, the individual with the problem behavior learns to make a communication repsonse that is functionally equivalent to the problem behavior. When the communication produces the same reinforcing outcome as the problem behavior, there is no longer any reason for the problem behavior to occur. In functional communication training, an individual with a problem behavior reinforced by attention would learn to ask for attention. An individual with a problem behavior reinforced by escape from a particular situation would learn to ask for a break from the situation The communication response that is reinforced in this variation of DRA is more efficient than the problem behavior; that is one of the advantages of communication as an alternative behavior.

Research on DRA

Leitenberg and his colleagues investigated DRA procedures for increasing appropriate behaviors and decreasing sibling conflict involving physical aggression, verbal attacks, screaming, and crying (Leitenberg, Burchard, Burchard, Fuller, & Lysaght, 1977). Six families participated. The mothers were instructed to use praise and pennies to reinforce their children's appropriate behaviors (such as playing together, helping, sharing, and talking to each other). At the same time, the mothers ignored the conflicts between their children. The researchers found that DRA decreased conflict behavior in the siblings and increased appropriate behavior.

Allen and Stokes (1987) used DRA procedures to increase cooperative behavior and decrease disruptive behavior exhibited by children during dental treatment. The five children (ages 3-6) participating in this study exhibited disruptive behaviors, such as head and body movements, crying, gagging, and moaning, while the dentist was providing treatment. Allen and Stokes used positive and negative reinforcement when the child exhibited cooperative behavior in the dentist's chair (that is, being still and quiet). When the child was still and quiet in the chair for an interval of time, the dentist negatively reinforced this behavior by turning off the drill for a brief period. Over the course of treatment sessions, the interval of time that the child had to engage in the incompatible behavior was lengthened gradually. The child also received praise and stickers as positive reinforcers for being still and quiet. Allen and Stokes demonstrated a reduction in disruptive behavior for all five children with this DRA procedure. In a similar study, Stokes and Kennedy (1980) used small trinkets to reinforce the cooperative behavior of young children during dental visits and found that their disruptive behavior decreased as a result.

Differential reinforcement of communication, or functional communication training, has been evaluated in a number of studies by Carr and Durand (Carr & Durand, 1985; Durand & Carr, 1987, 1991). The procedure is similar across studies. The researchers conduct a functional analysis to identify the reinforcer for the problem behavior exhibited by students with developmental disabilities in classroom settings. When a child's problem behavior is reinforced by attention, the child is taught to ask for attention as an alternative response. The child says, "How am I doing?" and the teacher responds to this behavior with attention. Therefore, this communication behavior increases and the problem behavior decreases. If the problem behavior is reinforced by escape when difficult academic material is presented, the child is taught to ask for assistance. The child says, "I don't understand," and the teacher responds by providing assistance. As a result, the child is less likely to engage in the problem behavior to escape from the academic task. Across their studies, Durand and Carr have shown decreases in problem behaviors maintained by attention and escape and have demonstrated increases in communication as a functionally equivalent alternative behavior. Books by both Durand and Carr describe the functional communication training procedure in detail (Carr et al., 1994; Durand, 1990).

Many other behavior modification experiments have demonstrated the value of DRA for increasing various socially significant behaviors. In a study with preschoolers, Goetz and Baer (1973) showed that they could increase the frequency of the children's creative play behaviors through social reinforcement by the teacher. Each time a child played creatively with blocks (defined as creating novel structures), the teacher showed interest and enthusiasm. However, when the children built the same structures again, the teacher did not show interest or enthusiasm. As a result, the children created more novel structures with the blocks and built fewer identical structures (Figure 15-1). These results suggest that creativity, often considered a trait, could actually be a response class that could be increased through DRA. Many studies have documented the value of DRA for increasing desirable behaviors in children (Sulzer-Azaroff et al., 1988).

DRA has also been used to increase a variety of worker behaviors in job situations (Hermann, Montes, Dominguez, Montes, & Hopkins, 1973; Reid, Parsons, & Green, 1989). Improving worker performance by differential reinforcement is one aspect of organizational behavior modification (Luthans & Kreitner, 1985).

Other studies have used DRA with people with mental retardation (Bailey & Meyerson, 1969; Whitman, Mercurio, & Capronigri, 1970), college students (Azrin, Holz, Ulrich, & Goldiamond, 1973), people with mental illness (Kale, Kaye, Whelan, & Hopkins, 1968; Mitchell & Stoffelmayr, 1973), welfare recipients (Miller & Miller, 1970), underachieving students (Chadwick & Day, 1971), and hypertensive adults (Elder, Ruiz, Deabler, & Dillenhofer, 1973). In each case, researchers were interested in helping people increase desirable behaviors to more healthy or socially appropriate levels while decreasing interfering undesirable behaviors.

Mitchell and Stoffelmayr (1973) applied the Premack principle in a DRA program to increase the work behavior of two people with schizophrenia. They differentially reinforced work performance (a low-probability behavior) by allowing the patients to sit down and do nothing (high-probability behavior) for a brief time only after completing a certain amount of work. If they did not complete the work, they were not allowed to sit down and do nothing. The results showed that the work performance of both people increased dramatically with the use of DRA.

Differential Reinforcement of Other Behavior

Knight and McKenzie (1974) conducted a study to evaluate the effects of differential reinforcement for decreasing bedtime thumb-sucking in children. The procedure they used is called **differential reinforcement of other behavior (DRO).** One of the subjects,

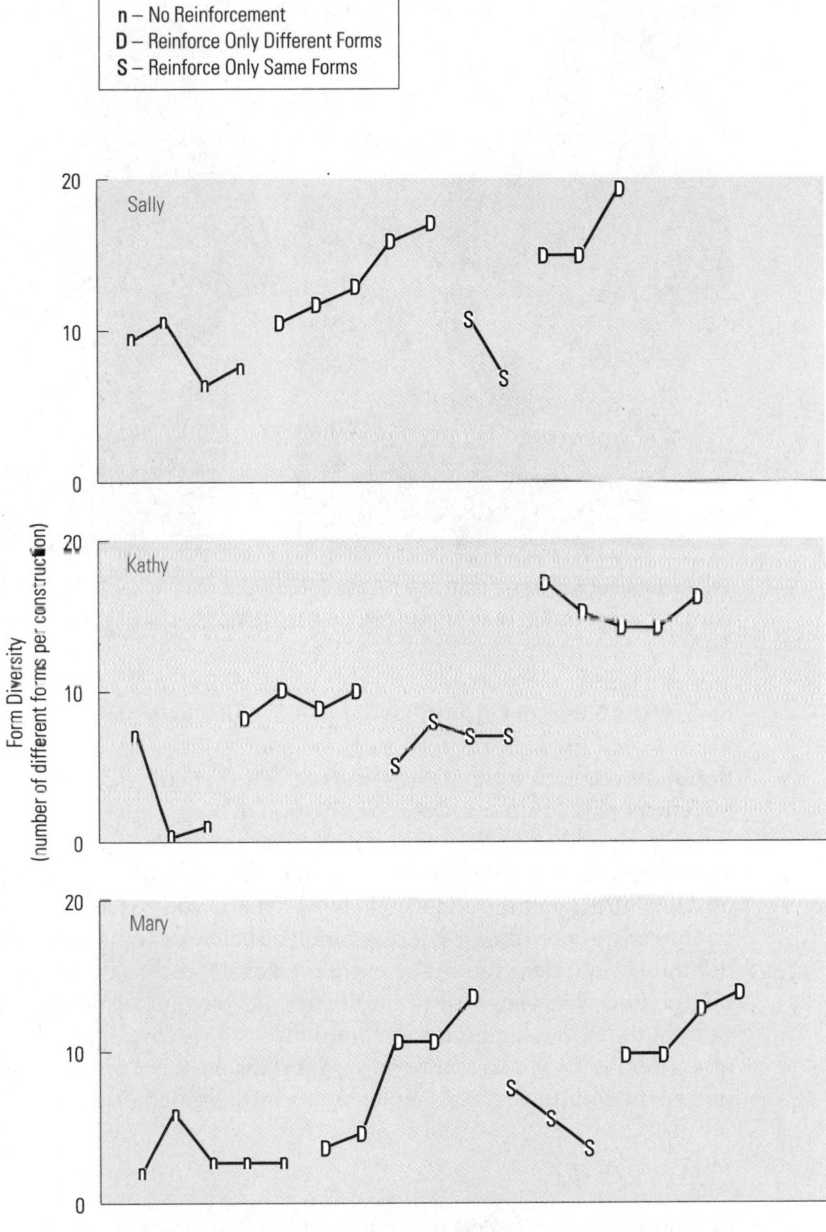

FIGURE 15-1 The form diversity scores of three children in the course of block-building training (from Goetz & Baer, 1973). Data points labeled *D* represent scores produced when reinforcement was programmed only for different (nonrepetitive) forms; points labeled *S* represent scores produced when reinforcement was programmed only for repetition of the same forms used previously in that session.

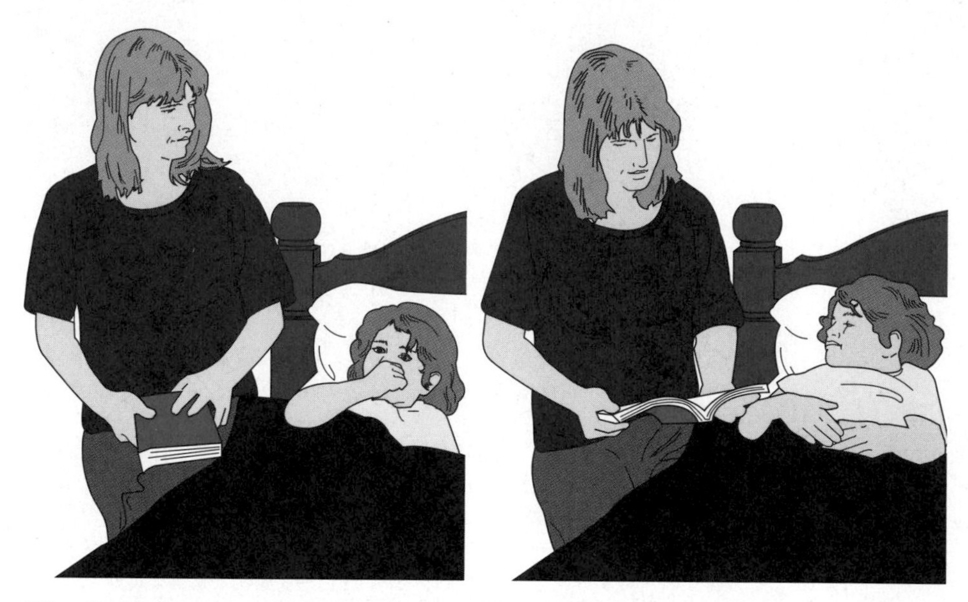

FIGURE 15-2 When Sara sucked her thumb, the researcher did not read to her. When Sara did not suck her thumb, the researcher read to her. This reinforced the absence of the behavior.

Sara, was a 3-year-old girl who spent her days in a day care program while her parents were at work. In day care, Sara took a nap for an hour each afternoon and sucked her thumb throughout most of the nap time. The experimenters used a differential reinforcement procedure to reduce the duration of Sara's thumb-sucking during nap time. Because Sara liked to have stories read to her at nap time, they used reading to her as a reinforcer. In this differential reinforcement procedure, the experimenter sat down next to Sara at nap time and read to her whenever she was not sucking her thumb. The reinforcer was delivered when the problem behavior was absent. Whenever Sara put her thumb into her mouth, the experimenter stopped reading (Figure 15-2). Because the reinforcer was contingent on the absence of thumb-sucking, the length of time without thumb-sucking increased until there was no more thumb-sucking during nap time (Figure 15-3). This same procedure was effective with two other children who sucked their thumbs. It was implemented by their mothers in their homes at bedtime.

Defining DRO

In DRO, the reinforcer is contingent on the absence of the problem behavior (Reynolds, 1961). This means that the reinforcer is no longer delivered after the problem behavior (extinction) but the reinforcer is delivered after an interval of time in which the problem behavior does not occur. The logic behind the DRO procedure is that if the reinforcer is delivered only after periods of time in which the problem behavior is absent, the problem behavior decreases through extinction, and time periods without the problem behavior should increase. If periods of time without the problem behavior increase, the occurrence of the problem behavior must naturally decrease.

It is important to note that the term *differential reinforcement of other behavior* may be confusing. Although the name of the procedure suggests that you will reinforce

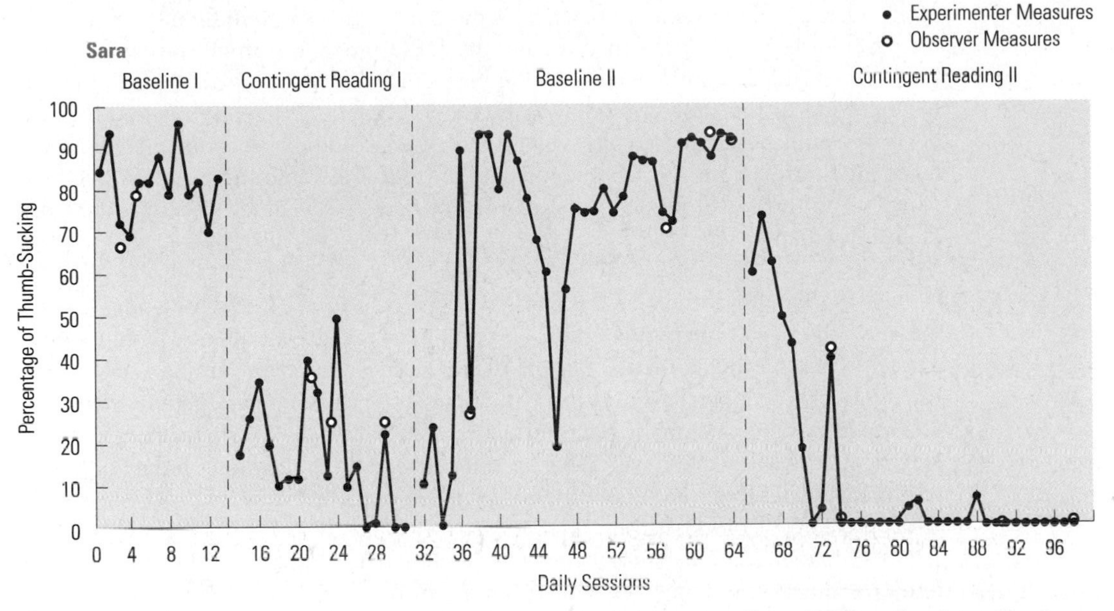

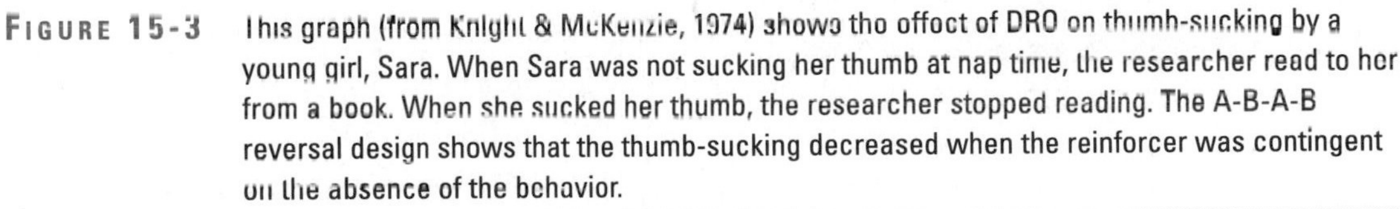

FIGURE 15-3 This graph (from Knight & McKenzie, 1974) shows the effect of DRO on thumb-sucking by a young girl, Sara. When Sara was not sucking her thumb at nap time, the researcher read to her from a book. When she sucked her thumb, the researcher stopped reading. The A-B-A-B reversal design shows that the thumb-sucking decreased when the reinforcer was contingent on the absence of the behavior.

other behavior, in fact, you will reinforce the absence of the problem behavior. Although other behaviors may occur when the problem behavior is not occurring, you do not identify other behavior to reinforce in place of the problem behavior. DRO can also be seen as differential reinforcement of zero rate of the behavior. According to Reynolds (1961), DRO involves "reinforcement for not responding" (p. 59). Recall the case in which the experimenter read stories to Sara when she was not sucking her thumb. Reading stories was the reinforcer; it was delivered when the problem behavior, thumb-sucking, was not occurring. Make note of this distinction so that you do not confuse DRO with the other differential reinforcement procedures. Let's examine the sequence of steps involved in implementing the DRO procedure.

Identifying the Reinforcer for the Problem Behavior Extinction of the problem behavior is a component of the DRO procedure. As we saw in Chapter 13, you must conduct a functional assessment to identify the reinforcer for the problem behavior before you can implement an extinction procedure. Research demonstrates clearly that you must eliminate the reinforcer maintaining the problem behavior for a DRO procedure to be successful (Mazaleski, Iwata, Vollmer, Zarcone, & Smith, 1993). Reinforcing the absence of the problem behavior would not be very effective if instances of the problem behavior continued to be reinforced. If it is not possible to use extinction for the problem behavior (for the reasons discussed in Chapter 14), it usually will not be possible to use DRO effectively. One exception would be the case in which the reinforcer for the absence of the problem behavior is more powerful or potent than the reinforcer for problem behavior itself. In this case, the DRO procedure might be effective because the payoff for not engaging in the problem behavior is bigger than the payoff for engaging in the problem behavior (Cowdery, Iwata, & Pace, 1990). Another exception would be a situation in which you use some other procedure (such as antecedent control, time-out, or guided compliance) to decrease the problem behavior while using the DRO procedure (Repp & Deitz, 1974). These procedures are discussed in Chapters 16–18.

Identifying the Reinforcer to Use in the DRO Procedure If you are going to reinforce the absence of the problem behavior, you must use a consequence that functions as a reinforcer for that particular person. As you learned, there are various ways to identify reinforcers that you can use with particular people. You can ask people their preferences for various potentially reinforcing events. You can observe what activities or objects people choose when given choices. You can experimentally manipulate potential reinforcers to observe which ones increase the behaviors that they follow (Fisher et al., 1992; Green et al., 1988; Mason, McGee, Farmer-Dougan, & Risley, 1989; Pace et al., 1985). One consequence that is certain to function as a reinforcer for the person is the reinforcer for the problem behavior identified in the functional assessment (Durand et al., 1989). If a reinforcing event is maintaining the problem behavior, this reinforcer should be effective in a DRO procedure when it is made contingent on the absence of the problem behavior.

Choosing the Initial DRO Time Interval DRO involves delivering the reinforcer after an interval of time in which the problem behavior does not occur. Thus, to implement DRO, you must choose the initial time interval for delivering the reinforcer. The length of the interval should be tied to the baseline rate of the problem behavior: If the problem behavior occurs frequently, the DRO interval will be short; if the problem behavior occurs infrequently, the DRO interval will be longer. You should choose an interval length that will result in a high probability of reinforcement (Repp, 1983). For example, suppose that a problem behavior occurs at an average rate of ten times an hour in a given situation. That means that, on the average, 6 minutes elapse between each occurrence of the problem behavior. For this particular problem behavior, the DRO interval must be set at less than 6 minutes so that there is a good probability that the problem behavior will not occur in the interval and the reinforcer can be delivered. As the frequency of the problem behavior decreases, the DRO intervals can be lengthened gradually.

Implementing DRO After you identify the reinforcer for the problem behavior, choose a reinforcer to use in the DRO procedure, and establish the initial interval length, you are ready to implement the DRO procedure. First, the change agent (e.g., the parent or teacher) must be taught how to implement the procedure. The change agent is instructed to eliminate the reinforcer for the problem behavior and to deliver the reinforcer at the end of every interval in which the problem behavior does not occur. The change agent has a stopwatch (or other timing device) to time the DRO interval. At the end of each interval, the stopwatch cues the change agent to deliver the reinforcer if the problem behavior has not occurred. If the problem behavior does occur at some point, the reinforcer is not delivered, and the interval for reinforcement is

IMPLEMENTING DRO

1. Identify the reinforcer for the problem behavior.
2. Identify the reinforcer to use in the DRO procedure.
3. Choose the initial DRO time interval.
4. Eliminate the reinforcer for the problem behavior and deliver the reinforcer for the absence of the problem behavior.

reset. Suppose that the DRO interval is 10 minutes. Then, any time the problem behavior occurs before the 10-minute interval is up, the change agent resets the interval for 10 minutes. After 10 minutes, if the problem behavior has not occurred, the reinforcer is delivered. Once the reinforcer is delivered, the interval is reset for another 10 minutes. If the person with the problem behavior can understand instructions, you should tell the person that the reinforcer will be given when the target behavior does not occur for a specific period of time.

After the problem behavior is decreased and the client is receiving the reinforcer after almost all intervals, it is time to increase the length of the intervals. The interval length is increased slowly to maintain the reduction in the problem behavior. Eventually, the DRO interval is increased to a level that will be manageable for the change agent in the long term. Depending on the person and the particular problem behavior, it is not uncommon to increase the DRO interval to an hour or two or to an entire day. This would mean that the client would have to refrain from engaging in the problem behavior for the entire day to receive the reinforcer at the end of the day. For many clients, the DRO procedure is eventually eliminated after an extended period of time in which the problem behavior no longer occurs.

Research Evaluating DRO Procedures

We now review some of the extensive research on DRO for treating various problem behaviors.

Bostow and Bailey (1969) implemented DRO with Ruth, a 58-year-old woman with mental retardation who lived in a state institution and screamed loudly and violently to get what she wanted (e.g., her meal tray, a cup of coffee, articles of clothing, favorite objects). Before using DRO, the staff had inadvertently reinforced this problem behavior by getting things for her when she screamed. In the DRO procedure, staff provided the objects that Ruth wanted only after time periods in which she did not scream. The time periods were increased gradually from 5 minutes to 30 minutes as the screaming no longer occurred. When the screaming did occur, staff did not provide the reinforcing objects to her. Instead, they wheeled her wheelchair to a corner of the room, where her screaming did not disrupt other residents. (This is a time-out procedure; see Chapter 17.) The screaming was reduced to zero with the use of these procedures (Figure 15-4).

Cowdery, Iwata, and Pace (1990) worked with Jerry, a 9-year-old boy who engaged in a type of self-injurious behavior (SIB) in which he scratched or rubbed his skin until he produced open sores all over his body. Jerry did not exhibit mental retardation, but he had never attended school; the SIB was so severe that he had spent most of his time in hospitals. The researchers conducted a functional assessment that showed that

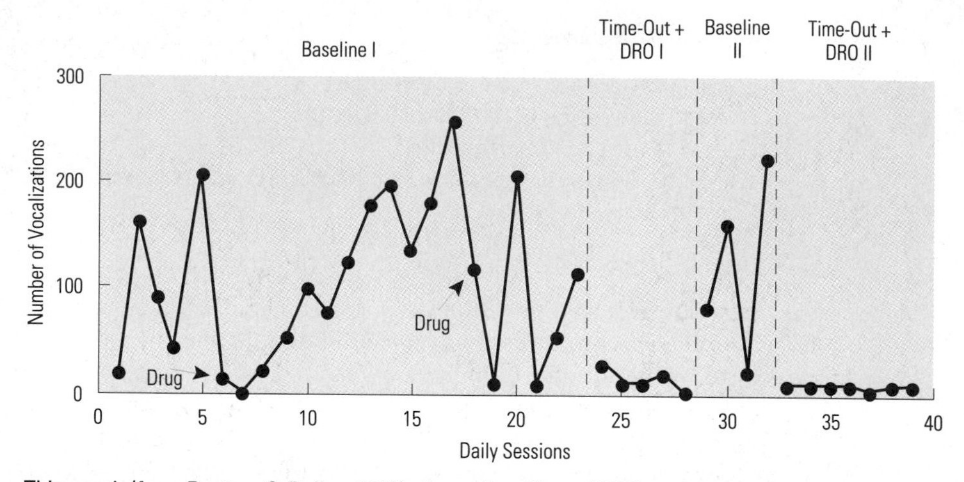

FIGURE 15-4 This graph (from Bostow & Bailey, 1969) shows the effect of DRO and time-out on the screaming of a 58-year-old woman with mental retardation who lived in an institution. When the woman stopped screaming for brief periods of time, the staff provided reinforcers. When she screamed, she was taken to another part of the room by herself, and no reinforcers were provided. Gradually, the DRO interval was lengthened, and she was able to go longer and longer without screaming. As you can see in the graph, each time the DRO procedure (and time-out) was implemented in an A-B-A-B reversal design, the screaming decreased to zero.

the SIB occurred exclusively when Jerry was alone. There was no social reinforcement for the problem behavior.

The researchers implemented a DRO procedure involving token reinforcement. Jerry received tokens for periods of time that he did not engage in SIB and later exchanged his tokens for access to TV, snacks, video games, and various play materials. The authors put Jerry into a room by himself and observed him through a one-way observation window. If Jerry went 2 minutes without scratching, an experimenter came in the room, looked at him briefly to inspect for scratches, and gave Jerry a token for not scratching. If Jerry scratched during the 2-minute interval, an experimenter went into the room, pointed to the spot where Jerry had scratched, and said that he could not have a token because he had scratched. However, the experimenter encouraged him to try again. When Jerry was successful with the 2-minute interval, it was increased to 4 minutes. Eventually, the DRO interval was increased to 15 minutes.

Once Jerry was successful in the short treatment sessions, the authors implemented the DRO procedure for 4–5 hours per day while Jerry was in activity areas on the hospital ward. The DRO interval in the activity area was 30 minutes. Each time Jerry went 30 minutes without scratching, he received a token. If he scratched, the 30-minute DRO interval was reset and he had to refrain from scratching for the next 30 minutes to get a token. Next, the DRO procedure was extended to the entire day. Finally, Jerry was discharged from the hospital and his parents continued to use the DRO procedure at home. This program greatly reduced Jerry's scratching. It was the first time Jerry had been out of the hospital in 2 years.

Whole-Interval DRO

- Behavior is absent throughout the entire interval.
- Reinforcer is delivered.

Momentary DRO

- Behavior is absent when the interval ends.
- Reinforcer is delivered.

In this study, the researchers were able to decrease Jerry's problem behavior using DRO without also using extinction for the problem behavior. The reinforcer for Jerry's scratching was its sensory consequences. Although the experimenters did not eliminate this reinforcer, the reinforcers for the absence of the scratching apparently were strong enough to produce a decrease in the behavior even though it continued to be reinforced. Whenever possible, extinction should be a component of the DRO procedure.

A study by Repp, Barton, and Brulle (1983) compared two variations of DRO: the whole-interval and momentary procedures. In **whole-interval DRO**, the problem behavior must be absent for the whole interval for the reinforcer to be delivered. In **momentary DRO**, the problem behavior must be absent at the end of the interval for the reinforcer to be delivered.

The researchers compared the effectiveness of the two types of DRO with three 7-year-old boys with mild mental retardation who engaged in disruptive behaviors (interruptions, out of seat, off task) in the classroom. In the whole-interval DRO, the child was given a small treat at the end of each 5-minute interval if the disruptive behavior did not occur at any time in the interval. In the momentary DRO procedure, the child received a small treat if the problem behavior was not occurring at the end of each 5-minute interval. The authors found that the whole-interval DRO procedure was more effective in reducing the disruptive behavior than was the momentary DRO procedure. The only time that the momentary DRO procedure resulted in a decrease in the problem behavior was when it was implemented after the whole-interval DRO procedure had already decreased the problem behavior. The results suggested that the momentary DRO procedure was not effective by itself but may be useful to maintain the behavior change produced by the whole-interval DRO procedure. The findings of Barton, Brulle, and Repp (1986) supported this conclusion. The benefit of momentary DRO is that the target behavior does not have to be observed throughout the entire interval.

The studies cited here, as well as other research, suggest that the DRO procedure is effective with a variety of problem behaviors in a variety of people (Mazaleski et al., 1993; Poling & Ryan, 1982; Repp, 1983; Vollmer & Iwata, 1992; Vollmer, Iwata, Zarcone, Smith, & Mazaleski, 1993; Zlutnick, Mayville, & Moffat, 1975). DRO is most effective when the reinforcer for the problem behavior can be identified and eliminated and when the length of the DRO interval is based on the baseline rate of the behavior. Furthermore, DRO is most effective when the reinforcer is delivered in response to the absence of the problem behavior for the entire interval (whole-interval DRO).

Differential Reinforcement of Low Rates of Responding

Deitz and Repp (1973) investigated another type of differential reinforcement called **differential reinforcement of low rates of responding (DRL).** They used the procedure to decrease disruptive behavior in special education and regular education classrooms. In one experiment, they used DRL to decrease talk-outs (talking in class without permission) in a classroom of students with mental retardation. Before treatment was implemented, the students averaged 32 talk-outs during a 50-minute class period. In the DRL procedure, the teacher told the students before class started that if they talked-out fewer than five times in the class period, they would all receive two pieces of candy at the end of the day. The reinforcer, candy, was contingent on a lower rate of the behavior. They conducted the DRL procedure for 15 days and, during this time, the average number of talk-outs decreased to about three per 50-minute class period. In the 15 days that they conducted the DRL procedure, the students went over five talk-outs in the class period only once and lost the reinforcer for that day.

Defining DRL

In DRL, the reinforcer is delivered when the rate of the problem behavior is decreased to a criterion level. In the DRL procedure you do not reinforce the absence of the behavior, as in the DRO procedure; rather, you reinforce a lower rate of the problem behavior. A DRL procedure is used when a low rate of the problem behavior can be tolerated or when the behavior is a problem only because of its high rate. Suppose that a student in second grade raises his hand to answer questions every few minutes. Raising his hand is not a problem behavior except for the fact that it occurs too frequently and the other students do not get a chance to participate. The teacher does not want to eliminate this behavior; she just wants to lower the rate of the behavior. DRL would be an ideal procedure to use in this case. To use DRL, the teacher would tell the student that she wants him to raise his hand only three times per class period and that if he does so, he will be allowed to read first in the reading group later in the day. (The teacher knows that this is a reinforcer for the student.) If he raises his hand more than three times in the class period, he will read last in the group that day. The teacher might make the DRL procedure more effective by telling the student to keep track of the times he raises his hand on a piece of paper on his desk. When he records the behavior a third time, he knows he must not raise his hand again. Alternatively, the teacher might make a mark on the board each time the student raises his hand; again, the student will see when he gets to three and must not raise his hand again.

Variations of DRL

There are two main ways in which DRL schedules can be programmed (Deitz, 1977). In one variation, reinforcement is delivered if fewer than a specified number of responses occurs in a period of time. This is called **full-session DRL.** The session might be a class period or some other appropriate period of time at home, school, work, or wherever the problem behavior occurs. The change agent specifies the maximum number of responses that can occur in the session for the reinforcer to be delivered. At the end of the session, if the number of responses is fewer than the specified number,

FULL-SESSION DRL

- Fewer than X responses occur in the session.
- Reinforcer is delivered.

SPACED-RESPONDING DRL

- Response occurs after an interval of time.
- Reinforcer is delivered.

the change agent delivers the reinforcer. The teacher who told the student he had to raise his hand in class no more than three times to receive the reinforcer was using full-session DRL. Contrast this procedure with a DRO procedure, in which the student would have to refrain completely from the behavior during the session in order to receive the reinforcer.

In a second variation of DRL, **spaced-responding DRL**, there must be a specified amount of time between responses for the reinforcer to be delivered. In spaced-responding DRL, the objective is to pace the behavior. Go back to the example of the student in second grade who raises his hand too frequently. To use spaced-responding DRL, the teacher would call on the student only if he raised his hand at least 15 minutes after the last time he raised his hand. (Being called on by the teacher is a reinforcer for raising his hand.) If he raised his hand before this 15-minute interval was up, the teacher would not call on him, and he would have to wait another 15 minutes before he could raise his hand and get called on by the teacher. When the behavior occurs after the DRL interval is up, the behavior is reinforced. However, if the behavior occurs before the DRL interval is up, the behavior is not reinforced, and the interval is reset.

How are DRO and spaced-responding DRL different?

In DRO, the reinforcer is delivered for the *absence* of the behavior after an interval of time has passed. If the behavior occurs, the reinforcer is not delivered. In spaced-responding DRL, the reinforcer is delivered for the *occurrence* of the behavior after an interval of time has passed since the last instance of the behavior. DRO is used when you want to eliminate a problem behavior; spaced-responding DRL is used when you want to decrease the rate of a behavior that occurs too frequently.

A third type of DRL, **interval DRL**, is similar to spaced-responding DRL. Interval DRL involves dividing a session into intervals and providing the reinforcer if no more than one response occurred in each interval. Whereas spaced-responding DRL entails a specific interval of time between each response, interval DRL entails an average time between each response. To simplify the discussion of DRL, the interval procedure will not be considered further; see Deitz (1977) for more information.

Implementing DRL Procedures

The first step is to determine whether DRL is the appropriate procedure to use. If the goal is to decrease the rate of a behavior but not to eliminate the behavior, DRL is appropriate. The next step is to determine an acceptable level of the behavior. In full-session DRL, you must decide how many responses per session are acceptable. In spaced-responding DRL, you must choose what interval of time should elapse between each occurrence of the behavior. Next you must decide whether to implement full-session DRL or spaced-responding DRL. If the timing of the behavior is important and it is necessary to have an interval of time between responses, spaced-responding DRL is most appropriate. For example, if you are trying to get an obese person to slow down his eating rate and you want 10 seconds to elapse between each bite of food, spaced-responding DRL would be most appropriate. However, if the timing of each response is less important and you simply want to decrease the overall rate of the behavior in a session, full-session DRL is most appropriate.

Before implementing the DRL procedure, you should inform the client about the procedure so that he or she knows the criterion for reinforcement. In full-session DRL, you should tell the client the maximum number of responses that is acceptable in the session. In spaced-responding DRL, you should tell the client how much time you expect between each instance of the behavior. In both cases, you should tell the client what the reinforcer is for achieving the criterion performance.

In addition to instructions, it is often useful to give the client feedback on his or her performance when implementing the DRL procedure. For example, in full-session DRL, the change agent or the client might keep track of the number of responses in the session so that the client can see when he or she is approaching the maximum. For example, Tony, a young man with mental retardation living in a group home, frequently asked staff what the weather was going to be like the next day. Each evening, from supper until he went to bed, Tony asked staff about the weather 10–12 times. The staff implemented a full-session DRL in which they provided a preferred activity at the end of the evening if Tony asked about the weather no more than four times. To help Tony keep track of the number of times he asked about the weather each evening, he carried a notecard with him and put a check mark on it each time he asked. He understood that once his notecard had four check marks on it, he could not ask about the weather any more that evening. He learned to look at his notecard whenever he was about to talk to staff and to ask about something other than the weather when he already had his four check marks. Eventually the criterion was decreased from four to two as Tony limited his questions about the weather.

When using spaced-responding DRL, it is helpful to provide some method that allows the client to keep track of the time between responses, to help him or her pace the behavior. For example, Jenny, a 5-year-old girl, had accidentally wet her pants in kindergarten one day. Although no one else had noticed, she was embarrassed. She started going to the bathroom frequently, up to five times an hour, when she was at school. The teacher implemented a spaced-responding DRL procedure in which Jenny received a star if she waited at least 30 minutes between trips to the bathroom. To help Jenny time the intervals, the teacher had a notebook with a big star on it and she put the notebook upright on her desk each half hour as a cue to Jenny that she could now go to the bathroom. When Jenny saw the notebook with the big star on the teacher's desk, she knew she could get a star for going to the bathroom. If she went before the notebook was put up on the teacher's desk, she would not get a star and would have to wait another 30 minutes before she could go to the bathroom and get a star. Eventually, as Jenny was successful with the 30-minute interval, the teacher increased the interval to an hour. By using the notebook as a cue, instead of a timer that the whole class could hear, the teacher was able to avoid drawing attention to Jenny and embarrassing her in front of the class.

Research Evaluating DRL Procedures

Studies by Deitz and Repp (1973, 1974) evaluated full-session DRL procedures for decreasing problem behaviors in children of school age. In addition to the experiment described earlier, in which they used DRL to decrease talk-outs in a class of ten elementary students with mental retardation, Deitz and Repp (1973) conducted an experiment evaluating full-session DRL with 15 high school senior girls in a business class. The target behavior was a subject change, in which a student changed the topic of class discussion from an academic topic to a nonacademic topic (e.g., a social topic). Before the DRL procedure was implemented, there were close to seven subject changes per 50-minute class period.

The DRL procedure was conducted in five phases. In the first phase, the students had to make fewer than six subject changes per class period. If they met this criterion for the first four days of the week, they received a free day, with no class on Friday, as the reinforcer. In the second phase, the criterion was fewer than four subject changes per class period. The criterion was fewer than two subject changes per class period in the third phase and zero in the final phase. In each phase, the class met the criterion and received the reinforcer, a free day on Friday. By the last phase, the DRL procedure had reduced the problem behavior to zero. Technically, the last phase was a DRO procedure rather than a DRL procedure because the absence of the behavior was required for reinforcement.

In another study, Deitz and Repp (1974) used full-session DRL to decrease classroom misbehavior in elementary school children. An 11-year-old boy who frequently talked out in class decreased this behavior when the DRL procedure was implemented. The teacher told him that he would receive a gold star each time he engaged in two or fewer talk-outs in a 45-minute class period. The behavior decreased from an average of six talk-outs per class period in two baseline conditions to less than two (an average of 1.5) in two treatment phases implemented in an A-B-A-B research design. The same procedure was effective in decreasing out-of-seat behavior and talk-outs in two other 11- and 12-year-old students.

A couple of studies have investigated the spaced-responding DRL procedure for decreasing the rate of problem behaviors in people with mental retardation. Singh, Dawson, and Manning (1981) used this type of DRL procedure to decrease the rate of stereotypic responding in adolescents with mental retardation living in an institution. **Stereotypic behavior** is repetitive behavior that does not serve any social function for the person. Such behaviors often are called self-stimulatory behaviors because they produce some form of sensory stimulation for the person. The three adolescents in this study engaged in body rocking, mouthing objects, and repetitive finger movements. Using praise as a reinforcer, the researchers praised the subjects when they emitted a stereotypic response if the time since the last response was at least 12 seconds. The 12 seconds between responses is called an **interresponse time (IRT)**. After the rate of stereotypic behavior decreased in the DRL procedure with the 12-second IRT, the IRT was increased to 30 seconds; the subjects received praise after a response each time

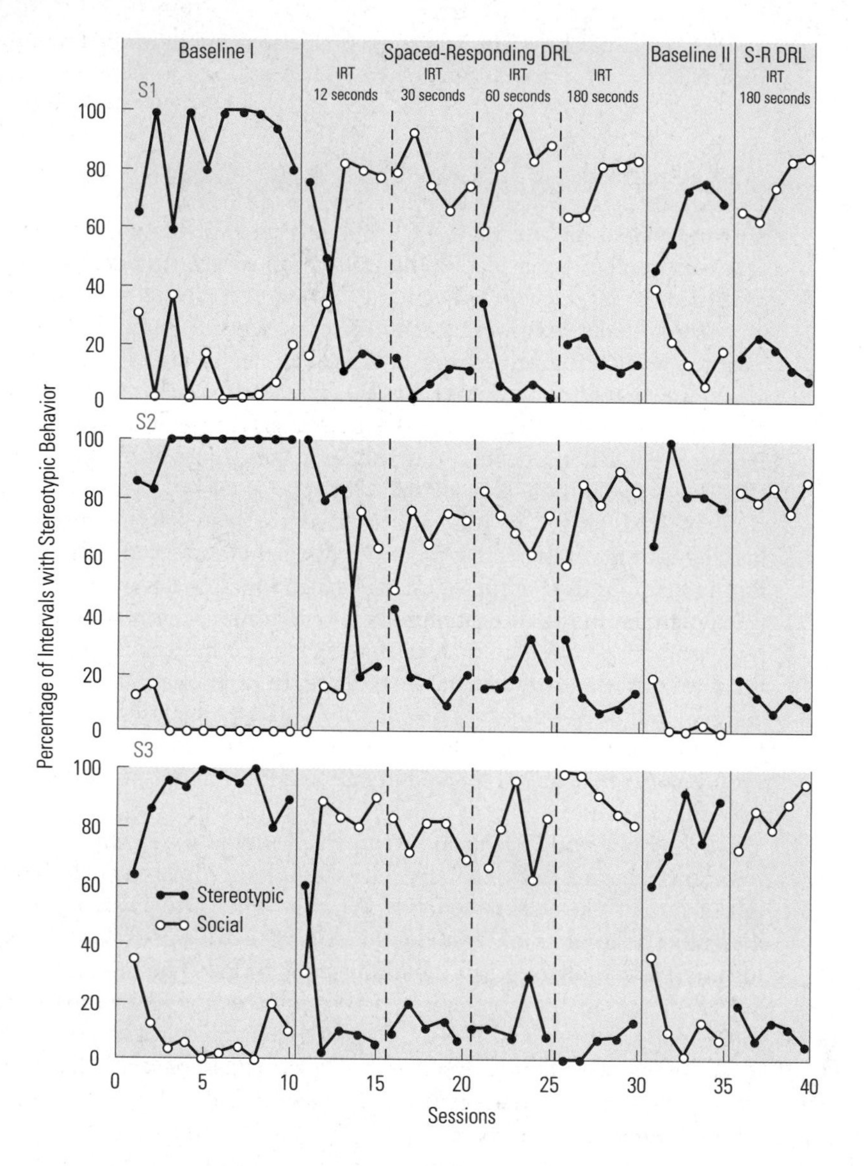

FIGURE 15-5 This graph (from Singh et al., 1981) shows the effects of spaced-responding DRL on the stereotypic behavior of three adolescent girls with mental retardation. After baseline, DRL was implemented and the IRT was increased gradually from 12 to 180 seconds. The stereotypic behavior decreased when the DRL procedure was implemented and remained low at each IRT. The graph also shows that appropriate behaviors increased as the stereotypic behavior decreased.

there was at least 30 seconds between responses. The IRT was then increased to 60 seconds and finally to 180 seconds. The results showed that the stereotypic behavior decreased with the use of the spaced-responding DRL procedure and more acceptable behavior (e.g., smiling, communicating, or playing with toys) increased. The results from this study are shown in Figure 15-5.

Lennox, Miltenberger, and Donnelly (1987) used a spaced-responding DRL procedure to decrease the eating rate of three people with profound mental retardation who ate their meals extremely rapidly. The rapid eating was a problem because it stigmatized the clients and it had potential negative health effects. The researchers observed other people eating and established that 15 seconds was an average time between bites of food (IRT) for those eaters. The researchers implemented the DRL procedure by sitting next to each subject at mealtimes and blocking the subject from taking a bite of food when the subject attempted to take a bite less than 15 seconds after the previous bite of food. If the time since the last bite of food was at least 15 seconds, the experimenters allowed the subject to take a bite. To help the subjects pace their bites of food, the experimenters prompted the subjects to put down the utensil and put their hands in their laps between each bite. This established a competing response that helped the subjects wait 15 seconds between each bite of food. The DRL procedure decreased the eating rate for all three subjects. However, one subject became aggressive when the experimenters blocked him from taking a bite. For this subject, they added a brief time-out procedure (Chapter 17) in which they sat across the table and pulled his plate out of reach each time he tried to take a bite of food before the IRT had reached 15 seconds. The addition of the brief time out allowed the experimenters to implement the DRL procedure successfully with this subject also. It is important to note that the subject was never deprived of food; he always finished his meal. It would be unethical to not allow him to finish his meal.

CHAPTER SUMMARY

1. DRA involves reinforcing a desirable behavior and extinguishing undesirable behaviors that may interfere with the desirable behavior. To use DRA, the desirable behavior must be occurring at least occasionally so that it can be reinforced.
2. DRO involves reinforcing the absence of the problem behavior during intervals of time. When the problem behavior does not occur in the interval, the reinforcer is delivered and when the problem behavior occurs, the interval for reinforcement is reset. DRL involves reinforcing a lower rate of the problem behavior. The reinforcer may be contingent on fewer than a set number of responses occurring in a time period or the reinforcer may be contingent on the behavior when a specified interresponse time occurs.
3. DRA should be used when you want to increase the frequency of an existing desirable behavior. DRO should be used when you want to eliminate a problem behavior. DRL may be used when you want to decrease but not necessarily eliminate a target behavior.
4. Reinforcement is involved when the alternative behavior (DRA), the absence of the behavior (DRO), or a lower rate of the behavior (DRL) is reinforced. Extinction is used when the problem behavior occurs (DRA and DRO) or when the rate of the behavior exceeds the criterion for reinforcement (DRL).
5. Negative reinforcement is used in DRO or DRA when termination of an aversive stimulus is the reinforcer for an alternative behavior (DRA) or the reinforcer for the absence of the problem behavior (DRO).

Practice Test

1. Define differential reinforcement of alternative behavior (DRA). (p. 311)
2. Provide an example of DRA that is not in the book.
3. What two behavioral principles are involved in differential reinforcement? Explain. (p. 311)
4. When is it appropriate to use DRA? (p. 313)
5. Provide an example of a situation in which you would not use DRA. (p. 313)
6. Describe three ways to identify reinforcers for a person. (pp. 314–315)
7. When using DRA, at what point do you use a continuous reinforcement schedule? Why? (p. 315)
8. When using DRA, at what point do you use an intermittent reinforcement schedule? Why? (p. 316)
9. What is the Premack principle? Provide an example. (p. 320)
10. What is generalization? How do you program for generalization when using DRA? (p. 316)
11. How does DRO differ from DRA? (pp. 322–323)
12. What does *DRO* stand for? Describe the implementation of the DRO procedure. (p. 322)
13. Provide an example of DRO.
14. Why is it important to use extinction for the problem behavior when implementing DRO? (p. 323)
15. How do you establish the length of the interval for reinforcement in the DRO procedure? Provide an example. (p. 324)
16. When implementing DRO, what do you do if the problem behavior occurs before the end of the interval for reinforcement? (pp. 324–325)
17. How is a whole-interval DRO procedure different from a momentary DRO procedure? Which one is preferable? Why? (p. 327)
18. What does DRL stand for? What are the two types of DRL procedures? (pp. 328–329)
19. Describe the implementation of full-session DRL. Provide an example. (p. 328)
20. Describe the implementation of spaced-responding DRL. Provide an example. (p. 329)
21. How does the purpose of DRO differ from that of DRL? (p. 329)
22. How does the implementation of DRO differ from the implementation of spaced-responding DRL? (p. 329)
23. When implementing the spaced-responding DRL procedure, what do you do if the behavior occurs before the end of the interval? (p. 329)

Applications

1. Describe how you might use one of the three types of differential reinforcement procedures in your self-management project to increase the rate of your target behavior or decrease a problem behavior. If you believe differential reinforcement is not an appropriate procedure for your self-management project, give your reasons.

2. Your friend Betty knows that you are taking a behavior modification class and comes to you for help. She is not doing well in her courses because she spends very little time studying. Every evening after supper, she spends time with her friends, talking, watching TV and videos, and playing games. She wants your advice on how to study more in the evening. Describe how you would apply DRA using the Premack principle to help Betty study more.

3. You are a staff member working in a residential program for juvenile delinquents. One of

the adolescents in the program, Charles, hates to be teased about his height. (He's quite tall.) Whenever another adolescent teases him, Charles gets into a fight. Although this makes the other person stop teasing him, the fighting is getting Charles in trouble and may lengthen the time he has to spend in the program. Charles wants you to help him with his problem of getting into fights. You consider using DRA. Answer the following questions to illustrate how you will use differential reinforcement.

a. What is currently reinforcing Charles' fighting? Is this positive or negative reinforcement?
b. What desirable behavior will you have Charles engage in to take the place of the fighting?
c. What will reinforce the desirable behavior?
d. How will you make sure the desirable behavior gets reinforced each time Charles exhibits that behavior?
e. How will you program for generalization to make sure Charles exhibits the desirable behavior whenever he gets teased?

4. Your friend Christina complains that she drinks way too much caffeine each day. She estimates that she drinks a total of ten cups of coffee or cans of cola. Not only is her habit expensive, but she has trouble getting to sleep at night. Christina wants to limit her caffeine to a combined total of four cups of coffee or cans of cola per day. Describe how you would instruct Christina to implement a full-session DRL procedure to decrease her daily coffee and cola consumption. Describe how you would instruct Christina to implement a spaced-responding DRL procedure to limit her daily coffee and cola consumption.

5. The Jacksons like to go out for supper a few nights a week. However, they don't go as often as they would like because their children, 4-year-old Jimmy and 5-year-old Jane, engage in disruptive behavior at restaurants while waiting for the food to arrive. The children tease each other, play with the table settings, get out of their seats, and complain about having to wait. The parents often reprimand them for their disruptive behavior, but Jimmy and Jane behave themselves only for a brief time afterward and then start engaging in disruptive behavior again. Describe the DRO procedure you would have the Jacksons implement to decrease their children's disruptive behavior in restaurants.

MISAPPLICATIONS

1. Elena went to see a counselor at the University Counseling Center because she was having trouble adjusting to school. Elena's main problem was that she was unsure of herself and didn't know what to say to people she met at parties or other gatherings. Instead, she said things that sounded stupid to her. The counselor decided to use DRA. He would let Elena practice appropriate social skills in role-plays in their counseling sessions and reinforce Elena's social skills with praise and positive feedback. He would withhold praise and positive feedback when Elena acted unsure of herself or said things that sounded stupid and would provide corrective feedback instead. Elena role-played talking to people as if she were in the cafeteria. After three sessions, she increased her social skills in the role-plays. The counselor thought Elena was doing so well that she did not need to come in and work on her social skills anymore. The counselor wished her luck and said goodbye.

a. What is the problem with the use of DRA in this example?
b. Describe what you would have done differently to make DRA more effective.

2. Jared was excited about teaching his dog, Puff, to roll over. His neighbor had taught her dog to roll over, and Jared knew he could use DRA to teach Puff to roll over, although he'd never seen Puff do so before. Knowing that Puff loved bacon, Jared fried some and cut it into pieces to use as reinforcers. He then took Puff into the living room and gave her the command to roll over. As soon as Puff rolled over, he was go-

ing to give her a big piece of bacon to reinforce that behavior. He would then give her the command again and immediately give her a piece of bacon when she rolled over again. Is this an appropriate application of DRA? Why or why not?

3. Lonnie, a 5-year-old boy, was an only child who lived with his parents. His mother, who was home with Lonnie during the day, was having trouble with Lonnie's disruptive behavior. He whined frequently, interrupted her when she was busy, and demanded that she play with him. His mother responded in various ways, sometimes playing with him, sometimes explaining to him that she was busy, and sometimes ignoring the disruptive behavior. She described the problem to the family doctor, who suggested the use of DRO to decrease the disruptive behavior. The doctor told Lonnie's mother to provide a reinforcer (praise, attention, and a treat) after Lonnie had gone 2 hours without disruptive behavior. If Lonnie engaged in the disruptive behavior, she was to ignore the behavior and wait another 2 hours (the DRO interval) and provide the reinforcer if Lonnie had not engaged in the problem behavior in that time. What is the problem with this DRO procedure? How would you make it better?

4. Marva, a 39-year-old woman with severe mental retardation, spent 23 years living in a state institution, where she began engaging in stereotypic behavior involving repetitive body rocking. Marva moved to a group home, where she continued to engage in the stereotypic behavior. Whenever she was not engaged in an activity or a task, she sat in a chair and rocked back and forth, or she stood and rocked back and forth from one foot to the other. Marva spent most of her time by herself, away from other people in the group home. The staff were going to implement a DRO procedure in which they would praise Marva each time she went 5 minutes without rocking. They planned to gradually increase the DRO interval once the stereotypic behavior was decreasing. What is the problem with this DRO procedure? How could you make it better?

CHAPTER 15 *Quiz 1* Name:

1. ______________________ is a procedure in which reinforcement is used to increase the frequency of a desirable behavior, and extinction is used decrease the frequency of undesirable behaviors.

2. Identify two different ways to identify reinforcers to use in a differential reinforcement procedure.

   ______________________________ and ______________________________

3. When using DRA, you will use continuous reinforcement initially, and then use

   ______________________ to maintain the behavior.

4. ________________ is a procedure in which you provide a reinforcer for the absence of the problem behavior.

5. What does DRO stand for? ______________________________

6. What does DRA stand for? ______________________________

7. What do you reinforce in a DRL procedure? ______________________________

Match the following procedures to the descriptions.

a. Spaced-responding DRL   b. Full-session DRL   c. DRO

8. ________ A reinforcer is delivered at the end of 30 seconds if the behavior did not occur in the interval.

9. ________ A reinforcer is delivered if the behavior occurred fewer than 5 times in the class period.

10. ________ A reinforcer is delivered if the behavior occurred at least 30 seconds after the last instance of the behavior.

CHAPTER 15 *Quiz 2*

Name:

1. What two behavioral principles are involved in DRA? ____________________ and ____________________

2. ____________________ is an appropriate procedure to use when you want to increase the rate of a desirable behavior, the behavior is occurring at least occasionally, and you have access to an effective reinforcer.

3. In the ______________ procedure, when the problem behavior occurs, you do not provide the reinforcer and instead reset the interval for reinforcement.

4. In ____________________ DRO, the reinforcer is delivered if the problem behavior was absent in the entire interval.

5. In ____________________ DRO, the reinforcer is delivered if the problem behavior was absent when the interval ended.

6. In __________________ DRL, the reinforcer is delivered when fewer than a specified number of responses occurs.

7. In __________________ DRL, the reinforcer is delivered when response occurs a specific amount of time after the previous response.

Match the following procedures to the descriptions.

a. DRA b. DRO c. DRL

8. _______ When Nelly raised her hand at least 10 minutes after the last time she raised her hand, her teacher called on her.

9. _______ When Nelly went 10 minutes without talking out in class, her teacher praised her.

10. _______ When Nelly asked her classmate for the scissors instead of grabbing the scissors from her classmate's hand, her teacher praised her.

CHAPTER 15 *Quiz 3* Name:

1. Which differential reinforcement procedure was used when staff reinforced Mrs. Williams' positive talk and ignored her complaining? ____________________

2. In differential negative reinforcement of alternative behavior (DNRA), what is the reinforcer for the desirable behavior? ________________________________

Match the appropriate procedure to the following examples.

a. DRI b. DRC or functional communication training

3. ________ In an attempt to decrease Jenny's hair pulling, each time Jenny holds her hands in her lap, her parents praise her.

4. ________ Jenny engages in disruptive behavior in an attempt to get out of doing her homework. In an attempt to decrease Jenny's disruptive behavior, each time Jenny asks for assistance instead of engaging in disruptive behavior, her parents help her with her homework.

5. In the DRO procedure, the reinforcer is contingent on ____________________.

6. When the baseline rate of the problem behavior is high, the DRO interval will be ______________ (shorter/longer), and when the baseline rate of the problem behavior is low, the DRO interval will be ____________ (shorter/longer).

7. In DRO, what do you do each time the problem behavior occurs?

____

Match the following procedures to the descriptions.

a. DRA b. DRO c. DRL

8. __________ Staff provided a reinforcer when Pete went 2 minutes without cursing.

9. __________ Staff provided a reinforcer each time Pete used the word "fudge" instead of a curse word.

10. __________ Staff provided Pete a reinforcer when he cursed fewer than two times each evening.

Antecedent Control Procedures

The procedures we discussed in the preceding chapters—functional assessment, extinction, and differential reinforcement—are used to increase desirable behaviors and decrease undesirable behaviors. Functional assessment procedures are used to identify the antecedents and consequences that maintain the desirable and undesirable target behaviors. With extinction procedures, the reinforcer for an undesirable behavior is removed; with differential reinforcement procedures, reinforcers are delivered for alternative desirable behaviors, for the absence of the problem behavior, or for a lower rate of the problem behavior. In **antecedent control procedures** (also called antecedent manipulations), antecedent stimuli are manipulated to evoke desirable behaviors, so that they can be differentially reinforced, and to decrease undesirable behaviors that interfere with the desirable behaviors.

- What is an antecedent control procedure?
- How can you influence a target behavior by manipulating a discriminative stimulus for the behavior?
- What is an establishing operation, and how does it influence a target behavior?
- What is the effect of response effort on a target behavior?
- What are the three functional, nonaversive approaches to intervention for a problem behavior?

Examples of Antecedent Control

Getting Marianne to Study More

Marianne was in the middle of her first semester of college. Because she was getting Ds and Fs in most of her classes, she went to the counseling center for help. As she talked to her counselor, it became clear that she was not studying enough. The only time that Marianne studied was the night before a test. She had many friends in the dorm and, instead of studying, they watched TV at night or went to parties or just spent hours talking. Every time Marianne started to study, she stopped and did something fun with her friends instead. As a result, she panicked when she had to take tests and stayed up all night studying and trying to catch up. The counselor decided that antecedent control procedures would help Marianne study more. Together, Marianne and the counselor decided on the following plan.

1. Marianne identified the 2 hours each day that would work best for her to study. She wrote these 2 hours down in her appointment book for each day of the week.
2. She decided that she would study in the library. She was distracted frequently by her friends in the dorm, so she knew she had to study in another location if she was

going to get any work done. She decided on the library because her classes were near the library and her friends never went there.

3. She identified a friend who studied every day. She called her friend and planned study sessions at least a few days a week.

4. She wrote down her study schedule on a sheet of paper and posted it on the refrigerator door at the beginning of each week. She told her friends that she intended to study at these times and asked them not to bother her.

5. She kept her books with her in a backpack so that she could study if she had some free time (e.g., if a class was canceled or between classes).

6. She wrote down the times of all her tests and assignments on a calendar in her room. Each evening she crossed the current day off the calendar, so that she could see how close she was getting to a test or assignment.

7. She made a written contract with her counselor in which she committed to do the hours of studying that she had scheduled.

These seven steps helped Marianne study more often. Each step involved manipulating an antecedent to studying or manipulating an antecedent to competing behaviors that interfered with studying. Consider another example.

Getting Cal to Eat Right

Cal was interested in improving his diet. He wanted to eat more complex carbohydrates, vegetables, fruits, and foods high in fiber. Currently, he was eating many foods high in fat and sugar and low in fiber (such as potato chips, candy, cookies, and soft drinks). Cal took a number of steps to make it more likely that he would eat healthful foods.

Identify the steps you believe Cal could take to make it more likely that he would eat healthful foods.

1. He got rid of all the unhealthful foods he had in his apartment and at work.

2. He went shopping only on a full stomach, so that he wasn't tempted to buy quick-to-eat but unhealthful foods.

3. He made a list of healthful foods to buy before shopping and never bought anything that was not on the list.

4. He packed a healthful lunch each day and brought it to work with him so that he wouldn't eat fast food or unhealthful snacks at lunchtime.

5. He never kept any change in his pocket when he went to work so that he couldn't buy any junk foods from the vending machines.

6. He bought a number of fruits and healthful snacks and kept them handy at home to replace the unhealthful snacks he used to have at home.

7. He told his roommate and his girlfriend that he was going to eat only healthful foods and asked them to remind him if they saw him eating unhealthful foods.

8. He bought a health food cookbook to learn how to make healthful foods that tasted good.

9. He made a graph on which he could record the number of days each month that he ate only healthful food. He put the graph on his refrigerator where he and his roommate and girlfriend could see it every day.

By making these nine straightforward changes, Cal was able to change the antecedent conditions that contributed to his eating behaviors. The changes made it more likely that he would eat healthful food and less likely that he would eat unhealthful food.

Defining Antecedent Control Procedures

Antecedent control procedures involve manipulating some aspect of the physical or social environment to evoke a desired response or to make a competing, undesirable behavior less likely. Six different antecedent control procedures are described here.

Presenting the S^D or Cues for the Desired Behavior

One reason that a desirable behavior may not occur very often is that the S^Ds for the behavior are not present in the person's environment. For example, the S^D for eating healthful foods is the presence of healthful foods in the kitchen or the person's lunch bag. If healthful foods are not present, the person will be less likely to eat such foods; if they are present and readily available, the person is more likely to eat them.

To increase the likelihood that he would eat healthful foods, Cal presented appropriate S^Ds. What were they?

Cal bought healthful foods and kept them available in his kitchen to eat. He also packed a healthful lunch and brought it to work with him each day. As a result, he was more likely to eat healthful foods.

Cal also presented cues for the appropriate behavior. In other words, he arranged for stimulus prompts or response prompts to evoke the desirable behavior.

What cues did Cal present to increase the likelihood that he would eat healthful foods?

Cal made a list of healthful foods to buy when he went shopping. The list was a cue (a stimulus prompt) for him to buy healthful foods. Cal asked his roommate and girlfriend to remind him to eat healthful foods. Their reminders were cues (response prompts) for eating healthful foods. Cal made a graph and put it up on the refrigerator. The graph was a reminder (a stimulus prompt) to eat right. Each time he saw the graph, it cued him to eat healthful foods.

In Marianne's attempt to increase her studying, what S^Ds and cues for studying did she present?

The S^D for studying is a desk or table in a quiet location, with books or notes available. When Marianne is at a desk by herself with her books, she is more likely to study. She arranged for this S^D to be present by going to the library to study and by keeping her books in her backpack (Figure 16-1). Marianne took a number of steps to present cues for study behavior. Writing down her planned study time each day in her appointment book is a stimulus prompt for studying. Posting her study schedule is also a stimulus prompt: When she sees the schedule, it cues (reminds) her to study. Finally, arranging to study with a friend sets up a response prompt that makes studying more likely. The friend will come by Marianne's room or will meet her at their study place and will be a cue for Marianne to study.

FIGURE 16-1 Marianne presented the S^D for studying and eliminated S^Ds for competing behavior (TV, talking, partying) by going to the library with her books.

When considering using antecedent control procedures to increase a behavior, ask yourself what circumstances or stimulus conditions you could arrange that would have stimulus control over the behavior. By presenting the S^D or cues for the behavior, you are arranging the right conditions for the behavior to occur. As you can see from the examples, you arrange the S^D or cues for the behavior by changing some aspect of the physical or social environment. Consider one other example of arranging an S^D for a desirable behavior to compete with an undesirable behavior.

Tony often got into fights in high school when he believed somebody was saying something to put him down. Because of his fighting, he was participating in an anger management group with other high school students who got into fights. The students were learning skills to respond assertively to provocations and to walk away from situations where a fight was likely. As part of the training program, the students learned how to cue each other to walk away when they saw a conflict developing. When Tony's buddy, Raphael, saw him getting involved in a conflict, he would say to Tony, "Walk away, now!" This cue prompted Tony to walk away with Raphael instead of fighting. As soon as they got out of the conflict situation, they praised each other for avoiding a fight and discussed the situation in the next group meeting. Raphael's cue had stimulus control over Tony's alternative behavior, walking away. The alternative behavior was then reinforced immediately by Raphael and later by the counselor who taught the anger management group.

Arranging Establishing Operations for the Desirable Behavior

As we already know, an establishing operation is an environmental event or biological condition that changes the value of a stimulus as a reinforcer. When an establishing operation is present, the behavior that results in that stimulus is strengthened. For example, running 5 miles and sweating profusely is an establishing operation that makes water more reinforcing and thus strengthens the behavior of getting and drinking water. Going without food for a day is an establishing operation that makes food more reinforcing and therefore strengthens the behavior of getting and eating food. One way to make a desirable behavior more likely to occur is to arrange an establishing operation for the outcome of that behavior. If you can increase the reinforcing value of the consequence of a behavior, you make it more likely that the behavior will occur.

When Cal bought a health food cookbook, he was making it more likely that he would cook food that tasted good. By buying and using the cookbook, Cal increased the reinforcing value of healthful food and made it more likely that he would eat healthful food.

How did Marianne arrange an establishing operation for studying?

Marianne did two things that made studying more reinforcing. First, she posted her schedule of tests on a calendar and crossed off each day that passed. Seeing the day of her tests getting closer on the calendar made studying more reinforcing. You can hypothesize that seeing the test getting closer and closer created an unpleasant state (feeling anxious, thinking about failing the test) and that studying removed that unpleasant state. Therefore, studying was negatively reinforced. However, feeling anxious and thinking unpleasant thoughts of failure are private behaviors (Skinner, 1974). Even though a person can report these private behaviors, they cannot be observed by another person, so we can only hypothesize about their role in making studying more reinforcing. Chapter 25 discusses the role of thoughts and feelings in behavior modification.

Second, Marianne made a contract with her counselor to study for 2 hours each day. The contract made studying more reinforcing by arranging for her counselor's approval if she succeeded in studying the 2 hours each day. We can also hypothesize that the contract created an aversive state (feeling anxious about failing to study, thinking about the counselor's disapproval for not studying) that could be removed by studying each day. Therefore, studying the 2 hours each day would be negatively reinforced by escaping from or avoiding the aversive state created by the contract (Malott, 1989; Malott, Malott, & Trojan, 2000).

Consider another example. You want to teach a skill to a young child with autism and you are using bites of food as a reinforcer. Training will be much more effective right before lunch than right after lunch because food will be more reinforcing before lunch. You are using a naturally occurring establishing operation (the food deprivation that precedes a meal) to increase the likelihood that a desirable behavior will occur during training (Vollmer & Iwata, 1991).

Consider one other example of how you can make an undesirable behavior less likely by arranging an establishing operation for a desirable competing behavior.

Matt, a 13-year-old adolescent with mild retardation, has been engaging in problem behaviors in the evening around 11 P.M. when his parents suggest that he should get to bed so that he can get up for school the next day. When Matt's parents ask him to get ready for bed, he argues and engages in verbally abusive behavior. He then continues to watch TV and does not go to bed until after 1 A.M. Because he stays up late, Matt has trouble getting up for school the next morning. In addition, he takes a 2- to 3-hour nap each afternoon as soon as he gets home from school. As a result, Matt is not tired at bedtime and is more likely to engage in the problem behavior and refuse to go to bed.

ANTECEDENT MANIPULATIONS THAT EVOKE A DESIRED RESPONSE

- Presenting the S^D or supplemental stimuli (cues) that have stimulus control over the desired behavior
- Arranging an establishing operation such that the consequence of the desirable behavior is more reinforcing
- Decreasing the response effort for the desirable behavior

How could the parents create an establishing operation to make the consequence for the alternative behavior (going to bed on time) more reinforcing?

To increase the likelihood of the alternative behavior, the parents start to keep him from taking a nap after school by occupying him with activities until supper time. Keeping him from taking a nap makes him more tired at bedtime. It creates an establishing operation that increases the reinforcing value of sleep and makes it more likely that he will engage in the desirable behavior by going to bed and going to sleep at 11 P.M.

Decreasing Response Effort for the Desirable Behavior

Another strategy for making a desirable behavior more likely is to arrange antecedent conditions such that less effort is needed to engage in the behavior. Behaviors that take less response effort are more likely to occur than are behaviors that take more response effort, if both result in fairly equal reinforcers. If you like Coke and Pepsi equally well, you are much more likely to drink a Pepsi from your refrigerator than to drive to the store to get a Coke. You choose the behavior that takes less response effort.

How did Cal decrease response effort to make it more likely that he would eat healthful food?

By keeping healthful foods available in the house and getting rid of the junk foods, he made it easier to eat the healthful food than to eat the junk food; eating healthful food took less response effort. By making a healthful lunch and taking it to work with him, he made it easier to eat healthful food. It would have taken more response effort to go to a restaurant (even a fast food restaurant) than to eat the lunch he had brought with him.

How did Marianne decrease response effort to make it more likely that she would study more often?

By bringing her books with her in her backpack, Marianne had easy access to them; she could take them out and study wherever the opportunity arose. If she had kept her books back at her dorm room, it would have taken much more response effort to go and get the books.

Consider another example of how you can make an undesirable behavior less likely to occur by decreasing the response effort for a desirable alternative behavior. To decrease pollution, city officials wanted to decrease the number of cars on the road. Their survey showed that most cars on the interstate at rush hour had only one person in them. The officials wanted to decrease the number of people driving alone in their cars by increasing the alternative behavior of carpooling. Drivers often avoid carpooling because of the effort involved; therefore, to increase carpooling, the city officials decided to make it easier (to decrease the response effort). At each interstate exit, the city built parking lots where people could leave their cars and get a ride with other people. The city designated one lane of the interstate for cars with at least three people in them, two passengers along with the driver. Cars in that lane could avoid much of the traffic in the other three lanes, making it easier to get to work. After implementing these measures to reduce the response effort involved in carpooling, city officials found that the number of cars with people driving alone decreased and the number of cars with multiple passengers increased.

As we have seen, there are a number of ways to use antecedent control to make it more likely that a desirable behavior will occur.

- You can present the S^D or arrange cues for the desirable behavior.
- You can arrange an establishing operation that will make the outcome of the behavior more reinforcing so that the behavior is more likely to occur.
- You can manipulate antecedent conditions that decrease the response effort so that the desirable behavior is more likely to occur.

These three strategies all focus on manipulating antecedents to the desirable behavior. They can be used individually or in combination. However, antecedent control procedures should always be used in conjunction with differential reinforcement that will strengthen the desirable behavior once it occurs.

Sometimes a behavior is not as frequent as desired because an undesirable competing behavior interferes with it. Competing behaviors are concurrent operants reinforced on concurrent schedules of reinforcement. Marianne did not study often enough because she watched TV, went to parties, and talked with her friends. These are all competing behaviors that are highly reinforcing. They prevented Marianne from studying because she could not do both at the same time. When Cal ate potato chips, donuts, and greasy cheeseburgers, he was engaging in competing behaviors that interfered with eating healthful foods.

One way to make a desirable behavior more likely to occur is to make undesirable competing behaviors less likely to occur. A number of antecedent control procedures can be used to decrease the likelihood that undesirable competing behaviors will occur.

Removing the S^D or Cues for Undesirable Behaviors

One way to decrease the likelihood of an undesirable behavior is to remove the antecedent conditions that have stimulus control over it. If the S^D or cues for an undesirable behavior are not present, it is less likely that the person will engage in the behavior.

In his attempts to eat more healthful food, how did Cal remove the S^D or cues for undesirable competing behaviors?

The presence of unhealthful food is an S^D for eating unhealthful foods. In other words, if junk food is around, Cal is more likely to eat it. Cal removed the S^D for eating unhealthful food by getting rid of all the unhealthful food from his apartment. In addition, Cal stopped bringing any change to work with him. When he had change in his pocket, he was more likely to get junk food from the vending machines. By not having any change with him, he made it less likely that he would engage in this competing behavior and more likely that he would eat the healthful food that he brought to work with him.

In her strategy for studying more, how did Marianne remove the S^D or cues for undesirable competing behavior?

The presence of her friends is an S^D for talking or partying. The TV is an S^D for watching TV. To remove the S^Ds for these competing behaviors, Marianne went to study at the library, where there is no TV and there are no disruptive friends around. In addition, by posting her study schedule and asking her friends to leave her alone at those times, Marianne removed S^Ds for competing behavior and thus made it more likely that she would study at those times.

Consider another example. Vicki, a student in an elementary classroom, typically engages in disruptive behavior (such as throwing spit balls and making funny noises) when she sits in the back of the classroom near Wanda, who laughs and pays attention to the disruptive behavior. Wanda's presence near Vicki in the back of the classroom is an S^D for the disruptive behavior because Wanda reinforces this behavior when it occurs and the teacher cannot see Vicki engaging in the behavior.

If you were the classroom teacher, how would you eliminate the S^D or cues for Vicki's undesirable behavior?

One strategy would be to move Vicki to the front of the class, away from Wanda, so that Wanda could no longer provide attention as a reinforcer for the problem behavior. In that case, Wanda would not be present as an S^D for the disruptive behavior. In addition, Vicki would be closer to the teacher, who is an S^D for paying attention and doing her work (Figure 16-2).

Removing Establishing Operations for Undesirable Behaviors

If you can make the outcome of the undesirable behavior less reinforcing, you will be less likely to engage in the behavior and therefore more likely to engage in the desirable behavior. You make the outcome of the undesirable behavior less reinforcing by removing the establishing operation for the reinforcer. This is not always possible, but in some cases it is a useful strategy.

Cal used this strategy to make it less likely that he would buy junk foods and more likely that he would buy healthful foods when he went shopping. Before he went shopping, he ate a meal so that he would not be hungry at the grocery store. In this way, the unhealthful foods were less reinforcing at the time he went shopping, and he was less likely to buy them. If he went shopping when he was hungry, he would be more likely to buy snacks and other junk food (unhealthful foods), which are displayed prominently in the store (as S^Ds for buying them) and are ready to eat. In addition, sugar, salt, and fat, the ingredients of many junk foods, are highly reinforcing to people who are even slightly hungry. By removing the establishing operation, Cal was less likely to buy unhealthful foods and more likely to buy the healthful foods on the list. Eating a meal before he went shopping ensured that his shopping list of healthful

FIGURE 16-2 Vicki engages in disruptive behavior when she is seated at the back of the classroom near Wanda. The teacher removes the S^Ds for disruptive behavior by placing Vicki at the front of the class, away from Wanda. As a result, her disruptive behavior decreases.

foods would have more stimulus control over the behavior than did the sight of the junk foods in the store. Conduct an experiment with yourself: Go shopping when you're really hungry and see whether you buy (or are tempted to buy) different foods than when you're not hungry.

Consider another example. Millea usually goes home on her lunch hour and runs 4 or 5 miles for exercise. Recently, however, she has been staying up late at night and watching TV. As a result, she feels tired when she goes home at lunchtime and takes a nap instead of going for a run.

To make it less likely that she would take a nap and more likely that she would run, Millea could remove an establishing operation for taking a nap. How would she do that?

What is the reinforcer for the competing behavior of taking a nap? The reinforcer is sleep. What is an establishing operation that makes sleep more reinforcing at a

Antecedent Manipulations That Make Undesirable Competing Responses Less Likely

- Removing the S^D or cues for the competing behaviors
- Eliminating establishing operations for the outcome of the competing behaviors
- Increasing the response effort for the competing behaviors

particular time? Going without sleep the night before and feeling tired is an establishing operation that makes sleep more reinforcing. So how does Millea remove the establishing operation for sleeping? She goes to bed at a reasonable time the night before so that she is not lacking sleep. When she does this, sleep is not as reinforcing at lunchtime, and Millea is less likely to nap and more likely to go running instead. Millea could also eliminate the S^D for the competing behavior by changing into her running clothes at the health club near her office and running from there. In this way, she is never near her bed (the S^D for sleeping) at lunchtime, and the competing behavior could not happen as easily. (She probably wouldn't take a nap on the bench in the locker room.)

Increasing the Response Effort for Undesirable Behaviors

One other strategy for decreasing the likelihood of an undesirable competing behavior is to increase the response effort for the behavior. If the competing behaviors take more effort, they are less likely to interfere with the desirable behavior. By going to the health club to run during her lunch hour, Millea increases the effort it would take to nap instead: She would have to get into her car and drive home to go to bed. For this reason, she probably would not take a nap and would be more likely to run during her lunch hour. As you can see, going to the health club to run removed the S^D for taking a nap and it increased the response effort for taking a nap.

In her strategy to study more, how did Marianne increase the response effort for the competing behavior?

By going to the library to study, Marianne made it harder to talk and watch TV with her friends. To engage in this competing behavior, she would have to pack up her books and walk back to her dorm from the library. This takes effort. When she studied in her room, it took little effort to stop studying and talk with her friends or turn on the TV. Going to the library to study served two functions. It removed the S^D for the undesirable competing behavior and it increased the response effort for engaging in the competing behavior.

In his attempts to eat more healthful food, how did Cal increase the response effort for the competing behavior?

Cal got rid of all the unhealthful food from his apartment. By doing this, he increased the response effort for eating unhealthful foods. Whereas previously he could simply walk into the kitchen to get some junk food, now Cal would have to go to the store to get some. Therefore, he is more likely to eat what is in his house (healthful foods) than to engage in the competing behavior of eating junk food. Also, by no longer bringing change to work with him, Cal increased the response effort for eating junk food because he would have to go find change before he could use the vending machine. If he had asked his co-workers to refuse his requests for change, this would have increased the response effort even more. As you can see, getting rid of junk foods from his house and not bringing change to work served two functions: They removed the S^Ds for the competing behavior of eating unhealthful foods and they increased the response effort for this competing behavior. Consider one other example.

Melanie had smoked cigarettes since graduating from high school. Now married, with a few children in grade school, she decided that she needed to quit smoking or at least cut down the number of cigarettes she smoked each day. She was trying to chew nicotine gum as an alternative behavior to smoking cigarettes. Melanie was at home during the day. Her husband drove the car to work, and the kids walked to the neighborhood school. Melanie devised a plan to help her decrease the number of cigarettes she smoked. Each day before the children went to school at 8 A.M., she asked one of them to hide her pack of cigarettes somewhere in the house. She kept plenty of nicotine gum in the house but kept only one pack of cigarettes in the house at one time. As a result, once the children were off to school, Melanie couldn't smoke unless she searched the house to find the pack or else walked to the store to buy a new pack. However, the nicotine gum was readily available to her. This strategy greatly increased the response effort involved in smoking relative to the response effort involved in chewing the nicotine gum and, as a result, decreased the number of cigarettes that she smoked each day.

As you have seen, you can implement three antecedent control strategies to decrease the likelihood that undesirable competing responses will interfere with the desirable behavior.

- You can remove the S^D or cues for the undesirable behaviors.
- You can eliminate the establishing operation for undesirable behaviors.
- You can increase the response effort for the undesirable behaviors.

Research on Antecedent Control Strategies

Research has demonstrated that antecedent control strategies are effective in increasing a variety of behaviors. A number of studies have evaluated strategies in which S^Ds or cues for the desirable behavior are presented.

O'Neill, Blanck, and Joyner (1980) implemented an antecedent control procedure to increase the use of trash receptacles and decrease litter at college football games. They modified a trash can by putting a cover over it that resembled the hats worn by many of the university's football fans. In addition, when someone pushed the door covering the trash can, a mechanical device lifted the cover to expose the word *Thanks*. The modification of the trash can was a cue (stimulus prompt) to put trash in the can. The fans at football games put more than twice as much trash in the modified trash can as they did in the unmodified trash can.

Researchers have demonstrated that antecedent control procedures can lead to increases in recreational activities and social interactions in older adults in a nursing home or a hospital ward. McClannahan and Risley (1975) found that residents in a nursing home did not spend much time engaging in recreational activities even though the activities were readily available. To increase participation, an activity leader gave the residents some recreational materials or prompted them to engage in some recreational activities whenever they were in a recreational lounge area. Using these cues to participate resulted in a large increase in recreational activities among the residents. In a similar study, Melin and Gotestam (1981) rearranged furniture in the coffee room in a hospital ward to increase social interactions between older adults with dementia or schizophrenia. When the furniture was arranged to facilitate conversation, the social contacts among residents increased greatly (Figure 16-3).

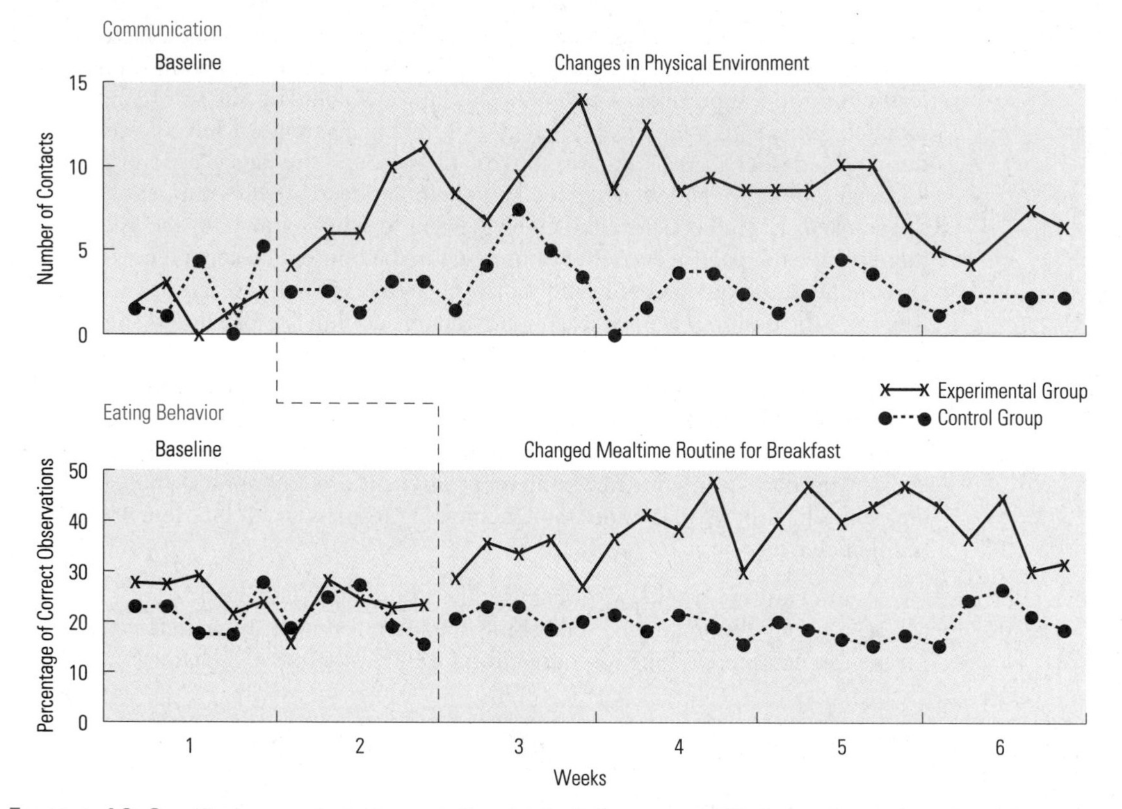

FIGURE 16-3 The top panel of this graph (from Melin & Gotestam, 1981) shows the number of social contacts made by two groups of older adults in a hospital ward. After baseline, the physical environment was changed for the experimental group to be more conducive to social interaction. The environment was not changed for the control group. The graph shows that social contacts increased for the experimental group after the antecedent manipulation. The bottom panel shows the percentage of correct eating behaviors exhibited by the experimental group and the control group at mealtimes. People in the control group received their meals on trays and ate alone. The people in the experimental group ate their meals together around small tables, with food in serving dishes on the tables. The antecedent manipulation, introduction of a family-style eating arrangement, resulted in improved eating behaviors by the residents. This graph shows a multiple-baseline-across-behaviors design, with data on groups rather than individuals.

Other researchers have shown that antecedent control procedures can be used to increase seat belt use. Rogers and his colleagues used cues to increase seat belt use by employees at state agencies when they drove agency-owned vehicles (Rogers, Rogers, Bailey, Runkle, & Moore, 1988). To the dashboard of each vehicle was affixed a sticker reminding the driver to use the seat belt, along with a warning that there could be a reduction in insurance coverage if the driver had an accident while not wearing a seat belt. In addition, each driver had to read a memo describing the regulation about the mandatory use of seat belts in agency vehicles. Rogers demonstrated large increases in the number of employees wearing seat belts when the antecedent control procedure was introduced (Figure 16-4). Other researchers (e.g., Berry & Geller, 1991) have

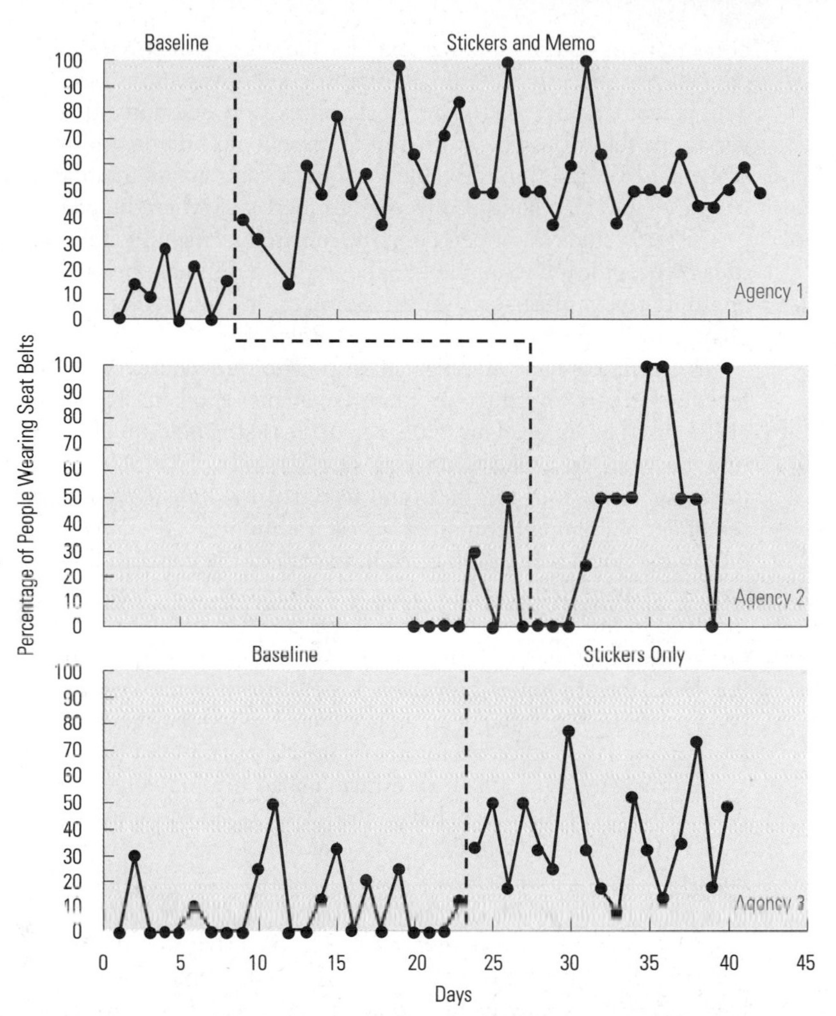

FIGURE 16-4 This graph (from Rogers et al., 1988) shows the percentage of people in state vehicles who wore their seat belts before and after a stimulus control procedure was implemented. The percentage of people wearing seat belts increased when the procedure was implemented with people from three different agencies. The top two panels show the effects of the stickers in the cars and the memo. The bottom panel shows the effect of the stickers only. The graph illustrates a multiple-baseline design across subjects from the three agencies. The percentage of people engaging in the behavior is shown rather than the behavior of individual subjects.

shown that using cues, such as auditory or visual signals in the car, can result in increases in seat belt use.

Green, Hardison, and Greene (1984) used antecedent control procedures to enrich interactions between family members when they ate at family restaurants. The purpose of the study was to evoke meaningful conversations between preschool children and their parents while they waited for their food in restaurants. The researchers believed that the children would be less likely to get bored or engage in disruptive behavior if they had interesting conversations with their parents. In addition, mealtime conversations could be educational for the preschool children. The researchers used educational placemats in an attempt to cue conversations between family members. The placemats included pictures, activities, and questions to generate topics of conversations that would be of interest to preschool children and their parents. Identical placemats were put on the table in front of each family member. Green and his colleagues found that family conversations increased when the placemats were used.

In each study described here, the researchers manipulated some antecedent stimulus or event to increase the likelihood that a desirable behavior would occur in the appropriate circumstances. In these studies, the antecedent manipulation involved a change in the physical or social environment.

Researchers have investigated a variety of procedures involving manipulating antecedent events to reduce problem behaviors. Brothers, Krantz, and McClannahan (1994) used an antecedent strategy to decrease the amount of recyclable paper thrown into trash cans in a social service agency. To get the 25 employees of the agency to stop throwing paper into the trash and to put it in recycling containers instead, the researchers put a small container on each employee's desk. The container served two functions: It was a cue for the employee to put the paper in the container, as an alternative behavior to throwing the paper in the trash; and it decreased the response effort involved in the desirable behavior. It was easier to put the used paper in the container on the desk than to put it in a wastebasket. When they put the recycling containers on the desks, the amount of recyclable paper thrown in trash cans decreased dramatically (Figure 16-5). The value of an antecedent manipulation such as this is that it is simple to implement and effective in producing a change in the problem behavior.

Horner and Day (1991) also investigated the influence of response effort on the occurrence of a desirable behavior that was functionally equivalent to the problem behavior. They worked with Paul, a 12-year-old boy with severe mental retardation. Paul engaged in aggressive behavior (hitting, biting, and scratching) in teaching situations. The problem behavior was reinforced by escape from the task being taught. Horner and Day taught Paul two alternative behaviors that would also result in escape from the task. One alternative behavior involved signing the word *break*. This simple behavior took less response effort than engaging in the aggressive behavior. When Paul signed *break*, staff members immediately terminated the teaching trial for a brief period of time. The other alternative behavior was to sign, "I want to go, please." When Paul signed the full sentence, the staff immediately stopped the teaching session for a brief time. However, this behavior took more time and effort than the aggressive behavior. The researchers found that when Paul had to sign *break* as a functionally equivalent alternative behavior, he was much less likely to engage in aggressive behavior because the alternative behavior took less response effort. However, when Paul had to sign the full sentence to escape from the task, he continued to engage in aggressive behavior because the aggressive behavior took less response effort than the alternative behavior. Research by Horner, Sprague, O'Brien, and Heathfield (1990) produced similar results showing that an alternative behavior is more likely to occur and replace the problem behavior when it takes less response effort.

A number of researchers have manipulated curriculum variables or teacher behaviors as antecedents to students' problem behaviors in classroom settings. (For a review, see Munk & Repp, 1994.) Kennedy (1994) worked with three students with disabilities who engaged in problem behaviors (aggression, self-injury, and stereotypic behavior) in a special education classroom. Kennedy conducted a functional assess-

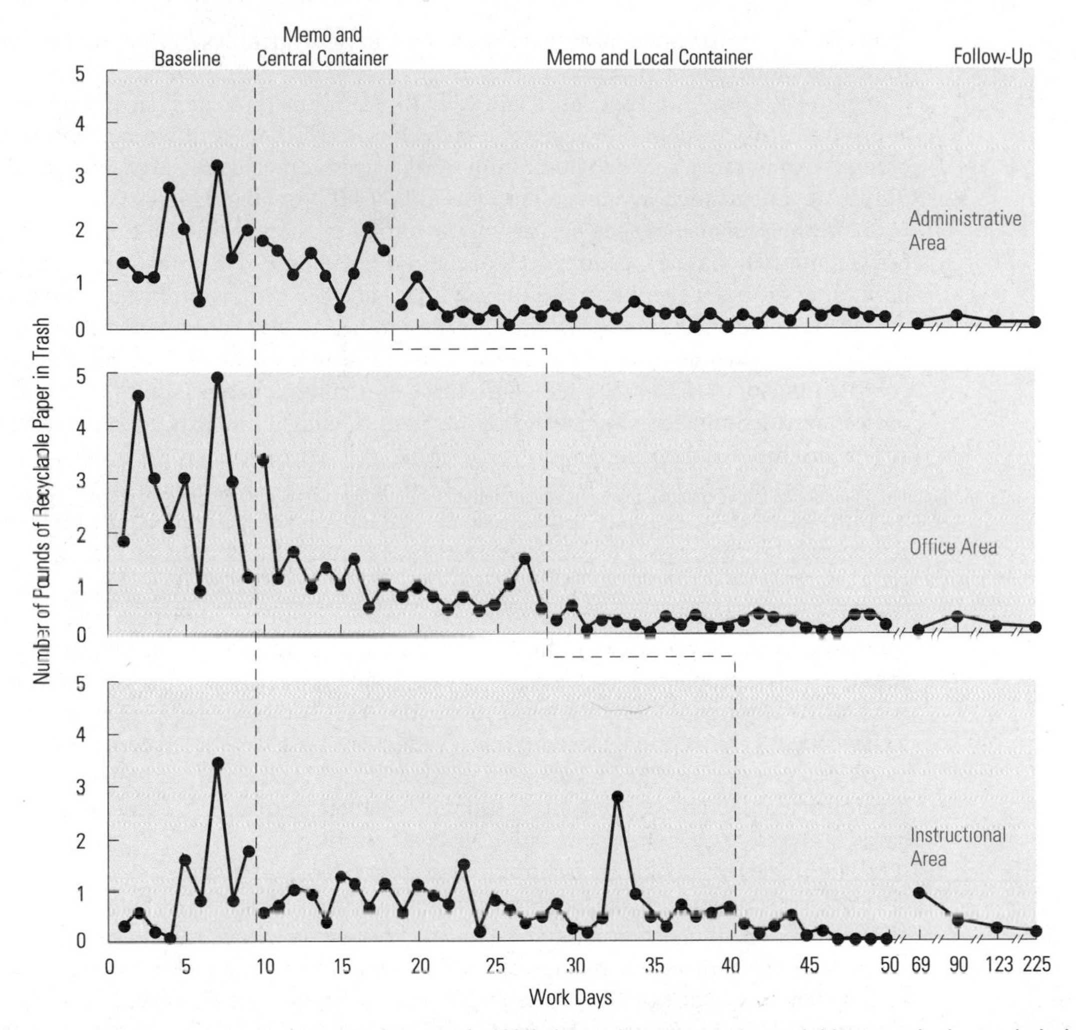

This graph (from Brothers et al., 1994) shows the pounds of recyclable paper in the trash during baseline and two intervention conditions implemented in a multiple-baseline-across-settings design. After baseline, a memo was sent to employees asking them to recycle paper by putting it in a large bin located in a utility room near the center of the building. In the next phase, a memo was sent to employees asking them to recycle paper by putting it into boxes that were placed directly on their desks and countertops. The results showed that the amount of paper in the trash decreased greatly when the boxes were placed on the employees' desks. The boxes on their desks cued them to recycle, and they decreased the response effort involved in recycling.

ment and found that the problem behaviors occurred when the teacher made a high rate of task demands but did not occur when the teacher made social comments to the students. In light of these findings, Kennedy had the teacher decrease the task demands and increase the social comments she made in the classroom. This resulted in a large decrease in the problem behaviors for each student. The teacher then gradually increased the rate of task demands while keeping the social comments at a high level. As the task demands were increased back to the typical level, the problem behaviors remained low.

Dunlap, Kern-Dunlap, Clarke, and Robbins (1991) manipulated curriculum variables to decrease problem behaviors (such as kicking, hitting, spitting, and throwing objects) exhibited by a grade school student who had been categorized as emotionally disturbed. Their functional assessment found that Jill's problem behaviors were most likely in the presence of specific curriculum variables, such as fine motor tasks, long tasks, nonfunctional tasks, and tasks that she did not choose. Treatment involved manipulating the antecedent curriculum variables. The teacher gave Jill academic tasks that were shorter and more functional (related to her interests or daily activities) and that involved gross motor activities as opposed to fine motor activities. In addition, Jill got to choose her tasks more often. With these curriculum changes, Jill's problem behaviors were eliminated. Another study by Kern, Childs, Dunlap, Clarke, and Falk (1994) produced similar findings.

Horner, Day, Sprague, O'Brien, and Heathfield (1991) manipulated another curriculum variable to produce a decrease in problem behaviors (aggression and self-injury) exhibited by four adolescents with severe mental retardation. Their functional assessment showed that these students were most likely to engage in problem behaviors when hard academic tasks were presented to them but did not engage in problem behaviors when easy tasks were presented. Horner used an antecedent manipulation to decrease the problem behaviors. He had the teachers intersperse easy tasks with the hard tasks. Throughout the training sessions, the teacher provided a few easy tasks after the student completed a few hard tasks. When easy tasks were interspersed with the hard tasks, the problem behaviors were greatly reduced. Mace and his colleagues also demonstrated that problem behaviors (noncompliance) were less likely to occur when hard tasks were preceded by easy tasks (Mace et al., 1988).

The studies of problem behaviors in classroom settings all changed some aspect of the teaching situation to make problem behaviors less likely. Before these antecedent manipulations, the students' problem behaviors were reinforced by escape from the academic tasks. The antecedent manipulations made the academic situation less aversive for the students, so escape from the academic situation was no longer reinforcing. As you can see, the antecedent manipulations that altered some aspect of the teacher's behavior or the curriculum eliminated the establishing operation that made escape from the situation reinforcing. Because escape was no longer reinforcing, the students no longer engaged in problem behaviors that resulted in escape (see also Smith, Iwata, Goh, & Shore, 1995).

Another antecedent manipulation to decrease problem behaviors maintained by escape from instructional situations is noncontingent escape (Coleman & Holmes, 1998; Vollmer, Marcus, & Ringdahl, 1995; Vollmer et al., 1998; Wesolowski, Zencius, & Rodriguez, 1999). In this procedure, the people are given frequent breaks from aversive instructional activities or tasks. As a result, they are less likely to engage in problem behaviors to escape from the tasks because escape from the tasks is no longer reinforcing.

Working with adults with profound retardation who engaged in self-injurious behavior, Vollmer and his colleagues manipulated the level of attention to these individuals, in an attempt to decrease the rate of self-injury (Vollmer, Iwata, Zarcone, Smith, & Mazaleski, 1993). Their functional assessment showed that the self-injury was reinforced by attention. To decrease the likelihood of self-injury, the researchers provided noncontingent attention, which means that the attention was provided in-

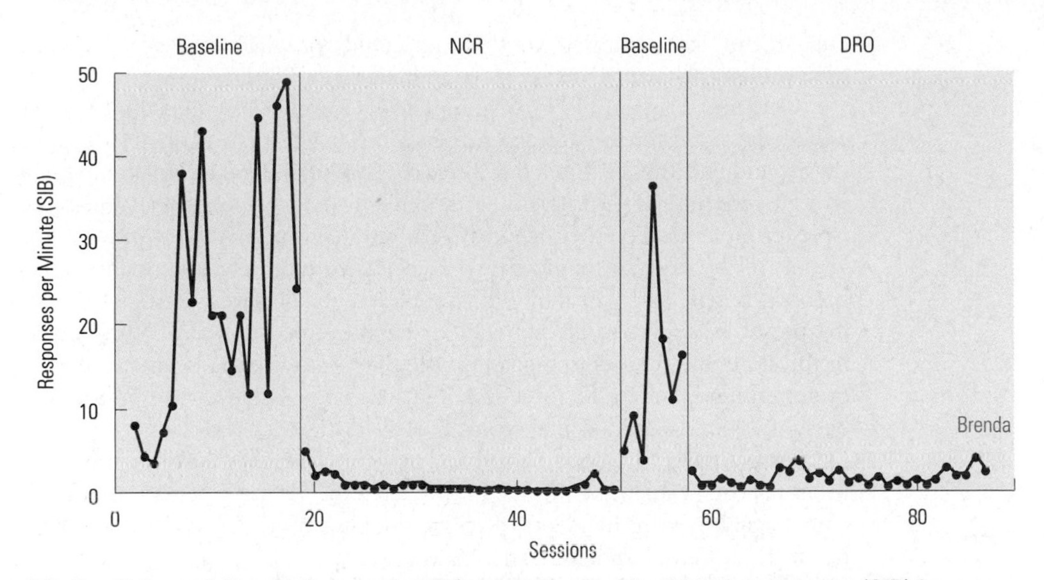

FIGURE 16-6 This graph (from Vollmer et al., 1993) shows the rate of self-injurious behavior (SIB) for one subject in baseline, a noncontingent reinforcement (NCR) condition, a second baseline condition, and a differential reinforcement of other behavior (DRO) condition. This subject's SIB was maintained by attention. When attention was provided frequently in the NCR condition, the SIB decreased almost to zero. The SIB also decreased to near zero in the DRO condition, when attention was provided for the absence of SIB. The data suggest that one way to decrease a problem behavior maintained by attention is to provide attention at frequent intervals independent of the behavior.

dependent of the self-injury. They found that the self-injurious behavior decreased for each person when they provided noncontingent attention at least once every 5 minutes (Figure 16-6). Providing attention at frequent intervals diminished the establishing operation that made attention a potent reinforcer for the self-injury. The people were less likely to engage in self-injury for attention now that they received substantial attention without engaging in the self-injury.

A number of other studies have shown that noncontingent reinforcement can be an effective treatment for problem behaviors maintained by attention and or by escape (Wilder & Carr, 1998; Fisher, Iwata, & Mazaleski, 1997; Hagopian, Fisher, & Legacy, 1994; Hanley, Piazza, & Fisher, 1997; Lalli, Casey, & Cates, 1997; Tucker, Sigafoos, & Bushell, 1998; Vollmer et al., 1998; Vollmer, Ringdahl, Roane, & Marcus, 1997).

Dyer, Dunlap, and Winterling (1990) investigated the influence of choice making on the problem behaviors of children with developmental delays. The three children in this study engaged in a variety of problem behaviors in the classroom, including aggression, throwing objects, screaming, and self-injury. The researchers manipulated two antecedent conditions. In one condition, the child could choose the educational task to work on in a session and the reinforcer for appropriate performance in the session. In the other condition, the child did not have a choice of materials or reinforcers. The researchers found that problem behaviors were less likely to occur when the children were given choices. These results suggest that choosing tasks and reinforcers increased the reinforcing value of the educational task and therefore increased the likelihood that the students would complete the task as an alternative to the problem behavior (Romaniuk & Miltenberger, 2001).

Carr and Carlson (1993) manipulated a number of antecedent variables to decrease the occurrence of problem behaviors (aggression, property destruction, self-injury, and tantrums) exhibited by three adults with mental retardation while shopping in a grocery store. The problem behaviors were severe enough that the shopping trips were terminated when they occurred. Carr and Carlson wanted to prevent problem behaviors in the store by manipulating antecedents that were functionally related to the problem behaviors. They found that problem behaviors were less likely to occur when the person was given choices of which activities to pursue or which items to buy first in the store, the request to buy a nonpreferred item was made after a request to buy a preferred item, and an S^D for a desirable alternative behavior was presented when the person was in a situation that typically evoked the occurrence of the problem behavior. For example, when one person had to wait in the checkout line, he often engaged in one of the problem behaviors. In this situation, he was given a preferred magazine. The magazine in his hands was an S^D for looking at the magazine as an alternative behavior to the problem behavior. This is a strategy many people use to keep from getting impatient while waiting in a checkout line. When Carr and Carlson implemented these and other procedures, the clients were able to go on shopping trips without engaging in the problem behaviors. Kemp and Carr (1995) conducted similar antecedent manipulations to decrease problem behaviors exhibited by adults with mental retardation at their jobs in the community.

Using Antecedent Control Strategies

The six different antecedent control strategies described here for making a desirable behavior more likely and undesirable behaviors less likely are summarized in Table 16-1. It is appropriate to use one or more of these strategies whenever the goal is to increase a desirable behavior or decrease an undesirable behavior. If the

Table 16-1 Antecedent Manipulations to Decrease Problem Behaviors and Increase Desirable Behaviors

Manipulating S^Ds or cues

- Eliminating the S^D or cues for the problem behavior
- Providing the S^D or cues for desirable alternative behaviors

Manipulating establishing operations

- Eliminating or diminishing an establishing operation for the reinforcer that is maintaining the problem behavior
- Creating or enhancing an establishing operation for the reinforcer that is maintaining desirable alternative behaviors

Manipulating response effort

- Increasing response effort for the problem behavior
- Decreasing response effort for desirable alternative behaviors

person is engaging in the behavior at least occasionally, antecedent control strategies may be used to make it more likely that the person will engage in the behavior at the appropriate times. Differential reinforcement procedures are used in conjunction with antecedent control procedures to maintain the behavior. Likewise, if a person is engaging in a behavioral excess, antecedent control strategies can make it less likely that this undesirable behavior will occur. Extinction and differential reinforcement often are used in conjunction with antecedent control procedures to decrease behavioral excesses.

How do you determine which antecedent control procedures to use in any given situation? There are no easy answers to this question. The best answer is that you should know how to use the various antecedent control procedures and choose the ones that best fit the situation. To understand the situation, you should conduct a functional assessment to analyze the three-term contingency (antecedents, behavior, and consequences) involved in maintaining the desirable behavior and the undesirable behaviors.

Analysis of the Three-Term Contingency for the Desirable Behavior

Answers to the following questions will provide information about the desirable behavior and its antecedents and consequences.

- Identify and define the desirable behavior that you want to increase. Can you reduce the response effort involved in this behavior?
- Analyze the antecedent situations related to the desirable behavior. What are the S^Ds for the desirable behavior, and what cues might evoke the desirable behavior? Which of these S^Ds and cues are present in the environment, and which ones are not? Which of these S^Ds and cues do you have access to in an antecedent control strategy, and which ones do you not have access to?
- Identify the reinforcer for the desirable behavior. Is this reinforcer contingent on the desirable behavior? Is the reinforcer strong enough to maintain the behavior? Can you manipulate the establishing operation to increase the effectiveness of this reinforcer? Are there other reinforcers that could be used contingent on the desirable behavior?

The answers to these questions will help you decide which antecedent control strategies might be useful for evoking the desirable behavior and which reinforcers might be used in a differential reinforcement procedure.

Analysis of the Three-Term Contingency for the Undesirable Behavior

Answers to the following questions will provide information about the undesirable competing behaviors and the antecedents and consequences of these behaviors.

- Identify and define the undesirable competing behaviors that may interfere with the desirable behavior. Can you increase the response effort of these competing behaviors?
- Analyze the antecedent stimuli associated with the undesirable behaviors. What are the S^Ds for the competing behaviors, and what cues might evoke the competing be-

haviors? Which of these S^Ds and cues are present in the environment, and which are not? Which of these S^Ds and cues can you manipulate in an antecedent control strategy and which ones are outside your control?

- Identify the reinforcers for the undesirable competing behaviors. Are these reinforcers contingent on the competing behaviors, and are they strong enough to maintain the behaviors? Can you manipulate the establishing operations so as to decrease the effectiveness of the reinforcers for the competing behaviors? Can you eliminate these reinforcers to use extinction for the competing behaviors?

The answers to these questions will help you decide which antecedent control strategies you can use, in conjunction with extinction and differential reinforcement, to decrease the likelihood of the competing behaviors.

Functional, Nonaversive Interventions for Problem Behaviors

This chapter and the two preceding chapters (14 and 15) have described three approaches for decreasing problem behaviors: extinction, differential reinforcement, and antecedent control. These approaches are functional, nonaversive interventions. They are functional because they decrease problem behaviors by modifying the antecedent and consquent variables that control the behaviors. They are nonaversive because they do not rely on the use of punishment. Functional, nonaversive procedures should always be the first treatments utilized in an attempt to decrease a problem behavior because they change the conditions that are maintaining the behavior (they address the function of the behavior).

With extinction you are removing the reinforcer for the problem. When the behavior no longer serves a function for the person (when it no longer results in a reinforcing outcome), there is no reason for the behavior to continue to occur.

With differential reinforcement, the person can achieve the same outcome without engaging in the problem behavior. If the person is producing the same functional consequence through an alternative behavior, the absence of the problem behavior, or a lower rate of the problem behavior, there is no reason for the problem behavior to continue to occur.

With antecedent manipulations, the antecedent events that evoke the occurrence of the problem behavior are no longer present, the effectiveness of the reinforcer for the problem behavior is diminished, or the effort involved in the problem behavior is increased. When the antecedent conditions no longer favor the problem behavior, there is no longer any reason for the problem behavior to occur.

CHAPTER SUMMARY

1. In antecedent control strategies, antecedent stimuli are manipulated to evoke the occurrence of desirable behaviors and to decrease the likelihood of competing behaviors.
2. If you present an S^D for a desirable behavior, that behavior is more likely to occur, and if you remove the S^D for undesirable behavior, that behavior is less likely to occur.
3. The establishing operation for the outcome of a desirable behavior is a condition that makes that behavior more likely to occur; if you remove the establishing operation for

the outcome of the undesirable behavior, the undesirable behavior is less likely to occur.

4. When a desirable behavior takes less response effort than an alternative undesirable behavior, and both behaviors result in the same reinforcing outcome, the desirable behavior is more likely to occur.
5. The three functional, nonaversive approaches to intervention for a problem behavior are extinction, differential reinforcement, and antecedent control strategies.

PRACTICE TEST

1. In general terms, what are antecedent control procedures? (p. 341)
2. How is the occurrence of undesirable competing behaviors related to the occurrence of a desirable behavior? (p. 347)
3. What is the goal of antecedent control procedures with regard to the occurrence of undesirable competing behaviors? (p. 347)
4. Identify the three antecedent control strategies that can be used to evoke a desirable behavior. (pp. 343–347)
5. Identify the three antecedent control strategies that can be used to decrease the likelihood of undesirable competing behaviors. (pp. 347–351)
6. Describe how you would eliminate the S^D or cues for a problem behavior. Provide an example. (p. 347)
7. Provide an example of how you would provide the S^D or cues for a desirable behavior to get the behavior to occur. (p. 343)
8. What is an establishing operation? Provide an example of how you would eliminate an establishing operation to make it less likely that a problem behavior will occur. (pp. 348–349)
9. Provide an example of how you would arrange an establishing operation for a desirable behavior to get the behavior to occur. (pp. 344–345)
10. Provide an example of how you could increase the response effort for a problem behavior to decrease the frequency of the behavior. (pp. 350–351)
11. Provide an example of how you would decrease the response effort for a desirable behavior to get the behavior to occur. (pp. 346–347)
12. The instructor in your contemporary American history class has suggested that you read the local morning newspaper every day to keep up with current events. You decide to use antecedent control strategies to help you read the paper each day.
    a. How will you present the S^D or cues for this behavior?
    b. How will you decrease response effort for this behavior?
    c. How will you eliminate the S^D or cues for competing behavior that interferes with reading the newspaper?
13. Why is it important to use differential reinforcement in conjunction with antecedent control procedures when you want to increase a desirable behavior? (p. 360)
14. Your young son eats a lot of hot dogs, chips, and desserts, but often refuses to eat fruit and vegetables and other foods you prepare. You want him to eat more of these healthful foods.
    a. How will you arrange an establishing operation for eating the healthful foods?
    b. How will you increase response effort for the competing behavior (eating hot dogs, chips, and desserts)?
15. What does it mean to say that an intervention is functional and nonaversive? (p. 360)
16. Besides antecedent manipulations, what are two other functional nonaversive interventions for problem behaviors? (p. 360)

APPLICATIONS

1. Describe how you could use antecedent control procedures in your self-management project. Consider each of the six strategies and describe the ones you would implement.

2. Melanie's physician suggested that she needed to drink six 8-ounce glasses of water per day. Melanie is a graduate student who comes to school in the morning and goes back home after 5 P.M. She has an office where she spends most of her time when she is not in class. Right across the hall, there are a number of vending machines. She gets coffee and soda from these machines four or five times per day. Describe how Melanie could apply four of the six antecedent control strategies to help herself drink the six glasses of water per day.

3. Ever since Stanley left home and came to school, family and friends have written letters to him. However, he rarely writes back. He wants to, but he never seems to get around to it. He is in school most of the day and he spends about 1–2 hours studying per evening. The rest of the evening, he watches TV (he has 54 channels on cable) or videos, or he spends time in the game room playing pool, Ping-Pong, or video games. Describe how Stanley could apply antecedent control procedures to help himself write letters to the people who write letters to him. Describe as many of the six antecedent control procedures as possible that you can apply to Stanley's problem.

4. Assume that you bought a treadmill and that you want to walk on it for 20–30 minutes, five times per week. You want to use antecedent control procedures and differential reinforcement to help you meet your goal. Before using these procedures, you must first analyze the three-term contingency for the desirable behavior (walking on the treadmill) and the three-term contingency for the competing behaviors that might interfere with your goal. Describe the three-term contingency for walking on the treadmill and for competing behaviors that would exist in your life if you were going to adopt this goal.

5. Merle is a young adult with autism who lives in a group home with five other adults. Merle engages in disruptive and self-injurious behavior (head-slapping, screaming, and rocking back and forth). Functional assessment results indicate that the behavior is most likely to happen when he is in the midst of commotion and activity. The problem is least likely to occur when Merle is in his room by himself listening to music or thumbing through his baseball card collection. The worst times are transition times to and from work, when the other residents are all present in the living and dining area, waiting to get on the van or having just gotten off the van. When Merle exhibits the problem behavior, the other residents usually disperse and the commotion and activity diminish. Describe how you would implement an antecedent procedure by eliminating the establishing operation for the behavior. Describe how you would implement an antecedent manipulation in which you presented the S^D for alternative behavior in an attempt to decrease the problem behavior.

6. Calvin worked on highway construction jobs in Florida. On the hottest days, he drank up to ten cans of soda. Calvin was concerned with all the sugar he was taking in; also, all the calories from the sodas were starting to make him bigger around the waist. He loved his sodas but he wanted to cut down to no more than three a day. Describe how Calvin could implement three of the antecedent control procedures described in this chapter to decrease the number of sodas he drank each day.

MISAPPLICATIONS

1. A teacher in a special education classroom was working with a child with severe retardation. The teacher was using small bites of food as reinforcers in a training program to help the child make correct letter discriminations. The teacher decided to arrange an establishing operation that

would make food a more powerful reinforcer so that the child would be more likely to respond correctly in training sessions. Because training sessions were in the early afternoon, the teacher decided to keep the child from eating lunch at noon. The teacher reasoned that if the child did not eat lunch, food would be a more effective reinforcer in the afternoon. What is wrong with this antecedent control strategy? What would be a better antecedent control strategy to use in this case?

2. Milt wanted to start working out more often. He decided that the best way to get into a regular workout routine would be to join a health club. He joined a club that was a 20-minute drive away. Milt reasoned that once he paid the membership fee for a year, he would be more likely to drive there and work out at least a few times a week. And because he paid the fee for the full year, he believed that he would continue to work out at the club for the whole year. What is wrong with this strategy? What could Milt do to make it more likely that he would work out regularly?

3. Dr. Drake, the dentist, was concerned that many of her patients did not floss their teeth regularly and were therefore at risk for gum disease. Dr. Drake devised a plan to get her patients to floss every day. Every time patients came in for a checkup or cleaning, Dr. Drake showed them awful pictures of people with gum disease and pictures of painful surgery that the people with gum disease had to endure because they did not floss regularly. Before the patients left the office, she told them that they could avoid the awful gum disease and the painful surgery by flossing their teeth for 2 minutes every day. What antecedent control strategy was Dr. Drake using to get her patients to floss their teeth? Why is this strategy, by itself, not enough to keep people flossing? What other strategies would you add to make it more likely that people would keep flossing their teeth regularly?

4. Sandy, a third grade student with learning problems, attended a special class. She usually engaged in disruptive behaviors in the classroom when required to complete math problems. The teacher conducted a functional assessment and found that the request to do math problems was the primary antecedent to the disruptive behavior. The teacher decided to use an antecedent manipulation and no longer asked Sandy to do math problems. The teacher reasoned that if Sandy was no longer asked to do math problems, the disruptive behavior would be less likely to occur. What is the problem with this procedure?

5. Phyllis and Fred, two medical students who lived together, had to study every day. They both liked to relax by watching TV. Fred watched baseball, football, basketball, and other ball games broadcast on cable channels. Phyllis watched old movies on cable. The problem started to emerge as Phyllis spent time watching movies instead of studying. Her work was suffering, but she continued to watch the old movies and convinced herself that she would catch up with her studying later. On the other hand, Fred watched his ball games only after he had his work done. Phyllis finally realized she had a problem and decided that one way to help her watch TV less often, and therefore study more often, would be to discontinue cable. If she got rid of cable, she would be eliminating the antecedent (movies on cable) for the problem behavior, so that the problem behavior would be less likely to occur. What is the problem with the antecedent manipulation in this case?

6. Patrick, an adult with mental retardation, lived in a group home and worked in a community job. A problem that Patrick exhibited in the group home was refusal to complete training activities such as grooming and household tasks. He was most likely to refuse when younger staff made requests to him. When older staff made requests, he was typically compliant. Because requests from younger staff appeared to be a reliable antecedent to the problem behavior, the supervisor decided to have only the older staff work with Patrick. What is the problem with this antecedent procedure?

CHAPTER 16 *Quiz 1* Name:

1. Identify the three functional, nonaversive interventions for behavior problems.

   ______________________, ______________________, ______________________

2. In order to evoke the desirable behavior, you would present the ____________________ for the desirable behavior.

3. In order to make the desirable behavior more likely, you could make the reinforcer for the behavior more potent by arranging a(n) ______________________.

4. In order to make a desirable behavior more likely, you could ____________________ response effort for the behavior.

Match the following procedure to the descriptions.

a. Present the S^D or cues b. Arrange an establishing operation
c. Decrease response effort

5. _____ To make it more likely that you will study, schedule study time in your appointment book each day.

6. _____ To make it more likely that you will sleep at night, get up early and don't take a nap during the day.

7. _____ To make it more likely that you will exercise regularly, sign up at a gym close to your home.

8. Removing an establishing operation for a behavior will make the behavior less likely to occur because it makes the ________________ less potent.

9. You keep your nicotine gum on your desk at work in order to make it more likely that you will chew it instead of smoking. What two antecedent control procedures are you using in this case?______________________ and ______________________

10. Putting parking lots by interstate exits has helped make car pooling more likely to occur in some cities. What antecedent control strategy is exemplified in this case?

    ____

Chapter 16 *Quiz 2* Name:

1. ______________________ procedures are used to evoke desirable behaviors and decrease undesirable behaviors.

2. In order to decrease an undesirable behavior, you could remove the ____________________ for the undesirable behavior.

3. In order to decrease an undesirable behavior, you could make the reinforcer for the behavior less potent by removing a(n) _____________________________.

4. In order to make an undesirable behavior less likely, you could _________________ response effort for the behavior.

Match the following procedure to the descriptions.

a. Eliminate the S^D or cues b. Eliminate the establishing operation
c. Increase response effort

5. _____ To make it less likely that you will buy junk food at the store, only shop after you have eaten a meal.

6. _____ To make it less likely that you will buy junk food at the store, don't go down the junk food aisle.

7. _____ To make it less likely that you will eat junk food, do not keep any junk food in your home or at work.

8. Why is a behavior more likely to occur when you arrange an establishing operation for the behavior? ____

Fritz engages in disruptive behavior in the classroom when he has to do hard math problems. When he engages in disruptive behavior, he is sent to the principal and gets out of doing his math problems.

9. What is the reinforcer for Fritz's disruptive behavior? _________________.

10. How could you eliminate the establishing operation in this example to help Fritz decrease his disruptive behavior? ____

CHAPTER 16 *Quiz 3*

Name:

1. Extinction, differential reinforcement, and antecedent control are three

   ______________________________ interventions for problem behaviors.

2. What are three antecedent control procedures you could use to evoke a desired response?

   ______________________, ______________________,

   ____

3. What are three antecedent control procedures you could use to decrease the likelihood

   of an undesirable behavior? ______________________,

   ______________________, ______________________

4. ______________ response effort for a behavior will make the behavior more likely

   and, ______________ the response effort for a behavior will make the behavior less likely.

5. If a person engages in a problem behavior for attention, you could eliminate the establishing operation for the behavior by doing what?

   ____

Match the following procedures to the descriptions.

a. Remove the S^D or cues
b. Eliminate an establishing operation
c. Decrease response effort
d. Present the S^D or cues
e. Increase response effort
f. Arrange an establishing operation

6. _____ In order to eat less at supper, drink a lot of water before supper so you're not as hungry.

7. _____ In order to eat more vegetables, buy a dip for the vegetables that tastes great.

8. _____ In order to get yourself to floss regularly, leave the floss out on the bathroom counter where you see it.

9. _____ In order to recycle waste paper, put the recycle box on your desk instead of across the room next to the wastebasket.

10. _____ In order to eat less candy, take the candy off the kitchen table and put the candy away in the cupboard where you won't see it.

SEVENTEEN

Using Punishment: Time-Out and Response Cost

As we saw in Chapter 6, punishment is a basic behavioral principle. Punishment occurs when a behavior is followed by a consequence that results in a decrease in the future probability of the behavior. The consequence following the behavior may involve the presentation of a stimulus event (positive punishment) or the removal of a stimulus event (negative punishment). In both forms of punishment, the behavior is weakened.

A variety of punishment procedures can be used to decrease a problem behavior. However, punishment procedures typically are used only after functional nonaversive interventions—extinction, differential reinforcement, and antecedent manipulations—have been implemented or considered. When these procedures are implemented and result in a decrease in the problem behavior, punishment procedures are not necessary. However, if functional, nonaversive procedures are not effective (or not completely effective) or if their use is limited or impossible for whatever reason, punishment procedures should be considered.

- How does time-out work to decrease a problem behavior?
- What are the two types of time-out?
- What is response cost? How do you use it to decrease a problem behavior?
- Why is it important to use reinforcement procedures along with time-out or response cost?
- What issues must you consider when using time-out or response cost?

Using punishment procedures can be controversial. Some people believe that using punishment, the contingent presentation of an aversive event or the removal of a reinforcing event, may violate the rights of the person being treated (e.g., LaVigna & Donnelan, 1986). In addition, positive punishment involves presenting an aversive stimulus, which is often perceived to be painful or unpleasant, so some people believe that punishment produces unnecessary pain or discomfort for the person receiving treatment. (Note, however, that an aversive stimulus is not defined in terms of painful or unpleasant feelings. Rather, behavior modification adopts a functional definition, in terms of its effect on behavior: An aversive stimulus is any stimulus whose contingent presentation decreases the future probability of a behavior or whose contingent removal increases the future probability of a behavior; see, for example, Reynolds, 1968.)

For these and other reasons (Chapters 6 and 18), punishment procedures usually are not the first choice of interventions for decreasing problem behaviors. If a punishment procedure is used, it is often a negative punishment procedure involving the removal of reinforcing events after a problem behavior. This chapter describes two common negative punishment procedures: time-out and response cost.

TIME-OUT

Cheryl and the other kindergarten children were sitting around the table making figures out of clay, finger painting, and cutting shapes out of construction paper. After a little while, Cheryl threw one of her clay figures and smashed some figures made by other children. Seeing this, the teacher calmly walked up to Cheryl and said, "Cheryl come with me." She took her by the arm, and they walked to a chair across the room. When they got to the chair, she said, "Cheryl, you can't play when you throw things or break things. Sit here until I say you can play again." The teacher then walked back to the table and praised the other children for the figures they had made. After 2 minutes, the teacher walked back over to Cheryl and said, "Cheryl, you can come back to the table and play now" (Figure 17-1). When Cheryl came back and played without any further problems, the teacher talked to her and praised her for playing nicely. This procedure, in which Cheryl was removed from the reinforcing activity in the classroom for a few minutes contingent on an instance of the problem behavior, is called time-out. Once the teacher started using time-out, the rate of Cheryl's problem behaviors decreased greatly.

For about a year, 5-year-old Kenny had talked back to his parents and refused to do what they asked. Usually, Kenny was watching TV or playing a game when he engaged in these problem behaviors. Although his parents argued with him and gave him warnings about what might happen, he usually continued to watch TV or play and did not complete the task that was requested. The parents discussed the problem with a psychologist and decided to implement the following plan. First, when a parent wanted Kenny to do something, the parent went up to him, looked him in the eyes, and stated clearly what he or she wanted him to do. Second, the parent continued to stand there

FIGURE 17-1 When Cheryl engages in a problem behavior in the classroom, she has to sit off to the side and watch her classmates have fun for a few minutes. The procedure, a form of time-out called contingent observation, removes Cheryl from the reinforcement in the classroom for a few minutes contingent on the problem behavior.

and, if Kenny did not do what was requested within a short time (10–15 seconds), the parent said, "If you don't do what I tell you, you have to sit in your room." The parent then took Kenny's hand and walked him to his room. There were no toys, TV, or other recreational materials in Kenny's room. The parent told him to stay there until told he could leave. If Kenny argued, complained, or talked back during this process, the parent did not say anything to him in return. After a few minutes, the parent went to Kenny's room and made the same request that Kenny had earlier refused. If Kenny complied with the request this time, the parent thanked him for performing the task and let him watch TV or resume playing. If he refused again, however, the parent told him that he would have to stay in his room longer and left him there. After a few more minutes, the parent returned and repeated the process until Kenny finally complied with the request. Finally, on occasions when Kenny complied with the parents' request without protest, the parents smiled and praised him enthusiastically.

These two examples illustrate the use of time-out (and other procedures) to decrease the occurrence of different problem behaviors. In each example, after the problem behavior, the child was removed from the reinforcing situation for a brief period. Playing with the clay and finger paints and interacting with the other children are reinforcing activities for Cheryl, and time-out involved removing her from the situation where these reinforcing activities were present. Watching TV or playing a game is reinforcing for Kenny, and time-out involved removing him from the opportunity to continue these activities.

What other behavioral procedures were used in conjunction with time-out in these examples?

Differential reinforcement of alternative behavior was used in both examples. When Cheryl was playing appropriately, the teacher reinforced this behavior with attention. When Kenny complied with his parents' requests, this behavior was reinforced with praise and the opportunity to continue the reinforcing activities that he was engaging in before the request. In addition, Kenny's parents used a stimulus control procedure by standing directly in front of Kenny, looking him in the eyes, and stating the request clearly. The specific request, close proximity, and eye contact became a discriminative stimulus in the presence of which Kenny's refusal behavior was punished (with time-out). Thus, whenever the parents make a request in this way, Kenny is less likely to refuse because refusal has been punished by time-out.

Types of Time-Out

Time-out is defined as the loss of access to positive reinforcers for a brief period contingent on the problem behavior (Cooper, Heron, & Heward, 1987). The result is a decrease in the future probability of the problem behavior. Time-out here is short for **time-out from positive reinforcement.** There are two types of time-out: exclusionary and nonexclusionary.

The example of Cheryl illustrates **nonexclusionary time-out.** Cheryl remained in the classroom after the problem behavior but had to sit across the room from where the other children played and was thus removed from the reinforcing activity. The case of Kenny illustrates **exclusionary time-out.** Contingent on the problem behavior, Kenny was taken out of the room where he was watching TV or playing. He was taken to a room where these reinforcers were not available.

Nonexclusionary time-out is most likely to be used when the person can be removed from the reinforcing activities or interactions while still remaining in the room and the presence of the person in the room will not be disruptive to others in the environment. If either of these criteria cannot be met, exclusionary time-out would be used instead. For example, if Cheryl sat across the room in the time-out chair and disrupted the other students by continuing to engage in the problem behavior, nonexclusionary time-out would not be appropriate. Alternatively, if watching other children play were just as reinforcing for Cheryl as playing herself, nonexclusionary time-out would not be effective. For the procedure to be effective, the person must be removed from access to positive reinforcers. For Cheryl, exclusionary time-out could be implemented by having her sit in the principal's office or in another room adjacent to the classroom for a few minutes each time she engaged in the problem behavior. In addition, nonexclusionary time-out might be effective if Cheryl was made to sit in a chair facing the wall.

EXCLUSIONARY TIME-OUT

- The person is removed from the room (the reinforcing environment) where the problem behavior took place and is taken to another room. This removes the person from all sources of positive reinforcement.

NONEXCLUSIONARY TIME-OUT

- The person remains in the room while being removed from access to positive reinforcers.

Using Reinforcement with Time-Out

Whenever you use time-out (or any other punishment procedure), you should also use a reinforcement procedure. The time-out procedure decreases the rate of the problem behavior, and a differential reinforcement procedure increases an alternative behavior to replace the problem (differential reinforcement of alternative behavior, DRA) or provides the reinforcer for the absence of the problem behavior (differential reinforcement of other behavior, DRO). Because the time-out procedure eliminates access to positive reinforcers contingent on the problem behavior, it is important for the person to have access to positive reinforcers through a DRA or DRO procedure. If you used time-out without a differential reinforcement procedure, there could be a net loss in reinforcement and the problem behavior could be more likely to reemerge after treatment.

Considerations in Using Time-Out

To use time-out effectively, you must address a number of considerations.

What Is the Function of the Problem Behavior? Time-out is appropriate to use with problem behaviors that are maintained by positive reinforcement involving social or tangible reinforcers. Time-out removes access to these and other positive reinforcers contingent on the problem behavior and, as a result, the problem behavior is less likely to occur. In addition, the time-in environment (the environment where the problem behavior takes place) must consist of positively reinforcing activities or interactions for time-out to be effective. Removing the person from this environment is time-out from positive reinforcement only if the time-in environment is positively reinforcing and the time-out environment is not reinforcing or is less reinforcing (Solnick, Rincover, & Peterson, 1977).

Time-out is not appropriate to use with problem behaviors maintained by negative reinforcement or sensory stimulation (automatic reinforcement). Because time-out removes the person from the ongoing activities or interactions in the room, time-out would negatively reinforce any behavior that was maintained by escape (Plummer, Baer, & LeBlanc, 1977). For example, suppose that a student engages in aggressive behavior in the classroom and this behavior is negatively reinforced by escape from the educational demands. If the teacher used time-out, removing the student from the classroom would negatively reinforce the aggressive behavior. Time-out negatively reinforces the problem behavior when the time-out environment is less aversive than the ongoing activities.

Likewise, when a problem behavior is maintained by sensory stimulation, time-out is not appropriate because it would not function as time-out from positive reinforcement. The person would be removed from the activities or interactions in the time-in environment and would have the opportunity to engage in the problem behavior while alone in the time-out area (Solnick et al., 1977). Because the problem behavior is reinforced automatically by the sensory stimulation it produces, time out would be reinforcing: The person would have the opportunity to engage in the automatically reinforced behavior without interruption.

Is Time-Out Practical in the Given Situation? Time-out is practical when the change agents can implement the procedure successfully and the physical environment is conducive to its use. In the time-out procedure, the person often is removed from the room or from the area of the room where the problem behavior occurs. The change agent implementing time-out often must physically escort the client to the time-out room or area. In some cases the client may resist when being escorted to time-out. If the resistance involves physical confrontation or aggression, especially if the client is a large person (e.g., an adult with mental retardation or a psychiatric disorder), the change agent may not be able to implement the procedure. This factor must be considered before time-out is chosen as a treatment.

The second practical consideration is whether there is an appropriate room or area to use for time-out. For exclusionary time-out, another room or a hallway can be used. However, the time-out area must be a place where the client does not have access to any positive reinforcers. If a child is sent to his or her room for time-out and the room has a TV, a stereo, and toys, the room is not an appropriate place for time-out. If other people interact with the client during time-out, the time-out area is not appropriate. For example, if a student is sent to sit in a hallway where his or her friends are hanging out, time-out will not be effective. If no room or area exists where the client can be removed from positive reinforcers, time-out cannot be implemented.

Sometimes a room is built or an existing room is modified specifically for use as a time-out room. Such a room should be safe (free of sharp or breakable objects), well-lighted (with a ceiling light that cannot be broken), and barren (empty except for a chair). In addition, there should be an observation window so that the client can be observed during time-out. A one-way observation window is best so that the client cannot see the observer. Finally, the room should not have a lock so that the client cannot lock out the change agent and the change agent cannot lock in the client. This safeguards against the misuse of a time-out room. It would be a misuse of time-out for the change agent to lock the door and leave a client unattended in a time-out room.

Is Time-Out Safe? As already noted, the time-out room must not contain any objects that clients could use to hurt themselves. In addition, although the change agent must not interact with clients during time-out, the change agent should observe them throughout the duration of time-out to ensure that they do not harm themselves. This is especially important for clients who engage in violent, aggressive, or self-injurious behavior.

Is the Time-Out Period Brief? Time-out is a brief loss of access to positive reinforcers. The problem behavior should result in an immediate removal from the reinforcing time-in environment. However, the client should be returned to the time-in environment as soon as possible and allowed to resume normal activities (whether educational, vocational, or recreational). Time-out duration is typically 1–10 minutes. However, if the client is engaging in problem behaviors in the time-out area at the end of the time-out period, time-out is extended for a brief time (typically 10 seconds to 1 minute) until the client is no longer engaging in problem behaviors. The absence of the problem behavior is required at the end of time-out so that the termination of time-out does not negatively reinforce the problem behavior. This extension of time-out is called a contingent delay. The only study on this topic to date (Mace, Page, Ivancic, & O'Brien, 1986) found that time-out was equally effective with or without the contingent delay. However, a contingent delay is recommended, pending further studies. When the client is released from time-out, the change agent should identify the desirable behavior that will be reinforced in the time-in environment.

Can Escape from Time-Out Be Prevented? Whether using exclusionary or nonexclusionary time-out, the change agents should prevent the client from leaving the time-out room or area before the end of the time-out interval. If implemented correctly, time-out is aversive for the client, so the client may try to leave. However, for time-out to be effective, the client must not leave until the interval is up. For example, if a parent is using a time-out chair with a 5-year-old, the parent must keep the child in the chair during time-out. If the child gets up, the parent (who is standing near the child in the chair) should calmly give the child the instruction to sit back down. If the child does not comply or if the child gets up repeatedly, the parent should use physical guidance to keep the child in the chair. This may vary from a hand on the shoulder to physically restraining the child in the chair (McNeil, Clemens-Mowrer, Gurwitch, & Funderburk, 1994). When a time-out room is being used, the parent must return the child to the room if the child leaves prematurely; alternatively, the parent may hold the door closed as the child tries to open it. In either case, it is important to avoid a struggle, which may be reinforcing for the child and thus make time-out less effective. If the parent cannot prevent escape from time-out or cannot avoid a reinforcing struggle, time-out should not be used.

CONSIDERATIONS IN USING TIME-OUT

- What is the function of the problem behavior?
- Is time-out practical in the circumstances?
- Is time-out safe?
- Is the time-out period brief?
- Can escape from time-out be prevented?
- Can interactions be avoided during time-out?
- Is time-out acceptable in the circumstances?

Can Interactions Be Avoided During Time-Out? Time-out must be implemented calmly and without any emotional response from the change agent. In addition, while taking the client to time-out or during time-out, the change agent must not interact socially with the client. Reprimands, explanations, or any other form of attention must be avoided during time-out because they lessen its effectiveness. For example, if a child sitting in a time-out chair whines, cries, calls the parent names, or says, "I hate you," or if the child pleads to get out of the chair or promises to be good, the parent should stand nearby and ignore the child until the time out interval is up. If the child resists going to the time-out chair or room, the parent must not scold the child or try to talk the child into complying. The parent should simply provide the degree of physical guidance that is necessary to get the child to the time-out room or chair.

Is Time-Out Acceptable in the Given Situation? In some treatment settings, such as programs for people with mental retardation, rules and regulations govern the use of time-out and other punishment procedures. Before deciding whether to use time-out, you must be certain that the procedure is acceptable in the particular treatment environment. In addition, when working with parents, it is important to assess the degree to which they find time-out to be an acceptable procedure. Although acceptability may be increased through rationales and explanations about a particular treatment, ultimately the parents must accept the use of time-out if they are to implement it with their child.

Research Evaluating Time-Out Procedures

Numerous studies have demonstrated the effectiveness of time-out with children and with people with mental retardation (Adams & Kelley, 1992; Bostow & Bailey, 1969; Handen, Parrish, McClung, Kerwin, & Evans, 1992; Hobbs, Forehand, & Murray, 1978; Mace, Page, Ivancic, & O'Brien, 1986; McGimsey, Greene, & Lutzger, 1995; Roberts & Powers, 1990; Rolider & Van Houten, 1985).

Porterfield, Herbert-Jackson, and Risley (1976) and Foxx and Shapiro (1978) investigated two variations of nonexclusionary time-out. Porterfield and her colleagues evaluated time-out with young children who engaged in aggressive and disruptive behaviors in a day care program. When a child engaged in a problem behavior, the caregiver took the child outside the play area and had the child sit down on the floor and watch the other children play. After the child sat there for about a minute with no toys, activities, or interactions, the caregiver allowed the child to return to the play area. The caregiver also praised the children for playing appropriately. Porterfield called this procedure **contingent observation** because, contingent on the occurrence of the problem behavior, the child had to sit and watch the other children play appropriately. The procedure decreased the level of disruptive and aggressive behavior of the children in the day care program.

Foxx and Shapiro worked with five boys with mental retardation who engaged in a variety of problem behaviors (hitting, throwing objects, yelling, getting out of seat, banging objects) in a special education classroom. The boys sat around a table where the teacher worked with them on various educational activities. The teacher delivered edible and social reinforcers to each student at intervals of about 2 minutes when the student was not exhibiting a problem behavior. During the time-in condition, each student wore a different-colored ribbon around his neck. When the student engaged in a problem behavior, the teacher removed the ribbon and put it around her neck as a signal that time-out was in effect for that student. As long as the student was not wearing his ribbon, he could not engage in any activities and could not receive the reinforcers. The time-out lasted for 3 minutes. Using this nonexclusionary time-out procedure resulted in decreases in problem behaviors for all five boys.

Mathews, Friman, Barone, Ross, and Christophersen (1987) worked with mothers and their 1-year-old children. The researchers instructed the mothers to use exclusionary time-out when their children engaged in dangerous behaviors (e.g., touching electrical cords or appliances). The mothers first childproofed the home by eliminating as many hazards as possible. This antecedent manipulation should be used by all parents of young children to increase safety. They then used time-out and differential reinforcement when their children were playing. The mothers praised their children for playing appropriately and, when a child engaged in a dangerous behavior, the mother immediately implemented time-out (Figure 17-2). The mother said "No," took

FIGURE 17-2 The mother is using time-out with her young child. Whenever the child engages in dangerous behavior, she puts the child in the crib, away from reinforcers, for a brief period of time.

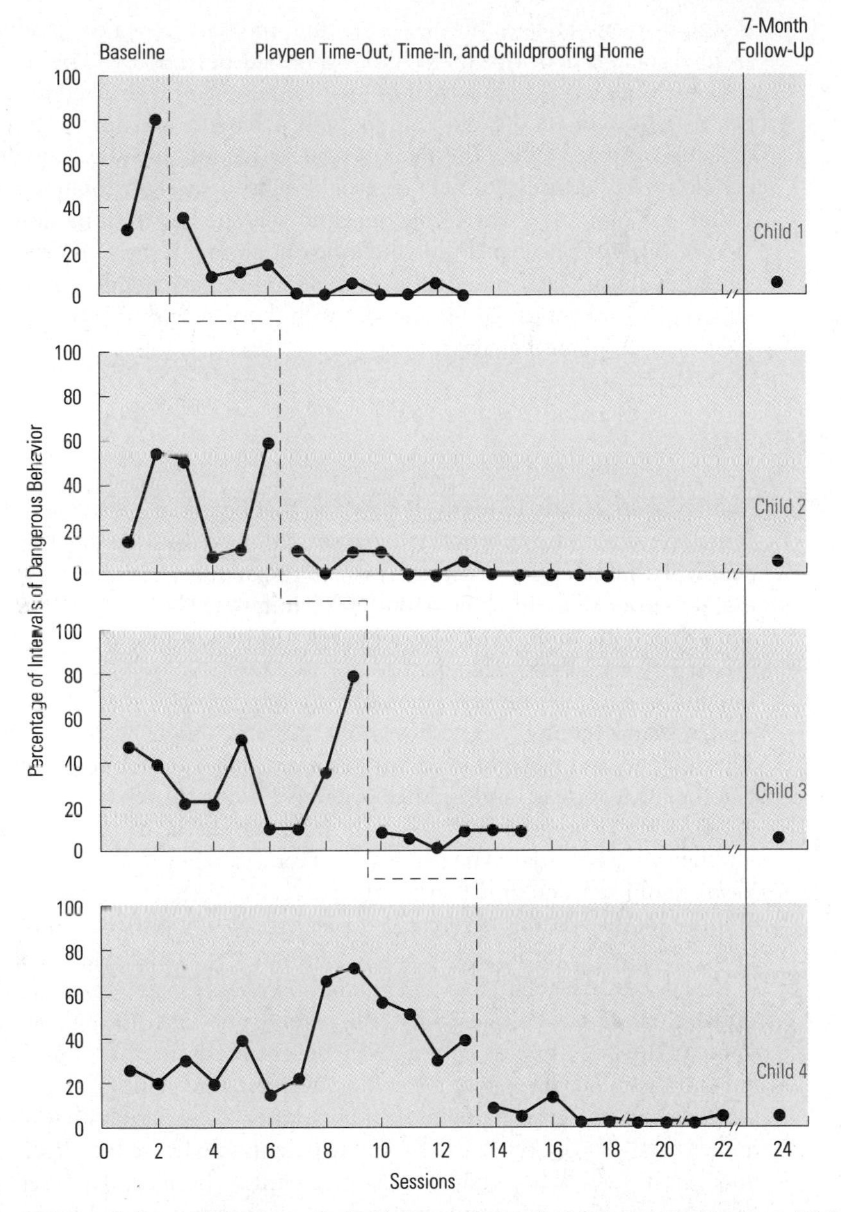

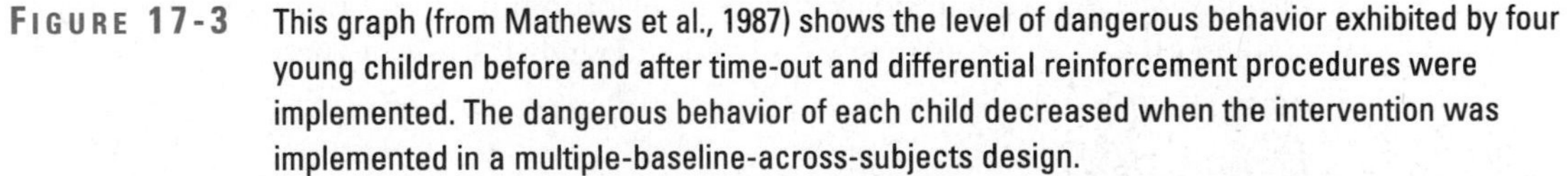

FIGURE 17-3 **This graph (from Mathews et al., 1987) shows the level of dangerous behavior exhibited by four young children before and after time-out and differential reinforcement procedures were implemented. The dangerous behavior of each child decreased when the intervention was implemented in a multiple-baseline-across-subjects design.**

her child from the play area, and put the child in the playpen for a brief period of time (until the child was quiet for 5–10 seconds). This time-out procedure resulted in a reduction in dangerous behavior for all the children (Figure 17-3).

Rortvedt and Miltenberger (1994) used exclusionary time-out to decrease noncompliance in two 4-year-old girls. The girls often refused to comply with their mothers' requests and, in response, the mothers repeated requests, threatened, scolded, or pleaded with them to do what had been asked. The researchers worked with each mother–daughter pair in their homes. They instructed the mother to praise her daughter when she did comply with a request and to use time-out when the daughter refused. When the mother made a request and the daughter did not comply within 20 seconds, the mother took the girl to another room and made her sit in a chair for 1 minute. After telling the child why she had to sit in the chair, the mother did not interact with her during the time-out period. If the child engaged in problem behaviors during time-out, the time-out period was extended until the child was quiet for at least 10 seconds. Using time-out with these two young children greatly reduced their noncompliant behavior.

Response Cost

Marty was in a hurry to finish shopping so that he could get home in time for the ball game. He pulled up in front of the store and parked in the parking spot reserved for people with disabilities. There were no other parking spaces close by, and he reasoned that he would be in the store for only a few minutes. Marty bought the items he needed and ran out the door. When he got to his car, he saw that he had a $150 ticket. After this incident, he never again parked in a spot reserved for people with disabilities. The fine for parking illegally is an example of a response cost procedure.

Jake and Jeremy, 7- and 8-year-old brothers, fought with each other frequently. They argued over who got to go first in games, yelled at each other when one had a toy that the other wanted, and wrestled over the TV remote control. Their parents decided to implement a program to decrease the frequency of the fighting. Both boys got a $2 allowance each Saturday. The parents told them that they would lose 25 cents of their allowance money each time they fought with each other. The parents defined fighting as arguing loudly, yelling, screaming, or crying, or any physical confrontation such as pushing, shoving, hitting, or wrestling. The parents put up a chart on the bulletin board in the kitchen. The chart had Jake's name and Jeremy's name, with eight quarters drawn under each name. For each fight, the parents put an X through a quarter under the name of the boy who was fighting. Whenever the parents saw or heard a fight, the parent calmly walked up to them and said, "You lost one quarter for fighting. I suggest you stop fighting, so that you don't lose more money." The parent then walked to the chart and crossed off a quarter. In addition, the parents taught the boys how to solve problems and compromise when they had disagreements. The parents praised them whenever they saw the boys engaging in problem-solving or compromise. Within a few weeks, Jake and Jeremy were fighting much less often and rarely lost any quarters.

Defining Response Cost

These two examples illustrate the behavioral procedure called **response cost,** which is defined as the removal of a specified amount of a reinforcer contingent on the occurrence of a problem behavior. Response cost is a negative punishment procedure when it results in a decrease in the future probability of the problem behavior. Marty lost $150 when he parked in the spot reserved for people with disabilities. As a result, he is much less likely to engage in this behavior again. Jake and Jeremy lost a quarter each time they engaged in the problem behavior, fighting. This resulted in a decrease in the rate of this behavior for the boys.

Response cost procedures are used widely by governments, law enforcement agencies, and other institutions. Governments rarely use positive reinforcement to control their citizens' behavior. If you don't pay your taxes or if you are caught cheating on your taxes, the IRS fines you. If you park illegally or get caught speeding, you get a ticket and pay a fine. If you write a bad check, you pay a fine to the bank. If you return books late to the library, you get fined. In each case, the fine is the loss of a quantity of a reinforcer (money) and is imposed to decrease the probability that you will engage in the inappropriate behavior. Money is commonly used in response cost procedures because it is a reinforcer for practically everyone and because it is easily quantified. The severity of the loss can be adjusted easily to fit the misbehavior. Other reinforcers that can be used in response cost procedures include tangible or material reinforcers, such as snacks, toys, tokens, or the opportunity to use the family car, or activity reinforcers, such as going to a movie, playing a game, or going out at recess. Any privilege that can be revoked contingent on the occurrence of a problem behavior may be used in a response cost procedure.

Using Differential Reinforcement with Response Cost

If a response cost procedure is being used to decrease a problem behavior, differential reinforcement should also be used to increase a desirable alternative behavior (DRA) or to reinforce the absence of the problem behavior (DRO). As stated previously, a differential reinforcement procedure should be used in conjunction with any punishment or extinction procedure.

Comparing Response Cost, Time-Out, and Extinction

Response cost, time-out, and extinction procedures are similar in that they are used to decrease a problem behavior. However, different processes are involved.

- With extinction, the problem behavior is no longer followed by the reinforcing event that previously maintained the behavior.
- With time-out, the person is removed from access to all sources of reinforcement contingent on the problem behavior.
- With response cost, a specific amount of a reinforcer the person already possesses is removed after the problem behavior.

The distinction between the three procedures may be clarified by means of an example.

Joey plays with various toys and crafts at a table with other preschool children. The teacher and teacher's aide play with the children, help them, and provide attention at periodic intervals. The reinforcers in this environment include toys, crafts, attention from the adults, and attention from the other children. In the classroom, Joey engages in disruptive behavior, which is reinforced by the teacher's attention. She explains to Joey why his behavior is not good, hugs him, and tells him to play nicely. This happens every time Joey engages in the disruptive behavior.

Describe how the teacher would implement extinction, time-out, and response cost procedures with Joey.

In extinction, the teacher would ignore Joey's disruptive behavior. Her attention is the reinforcer for the problem behavior, so if she ignored the behavior, she would be withholding the reinforcing consequence. Extinction probably is not the best procedure in this case because Joey's disruptive behavior might escalate and disrupt or hurt the other children.

In time-out, the teacher would remove Joey from the table and put him in a chair in the hallway, in another room, or across the room for a few minutes. By putting Joey in a chair away from the table, the teacher removes Joey from access to all the reinforcers present in the environment. Time-out would be an appropriate procedure because Joey could not continue to disrupt the other children while away from the table during time-out.

In response cost, the teacher would remove some reinforcer that Joey already possesses when he engages in disruptive behavior. For example, the teacher might take away his favorite toy for a short period when he is disruptive. The favorite toy is a reinforcer that Joey loses contingent on the problem behavior, but it is not the reinforcer for the problem behavior. Attention is the reinforcer for the problem behavior. Response cost might be an appropriate procedure, depending on whether Joey's disruptive behavior escalates when the toy is removed.

Considerations in Using Response Cost

To use response cost procedures successfully, you must consider a number of issues.

Which Reinforcer Will Be Removed? You must identify the reinforcer and the amount of the reinforcer you will remove in the response cost procedure. The reinforcer should be one that the change agent has control over so that it can be removed after the problem behavior. The quantity of the reinforcer must be large enough so that its loss contingent on the problem behavior will decrease the problem behavior. Although a quarter may be a large reinforcer for a child, most adults would not stop speeding if the fine were only a quarter. After identifying the reinforcer, you must decide whether the loss of the reinforcer is permanent or temporary. When you pay a fine for a speeding ticket, the loss of the money is permanent. However, sometimes the loss of a reinforcer is temporary. For example, a parent may take a child's bicycle away for a week as punishment for a problem behavior. Although the child loses a week of biking activity, the bike eventually is returned to the child.

Is the Reinforcer Loss Immediate or Delayed? In some cases, the reinforcer is removed immediately after the problem behavior in a response cost procedure. For example, a student who engages in disruptive behavior in the classroom loses a token immediately. However, when a token reinforcement program is not in use, the reinforcer loss in response cost usually is delayed. You pay the speeding fine later. The child loses allowance money at the end of the week, when the allowance is given. A child loses the opportunity to engage in an activity later in the day contingent on a problem behavior earlier in the day.

Although the reinforcer loss typically is delayed, the person is told about the loss immediately after the problem behavior. In addition, in some cases an immediate consequence occurs along with the delayed loss of the reinforcer. For example, Jake and Jeremy's parents put an X through a quarter on a chart to symbolize the loss of allowance money. The person caught speeding is given a ticket as an indication of the money to be lost later. An X is put by a student's name on the chalkboard to indicate the loss of recess. The immediate verbal statement about losing a reinforcer and the symbolic representation become conditioned punishers because they are paired with the eventual loss of the reinforcer. In this way, the actual loss of the reinforcer can be delayed yet still be an effective punisher.

If response cost is to be used with people with severe intellectual deficits, it is best to have an immediate reinforcer loss. For such people, a delay between the problem behavior and the loss of the reinforcer may make response cost less effective. Therefore, if response cost is going to be used with people with severe or profound retardation, it may best be used in conjunction with a token reinforcement program. In a token program, the person accumulates tokens as reinforcers for desirable behaviors, and a token can be taken immediately contingent on the occurrence of the problem behavior.

Is the Loss of Reinforcers Ethical? It is important that the removal of reinforcers in the response cost procedure does not violate the rights of the person being treated or result in harm to him or her. Although parents might take away a toy or other possession from their child as a consequence for a problem behavior, taking away a personal possession from an adult in a treatment program would be a violation of that person's rights. In addition, depriving a child or adult in a treatment program of a meal or food that is normally available to the person is also a violation of that person's rights. Although parents might not allow their child to have a dessert or a snack as a consequence for a problem behavior in a response cost program, parents should never deprive a child of nutritional requirements that could result in harm to the child.

Is Response Cost Practical and Acceptable? The response cost procedure must be practical. The change agent must be capable of carrying out the procedure. The response cost procedure must not stigmatize or embarrass the person with the problem behavior. The change agent implementing the procedure must find the procedure to be an acceptable method for decreasing a problem behavior. If the procedure is not practical or the change agent does not find it acceptable, alternative procedures must be considered.

CONSIDERATIONS IN USING RESPONSE COST

- Which reinforcer will be removed?
- Is the reinforcer loss immediate or delayed?
- Is the reinforcer loss ethical?
- Is response cost practical and acceptable?

Research Evaluating Response Cost Procedures

There have been numerous evaluations of response cost programs with various problem behaviors in a variety of populations. Response cost has been used to decrease child misbehavior during family shopping trips (Barnard, Christophersen, & Wolf, 1977), inappropriate behaviors in long-term patients in a psychiatric hospital (Doty, McInnis, & Paul, 1974), sleep problems in a young child (Ashbaugh & Peck, 1998), sleep problems in children and adolescents with mental retardation (Piazza & Fisher, 1991), off-task behavior in hyperactive children (Rapport, Murphy, & Bailey, 1982), noncompliance to parental requests (Little & Kelley, 1989), thumb-sucking and hair-pulling (Long, Miltenberger, & Rapp, 1999; Long, Miltenberger, Ellingson, & Ott, 1999), disruptive behavior in the classroom (Barrish, Saunders, & Wolf, 1969), and speech dysfluencies in college students (Siegal, Lenske, & Broen, 1969). A number of other evaluations of response cost procedures are described in more detail here.

Marholin and Gray (1976) investigated the effects of response cost on the cash shortages in a restaurant. Before response cost was implemented, the business had shortages from the cash register at the end of the day that averaged 4% of the day's income. Six cashiers participated in the study. During the response cost intervention, the shortage at the end of a day was calculated; if it was over 1%, it was divided between the cashiers for that day and taken out of their paychecks. The daily cash shortages during the group response cost condition decreased to well below the 1% criterion (Figure 17-4).

Aragona, Cassady, and Drabman (1975) used response cost as a component of a weight-loss program with children and their parents. The parents and their child attended 12 weekly group meetings. At the meetings, they learned a number of skills for managing caloric intake and initiating and maintaining an exercise program. At the beginning of the weight-loss program, the parents deposited a sum of money with the researchers. In the response cost component of the program, they lost a portion of this money if they did not show up for a weekly meeting, if they did not bring their graphs and charts to the meeting, and if their child did not lose the amount of weight specified in a contract for the week. All of the children lost weight across the 12 weeks of the program. In this study, the researchers used response cost contingent on weight loss, which is the outcome of a number of behaviors. Note that it is usually more effective to make the response cost contingent on specific behavior.

McSweeny (1978) reported an example of response cost used with the entire population of a major city. Before 1974, directory assistance calls in Cincinnati, Ohio, were free. From 1971 through 1973, between 70,000 and 80,000 directory assistance calls were made to phone company operators every day. In 1974, the telephone company instituted a 20-cent charge for each call to directory assistance, and the number of directory assistance calls per day dropped to around 20,000, a decrease of 50,000–60,000 calls per day. When telephone users had to pay to get a number through directory assistance, this behavior decreased and, presumably, the alternative behavior of using the phone book to get a number increased.

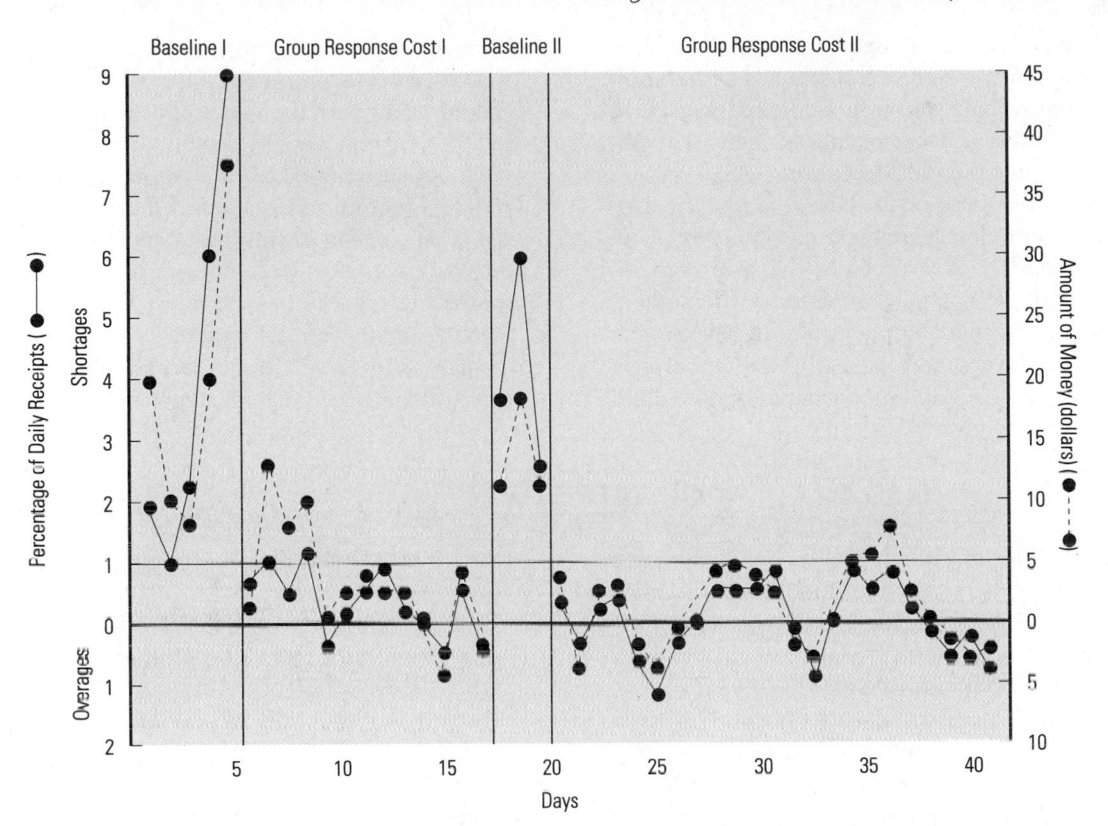

FIGURE 17-4 This graph (from Marholin & Gray, 1976), shows the effects of response cost on the daily cash shortages (or overages) from the cash register of a small business. The dotted line shows the total amount of money in the cash register that was under or over the expected amount at the end of the day. The solid line shows the percentage of the day's sales that was under or over at the end of each day. The response cost was implemented if the shortage was more than 1% of the day's sales. Response cost was implemented in an A-B-A-B design and decreased shortages to the criterion level each time it was implemented.

CHAPTER SUMMARY

1. In time-out, the person loses access to all sources of reinforcement contingent on the problem behavior. Time-out works as a form of negative punishment.
2. In nonexclusionary time-out, the person is removed from all sources of reinforcement while remaining in the environment where the problem behavior occurred. In exclusionary time-out, the person is removed from the environment and taken to a time-out room or area.
3. In response cost, the person loses a quantity of a specific reinforcer contingent on the occurrence of the problem behavior. Immediately after the problem behavior, the reinforcer is removed and the person is less likely to engage in the problem behavior in the future.

4. Reinforcement is used in conjunction with time-out or response cost so that a desirable alternative behavior is strengthened to replace the problem behavior that is decreased with these punishment procedures.
5. For time-out to be effective, the time-in environment must be reinforcing. Time-out is not appropriate for problem behaviors maintained by escape or sensory stimulation. Time-out must be practical, safe, acceptable to caregivers, and brief in duration. Escape from time-out and interactions with the child during time-out must be prevented. For response cost to be used successfully, the change agent must have control over the reinforcer to be removed. In addition, reinforcers must not be removed from a person if it will result in harm or a violation of that person's rights. The change agent must choose the appropriate reinforcer to remove during the response cost procedure and must determine whether the loss of the reinforcer will be immediate or delayed. Response cost must be practical and acceptable to caregivers.

PRACTICE TEST

1. What is punishment? What is the difference between positive punishment and negative punishment? (p. 369)
2. Describe time-out. Explain why time-out is a negative punishment procedure. (p. 371)
3. What is nonexclusionary time-out? What is exclusionary time-out? Provide an example of each type of time-out. (pp. 371–372)
4. Under what conditions would you use nonexclusionary time-out rather than exclusionary time-out? (p. 372)
5. Describe how the effectiveness of time-out is related to the function of the problem behavior and the nature of the time-in environment. (pp. 372–373)
6. Describe the characteristics of an appropriate time-out room or area. (pp. 373–374)
7. Why should the time-out period be brief? (p. 374)
8. If parents use time-out with their child, what must the parents do and not do while the child is in the time-out room or area? (pp. 374–375)
9. Describe response cost. Explain what makes response cost a negative punishment procedure. (pp. 378–379)
10. Describe two examples of response cost procedures. (p. 378)
11. Describe the difference between extinction, time-out, and response cost. (p. 379)
12. Describe the ethical issues involved in choosing which reinforcer to remove in a response cost procedure. (p. 381)
13. In a response cost procedure, the reinforcer often is removed some time after the problem behavior occurs. What happens immediately after the problem behavior? Provide an example. (pp. 380–381)
14. Why is differential reinforcement used in conjunction with time-out and response cost? (pp. 372, 379)

APPLICATIONS

1. Describe how you might implement a response cost procedure in your self-management project. Explain why this procedure is appropriate.

2. A family has three young children, ages 4, 5, and 6, who play together frequently. Often when one of the children, Hillary, doesn't get her way, or if one of the other children is playing with her favorite toy, she engages in tantrum behavior. She cries and demands to get her way or get her toy back and sometimes throws toys. As a result, she gets her way or one of the parents settles the dispute and the children continue to play. De-

scribe the time-out procedure you would teach Hillary's parents to decrease her tantrum behavior.

3. Describe the response cost procedure you would teach Hillary's parents to decrease her tantrum behavior.

4. Louis is a 10-year-old with severe mental retardation in a special education class with 12 other children. The teacher and teacher's aide run group and one-on-one teaching sessions with the students. Louis engages in aggressive behavior in which he pulls the other students' hair. You have been asked to consult with the teacher to develop treatment recommendations. You observe in the classroom for a few days and notice that the teacher and teacher's aide rarely praise the students or provide other sources of reinforcement. You also observe that Louis gets reprimanded and put in a chair each time he pulls hair. This has not decreased the hair-pulling, however. Describe the instructions you would give to the teacher to make the classroom environment more reinforcing in general. Also describe the time-out and differential reinforcement procedures the teacher should use with Louis for the aggressive behavior once the other changes are made in the classroom (time-in) environment.

MISAPPLICATIONS

1. Marybeth was a 5-year-old who had developed the problem behavior of ignoring her mother's requests and continuing to play or watch TV. For example, when her mother asked her to come in and wash up for lunch, she would ignore her mother or say "Later" and continue to play on the swing set. Marybeth continued to refuse to comply until her mother had repeated the request 10–12 times. To decrease Marybeth's noncompliance, her mother instituted a time-out procedure. Whenever Marybeth did not comply with a request, her mother walked up to her, took her to the dining room, and told her to sit in a chair for disobeying her. During Marybeth's 2-minute time-out, her mother stood nearby. Marybeth complained and argued while sitting in the time-out chair. In response, her mother told her to be quiet, explained why she had to sit there, and threatened that she would have to sit there longer if she did not be quiet. This interaction continued throughout every time-out period. What is the problem with the way Marybeth's mother is implementing time-out? How could she improve her use of time-out?

2. Felix, a 25-year-old man with profound mental retardation living in a group home, ate supper at a dining table with five other residents with mental retardation. Felix often grabbed food from other residents' plates and ate it. This upset the other residents and caused problems at meals. The staff implemented a response cost procedure to decrease the food stealing. As soon as Felix grabbed food from somebody's plate, the staff removed him from the table, and he lost the remaining portion of his meal. After this response cost procedure was implemented, the food stealing decreased to only a few occurrences per week. What is wrong with this response cost procedure?

3. Sam is a seventh grader who is failing most of his classes. He is often truant from school and claims that he hates to be in school. In the classroom, Sam engages in a problem behavior in which he picks on some of the other students. He grabs books or papers from their desks and pokes or pinches them during class. The teacher decided on a time-out program for Sam. Whenever he engaged in one of the problem behaviors, the teacher made him sit outside the classroom in the hallway for 15 minutes. After 15 minutes, the teacher went out and told him to come back in the classroom. Although the teacher used this time-out procedure for several weeks, the problem behaviors persisted. What is wrong with this use of time-out?

CHAPTER 17 *Quiz 1* Name:

1. Positive punishment involves the presentation of a(n) ____________________ following the behavior.

2. Negative punishment involves the removal of a(n) ____________________ following the behavior.

3. With the use of time-out, what happens following the occurrence of the problem behavior?

    ____

4. Time-out is an appropriate procedure to use with problem behaviors maintained by

    what type of reinforcement? ____________________

5. Time-out is not an appropriate procedure to use with problem behaviors maintained by

    what type of reinforcement? ____________________

6. For time-out to be most effective, what should the time-in environment be like?

    ____

7. In response cost, what happens following the occurrence of the problem behavior?

    ____

Match the following procedures to the descriptions.

a. Response cost b. Extinction c. Time-out

8. _____ The problem behavior is no longer followed by the reinforcing consequence that maintained the behavior.

9. _____ A specified amount of a reinforcer the person already possesses is removed following the occurrence of the problem behavior.

10. _____ The person is removed from access to all sources of reinforcement contingent on the problem behavior.

CHAPTER 17 *Quiz 2*

Name:

1. ______________________ is defined as the loss of access to positive reinforcers for a brief period contingent on the problem behavior.

2. What are two types of time-out? ______________________ and ______________________

3. A(n) ______________________ procedure should always be used in conjunction with time-out.

4. ______________________ punishment involves the presentation of an aversive stimulus following the behavior, and ______________________ punishment involves the removal of a reinforcing stimulus following the behavior.

5. What is the typical duration of the time-out period? ______________________

6. If the time-in environment is highly reinforcing, time-out is likely to be ______________________ (more/less) effective.

7. What procedure is the government using when it fines you for breaking the law (e.g., speeding, parking illegally) in an attempt to get you to stop breaking the law? ______________________

Match the following procedures to the descriptions.

a. Time-out   b. Extinction   c. Response cost

8. _____ Sunny cried and screamed when her mom was on the phone, and her mom usually got off the phone right away to see what was wrong, calm Sunny down, and comfort her. To try to get Sunny to stop screaming and crying when she was on the phone, mom walked away from Sunny whenever she started to scream and cry.

9. _____ Sunny cried and screamed when her mom was on the phone, and her mom usually got off the phone right away to see what was wrong, calm Sunny down, and comfort her. To try to get Sunny to stop screaming and crying when she was on the phone, mom had Sunny sit in her room by herself whenever she started to scream and cry.

10. _____ Sunny cried and screamed when her mom was on the phone, and her mom usually got off the phone right away to see what was wrong, calm Sunny down, and comfort her. To try to get Sunny to stop screaming and crying when she was on the phone, mom took away Sunny's favorite doll whenever she started to scream and cry.

CHAPTER 17 *Quiz 3* Name:

1. Time-out and response cost are examples of which type of punishment?

   ______________________________.

2. Punishment procedures are typically used in behavior modification only after what procedures have been used first? ______________________________

3. If punishment is used in behavior modification, ____________________ (positive/negative) punishment is most likely to be used.

4. When Betty hit another child in the kindergarten classroom, she had to sit in a chair off to the side of the classroom for 2 minutes. As a result she was less likely to hit other children. What type of time-out is illustrated in this example? ____________________

5. When Betty hit another child in the kindergarten classroom, she had to sit in a chair in the hallway for 2 minutes. As a result she was less likely to hit other children. What type of time-out is illustrated in this example? ____________________

6. What should you do if the child in time-out is engaging in problem behavior at the end of the time-out period? ______________________________

7. ____________________ is defined as the removal of a specified amount of a reinforcer contingent on the occurrence of the problem behavior.

8. A(n) ______________________________ procedure should always be used in conjunction with response cost.

9. In a(n) ____________________ procedure, the reinforcer for the problem behavior is withheld following the behavior, and in a(n) ____________________ procedure, a reinforcer the person already possesses is removed following the behavior.

10. In response cost, if you cannot remove the reinforcer immediately after the problem behavior, what should you do immediately after the problem behavior occurs?

    ____

EIGHTEEN

Positive Punishment Procedures and the Ethics of Punishment

Chapter 17 discussed negative punishment procedures, time-out and response cost, which involve removing reinforcing events contingent on the occurrence of the problem behavior. This chapter describes the use of positive punishment procedures to decrease problem behaviors. In positive punishment, aversive events are applied contingent on the occurrence of a problem behavior, and the result is a decrease in the future probability of the behavior. As described in Chapter 17, the use of punishment, especially positive punishment, is controversial. Functional nonaversive treatment approaches should always be used before punishment is considered, and reinforcement procedures should always be used in conjunction with punishment. Ethical considerations in using punishment procedures are discussed later in this chapter.

- What is the application of aversive activities?
- What are five positive punishment procedures involving the application of aversive activities?
- What is the application of aversive stimulation?
- What issues must you consider before using positive punishment procedures?
- What ethical issues are involved in using punishment procedures?

Two major categories of aversive events are used in positive punishment procedures: the application of aversive activities and the application of aversive stimulation (Sulzer-Azaroff & Mayer, 1991).

Application of Aversive Activities

One Saturday morning, 5-year-old Allison was using crayons in her coloring book. Her father was busy in another part of the house. Allison was mad at her father because he wouldn't take her to the park. She got her crayon and started to scribble in big circles on the white kitchen wall. When she had colored a large portion of one wall, her father walked in the room and saw what she'd done. Allison started crying and saying she was sorry. Her father calmly walked up to her and said in a firm voice, "You don't write on walls. Now you have to clean this up." He got a bucket of detergent and water, took Allison to the place that she had marked on the wall, gave her a soapy rag, and told her to clean the wall. He stood and watched her clean but did not say anything more to her. He ignored her complaining and physically prompted her to continue if she stopped cleaning. Once Allison had cleaned the crayon marks off the wall, he took her to another wall in the kitchen and told her to clean that wall also. Again, he did not interact with her except to provide physical guidance if she stopped. After about 15 minutes of cleaning, he told Allison she was done and that she could play again. As a result of this procedure, Allison was less likely to mark on the walls again when she was angry in the future.

It was 2 A.M. and the buzzer next to Simon's bed woke him just as he was starting to wet the bed. The buzzer is activated by a sensor in a pad placed under the sheets on his bed; the sensor detects liquid (urine). Also woken by the buzzer, Simon's mother came to his room and told him to change his pajamas and sheets, take them to the laundry room, wipe off the pad, and put clean sheets on the bed. After Simon had done this, his mother told him that he had to practice getting out of bed at night and going to the bathroom. According to her instructions, Simon got in bed under the covers and then pulled off his covers, got up, walked to the bathroom, and stood in front of the toilet. Although Simon complained, his mother made him complete this behavior ten times before going back to sleep. After he had finished practicing, she said good night and reminded him to get up and go to the bathroom next time he had to go at night. After a few weeks of this procedure, Simon was rarely wetting his bed anymore.

In each of these two cases, a problem behavior was decreased by the contingent **application of aversive activities.** Contingent on the problem behavior, the child was made to engage in an aversive activity. As a result, the problem behavior was less likely to occur in the future. An aversive activity is a low-probability behavior the person typically would not choose to engage in. For Allison, the aversive activity was cleaning the walls. For Simon, it was the repeated practice of getting out of bed and going to the bathroom. This form of positive punishment is based on the Premack principle, which states that when the requirement to engage in a low-probability behavior (the aversive activity) is made contingent on the occurrence of a high-probability behavior (the problem behavior), the high-probability behavior will decrease in the future (Miltenberger & Fuqua, 1981).

Although an aversive stimulus is an environmental event that can be a punisher, an aversive activity is a behavior that can be a punisher for another behavior. A person will try to avoid or escape from performing an aversive activity. As a result, the change agent often has to use physical guidance to get the person to engage in the aversive activity contingent on the problem behavior. When Allison complained about washing the walls and tried to quit, this was evidence that washing walls was an aversive activity. In response, her father used physical guidance to make Allison wash the walls. When Simon complained about the repeated practice of going to the toilet at night, this too was an indication that the behavior was an aversive activity. Even though practicing this routine was aversive, Simon did not stop because his mother's instructions had stimulus control over the behavior.

When applying an aversive activity as a positive punisher, the change agent instructs the client to engage in the aversive activity immediately contingent on the problem behavior. If the client does not engage in the activity upon command, the change agent then uses physical guidance to make the client engage in the behavior. Eventually, the client should engage in the activity upon command to avoid the physical guidance that previously followed the command. For example, Allison stopped washing walls and her father immediately used physical guidance to make her continue washing. As a result, she continued to wash the walls when instructed in order to avoid further physical guidance from her father.

Various types of positive punishment procedures use different types of aversive activity, as follows.

Overcorrection

Overcorrection is a procedure developed by Foxx and Azrin (1972, 1973) to decrease aggressive and disruptive behaviors exhibited by people with mental retardation in institutional settings. In overcorrection, the client is required to engage in an effortful behavior for an extended period contingent on each instance of the problem behavior. There are two forms of overcorrection: positive practice and restitution.

Positive Practice In **positive practice,** the client has to engage in correct forms of relevant behavior contingent on an instance of the problem behavior. The client engages in the correct behavior, with physical guidance if necessary, for an extended period (say, 5–15 minutes) or until the correct behavior has been repeated a number of times. This is said to be an overcorrection procedure because the client has to engage in the correct behavior many times in positive practice. Positive practice was used with Simon in our example. He had to practice the correct behavior of getting out of bed and going to the bathroom ten times contingent on an instance of the problem behavior: wetting his bed.

Consider another example. Assume that a grade school student makes numerous spelling errors on the written assignments that she hands in to her teacher. She makes errors because she rushes through the assignment and does not check her work.

How could the teacher implement positive practice overcorrection to decrease spelling errors from this student?

The teacher could mark each misspelled word on her assignment, give the assignment back to the student, and tell her to write the correct spelling of each word ten times. The repeated practice in correct spelling is an example of positive practice. Because this aversive activity is contingent on misspelling, the misspelling should decrease in future assignments.

Research has documented the effectiveness of positive practice overcorrection for decreasing problem behaviors, primarily in people with mental retardation (Foxx & Bechtel, 1983; Miltenberger & Fuqua, 1981). For example, Wells, Forehand, Hickey, and Green (1977) evaluated positive practice for treating stereotypic behavior (inappropriate object manipulation and other repetitive body movements) by two 10-year-old boys with severe retardation. Each time one of the boys engaged in the problem behavior in the playroom, the teacher implemented positive practice in which she physically guided the boy to play appropriately with toys for 2 minutes. Positive practice decreased the problem behaviors of both boys to zero.

Restitution **Restitution** is a procedure in which, contingent on each instance of the problem behavior, the client must correct the environmental effects of the problem behavior and restore the environment to a condition better than that before the problem behavior. Physical guidance is used as needed to get the client to engage in the restitutional activities. In restitution, the client overcorrects the environmental effects of the problem behavior.

Restitution was used with Allison in our example. When she wrote on the walls with the crayon, her father made her clean the wall she wrote on and another wall in the kitchen. The correction went beyond the damage done by the problem behavior. In the other example, Simon had to perform a simple correction procedure: remove his wet sheets, change his clothes, clean up, and put clean sheets on the bed. This corrected the environmental effects of the problem behavior but did not involve overcorrection.

Consider an example in which a student with a behavioral disorder has an outburst in the classroom and knocks over a desk during a detention period when no other students are in the classroom.

Describe how the teacher would implement a restitution procedure with this student.

The teacher would have the student pick up the desk and put it back in place in its row. In addition, the teacher might have the student go up each row of desks in the classroom and straighten all the desks so that they are perfectly in line in the rows. In this way, the student would correct the problem he caused and would restore the classroom environment to a condition better than that before the problem behavior.

Research also documents the effectiveness of restitution for decreasing problem behaviors in people with mental retardation (Foxx & Bechtel, 1983; Miltenberger & Fuqua, 1981). Restitution has been used with adults with mental retardation as part of a toilet training program to decrease toileting accidents (Azrin & Foxx, 1971), to stop food stealing (Azrin & Wesolowski, 1975), and to decrease aggressive, disruptive behavior and self-stimulatory behavior (Foxx & Azrin, 1972, 1973). Some of the results obtained by Foxx and Azrin (1973) are summarized in Figure 18-1.

Contingent Exercise

Contingent exercise is another positive punishment procedure involving the application of aversive activities. In the contingent exercise procedure, the client is made to engage in some form of physical exercise contingent on an instance of the problem behavior (Luce, Delquadri, & Hall, 1980; Luce & Hall, 1981). The result is a decrease in the future probability of the problem behavior. Contingent exercise differs from overcorrection in terms of the aversive activity. In overcorrection, as we have seen, the aversive activity is a correct form of behavior related to the problem behavior (positive practice) or a behavior that corrects a disruption to the environment created by the problem behavior (restitution). In contingent exercise, by contrast, the aversive activity involves physical exercise unrelated to the problem behavior. The exercise must be a physical activity that the client is capable of carrying out without harm. As with overcorrection and other procedures involving the application of aversive activities, physical guidance is used if necessary to get the client to engage in the contingent exercise. Consider the following example.

Johnny had started swearing around his younger brothers, and this concerned his parents. They asked him not to swear and, in particular, not to swear around his brothers. Johnny agreed to comply with his parents' request, but one day his father caught him swearing again. His father had Johnny immediately stop what he was doing, gave him a rag and a bottle of window cleaner, and told him to wash windows in the house for the next 10 minutes. Johnny grudgingly washed the windows under his father's supervision. When Johnny was done, his father said that he would do the same each time he caught Johnny swearing. Johnny's swearing around his family stopped almost immediately once his father implemented this contingent exercise procedure (adapted from Fisher & Neys, 1978).

Luce and his colleagues used contingent exercise to decrease aggressive behavior and threats in the classroom by two boys with developmental delay (Luce et al., 1980). Whenever one of the boys engaged in the problem behavior, the teacher required the

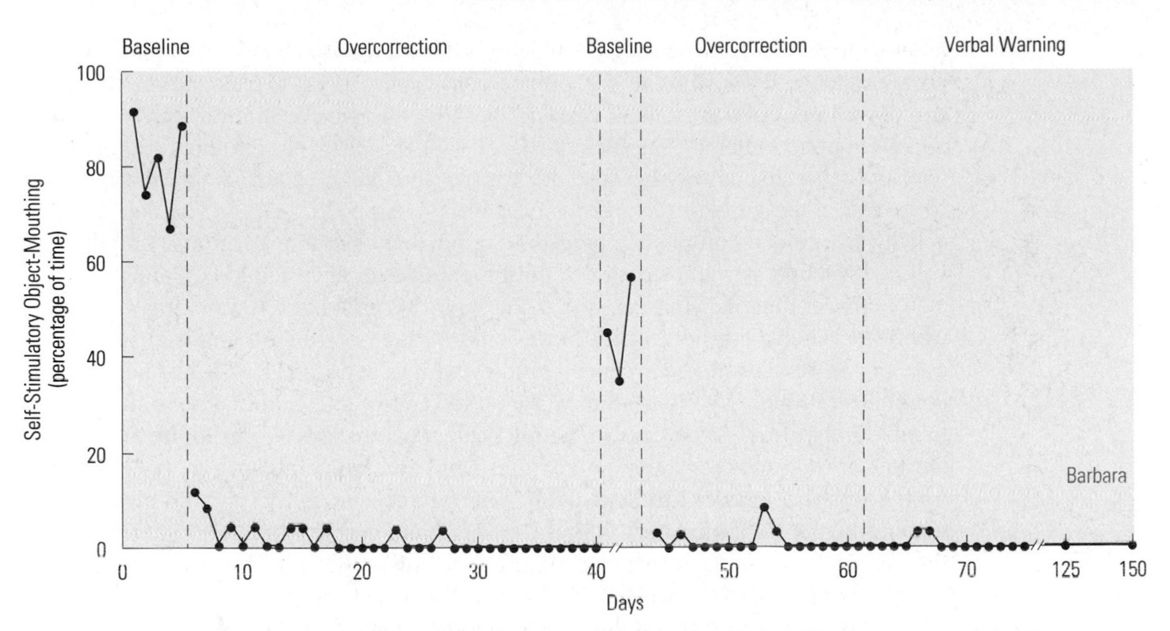

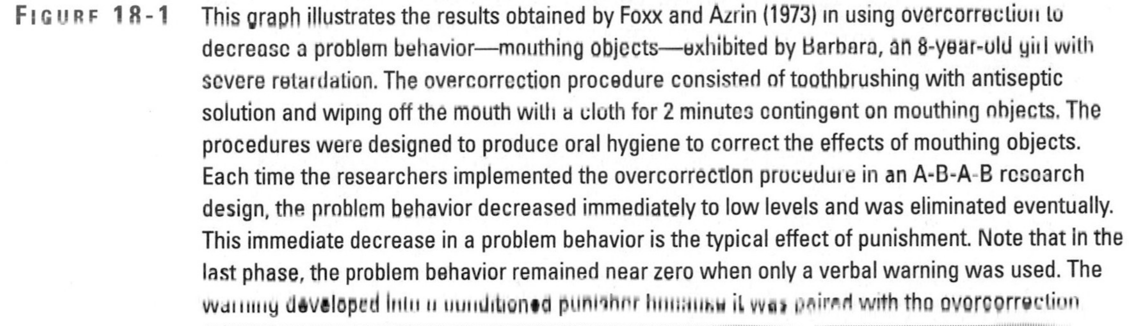
FIGURE 18-1 This graph illustrates the results obtained by Foxx and Azrin (1973) in using overcorrection to decrease a problem behavior—mouthing objects—exhibited by Barbara, an 8-year-old girl with severe retardation. The overcorrection procedure consisted of toothbrushing with antiseptic solution and wiping off the mouth with a cloth for 2 minutes contingent on mouthing objects. The procedures were designed to produce oral hygiene to correct the effects of mouthing objects. Each time the researchers implemented the overcorrection procedure in an A-B-A-B research design, the problem behavior decreased immediately to low levels and was eliminated eventually. This immediate decrease in a problem behavior is the typical effect of punishment. Note that in the last phase, the problem behavior remained near zero when only a verbal warning was used. The warning developed into a conditioned punisher because it was paired with the overcorrection

boy to stand up and sit down on the floor ten times in a row. The teacher verbally prompted the boy to stand up and sit down and physically guided the behavior when necessary. The problem behaviors decreased to low levels for both boys.

Guided Compliance

When a person is engaging in a problem behavior in a compliance situation (the person is instructed or asked to engage in an activity), **guided compliance** can be used as a positive punishment procedure to decrease the problem behavior. In a guided compliance procedure, the person is physically guided through the requested activity (such as an educational task) contingent on the occurrence of the problem behavior. For most people, physical guidance in a noncompliance situation is an aversive event. Because physical guidance of the requested activity occurs contingent on the problem behavior, it acts as a punisher for the problem behavior. (If the physical guidance is not a punisher for a particular client, guided compliance would not be used with that client.) Once initiated, however, physical guidance is withdrawn if the person begins to comply with the requested activity. Because the withdrawal of the physical guidance is contingent on the occurrence of the requested activity (compliance), compliance is negatively reinforced. As you can see, guided compliance serves two functions. It is positive punishment of the problem behavior because the aversive stimulus (physical guidance) is applied after the problem behavior, and it negatively reinforces compliance with the requested activity because the aversive stimulus is removed after compliance. Moreover, if the problem behavior is negatively reinforced by escape from a requested activity, the guided compliance procedure removes the reinforcer (escape) and thus involves extinction as well as positive punishment and negative reinforcement.

Consider the following example. Lindsey, an 8-year-old girl, is watching a TV show when her parents ask her to pick her toys up off the floor before guests arrive for the evening. In response to the request, Lindsey whines and argues with her parents and continues to watch TV. Her father walks up to Lindsey and calmly repeats the request to pick up her toys. As he does so, he physically guides Lindsey over to the area where her toys are spread across the floor and uses hand-over-hand guidance to make her pick up the toys. He ignores Lindsey's complaints but, as soon as she starts to pick up toys without his physical guidance, he releases her hand and lets her continue to pick up the toys on her own. Once she has finished picking up her toys, her father thanks her and lets her go back to what she was doing. If the parents use this procedure each time Lindsey is noncompliant, Lindsey is less likely to engage in problem behaviors when they make requests and more likely to comply with their requests.

Positive punishment

Antecedent	Behavior	Consequence
Lindsey's father tells her to pick up her toys.	Lindsey whines and argues.	Her father physically guides compliance.

Outcome: Lindsey is less likely to whine and argue when her father makes a request in the future because whining and arguing were followed by application of physical guidance.

Negative reinforcement

Antecedent	Behavior	Consequence
Her father makes a request and uses physical guidance.	Lindsey starts to comply with the request.	Her father withdraws the physical guidance.

Outcome: Lindsey is more likely to comply when her father makes a request in the future because compliance was followed by the removal of physical guidance.

Handen and his colleagues (Handen, Parrish, McClung, Kerwin, & Evans, 1992) evaluated the effectiveness of guided compliance for decreasing noncompliance in children with mental retardation. When the trainer made a request and the child did not comply, the trainer used hand-over-hand guidance to get the child to carry out the requested activity. The researchers also evaluated time-out and found that guided compliance and time-out were equally effective in decreasing noncompliance in the children participating in the study.

Physical Restraint

Physical restraint is a punishment procedure in which, contingent on a problem behavior, the change agent holds immobile the part of the client's body that is involved in the behavior. As a consequence, the client is physically restrained from continuing to engage in the problem behavior. For example, when a student with mental retardation engages in aggressive behavior (by slapping students sitting nearby), the teacher might respond by holding the student's arms down for 1 minute. While being physically restrained, the student cannot engage in the problem behavior or any other behavior. The teacher does not interact with the student while applying the physical restraint (Figure 18-2).

For many people, having their movement restrained as an aversive event; for these people, physical restraint functions as a punisher. However, for some people physical restraint may function as a reinforcer (Favell, McGimsey, & Jones, 1978). Therefore, it is important to determine whether physical restraint will function as a punisher or as a reinforcer for a particular person before planning to use physical restraint.

One variation of physical restraint involves response blocking, in which the change agent prevents the occurrence of a problem behavior by physically blocking the response (Lerman & Iwata, 1996a). As soon as the client initiates the problem behavior, the change agent blocks it so that the client cannot complete the response. For example, suppose that a student with mental retardation engages in hand-mouthing behavior; that is, the student puts his hand in his mouth, in an action similar to thumb-sucking. Response blocking in that case would mean that as soon as he brings his hand up to his mouth, the teacher puts his or her hand in front of the student's mouth to prevent the student from inserting his hand (Reid, Parsons, Phillips, & Green, 1993). Response blocking can also be used with brief restraint; in this case, the change agent blocks the response and then uses physical restraint for a brief period of time (Rapp, Miltenberger, Galensky, Ellingson, et al., 2000).

FIGURE 18-2 When the student slaps another student, the teacher applies physical restraint for 1 minute by holding the student's arms down. The student cannot engage in any reinforcing activities and cannot get attention from the teacher during this time.

Shapiro, Barrett, and Ollendick (1980) evaluated physical restraint as a treatment for hand-mouthing exhibited by three girls with mental retardation. Each time the girl put her hand in her mouth, the trainer removed it from her mouth and physically restrained the child's hands on the table in front of her for 30 seconds. This procedure decreased the problem behavior for all three children. Brief physical restraint has also been used as an effective intervention for pica behavior (ingesting nonfood objects) in people with mental retardation (Bucher, Reykdal, & Albin, 1976; Winton & Singh, 1983). With a behavior such as pica, it is preferable to block the response, so that the person does not get the inedible item into his or her mouth, and then to use the brief restraint.

Cautions in the Application of Aversive Activities

From the preceding discussion of the various aversive activities that can be applied in positive punishment procedures, it is clear that physical contact between the change agent and the client often is needed when implementing these procedures. Because the change agent often must physically guide the client through the aversive activity, a number of cautions are in order.

- The application of aversive activities should be used only when the change agent can provide physical guidance.
- The change agent must anticipate that the client may resist the physical guidance, at least initially, and must be certain that he or she can carry out the procedure if the client does resist physically.
- The change agent must be certain that the physical guidance involved in the procedure is not reinforcing to the client. If such physical contact is reinforcing, the procedure will not function as punishment.
- The change agent must be certain that the procedure can be carried out with no harm to the client or change agent. This is particularly important when the client resists and struggles with the change agent during the implementation of the procedure, with the risk of injury to both.

APPLICATION OF AVERSIVE STIMULATION

A woman with profound mental retardation engages in a behavior called bruxism, in which she grinds her upper and lower teeth together. It is so severe that it makes a loud noise and results in damage to the teeth. The staff implement a punishment procedure in which they put an ice cube against her jaw each time she engages in the bruxism. The ice cube is held against her jaw for 6–8 seconds. As a result of this procedure, the frequency of the bruxism decreases greatly (Blount, Drabman, Wilson, & Stewart, 1982).

A 6-month-old child is admitted to the hospital because she is underweight and malnourished. The infant engages in a life-threatening behavior called rumination in which, immediately after she eats, she regurgitates the food back into her mouth. The rumination continues for 20–40 minutes after each feeding until the infant loses most or all of the food she has just eaten. If she continues this behavior without medical intervention, she will die. A psychologist at the hospital implements a punishment procedure in which he instructs the nurse to squirt a small amount of concentrated lemon juice into the infant's mouth each time she starts to ruminate. The infant makes a face and smacks her lips and tongue when the sour lemon juice enters her mouth, and she stops the rumination. If she starts ruminating again, the nurse squirts another small amount of lemon juice into her mouth. This punishment procedure is implemented after each feeding when the infant ruminates, and the life-threatening rumination is eliminated. The child gains weight steadily while she is in the hospital and is discharged after a couple of months (Sajwaj, Libet, & Agras, 1974).

These two examples illustrate positive punishment procedures involving the **application of aversive stimulation** to decrease serious problem behaviors. In the first case, the aversive stimulation was an ice cube applied to the jaw; in the second case, it was lemon juice squirted into the mouth. Whereas in the application of aversive activities the client must engage in a particular behavior contingent on an instance of the problem behavior, the application of aversive stimulation involves delivering an aversive stimulus after the problem behavior. When the problem behavior results in the delivery of the aversive stimulus, the behavior is less likely to occur in the future. A variety of aversive stimuli have been used in positive punishment procedures. These include electric shock, aromatic ammonia, spray mist of water in the face, facial screening, noise, and reprimands.

Electric shock has been used as a punisher with severe behavior problems such as self-injurious behavior. Linscheid, Iwata, Ricketts, Williams, and Griffin (1990) evaluated the effectiveness of a remote control shock device to decrease head-hitting (a dangerous and potentially life-threatening behavior) exhibited by five children and adults with profound retardation. Each client wore a sensing device on his or her head. The sensor detected head-hits and sent a radio signal to a shock generator attached to the client's leg. Each head-hit resulted in an immediate brief shock to the leg. The shock was painful but did not harm the client. The head-hitting decreased immediately to nearly zero for all five clients when shock was used as the aversive stimulus. The results obtained for one of the clients are shown in Figure 18-3.

Aromatic ammonia has been used to decrease behavior problems such as self-injurious behavior (Tanner & Zeiler, 1975) and aggressive behavior (Doke, Wolery, & Sumberg, 1983). Contingent on the problem behavior, the change agent breaks open an ammonia capsule and waves the capsule under the client's nose. The smell of the ammonia is an aversive stimulus that decreases the problem behavior it follows. The ammonia capsule is the same as the smelling salts used to arouse an unconscious boxer or football player.

In the punishment procedure involving spray mist, the person who engages in the severe problem behavior is given a brief spray in the face from a water bottle contingent on an instance of the problem behavior. The spray mist is always clear water and causes no harm to the person. Dorsey, Iwata, Ong, and McSween (1980) used the spray mist procedure to decrease self-injurious behavior in nine children and adults with profound mental retardation.

Facial screening is a punishment procedure in which the client's face is covered briefly with a bib or with the change agent's hand. For example, facial screening was evaluated in a study by Singh, Watson, and Winton (1986). They worked with three institutionalized girls with mental retardation who engaged in self-injurious behavior involving hitting or rubbing their heads and faces. Each girl wore a terry cloth bib and, when the self-injury occurred, the experimenter took the bib and pulled it up over the girl's face for 5 seconds. The procedure was not painful and the girls could still breathe easily. This procedure reduced the self-injury to zero or almost zero for all three girls.

Recent research has shown that noise, similar to the sound of an alarm buzzer, may function as a punisher for hair-pulling and thumb-sucking when it is delivered contingent on the behavior (Ellingson et al., 2000; Rapp, Miltenberger, & Long, 1998;

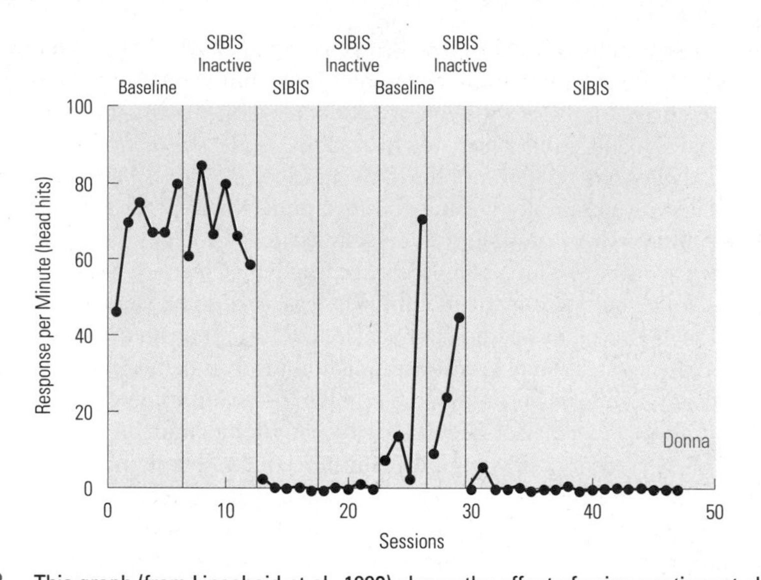

FIGURE 18-3 This graph (from Linscheid et al., 1990) shows the effect of using contingent electric shock as a punisher for self-injurious behavior (head-hits) exhibited by Donna, a 17-year-old teenager with profound retardation. The experimenters used the SIBIS (self-injurious behavior inhibiting system) device, which detects a head-hit and delivers a shock to the leg. The graph shows that during baseline and when Donna wore the SIBIS device but before it was activated, the head-hitting occurred at a rate of 50-80 responses per minute. In other words, she hit her head more than once per second on average. When contingent shock was used as a punisher, the head-hits decreased immediately to nearly zero and were eliminated quickly. The total number of shocks delivered to Donna was small because the head-hits decreased to near zero immediately. Notice that in the fourth phase, when SIBIS was inactive, the head-hits remained near zero. Because the SIBIS device delivered an electric shock for head-hits in the preceding phase, the device developed stimulus control over the behavior. Therefore, the behavior continued to be suppressed when the device was worn, even though it did not deliver a shock in this phase. After the head-hitting increased in the second baseline, the inactive device lost stimulus control and the shocks had to be readministered. The behavior quickly decreased to zero again when the shocks were delivered.

Stricker et al., 2001, 2003). Rapp, Miltenberger, and Long (1998) developed a treatment device with two parts, one worn on the wrist and one worn on the collar of a shirt. A woman who engaged in severe hair-pulling (she had pulled out half the hair on her head) wore the device and, when she raised her hand to pull her hair, the device sounded an alarm. The noise of the alarm did not stop until she lowered her hand away from her head. The woman's hair-pulling decreased to zero when she wore the device. Ellingson et al. (2000) and Stricker et al. (2001) showed that when children who sucked their thumbs or fingers wore the device, the noise produced by the device contingent on thumb- or finger-sucking decreased these behaviors to zero.

Research by Van Houten and his colleagues evaluated the effectiveness of reprimands as punishers (Van Houten, Nau, MacKenzie-Keating, Sameoto, & Colavecchia, 1982). They found that reprimands were effective as punishers with elementary school students when the reprimand instructed the student to stop a specific misbehavior and was delivered with eye contact and a firm grasp of the student's shoulder. Reprimands also decreased the problem behaviors of students who observed the reprimands but did not receive reprimands themselves. Doleys, Wells, Hobbs, Roberts, and Cartelli (1976) also found reprimands to be effective punishers for noncompliant behavior by children with mental retardation.

Positive Punishment: Treatment of Last Resort

Although many examples of punishment involving the application of aversive stimulation are described here, punishment procedures are being used less and less often. Research into functional nonaversive treatment approaches has provided alternatives to punishment, and changing philosophies in the field of behavior modification, especially when used with people with mental retardation, have reduced the acceptance of punishment as a form of treatment (Miltenberger, Lennox, & Erfanian, 1989). Professionals tend to use positive punishment procedures as treatments of last resort. Such procedures usually are reserved for problem behaviors that are the most difficult to treat and the most severe. Negative punishment procedures such as time-out and response cost, which do not involve the application of aversive events, are much more acceptable and more commonly used than positive punishment.

Considerations in Using Positive Punishment

A number of considerations must be addressed before positive punishment procedures are used.

- *Use functional nonaversive procedures first.* Any time you are considering using a punishment procedure, you should first use functional nonaversive procedures in an attempt to decrease the problem behavior and increase acceptable alternative behaviors. If extinction, differential reinforcement, and antecedent manipulations do not produce satisfactory changes in the problem behavior, punishment procedures may be considered.
- *Implement differential reinforcement with punishment.* Differential reinforcement of an alternative behavior (DRA) or the absence of the problem behavior (differential reinforcement of other behavior, DRO) should always be used in conjunction with punishment. In this way, the focus of intervention is on increasing desirable behavior to replace the problem behavior that is eliminated or decreased.
- *Consider the function of the problem behavior.* You will always conduct a functional assessment of the problem behavior before deciding on treatment. This allows you to choose the most appropriate functional treatment (extinction, differential reinforcement, antecedent manipulations). Functional assessment information also plays a role in determining the appropriate punishment procedure for the problem. Time-out would be appropriate for a problem behavior maintained by attention or other positive reinforcers. However, time-out would not be appropriate for problem behaviors maintained by escape. Likewise, the application of aversive activities would be appropriate for problem behaviors maintained by escape but might not be appropriate for problem behaviors maintained by attention. Because the change agent has to pay a certain amount of attention to the client to implement overcorrection, contingent exercise, guided compliance, or physical restraint, these procedures might reinforce a problem behavior maintained by attention. However, if the change agent implements the aversive activity with minimal attention and if the aversive activity is sufficiently aversive, such procedures may be effective for problem behaviors maintained by attention.

■ *Choose the aversive stimulus with care*. When planning to use positive punishment procedures involving an aversive stimulus, you must first determine that the stimulus is indeed aversive (Fisher et al., 1994). Different stimuli function as reinforcers and punishers for different people and in different contexts. For example, a reprimand may function as an aversive stimulus (punisher) for one student but as a reinforcing stimulus for another. Likewise, a reprimand may function as a punisher in a classroom in which the teacher provides praise for appropriate behavior but as a reinforcer in another classroom where a teacher does not provide attention for appropriate behavior. Spanking is another stimulus that may be aversive and thus function as a punisher for some people but may function as a reinforcer or a neutral stimulus for others. Remember that an aversive stimulus is always defined by its effect on the behavior it follows.

To enhance the effectiveness of aversive stimuli as punishers, it may be helpful to use varied punishers rather than a single punisher. Charlop, Burgio, Iwata, and Ivancic (1988) showed that using varied punishers (three different punishers were alternated) decreased aggressive and disruptive behaviors in children more than did using a single punisher.

■ *Collect data to make treatment decisions*. A punishment procedure should produce a rapid decrease in the problem behavior. If a punishment procedure is used and the data show that the problem behavior does not decrease immediately after the procedure is implemented, the procedure should be reevaluated and possibly discontinued. The lack of a decrease in the behavior suggests that the procedure did not function as punishment for the client (possibly because the punishing stimulus was not intense enough), that the procedure was not implemented properly, or that the behavior continued to be reinforced and the effect of the reinforcement was stronger than the effect of punishment. Further assessment is necessary to determine the nature of the treatment failure.

■ *Address the ethical considerations in the use of punishment*. Ethical aspects of the decision to use punishment are our next topic.

THE ETHICS OF PUNISHMENT

The decision to use a punishment procedure should be made carefully after alternative treatments have been considered. Because punishment involves the loss of reinforcers, forced activity, restriction of movement, or delivery of aversive stimulation, its use can result in the restriction of the client's rights. As a result, punishment procedures often are called restrictive procedures. In addition, misusing or overusing punishment procedures can harm the recipient (Gershoff, 2002). Finally, some individuals and organizations believe that the application of aversive stimulation is not humane and is not justified for any reason (LaVigna & Donnellan, 1986; The Association for Persons with Severe Handicaps, 1987). For these reasons, you should always consider the following ethical issues before deciding to implement a punishment procedure.

Informed Consent

A person must fully understand the punishment procedure, the rationale for its use, how and when it will be used, its intended effects and side effects, and possible treatment alternatives. The person must be fully informed and must willingly agree to be the recipient of the procedure before it is used. Only adults can give **informed consent.** Therefore, before a punishment procedure is used with a minor or an adult who cannot give consent (e.g., some people with mental retardation or psychiatric disorders), a legal guardian or legal representative must give consent on the person's behalf.

Alternative Treatments

As discussed in preceding sections, a punishment procedure will not be the first choice of treatment in most cases. Less restrictive nonaversive treatments are used before punishment is considered. In many cases, severe problem behaviors can be eliminated with nonaversive treatment procedures developed from a functional assessment of the problem. If punishment is to be used, less restrictive punishment procedures should be implemented, if possible, before the most restrictive punishment procedures are used. In addition, reinforcement procedures are always used in conjunction with punishment procedures.

Recipient Safety

A punishment procedure should never result in harm to the client. If physical guidance is used in the application of aversive activities, the change agent must not harm the client in the process of physically guiding the behavior. An aversive stimulus must never be used if it causes physical injury to the client.

Problem Severity

Punishment procedures should be reserved for more severe problem behaviors. The delivery of a painful, unpleasant, or annoying stimulus can be justified only if the problem behavior presents a threat to the person's well-being or harm to other people.

Implementation Guidelines

If a punishment procedure is to be implemented, there must be strict written guidelines for using the procedure. With written guidelines, there can be no ambiguity about how the procedure is conducted, when and where it is to be conducted, and by whom.

Training and Supervision

In addition to written guidelines explaining the use of the punishment procedure, all staff, teachers, or other personnel who will implement the procedure must receive behavioral skills training in the correct use of the procedure. This involves instructions, modeling, the opportunity for rehearsal, feedback, and continued rehearsal until the procedure is implemented without errors. Personnel implement the procedure only after they have demonstrated competence in its use. Once a punishment procedure is in use, there must be ongoing supervision of the personnel carrying out the procedure to ensure that they continue to implement it correctly.

Peer Review

The punishment procedure must be written into a detailed program and the written program must be reviewed by a panel of peers, which should include professionals in behavior analysis and behavior modification. The peer review panel will evaluate the punishment program and approve the procedure if it is well designed and justified for use in the particular case. Peer review ensures professional evaluation of the chosen procedure and prevents the misuse of punishment.

Accountability: Preventing Misuse and Overuse

Because the use of punishment may be negatively reinforced by the termination of the problem behavior, there is always the risk that punishment may be misused or overused. Therefore, it is important that each person who implements the punishment procedure be held accountable for its correct implementation and the avoidance of misuse or overuse. Implementation guidelines, training, and supervision contribute to accountability. Frequent review of data on the problem behavior and use of the punishment procedure also contributes to accountability. Foxx, McMorrow, Bittle, and Bechtel (1986, p. 184) have recommended the following steps to ensure accountability of a program involving the use of electric shock: "(a) testing everyone before they were allowed to use the program; (b) having each person who conducted the program experience the shock prior to using it; (c) assigning a specific individual to be responsible for implementing the program each shift or school day; and (d) requiring accurate record keeping that was verified each shift or school day by the staff's supervisor and one of the primary treatment personnel." Although these steps were developed for the use of a shock procedure, they are relevant for the use of any punishment procedure involving the application of aversive stimulation.

Chapter Summary

1. With the application of aversive activities, contingent on the occurrence of a problem behavior, the person is required to engage in an aversive (low probability or nonpreferred) activity in an attempt to decrease the problem behavior. Manual guidance is used as necessary to have the person engage in the aversive activity contingent on the problem behavior.
2. Punishment procedures involving the application of aversive activities include positive practice overcorrection, restitutional overcorrection, contingent exercise, guided compliance, and physical restraint.
3. In punishment procedures involving the application of aversive stimulation, an aversive stimulus is delivered contingent on the problem behavior. An aversive stimulus is defined functionally: When applied contingently, it will decrease the future occurrence of a problem behavior.
4. Punishment should be used only after functional nonaversive approaches have been implemented and proven ineffective or partially ineffective in decreasing the problem behavior. Differential reinforcement procedures must be used in conjunction with punishment. Data must be collected to document the effectiveness of punishment procedures. A punishing stimulus must be chosen with care and after consideration of the function of the problem behavior.
5. Ethical issues with the use of punishment involve informed consent, use of alternative treatments, recipient safety, problem severity, implementation guidelines, training and supervision, peer review, and accountability.

Practice Test

1. What is the difference between positive punishment and negative punishment? Provide examples that illustrate each. (p. 391)
2. Describe the application of aversive activities as a form of positive punishment. Describe how it is based on the Premack principle. (p. 392)

3. Describe the positive practice procedure. Provide an example. (p. 393)
4. Describe the restitution procedure. Provide an example. (pp. 393–394)
5. Describe the contingent exercise procedure. How does it differ from overcorrection? For each example you provided in Questions 3 and 4, describe how you would use contingent exercise instead of the overcorrection procedures. (pp. 394–395)
6. Do you think a teacher would find overcorrection or contingent exercise more acceptable for use in the classroom? Explain your answer.
7. Describe the guided compliance procedure. When is it used? Describe how guided compliance may be a component of overcorrection or contingent exercise procedures. (pp. 395–396)
8. Describe the physical restraint procedure. Provide an example. Provide an example of response blocking. (p. 397)
9. Describe the application of aversive stimulation as a form of positive punishment. (p. 398)
10. How do you know whether a particular stimulus is an aversive stimulus for a person? (p. 402)
11. Identify six different aversive stimuli that have been used in positive punishment procedures. (pp. 398–400)
12. Why is the use of punishment procedures decreasing? (p. 401)
13. Identify the five issues that must be addressed when using a punishment procedure. (pp. 401–402)
14. What is informed consent? (p. 402)
15. How is severity of the problem behavior related to the use of punishment? (p. 403)
16. What is peer review and how is it related to the use of punishment? (p. 403)
17. What steps can be taken to ensure accountability in the use of punishment? (p. 404)

APPLICATIONS

1. Describe how you would use a positive punishment procedure in your self-management project. If positive punishment is not applicable to your project, describe why not.

2. Tom and Dick grabbed half a dozen eggs from the refrigerator before they went out on Halloween night. They were going over to the school to egg the windows to their fifth grade classroom. They went around in the back of the school building in the dark to the classroom window and each threw three eggs at it. After they had covered the window with eggs, they walked back around the building and ran into Mr. Alvarez, their principal. Describe the restitution procedure Mr. Alvarez could use with Tom and Dick to decrease the probability that they will engage in this type of misbehavior again.

3. Geraldine is a kindergarten teacher with 20 students in her classroom. She runs a number of structured and unstructured activities in the classroom in which the children work individually and in groups. She has found that when the students are in group activities that are less structured (e.g., when engaged in arts and crafts activities around a large table) some students act out. They engage in minor disruptive behaviors that are reinforced by attention from the other children. Although the behaviors are not dangerous, they disrupt the class and set a bad example for the other students. Describe how Geraldine could use reprimands effectively to decrease the disruptive behavior.

4. An inner-city hospital sees a number of young children each year for lead detoxification. These young children are admitted to the hospital because they have eaten lead-based paint chips from the walls of their homes. The landlords do not maintain the apartments very well and, as a result, there is often peeling paint on the walls. When a child ingests lead (from peeling paint chips or any other source), it accumulates in the brain and can cause brain damage and mental retardation. The children spend a week in the hospital as the doctors use medical procedures to rid their bodies of the lead. While

the children are in the hospital, they spend much of their day in a playroom with other children that is staffed by child development specialists. Although the playroom is clean and safe, the children often put toys or other items in their mouth, a behavior that would be dangerous in an unsafe environment. Describe how the staff can use response interruption and brief restraint with these children to eliminate the problem behavior of putting objects in their mouths.

MISAPPLICATIONS

1. Ted is a young man with severe retardation and autism who engages in a stereotypic behavior involving paper shredding. Ted will pick up a piece of paper (newspaper, notepaper, a page from a report or program) and tear away thin strips until the piece is shredded. He gazes at the paper as he rips it and does not pay attention to other people or events in the environment. This behavior has been a concern for years because he is not involved in educational tasks while ripping paper and because he sometimes shreds important papers. Ted is not aggressive in obtaining paper to shred but he becomes aggressive if you try to take a piece of paper away from him once he has it in his hand. The staff have implemented a number of reinforcement procedures and antecedent manipulations but have not decreased the behavior. They are now planning a punishment procedure involving contingent electric shock. Ted will wear a shock device on his upper arm that can be activated by remote control. A staff person will have the control box and, anytime that Ted starts to rip a piece of paper, will activate a brief shock. The shock will be mildly painful but will cause no harm. The staff members delivering the shocks will be trained and supervised, and data will be collected to document the effects of the procedure. What is wrong with this punishment procedure?

2. Betty is a large woman (200 pounds) with severe mental retardation. She lives in a group home and rides a van to and from her work site each day. She does assembly work for a local factory with a job coach and a group of five other people with mental retardation. Betty has been exhibiting a problem behavior in which she refuses to get on the van in the morning and she refuses to leave the break room after her morning break and after lunch. Because of her size, Betty is intimidating and often gets what she wants. When the job coach asks her to get on the van or to come back to work, Betty yells "No," makes a fist and waves it at the job coach, and continues to sit where she is. Eventually, Betty does get on the van or come back to work, but only after the job coach talks her into it. Because Betty is exhibiting noncompliant behavior in work-related situations, the job coach has decided to implement guided compliance in which Betty will be physically guided onto the van and back to work when she refuses. What is wrong with using guided compliance in this situation?

3. JT is a teenager with mental retardation who lives in a group home with other teenagers with disabilities. He engages in self-injurious behavior involving face-slapping and ear-slapping. The staff are concerned that he will damage his hearing if he continues to slap himself in the ear. They report that he usually slaps himself when they are occupied in training programs with other residents. The group home manager has read a research study in which aromatic ammonia was shown to be an effective treatment for self-injurious behavior. He thinks it might work with JT. However, before going to the effort of writing up a program, having the program reviewed by the behavior intervention committee, and training staff to implement the procedure, he decides on a pilot program to see whether the procedure will work. He gives a box of ammonia capsules to the staff working with JT and instructs them to break open a capsule and wave it under JT's nose when he slaps himself. The manager tells the staff to use the procedure for a few days and see whether it decreases the face-slapping. If it does, he will take all the necessary steps and formally implement the punishment procedure. What is wrong with this approach?

CHAPTER 18 *Quiz 1* Name:

1. Two major categories of events used in positive punishment procedures are

   ____________________________ and ____________________________.

2. In ____________________________ overcorrection, the person is required to engage in a correct form of relevant behavior contingent on the problem behavior.

3. In ____________________________ overcorrection, the person has to correct the environmental effects of the problem behavior.

4. In the guided compliance procedure, what does the change agent do each time the problem

   behavior occurs? ____

5. In the guided compliance procedure, what does the change agent do each time the individual

   starts to comply with the requested activity? ____

6. Delivering a noise contingent on thumb sucking in order to decrease thumb sucking is an

   example of punishment by ________________________________.

7. ________________________________ should always be used in conjunction with punishment.

Match the following procedures to the descriptions.

a. Restitution	b. Positive practice	c. Contingent exercise
d. Guided compliance	e. Physical restraint	f. Response blocking

8. _____ Contingent on screaming in class, the student is made to stand up and sit down five times.

9. _____ Contingent on hand mouthing, the teacher holds the student's hand at her side for 30 seconds.

10. _____ Contingent on refusal to do a requested task, the teacher physically guides the student to do the task.

CHAPTER 18 *Quiz 2*

Name:

1. ________________________ procedures should always be used before punishment is considered for decreasing a problem behavior.

2. What are the two types of overcorrection procedures? ________________________

   and ________________________

3. In the ________________________ procedure, the person is physically guided through the requested activity contingent on the occurrence of the problem behavior.

4. In the contingent exercise procedure, what happens each time the problem behavior occurs?

   ____

5. In the ________________________ procedure, the change agent holds immobile the part of the client's body involved in the problem behavior.

6. In ________________________, the change agent prevents the occurrence of the problem behavior by physically blocking the response.

7. What are two ethical issues to consider before using punishment?

   ________________________ and ________________________

Match the following procedures to the descriptions.

a. Restitution
b. Positive practice
c. Contingent exercise
d. Guided compliance
e. Physical restraint
f. Response blocking

8. _____ Contingent on wetting his pants on the playground, the student is required to come in from the playground and walk into the bathroom five times in a row.

9. _____ When a child raises her hand to her mouth in an attempt to suck her thumb, her dad puts his hand in front of the child's hand to prevent the thumb sucking from occurring.

10. _____ When a child makes a mess with his food on the kitchen floor, the child has to clean the kitchen floor and the bathroom floor as well.

CHAPTER 18 *Quiz 3* Name:

1. Positive punishment involves the application of ______________________ or the application of ______________________.
2. Restitution and positive practice are two types of ______________________ procedures.
3. In the ______________________ procedure, the individual has to engage in physical exercise that is unrelated to the problem behavior each time the problem behavior occurs.
4. Guided compliance serves two functions: ______________________ for the problem behavior because physical guidance is applied and ______________________ for compliance because physical guidance is withdrawn.
5. In the physical restraint procedure, what does the change agent do each time the problem behavior occurs? ______________________
6. What are two examples of aversive stimuli that have been used in punishment by the application of aversive stimulation? ______________________ and ______________________
7. Positive punishment involves the ______________________ of an aversive stimulus following a behavior to be decreased, and negative reinforcement involves the ______________________ of an aversive stimulus following the behavior to be increased.

Match the following procedures to the descriptions.

a. Restitution b. Positive practice c. Contingent exercise
d. Guided compliance e. Physical restraint f. Response blocking

8. _____ When a teenager curses at home, his parents make him wash windows for 10 minutes.
9. _____ Sally screams and cries when her parent asks her to put her toy down and come to the kitchen for supper. In response, her parent takes her hand and physically prompts her to put the toy down and then leads her by the hand to the kitchen.
10. _____ When Sally tries to hit her sister, dad puts his hand in front of Sally's hand to prevent her from hitting.

Promoting Generalization

It is always important to program for generalization of the behavior changes produced by a behavior modification program. Programming for generalization increases the likelihood that the behavior change will occur in all relevant situations or circumstances in the person's life.

Examples of Generalization Programming

- What strategies can be used to promote generalization of behavior change?
- What role do natural contingencies of reinforcement have in generalization?
- What aspects of the stimuli used in training are important in promoting generalization?
- How are functionally equivalent responses involved in generalization?
- What are procedures for promoting generalized reductions in problem behaviors?

Recall from Chapter 15 the case of Mrs. Williams, the nursing home resident who rarely engaged in positive conversation and often complained to the staff. The staff used differential reinforcement of alternative behavior to increase the frequency of positive conversation and to decrease the frequency of complaining. Successful generalization of Mrs. Williams' behavior change is defined as an increase in positive conversation and a decrease in complaining with all the people she talks to, in all situations. To accomplish this goal, all staff (nurses, nursing assistants, physicians, and others), visitors, and other residents would have to use differential reinforcement consistently with Mrs. Williams. If some people continued to reinforce her complaining with their attention, the complaining would continue and the positive conversation would occur less often with those people and possibly with others. The psychologist who taught the staff to use differential reinforcement with Mrs. Williams programmed for generalization by training all staff how to use the procedure successfully and instructing them to use it at all times. Furthermore, the psychologist held a meeting with Mrs. Williams' family and taught them the importance of using differential reinforcement and how to use it. Finally, the psychologist taught the nurses how to prompt other residents to ignore Mrs. Williams' complaining and to pay attention to positive conversation. The head nurse was responsible for monitoring the use of differential reinforcement and providing further training if needed. Successful generalization of the behavior change occurred with Mrs. Williams because all relevant people carried out the differential reinforcement procedure as planned.

Recall the case of Marcia (Chapter 12), who was learning assertiveness skills through behavioral skills training procedures. Generalization of Marcia's assertiveness skills is defined as the occurrence of an appropriate assertive response to any unreasonable request made by a co-worker. In other words, there would be evidence of generalization if she used an assertive response in all the situations in which one was needed. The psychologist, Dr. Mills, programmed for generalization by teaching Marcia to respond to a wide range of possible unreasonable requests. All unreasonable requests from a co-worker that Marcia could recall or anticipate were used in training. Marcia successfully rehearsed appropriate assertive behavior in realistic role-plays of all the situations she identified. Dr. Mills made the role-plays progressively more difficult; he role-played her co-workers becoming more and more persistent in their unreasonable requests. When Marcia responded assertively to all the difficult situations that Dr. Mills could simulate in role-plays, he believed the assertiveness skills would generalize to the job situation. However, because the assertiveness skills were reinforced only in the context of role-plays, generalization to the actual job situation is not ensured.

Consider the following example of a generalization failure. Recall our example in Chapter 10, where coach McCall used physical prompts to help Trevor hit a baseball thrown by a particular pitcher, Dave. When Dave pitched, coach McCall helped Trevor swing the bat correctly to hit the ball. Eventually, coach McCall faded the physical prompts until Trevor was hitting the ball without any assistance. Dave then threw the ball faster and in more difficult locations to teach Trevor how to hit more difficult pitches. Although Trevor hit the ball successfully in practice, he could not hit the ball in a game when it was thrown by the opposing team's pitcher. Trevor's ability to hit the ball in practice did not generalize to the game situation. One reason that the behavior did not generalize is that the pitches in the game were different from those Trevor learned to hit in practice. In other words, the training stimuli (in practice) were not similar enough to the stimuli in the target situation (a real game) for the behavior to generalize to the target situation. To program for generalization, coach McCall must make the pitches Trevor learns to hit in practice (the training stimuli) as similar as possible to the pitches that Trevor must hit in games (the target stimuli). Coach McCall could do this by having a variety of pitchers pitch to Trevor during practice.

DEFINING GENERALIZATION

During discrimination training, as we saw in Chapter 7, the occurrence of a behavior is reinforced only in the presence of a certain stimulus (the discriminative stimulus, S^D). Stimulus control develops through this process, and the behavior is more likely to occur in the future when the S^D is present. **Generalization** is defined as the occurrence of the behavior in the presence of stimuli that are similar in some way to the S^D that was present during training. In other words, a class of similar stimuli develops stimulus control over the behavior. In behavior modification, generalization is defined as the occurrence of the behavior in the presence of all relevant stimuli outside the training situation.

Generalization of behavior change is an important issue in behavior modification. When behavior modification procedures are used to develop, increase, or maintain desirable behaviors, you want the behaviors to occur beyond the training circumstances, in all the relevant stimulus situations. For example, it is an example of generalization when Marcia makes an assertive response to one of her co-workers who makes an unreasonable request to her. Her assertive responses were developed under the stimulus control of the training situation (the role-plays) and now occur outside training in similar situations. If Trevor hits the baseball when it is thrown by the opposing pitcher in a game, generalization has occurred. His behavior of hitting the ball was developed under the stimulus control of the practice pitches thrown by Dave. Training is not successful until the behavior generalizes to similar situations (pitches thrown in a game).

Strategies for Promoting Generalization of Behavior Change

This chapter outlines strategies that can be used to program for generalization of behavior change (Table 19-1). The strategies discussed are based on those reviewed by Stokes and Baer (1977) and Stokes and Osnes (1989).

Table 19-1 Strategies for Promoting Generalization of Behavior Change

- Reinforcing instances of generalization
- Training skills that contact natural contingencies of reinforcement
- Modifying natural contingencies of reinforcement and punishment
- Incorporating a wide range of relevant stimulus situations in training
- Incorporating common stimuli
- Teaching a range of functionally equivalent responses
- Incorporating self-generated mediators of generalization

Reinforcing Occurrences of Generalization

One way to promote generalization is to reinforce the behavior when generalization occurs—in other words, to reinforce the behavior when it occurs outside the training situation in the presence of relevant stimuli. In this way, all relevant stimuli develop stimulus control over the behavior. Bakken, Miltenberger, and Schauss (1993) implemented this generalization strategy when they taught parenting skills to parents with mental retardation. The goal was for the parents to use the parenting skills in the home, where they were needed. To promote generalization of the parenting skills to the home environment, the researchers conducted training sessions in the homes and provided reinforcers when the clients exhibited the parenting skills in this setting. As a result, the skills generalized to the home setting.

When teaching clinical psychology graduate students how to conduct therapy sessions, the professor provides instructions and modeling and then has the students rehearse the skills in role-plays of therapy sessions. After each rehearsal, the professor provides feedback: praise to reinforce the correct behavior and instructions for improvement.

How would the professor promote generalization of the skills to actual therapy situations?

One method would be to reinforce instances of generalization. The professor could sit in the therapy session with the student and nod or smile approval for each correct therapy skill. Another strategy would be to watch through an observation window as the student conducts a therapy session with a client. Immediately after the session, the professor would praise the student for all of the skills that were executed correctly in the session. Alternatively, the professor could use a bug-in-ear technique in which the student wears a small speaker device in one ear and the professor delivers praise to the student immediately after each skill is executed correctly in the session. Correctly executing the therapy skills in actual therapy sessions is an instance of generalization. Reinforcing instances of generalization is perhaps the most straightforward approach to promoting generalization. This strategy blurs the distinction between training and generalization conditions because training occurs in all relevant situations. Stokes and Baer (1977, p. 350) defined generalization as "the occurrence of relevant behavior under different, nontraining conditions," but in this strategy, in effect, there is no condition in which training does not occur.

One drawback to this strategy is that it is not always possible to provide reinforcement for the behavior outside the training situation. For example, Dr. Mills cannot go to Marcia's office and praise her each time she engages in assertive behavior. In most parenting classes, the teacher cannot go to the parents' homes and provide reinforcers for the parenting skills they exhibit there. If you cannot reinforce instances of generalization, you must use other strategies to promote generalization.

Training Skills That Contact Natural Contingencies of Reinforcement

Another strategy to promote generalization is to train skills that will result in natural contingencies of reinforcement in relevant situations. If you cannot provide reinforcement for the behavior in relevant situations outside the training situation, it is important for natural reinforcers to be present. For example, when deciding what leisure skills to teach to young adults with disabilities who will be graduating from high school and living in community apartments or group homes, it is important to teach the preferred leisure activities that will be available to them in their communities. In this way, the clients will have opportunities to engage in the activities that are reinforcing to them. If the clients are trained in activities that are not reinforcing or not available, the leisure skills are unlikely to generalize to the community setting. When teaching dating skills to shy adolescents, it is important to teach approaches to which members of the other sex will respond favorably. In this way, the skills will be reinforced in relevant situations in the natural environment (because they will result in pleasant interactions and dates).

Research by Durand and Carr (1992) demonstrated the generalization of communication skills outside the training situation by students with developmental disabilities. The students in the study exhibited behavior problems that were reinforced by teacher attention. Durand and Carr wanted to teach the students how to get their teacher's attention through more desirable behavior. They taught the students to ask the teacher, "Am I doing good work?" When the students asked this question, the teacher responded with attention. The teacher differentially reinforced the children's communication behavior; this behavior increased, and the behavior problems decreased. Generalization occurred when teachers who did not know that the students had learned the communication skills were present. When the students asked the same question to the new teachers, they responded to the questions with attention, in the same way as the teachers who were trained. Generalization occurred because the students' questions drew on natural contingencies of reinforcement.

Although you should strive to teach skills that will contact natural contingencies of reinforcement, this is not always possible. For example, when Marcia first makes an assertive response to a co-worker, the co-worker might react in an angry fashion or might repeat the unreasonable request. If a nonspeaking student learns sign language as a way to communicate with the teacher, this skill may not generalize to other people: If other people do not know sign language, they will not respond to the student in ways that will reinforce the use of signs. It is not a skill that contacts natural contingencies of reinforcement. When skills are not naturally reinforced outside the training situation, other generalization strategies must be implemented.

Modifying Natural Contingencies of Reinforcement and Punishment

Desirable behaviors will occur in relevant situations outside the training situation if the behavior is reinforced in those situations (and if punishment contingencies are not operating in those situations). When the trainer is not able to reinforce occurrences of generalization and there are no existing natural contingencies of reinforcement, generalization may be promoted by modifying the contingencies of reinforcement in the relevant situations. Consider the following example.

Naomi, a 13-year-old girl in a juvenile detention center, often exhibited aggressive and disruptive behavior when the older girls in the center provoked her. Her counselor taught Naomi the skills to respond calmly to the provocations of her peers. Naomi learned in role-plays with her counselor how to say to herself, "Ignore them, walk away, and stay out of trouble," and then to walk away. To promote generalization, the counselor met with the staff who worked with Naomi and instructed them to praise Naomi any time they saw her walk away from a provocation. Because the residents were on a token reinforcement program (Chapter 22), the staff were also instructed to give Naomi a token whenever she exhibited this skill. As a result of this immediate reinforcement of her self-control skills by the staff, Naomi used the skills whenever she was provoked and managed to stay out of confrontations with her peers.

Recall the example of Mrs. Williams. When differential reinforcement was implemented, her rate of positive conversation increased with everyone in the nursing home.

What did the psychologist do to promote the generalization of Mrs. Williams' positive conversation?

The psychologist instructed all staff to use the differential reinforcement procedure with Mrs. Williams and taught the staff to teach everyone else who talked to Mrs. Williams to use the procedure. In this way, Mrs. Williams' positive conversation was reinforced by everyone who spoke with her. The psychologist had modified the natural contingencies of reinforcement for her positive conversation.

Sometimes, natural punishment contingencies make generalization of the desirable behavior less likely. Although a person might learn to perform a desirable behavior in training, the behavior is unlikely to generalize if it is punished outside the training situation. One way to promote generalization is to eliminate any punishment contingency that would suppress the desirable behavior outside the training situation. Consider the following example.

The school district decided to integrate students with disabilities into the regular classrooms. Mrs. Prunty's third grade class was going to get three new students with developmental disabilities. Before the new students were transferred to her class, she used behavioral skills training procedures to teach the students in her class how to treat the new students with respect and how to be helpful and make friends with them. After the new students arrived, Mrs. Prunty's third graders interacted well with them. The skills she had taught to her class were generalizing to the classroom with the new students. However, Mrs. Prunty noticed that students from the other third grade class were teasing and making fun of her students on the playground for being friendly with the new students. As a result of these punishment contingencies, Mrs. Prunty's third graders started to interact less and less with the new students. Mrs. Prunty decided that if she wanted the interactions with the new students to continue, she needed to eliminate the punishment contingency. In other words, she had to get the other third graders to stop teasing and making fun of her students when they interacted with the students with disabilities. Once Mrs. Prunty eliminated the mean comments from the other third graders, her students started interacting with the new students again in the classroom. In addition, their interactions with the new students generalized to the playground.

All three of the generalization strategies described thus far focus on reinforcing the behavior outside the training situation. Generalization can also be promoted by arranging appropriate stimulus situations and response variations during training. These strategies are described next.

Incorporating a Variety of Relevant Stimulus Situations in Training

If the goal of generalization programming is for the behavior to occur in all relevant situations after training is completed, one obvious method to promote generalization is to incorporate many of the relevant situations in training. Stokes and Baer (1977) and Stokes and Osnes (1989) referred to this strategy as training the learner to respond to sufficient stimulus exemplars. The logic is that if the learner is trained to respond correctly to a range of relevant stimulus situations (stimulus exemplars), the behavior is more likely to generalize to all relevant stimulus situations. For example, Dr. Mills taught Marcia to respond assertively to a wide range of unreasonable requests that he role-played during training. He chose the particular stimulus exemplars because they were the requests that the co-workers were most likely to make. When Cheryl Poche taught abduction prevention skills to preschool children, she incorporated a variety of abduction lures into the training procedures (Poche, Brouwer, & Swearengin, 1981; Poche, Yoder, & Miltenberger, 1988). Poche reasoned that if the children could respond correctly to all of the different lures in training, the abduction prevention skills would be more likely to generalize to an actual abduction situation.

Stokes, Baer, and Jackson (1974) used this strategy to promote generalization when they taught greeting responses to children with mental retardation. When one experimenter taught the students to wave as a greeting response, there was little generalization of this greeting to the 20 staff members who worked with the students. However, when the students learned to wave to a second experimenter, the greeting response soon generalized to the rest of the staff. When only one person reinforced the greeting response initially, that person developed stimulus control over the greeting. However, once a different person reinforced the greeting response (a second exemplar was incorporated into training), the stimulus class that developed stimulus control over the behavior included all of the staff in the institution.

Suppose that the greeting response failed to generalize to all staff after it was reinforced by a second experimenter. What else could Stokes and his colleagues do to promote generalization?

To promote generalization, they could have additional staff prompt and reinforce the greeting response and assess generalization to the other staff. Each additional staff member who reinforces the greeting response is another stimulus exemplar. Eventually, when sufficient stimulus exemplars are introduced into training, the response will generalize to all the members of the stimulus class from which the exemplars were chosen. Unfortunately, you cannot determine in advance how many exemplars are sufficient for generalization to occur. Consider the study by Davis, Brady, Williams, and Hamilton (1992). They used a treatment procedure with two young boys with disabilities to increase their compliance to adult requests. In the procedure, the trainer first made a few high-probability requests (easy requests that would be fun for the child), and then made the request to which the child was usually noncompliant (a low-probability request). When one trainer used this procedure, the child became more compliant with that trainer but not with other trainers. In other words, there was no generalization of the child's increased compliance. Davis was interested in determining how many trainers had to use the procedure before the increase in compliance would generalize to trainers who had not used the procedure with the child. They found that the behavior generalized after two trainers used the procedure with one child and after three trainers used the procedure with the other child. The results from this study are summarized in Figure 19-1.

Horner has described a strategy for promoting generalization called **general case programming** (Horner, Sprague, & Wilcox, 1982). General case programming is defined as using multiple training examples (stimulus exemplars) that sample the range of relevant stimulus situations and response variations. Neef and her colleagues used general case programming to teach adults with mental retardation to use washing machines and dryers (Neef, Lensbower, Hockersmith, DePalma, & Gray, 1990). They trained some of the subjects to use a variety of machines so that they could learn all of the different ways to operate washing machines and dryers. Other subjects learned to use only one washing machine and dryer. Neef found that the subjects who were trained with a variety of machines were more successful in operating a novel machine than were the subjects who received training on only one machine. In other words, there was more generalization of the skills with the use of general case programming.

Incorporating Common Stimuli

Another strategy for promoting generalization is to incorporate stimuli from the generalization environment (target situation) into the training situation. In other words, if the training and generalization situations have some features or stimuli in common, generalization is more likely to take place. This strategy is similar to that in which a wide variety of relevant stimulus situations are incorporated into the training situation. However, in this strategy, some aspect of the target situation (a physical or social stimulus) is used in training. For example, when Poche used a variety of abduction lures in

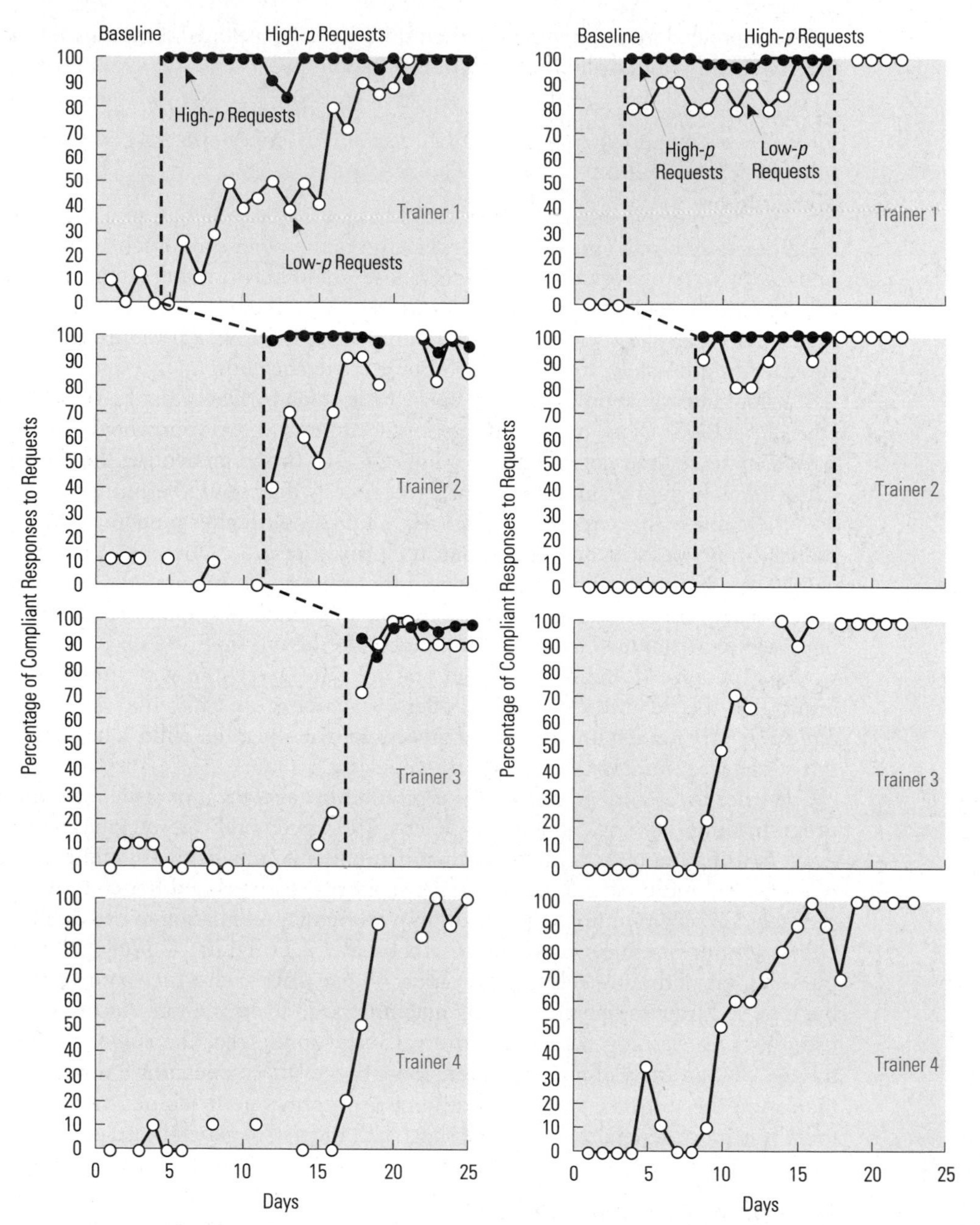

FIGURE 19-1 The left panel (from Davis et al., 1992) shows the percentage of Bobby's compliant behavior to high-probability (high-p) and low-probability (low-p) requests delivered by four different trainers. The authors used high-p requests to increase compliance to the low-p requests. In this case, generalization occurred after the use of three stimulus exemplars (trainers). The right panel shows the percentage of Darren's compliant behavior to low-p and high-p requests delivered by four trainers. For Darren, generalization occurred after the second exemplar was used.

training, she was incorporating relevant stimulus exemplars or situations. However, when she conducted training outside on the playground, she was incorporating a common physical stimulus (being outside, where an abduction attempt is more likely to take place) into the training situation.

How could Dr. Mills incorporate a common stimulus into the training sessions with Marcia to promote the generalization of her assertiveness skills?

If Dr. Mills took Marcia to her office and had her rehearse her assertiveness skills in role-plays there, he would be incorporating a common stimulus (the office environment). The logic of this strategy is that the stimulus from the target situation will develop stimulus control over the behavior during training. Later, the behavior will occur in the target situation when this stimulus is present.

Sometimes during social skills training, other therapists or therapy assistants are introduced into the training sessions so that the client can rehearse the skills with novel people. For example, a female therapist may role-play with a male client who is trying to develop the skills to interact more effectively with women. If the client can perform the skills successfully in a role-play with a woman he meets in the session, it is more likely that the skills will generalize to other situations in which he is introduced to a woman (e.g., at a party). In this case, the common stimulus incorporated into the training situation was a woman the client had never met before.

Teaching a Range of Functionally Equivalent Responses

In addition to incorporating a variety of stimulus exemplars and common stimuli into the training situation, it is often useful to teach a variety of responses that may all achieve the same outcome for the client. Different responses that achieve the same outcome are called **functionally equivalent responses.** In other words, each response serves the same function for the person. For example, if you were teaching a person with mental retardation to use vending machines, you would teach a variety of responses that would operate the machines. On some machines you push a button to make a selection; on others, you pull a knob. Both responses produce the same outcome. If you taught both responses, the person would be able to use a wider variety of machines after training. In other words, there would be greater generalization.

As we have seen, general case programming samples the range of relevant stimulus and response variations so that the learner learns all the variations that may be needed in the natural situation. Sprague and Horner (1984) used general case programming to teach adolescents with mental retardation to use vending machines. They found that more generalization occurred when they used general case programming than when they used other teaching methods. In the general case training, the students learned all the different responses they needed to operate any available vending machine.

Consider another example. In social skills training, people will learn a range of skills to use in a variety of situations. The person will then have a number of different responses that may produce the same outcome. For instance, a shy young man may learn a number of different ways to ask a woman out on a date. If asking in one way fails in a particular situation, asking in another way may be successful. If the young man had learned to ask for a date in only one way, he may have been unsuccessful, and there would be less likelihood that the skills would generalize to other situations with other women. In assertiveness training, Marcia learned to say no to unreasonable requests in a variety of ways. If one assertive response did not work, she could use another assertive response and then another until she was successful.

Incorporating Self-Generated Mediators of Generalization

Stokes and Osnes (1989, p. 349) defined a mediator of generalization as "a stimulus that is maintained and transported by the client as part of treatment." The mediator may be a physical stimulus or a behavior exhibited by the person. The mediator has stimulus control over the target behavior, so the behavior generalizes beyond the training situation when the mediator is present. For example, parents attend a lecture on child management techniques and take notes. Later the parents review the notes to guide their behavior as they implement the techniques with their own child. The notes are a **self-generated mediator of generalization;** they promote generalization of the child management skills to the home setting. In a similar fashion, the parents could memorize a few rules from the lecture, such as "Catch your child being good and praise him" and "Ignore minor problems." Later at home, when repeating the rules to themselves, they are more likely to praise their child when the child engages in desirable behavior and to ignore minor problems. The rules that they recite to themselves are self-generated mediators of generalization of their child management skills.

A study by Ayllon, Kuhlman, and Warzak (1983) illustrates how a physical stimulus can function as a self-generated mediator to enhance generalization. The researchers worked with students with behavior disorders who received training in reading and math in a Resource Room, a special class where extra assistance is provided. The students completed almost 100% of reading and math assignments correctly in the Resource Room, but the behavior did not generalize well to the regular math and reading classes. They got only about 60% of their assignments correct in the regular classes. Ayllon programmed for generalization in the following way. Each student brought a personal item from home—a small photo, a medal, or some other trinket—as a good luck charm and kept it on his or her desk in the Resource Room. After the students successfully completed math and reading in the Resource Room with the good luck charms on their desks, they took the good luck charms with them to their regular reading and math classes. As a result, their performance improved in the regular classes. Because the good luck charm was associated with successful performance in one setting, it facilitated generalization of successful performance to another setting. The graphs from this study in Figure 19-2 show the improvement in math and reading for four students once the good luck charms were used as mediators of generalization. A multiple-baseline design across settings (math and reading classes) was used with each student.

Self-recording is another example of a self-generated mediator of generalization. For example, a young woman is seeing a psychologist for help with a stuttering problem. The treatment involves a regulated breathing technique that the woman learns from the psychologist and must practice each day. The client performs the regulated breathing technique well in sessions but fails to practice the technique outside the sessions. To promote generalization outside the treatment sessions, the psychologist instructs the client to implement self-recording. The client puts a recording sheet on her

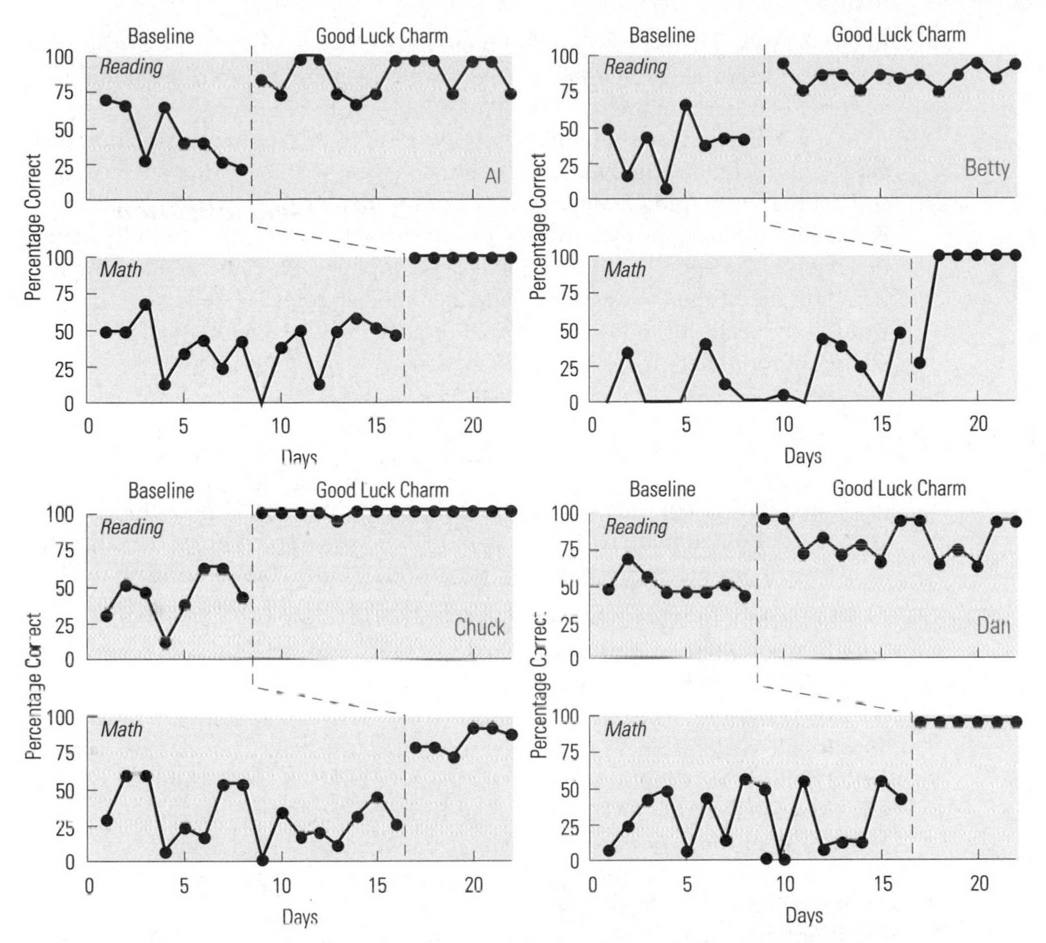

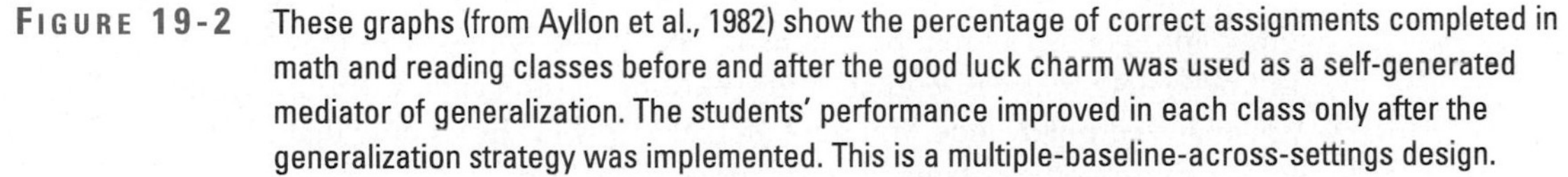

FIGURE 19-2 These graphs (from Ayllon et al., 1982) show the percentage of correct assignments completed in math and reading classes before and after the good luck charm was used as a self-generated mediator of generalization. The students' performance improved in each class only after the generalization strategy was implemented. This is a multiple-baseline-across-settings design.

desk at work and on her refrigerator at home and records on the sheet the time that she practices. The presence of the recording sheet and the act of self-recording are self-generated mediators that make it more likely that the client will practice the technique outside the sessions.

Self-instruction is another mediator of generalization. When a person recites a self-instruction, it acts as a cue to engage in the appropriate behavior at the appropriate time. The parents described earlier recited self-instructions to use the child management techniques they had learned in the lecture. The use of self-instructions helped the child management skills generalize to the home with their own kids. In our earlier example, Naomi was using self-instructions when she said to herself, "Ignore them, walk away, and stay out of trouble," in response to provocations from her peers.

Reciting this self-instruction made it more likely that she would walk away from a fight. It made it more likely that this behavior would generalize from the training sessions with her counselor to the real problem situation with her peers.

Any behavior that cues the appropriate behavior in the target situation can be regarded as a self-generated mediator of generalization. Some of the antecedent control strategies discussed in Chapter 16 may be considered self-generated mediators of generalization because they involve the occurrence of one behavior to influence another behavior in the appropriate situation. For example, when Cal made a shopping list of healthful foods, the list was a self-generated mediator that made it more likely that he would buy healthful foods. Chapter 20 discusses self-generated mediators of generalization in more detail.

Implementing Strategies to Promote Generalization

It is important to consider the generalization of behavior change before, during, and after the implementation of behavior modification procedures. In implementing strategies to promote generalization, you should observe the following guidelines.

1. *Identify the target stimulus situations for the behavior.* The goal of a behavior modification program is for the behavior change to generalize to all relevant stimulus situations. In other words, if you are establishing a new behavior or strengthening an existing behavior, you want that behavior to occur at the appropriate times and in the appropriate circumstances (the target stimulus situations). To promote generalization of the behavior to those situations, you must identify the target stimulus situations before the start of training. Once you identify the relevant situations, you can implement generalization strategies to increase the likelihood that the behavior will occur in those situations. If you do not identify the target stimulus situations before training, generalization will be left to chance.

2. *Identify natural contingencies of reinforcement for the behavior.* Once the natural contingencies of reinforcement are identified, training can focus on strengthening the behaviors that will contact those existing contingencies. If the contingencies are not analyzed in advance, you might target behaviors in training that are not functional for the person outside the training situation. As a result, generalization would be much less likely to occur.

3. *Implement appropriate strategies to promote generalization.* Once you have analyzed the three-term contingency for the behavior outside the training situation, you are in a position to choose appropriate strategies to promote generalization.

Analyzing the target stimulus situations allows you to incorporate a variety of these situations into training sessions. In addition, it permits you to choose common stimuli that might be incorporated into training or to choose mediators that facilitate generalization of the behavior to these situations. Finally, as a result of identifying stimulus situations before training, you can identify instances of generalization and provide reinforcers for the behavior when it occurs in these situations.

Analyzing existing reinforcement contingencies helps you choose the variations in the behavior that are most likely to be reinforced. By training the skills that are most likely to contact natural reinforcement contingencies, you are enhancing the likelihood of generalization. In addition, you must understand the natural contingencies of reinforcement and punishment to determine when and how to modify those contingencies to promote generalization.

4. *Measure generalization of behavior change.* You must collect data on the occurrence of the behavior in the target stimulus situations to determine whether your efforts to promote generalization have been successful. If the behavior does generalize to the target situations, continue to assess the behavior periodically in these situations to ensure that the generalized behavior change has maintained over time. Your assessment should also include information on natural contingencies, to determine whether the behavior continues to be reinforced in the target situations. If your assessment indicates that the behavior has not generalized to the target situations, you must implement further strategies to promote generalization and continue to assess the behavior and the natural contingencies until there is evidence of generalization and maintenance of the behavior.

Promoting Generalized Reductions in Problem Behaviors

The outcome of treatment for problem behaviors should be an improvement in the client's functioning. Improvement in functioning is defined not only by a decrease in or elimination of the problem behavior but, more importantly, by the development and maintenance of new skills or the strengthening of existing alternative behaviors and an increase in the quantity of positive reinforcement. For example, behavior modification for a third grader, Warren, who is considered a bully (because he starts fights with his classmates) would be successful when he develops more appropriate social skills and uses these skills regularly with his peers, receives social reinforcement from his peers, and no longer gets into fights with his peers. Eliminating Warren's problem behavior (fighting) is but one desired outcome of treatment. Enhancing social skills and increasing social reinforcement from his peers are also desired outcomes because they improve the quality of Warren's life and help prevent recurrence of the problem behavior.

One additional outcome that defines successful treatment for problem behaviors is the generalization of the behavior changes across all relevant situations and over time after treatment is discontinued (Horner, Dunlap, & Koegel, 1988). In the example just considered, generalization has occurred when Warren exhibits appropriate social skills and no longer gets into fights at school, at home, at his friends' homes, on the playground in his neighborhood, at camp, and in any other situation with peers. In addition, treatment is successful if he refrains from fighting and exhibits good social skills in all relevant situations long after the treatment has ended.

To achieve a generalized reduction in a problem behavior, the focus of the intervention efforts should be on developing appropriate functionally equivalent alternative behaviors as replacements for the problem behavior (Carr et al., 1994; Durand, 1990; Reichle & Wacker, 1993). When a person has developed functionally equivalent alternative behaviors, these behaviors can occur and receive reinforcement in all the situations in which the problem behavior occurred previously. When the intervention consists only of an extinction or punishment procedure designed to eliminate the problem behavior, a generalized reduction in the problem is unlikely (Durand & Carr, 1992). This is because the extinction or punishment procedure might not be used in all situations in which the problem behavior occurs, so the behavior will continue to be reinforced at least occasionally. In addition, without functionally equivalent alternative behaviors to replace the problem, the problem behavior is more likely to recur in situations in which it was previously reinforced.

The focus on developing and increasing appropriate replacement behaviors is known as the constructional approach to treating problem behaviors (Goldiamond, 1974). The objective is to develop repertoires of more appropriate behavior that are functional for the person. To develop a repertoire is to teach functional skills and reinforce the occurrence of those behaviors in natural contexts. Although the focus is on increasing desirable alternatives through this constructional approach, extinction (and sometimes punishment) of the problem behavior is also used and must be continued over time so that the problem behavior is no longer functional for the person (Wacker et al., 1990). Desirable alternative behaviors are more likely to replace the problem behavior if it is no longer reinforced.

To achieve a generalized reduction in problem behaviors, attention must be paid to the following guidelines (Dunlap, 1993).

1. *Conduct a functional assessment of the problem behavior.* As you have seen, a functional assessment is always the first step in treating problem behaviors. A thorough understanding of the antecedents and consequences of the problem behavior and alternative behaviors is critical for the success of any behavior modification intervention. A complete functional assessment is also necessary for programming successful generalization of behavior change. Functional assessment information should be used to develop appropriate interventions that will be implemented in all the situations in which the behavior occurs.

2. *Plan for generalization in advance.* The intervention for the problem behavior should be planned from the beginning to maximize the likelihood of producing a generalized reduction in the behavior. When planning an intervention, you should use the known strategies for promoting generalization. Seven different procedures for promoting generalization have been discussed in this chapter. All of these procedures that are applicable to a client's problem behavior should be implemented to achieve a generalized reduction in the problem behavior.

3. *Focus on functionally equivalent alternative behaviors to replace the problem behaviors.* Generalized reductions in problem behaviors are best achieved when there are generalized increases in appropriate alternative behaviors that serve the same function as the problem behavior (Carr, 1988). Warren is less likely to get into fights because he learned desirable social skills that result in social reinforcement from his peers. If the use of these social skills generalizes to all relevant situations with peers, the problem behaviors should be decreased in all relevant situations with peers.

4. *Maintain extinction (or punishment) contingencies across situations and over time.* It is important that reinforcement for the problem behavior be eliminated (or minimized) in all situations for as long as the person continues to engage in the problem behavior. If extinction (or punishment) contingencies are discontinued prematurely, there is a risk that the problem behavior may begin to occur more frequently. A long history of reinforcement for problem behaviors often precedes the beginning of a behavior modification intervention. Therefore, even after the frequency of the prob-

lem behavior has been reduced to zero, the behavior may occur again in situations that previously exerted strong stimulus control over the behavior (spontaneous recovery). If this happens and the behavior is reinforced because extinction (or punishment) procedures were discontinued prematurely or implemented inconsistently, the frequency of the behavior is likely to increase again.

CHAPTER SUMMARY

1. The strategies for promoting generalization are found in Table 19-1. They involve manipulating the stimuli used during training, the range of responses trained, and the contingencies of reinforcement in the generalization settings.
2. If the behavior being trained is one that will contact natural contingencies of reinforcement in the target situation, then the behavior is more likely to generalize to the target situation and continue to occur in that situation.
3. The stimuli used in training should be similar to the stimuli in the target situation so that they have stimulus control over the target behavior in the target situation. The more similar the stimuli in the training situation are to the stimuli in the target situation, the more likely the behavior is to generalize to the target situation.
4. If a variety of different responses can all produce a reinforcing outcome in the target situation, then the behavior is more likely to generalize to the target situation. Also, if a desirable behavior produces the same reinforcing outcome as the problem behavior does in the target situation, then the desirable behavior is more likely to occur in the target situation.
5. To promote generalized reductions in a problem behavior, you should conduct a functional assessment of the problem behavior to determine the antecedents and reinforcing consequences, plan for generalization in advance using the seven generalization strategies identified in this chapter, focus on functionally equivalent alternative behaviors to replace the problem behavior, and maintain extinction or punishment procedures across situations and over time.

PRACTICE TEST

1. What is generalization? Why is generalization important in a behavior modification program? (pp. 412–413)
2. Provide an example of generalization (not from the chapter). Provide an example of a failure of generalization (not from the chapter).
3. Seven strategies for promoting generalization were described in this chapter. Identify and describe each strategy. Provide an example of each strategy. (pp. 413–422)
4. One generalization strategy is to reinforce instances of generalization; another is to train skills that contact natural contingencies of reinforcement. Which strategy is preferable? Why? (pp. 413–415)
5. You are teaching a child with mental retardation how to get a drink of water from a faucet. Describe the variety of stimulus exemplars and response variations you would use during training.
6. What is general case programming? Provide an example. (pp. 417–419)
7. To promote generalization, it is important to teach a range of functionally equivalent responses. Why? (pp. 419–420)
8. How does using common stimuli in training facilitate generalization? (pp. 417–419)
9. Why is it important to analyze the three-term contingency for the behavior in the

natural situation before starting a behavior modification program? (p. 422)

10. What can you do to promote generalization if there are no natural contingencies of reinforcement for the behavior? (p. 415)
11. Describe how you could use self-generated mediators of generalization to promote the generalization of the skills you learn in this class. (pp. 420–421)
12. What is a constructional approach to treating a problem behavior? (p. 424)
13. What is a generalized reduction in a problem behavior? (pp. 423–424)
14. Identify and describe the four guidelines for achieving a generalized reduction in a problem behavior. (pp. 424–425)
15. Why should an extinction (or punishment) contingency be continued beyond the point at which the frequency of the problem behavior has reached zero? (p. 424)

APPLICATIONS

1. Describe the strategies you will use to promote generalization and maintenance of the behavior change resulting from your self-management project. Identify the generalization strategies and describe how you will implement them.

2. Coach Knight wants to teach her basketball team a new play to use in games. The coach diagrams the play for the players and shows each player what to do in the play. Next, she has the team practice the play until they can execute it correctly. Describe what strategies coach Knight can use to promote generalization so that the team executes the play correctly in games.

3. Your behavior modification professor is teaching the class how graduated guidance is used to teach skills to children with mental retardation. Describe the strategies the professor can use to promote generalization so that each student in the class can use graduated guidance successfully when working with children with disabilities.

4. Your friend, a special education teacher, is teaching the students in her class to recognize words. She has flashcards with each of the important words that they need to learn for living in the community (e.g., *in, out, walk, don't walk, enter, men, women*). She is using prompting and fading to teach the adolescents how to read these words. Describe the advice you will give to your friend that will help her program for the generalization of the students' reading.

5. Heidi implemented a self-management project in which her goal was to stop using specific curse words. She self-monitored the daily frequency of the curse words by keeping a tally on an index card she kept in her pocket. She set daily goals for herself to reduce the frequency of curse words each day until she was no longer using the words. If the frequency of her curse words was more than her goal for the day, she had to put $2 into a jar in the kitchen. At the end of the week, her roommate counted up the money and gave it to charity. In addition to this response cost procedure, she asked friends from her behavior modification class to remind her whenever they heard her use a curse word. She was able to reach her goal every day, except on the days that she played softball. On softball days she cursed frequently with her teammates as they sat around and talked about the game once it was over. Describe procedures Heidi could use to promote generalization of the reduction in cursing to the softball days.

6. Professor Melvin was disliked by the office staff because she was rude and sarcastic in many of her interactions with them. She never smiled or engaged in conversation with the staff. When she wanted something done, she told the staff what to do in a demanding fashion without saying "please" and "thank you." The staff often stopped whatever they were doing and did Dr. Melvin's work immediately to avoid upsetting her. If the staff said that they could not do her work immediately because they had other work

to do or deadlines to meet, Dr. Melvin persisted in her demands until they agreed. If an assignment was not done correctly or on time, she made a sarcastic or critical comment, often in an angry tone of voice. After being advised by the department chairperson that she must stop interacting with staff in this way, Dr. Melvin sought help from a psychologist. Describe the treatment procedures that the psychologist might use to help Dr. Melvin decrease her negative interactions with staff and to ensure a generalized reduction in the negative interactions.

MISAPPLICATIONS

1. For weeks, coach Anderson had been teaching his high school baseball team to hit an assortment of difficult pitches, and he wanted to prepare his players for the pitches they would face in games. The coach scheduled the first game of the season with the best team in the region. This team had much better players than coach Anderson's team. The pitchers would throw some of the most difficult pitches that the players would see all year. Coach Anderson thought that playing the hardest team first would be good for his players. Identify the good and bad aspects of coach Anderson's strategy for promoting generalization of his players' hitting.

2. Dr. Nolan conducts anger management training groups for adults with mental retardation living in group homes or apartments in the community. In the group training sessions, Dr. Nolan discusses anger management strategies (e.g., relaxation procedures, calming self-statements, and coping responses such as walking away), models the strategies, and has all participants rehearse the skills in a variety of role-plays. After each rehearsal, she provides feedback (reinforcement and instructions for improvement) to the participants. At the beginning of the training, she asks the participants to identify situations in which they had trouble controlling their anger; she then uses those situations as role-plays in the training. Sometimes particular people in the group have had anger difficulties with each other. When this happens, Dr. Nolan has the particular participants practice anger management skills in role-plays with each other. The group meets for ten sessions, and Dr. Nolan encourages all of the group members to participate actively in every session. What strategies is Dr. Nolan using to promote generalization? What other strategies could she use to promote generalization?

3. A community college offers an introductory course on personal computers. According to the course description, it is intended to prepare students to use personal computers for school, work, or home applications. The course meets twice a week for 10 weeks and covers word processing, spreadsheets, and some simple graphics and statistics. The computer lab has IBM computers and IBM-compatible software. The students practice on the computers in the lab what they have learned in lecture. What important strategy for promoting generalization is missing from this course?

4. Angie is an 8-year-old in a second grade classroom for children with behavior disorders. In this class there are ten students, a teacher, and a teacher's aide. Angie's problem behaviors include disruptive behaviors such as taking materials from other students, teasing other students by poking them and making faces, and pulling the hair or clothes of other students. The problem behaviors occur when the teacher's attention is directed to other students during independent work time. The consequence maintaining Angie's disruptive behavior is attention from the other students as they cry or tell her to stop and from the teacher as he scolds her for her misbehavior. The teacher implemented a time-out procedure in which he made Angie sit in a chair in the back of the room away from the other children for 5 minutes contingent on the problem behavior. Why is this treatment inadequate for promoting generalization? What would you add to the treatment to promote generalization of the behavior change?

5. Paige was an adolescent with severe mental retardation who lived with her parents. She was starting high school this year. Because the high school was near their house, her parents decided to let her walk to school. However, Paige walked into intersections without looking when her parents practiced walking to school with her. The parents wanted to eliminate Paige's behavior of walking into an intersection without looking and replace it with the behavior of stopping on the curb, looking at the walk sign, looking both ways, and walking only if the walk sign was lit and there was no traffic in the intersection. They practiced at the traffic light between their home and the high school. When Paige approached the intersection, the parents used prompts to get Paige to engage in the appropriate behavior. If she stepped off of the curb without looking or when the walk sign wasn't lit, the parent said "No" firmly and grabbed her arm. The parents gradually faded the prompts until Paige engaged in the correct behavior and no longer walked into the intersection without looking, even when they were not near her. Why is this street safety training inadequate to promote generalization? What should the parents do to promote generalization?

CHAPTER 19 *Quiz 1* Name:

1. Programming for ____________________ increases the likelihood that the behavior change will occur in all relevant situations or circumstances in the person's life.

2. When the trainer is not able to reinforce occurrences of generalization and when there are no natural contingencies of reinforcement for the behavior, generalization may be promoted by modifying ____________________ in the relevant situations.

3. Different responses that achieve the same outcome (they serve the same function) are called ____________________ responses.

4. If you teach a parent to use self-instructions at home to prompt herself to use the parenting skills that she learned in your parenting class, what generalization strategy are you using?

____

Match the following strategies to their definitions.

a. Reinforce instances of generalization
b. Train skills that contact natural contingencies of reinforcement
c. Modify natural contingencies of reinforcement and punishment
d. Incorporate a wide range of relevant stimulus situations in training
e. Incorporate common stimuli
f. Teach a range of functionally equivalent responses
g. Incorporate self-generated mediators of generalization

5. _____ Train behaviors that will result in reinforcement in relevant situations in the natural environment.

6. _____ Utilize as many relevant stimulus situations as possible in training.

7. _____ Reinforce the behavior when it occurs in the natural environment.

8. _____ Use stimuli from the generalization environment in the training environment.

9. _____ Teach people in the natural environment to use reinforcement or punishment for the behavior.

10. _____ Teach a variety of response that may all achieve the same outcome for the client.

CHAPTER 19 *Quiz 2* Name:

1. ____________________ is defined as the occurrence of the behavior in the presence of stimuli that are similar in some way to the S^D that was present during training.

2. Desirable behavior will occur in all relevant situations outside the training situation if the behavior is __________________ in those situations.

3. If the learner is trained to respond to a range of ______________________________, the behavior is more likely to generalize to all relevant situations.

4. ______________________ involves the use of multiple training examples that sample the range of relevant stimulus situations and response variations.

Match the following strategies to the examples.

a. Reinforce instances of generalization
b. Train skills that contact natural contingencies of reinforcement
c. Modify natural contingencies of reinforcement and punishment
d. Incorporate a wide range of relevant stimulus situations in training
e. Incorporate common stimuli
f. Teach a range of functionally equivalent responses
g. Incorporate self-generated mediators of generalization

5. _____ Teach a person to self-monitor each instance of nail biting at home to prompt her to use the competing response strategy you taught her in the training session.

6. _____ During social skills training with a shy teenager, have a couple of classmates come to the training session so the teenager can practice the skills with them.

7. _____ After teaching a first grader to raise her hand before speaking in class, teach the first-grade teacher to provide praise when the student raises her hand before speaking.

8. _____ After teaching a child to share in training sessions, praise the child each time you observe him sharing in the classroom.

9. _____ When teaching a person with mental retardation how to use vending machines, teach her all the different ways to make a selection from a vending machine.

10. _____ When teaching assertiveness skills to a person who often says 'yes' to unreasonable requests, role play as many unreasonable requests as possible and have her respond assertively during training.

CHAPTER 19 *Quiz 3* Name:

1. In behavior modification, ______________________________ is defined as the occurrence of the behavior in the presence of all relevant stimuli outside of training.

2. One way to promote generalization is to __________________________ the behavior when generalization occurs.

3. In the technique of incorporating common stimuli, stimuli from the ______________________ environment are incorporated into the training situation to promote generalization.

4. General case programming is defined as using multiple training examples that sample

   the range of ______________________________ and ______________________________.

5. What generalization strategy is being used when a trainer teaches the learner a number

   of different ways to make a correct response? ______________________________________

Match the following strategies to the examples.

a. Reinforce instances of generalization
b. Train skills that contact natural contingencies of reinforcement
c. Modify natural contingencies of reinforcement and punishment
d. Incorporate a wide range of relevant stimulus situations in training
e. Incorporate common stimuli
f. Teach a range of functionally equivalent responses
g. Incorporate self-generated mediators of generalization

6. _____ In an attempt to get parents to use the parenting skills they learned in a parent training class, the instructor asks the one parent to praise the other when he or she uses the parenting skills correctly at home.

7. _____ In an attempt to get parents to use the parenting skills they learned in a parent training class, the instructor teaches the parent a simple self-instruction to use at home to prompt the correct use of the parenting skills.

8. _____ In an attempt to get parents to use the parenting skills they learned in a parent training class, the instructor visits the parents' homes and praises them when they use the skills correctly.

9. _____ In an attempt to get parents to use the parenting skills they learned in a parent training class, the instructor teaches the parents skills that their children will naturally respond favorably to.

10. _____ In an attempt to get parents to use the parenting skills they learned in a parent training class, the instructor has the parents bring their children to the session and practice the skills with their children in the session.

Self-Management

This chapter describes behavior modification procedures people can use to influence their own behavior. Most often, behavior modification procedures are implemented by change agents to influence the behavior of another person—for example, a psychologist helping a client or parents modifying a child's behavior. When a person uses behavior modification procedures to change his or her own behavior, the process is called **self-management.**

- How do you define a self-management problem?
- What is self-management?
- What is social support? How is it beneficial as a component of self-management?
- What are the different types of self-management strategies?
- What steps are involved in a self-management program?

Examples of Self-Management

Getting Murray to Run Regularly

Murray had been running 3–5 miles about five days a week for a few years. This aerobic exercise helped him keep his weight and blood pressure down and made him feel better. Murray planned to run throughout his lifetime to stay healthy. Once Murray graduated from college and started working full time, however, he began to miss more and more runs each week. When he got home from work, he was tired and hungry and usually sat in front of the TV and ate some snacks. After that, he would skip his run for the day. Murray decided that he needed to make some changes. He remembered some self-management procedures from his behavior modification class and decided it was time to implement them.

The first thing that Murray did was to develop a data sheet on his computer. The data sheet included a space to record the time and distance that he ran each day of the week and another space to record his goal for the day. At the beginning of each week, Murray wrote down the number of miles he was going to run on each day that week. His ultimate goal was to run 5 miles on five days a week. He started with 3 miles on three days each week and increased the number of miles each day and then the number of runs each week until he had reached his goal. After each run, Murray recorded the time and distance of his run on the data sheet. He kept the data sheet in a prominent place on the desk in his study at home so that he noticed it frequently.

Murray also made a graph on which he plotted the number of miles he ran each week. On the graph, he made a mark to indicate his goal for that week. At the end of each week, Murray plotted the number of miles on his graph. He put the graph on the bulletin board in his study. The graph was there as a reminder to him to keep running. The data sheet and graph Murray used are shown in Figures 20-1 and 20-2.

The next thing Murray did to increase the likelihood that he would run after work was to eat a snack on his break at work at around 3 P.M. He did this so that he wouldn't be so hungry right after work. If he wasn't hungry, he would be less likely to eat after work and more likely to run instead.

Another part of Murray's plan was to find some friends to run with him. He joined the local running club and got to know some people from his part of town who also ran after work. Murray planned a number of his runs with some of these other runners. By planning his runs with other people, Murray was making a public commitment to run at a certain time and generating social support from his fellow runners. He was also making the runs more fun because he got to spend time with his new friends while he ran.

Getting Annette to Clean Up Her Mess

Annette lived with her friend Shannon in an apartment near campus. Annette and Shannon had been friends since they met in their first year of college. They moved into the apartment at the beginning of their junior year. After one semester in the apartment, Shannon was getting into arguments with Annette about her messiness. Annette rarely cleaned up after herself. She left dishes lying around, didn't put food back into the refrigerator or cupboards, didn't wash her dishes, and left her things lying around in the bathroom. Shannon often put things away or cleaned up after Annette. Annette's room was also a mess, but Shannon simply closed the door to Annette's room to keep from seeing the mess. Annette eventually realized that her messiness was causing a problem with Shannon and decided to modify her behavior. She implemented a number of self-management strategies.

First, she posted notes to herself in the kitchen and bathroom as reminders to clean up after herself. One note was on the bathroom mirror and the other was on the refrigerator. The note said, "Annette, clean up now!"

Second, Annette bought paper plates and cups to make it easier to clean up. She divided many of her foods into one-serving portions so that there was no food to put back into the refrigerator or cupboards after she had prepared a meal. She also bought a basket for all of her toiletries, so that she could take them out and put them back into the bathroom cabinet more easily.

Third, Annette signed a contract with Shannon in which she would lose $2 each time she left a mess in the kitchen, bathroom, or living room. The contract defined clearly what constituted a mess. Annette put a data sheet in the kitchen to monitor her behavior. Whenever Annette left a mess, she had to record the mess on the data sheet. If she then cleaned up the mess, she got $1 back. If Shannon found a mess and cleaned up for Annette, Shannon recorded it and Annette lost the full $2. With this contract, Annette lost money when she left a mess, but she lost less money if she eventually cleaned up her mess.

Finally, Annette asked Shannon to make a positive comment when she noticed that Annette had cleaned up after herself. In this way, Annette hoped to arrange social reinforcement from Shannon for cleaning up after herself.

Day	Date	Time	Distance	Goal (distance)
Monday				
Tuesday				
Wednesday				
Thursday				
Friday				
Saturday				
Sunday				

FIGURE 20-1 Murray used this data sheet to record his running behavior each day. The data sheet has a space for the distance and time of the run each day of the week and a space for Murray to write in his goal for that day.

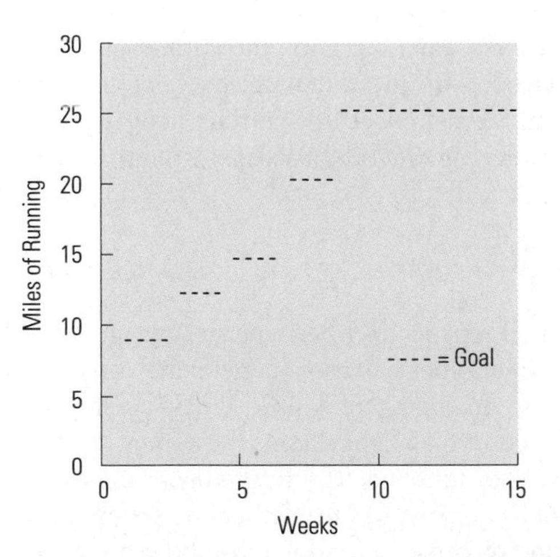

FIGURE 20-2 This graph will show the number of miles Murray runs each week. The marks on the graph indicate the weekly goals Murray has set for himself.

Defining Self-Management Problems

These two examples illustrate self-management problems and self-management strategies implemented by two different people. In each case, the people are exhibiting behavioral deficits; that is, they fail to engage in desirable behaviors. The behaviors are desirable because they will have a positive impact on the people's lives in the future. However, even though the future outcome of the behavior will be positive, the behavior does not occur because it is not reinforced immediately when it occurs or because competing behavior that is immediately reinforced interferes with its occurrence. Because the positive outcome is in the future, it does not exert an influence on the occurrence of the desirable behavior at present. Murray was not running as often or as far as he desired, and Annette was not cleaning up after herself when she made a mess. Running has a positive impact in the future in terms of improved health for Murray, but the competing behaviors of eating snacks and watching TV are immediately reinforced. Cleaning up in the apartment has a positive impact on Annette's friendship with Shannon in the future, but the competing behaviors of walking away from a mess and engaging in preferred activities are immediately reinforced. The goal of self-management strategies is to increase the current level of the deficit behavior so that the positive outcome can be achieved for the person in the future.

Another type of self-management problem is an excess of an undesirable behavior. The behavior is undesirable because it will have a negative impact on the person's life in the future. Examples of behavioral excesses include overeating, smoking, alcohol abuse, and gambling. Although it will have a negative outcome on a person's life in the future, the undesirable behavior continues because it is immediately reinforced when it occurs or because alternative behaviors are not present to compete with its occurrence. Because the negative outcome is in the future, it does not influence the occurrence of the undesirable behavior in the present. The goal of self-management is to decrease or eliminate the behavioral excess so that the negative outcome does not occur in the future.

Table 20-1 provides examples of behavioral deficits and excesses that represent self-management problems. For each behavior, the current contingency influences its occurrence, and the delayed or future outcome does not influence its occurrence. Many self-management problems reflect this conflict between short-term contingencies and long-term outcomes (Malott, 1989; Watson & Tharp, 1993).

Defining Self-Management

In its basic form, self-management occurs when a person engages in behavior at one time to control the occurrence of another behavior (target behavior) at a later time (Watson & Tharp, 1993; Yates, 1986). According to Skinner (1953a), self-management involves a controlling behavior and a controlled behavior. As the names imply, the person engages in the **controlling behavior** to influence the future occurrence of the **controlled behavior.** The controlling behavior involves implementing self-management strategies in which the antecedents and consequences of the target behavior or alternative behaviors are modified; these strategies make the controlled behavior (target behavior) more likely. In our example, Murray engaged in a number of controlling behaviors—such as setting goals, self-monitoring, eating a snack at work, and arranging to run with others—that made it more likely that he would run more often (the controlled behavior). Annette also

TABLE 20-1 Behavioral Deficits and Excesses as Self-Management Problems in Which Immediate Contingencies Contrast with Future Outcomes

Behavioral Deficit	**Immediate Contingency**	**Delayed Positive Outcome**
Studying	Lack of reinforcement Response effort Reinforcement of competing behavior (TV, parties, phone calls)	Good grades Graduation Job or graduate school
Exercise	Punishment (sore muscles) Response effort Reinforcement of competing behavior (eating, TV, naps)	Better health Weight loss Better physique
Healthful eating	Decreased reinforcement value Response effort to prepare healthful food Reinforcement for competing behavior (eating junk food)	Better health Weight loss More energy Less constipation
Behavioral Excess	**Immediate Contingency**	**Delayed Negative Outcome***
Smoking	Immediate reinforcement (alertness, relaxation) Little response effort Response effort for alternative behaviors	Lung cancer Emphysema Heart disease Stained teeth
Unprotected sex	Immediate reinforcement Less response effort Less reinforcement and more response effort for condom use	Pregnancy Exposure to HIV, diagnosis of AIDS Other sexually transmitted diseases
Eating junk food	Immediate reinforcement Increased reinforcement value Little response effort Prevalent cues (advertising)	Tooth decay Weight gain Pimples

*Many of these delayed outcomes are also uncertain outcomes because they may not occur for every person who engages in the excess behavior. For example, a smoker might not get lung cancer, and unprotected sex might not lead to HIV infection. However, the excess behaviors increase the probability of the delayed negative outcomes.

engaged in controlling behaviors to increase the likelihood that she would clean up after herself. These controlling behaviors included posting reminders, using paper plates and cups, arranging social reinforcement, self-monitoring, and writing a contract with her roommate. We now consider the types of self-management strategies that can be implemented as controlling behaviors to influence the future occurrence of a target behavior (Karoly & Kanfer, 1982; Thoreson & Mahoney, 1974).

TYPES OF SELF-MANAGEMENT STRATEGIES

In self-management, a person identifies and defines a target behavior and arranges for one or more behavior modification procedures to influence the occurrence of that behavior. The following types of procedures are commonly used in self-management.

Goal-Setting and Self-Monitoring

You can influence the likelihood that you will engage in a target behavior in the future by establishing a goal for yourself. **Goal-setting** involves writing down the criterion level of the target behavior and the time frame for the occurrence of the behavior. For example, Murray set a goal for the number of days he was going to run and the number of miles he would run each day for the upcoming week. The goal for each day, written down on a data sheet, acted as a cue for him to run on those days. As you recall, Murray also implemented a number of other self-management strategies. Although goal-setting by itself is not always an effective self-management strategy, it is effective when implemented with self-monitoring and other self-management strategies (Doerner, Miltenberger, & Bakken, 1989; Suda & Miltenberger, 1993).

You should set goals that are achievable. When a goal is achievable, you are more likely to be successful, to exhibit the desired level of the target behavior. Achieving the goal is particularly important early in a self-management program because it is often the criterion for a reinforcement contingency to be implemented, and early reinforcement generally increases the likelihood that the person will persevere in the program. In addition, goal achievement is a conditioned reinforcer for many people or may become a conditioned reinforcer if other reinforcers are delivered when the person achieves the goal.

Goal-setting is implemented most often in conjunction with self-monitoring. With self-monitoring, you record each instance of the target behavior as it occurs. This allows you to evaluate progress toward the goal. In addition, self-monitoring often is reactive; that is, the act of self-monitoring may result in a beneficial change in the target behavior that is being recorded (e.g., Latner & Wilson, 2002). For example, if Annette begins to self-monitor her cleaning behavior, she is more likely to increase this behavior, even before other self-management strategies are implemented. As you will see in a later section of this chapter, goal-setting and self-monitoring are both steps in the process of implementing a self-management program.

Antecedent Manipulations

A variety of antecedent manipulations for increasing or decreasing a target behavior were described in Chapter 16. Antecedent manipulations often are used by people in self-management programs to influence their own behavior. Recall that in an antecedent manipulation, you modify the environment in some way before the target behavior occurs to influence the future occurrence of the target behavior (Epstein, 1996). Six types of antecedent manipulations to increase the likelihood of a target behavior were described in Chapter 16:

- Presenting the S^D or cues for the desirable target behavior
- Removing the S^D or cues for competing undesirable behaviors
- Arranging an establishing operation for the desirable target behavior
- Removing establishing operations for the competing behaviors
- Decreasing the response effort for the desirable target behavior
- Increasing the response effort for the competing behaviors

Look again at Chapter 16 for detail on each of these antecedent manipulations. Identify the antecedent manipulations Annette used to increase the likelihood that she would clean up after herself.

First, Annette presented a cue for the target behavior by posting reminders to herself in the kitchen and bathroom and displaying the data sheet in the kitchen. Second, she decreased response effort for the target behavior by using paper plates and cups and single-serving portions of food. In this way, she had less to clean up. She also decreased response effort for cleaning up in the bathroom by buying the basket in which she kept her toiletries; it was easier to put them away in the basket. Third, she signed a contract with her roommate and arranged for her roommate to praise her when she cleaned up. These antecedent manipulations increased the likelihood that Annette would clean up after herself immediately.

The antecedent manipulations to decrease the likelihood of a target behavior are the opposite of those used to increase the likelihood of a target behavior (Chapter 16). They include removing the S^D or cues for the target behavior and presenting the S^D or cues for desirable alternative behaviors, removing establishing operations for the target behavior and presenting establishing operations for the alternative behaviors, and increasing response effort for the target behavior and decreasing response effort for the alternative behavior. These strategies are described in more detail in Chapter 16.

Note that all self-management procedures involve antecedent manipulations because the person engages in some controlling behaviors in advance of the target behavior to be controlled. In other words, the person plans the self-management strategy and arranges for its occurrence before the incidence of the target behavior. Even in a self-management strategy that involves manipulating response consequences rather than manipulating antecedents, the implementation of the response consequence is arranged in advance of the target behavior, so such a self-management strategy is technically an antecedent manipulation.

Behavioral Contracting

A **behavioral contract** is a written document in which you identify the target behavior and arrange consequences contingent on a specified level of the target behavior in a specific time period. Although another person (the contract manager) applies the consequences, a behavioral contract is considered to be a type of self-management strategy because the behavior of entering into the contract is a controlling behavior designed to influence the future occurrence of the target behavior. In a behavioral contract (Chapter 23), you identify and define the target behavior to be changed, establish a method of data collection, define the criterion level of the target behavior to be achieved in the time frame of the contract, and arrange the contingencies and the person to implement the contingencies to influence the target behavior. These are the controlling behaviors that you perform in a self-management strategy based on a behavioral contract.

One variation of a behavioral contract that can be used in a self-management plan is a contract written by the person without the assistance of a contract manager. In this variation, you would write a contract in the manner described, but you would implement the contract contingencies yourself. Although such a contract may be effective in helping you change a target behavior, it is likely to be less effective than a contract carried out with the assistance of a contract manager.

What problem may arise when you implement the contingencies in your own behavioral contract without the help of a contract manager?

The problem is that you might not implement the contingency as written. For example, suppose that you write a contract in which you state that you can watch an hour of TV in the evening as a reinforcer for completing 3 hours of homework. If you do not complete the homework, you might still watch the TV that evening. You would then have failed to implement the contingency as written in your contract. Martin and Pear (1992) call this **short-circuiting the contingency.** Short-circuiting occurs when a person arranges a reinforcer for a target behavior but then takes the reinforcer without first engaging in the target behavior. Alternatively, short-circuiting may occur when a person arranges a punisher for a target behavior but does not implement the punisher after engaging in the target behavior. This does not always happen when you write a contract by yourself, but it is important to be aware of the possibility. The benefit of having a contract manager is that the contract manager will implement the contingencies consistently and short-circuiting will be less likely.

Arranging Reinforcers and Punishers

A similar self-management strategy involves arranging contingencies of reinforcement or punishment without writing them into a contract. You might arrange a reinforcement or punishment contingency with yourself, such as a plan that you will eat breakfast only after you have studied for an hour in the morning. Eating breakfast is to be a reinforcer for studying. However, because you are implementing the reinforcement contingency yourself, you are able to short-circuit the contingency. You could eat breakfast even if you did not complete an hour of homework first. Although short-circuiting is a possible disadvantage, the advantage of arranging contingencies with yourself is that you do not have to rely on another person for assistance.

You can also arrange for reinforcers or punishers to be implemented by another person. If the other person is implementing the contingency, short-circuiting is less likely to be a problem. For example, a student who lives with his mother might tell her not to fix him any breakfast until she sees that he has studied for an hour. His mother is more likely to implement the reinforcement contingency correctly—to give him breakfast only after he has studied for an hour—than he would himself.

What problems might arise if you ask another person to implement your reinforcement or punishment contingencies?

One problem is that you might not have friends or family members who are willing to get involved in a behavior modification program. Another is that you might get angry with a friend or family member who withholds a reinforcer or implements a punishment contingency, even though you agreed to it in advance. These potential problems aside, enlisting another person to implement reinforcement or punishment contingencies is going to increase the likelihood that your self-management efforts will be successful. Without the help of another person, you are more likely to ignore the reinforcement or punishment contingencies you have arranged for your target behavior.

Besides positive reinforcement contingencies, you can also arrange punishment or negative reinforcement contingencies. Common punishment or negative reinforcement contingencies involve response cost or the application or removal of aversive activities. For example, a student living in a house with two roommates says that she will pay $10 to her roommates if she smokes a cigarette that day. She arranged for the loss of money (response cost) to serve as a punisher for smoking to decrease her rate of smoking in the future. She might also agree to clean the house by herself if she smokes a cigarette that day. Cleaning the house will act as an aversive activity that decreases the likelihood that she will smoke. The student might arrange a negative reinforcement contingency that states that if she does not study for 3 hours on a particular day, she has to wash all the dishes that evening (or pay her roommates $10). Completing the 3 hours of homework results in avoiding washing the dishes (or losing $10); thus, the behavior of doing homework is negatively reinforced.

Social Support

Social support occurs when significant others in a person's life provide a natural context or cues for the occurrence of the target behavior or when they naturally provide reinforcing consequences for the occurrence of the target behavior. Social support is a self-management strategy when you specifically arrange for social support to influence the target behavior.

How did Murray arrange for social support to increase the likelihood that he would run more often?

Murray made arrangements to run a few days a week with other people from the local running club. When Murray scheduled his runs with his friends from the running club, he was creating a natural context for the occurrence of the target behavior. On the days that he scheduled these runs with his friends, he was more likely to run. There was also natural reinforcement for running with his friends: Spending time with his friends was a positive reinforcer that occurred contingent on running with them. Scheduling runs with his friends created natural antecedents and consequences for Murray's running.

Consider a few other examples of how people use social support as a self-management strategy. When Martha wanted to decrease her beer drinking, she scheduled more social events with her nondrinking friends and did not schedule any activities with her friends who drink. As a result, she was less likely to drink beer at social events because the natural contingencies when she was with her nondrinking friends promoted the consumption of nonalcoholic beverages. Roger needed to get a lot of studying done in the last four weeks of the semester. He had one group of friends who rarely studied. They usually watched TV, played video games, or sat around and talked. Another group of friends, who shared a large house, spent most of their time studying on weeknights. Roger went over to their house each night during the week and, as a result of the natural social contingencies there, was more likely to study.

Whenever possible, it is a good idea to include a social support component in a self-management program. The involvement of others increases the likelihood of success by helping to prevent the short-circuiting of contingencies. Short-circuiting is less likely to occur when other people implement the contingencies or watch the person implement the contingencies as part of a self-management program.

Self-Instructions and Self-Praise

You can often influence your own behavior by talking to yourself in specific ways (Malott, 1989). As you will learn in Chapter 25, you can influence your own behavior by reciting self-instructions that cue the appropriate behavior at the appropriate time. In essence, with **self-instructions** you are telling yourself what to do or how to do it in situations that call for a specific target behavior. Immediately after the appropriate behavior occurs, you can recite **self-praise** statements in which you provide positive evaluations of your own behavior. For example, as Rolanda walks to her boss's office, she says to herself, "Remember to make eye contact, use a firm tone of voice, and ask the question directly." Once Rolanda engages in these assertive behaviors, she says to herself, "Way to go! I was assertive and said what I wanted to say." Rolanda's self-instructions and self-praise statements made it more likely that she would behave assertively in her boss's office. However, for Rolanda to be able to recite the self-instructions and self-praise statements in her boss's office, she had to rehearse them in advance. Self-instructions and self-praise are behaviors themselves, and they must be learned before they will occur in a criterion situation to influence other target behaviors.

As we will see in Chapter 25, a person typically learns self-instructions and self-praise by rehearsing them in role-play situations that simulate real problem situations. To use self-instructions and self-praise statements in a self-management program, you must identify the self-statements, determine the most appropriate time and place to use them, rehearse them in a role-play or as you imagine the problem situation, and plan to use them only after they are well learned.

Steps in a Self-Management Plan

A self-management plan based on one or more of the strategies just described should include nine basic steps, as follows.

1. *Making the decision to engage in self-management.* You typically make the decision to engage in a self-management program after a period of dissatisfaction with some aspect of your own behavior. As you start to think about the unsatisfactory behavior and imagine how the behavior could be improved, you become motivated to take some action (Kanfer & Gaelick-Buys, 1991). If you have learned how to carry out a self-management program, as a result of taking a class or reading a book, you would be likely to begin the process at this time. The event that gets the process of self-management started is anticipation of beneficial changes in the target behavior. You are more likely to take steps to change if you anticipate a positive outcome of your efforts.

2. *Defining the target behavior and competing behaviors.* The purpose of a self-management program is to increase or decrease the level of a target behavior. You must first define the target behavior to be changed so that you can record it accurately and implement the self-management strategy correctly. It is also important to identify and define the behaviors that compete with the target behavior. When the target behavior is a behavioral deficit to be increased, you will seek to decrease undesirable competing behaviors. When the target behavior is a behavioral excess to be decreased, you will seek to increase desirable competing behaviors.

Steps in a Self-Management Plan

1. Making the decision to engage in self-management
2. Defining the target behavior and competing behaviors
3. Goal-setting
4. Self-monitoring
5. Functional assessment
6. Choosing appropriate self-management strategies
7. Evaluating change
8. Reevaluating self-management strategies
9. Implementing maintenance strategies

3. *Goal-setting*. Your goal is the desirable level of the target behavior to be achieved in the self-management project. In setting the goal, you identify an appropriate level of the target behavior that will reflect an improvement in some aspect of your life. Once you decide on the goal, you should write it down so that it becomes more salient. Making your goal public, so that significant others are aware of it, is also valuable. You might also write down a number of intermediate goals if you plan to achieve the final goal gradually. Sometimes the intermediate goals can be developed only after a period of self-monitoring to determine the baseline level of the target behavior. The intermediate goals build upon the baseline level of the behavior in gradual approximations to the final goal.

4. *Self-monitoring*. After defining the target behavior, you develop and implement a self-monitoring plan. Using a data sheet or some recording device (Chapter 2), you record each occurrence of the target behavior immediately after it occurs. You record the target behavior for a period of time (say, 1–2 weeks) to establish a baseline level of the behavior before implementing the self-management procedures. It is possible that the target behavior will change in the desired direction as a result of self-monitoring and goal-setting. You should not implement the self-management strategies until the level of the target behavior is stable. If the target behavior reaches the goal level as a result of the goal-setting and self-monitoring procedures, you can postpone implementing any further self-management strategies and continue to set goals and self-monitor. If the target behavior is not maintained at the goal level with self-monitoring, further self-management strategies can then be implemented. Self-monitoring is continued throughout the self-management program to judge the effectiveness of the program and the maintenance of changes over time.

5. *Functional assessment*. Concurrently with the implementation of self-monitoring during baseline, you should conduct a functional assessment to determine the antecedents and consequences of the target behavior and competing alternative behaviors. Chapter 13 describes how to conduct a functional assessment. The purpose of the functional assessment is to understand the variables that contribute to the occurrence or nonoccurrence of the target behavior and alternative behaviors. Specific self-management strategies that alter the antecedent and consequent variables identified in the functional assessment are then chosen.

6. *Choosing appropriate self-management strategies*. At this point in the process, you must choose the self-management strategies to modify your target behavior. First,

choose strategies that manipulate antecedents to the target behavior or manipulate antecedents to alternative behaviors that compete with the target behavior. The antecedents you manipulate are chosen on the basis of the functional assessment information. Types of antecedent manipulations are described briefly in this chapter and in detail in Chapter 16. Second, choose strategies that alter consequences of the target behavior or of the alternative behaviors. If you want to decrease an undesirable target behavior, you should do one or more of the following: eliminate the reinforcer for the target behavior, arrange punishers for the occurrence of the target behavior, provide reinforcers for the alternative behaviors, eliminate punishment contingencies for the alternative behaviors, or use behavior skills training procedures to teach the alternative behaviors. If you want to increase a desirable target behavior, you should do one or more of the following: arrange reinforcers for the target behavior, eliminate any punishment contingencies operating for the target behavior, eliminate the reinforcers for the alternative behaviors, or provide punishers for the alternative behaviors. These strategies are summarized in Table 20-2.

As you can see, in a self-management plan you should choose antecedent and consequence manipulations that affect the target behavior directly or antecedent and consequence manipulations that affect alternative behaviors as a way to influence the target behavior indirectly.

7. *Evaluating change.* Once you have implemented the self-management strategies, continue to collect data through self-monitoring and evaluate whether your target behavior is changing in the desired direction. If the target behavior is changing as expected, continue to implement the self-management strategies and self-monitoring procedure to see whether you reach your goal. Once you achieve your goal, it is time to implement maintenance strategies. If the target behavior is not changing in the desired direction, it is time to reevaluate the self-management strategies and make any necessary changes.

TABLE 20-2 Categories of Self-Management Strategies Used to Decrease or Increase the Level of a Target Behavior

Antecedent manipulations to increase a desirable behavior and decrease an undesirable behavior

- Present S^D or cues for the desirable behavior.
- Eliminate S^D or cues for the undesirable behaviors.
- Arrange establishing operations for the desirable behavior.
- Eliminate establishing operations for the undesirable behaviors.
- Decrease response effort for the desirable behavior.
- Increase response effort for the undesirable behaviors.

Consequence manipulations to increase a desirable behavior and decrease an undesirable behavior

- Provide reinforcers for the desirable behavior.
- Eliminate reinforcers for the undesirable behaviors.
- Eliminate punishers for the desirable behavior.
- Provide punishers for the undesirable behaviors.
- Use skills training procedures to teach desirable behaviors.

8. *Reevaluating self-management strategies.* If the target behavior is not char in the desired direction after you implement the self-management strategies, you should consider two types of problems that may have contributed to the ineffectiveness of the self-management strategies. First, you may not have implemented the self-management procedures correctly. In the case of incorrect implementation (e.g., short-circuiting of the contingencies), the self-management procedures are unlikely to be effective in changing the target behavior in the desired direction. If you find that you did not implement the self-management procedures correctly, you must take whatever steps are necessary to implement them correctly in the future. If you find that it is impossible to implement the procedures correctly, you must choose other self-management procedures that you are capable of implementing. For example, if you write a contract with yourself but you always short-circuit the contingencies, you might consider writing the contract with another person who will implement the contingencies for you.

Second, you may have chosen inappropriate self-management strategies to implement in the first place. If you find that you are implementing the procedures correctly but that they are not resulting in the desired behavior change, you must reevaluate the procedures themselves. You may not have chosen relevant antecedents or consequences to manipulate in your self-management plan. You need to look again at your functional assessment information or conduct another functional assessment to determine which are the relevant antecedents and consequences.

9. *Implementing maintenance strategies.* Once you achieve your goal in your self-management program, it is time to implement strategies to maintain the target behavior at the desired level. In the ideal situation, you can stop using the self-management strategies and let natural contingencies of reinforcement or punishment maintain the target behavior or alternative behaviors. For example, when Annette cleans up after herself regularly, her roommate thanks her and generally interacts more positively with her. These are natural reinforcers for the behavior of cleaning up. In addition, a clean kitchen, living room, and bathroom have become conditioned reinforcers because the state of cleanliness has been paired with other reinforcers over the course of the self-management program. For Murray, natural contingencies of reinforcement are associated with his running. He has the social support of his friends to cue him to run and to socially reinforce his running. In addition, as he runs more, he gets into better shape, which reduces the response effort and makes running itself more reinforcing. For many people, however, the natural contingencies may not maintain the target behavior over the long run; in some cases, the natural contingencies may be a problem. Consider someone trying to maintain weight loss. It is often naturally reinforcing to go out with friends for pizza or burgers, to cookouts, or to parties where excessive eating is the norm. Therefore, it is necessary to continue to implement some self-management procedures, at least periodically. It is useful for people to continue to set goals and engage in self-monitoring. These self-management strategies are not time-consuming and are simple to carry out. Often, the continuation of goal-setting and self-monitoring is sufficient to maintain the target behavior. Self-monitoring is particularly important because it provides information about the occurrence of the target behavior over time. In this way, you can tell immediately whether there are problems in maintaining the target behavior, and you can then implement further self-management procedures as needed.

Chapter Summary

1. Most self-management problems involve target behaviors in which the immediate consequences are in conflict with the long-term outcome. In particular, undesirable target behaviors to be decreased are reinforced by immediate consequences, even though the long-term outcome is negative, or desirable target behaviors to be increased are suppressed by immediate consequences but have positive outcomes for the person in the long run.
2. Self-management is the use of behavior modification strategies to change your own behavior. Specifically, it is a process in which a person engages in controlling behaviors to influence the future occurrence of a controlled behavior. The controlling behaviors are self-management strategies, and the controlled behavior is the target behavior to be modified.
3. Social support involves significant others providing antecedents and or consequences to promote the occurrence of appropriate behavior. Social support is beneficial as part of self-management because the involvement of significant others can help prevent short-circuiting of self-management contingencies and make self-management more successful.
4. Self-management strategies include antecedent manipulations, behavioral contracts, arranging reinforcement or punishment contingencies, social support, self-instructions and self-praise, goal-setting, and self-monitoring.
5. Self-management programs typically are implemented in a sequence of steps: (1) making the commitment to change a particular behavior, (2) defining the target behavior and competing behaviors, (3) setting goals for the outcome of the self-management program, (4) implementing a self-monitoring plan, (5) conducting a functional assessment of the antecedents and consequences of the target behavior and alternative behaviors, (6) selecting and implementing the self-management strategies, (7) evaluating change in the target behavior, (8) reevaluating the self-management strategies if the target behavior does not change in the desired direction, and (9) implementing maintenance strategies.

Practice Test

1. What is a behavioral deficit? Describe a self-management problem that consists of a behavioral deficit. (pp. 436–437)
2. In your example, identify the immediate contingencies responsible for the behavioral deficit and the long-term outcome of the behavior.
3. What is a behavioral excess? Describe a self-management problem that consists of a behavioral excess. (pp. 436–437)
4. In your example, identify the immediate contingencies responsible for the target behavior and the long-term outcome of the behavior.
5. Identify the basic elements of self-management. (pp. 436–437)
6. What are controlling behaviors? Provide an example. (p. 436)
7. What is a controlled behavior? Provide an example. (p. 436)
8. What is the relationship between the target behavior and alternative behaviors in a self-management problem involving a behavioral deficit? (p. 436)
9. What is the relationship between the target behavior and the alternative behaviors in a self-management problem involving a behavioral excess? (p. 436)
10. Identify the various types of antecedent manipulations that can be used in a self-management program. (p. 438)

11. Provide an example of a person using a behavioral contract in a self-management program. (p. 439)
12. How is the strategy of arranging reinforcers or punishers different from a behavioral contract? How is it similar? (pp. 439–441)
13. What is social support? Provide an example of social support in a self-management program. (p. 441)
14. Provide an example of the use of self-instructions in a self-management program. How do you learn self-instructions to use in self-management? (p. 442)
15. Identify and describe the nine steps you go through in carrying out a self-management program. (pp. 442–445)

APPLICATIONS

1. Chris has been complaining recently that she can't get any homework done. She says that she wants to study every day but just can't get herself to do it. Although she took a behavior modification course, she doesn't think that she can carry out a self-management program successfully. Describe what you would say to Chris that would make it more likely that she would implement a self-management program to change her study behavior.

2. You are going to help Chris get her self-management program going. She defines her target behavior of studying and begins to self-monitor her studying behavior. Before she can choose self-management strategies to modify her study behavior, she must conduct a functional assessment of her study behavior and alternative behaviors that interfere with her studying. Identify the questions that you would ask Chris to get functional assessment information.

3. Chris tells you that she studies in her dorm room in the evening with the TV on. Often her roommates or friends come over while she is trying to study. She stops and talks to them and sometimes goes out with them. Often she stops studying to watch something on TV or to get herself something to eat or drink. On many days, she does not even try to study and spends time with her friends instead. When she does try to study, her friends call her boring and tell her that she is missing out on fun things. Identify self-management strategies involving antecedent and consequence manipulations that Chris could use to increase her study behavior.

4. You have a problem with biting your fingernails. You bite the nails whenever you see the white part of the nail that extends out at the end of the nail. Once you bite the white part off, you typically don't bite again until the nail grows and more white part shows. However, you also bite the nail when it is uneven or there is a rough edge from previous biting. The biting most often occurs when you are watching TV or a movie, during lectures, or when you are studying. Describe the self-management strategies (antecedent and consequence manipulations) that you would use to stop your nail-biting.

MISAPPLICATIONS

1. Courtney had smoked throughout college. She smoked when she studied, when she drove in her car, when she got up in the morning, after meals, when she was upset, and when she went out with friends. In her senior year, she began to read more about the health effects of smoking and decided to stop smoking. She planned to stop smoking on Monday. She would finish her current pack or throw the rest of a pack away if it wasn't finished by Monday. Her

plan was to use self-instructions. Starting Monday morning, every time that she had an urge to smoke, she would tell herself, "Don't smoke! It's bad for you!" She reasoned that if she made these statements to herself, she would be less likely to go out and buy a pack or get a cigarette from a friend. Courtney assumed that it would be difficult for a few days, but that it would get easier after that. What is the problem with Courtney's plan? What would you tell Courtney to do differently?

2. Lenny rarely did the dishes until they had piled up for days. He left dirty clothes lying around his apartment for more than a week until he finally did the laundry. He left his mail sitting on the kitchen counter until he opened it days later. He left books and other things from school lying on the floor and on the kitchen table. Although he lived alone, his messiness was starting to bother him. He wanted to stop making a mess and to put things away immediately, but he just didn't keep up with it. Lenny watched a lot of TV in the evenings after school. Whenever he wasn't studying, he was watching TV; sometimes he studied in front of the TV. He watched three or four shows every evening. Lenny decided to use TV watching as a reinforcer for his target behavior of putting things away and cleaning up after himself. He decided that he would put his books on the desk, put his laundry in the hamper, wash dishes after he used them, put food away immediately after he prepared it, and read his mail and put it on his desk right away. He would watch TV only after he had done all of these things, as a reinforcer for these behaviors. What is the problem with this plan? What could Lenny do differently to improve his plan?

3. George had been drinking heavily for a number of years. His drinking had gotten to the point that he was getting drunk every night, often by himself, and he had a hangover just about every day. Some days, he would have a drink in the morning to try to feel better from the night before. George decided that his drinking had become a problem. He decided to implement a self-management program to stop or limit his drinking. He got out his behavior modification textbook from college and read the self-management chapter again. He then designed a self-management plan based on the steps outlined in the chapter. What is the problem in this example? What should George do differently?

CHAPTER 20 *Quiz 1* Name:

1. When a person uses behavior modification to change his or her own behavior, the process is called ______________________.

2. An individual may use self-management procedures to increase a behavioral ______________________ or decrease a behavioral ______________________.

3. In self-management, a person engages in a(n) ______________________ behavior to influence the future occurrence of the controlled behavior.

4. ______________________ is a type of self-management strategy in which you modify the environment in some way before the target behavior occurs to influence the future occurrence of the target behavior.

5. If you want to decrease the likelihood of a target behavior, you could ______________________ the S^D or establishing operation for the behavior or ______________________ response effort for the behavior.

6. ______________________ occurs if a person arranges a reinforcer for a target behavior and then takes the reinforcer without first engaging in the target behavior.

7. ______________________ occurs when significant others provide a natural context or cues for the occurrence of the target behavior or naturally reinforce the target behavior.

8. If you want to increase a target behavior, you can provide ______________________ for the behavior or eliminate ______________________ for the behavior.

9. If you want to decrease a target behavior, you can provide ______________________ for the behavior or eliminate ______________________ for the behavior.

10. Why is it best to have a contract manager when writing a behavioral contract?

____

CHAPTER 20 *Quiz 2* Name:

1. If a person fails to engage in a desirable behavior, the person is exhibiting a behavioral

 ______________.

2. If a person engages in too much of an undesirable behavior, the person is exhibiting a

 behavioral ________________.

3. In self-management, the ________________ behavior is the behavior that is influenced when a person engages in the controlling behavior.

4. Presenting an S^D for the desirable behavior and increasing response effort for the undesirable behavior are examples of what self-management strategy? ____________________

5. A(n) ____________________ is a written document in which you identify the target behavior and arrange consequences contingent on a specified level of the target behavior.

6. _________________________ occurs if a person arranges a punisher for a target behavior and then does not implement the punisher after engaging in the target behavior.

7. What is one antecedent manipulation for decreasing a target behavior?

 ____

8. What is one antecedent manipulation for increasing a target behavior?

 ____

9. What self-management strategy involves telling yourself what to do or how to do it in situations

 that call for a specific target behavior? ____________________

10. After using self-management strategies to change your behavior, what two self-management strategies should you continue to use over time to promote maintenance of the behavior

 change? ________________ and ____________________

CHAPTER 20 *Quiz 3* Name:

1. ______________________________ is the process of using behavior modification to change your own behavior.
2. A person may use self-management procedures to ______________________ a behavioral deficit or ______________________ a behavioral excess.
3. A behavioral excess typically occurs because it is immediately ____________________ whereas a behavioral deficit typically does not occur because it is not immediately ____________________.
4. If you want to increase the likelihood of a target behavior, you could ________________ an S^D or establishing operation for the behavior or ________________ response effort for the behavior.
5. ______________________________ is said to occur when you fail to implement the contingencies that you have written into your behavioral contract.
6. If you arrange a contingency to increase the amount of homework you do, and you have to do 2 hours of homework or you will lose $10, doing homework is ________________________ by avoiding the loss of the money.
7. If you arrange a contingency in which you lose $10 dollars every time you smoke a cigarette in order to stop smoking , smoking is ______________________ by the loss of the money.
8. If you want to _______________a target behavior, you can provide reinforcers for the behavior or eliminate punishers for the behavior.
9. If you want to _______________ a target behavior, you can provide punishers for the behavior or eliminate reinforcers for the behavior.
10. What is likely to happen to the target behavior once you start self-monitoring the behavior?

____

TWENTY-ONE

Habit Reversal Procedures

This chapter focuses on a type of treatment procedure that is implemented by a person with a habit behavior. These treatments, called **habit reversal** procedures, are used to decrease the frequency of undesirable habit behaviors. Habit behaviors often do not interfere to any great extent with the person's social functioning; they tend to be more of an annoyance to the person or to significant others in the person's life. However, in some cases, the frequency or intensity of the habit behavior can become extreme and lead to negative perceptions of the person or decrease the person's social acceptability (Boudjouk, Woods, Miltenberger, & Long, 2000; Friedrich, Morgan, & Devine, 1996; Friman, McPherson, Warzak, & Evans, 1993; Long, Woods, Miltenberger, Fuqua, & Boudjouk, 1999). When the habit behavior occurs frequently or with high intensity, the person may seek treatment for the problem. In such cases, a habit behavior may be seen as a **habit disorder** (Hansen, Tishelman, Hawkins, & Doepke, 1990).

- What is a habit behavior and when does a habit behavior become a habit disorder?
- What are three categories of habit behaviors?
- What are the components of the habit reversal procedure?
- How do you apply the habit reversal procedure to each category of habit behavior?
- What makes habit reversal procedures work?

Examples of Habit Behaviors

Joel sat in his psychology class and listened intently to what the professor was saying. Throughout most of the class, he was biting his fingernails. Without thinking, he put his finger up to his mouth and chewed on the edges of the nail. He worked his way around the nail and kept chewing around the edges until it was even. He often went back over the nail and chewed on parts of the nail that were uneven. He usually stopped biting a particular nail after it was so short that he could not bite it any more. Joel was not particularly bothered by his nail-biting behavior, but his girlfriend often told him how awful his chewed-up fingernails looked.

Jose was a college baseball player who worked out in the weight room to build strength and took extra batting practice each day. After hard practices or workouts, he could feel tension in his neck and shoulders. When he felt the tension, he moved his head quickly to one side and then back in a rotating motion. This head-snapping movement usually relieved the tension, at least momentarily. Over the course of the season, Jose found that he was doing the head-snapping more and more frequently as he waited for his turn to bat or waited between pitches as he batted. When he watched videotapes of the games, he noticed how much he engaged in this behavior. Although the head-snapping behavior had not detracted from his performance, it seemed to him that there was something abnormal about how frequently it occurred.

Barbara was a medical student in her final year. She was on a pediatric rotation in which she was learning medical procedures from pediatricians in a children's hospital. She walked with the pediatricians as they made rounds in the hospital. After seeing each patient, the pediatrician quizzed Barbara and the other medical students about the patient's medical problem. Barbara often was nervous in these situations, and sometimes she stuttered some of her words as she answered the pediatrician's questions. When she stuttered, she got stuck on a word and repeated the word or syllables in the word a number of times before she finished the sentence. For example, she might say, "I think we need to take fur-fur-further X-rays to confirm that, Doctor." Although the stuttering had not negatively affected her in school, she was becoming concerned about it. The stuttering could affect her performance or professional opportunities in the future.

Defining Habit Behaviors

The three examples above illustrate three types of **habit behaviors:** nervous habits, motor tics, and stuttering (Woods & Miltenberger, 1995).

Nervous Habits

The behavior in the first example, nail-biting, is a common type of **nervous habit.** Other examples of nervous habits include twirling or stroking hair (or a moustache or beard), tapping a pencil, chewing on a pen or pencil, cracking knuckles, thumbsucking, repetitively manipulating a paper clip or similar item, jingling money in a pocket, folding or ripping paper (such as a napkin in a restaurant), fingernail-picking, and other repetitive manipulation of objects or body parts (Woods, Miltenberger, & Flach, 1996). Nervous habits involve repetitive, manipulative behaviors that are believed to be most likely to occur when the person experiences heightened nervous tension. Nervous habits do not typically serve any social function for the person; for example, they are not reinforced by others in the person's life. Instead, it is believed that they diminish nervous tension. In some cases, nervous habits may serve a self-stimulatory function (Ellingson, Miltenberger, Stricker, Garlinghouse, et al., 2000; Rapp, Miltenberger, Galensky, Ellingson & Long, 1999; Woods & Miltenberger, 1996b). Nervous habits can occur while other voluntary functional activities are occurring. In most cases, nervous habits involve the use of the hands. They may also in-

Habit Behaviors	Examples
Nervous habits	Nail-biting, hair-pulling
Motor tics	Head-jerking, facial grimacing
Stuttering	Word repetitions, prolongations

volve oral behaviors such as lip-biting or bruxism, in which a person grinds or clenches the upper and lower teeth together.

Many nervous habits do not cause any problems for the person unless the frequency or the intensity of the behavior becomes extreme. For example, occasionally chewing on a pen or unfolding a paper clip presents no problem, but chewing on pens throughout the day or unfolding hundreds of paper clips a day is a problem because of the excessive frequency of the behavior. Likewise, occasional nail-biting or fingernail-picking might not be a problem for most people, but biting or picking until the nails bleed or hurt is a problem. Intensity is also a problem in hair-pulling: Although twirling or stroking hair might not be a problem, hair-pulling in which strands of hair are pulled out of the scalp is a problem. Likewise, bruxism in which teeth are damaged or pain is produced in the jaw muscles is a problem because of the intensity of the behavior. When the frequency or intensity of a nervous habit becomes extreme, people often seek help to eliminate it. Teng, Woods, Twohig, and Marcks (2002) have used the term *body-focused repetitive behavior problems* to refer to nervous habits (such as nail biting, skin picking, skin biting, skin scratching, and mouth biting) that result in physical damage or negative social evaluations.

Motor and Vocal Tics

Jose, the baseball player who snaps his head back, exhibits a motor tic. **Motor tics** are repetitive, jerking movements of a particular muscle group in the body. They usually involve muscles in the neck or face but may also involve the shoulders, arms, legs, or torso. Motor tics involving the neck might include movements of the head forward, backward, or to the side, rotating movements involving twisting of the neck, or some combination. Facial tics might include squinting, forceful blinking, eyebrow-raising, grimacing in which a corner of the mouth is pulled back, or some combination. Other types of motor tics might include shoulder-raising, jerking the arm to the side, torso-twisting, or other repetitive body movements.

Motor tics are believed to be associated with heightened muscle tension (Evers & Van de Wetering, 1994). Sometimes the development of a tic is related to an injury or an event that increases the tension in a particular muscle group, but the tic movements continue to occur once the original injury or event has passed (Azrin & Nunn, 1973). For example, a person with tension in the lower back might get relief by twisting the torso in a particular way. However, the person continues to engage in the torso-twisting long after the back problem is resolved. This would be an example of a tic. It is not uncommon for children to develop simple motor tics and then to grow out of them. Motor tics are a problem when they are long-standing or extreme in frequency or intensity. In such cases, people often seek treatment.

In addition to motor tics, some people exhibit vocal tics. A **vocal tic** is a repetitive vocal sound that does not serve a social function. Examples of vocal tics are throat-clearing when there is no reason to clear the throat and coughing when the person is not sick. Vocal tics may also involve other sounds or words. In one case, a grade school boy who had had a cold for a long period continued to cough and clear his throat frequently months after the cold was gone (Wagaman, Miltenberger, & Williams, 1995). Although the coughing and throat-clearing initially were related to the boy's cold, they would be classified as vocal tics when they continued to occur months later.

Tourette's disorder is a tic disorder involving multiple motor and vocal tics. Tourette's disorder and other tic disorders are currently believed to be caused by a complex interaction of a genetic and neurobiological factors as well as enviornmental events (Lechman & Cohen, 1999). A child is diagnosed with Tourette's disorder when two or more tics (including at least one vocal tic) occur for at least 1 year. Tourette's disorder is considered a lifelong disorder with an onset in childhood.

Stuttering

In our third example, Barbara exhibited **stuttering,** a type of speech dysfluency in which the person repeats words or syllables, prolongs the sound of a word or syllable, or blocks on a word (makes no sound for a period of time while trying to say a word). Stuttering may occur in young children as they are first learning to use language. However, most children grow out of it without a problem. Stuttering sometimes persists in children and adults in various degrees of severity. In some cases, it is barely noticeable; in others, it interferes with speech production. People often seek treatment when their stuttering is severe enough to draw attention to them as they speak.

Each of these habit disorders has been treated successfully with behavior modification procedures called habit reversal procedures (Miltenberger, Fuqua, & Woods, 1998; Miltenberger & Woods, 1998; Woods & Miltenberger, 1995, 2001).

HABIT REVERSAL PROCEDURES

Azrin and Nunn (1973) developed a treatment program for eliminating nervous habits and tics. They called the multicomponent treatment habit reversal. In subsequent research, Azrin and Nunn and numerous other researchers demonstrated the effectiveness of habit reversal procedures for treating a variety of habit disorders including nervous habits, tics, and stuttering (Azrin & Nunn, 1974, 1977; Azrin, Nunn, & Frantz, 1980a; Finney, Rapoff, Hall, & Christopherson, 1983; Miltenberger & Fuqua, 1985a; Wagaman, Miltenberger, & Arndorfer, 1993).

The habit reversal procedure is implemented in a therapy session with the client who exhibits the habit disorder. The client then implements the procedures that are taught in session to control the habit as it occurs outside the session. In the habit reversal procedure, the person with the habit (or tic or stuttering) is first taught to describe the behaviors that are involved in the habit. After learning the behavioral definition of the habit, the client learns to identify when the habit occurs or when it is about to occur. These procedures constitute the **awareness training** component of habit reversal. The client then learns a **competing response** (a behavior incompatible with the habit behavior) and practices the competing response in session after each occurrence of the habit. Next, the client imagines the situations in which he or she will use the competing response outside the session to inhibit the habit. Finally, the client is instructed to use the competing response outside the session whenever the habit occurs or is about to occur. These procedures constitute the **competing response training.** Significant others (such as a parent or spouse) are instructed to prompt the client to use the competing response when the habit occurs outside the session. They are also instructed to praise the client for not engaging in the habit and for using the competing response successfully. The involvement of the significant others is called **social**

Habit Reversal Components

- Awareness training
- Competing response training
- Social support
- Motivation procedures

support. Finally, the therapist reviews with the client all the situations in which the habit occurs and how the habit may have caused inconvenience or embarrassment. This review is a **motivation strategy,** which increases the likelihood that the client will use the competing response outside the treatment session to control the habit.

In the habit reversal therapy session, the client learns two basic skills: to discriminate each occurrence of the habit (awareness training) and to use the competing response contingent on the occurrence of the habit or in anticipation of the occurrence of the habit (competing response training). Awareness of the habit is a necessary condition for the use of the competing response. The client must be trained to become aware of each instance of the habit so that he or she can institute the competing response immediately. The competing response typically is an unobtrusive behavior (not easily identified by others) that the person engages in for 1–3 minutes. Significant others continue to help the client to use these skills through reminders and reinforcement outside the therapy session (social support).

Applications of Habit Reversal

The main difference between the habit reversal procedures for different types of habit disorders is the nature of the competing response. A different competing response must be chosen specifically for the particular habit, tic, or stuttering problem that the client exhibits. We now consider the different ways in which habit reversal is applied to the various types of habit disorders. (For a review of habit reversal procedures, see Woods & Miltenberger, 1995, 2001.)

Nervous Habits

A number of researchers have evaluated habit reversal for treating nervous habits (Azrin, Nunn, & Frantz-Renshaw, 1980, 1982; Miltenberger & Fuqua, 1985a; Nunn & Azrin, 1976; Rapp, Miltenberger, Long, Elliott, & Lumley, 1998; Rosenbaum & Ayllon, 1981a, 1981b; Twohig & Woods, 2002; Woods, Miltenberger, & Lumley, 1996b; Woods et al., 1999). The nervous habits treated with habit reversal procedures include fingernail-biting, hair-pulling, thumb-sucking, and oral habits such as lip-biting and bruxism. In each case, the competing response was a behavior that the subject could perform easily but that was physically incompatible with the nervous habit. For example, a competing response for a student who bites his fingernails in the classroom could be to grasp a pencil for 1–3 minutes or to clench his fists for 1–3 minutes. The student would first learn to identify each time that he started to bite his fingernails. As soon as he detected the nail-biting behavior (e.g., when his finger touched his teeth, when his hand was moving toward his mouth), he would immediately terminate the behavior and grasp the pencil. Because holding a pencil is a natural activity in a classroom, the competing response does not draw attention to the student. A similar competing response could be used for hair-pulling or any nervous habit involving the use of the hands. If the person is not in a classroom or if a pencil or pen is not available, a competing response for nail-biting or hair-pulling could be to make a fist and hold it by his side for 1–3 minutes or to put his hand in his pocket for 1–3 minutes. Alternatively, the student could sit on his hands, fold his arms across his chest, fold his hands in his lap, or occupy his hands in any way that physically prevents nail-biting.

For an oral habit such as lip-biting or bruxism, a competing response might be to hold the top and bottom teeth together lightly for a couple minutes, which would be incompatible with either behavior.

When habit reversal is used with children, the parent might use physical guidance to get the child to engage in the competing response. For example, in one case, a 5-year-old girl engaged in hair-pulling and nail-biting, usually when she was inactive (e.g., watching TV or sitting and waiting). The competing response was to fold her hands together and lay them in her lap. Her mother was instructed to say, "Hands in lap," and physically guide her daughter's hands to her lap whenever she saw her daughter pulling her hair or biting her nails. Before long, the daughter began to put her hands in her lap as soon as her mother said, "Hands in lap." Eventually, she started to put her hands in her lap as soon as she began to bite her nails or pull her hair. Whenever she was sitting with her hands in her lap, her mother praised her. Both habit behaviors decreased with the competing response treatment, which was implemented with the parent's assistance (social support).

Motor and Vocal Tics

Habit reversal procedures have been evaluated for treating motor and vocal tics (Azrin & Nunn, 1973; Azrin, Nunn, & Frantz, 1980b; Azrin & Peterson, 1989, 1990; Finney et al., 1983; Miltenberger, Fuqua, & McKinley, 1985; Sharenow, Fuqua, & Miltenberger, 1989; Woods, Miltenberger, & Lumley, 1996a; Woods & Twohig, 2002). The competing response used in habit reversal procedures with motor tics involves tensing the muscles involved in the tic such that the body part involved is held motionless (Carr, 1995). For example, Jose, the baseball player who engages in head-snapping, would tense his neck muscles to a moderate degree as he held his head in a forward position. He would first learn to discriminate each time that he exhibited the tic or anticipated that he was about to exhibit the tic. Then, contingent on the occurrence of the tic or in anticipation of it, he would engage in the competing response for a couple of minutes. Moderately tensing the neck muscles and holding the head straight is not an obtrusive behavior, so it should not draw attention to him. Azrin and Peterson (1990, page 310) described a competing response for vocal tics such as coughing, throat clearing, and barking noises: "Slow rhythmic deep breathing through the nose while keeping the mouth closed. Exhalation should be slightly longer than inhalation (e.g., 5 sec. inhalation, 7 sec. exhalation)." Azrin and Peterson showed that the habit reversal procedure can be used successfully to treat motor tics and vocal tics associated with Tourette disorder, which is thought to have a neurological cause and is sometimes treated with medication (Shapiro, Shapiro, Bruun, & Sweet, 1978). The

TABLE 21-1 Response Definitions and Competing Responses

Tic	Response Definition	Competing Response
Head-shaking	Any back-and-forth lateral movement of the head	Tensing the neck muscles while holding the chin down and in toward the neck
Eye-blinking	Any eyeblink occurring less than 3 seconds after the previous blink	Opening eyes wide and blinking deliberately every 5 seconds while shifting gaze about every 10 seconds
Facial tic	Any outward movement of the lips	Tightly pursing or pressing the lips together
Facial tic	Pulling back either or both corners of the mouth	Clenching the jaw while pressing the lips together with upward movement of the cheek(s)
Head-jerking	Any jerking downward motion of the head	As for head-shaking
Shoulder-jerking	Any jerking motion of either shoulder or arm with the arm moving upward or toward the body	Pressing arms tightly against the sides of the body while pulling the shoulders downward

Source: Miltenberger et al., 1985.

tics exhibited by most people are not associated with Tourette syndrome and are treated effectively with habit reversal procedures.

Miltenberger et al. (1985) applied habit reversal procedures to six different motor tics exhibited by nine people. Table 21-1 provides behavioral definitions of the six different motor tics and the competing responses used with these tics. In each case, the competing response involved tensing opposing muscles to inhibit the tic behaviors.

Stuttering

Many studies have documented the effectiveness of habit reversal procedures with stuttering (Azrin & Nunn, 1974; Azrin, Nunn, & Frantz, 1979; Elliott, Miltenberger, Rapp, Long, & McDonald, 1998; Ladoucher & Martineau, 1982; Miltenberger, Wagaman, & Arndorfer, 1996; Wagaman et al., 1993; Wagaman, Miltenberger, & Woods, 1995; Waterloo & Gotestam, 1988). The competing response used with stuttering is very different from the competing response used with nervous habits or tics. Because stuttering involves interrupted airflow through the vocal cords that interferes with the production of fluent speech, a competing response would involve relaxation and uninterrupted airflow over the vocal cords during speech. The competing response in the habit reversal procedure with stuttering is also called **regulated breathing.** Clients are first taught to detect each instance of stuttering. The clients learn to describe the types of stuttering they exhibit and, with the therapist's help, they identify each instance of stuttering as they speak in session. Once clients are aware of most occurrences of stuttering, the therapist teaches the regulated breathing.

The first component is a quick relaxation procedure called **diaphragmatic breathing.** The client learns to breathe in a rhythmic pattern using the muscles of the diaphragm to pull air deep into the lungs. As the client is breathing smoothly and rhythmically, the therapist instructs the client to say a word as he or she starts to exhale. Because the client is relaxed and the air is flowing over the larynx in an exhalation, the client does not stutter the word. This speaking pattern is incompatible with the pattern involved in stuttering. The client practices this pattern with one word, then two, then short sentences, and so on. If the client starts to stutter at any point, the client stops talking immediately, breathes diaphragmatically, starts the airflow, and continues speaking. The client is then instructed to practice this method of speaking outside the session. A significant other such as a parent or spouse provides social support by prompting the client to practice and by praising the client for speaking fluently. The success of the treatment depends on whether the client practices every day, detects most instances of stuttering, and uses the regulated breathing method reliably (Elliott et al., 1998; Miltenberger et al., 1996; Wagaman, Miltenberger, & Woods, 1995; Woods, Twohig, Fuqua, & Hanley, 2000). The results of stuttering treatment for four children are shown in Figure 21-1 (from Wagaman et al., 1993).

WHY DO HABIT REVERSAL PROCEDURES WORK?

Researchers have demonstrated that the components of the habit reversal procedure most responsible for its effectiveness in decreasing nervous habits, motor and vocal tics, and stuttering are awareness training and the use of a competing response (Elliott et al., 1998; Miltenberger & Fuqua, 1985a; Miltenberger et al., 1985; Rapp, Miltenberger, Long, Elliott, & Lumley, 1998; Wagaman et al., 1993; Woods et al., 1996a). Awareness training is a critical component because the client must be able to discriminate each instance of the nervous habit, tic, or stuttering to implement the competing response. The use of the competing response then serves two possible functions. One function is to inhibit the habit behavior and provide an alternative behavior to replace it. A second is that the competing response may serve as a punisher, as in the application of aversive activities such as overcorrection and contingent exercise (Chapter 18).

Research by Miltenberger and his colleagues (Miltenberger & Fuqua, 1985a; Miltenberger et al., 1985; Sharenow et al., 1989, and Woods, Murray, Fuqua, Seif, Boyer, & Siah, 1999) suggests that the competing response does serve as a punisher in the case of motor tics and nervous habits. They found that the competing response was effective in decreasing habits and tics when it was contingent on the habit or tic but that the competing response did not have to be incompatible with the habit or tic. In other words, if the client engaged in some moderately effortful behavior (tensing a set of muscles for 3 minutes) contingent on an instance of the habit or tic, the habit or tic would decrease regardless of whether the behavior was related to the habit or tic. For example, when a person with a facial tic engaged in a competing response that involved tensing the bicep contingent on each instance of the facial tic, the frequency of the facial tic decreased (Sharenow et al., 1989). It should be noted, however, that awareness training was always used in conjunction with the competing response. Therefore, the effects of awareness training without the competing response cannot be determined. Ladoucher (1979) suggests that it is the increase in awareness of the habit or tic that is responsible for the success of the habit reversal procedure.

Awareness training was effective in decreasing motor tics without the addition of a competing response for three people: a college student (Wright & Miltenberger, 1987) and two grade school students (Ollendick, 1981; Woods et al., 1996a). In all three

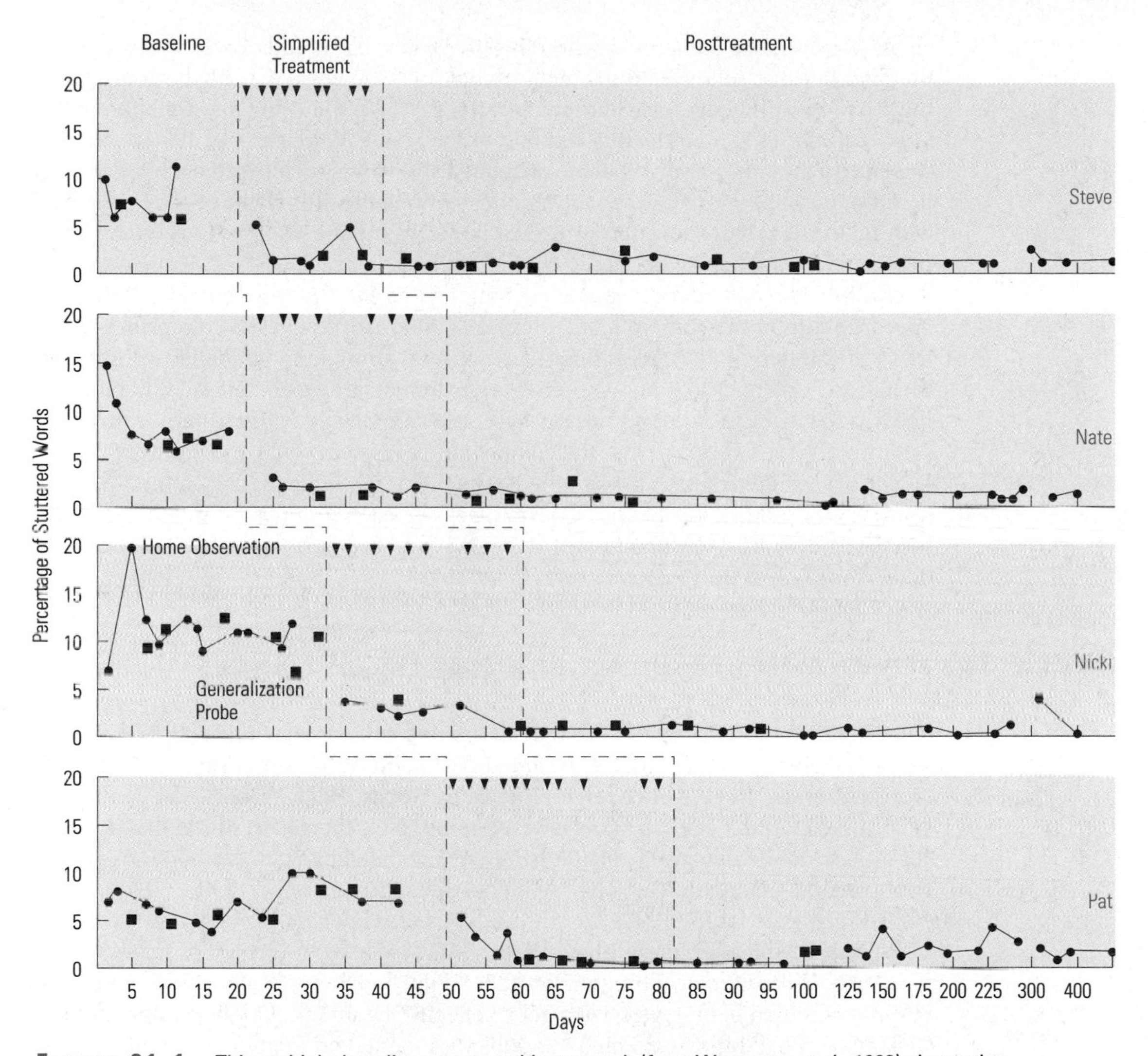

FIGURE 21-1 This multiple-baseline-across-subjects graph (from Wagaman et al., 1993) shows the percentage of stuttered words exhibited by four children before and after treatment. The treatment consisted of awareness training, competing response training, and social support from the parents. Stuttering decreased to low levels for all children once treatment was implemented. The round data points are from observations of stuttering at the child's home, and the square data points are from school observations. The school observations were conducted to measure generalization of changes in stuttering from home to school. During the simplified treatment phase, the arrowheads indicate days on which treatment sessions were implemented.

cases, however, the subjects engaged in self-monitoring in addition to the awareness training. Because self-monitoring requires the subject to engage in a behavior (recording the tic) contingent on each instance of the tic, self-monitoring may function in the same manner as the competing response. One study (Woods et al., 1996a) demonstrated that awareness training alone decreased and virtually eliminated a head-jerking tic for one child but that awareness training was not effective for three other children with motor tics. More research is needed to determine the effects of awareness training in decreasing habits and tics.

In the case of stuttering, awareness training and the use of a competing response appear to inhibit the stuttering and provide an alternative behavior to replace stuttering. With stuttering, the competing response is not a simple motor behavior involving the tensing of a muscle group; rather, it is an alternative speech pattern. Clients practice this speech pattern each time they talk, as an alternative to the pattern involved in stuttering. With habits and tics, the competing response is used contingent on the behavior; with stuttering, by contrast, the competing response is used each time the person speaks, in addition to being used contingent on each instance of stuttering. Therefore, it appears that the function of the competing response for habits and tics may differ from its function for stuttering.

Other Treatment Procedures for Habit Disorders

Habit reversal procedures have been demonstrated consistently to be effective in treating habit disorders and are the preferred treatment approach (Friman, Finney, & Christopherson, 1984; Miltenberger, Fuqua, & Woods, 1998; Woods & Miltenberger, 1995, 1996a; Woods et al., 2000). However, some researchers have shown that habit reversal may not be effective for habit behaviors exhibited by young children or people with mental retardation (Long, Miltenberger, Ellingson, & Ott, 1999; Long, Miltenberger, & Rapp, 1999; Rapp, Miltenberger, Galensky, Roberts, & Ellingson, 1999; Rapp, Miltenberger, & Long, 1998).

Long, Miltenberger, Ellingson, and Ott (1999) and Rapp, Miltenberger, and Long (1998) found that habit reversal was not an effective treatment for hair-pulling, thumb-sucking, and nail-biting exhibited by adults with mental retardation. After habit reversal was ineffective, Rapp, Miltenberger, and Long (1998) evaluated an awareness enhancement device that sounded an alarm each time a woman with mental retardation reached up to pull her hair. The woman wore a small electronic device on her wrist and near her neck. When she raised her hand to pull her hair, the device detected the movement and activated the alarm. The alarm then stopped when she moved her hand away from her head. The use of this device eliminated her hair-pulling. Ellingson, Miltenberger, Stricker, Garlinghouse, et al. (2000); Stricker et al. (2000); and Stricker, Miltenberger, Garlinghouse, & Tulloch (2003) also showed that the awareness enhancement device was an effective treatment for thumb-sucking and finger-sucking in children.

Long, Miltenberger, Ellingson, and Ott (1999) used differential reinforcement of other behavior (DRO) and response cost to eliminate thumb-sucking and nail-biting exhibited by adults with mental retardation after habit reversal did not eliminate the

TABLE 21-2 Other Behavior Modification Procedures used with Habit Disorders

Treatment Procedure	Habit Disorder	Authors
Aversive taste treatment	Thumb-sucking	Friman & Hove (1987)
Response prevention	Thumb-sucking	Watson & Allen (1993)
Response prevention and DRO (various reinforcers)	Thumb-sucking	Van Houten & Rolider (1984)
DRO (candy)	Thumb-sucking	Hughes, Hughes, & Dial (1979)
DRO (money)	Verbal tics	Wagaman, Miltenberger, & Williams (1995)
Time-out	Verbal tic	Lahey, McNees, & McNees (1973)
Time-out	Stuttering	James (1981)
Time-out and token reinforcement	Hair-pulling	Evans (1976)
Response cost	Stuttering	Halvorson (1971)
Response cost and token reinforcement	Stuttering	Ingham & Andrews (1973)
Contingent slap and token reinforcement	Hair-pulling	Gray (1979)
Snapping rubber band on wrist	Hair-pulling	Mastellone (1974)
Behavioral contracting	Hair-pulling	Stabler & Warren (1974)

behaviors. Long observed the clients via video from a separate room, and when the habit did not occur for a period of time, Long entered the room and delivered a reinforcer (e.g., a token). When the habit was observed to occur, Long entered the room and removed one of the reinforcers. Long, Miltenberger, and Rapp (1999) used a similar procedure to eliminate thumb-sucking and hair-pulling exhibited by a 6-year-old after habit reversal was ineffective. Similarly, Rapp, Miltenberger, Galensky, Roberts, and Ellingson (1999) found that DRO and social disapproval for thumb-sucking greatly decreased the behavior for a 5-year-old after habit reversal was not effective.

In other studies, response prevention was found to eliminate hair pulling and finger sucking by children (Deaver, Miltenberger, & Stricker, 2001; Ellingson, Miltenberger, Stricker, et al., 2000). For example, Deaver and colleagues (2001) used response prevention with a young child who twirled and pulled her hair when she was lying in her bed at night or at nap time. Each time the girl went to bed, her parents or the daycare provider placed thin mittens on her hands, and the mittens prevented hair twirling or pulling from occuring.

Finally, Rapp, Miltenberger, et al. (2000) found DRO, response interruption, and brief restraint to be an effective treatment for hair-pulling exhibited by an adolescent with mental retardation. Rapp provided praise for the absence of hair-pulling and, each time the client started to pull her hair, Rapp interrupted the response and held her arm at her side for 30 seconds.

In addition to the procedures described here, various other behavior modification procedures, based on differential reinforcement, antecedent control, and punishment, have been evaluated for habit disorder treatment. Examples of these procedures are listed in Table 21-2.

Chapter Summary

1. Habit behaviors are repetitive, automatically reinforced behaviors that often occur outside of the person's awareness; that is, the person does not discriminate each instance of the behavior. When the frequency or intensity of a habit behavior becomes extreme, it may be considered a habit disorder.
2. Nervous habits, tics, and stuttering are three categories of habit behaviors.
3. Habit reversal procedures consist of a number of treatment components, including awareness training to teach the person to discriminate each instance of the habit behavior, the use of a competing response contingent on the habit behavior, and social support procedures that motivate the person to continue using the competing response to eliminate the habit behavior.
4. For each category of habit behavior, the competing response is different. For motor tics, the person engages in a competing response by tensing the muscles involved in the tic. For a nervous habit, the person engages in an incompatible behavior using the muscles used in performing the habit behavior (e.g., holding an object to compete with nail-biting). In a competing response for stuttering, the person engages in an incompatible pattern of breathing and speaking called regulated breathing.
5. The effectiveness of habit reversal procedures is related to the use of the competing response, which functions as a punisher (for habits and tics) or as an alternative behavior to replace the habit behavior (in the case of stuttering). The effectiveness of increased awareness by itself has not been fully investigated.

Practice Test

1. What is a habit disorder? How do habit disorders differ from other problem behaviors discussed in this book? (p. 453)
2. What are nervous habits? Provide examples of various nervous habits. (pp. 454–455)
3. What are motor tics? What are vocal tics? How do tics differ from nervous habits? Provide examples of various types of motor tics. (p. 455)
4. Describe the different types of speech dysfluencies involved in stuttering. (p. 456)
5. Describe the habit reversal procedure. (pp. 456–457)
6. Describe the competing response that would be used for a nervous habit of knuckle-cracking. (pp. 457–458)
7. Describe the competing response that would be used with bruxism. (p. 458)
8. Describe the competing response that would be used with a motor tic involving head-jerking. What competing response would be used with a vocal tic such as throat-clearing? (pp. 458–459)
9. Describe regulated breathing, the competing response that is used with stuttering. (pp. 459–460)
10. What is involved in the social support component of the habit reversal procedure? (p. 456)
11. Describe awareness training. What is its purpose? (pp. 456, 460)
12. What are the two possible functions of the competing response in the habit reversal procedure? How does the function of the competing response for nervous habits and tics differ from its function for stuttering? (pp. 460, 462)
13. Name some of the other reinforcement and punishment procedures that have been used to eliminate habit disorders. (pp. 462–463)

Applications

1. Describe how you would implement habit reversal procedures in your own self-management project. If habit reversal procedures are not appropriate for your self-management project, explain why not.

2. Vicki is a college student who exhibits an eyeblink tic. The tic is more prevalent when she is around other people, especially in evaluative situations such as classes in which she is expected to participate actively. The tic involves rapid eyeblinking and squinting movements. Describe the implementation of the habit reversal procedure for this motor tic.

3. Dominic is a 4-year-old boy with a number of older brothers and sisters. Dominic began to stutter a couple of months ago. His stuttering involves repeating words or syllables. For example, he might say, "It's my-my-my turn to go next," or "I want more a-a-a-applesauce." He is most likely to stutter when he is excited. His siblings have made fun of him when he stutters and sometimes his parents finish his words or sentences for him. If this family came to you for advice, what would you advise them to do to help Dominic decrease his stuttering?

4. Tanya is a 5-year-old who sucks her thumb during the day when she is watching TV or not actively engaged in an activity and then as she falls asleep and at intervals throughout the night. Describe how the parents could use a differential reinforcement procedure and an antecedent control procedure (response prevention) to decrease Tanya's thumb-sucking at night and during the day.

Misapplications

1. Harvey saw a psychologist for a habit disorder involving hair-pulling. He was taught the habit reversal procedure, in which he became aware of each occurrence of the hair-pulling and learned to engage in a competing response involving grasping an object with his hands each time he pulled his hair. Harvey was an engineering student and found a couple of his classes particularly difficult. He decided that he couldn't take the time or energy to be aware of the hair-pulling and use the competing response in his two hardest classes. He used the procedures faithfully at other times, however. What is wrong with this use of habit reversal?

2. Shortly after Darlene moved with her family to another part of the country, she started to cough and clear her throat frequently. Her parents gave her cold medicine for a week but the coughing and throat-clearing did not decrease. After another few weeks, Darlene was still engaging in these behaviors. Her parents decided to use a habit reversal procedure in which they taught Darlene to become aware of each instance of coughing and throat-clearing and to engage in a competing response. They also implemented a DRO procedure and provided reinforcers for periods of time in which Darlene did not cough or clear her throat. What is wrong with the use of the habit reversal and DRO procedures in this case?

3. Marcus, a 10-year-old boy with severe mental retardation, lived at home with his family. Marcus engaged in a number of disruptive behaviors that were reinforced by his parents' attention. Because the problems were not too severe, his parents had not sought treatment for them. Marcus also had a nervous habit in which he bit his fingernails. The parents decided to use habit reversal procedures for the nail-biting. However, because of Marcus' intellectual disability, the parents would have to prompt the competing response each time Marcus bit his

nails. Whenever they observed nail-biting, one of the parents immediately walked up to him and said, "No nail-biting, Marcus," and placed his hands together in his lap. The parent held his hands together in his lap for 1–2 minutes, explained to him why nail-biting was bad for him, and told him he should hold his hands together instead of putting his fingers into his mouth. What is wrong with the use of the habit reversal procedure in this case?

CHAPTER 21 *Quiz 1* Name:

1. What are the three types of habit behaviors? ____________, ____________, and ____________.
2. When a habit behavior occurs frequently or with high intensity and leads the person to seek treatment, the habit behavior may be seen as a(n) ____________.
3. What is an example of a body-focused repetitive behavior problem? ____________
4. A(n) ____________ is a behavior that is incompatible with the habit behavior.
5. ____________ is a tic disorder involving multiple motor and vocal tics.
6. Describe the competing response that could be used for an individual with a motor tic involving twisting the head to the side. ____________
7. The competing response in the habit reversal treatment for stuttering is also called ____________.
8. In the social support procedure, what is the significant other supposed to do when the client engages in the habit behavior? ____________
9. In the social support procedure, what is the significant other supposed to do when the client is not engaging in the habit behavior or when the client uses the competing response?

   ____
10. Research has shown that habit reversal may not be effective for habit behavior exhibited by ____________.

CHAPTER 21 *Quiz 2*

Name:

1. Provide an example of a nervous habit ______________________ and provide an example of a motor tic. ______________________
2. ______________________ is used to treat nervous habits, tics, and stuttering.
3. Provide an example of two different competing responses that might be used in the treatment of nail biting. ______________________ and ______________________
4. What are the four major components of the habit reversal procedure?

   ______________________, ______________________, ______________________, and ______________________
5. When does a habit behavior become a habit disorder?

   ____
6. The competing response for ______________________ involves slow, rhythmic deep breathing through the nose while keeping the mouth closed.
7. Research has shown that the habit reversal components most responsible for its effectiveness are ______________________ and ______________________.
8. In competing response training, the person learns to engage in a(n) ______________________ each time the habit behavior occurs or is about to occur.
9. In awareness training what does the client learn to do?

   ____
10. One way that the competing response may work in habit reversal is to inhibit the habit behavior and provide a(n) ______________________.

CHAPTER 21 *Quiz 3* Name:

1. Nervous habits, tics, and stuttering are three types of ____________________.

2. Provide an example of a vocal tic. ____________________

3. What behaviors are involved in stuttering? ____________________

____

4. In the habit reversal procedure, ____________________ is the treatment component in which the person learns to identify each occurrence of the habit behavior.

5. In the habit reversal procedure, ____________________ is the treatment component in which the person learns to engage in an incompatible behavior contingent on the occurrence of the habit.

6. In the habit reversal procedure, ____________________ is the treatment component in which significant others help the client use the competing response outside of the therapy session through reminders and reinforcement.

7. In habit reversal, what does the therapist do as a motivational strategy to increase the likelihood that the client will use the competing response outside of the treatment session?

____

8. The use of the competing response in habit reversal serves two possible functions. One is to inhibit the habit and provide an alternative behavior to replace it. Alternatively, the competing response may serve as a(n) ____________________ for the habit behavior.

9. Identify two procedures other than habit reversal that may be effective for treating habit disorders. ____________________ and ____________________

10. How might you use response prevention to treat hair pulling exhibited by a young child while she is in bed at night? ____________________

TWENTY-TWO

The Token Economy

This chapter will describe a behavior modification program in which conditioned reinforcers are used systematically to strengthen the desirable behaviors of individuals participating in educational or treatment programs. Consider the following example.

Rehabilitating Sammy

Sammy, a 14-year-old girl, was placed in a treatment program for juvenile offenders because she had been involved in vandalism, burglary, and assault. The goal of the residential treatment program was to teach and maintain desirable prosocial behaviors in the residents and to eliminate antisocial behaviors similar to those that had resulted in their placement. Each resident was expected to engage in a number of desirable behaviors on a daily basis. These included getting out of bed on time, showering, grooming, making their beds, attending meals on time, attending classes on time, completing assigned chores (such as meal preparation and cleanup), attending group treatment sessions, and getting to bed on time. These prosocial behaviors were listed for the residents on a card they carried with them and were monitored by the program counselors. Each resident received a point for completing each behavior on a daily basis. Whenever the counselor saw the resident engage in the behaviors, the counselor added points to the resident's card and also recorded the points on a master list. The residents exchanged the points that they earned for privileges such as playing video games, pinball, or pool in the game room; later bedtimes; supervised outings away from the program; extra TV time; and passes for unsupervised leaves for the day. These privileges could be obtained only for points earned for prosocial behavior.

- What is a token economy?
- What steps are involved in implementing a token economy?
- When would you decide to use response cost as part of a token economy?
- What items might you use as tokens in a token economy?
- What are the advantages and disadvantages of a token economy?

In addition to their use as reinforcers for prosocial behaviors, points were taken away as a punisher for antisocial behavior exhibited by the residents. Point loss was a response cost procedure. The residents all received a list of antisocial behaviors that would result in the loss of points and the number of points that would be lost. For example, points were lost for swearing, fighting, stealing, lying, gang-related talk or action, cheating in class, threatening or assaulting a counselor, leaving without permission, and coming back late from an outing. Whenever a resident engaged in an antisocial behavior, the counselor took the resident's card and crossed off the points that were lost for that infraction. The counselor also recorded the point loss on the master list.

As Sammy progressed through the program, she engaged in more prosocial behaviors on a daily basis because these behaviors resulted in points and praise from the counselors. Initially, she engaged in a number of antisocial behaviors, such as swearing, threatening, fighting, and cheating in class, but these behaviors decreased over time as she lost points and, therefore, lost privileges each time they occurred. Once Sammy was receiving the maximum number of points for the day with no point loss for 2 consecutive weeks, she was allowed to stop carrying her card and was given free access to the game room and the TV. Counselors continued to monitor her behavior and praise her for prosocial behavior. If she failed to continue the prosocial behavior or started to exhibit antisocial behavior, the privileges were revoked and she carried the card once again and had to earn points for the privileges. Again, after 2 weeks of maximum points and no point loss, she stopped carrying the card and got free access to the game room and TV. For each additional 2 weeks that she went without problems, more privileges were added (such as hour passes from the program, outings, full day passes, overnight passes, and full weekend passes). After Sammy had displayed prosocial behaviors for 4 months without any problems, she was released from the program, with weekly follow-up by a counselor in her home.

Defining a Token Economy

This example illustrates a **token economy** used with adolescents in a residential treatment program. The purpose of a token economy is to strengthen clients' desirable behaviors that occur too infrequently and to decrease their undesirable behaviors in a structured treatment environment or educational setting. Each point received by the adolescents for desirable behavior is a **token.** A token is delivered immediately after a desirable behavior and is later exchanged for **backup reinforcers.** Because the token is paired with other reinforcers, it becomes a conditioned reinforcer that strengthens the desirable behavior it follows. Backup reinforcers can be obtained only by paying for them with tokens, and tokens can be obtained only by exhibiting desirable behaviors. The backup reinforcers are chosen because they are known to be powerful reinforcers for the clients in the treatment environment and, therefore, the clients are motivated to engage in the desirable behaviors and avoid the undesirable behaviors.

The following are basic components of a token economy:

- The desirable target behaviors to be strengthened
- The tokens to be used as conditioned reinforcers
- The backup reinforcers to be exchanged for the tokens
- A reinforcement schedule for token delivery
- The rate at which tokens are exchanged for the backup reinforcers

- A time and place for exchanging tokens for backup reinforcers
- In some cases, a response cost component, in which the undesirable target behaviors to be eliminated are identified, along with the rate of token loss for each instance of these behaviors

Table 22-1 shows the components of the token economy for Sammy.

TABLE 22-1 Components of the Token Economy for Sammy

Target Behaviors (Positive)	Points Earned	Target Behaviors (Negative)	Points Lost
Out of bed at 7 A.M.	2	Swearing	1
Shower	1	Yelling, threatening others	1
Hair combed	1	Fighting	4
Clean clothes	1	Stealing	4
Bed made	1	Lying	4
Breakfast on time	1	Gang talk	2
Class on time (morning)	1	Gang actions	2
Lunch on time	1	Cheating in class	4
Class on time (afternoon)	1	Threatening a counselor	1
Group counseling on time	1	Assaulting a counselor	5
Completed chore	1	Leaving without permission	5
Room clean at bedtime	1	Back late from an outing	3
In bed on time	1	Each hour gone or late	2
Completed homework	6		
Total daily points	20		
Extra Points			
A on a test	10		
A on a quiz	5		
B on a test	5		
B on a quiz	2		

Backup Reinforcers	Cost
30 minutes of pool	10
30 minutes of video games	10
30 minutes of computer games	10
30 minutes of pinball	10
30 minutes of Ping-Pong	10
30 minutes of TV	10
Movie rental	15
Choice of chore	5
Outing (supervised)	10
■ Dairy Queen	
■ Miniature golf	
■ Fast food	
■ Other	

Privilege Level and Criterion Behavior

1. Free access to game room: 2 weeks at maximum daily points
2. Daily one-hour pass: 4 weeks at maximum daily points
3. Full day pass (Saturday or Sunday): 6 weeks at maximum daily points
4. Overnight pass (Friday or Saturday): 8 weeks at maximum daily points
5. Full weekend passes: 10 weeks at maximum daily points

IMPLEMENTING A TOKEN ECONOMY

After deciding to use a token economy to strengthen desirable behaviors of clients in a treatment program, you must plan the components of the token economy carefully to ensure the success of the program. Let's examine those components one by one.

Defining the Target Behaviors

The purpose of the token economy is to strengthen desirable behaviors in clients; therefore, the first step in planning the token economy is to identify and define the desirable behaviors that will be reinforced in the program. In the case of Sammy, the target behaviors were prosocial behaviors that adolescents need to function effectively with their families and peers; they were behaviors that demonstrated responsible living within the norms or rules of society. The target behaviors will vary in a token economy depending on the people being treated and the nature of the treatment environment. Target behaviors might include academic skills in an educational setting, vocational skills in a work setting, self-help skills in a rehabilitation setting, and social skills in a residential setting. The main criterion for choosing the target behaviors is that they are socially significant or meaningful for the people involved in the program.

Once the target behaviors have been identified, it is important to define them carefully. Objective behavioral definitions of the target behaviors ensure that the clients know what behaviors are expected of them. Behavioral definitions of the target behaviors are also important, so that the change agents can record the behaviors and implement the token reinforcement reliably.

Identifying the Items to Use as Tokens

The token must be something tangible that the change agent can deliver immediately after each instance of the target behaviors. Tokens must be practical and convenient for the change agent to carry and to dispense in the treatment environment when the target behaviors occur. They must be in a form that clients can accumulate and, in most cases, carry with them. In some cases, clients may accumulate tokens but not keep the tokens in their possession. Examples might include check marks on a chart on the wall, points on a chalkboard, or poker chips kept in a container at the nurse's station. In the case of Sammy, points on a card carried by the adolescents were used as tokens. The point written on the card is tangible, easily dispensed by the change agent, and easily accumulated by the adolescent in the program.

Identify some other items that could be used as tokens in a token economy.

Some of the many possibilities are listed in Table 22-2.

The tokens chosen should not be available from any source other than the change agent. Tokens are not very effective if clients can get them from outside sources. This means that the change agents must prevent clients from stealing tokens from one another or from the change agents, counterfeiting tokens, and acquiring tokens from other sources within or outside of the program.

In Sammy's case, the counselors wrote points on the adolescents' cards as tokens, which were delivered for desirable behavior. As a precaution, the counselor also marked the number of points down on a master list for each adolescent. In this way,

TABLE 22-2 Examples of Tokens Used in Token Economies

Examples of Tokens Used in Token Economies
Poker chips
Smiley faces
Pennies or other coins
Replicas of dollar bills
Stamps, stickers, or stars
Check marks on an index card
Check marks on the chalk board
Beads, marbles
Plastic or cardboard cut into geometric shapes (circles, squares, etc.)
Printed cards or coupons
Hole punches in a card
An ink stamp on a card
Puzzle pieces that can be accumulated and put together in a puzzle

there was a separate record of the points earned by each adolescent in the program. If an adolescent tried to add points to his or her own card, this would be detected and dealt with by the counselor.

Identifying Backup Reinforcers

Tokens acquire their effectiveness as conditioned reinforcers because they are paired with the backup reinforcers; therefore, the effectiveness of a token economy depends on the backup reinforcers. Because different reinforcers are effective for different people, backup reinforcers must be chosen specifically for the people in the treatment program (Maag, 1999). Backup reinforcers may include consumables such as snacks or drinks; toys or other tangible objects; activity reinforcers such as games, videos, or TV time; and privileges. In the case of Sammy, the backup reinforcers were mostly activity reinforcers that are desirable to the adolescents participating in the program. See Table 22-3 for examples of backup reinforcers for elementary school students and Table 22-4 for examples of backup reinforcers for adolescents (Maag, 1999).

Backup reinforcers are not available to the clients except for purchase with tokens. Limiting access to the backup reinforcers increases their reinforcing value because a relative state of deprivation is established. However, clients cannot be deprived of the things to which they have a right. Such basic rights as nutritious meals, a comfortable physical environment, freedom from harm, reasonable leisure activities, training activities, and reasonable freedom of movement cannot be taken away from a person and used in a token economy. The reinforcers used in a token economy must be those that are above and beyond the client's basic needs or rights. For example, although a person cannot be deprived of a nutritious meal, the person might be able to exchange tokens for a special meal or dessert or snack. Likewise, although a person cannot be deprived of reasonable leisure activities (e.g., access to library books or exercise equipment), the person might be able to exchange tokens for access to video games, movies, or time in a game room with a pool table and Ping-Pong.

TABLE 22-3 Examples of Backup Reinforcers for Elementary School-Age Children

Listening to music	Choosing a game for the class
Cutting and pasting	Moving desk
Finger painting	Eating lunch with teacher
Playing marbles	Extra free time
Showing hobby to classmates	Visiting the nurse
Reading a story out loud to classmates	Reading morning announcements
Visiting another class	Having a project displayed
Running an errand	Erasing the chalkboard
Helping the librarian	Positive note home to parents
Getting first selection of recess toys	Using a learning center
Decorating bulletin board	Calling home
Borrowing a book	Visiting the principal
Leading student groups	

TABLE 22-4 Examples of Backup Reinforcers for Adolescents

Listening to music	Sitting out an activity
Writing a note to a friend	Moving desk
Borrowing a book	Telling a secret to a friend
Watching a music video	Making a phone call
Talking to a friend	Eating a snack or drinking a pop
Showing hobby to classmates	Getting free time
Eating lunch with a friend	Playing a game
Delivering a note to a friend	Excused from a quiz
Using the gym equipment after school	Visiting another class
Choosing an activity for the class	Rearranging the room
Running the film projector	Playing a computer game
Running an errand	Working on a hobby
Helping a teacher	Excused from homework assignment

Deciding on the Appropriate Schedule of Reinforcement

The change agents deliver tokens contingent on instances of the desirable target behaviors. Before the token economy is implemented, they must determine the schedule of reinforcement for token delivery. Often the program begins with continuous reinforcement, in which each instance of the target behaviors results in the delivery of a token. Later, after the target behaviors are occurring with more regularity, an intermittent reinforcement schedule, such as a fixed ratio (FR) or variable ratio schedule, may be incorporated to maintain the behavior. For example, suppose that a student in a special education class receives a token for every correct answer during a one-to-one training session. As the student's performance improves, the trainer may implement an FR 2 schedule and then increase the ratio further until the student receives a token for every fifth or every tenth correct response (FR 5 and FR 10, respectively), depending on the student's ability.

It is important to ensure that the student earns enough tokens in the early phases of the token economy so that he or she can exchange them for backup reinforcers regularly. In this way, the tokens acquire their value as conditioned reinforcers quickly, and the student receives reinforcement for desirable target behaviors.

Establishing the Token Exchange Rate

The backup reinforcers must be purchased with tokens earned for desirable behaviors; thus, each backup reinforcer must have a price, or the rate at which tokens are exchanged for them. Smaller items are exchanged for fewer tokens and larger items for more tokens. In addition, the change agents must determine the maximum number of tokens that the client can earn in a day and set the exchange rate accordingly. The exchange rate must be such that the client can acquire some backup reinforcers for exhibiting a reasonable level of desirable behavior but does not acquire so much of the reinforcers that satiation occurs. Setting the exchange rate is a matter of striking a balance for each person participating in the token economy. Often the change agents must adjust the exchange rate after beginning a token economy to produce the best results.

For example, if Sammy could earn a maximum of 15 points a day for perfect behavior in the adolescent treatment program but an hour of TV time cost 30 points, she would have to have two perfect days just to watch an hour of TV. In addition, she would not have any points left to purchase other backup reinforcers. She would not have access to reinforcers often enough with this stringent exchange rate. On the other hand, if an hour of TV cost 2 points and other reinforcers cost 1–2 points, Sammy would not have to engage in much desirable prosocial behavior to earn a variety of reinforcers each day. This exchange rate would be too lenient and would not motivate Sammy to engage in much prosocial behavior.

Establishing the Time and Place for Exchanging Tokens

The clients accumulate tokens for desirable behavior over time as they participate in the treatment program. Periodically, the clients are allowed to exchange their tokens for backup reinforcers. The time and place for exchange are planned in advance. In some cases, there is a token store, that is, a specific room where backup reinforcers are stored. The clients earning tokens do not have access to this room except at designated times. At the designated times, the clients come to the token store and look at the various backup reinforcers that are available for purchase. When they decide what they want to purchase, they exchange the appropriate number of tokens and receive the items. This process may vary depending on the nature of the token economy for a particular program. In some cases, the token store may be open for hours at a time, and the clients can choose when they want to make a purchase with their tokens. Sometimes there is no token store at all. Rather, the client identifies a specific activity or privilege that he or she would like to purchase and makes the arrangement with the staff running the program. For example, when Sammy had enough tokens to purchase TV time, she notified a staff person and made an arrangement to watch TV at the particular time that her favorite show was on. The staff person met her at the TV room at that time and let her in to watch the show.

In a psychiatric hospital, patients who earn tokens for appropriate behavior may exchange their tokens for snacks, soft drinks, cigarettes, and other items at a hospital canteen. The canteen is a small store that is open a few hours a day at specified times. The patients save their tokens and go to the canteen during business hours to buy the items (backup reinforcers) they want. They cannot get these items anywhere except at the canteen during business hours.

In a special education classroom, students receive poker chips for correct academic performance. Once in the morning and once in the afternoon, the students take their poker chips to the token store to exchange for backup reinforcers. The token store is in a converted storeroom. It contains toys, games, edibles, and vouchers for activities. Each item has a price attached. One at a time, the students go into the token store, choose an item, and buy it by giving the correct number of tokens to the storekeeper (the teacher's aide). The poker chips maintain their value as conditioned reinforcers because they are regularly paired with backup reinforcers. In addition, the students use math skills when they buy items from the store with their tokens.

Although the arrangements may vary between token economies, some specific arrangement must be made in advance for the time and place that tokens can be exchanged for backup reinforcers. Creating such a structure in advance results in more consistent implementation of the program.

Deciding Whether to Use Response Cost

A response cost component is not always used with a token economy. If the goal of the token economy is to strengthen desirable behaviors and there are no competing problem behaviors, the token economy will not include a response cost component. If there are undesirable behaviors that compete with the desirable behaviors, response cost may be included in the token economy.

When a response cost program is included, it should be introduced after the token economy has been in place for a period of time. The loss of tokens in the response cost component will be effective as a punisher only after the tokens have been firmly established as conditioned reinforcers for the participants.

Response cost is used only if the change agent can get the tokens back. If clients resist or become aggressive when the change agent attempts to take back tokens, it may be impossible to use response cost. In such cases, the change agent may consider the use of different tokens that the clients do not keep in their possession (e.g., points on a chart or on the chalkboard). This may prevent a struggle or aggressive behavior during the use of response cost.

To implement response cost, the change agents must define the undesirable target behaviors they hope to decrease and the number of tokens that will be lost for an instance of each identified problem behavior. The problem behaviors identified for inclusion in the response cost program must be socially significant problems that warrant the use of the response cost. The number of tokens lost for each instance of a problem behavior is determined by the severity of the problem, the number of tokens that the client can earn in a day, and the cost of the backup reinforcers. The loss of tokens in the response cost program must result in less opportunity to purchase backup reinforcers but must not result in the loss of all tokens (except for very serious problem behaviors). The loss of all tokens through response cost would negate the positive reinforcement of the desirable behaviors because the client does not have tokens to exchange for backup reinforcers. In addition, if a client loses all of the accumulated tokens through response cost, problem behaviors may continue because the client has nothing left to lose.

Staff Training and Management

Before a token economy is implemented for the first time, staff must receive training in its proper use. Written instructions in all components of the program and behavioral skills training are needed to conduct the program as planned. As new staff members are hired, each must undergo similar training. Supervisors or managers must monitor the implementation and provide appropriate staff management procedures (such as praise, feedback, or retraining) to ensure consistent implementation over time.

A token economy must be implemented consistently if it is to result in improvements in the target behaviors. This means that the staff must fulfill the following responsibilities:

- Discriminate each instance of all of the target behaviors
- Deliver tokens immediately after the target behavior, according to the correct schedule of reinforcement
- Discriminate each instance of all identified problem behaviors
- Implement response cost immediately when problem behaviors occur
- Preserve the integrity of the tokens and prevent theft or counterfeiting
- Know the exchange rate and times and adhere to the rules of exchange

PRACTICAL CONSIDERATIONS

In addition to the basic components of the token economy already described, successful implementation of a token economy depends on certain other considerations.

First, the change agent should always deliver the tokens immediately after the desirable target behavior. The portability and ease of delivery of tokens allows the change agent to reinforce desirable behaviors immediately after they occur.

Second, the change agent should praise the client while delivering the tokens for desirable behavior. Praise is a natural conditioned reinforcer for most people and becomes more potent as a reinforcer when paired with tokens. Once the token reinforcement is discontinued, the change agents will continue to deliver praise as a reinforcer for the desirable behavior.

Third, for young children or individuals with severe intellectual disabilities, early in the program, backup reinforcers should be given to the client at the same time the token is given so that the pairing is immediate and the token is more likely to become a conditioned reinforcer.

Finally, because a token economy is artificial and not found in most everyday environments, such as school, work, and home settings, it should always be faded out before the client leaves the treatment program. Once the clients are achieving success consistently, the token economy is discontinued, and natural contingencies of reinforcement (e.g., praise, good grades, and work outcomes) are used to maintain the desirable behavior. Fading increases the likelihood that the behavior change will be generalized from the treatment program to the everyday environment. In the example of Sammy, the token economy is discontinued each time she achieves 2 weeks of earning maximum points for desirable behavior. When the token reinforcement is no longer in place, natural reinforcers such as praise, accomplishments, and increased privileges maintain the behavior. These are the types of reinforcement she is most likely to find in her home environment when she leaves the program.

Phillips, Phillips, Fixsen, and Wolf (1971) demonstrated one way to fade the use of tokens in a token economy. They delivered tokens for room-cleaning on a daily basis to predelinquent boys in a residential treatment program. After delivering tokens for room-cleaning every day for 2 weeks, they delivered tokens every other day. After 8 days, they delivered tokens every third day. The fading routine continued in four steps until the boys received tokens for room cleaning every twelfth day. The boys continued to clean their rooms as the tokens were faded from every day to every twelfth day over a period of 2 months.

Applications of a Token Economy

The token economy has been used widely in behavior modification with a variety of populations and in a variety of settings (Glynn, 1990; Kazdin, 1977, 1982; Kazdin & Bootzin, 1972). Variations of a token economy have been implemented with hospitalized psychotic patients (Ayllon & Azrin, 1965, 1968; Nelson & Cone, 1979; Paul & Lentz, 1977), adolescents with behavior disorders (Foxx, 1998), hyperactive children (Ayllon, Layman, & Kandel, 1975; Hupp & Reitman, 1999; Robinson, Newby, & Ganzell, 1981), preschoolers (Swiezy, Matson, & Box, 1992), grade school students (McGinnis, Friman, & Carlyon, 1999; McLaughlin & Malaby, 1972; Swain & McLaughlin, 1998), students with learning disabilities (Cavalier, Ferretti, & Hodges, 1997), university students (Everett, Hayward, & Meyers, 1974), prison inmates (Milan & McKee, 1976), juvenile delinquents in correctional facilities or treatment programs (Hobbs & Holt, 1976; Phillips, 1968; Phillips et al., 1971), workers in industrial settings (Fox, Hopkins, & Anger, 1987), and hospitalized patients (Carton & Schweitzer, 1996; Magrab & Papadopoulou, 1977). A few of these studies are described in more detail here to illustrate the variations in the use of a token economy.

Robinson and his colleagues (1981) used token reinforcement with 18 hyperactive and underachieving boys in third grade to increase their academic performance in reading and vocabulary. The tokens were colored cardboard disks that each boy received for completing academic assignments and wore on a string around his wrist. They exchanged the tokens for 15 minutes of pinball or video games. The researchers showed that the number of academic assignments completed by the students increased dramatically when the tokens were used as reinforcers. Another study with three hyperactive children showed that using token reinforcement for math and reading performance increased the number of problems completed correctly and decreased the level of hyperactive behavior in all children (Ayllon et al., 1975). The results showed that the token reinforcement program decreased hyperactive behavior as much as the use of the drug Ritalin. However, token reinforcement increased academic performance, whereas

Ritalin did not improve academic performance. In this study, tokens (check marks on an index card) were exchanged for tangible reinforcers and activity reinforcers.

Milan and McKee (1976) implemented a token economy with 33 inmates in a maximum security prison. The inmates received tokens for completing daily living routines, educational activities, and other tasks. The tokens were points that they recorded in a checkbook banking system. They could then spend the points (by writing checks) for various tangible and activity reinforcers. The target behaviors and backup reinforcers are listed in Table 22-5. Milan and McKee showed that the inmates' targeted behaviors improved with the use of the token economy.

TABLE 22-5 Point Values of Representative Target Behaviors and Backup Reinforcers

Target Behaviors	**Points Awarded**
Morning activities:	
Arising on time	60
Bed made	60
Living area neat and clean	60
Personal appearance	60
Educational activities:[a]	
Student performance	Two per minute (estimated)
Tutor performance	Two per minute (estimated)
Assigned maintenance tasks:[b]	
Sweep main hall (back half)	60
Empty trash cans in recreation room	60
Mop front steps and landing	120
Dust and arrange furniture in television room	120
Backup Reinforcers	**Points Charged**
Activities available on the token economy cellblock	
Access to television room	60 per hour
Access to pool room	60 per hour
Access to lounge	60 per hour
Canteen items available:[c]	
Cup of coffee	50
Can of soft drink	150
Ham and cheese sandwich	300
Pack of cigarettes	450
Leisure time away from token economy cellblock	One per minute

Source: Milan & McKee (1976).

[a]Students were paid on a performance-contingent rather than time-contingent basis. Point values for units of academic material were based on an empirically derived estimated study time per unit and awarded when unit tests were passed.

[b]Although only four are presented here, there were sufficient maintenance tasks to ensure that all residents could earn 120 points by completing their assignments. Additionally, residents could volunteer for supplementary maintenance tasks to increase their daily point earnings.

[c]Although only four are listed here, a large variety of items were available in the token economy canteen.

McLaughlin and Malaby (1972) used a token economy with students in a fifth and sixth grade classroom. In the token economy, students earned points for academic performance. In addition, a response cost program was implemented in which students lost points for a variety of problem behaviors. The authors used classroom privileges as backup reinforcers with the students. The point schedule used in their token economy is shown in Table 22-6. In addition, the point chart McLaughlin and Malaby used to record the points earned and lost by each student is shown in Figure 22-1. The students' academic performance improved with the implementation of the token economy.

Another study demonstrated the long-term effect of a token economy on the number of accidents and injuries in an industrial setting (Fox et al., 1987). Miners working in open-pit mines participated in a token economy in which they earned tokens when members of their work group had no equipment accidents or lost time injuries (that is, injuries that resulted in a loss of production time) or when they made safety suggestions that were adopted by management. Members of the work group lost tokens in the event of a lost time injury, accident, or failure to report an accident or injury. The tokens were stamps that could be exchanged for thousands of items at a redemption store. The token economy was in place for 10 years and resulted in decreases in lost time injuries. Furthermore, the token economy resulted in a reduction in the cost of accidents and injuries by about $300,000 per year.

TABLE 22-6 Point Values of Target Behaviors and Undesirable Behaviors

Target Behaviors	**Points Earned**
Items correct	6–12
Study behavior 8:50–9:15 A.M.	5 per day
Bring food for animals	1–10
Bring sawdust for animals	1–10
Art	1–4
Listening points	1–2 per lesson
Extra credit	Assigned value
Neatness	1–2
Taking home assignments	5
Taking notes	1–3
Quiet in lunch line	2
Quiet in cafeteria	2
Appropriate noon hour behavior	3
Undesirable Behaviors	**Points Lost**
Assignments incomplete	25 per assignment
Have gum or candy in class	100
Inappropriate verbal behavior	15
Inappropriate motor behavior	15
Fighting	100
Cheating	100

Source: McLaughlin & Malaby (1972).

			Points Earned				Points Lost
Language							Assignments
Spelling							
Handwriting							Talking
Science							
Social Studies							
Reading							Break
Math							
Notes							Gum
Taking Home Work							
Sawdust for Rats							
Food for Rats							Library
Quiet Behavior							
Spelling Test							
Study							Out-of-Seat
Other							
						Total	Total Lost

Name____________________________

Row_____________________________

FIGURE 22-1 This chart (from McLaughlin & Malaby, 1972) was used by students to record the points that they earned and lost during their participation in the token economy in the classroom. The desirable target behaviors are listed, with spaces to record the points earned. Likewise, the undesirable behaviors are listed, with spaces to record the points taken away. A chart like this makes it clear to the students what behaviors are expected of them and how well they are doing in the program.

Hobbs and Holt (1976) demonstrated the effectiveness of a token economy with 125 adolescent boys in a correctional facility. Tokens were used to reinforce such behaviors as following rules, completing chores, engaging in acceptable social behavior, and engaging in appropriate line behavior (e.g., while waiting in line for meals). At the end of the day, each adolescent received a certificate that listed the number of tokens he earned for that day. The adolescents could save their certificates in a bank and earn interest or spend them on tangible reinforcers (e.g., sodas, candy, snacks, toys, games, and cigarettes) and activity reinforcers (e.g., recreational activities and home passes). The program resulted in an improvement in the adolescents' behavior (Figure 22-2).

Some of the earliest applications of the token economy were with patients in psychiatric hospitals (Ayllon & Azrin, 1965, 1968). Often such patients exhibit severe

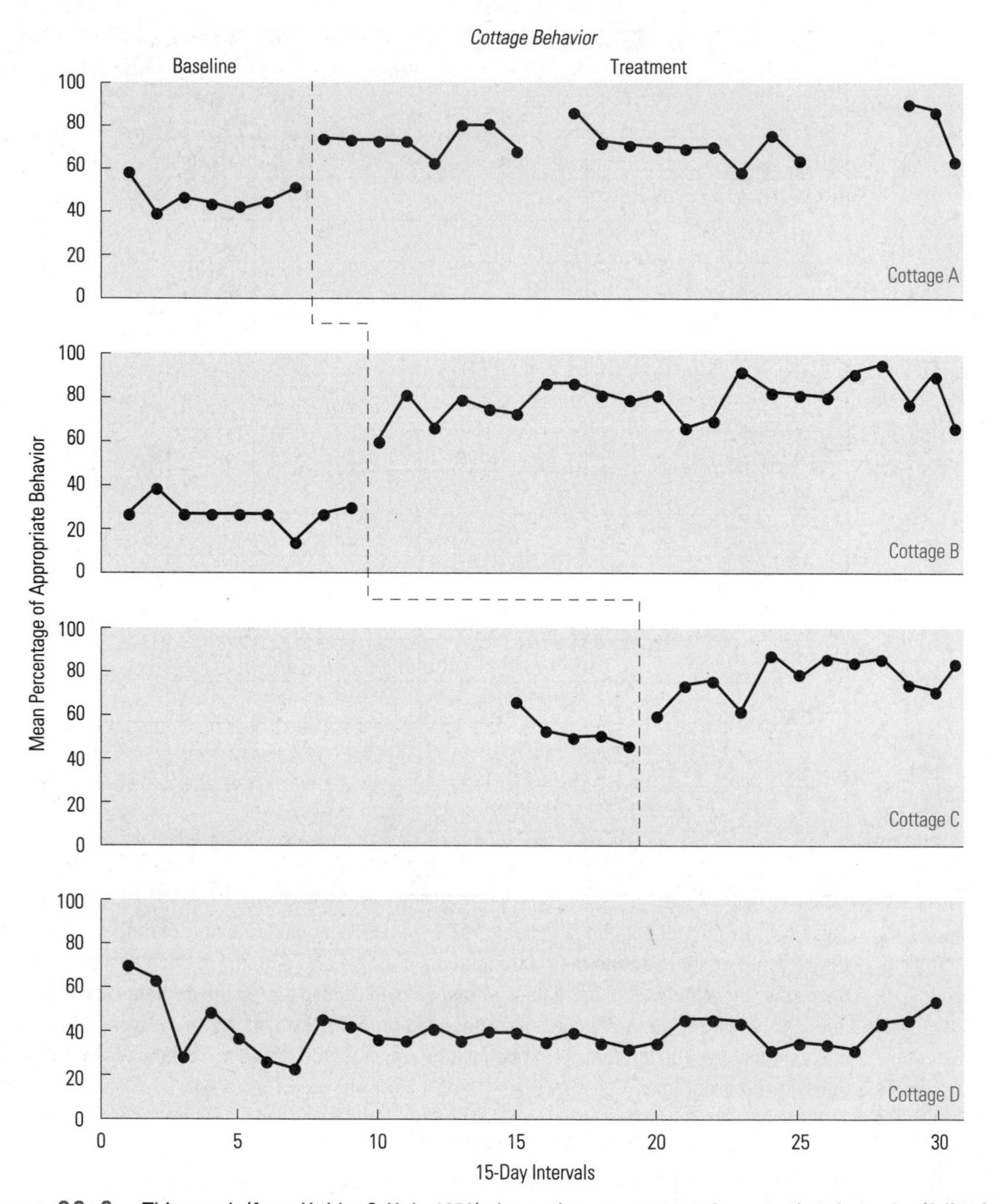

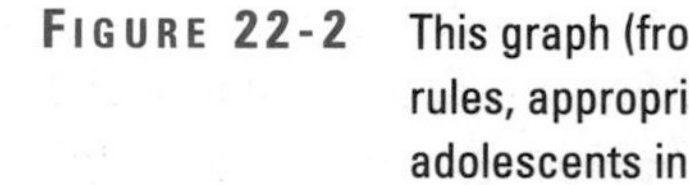

FIGURE 22-2 This graph (from Hobbs & Holt, 1976) shows the percentage of appropriate behavior (following rules, appropriate social behavior, and refraining from assaultive behavior) exhibited by adolescents in a correctional facility before and after the implementation of a token economy. The graph shows the effects of the token economy implemented sequentially across three cottages in the facility. As you can see, the behavior improved for the adolescents in each cottage only when the token economy was implemented in that cottage. The behavior of adolescents in cottage D did not improve because they did not participate in the token economy.

problem behaviors. However, they also lack the skills needed to function outside the hospital setting. Token economies have been used in institutional settings to decrease problem behaviors and to increase skills such as personal hygiene, personal management, social skills, and work skills. Table 22-7 lists and defines the target behaviors in each of these areas that were increased in a token economy implemented by Nelson and Cone (1979) with 16 men in a psychiatric hospital.

TABLE 22-7 Target Behaviors, Tokens Earned, and Response Definitions

Target Behavior	Tokens	Response Definition
Personal hygiene		
Washing face	1	Applying water to at least two-thirds of facial area (followed by drying with towel).
Combing hair	1	One or more strokes through hair with a comb or brush (resulting in hair appearing neat).
Shaving	1	(1) One or more strokes of razor across face or neck area (followed by removal of excess shaving cream and drying with a towel, resulting in clean-shaven appearance). (2) Applying electric razor to face or neck area (resulting in clean-shaven appearance).
Brushing teeth	1	(1) Inserting toothbrush into mouth accompanied by brushing motion (followed by rinsing mouth and wiping mouth area with towel). (2) Washing dentures in tap water.
Personal management		
Dressing neatly	1	Shirt buttoned (except for top button) and tucked in; pants zipped, with belt (buckled); shoes tied, with socks. Exceptions were made for shirts or sweaters that would not normally be tucked in and for pants that required no belt.
Making bed	1 or 2	Sheet and blanket covered completely by bedspread; bedspread tucked under front of pillow, then folded to headboard. After implementation of token reinforcement, a second token was given if the bedspread was even within 3 inches and not touching the floor and no obvious wrinkles were visible from 20 feet.
Cleaning bed drawer	1	All objects stacked or placed in orderly fashion; all clothes folded; no obvious dirt or dust.
Exercising	1 or 2	Physical activity of 2 or more minutes' duration that would be likely to increase fitness (strength, endurance, or flexibility) beyond the level expected from normal walking. After implementation of token reinforcement, subjects were paid 1 token for performing at least half and 2 tokens for performing all of the exercises during a daily 10-minute group exercise session.
Ward work (examples)		
Ashtray cleaner	1	Activity of 2 or more minutes' duration that would be helpful to housekeeping or ward staff in maintaining or managing the ward. After implementation of token reinforcement, more than 25 job descriptions were used to specify the times, locations, materials needed, tasks, and supervisor review procedures for various work tasks. Pay for jobs ranged from 1 to 4 tokens.
Cigarette roller	2	
Linen folder	4	
Dorm duster	2	
Social skills		
Greeting staff	1	Initiating an appropriate verbal greeting such as "Good morning," "Hello," or "How are you?" within 30 minutes of the director's or assistant's arrival on the ward.
Answering awareness questions correctly	3	Giving a correct answer to a preselected question about the immediate hospital environment or current news events (e.g., What is one advantage of moving to an open ward? Who is running for governor?).
Verbal participation in group discussions	1 or 2	Providing information about specific aspects of other residents' daily behavior during a weekly ward meeting. One token was given for one instance of verbal participation, and 2 tokens were given for two or more instances.

Source: Nelson & Cone (1979).

Advantages and Disadvantages of a Token Economy

Using token reinforcement programs has many advantages (Ayllon & Azrin, 1965; Kazdin & Bootzin, 1972; Maag, 1999).

- Tokens can be used to reinforce the target behavior immediately after it occurs.
- A token economy is highly structured; therefore, desirable target behaviors often are reinforced more consistently.
- Tokens are generalized conditioned reinforcers because they are paired with a variety of other reinforcers. As a result, tokens function as reinforcers regardless of any specific establishing operation that may exist for a client at any time.
- Tokens are easy to dispense and easy for the recipients to accumulate.
- Token reinforcement can be quantified easily, so different behaviors can receive a greater or lesser magnitude of reinforcement (more or fewer tokens).
- Response cost is easier to implement in a token economy because the recipient has accumulated tokens that may be removed contingent on the occurrence of the problem behavior.
- The recipient can learn the skills involved in planning for the future by saving tokens for larger purchases.

The disadvantages involved in the use of a token economy include the time and effort involved in organizing and conducting the program and the cost of purchasing the backup reinforcers. Staff training and management are also issues, especially when the token economy has complex components or when it is conducted on a large scale.

When considering the use of a token economy, you should address three basic questions. First, can staff or other change agents be trained to carry out the program consistently on a daily basis? Second, are there sufficient financial resources to conduct the program? Although the cost of backup reinforcers is important, McLaughlin and Malaby (1972) demonstrated that commonly available activities that do not cost anything can be used as reinforcers. Finally, do the expected benefits (improvement in behavior) justify the time, effort, and cost of conducting the program?

Chapter Summary

1. A token economy is a behavior modification procedure in which conditioned reinforcers called tokens are used to strengthen desirable behaviors in clients participating in a treatment or educational program. Research has demonstrated that the token economy can be used successfully with children and adults in a variety of treatment settings.
2. In a token economy, target behaviors are identified and tokens are delivered contingent on their occurrence. Tokens are later exchanged for backup reinforcers at a predetermined exchange rate.
3. Response cost, in which the occurrence of problem behaviors results in the loss of tokens, may be implemented as a component of a token economy when one goal is to decrease the occurrence of undesirable behaviors.
4. A variety of items may be used as tokens in a token economy (see Table 22-2 for examples). Tokens must be easy to carry and deliver by the change agent immediately following the target behaviors. The client must be able to accumulate tokens earned in a token economy.

5. The advantages of a token economy are that tokens can be delivered immediately after the target behavior, they are easy to dispense and accumulate, they can be quantified, and they don't lose their value as reinforcers. The token economy is highly structured, can accommodate a response cost procedure, and can teach the recipient planning skills. Disadvantages of a token economy include time, effort, and cost.

PRACTICE TEST

1. What is a token? Identify some items that can be used as tokens. Describe how tokens are used in a token economy. (pp. 472–475)
2. What is a generalized conditioned reinforcer? How does a token become a generalized conditioned reinforcer? (p. 475)
3. Why is it important to deliver a token immediately after an instance of the desirable target behavior? (p. 474)
4. What are the essential components of a token economy? Identify each of these components in the example of Sammy presented at the beginning of the chapter. (pp. 472–479)
5. What are backup reinforcers? Provide examples of backup reinforcers. How are backup reinforcers chosen? (pp. 475–476)
6. When would a continuous reinforcement schedule be used in a token economy? When would an intermittent schedule be used? (pp. 476–477)
7. What are the important considerations in establishing the exchange rate for backup reinforcers? (p. 477)
8. Why is it important to pair praise with the delivery of tokens? (p. 479)
9. Why is it important to fade the use of tokens over time? When is the appropriate time to fade the use of tokens? Explain how the use of tokens was faded with Sammy. (pp. 479–480)
10. Describe the advantages of a token economy. Describe the disadvantages. (p. 486)
11. Describe five different applications of a token economy. For each, identify the target behaviors, the items that were used as tokens, and the backup reinforcers.

APPLICATIONS

1. Describe how you might use token reinforcement, if appropriate, in your self-management project.

2. You are conducting a remedial reading program with a group of four third graders who are reading behind grade level. You are using a standardized reading program in which the students identify words and word sounds, read short passages aloud, and answer comprehension questions. You sit in front of the students as you conduct the lesson, and the students have many opportunities to respond in each group session. The students tend to be distracted and pay attention to things in the room other than the instructional items that are being presented. Describe the token economy you will implement with these students.

3. All of the students in the remedial reading group have some disruptive behaviors that may interfere with learning, such as pushing or shoving each other, getting out of seat, talking while the teacher is teaching, and making loud noises. Describe the response cost procedure you will implement as part of the token economy with the reading group to decrease the frequency of these problem behaviors.

4. After a couple months of participation in the token economy, the students are paying attention, answering correctly, and refraining from any problem behaviors. Describe how you will fade the token economy so that it is no longer used with these students.

MISAPPLICATIONS

1. Mr. O'Malley was in the teacher's lounge talking about the difficulty he was having with the students in his classroom. He was teaching six special education students, and they were exhibiting a number of behavior problems. A fellow special education teacher told Mr. O'Malley that he had had success with a token economy. He suggested that Mr. O'Malley put the students' names on the board, put a point after their names when they were being good, and erase points when they were exhibiting problems. After each class, the student with the most points would get a special privilege. Mr. O'Malley decided that this was a great idea and implemented it the next day. What is wrong with this use of a token economy?

2. The Tanners were running a group home for six adolescent boys who had been in trouble with the law. All the adolescents were expected to engage in a number of desirable behaviors on a daily basis. In addition, some problem behaviors were defined for each adolescent. The Tanners decided to use a token economy to help the adolescents increase their desirable behaviors and decrease the problem behaviors. They defined the target behaviors and used points as reinforcers. They reinforced the desirable behaviors on a specific schedule of reinforcement and removed points when problem behaviors were exhibited. The Tanners bought a pinball machine and a video game to use as backup reinforcers in the token economy. The machines were in the reinforcement room, and the adolescents could buy access to the room in the evening by exchanging tokens for *x* minutes of time. What is wrong with this use of a token economy?

3. Warden French at the maximum security federal prison decided that he needed a better motivational system for the inmates. After doing some reading on the topic, he decided to implement a token economy to get the inmates to engage in more desirable behaviors on a daily basis. He defined a number of desirable target behaviors related to rehabilitation and a number of undesirable behaviors that were interfering with rehabilitation. All of the inmates received a list of the behaviors that were expected of them. The warden instituted a high-tech system in which each inmate carried an electronic device that could be used to receive points as tokens. Each guard carried an electronic device that could be used to deliver points. Whenever the inmate engaged in one of the target behaviors, the guard used his scanner to read the code from the inmate's device and deliver points electronically (much as the scanner used at the supermarket reads the price of items being purchased). Whenever the inmate engaged in problem behaviors, the guard used the scanner to subtract points. The warden identified the number of points for each target behavior and the exchange rate for backup reinforcers. The warden wanted backup reinforcers that would be powerful reinforcers for the inmates so that the token system would produce beneficial changes in the inmates' behavior. The warden decided that the inmates had to have a specified number of tokens to enter the cafeteria at each mealtime. He set the number of tokens at a reasonable level so that the inmates could earn the tokens needed for each meal with a reasonable level of appropriate behavior. He wanted the inmates to be successful, especially at the beginning of the program. If they did not have the specified number of tokens at a mealtime, they could not eat and had to earn enough tokens by the next mealtime. The warden reasoned that food is always a reinforcer and that there were four opportunities for reinforcement each day: three meals and evening snack. He also reasoned that inmates who missed a meal or two would be even more motivated to earn tokens toward the next meal. In addition, the inmates could eat all that they wanted and, therefore, they could make up for any nutrition that they lost by missing a previous meal. What is wrong with this use of a token economy?

CHAPTER 22 *Quiz 1* Name:

1. The purpose of a(n) ________________ is to strengthen clients' desirable behaviors that occur too infrequently and decrease their undesirable behavior in a structured treatment environment or educational setting.

2. In a token economy, a(n) ________________ is delivered immediately after desirable behavior.

3. In a token economy, how is a token established as a conditioned reinforcer?

____

4. What are three examples of items that could be used as tokens in a token economy?

________________, ________________, ________________

5. A(n) ________________ schedule of reinforcement is used early in a token economy,

and a(n) ________________ schedule of reinforcement is used later in the program after the target behaviors are occurring consistently.

6. Limiting access to backup reinforcers increases their ________________ because a relative state of deprivation is established.

7. When would it be appropriate to add a response cost procedure to a token economy?

____

8. What do clients do with the tokens that they earn in a token economy?

____

9. Tony is a prison inmate who earns tokens each day for a number of desirable target behaviors. The prison guards use money as tokens, and Tony can earn a quarter for each of 10 different desirable behaviors each day. At the end of each day, Tony can spend the money he earned that day in a prison store. What is wrong with the token economy described in this example?

____

10. What would you change in the token economy described in question 9 to fix the problem?

____

CHAPTER 22 *Quiz 2* Name:

1. A token is delivered for desirable behavior and later exchanged for ____________________.

2. Provide three examples of items that could be used as tokens. ____________________,

   ____________________, ____________________

3. How does a client get backup reinforcers in a token economy?

   ____

4. When a token economy first begins, tokens are given on a ____________________ schedule of reinforcement.

5. If backup reinforcers are freely available to the client, their value as reinforcers in a token

   economy will be ____________________ (increased/decreased).

6. In a(n) ____________________ procedure, tokens are taken away when undesirable behaviors occur.

7. What is the goal of a response cost procedure in a token economy?

   ____

8. What is one advantage of using a token economy?

   ____

9. What is one disadvantage of using a token economy?

   ____

10. The director of a treatment program for juvenile delinquents started a token economy in which residents received tokens for prosocial behavior throughout the day and exchanged the tokens for backup reinforcers at the end of the day. A response cost program was also added in which any inappropriate behavior that a resident displayed resulted in the loss of all of the resident's tokens for that day. What is wrong with this program?

    ____

CHAPTER 22 *Quiz 3* Name:

1. A(n) ______________________ is something tangible that can be delivered after each instance of the desired behavior.
2. Clients use their tokens to pay for ______________________________ in a token economy.
3. Identify three different items that could be used as tokens in a token economy.

   _____________________, _____________________, ___________________________

4. In a(n) ________________________, a client earns tokens for desirable behaviors and later exchanges the tokens for backup reinforcers.
5. How can you increase the reinforcing value of backup reinforcers in a token economy?

   ____

6. When a response cost procedure is used in a token economy, what happens when an undesirable behavior occurs? ____

Johnny is in a special education classroom. Whenever he answers questions correctly in class, his teacher puts a poker chip into a coffee can he keeps with him. He accumulates poker chips, and, at the end of the school day, he uses his poker chips to buy items such as candy, small toys, stickers, or time in preferred activities.

7. In this example, what is the token? __________________________
8. In this example, what are the backup reinforcers? __________________________
9. In this example, what is the target behavior? __________________________
10. In this example, what schedule of reinforcement is illustrated? __________________________

TWENTY-THREE

Behavioral Contracts

As we have seen, the token economy is a procedure through which reinforcement and punishment contingencies can be applied systematically to manage the behavior of clients in a structured treatment environment. This chapter describes the behavioral contract, another procedure used to apply reinforcement and punishment contingencies to help people manage their own behavior.

- What is a behavioral contract?
- What are the components of a behavioral contract?
- What are the two types of behavioral contracts, and how do they differ?
- How do you negotiate a behavioral contract?
- How do behavioral contracts influence behavior?

Examples of Behavioral Contracting

Getting Steve to Complete His Dissertation

Steve was a graduate student who had completed all of his course work but had not finished writing his dissertation and a major review paper. Even though he could not graduate until he finished both projects, he had not done any writing on them for more than a year. Steve kept telling himself that he needed to write these papers after work in the evenings and on the weekends, but he always found something else to do instead. Steve decided to visit the university psychology clinic to see whether a psychologist could help him get his work done. A graduate student intern at the clinic, Rae, worked out a behavioral contract with Steve.

First, Rae asked Steve to set some reasonable goals for himself. Steve decided that writing an average of nine pages (typed, double-spaced) a week would be a reasonable goal. This amounted to one page per day Monday through Friday and two pages each day on the weekend, although Steve could actually write the nine pages on any days that he chose. To document that he had written the nine pages, Steve agreed to bring the typed pages to his meeting with Rae each week. Next, Steve and Rae had to agree on a reinforcement contingency that would motivate Steve to write the nine pages each week. They agreed on the following plan. Steve had a collection of vintage jazz albums that he cherished. Each week that he came to the meeting with Rae, he had to give one of his albums away to the university library if he did not have his nine pages written.

Describe how this is a negative reinforcement contingency.

This is a negative reinforcement contingency because by writing the nine pages and showing them to Rae, Steve avoids the aversive event (giving away an album). This

Behavioral Contract

I, Steve Smith, agree to write nine pages of my dissertation or review paper for the week beginning ______ and ending ______.

Nine pages of writing is defined as double-spaced typing on eight full pages and typing on any part of the ninth page.

Furthermore, I agree to bring the nine typed, double-spaced pages to my weekly meeting with Rae Jones (therapist) on ______ (date) to document that I have written the nine pages.

If I do not bring the nine pages of writing to Rae at the weekly meeting, Rae will choose one album from my box of albums and give the album to the university library.

Signed: ______________________________ ______________________________

Steve Smith, Client Rae Jones, Therapist

FIGURE 23-1 The one-party contract Steve wrote with Rae, the therapist, to increase the number of pages he wrote each week on his dissertation.

should strengthen Steve's writing behavior. Once Steve and Rae agreed on this plan, they put it in writing in a contract and they both signed the contract. The form of the contract is shown in Figure 23-1.

Steve brought the box of his vintage jazz albums to the clinic and kept them there so that the contingency could be implemented if necessary. He brought nine pages in the first week and Rae praised him for writing for the first time in a year. Rae asked him whether the goal was still reasonable and, when Steve assured her that it was, they wrote the same contract for the upcoming week. The next week Steve failed to write the nine pages. When he came to his meeting with Rae, he showed her five pages that he had written and made a number of excuses why he could not get his writing done. Rae showed him his signed contract and reminded him that they agreed that she would not accept any excuses. She then got the box of albums from the locked cabinet, chose an album from the box, and told him she would send it to the library.

After she had implemented the contingency, Rae asked Steve to describe the obstacles that had interfered with his writing. It became clear to Steve and Rae that there were no obstacles and that Steve had watched TV or read novels for many hours during the week when he could have been writing. On the basis of this discussion, Steve signed another contract similar to the first one. Steve never lost another album for failing to write the nine pages he committed to write each week. In fact, he averaged eleven pages a week until he had finished both papers. Each weekly meeting with Rae lasted only about 10 minutes as she checked his work to document that he had completed his writing, praised him for his success, and signed a new contract for the upcoming week. Whenever Steve thought about the writing that he needed to do, he thought about the album that he had given away in the second session. This made it more likely that Steve would sit down and write rather than engage in a competing behavior such as watching TV. Consider another example of a behavioral contract.

Helping Dan and His Parents Get Along Better

Dan grew up in a small town and never got into much trouble until he was 16 years old. When he and his friends turned 16, they started to spend time driving around and hanging out on the main street until late at night. About this time, Dan was missing supper with his family, staying out late, refusing to clean his room, and not doing his homework regularly. He also argued regularly with his parents and went out at night even when they told him he could not leave the house. His parents brought Dan in to see a psychologist to work out the problems.

As Dr. Houlihan talked with the family, it became clear that Dan was unhappy with his parents as much as his parents were unhappy with his behavior. Dan complained that his parents yelled at him all the time about cleaning his room, staying out late, and being home for supper. He was also displeased that they tried to ground him and didn't let him use the car to go on dates. His parents said that he couldn't use the car as long as he didn't obey them and that it was his fault that they were yelling at him frequently. Dan wanted his parents to change their behavior toward him, and the parents wanted Dan to change his behavior. Dr. Houlihan negotiated a behavioral contract between Dan and his parents.

First, Dr. Houlihan helped Dan and his parents see that if they both compromised a little they could all be happier. Then he helped Dan and his parents identify the behavior changes that they wanted in each other and come to agreements that they could all accept. For example, the parents wanted Dan to be in at 9 P.M. on weekdays, and Dan wanted to stay out past midnight. Dan was already staying out past midnight, so the parents agreed that 11 P.M. would be a reasonable compromise for a 16-year-old. Dan wanted his parents to quit nagging him about cleaning his room and doing his homework, but his parents wanted the homework done and the room cleaned. The parents agreed to stop telling him to clean his room and to stop telling him to do his homework every day. In return, Dan agreed to do his homework after school and clean his room every 2 weeks. They agreed that the room cleaning was less important than the homework, so they did not mind if it was not cleaned very often. Under the guidance of Dr. Houlihan, Dan and his parents came to a number of other agreements. Dr. Houlihan helped them see that they would all benefit from mutual changes in behavior. The form of the behavioral contract that Dr. Houlihan negotiated with Dan and his parents is shown in Figure 23-2.

Behavioral Contract

Contract date: ______ to ________

I, Dan Henderson, agree to engage in the following behaviors this week.

1. I will be home by 11 PM Sunday through Thursday nights.
2. I will do my homework right after school before I go out and I will leave the completed homework on the dining room table for my parents to check.

In return, we, Pete and Paula Henderson, agree to the following: If Dan is home by 11 PM and completes his homework each day, he can use the car for dates on Friday and Saturday night. Dan can use the car only one weekend night if he has one infraction (home late one night or homework not completed on one day).

We, Pete and Paula Henderson, agree to the following behaviors this week.

1. We will not ask Dan about his homework or about cleaning his room.
2. We will not demand that Dan be home for supper.

In return, I, Dan Henderson, agree to the following: If my parents do not ask me about my homework or about cleaning my room, I will clean my room once every 2 weeks. This is defined as putting everything away, vacuuming, and dusting. In addition, I will be home for supper at least 3 days a week.

All the target behaviors in this contract will be documented on a data sheet by Dan and his parents at the time that they occur.

Signed: ______________________ ______________________
Dan Henderson Pete and Paula Henderson

FIGURE 23-2 A two-party contract (parallel contracts) between Dan and his parents. Each party specifies behavior to change and a consequence for the behavior change.

Defining the Behavioral Contract

A **behavioral contract** (also called a contingency contract) is a written agreement between two parties in which one or both parties agree to engage in a specified level of a target behavior or behaviors. Furthermore, the contract states the consequence that will be administered contingent on the occurrence (or nonoccurrence) of the behavior (Homme, Csany, Gonzales, & Rechs, 1970; Kirschenbaum & Flanery, 1983; O'Banion & Whaley, 1981).

In the first example, Steve agreed to write nine pages a week (the specified level of the target behavior). The stated consequence was the loss of a record album for failure to engage in the target behavior. Another way to look at it is that Steve avoided the loss of an album by engaging in the target behavior; thus, the behavior was negatively reinforced. As you can see in this example, the contract states the time frame of the agreement (1 week) and identifies the person responsible for administering the consequence (Rae, the therapist).

In the second example, both parties agreed to engage in specific target behaviors. Dan agreed to two target behaviors desired by his parents, and the parents agreed to two target behaviors desired by Dan. The behavior of one party (Dan) is reinforced by the behavior of the second party (the parents), and vice versa. In this example, as in the first, the contract is time-limited: A period of 1 week is specified. In this way, the contract is renegotiated and rewritten frequently so that any problems in the contract can be corrected.

Components of a Behavioral Contract

There are five essential components of a behavioral contract, as follows.

1. *Identifying the target behaviors*. The first step in writing a behavioral contract is to define clearly the target behaviors involved in the contract. As with any behavior modification intervention, the target behaviors in the contract must be stated in clear objective terms. Target behaviors may include undesirable behaviors to be decreased or desirable behaviors to be increased, or both. With the assistance of the contract manager, the client chooses target behaviors that are meaningful and in need of change. Steve's target behavior was to write nine pages each week. Dan's target behaviors were to be home at 11 P.M. and to do his homework each day. Dan's parents' target behaviors were not asking Dan about his homework or about cleaning his room and not demanding that he be home for supper every day. A change in these target behaviors for these people would improve various aspects of their lives.

2. *Stating how the target behaviors will be measured*. The people responsible for implementing the behavioral contract (the contract manager or contract participants) must have objective evidence of the occurrence of the target behaviors. In other words, clients must be able to prove that the target behaviors did or did not occur so that the contingencies can be implemented correctly. Therefore, at the time the contract is written, the clients and the contract manager must agree on the method for measuring the target behavior. Acceptable methods include permanent products of the behaviors or direct observation and documentation of the behavior by the contract manager or by an agreed-upon third party. In the first example, Steve used a permanent product measure in his contract. He showed Rae, the contract manager, the

pages he had typed for the week. Other types of permanent product measures that may be used include body weight in a contract for weight loss, fingernail length in a contract to stop fingernail-biting, and number of units assembled in a contract to increase work productivity.

In the second example, how did Dan and his parents measure the target behaviors agreed upon in the contract?

They used direct observation and permanent product measures. Dan's completed homework left on the dining room table was a permanent product that documented the occurrence of the behavior. The target behavior of being home on time at night was directly observed by Dan and his parents when the behavior occurred. His parents' target behaviors were also directly observed by Dan and his parents. When the behaviors were observed, they were recorded on a data sheet provided by Dr. Houlihan.

If the target behaviors are measured objectively, there can be no ambiguity about their occurrence or nonoccurrence. As a result, there is no conflict in implementing the contract contingencies.

3. *Stating when the behavior must be performed.* Each contract must have a time frame that states when the behavior must occur (or not occur) for the contingencies to be implemented. Steve had 1 week to write nine pages. He could write the pages at any time in the week, but he had to show the typed pages to Rae at the scheduled meeting time for Steve to avoid the aversive consequence. The time frame of Dan's contract was 1 week. In addition, because Dan's target behaviors were time related (home on time each night and homework completed each day), the time frame was a part of the definition of the target behaviors.

4. *Identifying the reinforcement or punishment contingency.* The contract manager uses positive or negative reinforcement or positive or negative punishment to help the client perform (or refrain from) the target behavior stated in the contract. The reinforcement or punishment contingency is written clearly in the contract. The client agrees to a specified level of the target behavior and further agrees that a specific reinforcing or punishing consequence will be administered contingent on the target behavior. The four types of contingencies possible in a behavioral contract are illustrated in Table 23-1.

TABLE 23-1 Types of Contingencies in a Behavioral Contract

Positive Reinforcement
If a desirable behavior is performed, a reinforcer will be provided to strengthen the behavior.

Negative Reinforcement
If a desirable behavior is performed, an aversive stimulus will be removed or prevented to strengthen the behavior.

Positive Punishment
If an undesirable behavior is performed, an aversive stimulus will be provided to decrease the behavior.

Negative Punishment
If an undesirable behavior is performed, a reinforcer will be lost to decrease the behavior.

5. *Identifying who will implement the contingency.* A contract necessarily involves two parties. One party agrees to engage in a specified level of the target behavior and the other party implements the reinforcement or punishment contingency stated in the contract. The contract states clearly who will implement the contingency for the target behavior. In the first example, Rae served as the contract manager, the person responsible for implementing the contingency. She determined whether the requirements of the contract had been met (nine pages written) and took one of Steve's jazz albums if he did not show her the nine pages at their weekly meeting (the contract contingency).

COMPONENTS OF A BEHAVIORAL CONTRACT

1. Identifying the target behavior.
2. Stating how the target behavior will be measured.
3. Stating when the behavior must be performed.
4. Identifying the reinforcement or punishment contingency.
5. Identifying who will implement the contingency.

Sometimes in a behavioral contract, both parties agree to engage in specified levels of a target behavior, and each party's behavior change reinforces the behavior change of the other party. Such was the case with Dan and his parents. Dan agreed to two target behaviors, and the parents agreed to let him use the car in return. The parents agreed to two target behaviors and Dan agreed to clean his room and be home for dinner three times a week in return. In this case, the parents implement a contingency for Dan's target behaviors, and Dan implements a contingency for his parents' target behaviors.

TYPES OF BEHAVIORAL CONTRACTS

As illustrated in our examples, there are two types of behavioral contracts: one-party contracts and two-party contracts.

One-Party Contracts

In a **one-party contract** (also called a unilateral contract by Kirschenbaum & Flanery, 1984), one person seeks to change a target behavior and arranges reinforcement or punishment contingencies with a contract manager who implements the contingencies. A one-party contract is used when the person wants to increase desirable behaviors (e.g., exercise, studying or other school-related behaviors, good eating habits, or work-related behaviors) or to decrease undesirable behaviors (e.g., overeating, nail-biting, excessive TV watching, or arriving late to class or work). The contract manager may be a psychologist, counselor, or other helping professional, or the contract manager may be a friend or family member who agrees to carry out the terms of the contract.

In a one-party contract, the contract manager must not stand to gain from the contract contingencies. For example, it would not be ethical for Rae to take one of Steve's jazz albums for her own collection when Steve failed to write his nine pages for the week. If Rae were able to keep the album herself, she would benefit from the contract and, as a result, may not implement the contingencies fairly.

The contract manager must implement the contingencies as written. Sometimes it is difficult, especially for family or friends, to implement the contract contingencies. Therefore, it may not be wise for friends or family members to serve as contract managers. On failing to meet the requirements of the contract, the person might plead with the friend or family member not to implement the contingency or might get angry when the friend or family member does implement the contingency. The pleading or angry response may make it impossible for the friend or family member to follow through with the punishment or withhold the reinforcer. Therefore, the person best suited to act as a contract manager is someone trained in behavior modification who has no personal relationship with the person writing the contract (the contractee). If the contract manager does have a personal relationship with the contractee, the contract manager must be taught to adhere to the terms of the contract despite the relationship. This is less of a problem when the contract manager has some authority in the relationship, as when a parent manages a contract with a son or daughter.

Two-Party Contracts

Sometimes a behavioral contract is written between two parties, each of whom wants to change a target behavior. In a **two-party contract** or bilateral contract (Kirschenbaum & Flanery, 1984), both parties identify target behaviors for change and the contingencies that will be implemented for the target behaviors. Two-party contracts are written between people who have some relationship with each other, such as spouses, parents and a child, siblings, friends, or co-workers. Typically, each party is displeased with some behavior of the other party, and the contract identifies behavior changes that will be pleasing to both parties. Consider the example of a husband and wife who are displeased with each other because neither is doing much work around the house. They might enter into a behavioral contract of the form in Figure 23-3.

The contract between Bob and Barb Smith (Figure 23-3) is a two-party contract in which both parties identify specific target behaviors to perform, and the behavior change of one party acts as the reinforcer for the behavior change of the other party. Bob's target

Behavioral Contract

Date :________ to ________

For the coming week, I, Bob Smith, agree to the following tasks:

- I will take the trash to the curb on pick-up day.
- I will vacuum all of the carpets.
- I will mow the lawn.

In return, I, Barb Smith, agree to the following tasks:

- I will clean the bathroom.
- I will water the plants.
- I will load the dishwasher once per day and run it when it is full.

Signed: ______________________________ ______________________________

Barb Smith Bob Smith

FIGURE 23-3 A quid pro quo two-party contract between Bob and Barb Smith, in which they both specify a behavior to change and the behavior change of one person reinforces the behavior change of the other.

Behavioral Contract

Date :________ to ________

For the coming week, I, Bob Smith, agree to the following tasks:

- I will take the trash to the curb on pick-up day.
- I will vacuum all of the carpets.
- I will mow the lawn.

If I perform the tasks listed above by Saturday, I can play 18 holes of golf on Saturday afternoon or Sunday morning with my friends.

For the coming week, I, Barb Smith, agree to the following tasks:

- I will clean the bathroom.
- I will water the plants.
- I will load the dishwasher once per day and run it when it is full.

If I perform the tasks listed above by Saturday, I can play 18 holes of golf on Saturday afternoon or Sunday morning with my friends.

Signed: ______________________________ ______________________________
Barb Smith Bob Smith

FIGURE 23-4 The two-party contract between Barb and Bob Smith rewritten in the form of a parallel contract.

behaviors are desirable to Barb, and Barb's target behaviors are desirable to Bob. Therefore, Bob performs his target behaviors with the expectation that Barb will perform her target behaviors, and vice versa. Jacobson and Margolin (1979) call this a **quid pro quo contract** (meaning that one thing is given in return for another). Problems may arise if one party fails to perform the behavior identified in the contract. This may lead the other party to refuse to perform his or her target behaviors. For example, if Bob does not mow the lawn and vacuum the carpets, Barb may refuse to carry out all or part of her target behaviors. When one person's target behaviors are tied to the other person's target behaviors, one person's failure can result in the failure of the whole contract. This situation can be avoided if a separate contingency is established for each person's target behaviors rather than making one person's target behavior the consequence for the other person's target behavior. Figure 23-4 shows a rewritten form of the contract between Barb and Bob in which there is a separate contingency for each person's target behaviors. This type of two-party contract is called a **parallel contract** (Jacobson & Margolin, 1979).

In this contract, the target behaviors for Barb and Bob are the same as in the original contract. However, the contingency for the target behaviors for both parties is the opportunity to play a round of golf on the weekend with their friends. Both Barb and Bob love to play golf, so the opportunity to play should be an incentive for each party to perform his or her target behaviors. Moreover, if one party fails to perform the target behaviors, it should not influence the target behaviors of the other person because each person's target behavior is not contingent on the other person's target behavior. Rather, there is a separate contingency for each person's behavior.

NEGOTIATING A BEHAVIORAL CONTRACT

The parties involved in a behavioral contract must negotiate the components of the contract so that the contract is acceptable to all involved. In a one-party contract, the contract manager negotiates with the client until they agree upon an acceptable level of the target behavior, the appropriate consequences, and the time frame of the contract. The contract manager, who has training in behavior modification, helps the client choose target behaviors that are relevant and attainable in the time frame of the contract and helps the client choose a consequence that is strong enough to result in successful performance of the target behaviors. If they negotiate a level of the target behavior that the client can perform successfully, the client's efforts will be reinforced, and the client is more likely to enter into further contracts. If the level of the target behavior is too difficult to attain, the client may become discouraged and decline to enter into further contracts. If the level of the target behavior is too easy to attain, it will take more time than necessary to reach an ultimate behavior change goal.

Negotiating a two-party contract may be more difficult. Often the parties involved are engaged in a conflict or are experiencing interpersonal difficulties such that they are displeased with each others' actions. Each party may think that the other party is at fault while also believing that there is no problem with his or her own actions. As a result, each party may expect change in the other party's behavior while seeing no reason to change his or her own behavior. The psychologist must negotiate a contract that is acceptable to both parties. This means that the psychologist must help each party see that he or she will benefit from changing some aspect of his or her own behavior. The psychologist helps both parties understand that the conflict situation will improve only if both parties agree to participate and make changes that are pleasing to the other person. Only people with specific training in this area should negotiate two-party contracts with people in conflict (Jacobson & Margolin, 1979; Stuart, 1980).

Why Do Behavioral Contracts Influence Behavior?

Behavioral contracts specify target behaviors that the person wants to change and the consequences for those target behaviors. However, the consequences for the target behavior are delayed consequences; they do not immediately follow instances of the target behavior. Remember that a reinforcer or punisher must follow a target behavior immediately to strengthen or weaken the target behavior. Therefore, behavioral contracts cannot produce behavior change through a simple reinforcement or punishment process alone; they must be based on other behavioral processes, as well.

As stated in Chapter 16, a behavioral contract is a type of antecedent manipulation. The contractee states in writing that he or she will engage in a specific target behavior and signs the contract in the hopes of influencing the future occurrence of the target behavior. Therefore, the behavioral contract can act as a form of public commitment in which the contractee commits to engage in the target behavior. For people who have a history of reinforcement for correspondence between saying and doing (for doing what they say they are going to do), the act of stating that they plan to engage in the target behavior should increase the likelihood of engaging in the target behavior (Stokes, Osnes, & DaVerne, 1993). In addition, the contract manager, contract participants, or other people who are aware of the contract commitment may then prompt or cue the contractee to engage in the target behavior at appropriate times or provide reinforcing or punishing consequences when they observe the contractee engaging in the behavior. In this way, there are cues in the environment at the time that the target behavior is needed, and the consequences of the target behavior are immediate. This is a form of social support.

A second mechanism by which a contract may influence the target behavior is through **rule-governed behavior.** The contract establishes a rule that the contractee states later in the appropriate circumstances as a prompt or self-instruction to engage in the target behavior. For example, after developing his contract, Steve's rule was, "Write nine pages this week or you're going to lose an album." When Steve is at home at a time that he could be writing his dissertation, he states the rule to himself and it cues him to start writing. The rule is a form of self-instruction that cues or prompts the target behavior. To put it another way, signing a contract at an earlier time makes it more likely that you will think about the target behavior and talk yourself into engaging in the target behavior at the appropriate time.

Rule-governed behavior may operate another way to influence the target behavior. When the contractee states the rule, it may create an aversive physiological state (anxiety). Then, engaging in the target behavior results in escape from this aversive state (Malott, 1986). For example, when Steve says to himself, "I have to write nine pages or I'm going to lose an album," it creates an unpleasant state. He gets nervous or anxious about the writing that he committed to get done for the week. As soon as he starts to write, the anxiety decreases, and thus his writing behavior is negatively reinforced. As soon as he finishes his nine pages for the week, he no longer experiences the unpleasant state until he signs a contract for the next week. In this example, stating the rule is an establishing operation that makes it more likely that Steve will write because the writing behavior decreases the aversive (anxiety) state generated by stating the rule.

Why Do Behavioral Contracts Work?

- Behavioral consequences
- Public commitment
- Rule-governed behavior
- Establishing operations

Applications of Behavioral Contracts

Behavioral contracts have been used for a variety of target behaviors with children and adults (Allen, Howard, Sweeney, & McLaughlin, 1993; Carns & Carns, 1994; Leal & Galanter, 1995; Ruth, 1996). A number of researchers have used behavioral contracting to help adults lose weight and maintain weight loss (Jeffery, Bjornson-Benson, Rosenthal, Kurth, & Dunn, 1984; Kramer, Jeffery, Snell, & Forster, 1986; Mann, 1972). In the study by Mann, subjects in a weight-loss program brought valuable items (e.g., clothes, jewelry, and trophies) to the clinic for use in their behavioral contracts. The subjects then wrote behavioral contracts with the experimenter that stated that they could earn their valuables back for specified amounts of weight loss. The contracts resulted in weight loss for all subjects. Jeffery and his colleagues had subjects make a monetary deposit of $150 at the beginning of the weight-loss program. Subjects then signed behavioral contracts that stated that they could earn portions of the money each week for specified amounts of weight loss for that week. Although the subjects lost weight as a result of participating in the behavioral contracting program, subjects gained at least some of the weight back when the program was terminated. Note that these studies measured weight rather than eating behaviors.

Why does a behavioral contract target weight loss instead of eating behaviors such as calorie intake or fat consumption?

Although change in eating behavior is important to achieve weight loss, eating behavior cannot be verified by the contract manager, who is not present when the contractee eats. Therefore, the contract contingency is based on weight loss because weight can be measured by the contract manager in the session.

Wysocki, Hall, Iwata, and Riordan (1979) used behavioral contracts to help university students increase the amount of aerobic exercise they participated in each week. Each student deposited items of personal value with the experimenters. They developed behavioral contracts that stated that they could earn the items back by engaging in specific amounts of aerobic exercise each week. The aerobic exercise was recorded by another participant or by the experimenter to verify the occurrence of the target behavior. The students increased their participation in aerobic exercise routines after they started using the behavioral contracts.

Behavioral contracts have been used in a number of studies to improve school performance in children, adolescents, and college students (Bristol & Sloane, 1974; Kelley & Stokes, 1982, 1984; Miller & Kelley, 1994). Kelley and Stokes (1982) used contracts with disadvantaged high school dropouts enrolled in a vocational and educational program to help them complete academic work. Each student wrote a behavioral contract that specified daily and weekly goals for completing items correctly from workbooks. They earned specified amounts of money for achieving the goals stated in their contracts. The performance of all the students improved with the use of contracts.

Miller and Kelley (1994) taught parents to develop behavioral contracts with their fourth, fifth, and sixth grade children to improve their homework performance. The contracts stated the homework activities that were expected, the rewards for successful homework performance, and the consequences for failure to perform the behaviors stated in the contract. All children improved their homework performance with the use of contracts developed by the parents. An example of the contract is shown in Figure 23-5; the results of the study are shown in Figure 23-6.

Behavioral Contract

The following materials need to be brought home every day: homework pad, workbooks, text books, pencils.

If Ann remembers to bring home all of these materials, then she may choose one of the following rewards: gumballs, a dime.

However, if Ann forgets to bring home some of her homework materials, then she: does not get a snack before bed.

Ann may choose one of the following rewards if she meets 90% to 100% of her goals: late bedtime (by 20 minutes), 2 stickers or one of these if she meets 75% to 80% of her goals: soda, 1 sticker.

If Ann meets 80% or more of her goals on at least 3 days this week, she may choose one of the following BONUS rewards: renting a videotape, having a friend from school over to play.

Child's signature ____________________ Parent's signature ____________________

FIGURE 23-5 A one-party contract (from Miller & Kelley, 1994) used with grade school children to improve their homework.

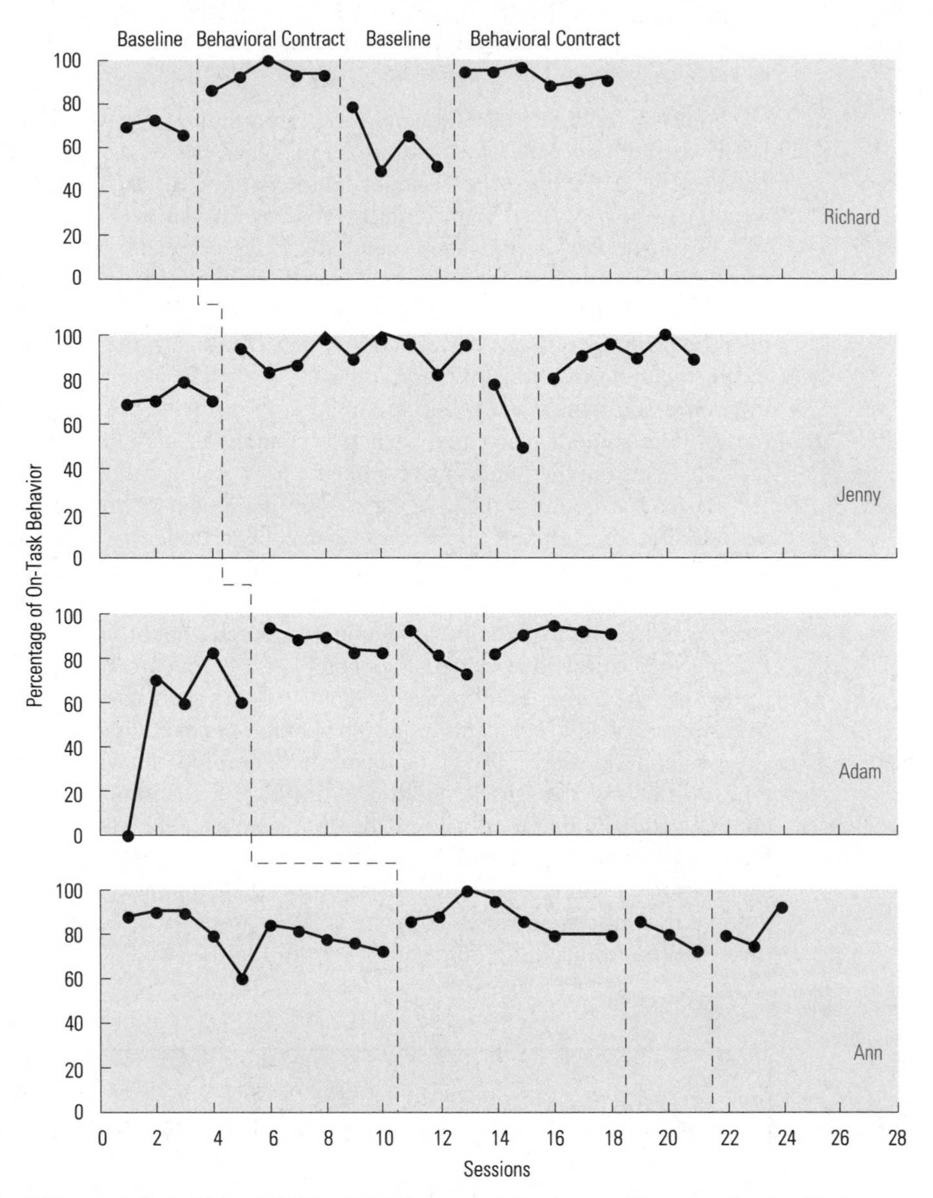

FIGURE 23-6 This graph (from Miller & Kelley, 1994) shows the percentage of homework completed accurately for four students during baseline and when the behavioral contracts were used. An A-B-A-B reversal design is used here to demonstrate the effectiveness of the behavioral contracts.

One other area in which behavioral contracts are used frequently is marital or couple therapy (Jacobson & Margolin, 1979; Stuart, 1980). Two-party contracts are negotiated by the marital therapist between the partners in conflict. Each partner agrees to engage in behaviors desired by the other partner, and the agreements are written into parallel or quid pro quo contracts. Once the behavioral contracts are implemented, the behavior of each partner changes, and the partners become more satisfied with the relationship.

Chapter Summary

1. Behavioral contracts are written agreements used by people who want to increase or decrease the level of desirable or undesirable target behaviors.
2. A contract is a written document that states the target behavior, the consequences for the occurrence or nonoccurrence of the target behavior, the time frame of the agreement, how the target behavior will be measured, and who will implement the consequences for the target behavior.
3. A one-party contract is an agreement between the contractee, who identifies a target behavior for modification, and a contract manager, who implements the contingencies stated in the contract. In a two-party contract, two parties each identify mutually desirable target behaviors for change. In quid pro quo contracts, the behavior change of one party is the reinforcer for the behavior change of the other party. In parallel contracts, each party agrees to behavior change desired by the other party and both parties arrange consequences for their respective behavior changes.
4. To negotiate a one-party contract, the contract manager helps the contractee identify a desirable level of the target behavior, a reasonable consequence, and a time frame for completing the target behavior. To negotiate a two-party contract, the contract manager has to help both parties identify the desirable target behaviors, consequences, and time frame of the contract. The manager must help the parties decide on a quid pro quo contract or parallel contracts and must get both parties to agree to the terms of the contract.
5. Writing a behavioral contract is an antecedent manipulation that makes it more likely that the person will engage in the target behavior specified in the contract. Behavioral contracts may work through a process of public commitment, rule-governed behavior, or creating an establishing operation that makes completing the behavior in the contract more reinforcing.

Practice Test

1. What is a behavioral contract? (p. 496)
2. Identify and describe the components of a behavioral contract. (pp. 496–498)
3. Identify each of the components of the behavioral contract written between Steve and Rae in the first example in this chapter.
4. What are two ways in which a target behavior can be measured in a behavioral contract? Provide an example of each. (p. 496)
5. What is a one-party contract? What is another name for a one-party contract? Provide an example. (p. 498)
6. What is a two-party contract? What is another name for a two-party contract? Provide an example. (pp. 499–500)
7. How does a quid pro quo contract differ from a parallel contract? (p. 500)
8. What is public commitment and how might public commitment be involved in the success of a behavioral contract? (p. 501)
9. Describe the role that rule-governed behavior may play in the effectiveness of behavioral contracts. (p. 502)
10. Describe how behavioral contracts are used in weight-loss programs for adults. (p. 502)
11. Describe how behavioral contracts may be used with school-age children to improve academic performance. (p. 503)

Applications

1. Describe how you could use a behavioral contract in your own self-management program. If the use of a behavioral contract is not appropriate for your self-management program, state why not.

2. Marty is a 17-year-old high school senior who lives on a farm with his parents. He uses one of the family cars each weekend evening to go out with his friends or to go out on dates. His parents have put him in charge of taking care of the cars. Each week, he is supposed to wash the cars, vacuum the insides, and wipe all of the inside surfaces because the cars get quite dusty going up and down the gravel road to their house. Lately, Marty has been failing to carry out his responsibility to clean the cars. Provide an example of a behavioral contract his parents could use with Marty to get him to care for the cars each week.

3. In an effort to get her students to read books during the summer vacation from school, Mrs. Steen, the third grade teacher, wrote a behavioral contract with each student in the class on the last day of class before summer vacation. In the contract, each student agreed to read six books during the 3 months of summer vacation. Mrs. Steen got local fast food restaurants to donate coupons for use as rewards in the contracts. The contract said that if students read the six books for the summer, they would receive a booklet of fast food coupons when they returned to school in the fall. Describe the ways that Mrs. Steen could measure the target behavior (reading six books) to determine whether the children had earned the fast food coupons.

4. Bill and Ruth both worked full-time and both shared household responsibilities and child-raising duties. The problem they encountered is that Bill often failed to complete his weekend chores. His chores consisted of sweeping and mopping the kitchen and bathroom floors, vacuuming the carpets in the house, and cleaning the kitchen. When the weekend came around, Bill often occupied his time on his computer, playing golf, watching football, baseball, or basketball games, and playing with the kids. As a result, his chores went undone or Ruth did them for him. Bill stated that he wanted to get his chores done, but something else always came up. He agreed with Ruth that it was important to share the responsibility and do his chores, so he agreed to develop a behavioral contract with her to make it more likely that he would do his chores each week. Provide an example of the behavioral contract that Bill might develop with Ruth to make it more likely that he would do his chores.

Misapplications

1. Dr. Campbell ran a behavioral contracting service out of the student counseling center at the university. He used behavioral contracts to help students study more and complete their academic assignments. Each student who worked with him wrote a one-party contract each week; the contract stated the target behavior (e.g., the amount of studying, the completed assignments) to be achieved for the week. The student wrote a check to Dr. Campbell for an agreed-upon amount of money each week. If the student failed to complete the contract requirement, Dr. Campbell cashed the check and kept the money. As a result, students were more likely to complete the contract assignments to avoid the loss of the money. Most students improved their academic performance and their grades as a result of the behavioral contracts with Dr. Campbell. What is wrong with the behavioral contracts in this example?

2. Larry had fought a battle with his weight for years. At a recent physical, his physician told him that he was 50 pounds overweight and that he had to do something about it. He talked to a nutritionist, who told him that he needed to

change his diet and eat less fat, drink less beer, and eat more complex carbohydrates. Larry's friend Jane, who was taking a behavior modification class, offered to work out a behavioral contract with Larry to help him change his diet and lose weight. The target behaviors that Larry identified were to drink no more than six beers per week, to eat only lean meats, to stop having second helpings at meals, to eat three servings of complex carbohydrates (e.g., vegetables, fruit, salad, rice, potato, and macaroni) at lunch and supper, and to replace butter with low-fat margarine. Larry wrote down everything that he ate each day on a recording sheet. He gave Jane a $200 deposit and wrote a contract that stated that he would lose $20 for each violation of his contract commitments each week. When he met with Jane each week, they reviewed his recording sheet for the week to see whether he had any violations. If he did, Jane subtracted the appropriate amount of money from Larry's deposit and sent the money to a local charity. What is wrong with the implementation of the behavioral contract in this example?

3. Claudia was smoking a pack and a half of cigarettes every day when she decided to quit for health reasons. She saw a counselor, who worked out a behavioral contract. Claudia gave the counselor a $500 deposit and signed a contract that stated that she would stop smoking completely on the following Monday. If she smoked at all on any day of the week, she would lose $100 for each infraction. As a measure of whether she smoked a cigarette, the counselor had a lab do a chemical analysis test on Claudia's urine; the test would detect the presence of nicotine and other byproducts of smoking if she had smoked a cigarette within the last 24 hours. Claudia dropped off a urine sample at the lab each day of the week for testing. Because she worked at the hospital that housed the lab, it was no effort to give a urine sample each day. Claudia met with her counselor once a week and reviewed the lab results to see whether she had refrained from smoking and to determine whether the contract contingency had to be implemented. What is wrong with the implementation of the behavioral contract in this case?

CHAPTER 23 *Quiz 1*

Name:

1. A(n) ______________________ is a written agreement between two parties in which one or both parties agree to engage in a specific level of a target behavior.

2. The first step in writing a behavioral contract is to clearly define the ______________________ to be modified.

3. When Rae counted the number of pages that Steve had written each week to document his target behavior in the behavioral contract, she was using a ______________________ measure.

4. What are the two types of behavioral contracts? ______________________ and ______________________

5. In a(n) ______________________ contract, the contract manager implements the contract contingency.

6. In a(n) ______________________ contract, if one party fails to perform the behavior identified in the contract, the other party may then refuse to perform his or her target behaviors, resulting in a failure of the whole contract.

Match the following terms to the description of the contract contingency.

a. Positive reinforcement
b. Negative reinforcement
c. Positive punishment
d. Negative punishment

7. _____ If the contractee engages in the undesirable behavior, an aversive stimulus is delivered

8. _____ If the contractee engages in the desirable behavior, an aversive stimulus is removed.

9. _____ If the contractee engages in the undesirable behavior, a reinforcer is removed.

10. If a person writes a behavioral contract and later states the contract contingency to himself and gets anxious, the person is more likely to engage in the target behavior to reduce the anxiety. In this case, stating the contract contingency and getting anxious is a(n) ______________________ that makes it more likely that the person will engage in the target behavior.

CHAPTER 23 *Quiz 2* Name:

1. What is another name for a behavioral contract? ______________________

2. Identify two types of consequences you could implement in a behavioral contract to increase a target behavior. ______________________ and ______________________

3. In addition to the use of permanent product measures, you can measure the target behavior in a behavioral contract through ______________________ by the contract manager or by an agreed-upon third party.

4. What are two types of two-party contracts? ______________________ and ______________________

5. What is a potential problem with the use of a quid pro quo contract?

   ____

6. In a(n) ______________________ contract, one person seeks to change a target behavior and arranges reinforcement or punishment contingencies with a contract manager.

Match the following terms to the description of the contract contingency.

a. Positive reinforcement b. Negative reinforcement
c. Positive punishment d. Negative punishment

7. _____ You agree to mow the lawn each weekend, and, if you do, your partner agrees to let you out of cleaning the bathroom that week.

8. _____ You agree that if you smoke any cigarettes during the week, you will lose the $10 you have given your roommate to hold for you.

9. _____ You agree to mow the lawn each weekend, and, if you do, your partner agrees to give you a massage.

10. What is one way a behavioral contract can influence behavior other than through a reinforcement or punishment process?

    ____

CHAPTER 23 *Quiz 3* Name:

1. A behavioral contract identifies one or more target behaviors and the ________________ for engaging in or not engaging in the target behavior(s).

2. Identify two types of consequences you could implement in a behavioral contract to decrease a target behavior.

   ________________________ and ________________________

3. In a one-party contract, who implements the contract contingency?

   ____

4. A(n) ________________ contract is a two-party contract in which the behavior change of one party serves as the reinforcer for the behavior change for the other party and vice-versa.

5. A(n) ________________ contract is a two-party contract in which both parties have separate contingencies for their target behaviors.

What type of contract is illustrated in each of the following examples?

a. One party   b. Quid pro quo   c. Parallel

6. _____ Martha agrees to mow the lawn each week, and, in return, Manny agrees to clean both bathrooms each week.

7. _____ Martha agrees to mow the lawn each week, and, if she does, she gets to go bowling on Sunday. Manny agrees to clean both bathrooms each week, and, if he does, he gets to go fishing on Sunday.

8. _____ Maggie agrees to complete two practice tests each week while studying for the GRE, and, if she does, she does not lose the $10 she gave the contract manager to hold.

Match the following terms to the description of the contract contingency.

a. Positive reinforcement   b. Negative reinforcement
c. Positive punishment   d. Negative punishment

9. _____ Sally agrees to lose 1 pound each week, and, if she does, she avoids losing the $10 deposit she gave her weight loss therapist.

10. _____ Sammy agrees to a contract in which she loses $10 each time she yells at her kids.

TWENTY-FOUR

Fear and Anxiety Reduction Procedures

This chapter describes procedures used to help people overcome fears and anxiety-related disorders. First, problems involving fear and anxiety are described in terms of operant and respondent behaviors. Next, procedures used to treat these problems are discussed. Fear and anxiety reduction procedures are based on principles of operant and respondent conditioning, so they address both types of behavior involved in fear and anxiety problems.

- What is fear? What is anxiety?
- How does relaxation training work to decrease fear and anxiety?
- What are the different types of relaxation training procedures? What features do they have in common?
- What is systematic desensitization? How does it work to alleviate a fear?
- How does in vivo desensitization differ from systematic desensitization? What are the advantages and disadvantages of each?

Examples of Fear and Anxiety Reduction

Overcoming Trisha's Fear of Public Speaking

Trisha was taking a class in which the students had to do an oral presentation. Trisha had never done a class presentation, and when she thought about it, she started to get nervous. Her heart beat faster, her stomach felt queasy, and her palms began to sweat a little. She did not have to give her talk until the end of the semester, so she tried not to think about it. When she didn't think about it, she felt better. As the end of the semester approached, she thought about the talk more often and experienced the unpleasant nervous sensations more frequently. Sometimes she imagined herself in front of the class giving the talk and forgetting what to say. When she had these images, she experienced the nervous sensations. On the day that she had to give her talk, Trisha's heart beat faster, her palms were cold and covered with sweat, her stomach hurt, and her muscles were tense. She experienced these sensations as she gave her talk and told herself that everyone could see that she was nervous. This thought made her more nervous. Trisha did not feel better until she was done and was back in her own seat at the back of the class. This was the first talk she had given. In the past, she had dropped other courses when she found out that she had to give a talk in the class. When she dropped these courses, she felt relieved that she didn't have to give the talk.

Trisha decided to see a psychologist about her fear of talking in front of the class. In upcoming semesters, she had to take a number of classes in which students were

FIGURE 24-1 Trisha practices her public speaking in front of an increasing number of people while maintaining relaxation.

required to give class presentations, and she didn't want to experience the same unpleasant fear reaction in the future. The psychologist, Dr. Gonzalez, first taught Trisha relaxation exercises that she could use to relax herself when she experienced the nervous sensations that Dr. Gonzalez called anxiety. Through a combination of breathing and muscle exercises, Trisha was able to relax herself when she experienced low levels of anxiety. Next Dr. Gonzalez had Trisha practice her relaxation exercises as she gave a talk to him in his office. Once Trisha could give her talk to him in the clinic office without experiencing anxiety, Dr. Gonzalez had Trisha give the talk to a friend of hers in an empty classroom. Again, Trisha was able to relax herself and give the talk with minimal anxiety. Next, Trisha was instructed to give her talk to two friends in an empty classroom as she practiced her relaxation exercises. As Trisha was successful, Dr. Gonzalez had her give the talk to more and more friends in a classroom, until she was talking to as many people as were in her class. Finally, Trisha gave the talk to her friends in the room where her class was held. When the day came for Trisha to give her talk to the class, she used the relaxation exercises, gave her talk with very little anxiety, and felt confident in front of the class (Figure 24-1).

Overcoming Allison's Fear of Spiders

Allison came in to see Dr. Wright at the student counseling center complaining of an intense fear of spiders. Whenever she saw a spider, she screamed for her husband to come and kill it. If she was alone when she saw a spider, she ran out of the room and did not go back into the room until she was certain that someone had killed the spider. She once climbed out of a window to get away from a spider that was hanging in a doorway. Allison reported intense fear reactions when she saw a spider. She experienced many of the same sensations Trisha experienced: rapid heart rate, muscle tension, sweating, upset stomach and nausea, tense muscles, light-headedness, and a flushed face. These sensations were extremely unpleasant; the only way that Allison could get relief was to get away from the spider or see it killed.

Dr. Wright started by assessing Allison's fear. She put a spider in a jar and placed it on a table in a large room. Dr. Wright then asked Allison to get as close to the spider as she could and to report the level of fear that she experienced as she approached the spider in the jar. Allison used a rating scale from 0 to 100 to report the intensity of the fear sensations. Before treatment, she could get within a few feet of the spider in the jar, but she reported the highest fear rating of 100. Standing that close to the spider, she felt terrified, even though it was in a jar and could not get out. Dr. Wright began treatment by teaching relaxation exercises to Allison. Once Allison learned these exercises, she used the exercises to relax herself as she gradually approached the spider with Dr. Wright at her side for support. First, Allison stood 20 feet from the spider and relaxed herself. When she reported feeling comfortable (a rating of about 25 on the fear scale), she took one step closer to the spider. With Dr. Wright at her side, she used the relaxation exercises until she reported feeling comfortable again. Allison and Dr. Wright continued this process, using the relaxation exercises and very gradually approaching the spider, in treatment sessions over a 3-month period. By the end of treatment, Allison could get close enough to a spider to kill it herself while reporting a low fear rating. This was her goal: to be able to kill a spider when she saw one, without experiencing the intense fear reaction. (This case is from Miltenberger, Wright, & Fuqua, 1986.)

DEFINING FEAR AND ANXIETY PROBLEMS

Many people seek treatment from psychologists for problems of fear and anxiety. Before talking about treatments for fears and anxiety problems, it is important to provide operational definitions of the behaviors involved.

A **fear** is composed of both operant and respondent behavior. Typically, a person is afraid of a particular stimulus or stimulus situation. When the stimulus is present, the person experiences unpleasant bodily responses (autonomic nervous system arousal) and engages in escape or avoidance behavior. The bodily responses are respondent behaviors we call **anxiety.** The autonomic nervous system arousal involved in anxiety is an establishing operation that makes it more likely that the person will engage in escape or avoidance behavior at that time.

In the case of Allison, identify the conditioned stimulus and conditioned response that make up the respondent behavior involved in her fear.

The presence of a spider is a conditioned stimulus (CS) that elicits a conditioned response (CR) of autonomic nervous system arousal involving rapid heart rate, sweating hands, muscle tension, upset stomach, light-headedness, and a flushed face. The CR involves unpleasant sensations that people call anxiety.

In the case of Allison, identify the operant behavior and the reinforcement for this behavior.

The operant behavior involved in Allison's fear of spiders involves screaming for her husband to come and kill the spider and running away when she sees the spider. Screaming for her husband is reinforced by the removal of the spider (her husband kills it); running away is also reinforced by escape from the spider, as she removes herself from the location where she saw the spider. When the spider is no longer present, there is a corresponding reduction in the anxiety (unpleasant bodily sensations) that was elicited by the presence of the spider. Thus, the behaviors of screaming and running away are negatively reinforced by the removal of, or escape from, the spider and the reduction in anxiety.

Identify the operant and respondent behaviors involved in Trisha's fear of public speaking.

In Trisha's case, being in front of the class to give a talk is a CS that elicits a CR of autonomic arousal. However, thinking about the talk and imagining herself giving the talk are also CSs that elicit the CR. As you can see, her own covert behavior (thoughts, images) can function as a CS that elicits anxiety as a CR. In this case, the operant behavior involves dropping classes in which she would have to give a talk. Dropping the classes is reinforced by elimination of the anxiety associated with giving the talk. Also, when she is thinking about the talk she has to give, replacing those anxiety-producing thoughts with other thoughts or behaviors is negatively reinforced by a reduction in the anxiety. For example, when Trisha is thinking about her talk and experiences anxiety, she calls her friend on the phone. As soon as she calls her friend, the anxiety-producing thoughts stop and the behavior of calling her friend is reinforced.

Most problems that we would label as fears or anxiety disorders are characterized by a combination of respondent behavior, in which the bodily response of anxiety is elicited by a particular CS, and operant behavior, in which escape or avoidance behaviors are reinforced by removal of the feared stimulus and reduction in the unpleasant anxiety. Because both operant and respondent behaviors are involved in the problem, most treatment approaches involve components that address both the operant and respondent behaviors.

Describe the operant and respondent behaviors involved in a child's fear of the dark.

Being in a room with the lights out (darkness) is a CS that elicits the CR of anxiety or autonomic arousal. When the child reports being scared or afraid of the dark, the child is identifying the unpleasant bodily responses that he or she experiences in the dark. The operant behavior may involve turning on a night light or leaving the door open so that the room is lit from the hallway. The outcome of these behaviors is that darkness is decreased or eliminated, and thus the anxiety is reduced. Another behavior might be crying or calling out for the parents. This behavior is reinforced by the presence of the parents, which decreases the anxiety associated with being in the dark.

Although it is clear that respondent behavior is a component of a fear, often it is not known how the fear developed through respondent conditioning; that is, it may not be known how the CS (the feared stimulus) became conditioned to elicit the CR of anxiety. Recall from Chapter 8 that a neutral stimulus becomes a CS when it is paired with an unconditioned stimulus (US) or another CS. As a result of this pairing, the neutral stimulus becomes a CS and elicits the same response that is elicited by the US. For example, a child who gets knocked down or bitten by a dog may then develop a fear of dogs. The painful stimulus (being knocked down or bitten) is a US that elicits autonomic arousal, an unconditioned response (UR). The dog itself is a neutral stimulus that becomes a CS because the dog's presence is paired with the painful stimulus. Therefore, when the child who was bitten sees a dog (a CS), it elicits a CR similar to the UR that was elicited by the painful stimulus of the dog bite.

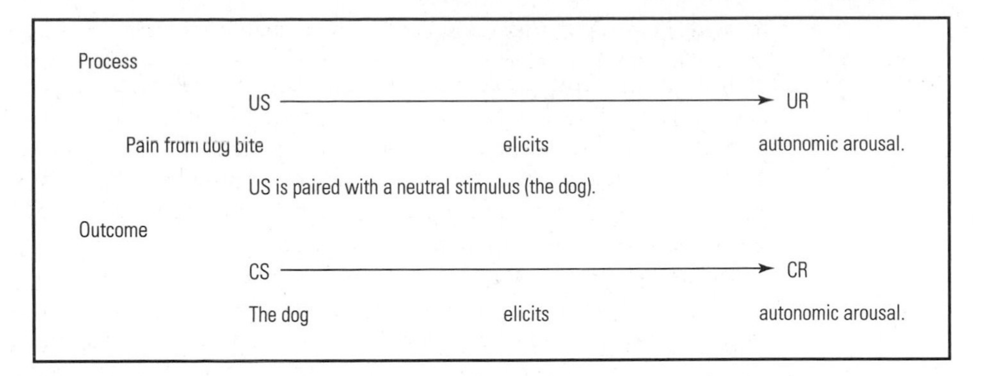

In the case of a dog bite, the role of respondent conditioning in the development of the fear is obvious. In many other cases, the person with the fear cannot remember a past event that may have conditioned the feared stimulus. Although the feared stimulus clearly elicits anxiety as a CR, how that feared stimulus became a CS may be unknown. However, knowledge of how the fear was conditioned is unnecessary to help the person overcome the fear. What is important is to identify all the stimuli that currently function as CSs and elicit the fear responses (the CRs).

One other issue to consider in understanding fears and anxiety problems is that sometimes a problem that appears to be a fear or anxiety problem is simply an operant behavior with no respondent behavior or fear component. For example, a child who screams and cries and claims to be afraid to go to school may have a school phobia or may simply be exhibiting operant behavior that is being positively reinforced (Kearney & Silverman, 1990). If it is a fear, the child experiences the respondent behavior of autonomic arousal that we call anxiety. This anxiety is elicited by school or school-related stimuli. Screaming, crying, and refusing to go to school are operant behaviors that are reinforced by escape from or avoidance of school and the reduction in anxiety associated with school. However, there may not be any anxiety associated with school, and the behavior of screaming, crying, claiming to be scared, and refusing to go to school may be positively reinforced by attention from a parent, watching TV, eating snacks, and playing games during the day. It is important to conduct a functional assessment of the supposed fear behavior to determine what function it serves for the child (Lee & Miltenberger, 1996).

Another example might be a fear of the dark. A true fear would include a CR of autonomic arousal (anxiety) elicited by the dark and escape or avoidance behavior reinforced by removal of darkness and a reduction in anxiety. However, the child's behavior of crying at night and claiming to be afraid may be reinforced by having a parent provide attention and comfort. The report of fear may not be an accurate identification of a bodily response of anxiety.

Procedures to Reduce Fear and Anxiety

A number of behavior modification procedures are used to help people overcome problems of fear or anxiety. These procedures involve relaxation training, systematic desensitization, and in vivo desensitization (Masters, Burish, Hollon, & Rimm, 1987; Spiegler & Guevremont, 1998) and are based on principles of respondent conditioning, operant conditioning, or a combination of the two.

Relaxation Training

Relaxation training procedures are strategies that people use to decrease the autonomic arousal that they experience as a component of fear and anxiety problems. The person engages in specific relaxation behaviors that result in bodily responses opposite to the autonomic arousal. Whereas bodily responses such as tense muscles, rapid heart rate, cold hands, and rapid breathing are part of autonomic arousal, relaxation exercises produce bodily responses such as decreases in muscle tension, heart rate, and breathing rate and warming of the hands. Once the person produces these opposite bodily responses, he or she reports a decrease in anxiety. Four common relaxation training approaches are progressive muscle relaxation, diaphragmatic breathing, attention-focusing exercises (Davis, Eshelman, & McKay, 1988), and behavioral relaxation training (Poppen, 1988).

Progressive Muscle Relaxation

In **progressive muscle relaxation** (PMR), the person systematically tenses and relaxes each of the major muscle groups in the body. Tensing and relaxing the muscles leaves them more relaxed than in their initial state. Progressive muscle relaxation was first described by Edmund Jacobson (1938) and has been used widely since then (Benson, 1975; Bernstein & Borkovec, 1973).

To use PMR, the person must first learn how to tense and relax each of the major muscles of the body. The person can learn to do this from a therapist, from listening to an audiotape of the procedure, or from reading a description. Table 24-1 identifies one set of muscle groups and describes how to tense these muscles when using the PMR procedure (Masters et al., 1987).

Having learned how to tense each of the muscle groups, the client can begin the relaxation procedure. First, the client gets into a comfortable position in a comfortable chair such as a recliner. The relaxation exercise should be conducted in a quiet room or some other place that has no major distractions. Next, the client closes his or her eyes and tenses and relaxes each muscle group identified in Table 24-1. Starting with the first muscle group, the dominant hand and arm, the client tenses the muscles tightly for about 5 seconds and then abruptly releases the tension. This allows the client to feel the contrast between the tension and relaxation in that particular muscle group. The client focuses on the decreased level of tension in the muscle group for 5–10 seconds and then moves to the next muscle group on the list: the other hand and arm. Again the client tenses the muscles tightly and then abruptly releases the muscles and throws off the tension. After the client tenses the muscles, the decreased level of tension or relaxed state of the muscles is pleasant and easily discriminable. The client repeats this process until all of the muscle groups have been tensed and relaxed. When the process is complete, the muscles of the body should be less tense or more relaxed than they were at the beginning of the relaxation exercise.

Relaxation Training Procedures

- Progressive muscle relaxation
- Diaphragmatic breathing
- Attention-focusing exercises
- Behavioral relaxation training

TABLE 24-1 Some Muscle Groups and Methods of Tensing Them for the PMR Procedure

Muscle Group	Method of Tensing
Dominant hand and arm	Make a tight fist, curl toward shoulder, bend arm to elbow.
Nondominant hand and arm	Same as dominant.
Forehead and eyes	Open eyes wide and raise eyebrows. Make as many wrinkles as possible on your forehead.
Upper cheeks and nose	Frown, squint eyes, wrinkle nose.
Jaw, lower face, neck	Clench teeth, protrude chin. Corners of mouth should be pulled down.
Shoulders, upper back, chest	Shrug shoulders and pull shoulder blades back as far as possible, as though trying to have them touch one another.
Abdomen	Bend forward slightly at waist, protrude stomach, tighten muscles as much as possible, making them very hard.
Buttocks	Squeeze buttocks together, push down into chair at same time.
Dominant upper leg	Push large muscle on top of thigh against smaller areas on bottom of thigh. Make muscles hard, press them against each other.
Dominant lower leg	Pull toes up till they point toward head. Stretch and harden muscles in calf.
Dominant foot	Point toes outward and downward, stretching foot.
Nondominant upper leg	Same as dominant.
Nondominant lower leg	Same as dominant.
Nondominant foot	Same as dominant.

Source: Masters et al. (1987).

Many people do PMR for the first time by listening to a relaxation tape or by listening to the relaxation instructions provided by a therapist. When a person tries PMR without the help of a therapist or audiotape, he or she must first practice tensing and relaxing each muscle group and then memorize the sequence to do the procedure correctly.

Once people have practiced PMR many times, they can begin to relax themselves without tensing and relaxing each muscle group. Because the PMR procedure teaches people to control their own muscle tension, they can then decrease muscle tension in situations in which they are likely to experience more tension. To facilitate this process, people often use a cue word when practicing PMR and then later recite the cue word to help themselves relax. For example, while practicing PMR in her own dorm room, Trisha repeated the cue word "Relax" to herself. The cue word became associated with the relaxation response and later, when Trisha was about to give her class presentation, she said "Relax" to herself as she relaxed her muscles. The cue word develops into a CS that elicits relaxation as a CR. Reciting the cue word also helps the person avoid thoughts that might elicit anxiety. If Trisha is saying "Relax" to herself while waiting for her turn to talk in class, it is more difficult for her to think about failing or to have other anxiety-producing thoughts.

Diaphragmatic Breathing Another relaxation exercise involves **diaphragmatic breathing** (Poppen, 1988)—also called deep breathing (Davis et al., 1988) or relaxed breathing (Mayo Clinic Foundation, 1989)—in which the person breathes deeply in a slow rhythmic fashion. At each inhalation, the person uses the muscles of the diaphragm to pull oxygen deep into the lungs. Because anxiety or autonomic arousal most often involves shallow, rapid breathing, diaphragmatic breathing decreases anxiety by replacing this breathing pattern with a more relaxed pattern. To illustrate this point, think about what happens when people are startled or frightened: Their breathing becomes rapid and shallow, and they have trouble catching their breath. A person experiences similar sensations when hyperventilating. Contrast this with the slow and deep breathing from a person about to fall asleep, an extreme state of relaxation.

To learn diaphragmatic breathing, a person should get in a comfortable sitting position and place a hand on the abdomen, just below the rib cage. This is the location of the diaphragm muscle. On inhaling, the person should feel the abdomen move outward as the diaphragm pulls the breath of air deep into the lungs (Poppen, 1988). The shoulders should be motionless in diaphragmatic breathing. Upward movement of the shoulders during inhalation indicates shallow breathing in the upper portion of the lungs rather than deep breathing into the lungs. Many people believe that the abdomen should be pulled in during inhalation. The opposite is true: The abdomen moves outward when a person breathes deeply using the muscles of the diaphragm (Mayo Clinic Foundation, 1989). After learning to breathe correctly, with the abdomen expanding at each inhalation, the person is ready to begin the breathing exercise.

To practice deep or diaphragmatic breathing to decrease anxiety, the person sits, stands, or lies down in a comfortable position, with eyes closed, and inhales slowly for 3–5 seconds until the lungs are comfortably filled with air. The diaphragm muscle extends the abdomen as the air is inhaled. The person then exhales slowly for 3–5 seconds. The diaphragm muscle pulls in the abdomen as the air is exhaled. It is best to inhale and exhale through the nose during diaphragmatic breathing exercises. On inhaling and exhaling, the person should focus attention on the sensations involved in breathing (e.g., the feelings of the lungs expanding and contracting, the air flowing in and out, and the movement of the abdomen). By focusing attention on these sensations, the person is less likely to think anxiety-provoking thoughts. Once the person can produce a decrease in anxiety by engaging in the diaphragmatic breathing during practice sessions, he or she can then use deep breathing to decrease arousal in anxiety-producing situations. For example, as Allison is standing 10 feet from the spider during treatment sessions, she engages in diaphragmatic breathing to lower her arousal or maintain a low level of arousal.

Note that diaphragmatic breathing exercises are a component of most other relaxation procedures. In PMR, for example, the person first learns to breathe correctly so as to enhance the effectiveness of the muscle tensing and relaxing exercises. PMR is not as effective if the person is breathing in a rapid and shallow fashion. As we see next, deep breathing is also a component of attention-focusing exercises.

Attention-Focusing Exercises **Attention-focusing exercises** produce relaxation by directing attention to a neutral or pleasant stimulus to remove the person's attention from the anxiety-producing stimulus. Procedures such as meditation, guided imagery, and hypnosis all produce relaxation through a mechanism of attention focusing (Davis et al., 1988). In meditation, the person focuses attention on a visual stimulus, an auditory stimulus, or a kinesthetic stimulus. For example, the person gazes at an object, focuses attention on repetitive mantras (word sounds), or focuses on his or her own breathing movements. Once focused on the object, mantra, or breathing during the meditation exercise, the person's attention cannot be focused on stimuli that produce anxiety.

In guided imagery or visualization exercises, the person visualizes or imagines pleasant scenes or images. Once again, this exercise focuses the person's attention so that it cannot be focused on anxiety-producing thoughts or images. The person listens to an audiotape or to a therapist who describes a scene or image. The person gets into a comfortable sitting or lying position, with eyes closed, and imagines the scene. The audiotape or the therapist describes sights, sounds, and smells when creating the image. For example, in describing a scene at the beach, the therapist might say, "Feel the warm sun on your skin; feel the warm sand under your feet; hear the waves gently rolling up on to the beach; smell the sweet scent of suntan oil." If many senses are engaged, the person is more likely to imagine the scene fully and to displace any anxiety-provoking thoughts or images.

In hypnosis, the person focuses attention on the hypnotic suggestions from the therapist or from an audiotape. In the hypnotic trance, attention is simply focused on the therapist's words so that the person is less aware of external stimuli, including anxiety provoking thoughts and images. A person can practice self-hypnosis by reciting hypnotic suggestions from a script to induce a state of relaxation.

Note that attention focusing procedures typically are used as components of other relaxation procedures. In PMR, the person focuses attention on each muscle group that is being tensed and relaxed. In diaphragmatic breathing exercises, the person focuses attention on the physical sensations of each inhalation and exhalation. At the same time, a relaxed posture is a component of diaphragmatic breathing exercises, guided imagery exercises, and PMR. As you can see, these three approaches to relaxation have many components in common.

Behavioral Relaxation Training In **behavioral relaxation training,** described by Poppen (1988), the person is taught to relax each muscle group in the body by assuming relaxed postures. This is similar to PMR, except that the person does not tense and relax each muscle group. The person sits in a recliner, with all parts of his or her body supported by the chair, and the therapist provides instructions for the client to put each part of his or her body into the correct posture. Table 24-2 presents the ten relaxed behaviors described by Poppen (1988).

Behavioral relaxation training includes components of the other relaxation procedures. The person is taught to breathe correctly, and his or her attention is focused on each of the ten relaxation behaviors involved in the procedure. As you can see, there are three components to this relaxation procedure: focus on muscle tension, correct breathing, and attention focusing.

It is important to learn relaxation procedures because relaxation training is a component of fear reduction procedures. The various fear reduction procedures are described next.

TABLE 24-2 Ten Relaxed Behaviors

Behavioral relaxation training consists of a description of ten postures and activities characteristic of a fully relaxed person whose body is fully supported by a reclining chair or similar device. Each behavior consists of an overt posture or activity of a particular region of the body. To enhance discrimination, both relaxed and some commonly occurring unrelaxed behaviors are presented for each item.

1. Head

Relaxed. The head is motionless and supported by the recliner, with the nose in the midline of the body. Body midline usually can be determined by clothing features such as shirt buttons or apex of V neckline. part of the nostrils and the underside of the chin are visible.

Unrelaxed. (a) Movement of the head. (b) Head turned from body midline; the entire nose is beyond midline. (c) Head tilted downward; the nostrils and underside of the chin are not visible. (d) Head unsupported by the recliner. (e) Head tilted upward; the entire underside of the chin is visible.

2. Eyes

Relaxed. The eyelids are lightly closed, with a smooth appearance and no motion of the eyes beneath the lids.

Unrelaxed. (a) Eyes open. (b) Eyelids closed but wrinkled or fluttering. (c) Eyes moving under the lids.

3. Mouth

Relaxed. The lips are parted at the center of the mouth from ¼ to 1 inch (7 to 25 mm), with the front teeth also parted.

Unrelaxed. (a) Teeth in occlusion. (b) Lips closed. (c) Mouth open more than 1 inch (25 mm); in most cases the corners of the mouth separate when the mouth is open beyond criterion. (d) Tongue motion, such as licking lips.

4. Throat

Relaxed. Absence of motion.

Unrelaxed. Any movement in the throat and neck, such as swallowing or other larynx action, twitches in the neck muscles.

5. Shoulders

Relaxed. Both shoulders appear rounded and transect the same horizontal plane. They rest against the recliner with no motion other than respiration.

Unrelaxed. (a) Movement of shoulders. (b) Shoulders on a diagonal plane. (c) Shoulders are raised or lowered so as not to appear rounded.

Source: Poppen (1988).

Systematic Desensitization

Systematic desensitization is a procedure developed by Joseph Wolpe (1958, 1961, 1990) in which the person with a phobia practices relaxation while imagining scenes of the fear-producing stimulus. A **phobia** is a fear in which the level of anxiety or escape and avoidance behavior is severe enough to disrupt the person's life. Wolpe determined that a person could decrease fear responses by learning to relax while imagining progressively greater anxiety-producing scenes described by the therapist. For example, in a systematic desensitization session, Allison would relax

TABLE 24-2 Ten Relaxed Behaviors *(continued)*

6. Body

Relaxed. The body is relaxed when the torso, hips, and legs are symmetrical around midline, resting against the chair, with no movement.

Unrelaxed. (a) Any movement of the torso, excluding respiration. (b) Twisting of torso, hips, or legs out of midline. (c) Any movement of the hips, legs, or arms that does not result in movement of feet or hands. (These are scored separately.) (d) Any part of the back, buttocks, or legs not supported by the recliner.

7. Hands

Relaxed. Both hands are resting on the armrest of the chair or on the lap, with palms down and the fingers curled in a clawlike fashion. The fingers are sufficiently curled if a pencil can pass freely beneath the highest point of the arc (excluding the thumb).

Unrelaxed. (a) Hands gripping the armrest. (b) Fingers extended and straight. (c) Fingers curled so that nails touch the surface of the armrest. (d) Fingers intertwined. (e) Movement of the hands.

8. Feet

Relaxed. The feet are pointed away from each other at an angle between 60° and 90°.

Unrelaxed. (a) Movement of feet. (b) Feet pointing vertically or at angle less than 60°. (c) Feet pointing out at an angle greater than 90°. (d) Feet crossed at the ankles. (e) One heel placed more than 1 inch (25 mm) fore or aft of the other.

9. Quiet

Relaxed. No vocalizations or loud respiratory sounds.

Unrelaxed. Any verbalization or vocalization, such as talking, sighing, grunting, snoring, gasping, coughing.

10. Breathing

Relaxed. The breath frequency is less than that observed during baseline, with no breathing interruptions. One breath equals one complete cycle of inhalation and exhalation. A breath is counted if any part of the inhalation occurs on the cue starting the observation interval and any part of the exhalation occurs on the cue ending the observation interval.

Unrelaxed. (a) Breath frequency is equal to or greater than that during baseline. (b) Any irregularity that interrupts the regular rhythm of breathing, such as coughing, laughing, yawning, and sneezing.

herself and listen to the therapist describe a scene in which she saw a spider 25 feet away. After Allison listened to this scene and maintained relaxation, the therapist would describe a scene in which the spider was 20 feet away. If Allison maintained relaxation, the therapist would continue to describe scenes in which the spider was closer and closer. The key ingredient is for Allison to maintain her relaxation response as she imagines the fear-producing stimulus. Wolpe called the process reciprocal inhibition because the relaxation response inhibits or prevents the occurrence of the fear response.

There are three important steps in the use of the systematic desensitization procedure.

1. The client learns relaxation skills using one of the procedures described earlier.
2. The therapist and client develop a hierarchy of fear-producing stimuli.
3. The client practices the relaxation skills while the therapist describes scenes from the hierarchy.

Once the client can maintain the relaxation response while imagining every scene from the hierarchy, the systematic desensitization is complete. The client should then be free from the fear responses (anxiety and avoidance behavior) when the client encounters the fear-producing stimulus in real life.

Developing the Hierarchy Once the client learns the relaxation procedures, the therapist and client develop a hierarchy of the fear-producing stimuli. The client uses a fear rating scale and identifies the amount of fear that is produced by a variety of situations related to the feared stimulus. The fear rating scale is called a subjective units of discomfort scale (SUDS; Wolpe, 1990). On the 0–100 scale, a rating of 0 corresponds to the absence of fear or anxiety and 100 corresponds to the maximum amount of fear or anxiety. For example, Allison might report that a spider on her arm is a SUDS rating of 100, the most fear she could possibly imagine. She might report that seeing a spider 5 feet away is a SUDS rating of 75, seeing one 10 feet away is a SUDS rating of 50, seeing one 20 feet away is a SUDS rating of 25, and sitting in her living room with her husband with no spider present is a SUDS rating of 0, the absence of the fear. The hierarchy is complete when the client has identified 10–20 different situations that are progressively more fear producing. Fear-producing situations should be identified across the range of fear levels so that the hierarchy is composed of situations with low, middle, and high fear scores. Table 24-3 presents examples of four hierarchies used in systematic desensitization (Morris, 1991).

Progressing through the Hierarchy Having developed relaxation skills and constructed the hierarchy with the therapist, the client is ready to begin systematic desensitization and progress through the hierarchy. At the start of the session, the client practices relaxation exercises. After the client signals a state of relaxation, the therapist describes the first scene in the hierarchy, which produces very little anxiety. The client imagines this scene while continuing to relax. Once the client has successfully imagined this scene while maintaining relaxation, the process moves to the next step in the hierarchy. The therapist describes a slightly more fear-producing scene. Again the client imagines this scene while maintaining the relaxation response. The therapist might repeat the scene a few times, to be sure that the client can imagine the scene while maintaining the relaxation response. The therapist then describes the next scene in the hierarchy, which is again slightly more anxiety-provoking than the previous scene, and the client imagines the scene while maintaining relaxation. This process continues over the course of a number of treatment sessions until the client can maintain relaxation through all of the scenes in the hierarchy.

Thus, in systematic desensitization, the client relaxes while imagining the feared stimulus; the client does not make actual contact with the fear-producing

TABLE 24-3 Samples of Initial Anxiety Hierarchies

Fear of being alone

10. Being with a group of people at the lab, either at night or during the day.
20. Being alone in a room with another woman.
30. Thinking about the possibility of being alone in my house during the day.
40. Walking to class early in the morning when there are few people outside.
50. Actually alone in my bedroom at home and it's daylight.
60. Driving a car alone at night and feeling a man is following me.
70. Walking alone on a city street downtown at night with a girlfriend.
80. Being alone in a house with a young child for whom I am babysitting.
90. Thinking about being alone at night a few hours before I will actually be alone.
100. Sitting alone in the living room of my house at night with the doors closed.

Fear of flying in airplanes

10. Watching a movie of a plane moving up and down and banking.
20. Sitting in a private plane on the ground with the motor idling.
30. Sitting in a private plane on the ground and the pilot begins to taxi down the runway.
40. Sitting in a private plane on the ground, taxiing, and the pilot revs the engine.
50. Planning a trip with a friend on a commercial jet, 3 months before the trip.
60. One month before the trip by jet.
70. Three weeks before the trip by jet.
80. Three days before the trip by jet.
90. In a private plane at takeoff.
100. In a commercial jet over land.

Fear of driving in high places

10. Entering a ramp garage on ground level.
20. Going up to third level of the garage from the second level.
30. Riding with a friend in a car and approaching the bridge over the Chicago River on Michigan Avenue.
40. Driving a car with a friend and beginning to approach the bridge over the Chicago River.
50. Driving my car over the Chicago River bridge.
60. Driving a friend and crossing the bridge over the Mississippi River near Moline.
70. Driving my car on the bridge over the Mississippi River near Moline.
80. Driving my car with a friend on a hilly road in Wisconsin.
90. Driving my car with a friend on a hilly road in Wisconsin and going halfway up a fairly steep hill.
100. Driving my car with a friend up to the top of a fairly steep hill. We get to the top and get out of the car and look around at the valley below, then go into a restaurant nearby, and later drive back down the hill.

Fear of leaving the house

10. Going out the front door to my car to go to the store.
20. Getting in the car and starting it up.
30. In the car and pulling out of the driveway.
40. On the street and pulling away from my house.
50. Two blocks from my house on way to the store.
60. Arrive at the store and park.
70. Enter the store.
80. Get a shopping cart and begin looking for items on my list.
90. Have all the items and go to checkout counter.
100. Have all the items and have to wait in a long, slow line to go through checkout.

Source: Morris (1991).

stimulus. Contrast this procedure with in vivo (real life) desensitization, in which the client is gradually exposed to the actual fear-producing stimulus while maintaining relaxation.

In Vivo Desensitization

In vivo desensitization is similar to systematic desensitization, except that the client gradually approaches or is gradually exposed to the actual fear-producing stimulus (Walker, Hedberg, Clement, & Wright, 1981). To use the in vivo desensitization procedure, the client must first learn the relaxation response. Next, the client and therapist must develop a hierarchy of situations involving the fear-producing stimulus. In the in vivo desensitization procedure, the client does not imagine each scene in the hierarchy; rather, the client experiences each situation in the hierarchy while maintaining relaxation as an alternative response to replace the fear response. In the examples of Trisha and Allison, in vivo desensitization was used to help them overcome their fears.

Recall that Trisha was afraid to give a class presentation. Dr. Gonzalez first taught her relaxation exercises. Next, they developed a hierarchy of fear-producing situations, as follows. The fear (SUDS) rating of each item is given in parentheses.

1. Giving a talk to Dr. Gonzalez in his office (20)
2. Giving a talk to Dr. Gonzalez in a classroom (25)
3. Giving a talk to a friend in a classroom (30)
4. Giving a talk to two friends in a classroom (40)
5. Giving a talk to five friends in a classroom (50)
6. Giving a talk to ten friends in a classroom (60)
7. Giving a talk to 20 friends in a classroom (75)
8. Giving a talk to 20 friends in the actual room where the class is held (80)
9. Giving a talk to 20 students she did not know (90)
10. Giving a talk to the 20 students in her class (100)

In vivo desensitization required Trisha to experience each situation in the hierarchy while using the relaxation exercises Dr. Gonzalez had taught her. As she was successful at each step in the hierarchy, she was one step closer to overcoming her fear of giving a talk in class.

Describe how in vivo desensitization was used with Allison to help her overcome her fear of spiders.

Dr. Wright first taught Allison how to relax. Next, they developed a hierarchy of fear-producing situations. The hierarchy for Allison involved distance from a spider: Her fear was greater when she was closer to the spider. To begin the in vivo desensitization, Allison relaxed herself as she stood far away—20 feet—from the spider. This situation produced little fear, and the relaxation replaced any fear that she might have experienced. Allison then moved one step up the hierarchy: Standing 19 feet from the spider, she again practiced her relaxation exercises so that the relaxation response replaced her fear response. With the support of Dr. Wright, Allison repeated this process until she had advanced to the last step in the hierarchy, in which she killed the spider.

During in vivo desensitization, it is important for the client to advance through each step in the hierarchy without an increase in anxiety. As we have seen, one way to accomplish this is for the client to practice relaxation at each step in the hierarchy. However, relaxation training is not always used during in vivo desensitization. Instead, the therapist might simply provide reinforcement for approach behavior at each hierarchy step. (In fact, even when relaxation is used, the client should receive positive reinforcement at each new step of the hierarchy, in the form of praise from the therapist.) Alternatively, the therapist might have the client engage in other reinforcing activities (Croghan & Musante, 1975; Erfanian & Miltenberger, 1990) or in distracting activities at each hierarchy step; for example, the client might recite coping statements (Miltenberger et al., 1986). Finally, the therapist might provide reassuring physical contact by holding the client's hand or placing a hand on the client's back as the client progresses through the hierarchy. This variation of in vivo desensitization is called *contact desensitization* (Ritter, 1968; 1969).

Erfanian and Miltenberger (1990) used in vivo desensitization with people with mental retardation who were dog-phobic. In this study, the clients did not learn relaxation procedures; rather, they engaged in activities that were positively reinforcing, as an alternative to running away, when a dog was introduced into their environment. Over the course of a number of treatment sessions, the experimenters moved the dog progressively closer to the clients in the recreation room of their own residence as they engaged in reinforcing activities such as playing cards or eating a snack. Results for two clients are shown in Figure 24-2.

Advantages and Disadvantages of Systematic and In Vivo Desensitization

The advantage of in vivo desensitization is that the client makes actual contact with the feared stimulus. Desirable behavior (e.g., approach behavior) in the presence of the feared stimulus is reinforced as an alternative behavior to escape or avoidance; there is no problem with generalization from imagination to the actual fear situation. Once the client has progressed through the hierarchy, he or she has demonstrated successful performance in the fear-producing situation. However, one disadvantage of in vivo desensitization is that it is more difficult and possibly more time-consuming and costly than systematic desensitization. This is because the therapist has to arrange actual contact with the fear-producing situations in the hierarchy; the therapist must leave his or her office to accompany the client as the client is exposed to the actual fear-producing stimuli. In some cases, it may not be possible to arrange contact with the fear-producing stimulus. For example, it may not be possible to find spiders in the winter in some parts of the country. However, whenever possible, in vivo desensitization is preferred over systematic desensitization in treating a fear or phobia because successful behavior is demonstrated in real life rather than in the imagination, and the successful behavior is reinforced, so that the behavior is strengthened in real-life situations.

The advantage of systematic desensitization is that it is easier and more convenient for the client to imagine the feared stimulus than to come into contact with it. For example, if the client has a fear of flying, the therapist can describe scenes of being in an airport, on an airplane on the ground, or on the plane in the air. It would be much more time-consuming and difficult to conduct treatment that involved actual

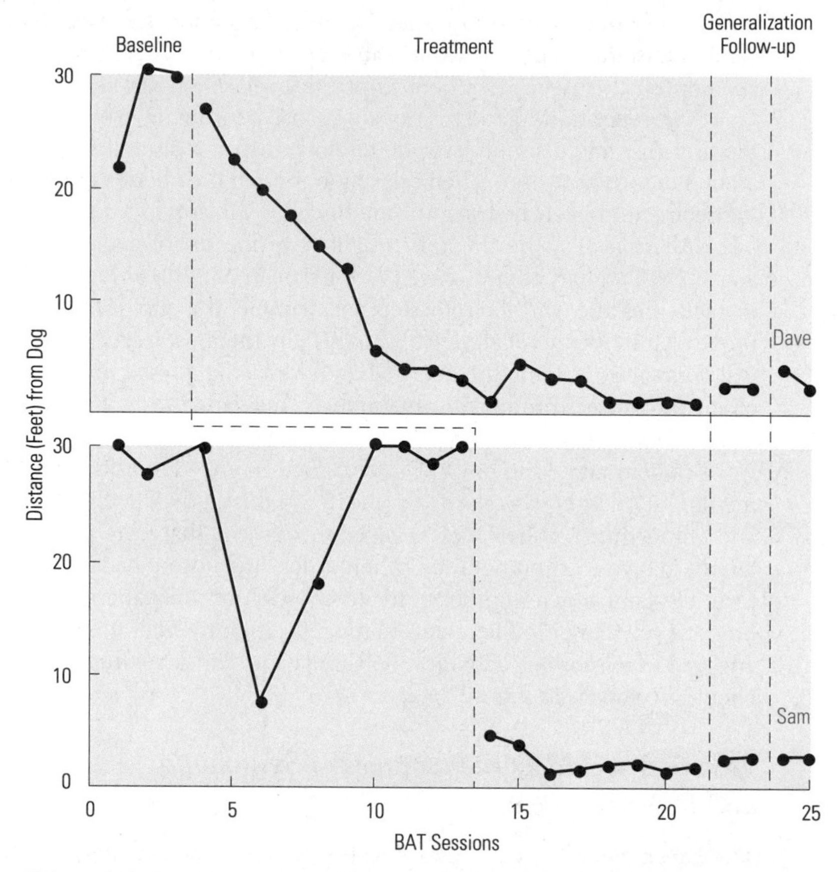

FIGURE 24-2 This multiple-baseline-across-subjects graph (from Erfanian & Miltenberger, 1990) illustrates the effect of in vivo desensitization on the dog phobias of two individuals with mental retardation. The graph shows the approach behavior of the two subjects during behavioral avoidance test (BAT) sessions, in which the subject was asked to get as close to the dog as he could. At the start of the BAT session, the dog was more than 30 feet away in a large room. The session ended when the subject stopped approaching the dog; the distance from the dog was measured at that time. The graph indicates how close to the dog the subjects could get, before and after treatment. In the generalization phase, the subjects walked past dogs positioned on a public sidewalk by a research assistant.

contact with the feared stimulus. However, one disadvantage of systematic desensitization is that the results may not fully generalize to the actual fear-producing situation. The client may be able to maintain relaxation while imagining the fear-producing situation but may not be able to do so while experiencing the actual situation.

It is important to assess the client's fear in the actual fear-producing situation to ensure that the results of systematic desensitization have generalized successfully. If the results of systematic desensitization do not fully generalize, in vivo desensitization may be used in addition to systematic desensitization to enhance its effectiveness and ensure generalization.

Other Treatments for Fears

In addition to systematic and in vivo desensitization treatments for fears, other treatments have been shown to be effective in treating fears exhibited by adults and children.

Flooding Flooding is a procedure in which the person is exposed to the feared stimulus at full intensity for a prolonged period of time (Barrios & O'Dell, 1989; Houlihan, Schwartz, Miltenberger, & Heuton, 1994). Initially, the person experiences heightened anxiety in the presence of the feared stimulus, but over time the level of anxiety decreases through a process of respondent extinction. For example, a person with a fear of dogs would sit in a room (with a therapist) with a dog present for a long period of time. Initially, the person would be highly anxious, but over time the anxiety would decrease and the person would be more comfortable with the dog. Because the CS (the dog, the feared stimulus) is presented without the US (being bitten or startled) over a period of time (e.g., a couple of hours), the CS no longer elicits the CR (anxiety).

Flooding should be conducted only by a professional. Because it is highly uncomfortable for the person with the fear to be exposed to the feared stimulus at first, he or she may escape from the situation during the flooding procedure and possibly worsen the fear. During in vivo desensitization, the person is exposed to the feared stimulus much more gradually, and thus he or she does not experience the discomfort that is experienced in the early stages of flooding.

Modeling Modeling has been used as a successful treatment for fears, especially in children. In the modeling procedure, the child observes another person approaching the feared stimulus or engaging in a feared activity, and the child is then more likely to engage in similar behavior. The person with the fear can observe a live model (Klesges, Malott, & Ugland, 1984) or a film or video model (Melamed & Siegel, 1975). Film and video modeling procedures have been widely used to help children overcome fear of surgery or fear of other medical and dental procedures (Melamed, 1979; Melamed & Siegel, 1975).

CLINICAL PROBLEMS

Although you can learn the basic components of anxiety and fear reduction procedures in a behavior modification class, you should not try to use these procedures for clinical problems with anxiety or fear experienced by yourself or others. You might use these procedures for minor fears or anxiety problems that do not disrupt your life in any meaningful ways. However, for more serious clinical problems that interfere significantly with your life, you should seek help from a behavior therapist, psychologist, or other licensed human service professional. When in doubt about the seriousness of a problem, it is best to seek assistance or consultation from a professional.

CHAPTER SUMMARY

1. A fear is composed of operant and respondent behaviors. A particular stimulus situation elicits autonomic arousal as a respondent behavior and the person engages in escape or avoidance responses as the operant behavior when the fear-producing stimulus is present. The bodily responses involved in autonomic arousal are called anxiety.
2. Relaxation exercises are used to help a person replace autonomic arousal with a relaxation response in the anxiety-producing situation.
3. Relaxation can be produced by four basic techniques: progressive muscle relaxation exercises, in which the person tenses and relaxes each major muscle group in the body; diaphragmatic breathing exercises, in which the person breathes slowly and deeply; attention-focusing exercises, in which attention is directed away from the anxiety-producing stimulus and toward a calming scene; and behavioral relaxation training, a technique that focuses on relaxed postures. All relaxation exercises address muscle tension, proper breathing, and attention focus.
4. Systematic desensitization and in vivo desensitization are procedures to help a person overcome a fear. In systematic desensitization the person relaxes and imagines scenes of fear-producing situations arranged in a hierarchy from least to most fear-producing.
5. In in vivo desensitization, the person is exposed gradually to the actual fear-producing situations (arranged in a hierarchy from least to most fear-producing) while maintaining relaxation or engaging in a behavior opposite to escape or avoidance. The important component of systematic and in vivo desensitization is the progression through a hierarchy that results in gradual exposure to more fear-producing scenes or situations. The advantage of in vivo desensitization is that the client makes actual contact with the feared stimulus, so generalization is enhanced. The disadvantage is the time and effort involved in conducting the procedure. The advantage of systematic desensitization is that it is easier and more convenient to carry out. The disadvantage is that the results may not fully generalize to the actual fear-producing situation.

PRACTICE TEST

1. Describe how respondent behavior is involved in a fear or anxiety problem. Provide an example, and identify the CS and CR in your example. (pp. 515–517)
2. Describe how operant behavior is involved in a fear or anxiety problem. Provide an example. Identify the operant behavior, and describe how the behavior is reinforced. (pp. 515–517)
3. Describe the respondent behavior Trisha exhibited as part of her fear of talking in front of the class. (p. 516)
4. Describe the operant behavior Allison exhibited as part of her fear of spiders. (p. 515)
5. Describe progressive muscle relaxation. (pp. 518–519)
6. Describe diaphragmatic breathing. (pp. 519–520)
7. Describe attention-focusing exercises. (pp. 520–521)
8. Describe behavioral relaxation training. (pp. 521–523)
9. In each of the four approaches to relaxation described in Questions 5–8, describe how muscle tension, breathing, and attention focus are addressed. (pp. 518–523)
10. Describe systematic desensitization. What is a hierarchy, and what role does it play in systematic desensitization? (pp. 522–526)
11. Describe in vivo desensitization. How does in vivo desensitization differ from systematic desensitization? (pp. 526–527)

12. What are the advantages and disadvantages of systematic desensitization? (pp. 527–528)
13. What are the advantages and disadvantages of in vivo desensitization? (pp. 527–528)
14. Would you choose systematic desensitization or in vivo desensitization to help a child overcome a fear of the dark? Why? (pp. 527–528)

APPLICATIONS

1. Jesse has a fear of heights. Whenever he looks out a window that is two stories or more above the ground, he experiences autonomic arousal. The higher he goes, the worse it gets. Jesse avoids heights as much as possible, and this has had a negative impact on his life. For example, when his friends got together recently at a seventh-floor restaurant, he declined to go out with them because of his fear. He has also refused to participate in other activities that involve heights. Describe how you would use in vivo desensitization to help Jesse overcome his fear of heights.

2. Martha has always been a little nervous about flying. Her anxiety has never interfered with her job; she flies about three times every week on business trips. However, she experiences an increase in heart rate and shallow rapid breathing when she is sitting on the plane before takeoff and just before landing. Martha would like to decrease her anxiety so that her experiences while flying are more pleasant. Describe the diaphragmatic breathing exercise you would teach Martha to help her relax on the plane.

3. Next semester, you have to take a psychology lab class in which you will use laboratory rats in experiments. This will involve transferring your rat from its home cage to the experimental chamber when you are working in the lab. You are very uncomfortable with the prospect of having to handle the lab rats. You want to overcome this fear before the semester starts. Describe the in vivo desensitization procedure you will use to decrease your fear of the lab rats. Assume that the professor will grant you access to the room where the rats are kept in their cages. Also assume that the rats are not aggressive and that they are used to being handled by people.

MISAPPLICATIONS

1. Christina, a 6-year-old girl, has developed a fear of the dark. In bed at night, she cries and calls for her parents to come into her room. If a parent comes to her room when she calls, she calms down. If the parent stays in her room until she falls asleep, she does not complain about being afraid. In addition, if her parents leave the light on in her room at night, she says she is not scared and does not cry or call for them. After a few months, her parents decide that they need to do something about her fear of the dark. They decide that they will turn off the light and leave her room at night before she is asleep. If she cries, calls for them, or indicates in some other way that she is afraid, they will ignore her and not come back to her room. The parents reason that she will eventually get over her fear of the dark. What is wrong with the parents' plan? What would be a better way to deal with Christina's fear?

2. Garth was a freshman at a university. He came from a small town and was not used to crowds of people. At parties or other large gatherings, he was nervous and uncomfortable. His muscles were tense, his heart beat faster, and sometimes his stomach felt upset. He stayed at parties for a while, but he felt better once he left. Garth decided to see a counselor about his anxiety. The counselor told him that he needed to learn relaxation skills and gave him an audiotape with instructions for progressive muscle relaxation (PMR). The counselor told Garth to listen to the tape and he would be more relaxed at parties. What is wrong with the use of PMR in this example? How could it be improved?

3. Louis had a fear of going to the dentist. He had not gone for 3 or 4 years. He avoided making appointments; the last time he had an appointment, he did not show up for it. Louis went to a psychologist, who used systematic desensitization with him. They developed a hierarchy of scenes related to going to the dentist. Louis learned relaxation skills and relaxed himself as the psychologist described each scene in the hierarchy. After six sessions of systematic desensitization, Louis was able to relax himself as he imagined sitting in the dentist's chair and submitting to dental work. After Louis could stay relaxed while imagining the dental treatment, the psychologist told him that they were done with treatment. What is wrong with the use of systematic desensitization in this case? How could it be improved?

CHAPTER 24 *Quiz 1* Name:

1. A fear is composed of both operant and ________________ behaviors.

2. The operant behavior in a fear involves ________________________ of the feared stimulus.

3. The bodily responses in a fear, which include rapid heart rate, tense muscles, and rapid, shallow breathing, are called ________________________.

4. In a fear of spiders, the spider is a(n) ____________________ that elicits a conditioned response of autonomic nervous system arousal.

5. In ________________________ relaxation, the person systematically tenses and relaxes each of the major muscle groups in the body.

6. In ________________________ relaxation, the person is taught to relax each muscle group by assuming relaxed postures.

7. During ______________________ desensitization, the client is exposed to the actual fear-provoking stimulus while progressing through the fear hierarchy.

8. During ______________________ desensitization, the client imagines the fear-provoking stimulus while progressing through the fear hierarchy.

9. What is one advantage of in vivo desensitization over systematic desensitization?

____

10. During ______________________ the person is exposed to the feared stimulus at full intensity for a prolonged period of time.

CHAPTER 24 *Quiz 2*

Name:

1. What is the operant behavior involved in a fear?

 ____

2. What is the respondent behavior involved in a fear?

 ____

3. A person with a fear of spiders sees a spider and experiences autonomic arousal. In this fear, the conditioned response is ______________ and the conditioned stimulus is ______________.

4. What is the reinforcer for the escape and avoidance behavior involved in a fear?

 ____

5. Identify two of the relaxation training procedures described in the chapter.

 ______________ and ______________

6. ______________ is a relaxation procedure in which the person learns to breathe in a slow, deep, rhythmic fashion.

7. ______________ produces relaxation by directing attention to a neutral or pleasant stimulus to remove the person's attention from the anxiety-producing stimulus.

8. A(n) ______________ is a series of feared stimuli ordered from least fear producing to most fear producing.

9. During systematic desensitization, what does the client do as the therapist describes each scene in the fear hierarchy? ______________

10. What is the name of the in vivo desensitization procedure in which the therapist may hold the client's hand or place a hand on the client's back to reassure the client as the client progresses through the fear hierarchy? ______________

CHAPTER 24 *Quiz 3* Name:

1. In a fear of public speaking, being in front of an audience elicits autonomic arousal. In this example, the conditioned stimulus is ______________ and the conditioned response is ______________.
2. What bodily responses are involved in anxiety?

   ____
3. Autonomic nervous system arousal involved in fear is a(n) ______________ that makes it more likely that the person will engage in escape or avoidance behavior.
4. Escape and avoidance behavior in a feared situation is ______________ (positively/negatively) reinforced.
5. ______________ procedures are strategies that people use to decrease the autonomic arousal they experience as a component of fear and anxiety problems.
6. What does the person do during the progressive muscle relaxation procedure to achieve relaxation? ______________
7. What does the person do during the behavioral relaxation procedure to achieve relaxation? ______________
8. What three steps are involved in the use of systematic desensitization?

   ______________, ______________

   and ______________
9. In which type of desensitization does the person have exposure to the actual feared stimulus?

   ____
10. What happens during flooding?

    ____

TWENTY-FIVE

Cognitive Behavior Modification

Behavior modification often is focused on analyzing and modifying overt behaviors. Most of the chapters in this text have described procedures for increasing or decreasing target behaviors that can be observed and recorded by an independent observer. However, some target behaviors may be covert, that is, not readily observable by another individual. Chapter 24 discussed one type of covert target behavior, the physiological responses involved in fear or anxiety problems. This chapter focuses on analyzing and modifying another type of covert behavior, **cognitive behavior.**

- What is cognitive behavior?
- What functions can cognitive behaviors serve?
- What is cognitive restructuring?
- How do you get people to change their thinking in cognitive restructuring procedures?
- How do you implement self-instructional training?

Note that people trained in behavior analysis do not favor the term *cognitive* for a variety of reasons (Skinner, 1974, 1977). However, the term is used widely in clinical psychology and behavior therapy and students are exposed to it regularly. Accordingly, the term is used in this text as a label for certain types of covert behaviors and behavior change procedures. In each case, operational definitions are provided for the behaviors that are labeled as cognitive and the procedures designed to change cognitive behaviors.

Examples of Cognitive Behavior Modification

Helping Deon Control His Anger

Deon, a junior in high school, was a recent immigrant to the United States; he had been at the high school since his sophomore year. Sometimes other students called Deon names or made racist comments to him. Deon often reacted to the name-calling or comments by getting into fights. He cursed at the other student and, if the other student did not stop or walk away, Deon began to throw punches or wrestle with him. Fights usually were broken up by teachers or other students. Deon had been suspended on a number of occasions for fighting. He was referred to a school counselor, Dr. Woods, to address this problem.

Through interviews with Deon, Dr. Woods identified a number of antecedents that preceded Deon's fighting. The primary antecedent was a situation in which another student called him a name or made a racist comment. However, some covert antecedents were also present. Deon experienced autonomic arousal (including rapid heart rate, tense muscles, and rapid breathing), which he labeled as anger. In these situations, he also made a number of angry statements to himself, such as "He can't say that to me!" or "I can't let him get away with that!" The name-calling or comments from the other student preceded his autonomic arousal (anger) and angry statements, which in turn preceded his fighting. The consequence for Deon's fighting varied. On some occasions, the other student backed down or ran away after Deon started fighting. On other occasions, the fighting was broken up by a teacher or other third party. In each case, the fighting terminated the name-calling or racist comments, at least temporarily; thus, the fighting was negatively reinforced. The decrease in autonomic arousal that Deon experienced after his fighting may also have been negatively reinforcing.

Dr. Woods could not easily apply any reinforcement or punishment procedures with Deon because she was not present when Deon got into fights. In addition, Dr. Woods could not remove the initial antecedent condition because she could not be there to stop other students from making comments or name-calling. (The high school did have rules against racist behavior and did provide training to reduce racist behavior, but this was not enough to stop the problem.) Dr. Woods decided to use cognitive behavior modification procedures to help Deon change his angry self-statements and autonomic arousal, the covert antecedents to his fighting. First, Dr. Woods helped Deon identify all of the angry self-statements he made in the fighting situations. He learned that his angry self-statements (thoughts) in response to the racist comments elicited more autonomic arousal, which made the fighting more likely to occur. Once Deon was aware of his angry thoughts and understood the role they played, he agreed to work with Dr. Woods to change his thoughts as one way to decrease his fighting.

Dr. Woods taught Deon to replace his angry thoughts with coping self-statements that would not lead to fighting. Deon learned a number of coping self-statements, such as "Don't fight, or you'll get suspended!" or "Walk away, he's a racist. It's not worth it!" or "Don't lower yourself to his level!" Using role-plays to simulate the fighting situations, Dr. Woods taught Deon to recite these coping statements out loud and then to walk away whenever someone called him a name or made racist comments to him. As Deon walked away from a fight in the role-play, he praised himself. He learned to say, for example, "Way to go, you walked away" or "It takes a real man not to fight" or "I'm in control here." Deon practiced in role-plays that simulated all of the racist comments and name-calling that he had heard over the year he had been in school. Dr. Woods provided instructions and modeling to teach Deon appropriate coping statements and provided praise and feedback for Deon's performance in the role-plays. Once Deon successfully recited a variety of coping statements out loud during the role-plays, he then learned to recite his coping statements silently instead of saying them out loud. He did this because it would not be appropriate to recite the coping statements out loud in a real conflict situation.

In addition to learning coping self-statements to replace his angry thoughts, Deon learned relaxation skills to calm himself when he was angry. Dr. Woods used behavioral skills training procedures to teach Deon appropriate assertiveness skills, that is, better ways to interact with the other students to decrease the likelihood of racist comments. Finally, Dr. Woods and Deon developed a behavioral contract that specified reinforcing consequences for Deon each time he went for a week without fighting. Deon enjoyed working with Dr. Woods and learning to control his behavior. It became reinforcing for him to walk away from a fight because of the self-praise statements he made and because of the praise he got from Dr. Woods when he recounted the situations in their meetings.

Which of the behavior modification procedures described previously in this text did Dr. Woods implement with Deon?

Dr. Woods first conducted a functional assessment by interviewing Deon to identify the antecedents and consequences of the fighting. She used behavioral skills training procedures (role-plays, rehearsal, modeling, praise, and feedback) to teach the coping self-statements and the assertiveness skills. Dr. Woods also taught Deon relaxation skills to decrease his autonomic arousal in the fighting situations. Finally, she used a behavioral contract to motivate Deon to avoid fighting. In this case, as in many others, multiple behavior modification procedures are used to address a problem.

Helping Claire Pay Attention in Class

Claire, a 7-year-old in second grade, often got into trouble with her teacher because she got out of her seat many times during each class period. When Claire got out of her seat, she would lean across the aisle to talk to a classmate, tease another student, grab something from another student's desk, or engage in some other disruptive behavior. Claire was given a diagnosis of attention deficit/hyperactivity disorder; her parents were considering having her put on Ritalin. Before they resorted to the medication, however, they wanted to find out whether behavior modification procedures could get Claire to stay in her seat and pay attention in class.

The family took Claire to a child psychologist, Dr. Cruz, who implemented self-instructional training. As Dr. Cruz described it to Claire and her parents, self-instructional training is a way to teach children how to talk to themselves to control their own behavior in the classroom. With this procedure, Claire would learn to give herself instructions to stay in her seat and pay attention to her teacher.

In his office, Dr. Cruz used behavioral skills training procedures to teach the self-instructions to Claire. First he modeled the behavior. He sat in a chair and pretended that he was in Mrs. Purdy's classroom. Whenever he started to get out of the chair, he stopped and said out loud, "Wait. I'm out of my seat. I have to stay in my seat or I'll get in trouble." As soon as he recited the self-instructions, he sat back down into the chair. Then he said out loud, "Good, I'm in my seat. Mrs. Purdy likes that!" After modeling the behavior and the self-instructions, Dr. Cruz asked Claire to do it just as he did it. When Claire rehearsed the behavior and the self-instructions in the role-play, Dr. Cruz provided praise and feedback. They practiced a number of times, until Claire was doing everything correctly. After Claire was giving herself instructions to sit down when she was out of her chair and then sitting back down immediately, Dr. Cruz had her repeat the instructions to herself more softly. They continued to practice until Claire was saying the instructions to herself covertly so that no one could hear her. Dr. Cruz provided praise and other reinforcers (such as stickers and treats) as Claire participated in the skills training in his office. At the end of the session, Dr. Cruz told Claire to use her self-instructions in class each time she started to get out of her seat, to sit back down immediately, and to praise herself just as they had practiced.

In addition to the self-instructional training, Dr. Cruz implemented two other procedures. He instructed the teacher to praise Claire periodically when she was in her seat paying attention in class. He told Mrs. Purdy to praise Claire at least two times an hour for being in her seat. She was to walk up to Claire's desk, whisper "Good job," and put a smiley face on a piece of paper on her desk. This way, Mrs. Purdy did not draw the attention of the whole class when she praised Claire. Whenever Claire got out of her seat and did not return immediately, Mrs. Purdy was to take Claire back to her seat immediately without saying anything to her. In this way, Claire was returned to her seat but did not get attention from the teacher that may have reinforced the out-of-seat behavior. The other procedure Dr. Cruz used was self-monitoring, in which Claire recorded at periodic intervals whether she was seated. Claire wore a wrist watch that beeped every 30 minutes. If she was seated when her watch beeped, she got to put a check mark on her self-monitoring chart at her desk. If she was not seated, it was a reminder to her to stay in her seat. Mrs. Purdy also kept track every half hour and, at the end of the day, Claire compared her recording to Mrs. Purdy's recording. This helped Claire record her own behavior accurately. After these procedures were implemented, Claire stayed in her seat and paid attention much more in class. As a result, her school work improved and she got better grades.

DEFINING COGNITIVE BEHAVIOR MODIFICATION

Cognitive behavior modification procedures are used to help people change behaviors that are labeled as cognitive. Before describing cognitive behavior modification procedures, it is important to provide a behavioral definition of cognitive behavior.

Defining Cognitive Behavior

When behavior modification procedures are used to change a target behavior, the target behavior must be identified and defined in objective terms so that its occurrence can be recorded. This is true for overt behaviors as well as covert behaviors such as cognitive behaviors. You can't change a target behavior unless you know exactly what the behavior is and when it is occurring. For overt behaviors, this involves direct observation and recording of the behavior by an independent observer or by the person exhibiting the target behavior (self-monitoring). Because cognitive behaviors are covert, they cannot be observed directly and recorded by an independent observer. Rather, the person engaging in the cognitive behavior must identify and record the occurrence of the behavior. Only the person can identify the occurrence of specific thoughts or self-statements because they are covert.

We know that people think, talk to themselves, solve problems, evaluate themselves, make plans, imagine specific behaviors or situations, and so forth. These are all instances of **cognitive behavior**; they are verbal or imaginal responses made by the person that are covert and thus not observable to others. To be able to work effectively with cognitive behaviors, we must work with the client to objectively define these behaviors. For example, a person can report the specific thoughts that he or she thinks at a particular time, people can describe the things that they say to themselves, a person can describe the situation or behavior that he or she was imagining, and people can tell you the evaluative statements that they make about themselves. To be

TABLE 25-1 Behavioral Definitions of Cognitive Behaviors and Their Corresponding Labels

Behavioral Definition	Label
When the client sees people talking, he thinks, "They're talking about me." When the client sees someone walking behind him he thinks, "That person is following me."	Paranoid thoughts
A person thinks, "I can do this! I can succeed at this job. I will do well."	Self-efficacy
A person thinks, "I wish I would just die. What's the point of going on? Nobody cares; it would be better for everyone if I was dead."	Suicidal thoughts
A batter in a softball game says to herself, "I can hit this pitcher. I'm better than she is. I'm going to win this game."	Self-confidence
The right fielder says to himself, "I hope he doesn't hit it to me. I don't know if I can catch it. I wish this game would end."	Low self-confidence
As a driver is looking for an address, she thinks, "I'm supposed to turn left at the first light and go three blocks to a stop sign. Then I turn left and go until I see the white house on the left."	Self-Instructions

a behavioral definition of a cognitive behavior, the thought, image, or self statement must be described clearly by the person engaging in the behavior. A label for the cognitive behavior is not a behavioral definition. For example, to say that a person has low self-esteem does not define the cognitive behavior. This is merely a label for a specific class of cognitive behaviors. It is a label for negative self-statements, such as "I can't do anything right" or "I'm fat and ugly and nobody likes me" or "I'll never amount to anything in life." These self-statements and others like them are the cognitive behaviors that are labeled as low self-esteem. You must be able to identify the specific cognitive behaviors (self-statements) to help the client change those behaviors using cognitive behavior modification procedures. Table 25-1 provides examples of behavioral definitions for cognitive behaviors and some possible labels for these behaviors.

The cognitive behaviors that make up the target behaviors for cognitive behavior modification include behavioral excesses and behavioral deficits. A behavioral excess is an undesirable cognitive behavior the person would seek to decrease. (The behaviors in Table 25-1 labeled as paranoid thoughts, suicidal thoughts, and low self-confidence are examples of cognitive behavioral excesses.) A behavioral deficit is a desirable cognitive behavior the person would seek to increase. (The behaviors in Table 25-1 labeled as self-efficacy, self-confidence, and self-instructions are examples of cognitive behavioral deficits.)

Functions of Cognitive Behavior

Why are we sometimes interested in modifying cognitive behavior? One reason is that cognitive behavior may be distressing to the person; it may function as a conditioned stimulus (CS) that elicits an unpleasant conditioned response (CR). For example, a person's fearful thoughts can function as a CS to elicit autonomic arousal (anxiety) as a CR. Deon's angry thoughts elicited autonomic arousal that he labeled as anger.

Cognitive behaviors that elicit undesirable CRs such as anxiety are behavioral excesses that can be decreased with cognitive behavior modification procedures.

Cognitive behaviors can also function as S^Ds for desirable behaviors. After reciting a rule or a self-instruction, a person may be more likely to engage in the desirable behavior specified by the rule or self-instruction. For example, a person who repeats a set of directions ("Turn left on Main Street and right on Fifth Avenue") may be more likely to arrive at the destination. Claire's self-instructions made it more likely that she would stay seated in her chair and pay attention in class. Self-instructions or rules sometimes are viewed as behavioral deficits that need to be increased in frequency through cognitive behavior modification procedures.

Cognitive behaviors may function as establishing operations (EOs) that influence the power of consequences to function as reinforcers or punishers. How we talk to ourselves about events in our lives may change the value of those events as reinforcers or punishers. For example, if an employee thinks, "My boss is a rotten guy and doesn't mean what he says," the boss' praise may not function as a reinforcer for the employee. On the other hand, if the employee does not negatively interpret the boss' actions or thinks more positive thoughts about the boss and his intentions, the boss' praise is more likely to function as a reinforcer for the employee.

Cognitive behaviors may also function as reinforcing or punishing consequences when they follow some other behavior. Praise statements or critical statements from others can serve as reinforcers or punishers. Likewise, praise statements or critical statements made by a person can serve as reinforcers or punishers for the person's own behavior. Both Deon and Claire learned to make praise statements to themselves after their own desirable behavior.

Cognitive Behavior Modification Procedures

Cognitive behavior modification procedures are used to help people change cognitive behaviors. Some procedures, called **cognitive restructuring,** are designed to replace specific maladaptive cognitive behaviors with more adaptive ones. Cognitive restructuring is used in the case of behavioral excesses, that is, when existing maladaptive cognitive behaviors contribute to a problem. Other procedures, called **cognitive coping skills training,** are designed to teach new cognitive behaviors that are then used to promote other desirable behaviors. These procedures are used in the case of behavioral deficits, that is, when a person does not have the cognitive behaviors needed to cope effectively with problem situations (Spiegler & Guevremont, 2003). We now consider these procedures in turn.

Note that in the remainder of this chapter, the term *thought* is used to refer to a cognitive behavior: thinking, making self-statements, or talking to oneself at the covert level (self-talk). The particular cognitive behavior meant by the term must be defined behaviorally in each case.

Cognitive Restructuring

In cognitive restructuring procedures, the therapist helps the client identify cognitive behaviors that are distressing and then helps the client get rid of these distressing thoughts or replace them with more desirable thoughts. Distressing thoughts might be those that elicit emotional responses such as fear, anxiety, or anger or those that are associated with unpleasant moods, problem behaviors, or poor performance. For example, when Trisha (from Chapter 24) thinks, "I know I'll be scared to death when I give my talk in class," she experiences anxiety and is more likely to engage in avoidance behavior (such as dropping the class). When Deon says to himself, "I can't let him get away with that!" he is more likely to experience autonomic arousal (anger) and to get into a fight. Cognitive restructuring consists of three basic steps.

1. *Helping the client identify the distressing thoughts and the situations in which they occur.* This can be done by asking clients to report what distressing thoughts they experience in specific situations. This relies on the clients' memory of the situations and associated thoughts. A second way to assess distressing thoughts is to have the client self-monitor, that is, write down a description of the situations and the thoughts as they occur.

2. *Helping the client identify the emotional response, unpleasant mood, or problem behavior that follows the distressing thought.* In this way, the client can see how the distressing thought is an antecedent to the unpleasant emotional response, mood, or problem behavior. The client must report this information from memory or must engage in self-monitoring to record the responses as they occur. Table 25-2 presents a data sheet that a client might use to record distressing thoughts, the situations in which they occur, and the emotional response or behavior that follows the distressing thought. This data sheet includes sample entries by four different people; in practice, of course, only one person would fill in any particular data sheet.

3. *Helping the client stop thinking the distressing thoughts or helping the client think more rational or desirable thoughts.* When the client thinks rational thoughts instead of the distressing thoughts in the problem situation, the client is less likely to have negative emotional responses or to engage in problem behaviors. It is not easy to help a client change his or her pattern of thinking. Cognitive restructuring typically is done by psychologists or other professionals with specific training in these procedures. The therapist challenges the client's distressing thoughts by asking questions that make the client analyze the logic or rationality of the thoughts or interpret the situation differently. Consider the second example from Table 25-2. This client, Danielle, has been feeling depressed, has been engaging in fewer and fewer activities outside of work, and has been reporting increasingly depressive thoughts. In the example, she had a number of distressing

TABLE 25-2 Example of a Data Sheet Used in Cognitive Restructuring

Situation	Thoughts	Emotional or Behavioral Outcome
Went to my history class.	"Oh my god! I hate to give a talk! I can't do it. I'll die!"	Experienced anxiety.
Getting ready to go out with my friends.	"They don't really like me. They call me because they feel sorry for me."	Felt depressed. Did not go out with my friends.
Husband came home late from work.	"I wonder who he's with. I bet he's at the bar. I bet he's flirting with other women."	Got angry. Ignored my husband when he came home. Yelled at him for being late.
Girlfriend talking and laughing with a football player at fraternity party.	"I bet he's hitting on her! How can she do this to me!"	Got jealous, angry. Got drunk. Called girlfriend names and left the party.

Steps in Cognitive Restructuring

1. Identify distressing thoughts and situations.
2. Identify emotional response or behavior that follows the thoughts.
3. Work to decrease distressing thoughts and replace them with more rational or desirable thinking.

thoughts when she was preparing to go out for an evening with her friends. Immediately after these thoughts, she felt more depressed and decided not to go out. To help her stop these distressing thoughts, the therapist might ask her the following questions: "How do you know that your friends don't really like you? Where is the evidence? What evidence do you have that they ask you out only because they feel sorry for you?" As the therapist poses these questions to her, she realizes that there is no evidence to support what she thinks. Eventually, it becomes clear that she is thinking in a distorted way. The therapist's questions challenge her to think more realistically or rationally and to dismiss the thoughts that are not rational or not accurate (Burns, 1980; Hollon & Jacobson, 1985). Cognitive restructuring occurs when she replaces these distorted thoughts with more appropriate thoughts that do not lead to depressed mood or behavior.

Cognitive Therapy Various authors have described the different variations of cognitive restructuring. These variations include rational–emotive therapy, systematic rational restructuring, and cognitive therapy (Beck, 1976; Beck & Freeman, 1989; Ellis & Bernard, 1985; Ellis & Dryden, 1987; Freeman, Simon, Beutler, & Arkowitz, 1989; Goldfried, 1988; Goldfried, Decenteceo, & Weinberg, 1974). This chapter focuses on **cognitive therapy**. David Burns (1980) provides an excellent description of cognitive therapy for depression based on the work of Aaron Beck (Beck, 1972; Beck, Rush, Shaw, & Emery, 1979).

As part of the treatment for depression, Burns uses one form of cognitive restructuring called cognitive therapy to help people change their distorted thoughts or self-talk. People who report that they are depressed engage in fewer reinforcing activities than they used to and engage in a type of distorted thinking in which they negatively evaluate or interpret events in their lives.

Cognitive therapy for depression involves first getting the person to engage in more reinforcing activities. The next step is to use cognitive restructuring to help the person change his or her distorted thinking. When the person engages in more reinforcing activities and replaces the distorted self-talk with more rational or accurate self-talk, the person is less likely to report that he or she is depressed.

Table 25-3 lists some types of distorted thinking that a depressed person may report. Burns calls these cognitive distortions.

After identifying the distorted thinking that a person engages in, the next step is to challenge the person to evaluate his or her thoughts and replace the distorted thinking with more accurate or logical thoughts. You challenge a person's distorted thinking by asking three types of questions.

- Where is the evidence?
- Are there any alternative explanations?
- What are the implications?

TABLE 25-3 Examples of Cognitive Distortions

All-or-nothing thinking
You see everything in terms of black or white with no shades of gray. If something is not perfect, it is not acceptable.

Overgeneralizaiton
You take a single negative event as evidence that something is all bad or is always going to be bad.

Disqualifying the positive
In a situation or event, there are usually some positive and negative aspects. You discount or ignore the positive aspects and instead focus on the negative aspect of the event, even when the situation or event was largely positive.

Jumping to conclusions
You arbitrarily jump to negative conclusions that are not supported by the facts. This may involve mind reading, making assumptions about what other people are thinking, or predicting negative future events without any evidence.

Magnification and minimization
You blow negative events out of proportion or minimize the importance of positive events.

Labeling and mislabeling
You put negative labels on events or on yourself, which influences how you view yourself or events in the world.

Personalization
You assume responsibility for the occurrence of negative events, even when there is no evidence that you are responsible.

Source: Burns (1980).

Consider the following example. Ruth went to see a psychologist because she was feeling depressed. She was recently hired as a midlevel manager in a large manufacturing firm. She often worried about her performance on the job, although she had never been told that she was not doing a good job. One day, she made a mistake on an order. Her boss told her about it and showed her how to do it correctly in the future. After this happened, Ruth said to herself, "I'm no good at this job, I'm too stupid. I know I'm going to get fired. My boss thinks I'm incompetent." She made these and similar statements to herself on the job and at home. When she made these statements to herself, she felt more depressed.

Identify the cognitive distortions in Ruth's self-statements.

Ruth is overgeneralizing from a single instance (making one mistake) and telling herself that she is no good at her job. She is labeling herself as stupid. She is jumping to conclusions when she tells herself that her boss thinks she is incompetent and that she is going to get fired. In the following script from a cognitive behavior modification session, notice how the psychologist (P) uses questions to challenge Ruth (R) to change her distorted thinking. Ruth has just made the statement that "I am no good at my job and I'm going to get fired" and says that she feels depressed when she thinks this way.

P: Ruth, where is the evidence that you're no good at your job?
R: Well, I just know that I'm no good at it.
P: Yes, you said that, but where is the evidence for this statement?
R: Well, my boss never tells me I'm doing a good job.
P: Okay, your boss doesn't tell you that you are doing well. Does this mean you are not doing a good job?
R: It must. If I was doing a good job, he would tell me.
P: Is there any other explanation for why your boss doesn't tell you that you are doing a good job?
R: I don't know.
P: Does he tell anybody else that they're doing a good job?
R: No.
P: Do you think your co-workers do a good job?
R: Yes.
P: But your boss doesn't tell them that they do. Is it possible that you are doing a good job even if your boss doesn't tell you that you are?
R: I suppose.
P: Yes, I suppose so too. Is there any other explanation for why your boss doesn't tell you or your co-workers that you are doing a good job?
R: Well, I suppose because he's too busy.
P: That's a very reasonable explanation. Is there any other explanation?
R: Well, maybe it's just not his supervisory style to tell people when they do a good job.
P: Great, so there may be a couple of other explanations for why your boss doesn't tell you that you do a good job at work. Now tell me, where is the evidence that you are going to get fired?

The psychologist would continue to ask Ruth such questions until she came to the conclusion that her original thoughts were not accurate and she made more reasonable or accurate self-statements to replace these inaccurate or distorted thoughts. As Ruth replaced her distorted, negative self-statements with more reasonable ones, she would be less likely to report a depressed mood. In addition, Ruth would learn the skill of questioning her own distorted thinking in this same way and would be able to use this skill in the future if she engaged in distorted thinking again.

Cognitive Coping Skills Training

In **cognitive coping skills training,** the therapist teaches clients specific self-statements that they can make in a problem situation to improve their performance or influence their behavior in the situation. In our examples, both Deon and Claire used cognitive coping skills to influence their behavior in a problem situation. Deon made coping self-statements when people called him names or made racist comments at school. When he made the coping statements to himself in these situations, he was less likely to get angry and more likely to walk away from a fight. Claire used a type of coping statement called self-instructions when she started to get out of her chair in the classroom. She instructed herself to sit back down in her chair and pay attention to the teacher. In each case, Deon and Claire learned the coping statements through instructions, modeling, rehearsal, and feedback, in role-play situations that simulated the problem situations. Once Deon and Claire started using the coping self-statements in the problem situations, their behavior in those situations improved.

Spiegler and Guevremont (2003) describe three types of procedures for cognitive coping skills training: self-instructional training, stress inoculation training, and problem-solving therapy. This chapter focuses on self-instructional training. (For information on other types of cognitive coping skills training, see Spiegler & Guevremont, 2003; or see D'Zurilla, 1986; D'Zurilla & Goldfried, 1971; Meichenbaum, 1977, 1985; Nezu, Nezu, & Perri, 1989; Novaco, 1977.)

Self-Instructional Training **Self-instructional training** consists of three basic steps.

1. *Identifying the problem situation and defining the desirable behavior most appropriate to the situation.* It is also important to identify any competing behavior that may interfere with the desirable behavior in the problem situation. For Deon, the desirable behavior was to walk away from a provocation by another student. The competing behaviors were fighting (overt behavior) and his anger-related self-statements in the problem situation (covert behavior). For Claire, the desirable behavior was to sit in her chair and pay attention to the teacher. The competing behavior was getting out of her chair and disrupting other students.
2. *Identifying the self-instructions that will be most helpful in the problem situation.* Deon learned self-statements that cued him to walk away from the provocation by another student. These self-statements also interfered with his existing self-statements, which elicited arousal (anger) in the problem situation. As a result, he was less likely to get angry and more likely to walk away. Claire learned self-statements in which she instructed herself to stay in her seat and look at the teacher during class. The self-statements were simple self-instructions appropriate to the developmental level of a 7-year-old child.
3. *Using behavioral skills training to teach the self-instructions.* The person must practice the self-instructions in role-plays that simulate the problem situation so that the self-instructions generalize to the problem situation after behavioral skills training is completed.

When conducting behavioral skills training, the therapist first models the self-instructions and the desirable behavior in the context of the role-play. For example, as Claire watched, Dr. Cruz sat in a chair at a desk and acted as if he were Claire in her classroom. Each time he started to get out of the chair, he recited the self-instructions

STEPS IN SELF-INSTRUCTIONAL TRAINING

1. Identify the problem situation, define the desirable behavior to be increased, and identify competing behaviors.
2. Identify the self-instructions to be used in the problem situation.
3. Use behavioral skills training to teach the self-instructions.

out loud and immediately sat back down in the chair. Each time he sat back down in the chair, he praised himself.

After modeling the self-instructions and desirable behavior a few times for Claire, he asked Claire to practice it with him. Now Claire sat down at a desk and, each time she started to get up, she recited the self-instructions and immediately sat back down. Then she praised herself for sitting. Dr. Cruz praised Claire after each rehearsal that she completed with him.

After Claire demonstrated the self-instructions and desirable behavior with Dr. Cruz, he asked her to do it by herself. This time, Claire recited the self-instructions out loud as she started to get up and then sat back down and praised herself. She engaged in this sequence of self-instructions and desirable behavior without any help from Dr. Cruz. He praised her each time for her performance.

Dr. Cruz had Claire participate in the same role-play a few more times; each time, she recited the self-instructions more quietly. Finally, Dr. Cruz told her to say the self-instructions to herself so that he could not hear her. In this way, the self-instructions and self-praise occurred covertly so that they did not draw attention to Claire in the classroom. The sequence of steps in behavioral skills training used to teach self-instructions is listed in Table 25-4.

Once the client learns the self-instructions in the context of role-plays that simulate the problem situation, the client is instructed to use the self-instructions in the actual problem situation. If self-instructional training is effective, the problem situation should be a discriminative stimulus for the self-instructions. Having recited the self-instructions in the problem situation, the client is more likely to engage in the desirable behavior because the desirable behavior was chained to the self-instruction in the role-plays. As a result, the self-instruction becomes a discriminative stimulus for the desirable behavior.

Donald Meichenbaum developed self-instructional training and evaluated its effectiveness for helping people control their own behavior. For example, Meichenbaum and Goodman (1971) taught young children to use self-instructions to control their own impulsive behavior. Other researchers have also demonstrated the effectiveness of self-instructional training with children (Bryant & Budd, 1982; Guevremont, Osnes, & Stokes, 1988; Kendall & Braswell, 1985). Meichenbaum has also implemented self-

TABLE 25-4 Steps in Behavioral Skills Training Used to Teach Self-Instructions

1. The therapist recites the self-instructions out loud and engages in the desirable behavior.
2. The therapist and the client recite the self-instructions out loud and engage in the desirable behavior.
3. The client recites the self-instructions out loud and engages in the desirable behavior without assistance from the therapist.
4. The client recites the self-instructions in a progressively softer voice and engages in the desirable behavior.
5. The client recites the self-instructions without producing any sound and engages in the desirable behavior.
6. The client recites the self-instructions covertly without moving her lips and engages in the desirable behavior.

instructional training with schizophrenic adults (Meichenbaum & Cameron, 1973). The patients in this study used self-instructions to increase the amount of "healthy talk" they engaged in and decrease the amount of "sick talk," to increase attention to task, and to improve performance on a variety of tasks. Other researchers have also shown that self-instructional training can be effective with schizophrenic patients (Meyers, Mercatoris, & Sirota, 1976). Self-instructional training has also been used effectively for a variety of problems in nonschizophrenic adults (Masters, Burish, Hollon, & Rimm, 1987; Spiegler & Guevremont, 2003).

Acceptance-Based Therapies

The goal of cognitive restructuring and cognitive coping skills training procedures, as described in this chapter, is to help people change their thinking in order to change their negative feelings or problem behavior for the better. However, other treatment approaches have the goal of helping people to accept their negative thoughts and feelings rather than to change them (Hayes, Strosahl, & Wilson, 1999; Hayes & Wilson, 1994; Kohlenberg & Tsai, 1991). Acceptance-based therapies have only recently been developed as an alternative to traditional cognitive behavior modification procedures described in this chapter. In one form of therapy called acceptance and commitment therapy (Hayes, 1995; Hayes, Strosahl, & Wilson, 1999), the client learns that he or she has not been able to control troublesome thoughts and feelings in the past and that attempts to control thoughts and feelings have made the client's problem worse. In the course of therapy, the client learns to accept that the thoughts and feelings can continue to occur but that he or she can still achieve meaningful behavior change goals (Paul, Marx, & Orsillo, 1999). When the client accepts the negative thoughts and feelings, they lose their ability to disrupt the client's life and he or she can commit to and work toward valued behavior changes.

Clinical Problems

This chapter is simply an introduction to cognitive behavior modification procedures and does not adequately teach a student to conduct cognitive behavior modification with real clinical problems. Anyone who is experiencing a serious emotional problem, such as depression, should seek help from a psychologist or other licensed mental health professional. Although you might use cognitive behavior modification for self-improvement, serious problems should always be referred to a professional.

Chapter Summary

1. Cognitive behavior is defined as thoughts, images, or self-statements that occur covertly.
2. A cognitive behavior can serve as a CS, an S^D, or an EO when it is an antecedent to another behavior, or it can serve as a reinforcer or punisher when it is a consequence of another behavior exhibited by the person.
3. In the cognitive restructuring procedure, the therapist helps the client identify distressing thoughts and replace them with more desirable thoughts.
4. To help people change their thinking, the therapist first helps the client identify maladaptive thoughts that contribute to emotional or

behavioral difficulties. The therapist then asks a series of questions to help the client critically evaluate the logic or accuracy of his or her thoughts. Through this process, the client begins to think in more accurate or logical ways, which alleviates emotional or behavioral problems.

5. The self-instructional training procedure includes two basic components. Using behavioral skills training procedures, the therapist teaches the client to make self-statements or self-instructions. Therapist and client practice the self-instructions and the desirable behaviors in role-play situations that simulate a problem situation. The client later recites the self-instructions and engages in the desirable behavior in the problem situation.

PRACTICE TEST

1. What are cognitive behaviors? Provide examples. (pp. 540–541)
2. Identify the cognitive behaviors that contributed to Deon's problem with fighting. (p. 538)
3. Provide examples of the cognitive behaviors that might be involved in what we call guilt.
4. Identify and briefly describe the two general categories of cognitive behavior modification procedures. (p. 542)
5. In cognitive restructuring, the therapist helps the client identify the distressing thoughts he or she experiences. What are the two ways in which the therapist can assess the clients thoughts? (p. 543)
6. What is a cognitive distortion? Describe a few of the types of cognitive distortions identified by Burns (1980). Provide an example of each. (pp. 544–545)
7. What is the goal of cognitive restructuring? (p. 543)
8. According to Burns (1980), what are the three types of questions a therapist uses to challenge a client's distorted thinking? (p. 544)
9. What is the goal of cognitive coping skills training? (p. 546)
10. Describe the behavioral skills training procedures used to teach self-instructions to a client. (pp. 547–548)
11. In self-instructional training, what is done to increase the likelihood that the self-instructions will generalize to the actual problem situation? (p. 548)
12. Name two types of problems for which self-instructional training has been used successfully. (pp. 548–549)
13. In the case of Claire, what other behavior modification procedures were used in addition to self-instructional training? (pp. 539–540)
14. How do cognitive behavior modification procedures differ from other behavior modification procedures described in this book? (p. 537)
15. What is the goal of acceptance and commitment therapy? How does it differ from the goal of cognitive behavior modification procedures? (p. 549)

APPLICATIONS

1. Describe how you would implement a cognitive behavior modification procedure as part of your own self-management project. If a cognitive behavior modification procedure is not appropriate for your project, describe why not.

2. Chad, a 22-year-old man with mild mental retardation, has good verbal abilities and can easily carry on a conversation and understand complex directions. Chad works in a factory. He does his job well, but he has been

caught stealing from the other workers' lockers. The problem occurs at break or other times when he is near the lockers and no one else is around. At these times, he opens people's lockers and takes cans of soda from them, or he takes change that he uses to buy a can of soda from the vending machine. He is going to lose his job if he does not stop stealing. When caught stealing, he says he is sorry and promises not to do it again, but the problem continues. Describe how you would conduct self-instructional training with Chad to help him stop stealing from other workers.

3. Describe other behavior modification procedures you would use in conjunction with self-instructions to help Chad stop stealing money and soda from other workers' lockers.

4. Vicki leaves the office each day at 5 P.M. and drives out to her home in the suburbs. The drive takes her 30 minutes in the rush hour traffic. As Vicki sits in traffic jams, she gets impatient and angry. (She experiences autonomic arousal.) She makes a number of angry statements to herself such as, "I hate this city! Why can't people learn to drive! I wish these idiots would speed up or move over! Stupid drivers!" As she makes these angry statements to herself, she becomes more angry and sometimes engages in aggressive behavior: making obscene gestures to other drivers, tailgating the cars in front of her, or yelling at other drivers. Describe the cognitive coping skills training that you would implement with Vicki to help decrease her anger and aggressive behavior in her car on the way home from work.

MISAPPLICATIONS

1. Wendy had pretty much kept to herself in the months since she started college. She didn't have any friends there and was uncomfortable around new people. She was not getting involved in activities and not making friends. When she thought about going to parties or other activities she told herself, "Nobody would want to talk to me. What's the use of trying? It's too difficult to meet new people. I'm not very interesting. People would be bored talking to me." When she had these thoughts, she felt depressed and decided not to go to the party or the activity. Wendy saw a counselor to help her overcome this problem. The counselor first conducted an assessment interview with Wendy to understand the problem that she was experiencing. The counselor decided that she had low self-esteem and that the low self-esteem was the cause of her problems. The therapist told Wendy that he would help her eliminate her low self-esteem and that she would be happier and more likely to get involved in activities and make friends. What is wrong in this example? What should the counselor do differently?

2. Arnie took a behavior modification course in which he learned about cognitive behavior modification. One chapter in the textbook described cognitive restructuring and other procedures. Arnie had a friend who reported that she was depressed. Arnie told her that he could help her overcome her depression with cognitive behavior modification. Arnie got out his book and studied the cognitive behavior modification chapter again. He paid particular attention to the section on cognitive distortions and the questions to use to help a person change distorted thinking. After reading the chapter again, Arnie got together with his friend and started using cognitive behavior modification to help her with her depression. What is wrong in this example? What should Arnie do differently?

3. Carol, a 4-year-old girl, was an only child until recently. After her baby brother was born, Carol began to engage in tantrum behavior. When Carol's mother, Judy, was attending to the new baby, sitting at her computer, or engaging in some other activity, Carol screamed and cried and demanded her mother's attention. Judy usually stopped what she was doing and spent some time with Carol until she'd calmed down. After a few months of this, Judy decided to do something

about Carol's tantrum behavior. She decided to implement self-instructional training with Carol. Judy set up pretend situations (role-plays) with Carol in which Carol started to tantrum and immediately said to herself, "Mommy's busy" or, "Calm down and be good" or, "Mommy likes it when I'm good." Judy taught Carol to say these self-instructions in the role-plays and, when Carol could say them to herself without any help, Judy told her to say the self-instructions when she really got mad. What is wrong in this example? What should Judy do differently?

4. Perry was a college student who was apprehensive about public speaking. He got nervous when he thought about giving a class presentation. He went to see a counselor, who started using cognitive restructuring with Perry to help him change some cognitive behaviors that contributed to his anxiety. First, the counselor assessed the self-statements that Perry made when he got anxious about giving a talk in class. An example of what he said to himself is, "People will see how nervous I am and think I'm stupid. I can't do as well as everybody else in the class." Then the counselor worked with Perry to change the distorted thinking in these self-statements. The following is a segment of a script from a session between Perry (P) and the counselor (C). What is wrong in this example? What should the counselor do differently?

C: Perry, you say that people will see that you are nervous. There is no evidence for that statement. People can't tell that you are nervous.

P: Yeah, I suppose you're right.

C: In addition, there is no evidence that people will think that you're stupid. They probably can't tell that you're nervous and, even if they could, being nervous is normal. They certainly won't think that you're stupid.

P: They won't?

C: Of course not. You don't need to think that way. You also said that you can't do as well as everybody else in class. Now, Perry, there is no evidence for that statement either. I'm sure that you can do just as well as the other students. They're all learning to give class presentations too. You're all in the same situation.

P: Yeah, I guess you're right.

CHAPTER 25 *Quiz 1* Name:

1. Because cognitive behaviors are ________________, they cannot be directly observed and recorded by independent observers.

2. A cognitive behavior functions as a conditioned stimulus when it

   ____.

3. A cognitive behavior functions as an establishing operation when it

   ____.

4. Cognitive behaviors can function as ______________________ or ______________________ consequences when they follow some other behavior.

5. Cognitive therapy is one type of cognitive ____________________ (restructuring/coping skills training) procedure.

6. In cognitive ____________________ (restructuring/coping skills training) the therapist helps the client identify cognitive behaviors that are distressing and then helps the client get rid of these distressing thoughts or replace them with more desirable thoughts.

7. The goal of ____________________ therapies is helping clients to accept their negative thoughts and feelings rather than to change them.

8. In self-instructional training, the therapist uses ____________________ procedures to teach the self-instructions.

9. The first step in cognitive restructuring is to identify the ____________________ and

   ____________________ .

10. When a client thinks ____________________ instead of the distressing thoughts in the problem situation, the client is less likely to have negative emotional responses or engage in problem behaviors.

CHAPTER 25 *Quiz 2* Name:

1. ____________________ behaviors are verbal or imaginal responses made by a person that are not observable to others.

2. A cognitive behavior may function as a(n) ____________________ when it influences the power of reinforcing or punishing consequences.

3. Cognitive ____________________ (restructuring/coping skills training) procedures are used in the case of a behavioral excess, when existing maladaptive cognitive behaviors contribute to a problem.

4. In cognitive ____________________ (restructuring/coping skills training) procedures, the therapist teaches clients specific self-statements they can make in a problem situation to improve their performance or influence their behavior in the situation.

5. ____________________ is one type of cognitive restructuring procedure.

6. ____________________ is one type of cognitive coping skills training procedure.

7. In the ____________________ procedure, the therapist asks three types of questions to challenge the client's distorted thinking.

8. ______________________________ is an example of a cognitive distortion that a therapist would seek to help the client change in cognitive therapy.

9. In the ____________________ procedure, the client learns self-statements or self-instructions to guide his or her behavior in a problem situation.

10. Cognitive therapy for depression involves first getting the client to engage in

    ____________________. The next step is to use cognitive restructuring to help the person change his or her distorted thinking.

CHAPTER 25 *Quiz 3* Name:

1. A cognitive behavior may consist of __________________ or __________________ responses.

2. A cognitive behavior functions as a(n) __________________ when it elicits an unpleasant conditioned response.

3. Cognitive __________________ (restructuring/coping skills training) procedures are used in the case of a behavioral deficit, when a person does not have the cognitive behaviors that are needed to deal with a problem situation.

4. Identify two possible antecedent functions of cognitive behavior.

   __________________ and __________________

5. Self-instructional training is a type of cognitive __________________ (restructuring/coping skills training) procedure.

6. The three steps involved in cognitive restructuring are (1) to identify the distressing thoughts and situations, (2) identify emotional responses or behaviors that follow the thoughts, and

   (3) ____.

7. All-or-nothing thinking, overgeneralization, and disqualifying the positive are examples of

   __________________.

8. Identify two of the three questions the therapist asks the client to challenge the client's distorted thinking during cognitive therapy.

   ______________________________ and ______________________________

9. In self-instructional training, the self-instruction becomes a(n) __________________ for the desirable behavior.

10. The goal of acceptance-based therapies is for clients to __________________ their negative thoughts and feelings rather than to change them.

GLOSSARY

A-B design A research design consisting of a baseline and a treatment phase. The A-B design is not a true experimental design because the treatment condition is not replicated. Used mostly to document behavior change in clinical practice.

A-B-A-B reversal design A research design consisting of a baseline and treatment phase followed by withdrawal of treatment (the second baseline) and a second implementation of the treatment.

ABC observation A functional assessment method involving direct observation of the antecedents, the target behavior, and the consequences of the behavior. Typically conducted in the natural environment where the target behavior occurs.

abscissa The horizontal axis (*x*-axis) on a graph. Shows the units of time.

acquisition The development of a new behavior through reinforcement.

alternating-treatments design (ATD) A research design in which baseline and treatment conditions (or two treatment conditions) are conducted in rapid succession, typically on alternating days or sessions. Baseline and treatment phases can be compared with each other within the same time period.

antecedent A stimulus or event that precedes the target behavior.

antecedent control procedure A procedure in which antecedents are manipulated to influence the target behavior. May involve manipulating a discriminative stimulus (S^D) or cues, establishing operations, or response effort for the target behavior or alternative behaviors.

anxiety A term used to describe respondent behavior involving the activation of the autonomic nervous system (including rapid heart rate, shallow rapid breathing, and increased muscle tension). Autonomic arousal is an establishing operation that increases the probability of operant behavior involving escape or avoidance responses. Typically, some event functions as a conditioned stimulus (CS) to elicit the autonomic arousal as a conditioned response (CR). The operant behavior functions to escape from or avoid the CS.

application of aversive activities A positive punishment procedure in which, contingent on the undesirable behavior, the client is required to engage in an aversive activity (a low-probability behavior) to decrease the future probability of the undesirable behavior.

application of aversive stimulation A positive punishment procedure in which an aversive stimulus is delivered contingent on the occurrence of the undesirable behavior to decrease the future probability of the undesirable behavior.

applied behavior analysis A term often used interchangeably with the term *behavior modification*; it involves analyzing and modifying human behavior.

attention-focusing exercises A type of anxiety reduction strategy in which one focuses attention on a pleasant or neutral stimulus to remove attention from the anxiety-producing stimulus.

aversive stimulus A stimulus that will decrease the future probability of a behavior when the stimulus is delivered contingent on the occurrence of the behavior. Also called a punisher.

avoidance behavior A behavior that prevents an aversive event. The behavior is negatively reinforced by the avoidance of the aversive event.

awareness training A component of the habit reversal procedure in which the person is taught to identify each instance of a particular habit behavior as it occurs.

backup reinforcer Reinforcers used in a token economy. A client receives tokens for desirable behaviors and exchanges a specified number of tokens for any of a variety of backup reinforcers.

backward chaining A type of chaining procedure in which the last component of the chain is taught first. Once the last response in the chain occurs consistently when the last S^D is presented, the next to last component is taught, and the last two components of the chain occur together. This training sequence proceeds until the client has learned all the components in the chain.

backward conditioning A respondent conditioning procedure in which the unconditioned stimulus (US) is presented before the conditioned stimulus (CS). This is the least effective type of respondent conditioning procedure.

baseline The condition or phase in which no treatment is implemented.

behavior The subject matter of behavior modification. Behavior is what a person says or does; it involves a person's actions.

behavior modification The field of psychology concerned with analyzing and modifying human behavior.

behavioral assessment Measurement of the target behavior (or behaviors) in behavior modification. May also refer to measurement of antecedents and consequences of the target behavior.

behavioral chain A complex behavior consisting of two or more component behaviors that occur together in a sequence. For each component behavior, there is a discriminative stimulus and response. A behavioral chain is sometimes called a stimulus–response chain.

behavioral contract A written document that specifies a particular target behavior for a client and the consequences that will be contingent on the occurrence or nonoccurrence of the behavior in a stated period of time.

behavioral deficit A desirable target behavior that a person seeks to increase in frequency, duration, or intensity.

behavioral excess An undesirable target behavior that a person seeks to decrease in frequency, duration, or intensity.

behavioral relaxation training A type of relaxation training in which one assumes a relaxed posture in all of the major muscle groups of the body to achieve relaxation.

behavioral skills training procedure (BST) A procedure consisting of instructions, modeling, behavioral rehearsal, and feedback that is used to teach new behaviors or skills.

chaining procedures Procedures used to teach a person to engage in a chain of behaviors. Includes backward chaining, forward chaining, total task presentation, written task analysis, picture prompts, and self-instructions.

changing-criterion design A research design in which a number of different criterion (goal) levels are set for the behavior during the treatment phase. When the behavior increases (or decreases) to the criterion level each time that the criterion changes, a functional relationship is established between the treatment and the target behavior.

cognitive behavior Covert verbal behavior or imaginal behavior. Examples include thinking, talking to yourself, imagining specific behaviors or situations, and recalling events of the past. Cognitive behavior is influenced by the same environmental variables that influence overt behavior.

cognitive behavior modification Procedures used to help people change some aspect of their cognitive behavior. Includes procedures to help people eliminate undesirable cognitive behaviors (that is, cognitive restructuring) and procedures to teach people more desirable cognitive behaviors (that is, cognitive coping skills training).

cognitive coping skills training A cognitive behavior modification procedure in which the person learns specific self-statements for use in a problem situation to improve his or her performance or influence his or her behavior. An example is self-instructional training.

cognitive restructuring A cognitive behavior modification procedure in which the client learns to identify thoughts that are distressing and then learns to get rid of those thoughts or to replace them with more desirable thoughts.

cognitive therapy A type of cognitive restructuring, originally developed by Beck, in which the therapist teaches the client to identify and change his or her distorted thoughts or self-talk.

competing response An alternative behavior that occurs in place of another target behavior. Typically, the competing response is physically incompatible with the target behavior, so its occurrence competes with the occurrence of the target behavior.

competing response training A component of the habit reversal procedure in which the client is taught to engage in a competing response contingent on the occurrence of the habit behavior or contingent on the urge to engage in the habit behavior.

concurrent schedules of reinforcement Schedules of reinforcement that exist at the same time for two or more different behaviors (which are called concurrent operants). Which particular behavior occurs at a particular time depends on the relative schedule of reinforcement, magnitude of reinforcement, delay of reinforcement, and response effort for the available behaviors.

conditioned emotional response (CER) A type of conditioned response in which an emotional response such as fear, anger, or happiness is elicited by a conditioned stimulus in the process of respondent conditioning.

conditioned punisher A previously neutral stimulus that has been paired a number of times with an established punisher and consequently functions as a punisher itself.

conditioned reinforcer A previously neutral stimulus that has been paired a number of times with an established reinforcer and consequently functions as a reinforcer itself.

conditioned response (CR) In respondent conditioning, a CR is elicited by a conditioned stimulus. The conditioned stimulus acquires the power to elicit the CR by its repeated pairing with an unconditioned stimulus or another conditioned stimulus.

conditioned stimulus (CS) A previously neutral stimulus that has been paired with an unconditioned stimulus. Once established in this way, the CS elicits a conditioned response similar to the unconditioned response elicited by the unconditioned stimulus.

consequence The stimulus or event occurring immediately after a behavior.

contact densensitization A form of in vivo desensitization in which the therapist provides reassuring physical contact, such as holding the client's hand or placing a hand on the client's back, as the client progresses through the hierarchy.

contingency A relationship between a response and a consequence in which the consequence is presented if and only if the response occurs. When such a relationship exists, the consequence is said to be contingent on the response.

contingent exercise A positive punishment procedure involving the application of aversive activities. Contingent on the problem behavior, the person is required to engage in some form of physical exercise.

contingent observation A type of nonexclusionary time-out in which, contingent on the occurrence of the problem behavior, the person is removed from a reinforcing activity for a brief time and required to sit and observe other people as they continue to engage in the activity.

continuous recording A type of recording procedure in which some aspect of the behavior is recorded each time the behavior occurs. Frequency, duration, latency, or intensity can be recorded in a continuous recording procedure.

continuous reinforcement (CRF) schedule A schedule of reinforcement in which each instance of the behavior is followed by the reinforcer.

contrived setting An observation setting that is not part of the client's normal daily routine.

controlled behavior The target behavior that is influenced in a self-management project.

controlling behavior The use of self-management strategies in which the antecedents and consequences of a target behavior are modified and/or alternative behaviors are modified.

controlling variables The environmental events (antecedents and consequences) that influence the probability of a particular behavior. The controlling variables are the antecedents and consequences that are functionally related to the behavior.

covert behavior Behavior that is not observable to others. Covert behaviors are also called private events.

criterion stimuli The discriminative stimulus and other stimuli present when the target behavior occurs in the relevant situations following training.

delay conditioning A type of respondent conditioning in which the conditioned stimulus (CS) is presented and the unconditioned stimulus (US) is then presented before the termination of the CS.

deprivation A condition in which the person has gone without a particular reinforcer for a period of time. Deprivation is a type of establishing operation; it makes the reinforcer the person has gone without more potent.

diaphragmatic breathing A type of relaxation exercise in which one engages in slow rhythmic breathing, using the diaphragm muscle to pull air deep into the lungs.

differential reinforcement A procedure in which a specific desirable behavior is followed by a reinforcer but other behaviors are not. The result is an increase in the desirable behavior and extinction of the other behaviors.

differential reinforcement of alternative behavior (DRA) A procedure for decreasing a problem behavior by reinforcing a functionally equivalent alternative behavior (a competing behavior) to replace the problem behavior.

differential reinforcement of communication (DRC) A type of DRA procedure in which a communication response is reinforced to replace the problem behavior. Also called functional communication training.

differential reinforcement of incompatible behavior (DRI) A type of DRA procedure in which a physically incompatible behavior is reinforced to replace the problem behavior.

differential reinforcement of low rates of responding (DRL) A procedure in which a lower rate of a particular behavior is reinforced to decrease the rate of the behavior. Used when the goal is to decrease but not necessarily to eliminate a target behavior.

differential reinforcement of other behavior (DRO) A procedure in which the reinforcer is delivered after intervals of time in which the problem behavior does not occur. DRO involves reinforcing the absence of the problem behavior.

dimension of behavior An aspect of the behavior that can be measured and modified. Relevant dimensions may include frequency, duration, intensity, and latency.

direct assessment Behavioral assessment involving direct observation and recording of the behavior as it occurs. Direct assessment may also refer to direct observation and recording of the antecedents and consequences of the behavior.

direct observation *See* direct assessment.

discriminative stimulus (S^D) The stimulus that is present when a particular behavior is reinforced.

duration A dimension of behavior, specifically the time from the onset of the behavior to the offset of the behavior. Duration is how long an instance of the behavior lasts.

escape behavior Behavior that results in the termination of an aversive stimulus. The termination of the aversive stimulus negatively reinforces the behavior.

establishing operation An event that increases the potency of a particular reinforcer at a particular time. Deprivation is a type of establishing operation.

exclusionary time-out A time-out procedure in which the person is briefly removed from the reinforcing environment—typically to another room—contingent on the occurrence of a problem behavior.

experimental analysis of behavior The scientific study of behavior and the types of environmental events that are functionally related to the occurrence of behavior. Involves laboratory research with nonhumans and humans.

extinction (operant) The process by which, when a previously reinforced behavior is no longer followed by the reinforcing consequences, the frequency of the behavior decreases in the future.

extinction (respondent) The process by which, when a conditioned stimulus (CS) is no longer paired with an unconditioned stimulus (US), the CS gradually ceases to elicit the conditioned response (CR).

extinction burst The phenomenon in which, when a behavior is no longer reinforced, the behavior temporarily increases in frequency, duration, or intensity before it decreases. Novel behaviors or emotional responses may also occur in an extinction burst.

extrastimulus prompt A type of stimulus prompt in which a stimulus is added to help a person make a correct discrimination.

fading The gradual removal of prompts as the behavior continues to occur in the presence of the S^D.

fear Occurs when a stimulus situation elicits autonomic nervous system arousal and the individual engages in behavior to avoid or escape from the stimulus situation.

fear hierarchy Used in systematic desensitization or in vivo desensitization procedures. In the fear hierarchy, various fearful situations are listed in order from least to most fear-provoking. Each new situation in the hierarchy is only slightly more fear-provoking than the previous situation.

feedback In behavioral skills training procedures, feedback involves delivering praise for successful performance in a behavioral rehearsal and instruction on ways to improve the performance in the future.

fixed interval (FI) schedule A schedule of reinforcement in which the reinforcer is delivered for the first response that occurs after an interval of time has elapsed. The interval is the same each time.

fixed ratio (FR) schedule A schedule of reinforcement in which a specific number of responses must occur before the reinforcer is delivered. The number of responses needed for reinforcement does not change.

forward chaining A procedure for teaching a chain of behaviors. The first component of the chain is taught through prompting and fading and, once the first component has been learned, the second component is added. Once the first two components have been learned, the third component is added. This training sequence continues until all components of the chain are learned.

frequency A dimension of behavior—specifically, the number of times a behavior occurs in a specific time period. The number of responses (frequency) divided by the time equals the rate of the behavior.

frequency-within-interval recording A recording method in which the number of times the target behavior occurs (frequency) is recorded within consecutive intervals of time during the observation period.

full-session DRL A DRL procedure in which the reinforcer is delivered if fewer than a specified number of responses occurs in a specific period of time (the session). Used to decrease the rate of a behavior.

functional analysis A functional assessment method in which environmental events (antecedents and consequences of the behavior) are manipulated to demonstrate a functional relationship between the environmental events and the behavior.

functional assessment The process of generating information on the events preceding and following the behavior in an attempt to determine which antecedents and consequences are reliably associated with the occurrence of the behavior. Includes indirect assessment through interviews and questionnaires, direct observation of the antecedents and consequences in the natural environment, and functional analysis methods involving the manipulation of environmental events.

functional communication training *See* differential reinforcement of communication.

functional relationship A relationship between a behavior and an environmental event (or events) in which the occurrence of the behavior is controlled by the occurrence of the environmental event. A functional relationship is demonstrated in a research design by manipulating the environmental event and showing that the behavior changes if and only if the environmental event occurs.

functionally equivalent response A response that results in the same reinforcing outcome as an alternative response. The response serves the same function as the alternative response.

general case programming A strategy for promoting generalization that involves the use of multiple training examples (stimulus exemplars) that sample the range of stimulus situations and response variations.

generalization A process in which the behavior occurs in the presence of antecedent stimuli that are similar in some way to the discriminative stimulus present when the behavior was reinforced. Generalization is also defined as the occurrence of a target behavior in a nontraining situation after training.

generalized conditioned punisher A conditioned punisher that has been paired with a variety of other punishers. The word *no* is a generalized conditioned punisher for many people.

generalized conditioned reinforcer A conditioned reinforcer that has been paired with a variety of other reinforcers. Money and praise generalized are conditioned reinforcers for many people.

gestural prompt A physical movement or gesture of another person that leads to the correct behavior in the presence of the discriminative stimulus.

goal setting A self-management strategy in which the person decides on and writes down the desired level of the target behavior he or she hopes to achieve as a result of self-management procedures.

graduated guidance A prompting strategy used with the total task presentation procedure in which you provide full hand-over-hand assistance as a prompt for the learner to complete the behavior. As the learner begins to engage in the behavior independently, you gradually fade your assistance but continue to shadow the learner's movements so that you can provide assistance whenever it becomes necessary. Eventually, the shadowing is eliminated, and the person engages in the behavior independently.

guided compliance A positive punishment procedure used with a person who displays noncompliant behavior. When you make a request and the person refuses to comply, you physically prompt the person to engage in the behavior. The physical prompt is removed as the person complies with the request on his or her own. Guided compliance prevents escape from the requested behavior and thus also serves as an extinction procedure when the noncompliant behavior is negatively reinforced by escape from the requested activity.

habit behavior A repetitive behavior in one of three categories: nervous habits, tics, and stuttering.

habit disorder A repetitive behavior that is distressing to the person. Habit disorders include nervous habits, motor and vocal tics, and stuttering.

habit reversal A procedure for treating habit disorders. Its component procedures include awareness training, competing response training, social support, generalization strategies, and motivational strategies. Research has shown that awareness training and competing response training are the most crucial components for treatment effectiveness.

higher-order conditioning The process by which, when a neutral stimulus is paired with a conditioned stimulus (CS) a number of times, the neutral stimulus becomes a CS that will then elicit the same conditioned response (CR).

in vivo desensitization A procedure for treating a fear or phobia. The client first learns relaxation. Next, the client develops a fear hierarchy in which fear-producing situations are ordered from least to most fear-producing. Finally, the client makes actual contact with the fear-producing situation at each step in the hierarchy in turn while maintaining relaxation as a response that is incompatible with the fear response.

indirect assessment Assessment that relies on information from others. The information on the problem behavior, antecedents, and consequences is not derived from direct observation but from retrospective report in interviews and questionnaires.

informed consent The process in which the client is informed of the behavior modification procedure to be used and agrees in writing to undergo the procedure. Necessary for the use of positive punishment procedures.

instructions Verbal descriptions of the behavior to be performed. A component of the behavioral skills training procedure. Instructions often are used in conjunction with modeling and are most effective when the person has an opportunity to rehearse the behavior immediately in a role-play.

intensity A dimension of behavior, specifically the physical force or magnitude of the behavior. Often measured with a recording instrument or on a rating scale.

intermittent reinforcement schedule A schedule of reinforcement in which not every instance of the behavior is followed by the delivery of the reinforcer. Includes fixed ratio, fixed interval, variable ratio, and variable interval schedules.

interobserver reliability Occurs when two observers independently observe and record a person's behavior at the same time and agree on the occurrence of the behavior.

interresponse time (IRT) The time between the occurrence of consecutive responses.

interval DRL A type of DRL procedure that involves dividing a session into consecutive intervals or time and providing the reinforcer if no more than one response occurred in each interval.

interval recording A type of behavior recording procedure in which the observation period is divided into a number of consecutive time intervals and the behavior is recorded as occurring or not occurring in each of the intervals.

latency A dimension of behavior, specifically the time from some stimulus to the onset of the behavior.

law of effect States that a behavior that produces a favorable effect on the environment will be more likely to be repeated in the future.

maintenance Continuation of the behavior change for a long period after the termination of a behavior modification program. Also, continuation of an operant behavior with intermittent reinforcement.

modeling (modeling prompt) A type of prompt in which the trainer demonstrates the target behavior for the learner. Modeling works best in conjunction with instructions, in situations in which the learner has an opportunity to rehearse the behavior immediately in a role-play.

momentary DRO A type of DRO procedure in which the reinforcer is delivered if the person is refraining from the problem behavior at the end of the DRO interval. The problem behavior does not have to be absent throughout the entire interval for the reinforce to be delivered. Momentary DRO typically is not effective unless it follows the use of a whole-interval DRO procedure.

motivation strategy Part of the habit reversal procedure used to increase the likelihood that the client will use the competing response outside the treatment sessions to control the habit.

motor tics Repetitive, jerking movements of a particular muscle group in the body.

multiple-baseline-across-behaviors design A research design in which there is a baseline and treatment phase for two or more behaviors of the same person. The implementation of treatment is staggered across time for each of the behaviors. The same treatment is implemented for each behavior.

multiple-baseline-across-settings design A research design in which there is a baseline and treatment phase for the same behavior of the same subject in two or more different settings. Treatment is staggered across time in each of the settings. The same treatment is used in each of the settings. The same treatment is used in each setting.

multiple-baseline-across-subjects design A research design in which there is a baseline and treatment phase for two or more people exhibiting the same target behavior. The implementation of treatment is staggered across time for each subject. The same treatment is used with each subject.

natural contingency of reinforcement The reinforcement contingency for the behavior of a particular person in the normal course of the person's life.

natural setting An observation setting that is part of the client's normal daily routine. The target behavior typically occurs in the natural setting.

negative punishment A type of punishment in which the occurrence of a behavior is followed by the removal of a reinforcing stimulus. It results in decrease in the future probability of the behavior.

negative reinforcement A type of reinforcement in which the occurrence of the behavior is followed by the removal or avoidance of an aversive stimulus. It results in increase in the future probability of the behavior.

nervous habit Repetitive, manipulative behaviors that are most likely to occur when a person experiences heightened tension. Nervous habits do not typically serve any social function for the individual.

nonexclusionary time-out A type of time-out procedure in which, contingent on the problem behavior, the person is removed from all sources of reinforcement but is not removed from the room where the problem behavior took place.

observation period The time period in which an observer observes and records the behavior of a client participating in a behavior modification program.

one-party contract A behavioral contract in which one person seeks to change a target behavior. The person arranges the contract with a contract manager, who implements the contingency.

operant behavior Behavior that acts on the environment to produce an immediate consequence and, in turn, is strengthened by that consequence.

operant conditioning Occurs when a behavior in a particular situation is followed by a reinforcing consequence, thus making the behavior more likely to occur in similar circumstances in the future.

ordinate The vertical axis (*y*-axis) on a graph. Shows the level of the behavior.

overcorrection A positive punishment procedure in which, contingent on the problem behavior, a person is required to engage in effortful activity for a brief period. Positive practice and restitution are two types of overcorrection.

overt behavior Behavior that can be observed and recorded by a person other than the one engaging in the behavior.

parallel contract A two-party contract in which two people each seek behavior change. Both people specify their behavior to be changed and the consequence for their behavior. However, the contract behaviors and consequences for each party are independent of each other. Contrast the quid pro quo contract, in which the behavior of one party is the reinforcer for the behavior of the other party.

phobia A fear in which the level anxiety or escape and avoidance behavior is severe enough to disrupt the person's life.

physical guidance Another term for physical prompting.

physical prompt A type of prompt in which the trainer physically assists the learner to engage in the correct behavior at the correct time. Most often involves hand-over-hand guidance of the behavior.

physical restraint A type of positive punishment procedure in which, contingent on the occurrence of the problem behavior, the change agent holds immobile the part of the client's body that is involved in the problem behavior so that the client cannot continue to engage in the behavior.

picture prompts A type of prompt in which the client is presented with a picture of a person engaging in the target behavior. The picture acts as a prompt for the client to engage in the correct behavior at the correct time. Often, a sequence of pictures is presented to prompt a client to engage in a chain of behaviors.

positive practice A type of overcorrection procedure in which, contingent on the problem behavior, the client is required to engage in correct forms of relevant behavior until the behavior has been repeated a number of times.

positive punishment A type of punishment in which, contingent on the behavior, an aversive stimulus or event is presented and the probability of the behavior decreases in the future.

positive reinforcement A type of reinforcement in which, contingent on the behavior, a stimulus or event is presented and the probability of the behavior increases in the future.

positive reinforcer A stimulus that will increase the future probability of a behavior when the stimulus is delivered contingent on the occurrence of the behavior.

Premack principle One type of positive reinforcement in which the opportunity to engage in a high probability behavior is made contingent on the occurrence of a low probability behavior in order to increase the low probability behavior.

product recording A type of behavior recording in which the outcome or permanent product of the behavior is recorded as an indication of the occurrence of the behavior.

progressive muscle relaxation (PMR) A relaxation procedure in which the client learns to tense and relax each of the major muscle groups of the body. By this means, the client decreases muscle tension and autonomic arousal in the body.

prompt A prompt is used to increase the likelihood that a person will engage in the correct behavior at the correct time. A prompt may involve the behavior of the trainer (response prompts) or supplemental environmental stimuli (stimulus prompts).

prompt delay In this procedure, the trainer presents the discriminative stimulus (S^D) and then, after a specific interval of time (say, 4 seconds), presents the prompt. The delay between the presentation of the S^D and the presentation of the prompt means that as training progresses, the person may make the response before the prompt is given.

prompt fading *See* fading.

punisher A stimulus or event that, when presented contingent on the occurrence of a behavior, decreases the future probability of the behavior.

punishment The process in which a behavior is followed by a consequence that results in a decrease in the future probability of the behavior.

quid pro quo contract A two-party contract in which two people each specify a behavior that they will change in return for the behavior change of the other person.

rate The frequency of the behavior divided by the time of the observation period. Typically reported as responses per minute.

reactivity The phenomenon in which the process of recording behavior causes the behavior to change even before treatment is implemented for the behavior.

real-time recording A recording method in which you record the exact time of each onset and offset of the target behavior in the observation period. Real-time recording results in information on the frequency and duration of the target behavior as well as the exact timing of each instance of the behavior in the observation period.

regulated breathing The competing response that is used in the habit reversal treatment for stuttering.

rehearsal Practice of the behavior in a role-play situation after instructions and modeling. Rehearsal is followed by feedback on the performance.

reinforcement The process in which the occurrence of a behavior is followed by a consequence that results in an increase in the future probability of the behavior.

reinforcer A stimulus or event that increases the future probability of a behavior when it occurs contingent on the occurrence of the behavior.

relaxation training A procedure for teaching a person the skills needed to decrease autonomic arousal (anxiety) by producing an incompatible state of relaxation. Progressive muscle relaxation, diaphragmatic breathing, attention-focusing exercises, and behavioral relaxation training are types of relaxation training procedures.

research design In behavior modification, a research design specifies the timing of the baseline and treatment phases for one or more people in an attempt to demonstrate a functional relationship between the treatment and the behavior.

resistance to extinction The tendency for a person to continue to respond after extinction is in effect for the behavior. Intermittent reinforcement schedules make the behavior more resistant to extinction than do continuous reinforcement schedules.

respondent behavior Behavior that is elicited by a prior stimulus. An unconditioned response (UR) and a conditioned response (CR) are respondent behaviors because they are elicited by unconditioned stimuli (US) and conditioned stimuli (CS), respectively.

respondent conditioning A process in which a neutral stimulus is paired with an unconditioned stimulus (US). The US elicits an unconditioned response (UR). As a result of pairing the neutral stimulus with the US, the neutral stimulus becomes a conditioned stimulus (CS) that will elicit a response similar to the UR, called a conditioned response (CR).

respondent extinction *See* extinction (respondent).

response A response is one instance or occurrence of a particular behavior.

response blocking A procedure in which the change agent physically blocks a problem behavior so that the client cannot complete the response. Often used in conjunction with brief restraint.

response cost A negative punishment procedure in which, contingent on a behavior, a specified amount of a reinforcer is removed.

response effort The amount of force, exertion, or time involved in executing a response. With an increase in response effort for one behavior, the probability of that behavior decreases relative to the probability of a functionally equivalent alternative behavior.

response prompt A type of prompt in which the trainer engages in a behavior to induce the client to engage in the target behavior in the presence of the discriminative stimulus. Includes verbal prompts, gestural prompts, modeling prompts, and physical prompts.

restitution A type of overcorrection procedure in which, contingent on the occurrence of the problem behavior, the client is required to correct the environmental effect of the problem behavior and to bring the environment to a condition better than that before the problem behavior.

rule-governed behavior Behavior that is controlled by a verbal statement (a rule) about a contingency between the behavior and a consequence.

S-delta (S^{Δ}) A stimulus that is present when a behavior is not reinforced. In discrimination training, the behavior is reinforced if it occurs in the presence of the S^{D} but not in the presence of the S^{Δ}.

salient A stimulus is salient when it is intense or easily detected by the individual.

satiation Progressive (and ultimately total) loss of effectiveness of a reinforcer. Satiation occurs when you have recently consumed a large amount of a particular reinforcer or when you have had substantial exposure to a reinforcing stimulus.

scatter plot A type of functional assessment procedure in which you record each half hour whether the behavior occurred in the preceding half hour. Used to establish the temporal pattern in the behavior.

schedule of reinforcement Specifies which responses will be followed by delivery of the reinforcer. In a continuous reinforcement schedule, every response is followed by the reinforcer. In an intermittent schedule, not every response is followed by the reinforcer.

self-generated mediator of generalization A behavior that makes it more likely that one will perform the target behavior at the right time. A self instruction that is used to cue the appropriate behavior at the appropriate time is an example.

self-instructional training A type of cognitive behavior modification procedure in which the client learns to make specific self-statements that increase the likelihood that a target behavior will occur in a specific situation.

self-instructions Self-statements that make it more likely that a target behavior will occur in a specific situation.

self-managment Behavior modification procedures used by a person to change his or her own behavior. In a self-management strategy, the person engages in a behavior that alters an antecedent or consequence of the target behavior or alternative behavior.

self-monitoring A type of direct observation data collection in which the client observes and records his or her own behavior as it occurs.

self-praise Making positive statements to yourself or providing positive evaluations of your own behavior after engaging in an appropriate behavior.

shaping The reinforcement of successive approximations to a target behavior. Used to establish a novel topography or dimension of a behavior.

short-circuitng the contingency Occurs when a person arranges a reinforcer for a target behavior in a self-management project but then takes the reinforcer without first engaging in the target behavior. May also occur when a person arranges a punisher for a target behavior but does not implement the punisher after engaging in the target behavior.

simultaneous conditioning The process in which the unconditioned stimulus (US) and conditioned stimulus (CS) are presented at the same time in respondent conditioning trials.

social support A component of the habit reversal procedure in which a significant other praises the client for correct use of the competing response and prompts the client to use the competing response when the habit behavior occurs. In general, social support occurs when significant others are involved in implementing contingencies in the natural environment to help a person reach a self-management goal.

spaced-responding DRL A type of DRL procedure in which the reinforcer is delivered when responses are separated by a specific time interval. If a response occurs before the interval has ended, the reinforcer is not delivered and the interval is reset. The interval between responses is called the interresponse time.

spontaneous recovery (operant) The process in which, when an operant behavior has been extinguished, the behavior may occur again in the future in circumstances in which it was previously reinforced.

spontaneous recovery (respondent) The process in which, when a conditioned response (CR) has been extinguished, the CR may occur at a later time when the conditioned stimulus (CS) is presented again.

stereotypic behavior Repetitive behaviors that do not serve any social function for the individual. They are often called self-stimulatory behaviors because they function to produce some form of sensory stimulation for the individual.

stimulus An environmental event that can be detected by one of the senses.

stimulus class A group of stimuli that all have the same functional effect on a particular behavior. For example, each stimulus in a stimulus class may function as an discriminative stimulus for a particular behavior.

stimulus control The outcome of stimulus discrimination training. A particular behavior is more likely to occur in the presence of a particular discriminative stimulus (the S^D) because the behavior has been reinforced only when the S^D was present. The S^D has stimulus control over the behavior.

stimulus discrimination training A process in which a behavior is reinforced when the discriminative stimulus (S^D) is present and is extinguished when the S^Δ is present. As a result, the behavior is more likely to occur only when the S^D is present. Also called discrimination training.

stimulus exemplars Stimuli that represent the range of relevant stimulus situations in which the response is to occur after training. One strategy for promoting generalization is to train sufficient stimulus exemplars.

stimulus fading The gradual elimination of a stimulus prompt as the behavior continues to occur in the presence of the discriminative stimulus.

stimulus prompt Some change in an antecedent stimulus or the addition or removal of an antecedent stimulus, with the goal of making a correct response more likely.

stimulus–response chain *See* behavioral chain.

stuttering A speech dysfluency in which the individual repeats words or syllables, prolongs a word sound, and or blocks on a word (makes no sound for a period of time when trying to say a word).

successive approximation In the process of shaping, each successive approximation is a behavior that more closely resembles the target behavior. The shaping process starts with reinforcement of the first approximation, a behavior currently exhibited by the person. After the first approximation is strengthened through reinforcement, it is extinguished. A closer approximation then occurs and is reinforced. This process continues until the person exhibits the target behavior.

systematic desensitization A procedure used to treat a fear or phobia. The person first learns relaxation. Next, the person develops a hierarchy of fear-producing situations. Finally, the person uses the relaxation procedure as he or she imagines each situation in the hierarchy, starting with the least fear-producing situation and gradually working up to the most fear-producing situation. The goal is to replace the fear response with the relaxation response as each situation is imagined.

target behavior In behavior modification, the behavior to be modified.

task analysis Identification of the discriminative stimulus and response for each component of a behavior chain.

textual prompts *See* written task analysis.

three-term contingency The antecedent that is present when the behavior occurs, the behavior, and the reinforcing consequence. Also called a contingency of reinforcement.

time-out from positive reinforcement A type of negative punishment in which, contingent on the occurrence of the problem behavior, the person loses access to positive reinforcers for a brief period. Typically, the person is removed from the reinforcing environment in a time-out procedure.

time sample recording A behavior recording procedure in which the observation period is divided into intervals, and the behavior is recorded during a part of each interval. In time sample recording, the observation intervals are discontinuous.

token A conditioned reinforcer used in a token economy. The token is something that can be given to another person and accumulated by that person. The token is a conditioned reinforcer because it is given to the person after a desirable behavior and is exchanged for established reinforcers called backup reinforcers.

token economy A reinforcement system in which conditioned reinforcers called tokens are delivered to people for desirable behaviors: the tokens are later exchanged for backup reinforcers.

total task presentation A procedure for teaching a chain of behavior in which the trainer physically prompts the learner through all steps in the chain. Eventually, the trainer fades the physical prompts and shadows the learner's movements as he or she completes the chain of behaviors. Eventually, the learner completes the chain without any assistance from the trainer.

Tourette's disorder A tic disorder involving multiple motor and vocal tics that have occurred for at least one year.

trace conditioning A type of respondent conditioning in which the conditioned stimulus (CS) is presented and then the unconditioned stimulus (US) is presented after the termination of the CS.

training stimuli The discriminative stimulus and other stimuli present during training sessions.

transfer of stimulus control A process in which prompts are removed once the target behavior is occurring in the presence of the discriminative stimulus (S^D). Prompt fading and prompt delay are procedures used to transfer stimulus control from the prompt to the S^D.

treatment acceptability Subjective judgments about how much people like a particular treatment procedure. Usually measured with rating scales.

two-party contract A type of behavioral contract in which two people both identify behavior to change and the consequences for the behavior change.

unconditioned punisher A stimulus or event that is naturally punishing because avoiding or minimizing contact with such a stimulus has survival value. No prior conditioning is needed for an unconditioned punisher to function as a punisher. Examples are painful stimuli or extreme levels of stimulation.

unconditioned reinforcer A stimulus that is naturally reinforcing because the capacity for our behavior to be strengthened by the stimulus has survival value. No prior conditioning is necessary for an unconditioned reinforcer to be a reinforcer. Examples include food, water, escape from extreme stimulation, and sexual contact.

unconditioned response (UR) The response that is elicited by an unconditioned stimulus (US).

unconditioned stimulus (US) A stimulus that naturally elicits an unconditioned response (UR) because the UR has survival value. No prior conditioning is needed for the US to elicit a UR.

variable interval (VI) schedule A schedule of reinforcement in which the first response that occurs after a specified time interval is reinforced. The time interval varies around an average value.

variable ratio (VR) schedule A schedule of reinforcement in which a specified number of responses is needed for the delivery of the reinforcer. The number of responses needed varies around an average number.

verbal prompt A type of prompt in which the verbal behavior of another person results in the correct behavior of the trainee in the presence of the discriminative stimulus.

vocal tic A repetitive vocal sound or word uttered by an individual that does not serve any communicative function.

whole-interval DRO A type of DRO procedure in which the problem behavior must be absent throughout the entire interval of time for the reinforcer to be delivered. Most DRO procedures involve whole-interval DRO.

within-stimulus prompt A type of stimulus prompt in which some aspect of the discriminative stimulus or S^{Δ} is changed to help a person make a correct discrimination.

written task analysis A written list of each discriminative stimulus and response in a chain of behaviors. Sometimes a written task analysis (also known as textual prompts) is given to the learner to guide the learner's behavior through the chain of behaviors.

REFERENCES

Ackerman, A. M., & Shapiro, E. S. (1984). Self-monitoring and work productivity with mentally retarded adults. *Journal of Applied Behavior Analysis, 17*, 403–407.

Adams, C. D., & Kelley, M. L. (1992). Managing sibling aggression: Overcorrection as an alternative to time out. *Behavior Therapy, 23*, 707–717.

Alavosius, M. P., & Sulzer-Azaroff, B. (1986). The effects of performance feedback on the safety of client lifting and transfer. *Journal of Applied Behavior Analysis, 19*, 261–267.

Alberto, P. A., & Troutman, A. C. (1986). *Applied behavior analysis for teachers*. Columbus, OH: Merrill.

Albion, F. M., & Salzburg, C. L. (1982). The effect of self-instruction on the rate of correct addition problems with mentally retarded children. *Education and Treatment of Children, 5*, 121–131.

Allen, K. D., & Stokes, T. F. (1987). Use of escape and reward in the management of young children during dental treatment. *Journal of Applied Behavior Analysis, 20*, 381–390.

Allen, L. J., Howard, V. F., Sweeney, W. J., & McLaughlin, T. F. (1993). Use of contingency contracting to increase on-task behavior with primary students. *Psychological Reports, 72*, 905–906.

Anderson, C. M., & Long, E. S. (2002). Use of a structured descriptive assessment methodology to identify variables affecting problem behavior. *Journal of Applied Behavior Analysis, 35*, 137–154.

Aragona, J., Cassady, J., & Drabman, R. S. (1975). Treating overweight children through parental training and contingency contracting. *Journal of Applied Behavior Analysis, 8*, 269–278.

Arndorfer, R., & Miltenberger, R. (1993). Functional assessment and treatment of challenging behavior: A review with implications for early childhood. *Topics in Early Childhood Special Education, 13*, 82–105.

Arndorfer, R. E., Miltenberger, R. G., Woster, S. H., Rortvedt, A. K., & Gaffaney, T. (1994). Home-based descriptive and experimental analysis of problem behaviors in children. *Topics in Early Childhood Special Education, 14*, 64–87.

Ashbaugh, R., & Peck, S. M. (1998). Treatment of sleep problems in a toddler: A replication of the faded bedtime with response cost protocol. *Journal of Applied Behavior Analysis, 31*, 127–129.

Asterita, M. F. (1985). *The physiology of stress*. New York: Human Sciences Press.

Axelrod, S. (1987). Functional and structural analyses of behavior: Approaches leading to reduced use of punishment procedures. *Research in Developmental Disabilities, 8*, 165–178.

Axelrod, S., & Apsche, J. (Eds.). (1983). *The effects of punishment on human behavior*. New York: Academic Press.

Ayllon, T. (1963). Intensive treatment of psychotic behavior by stimulus satiation and food reinforcement. *Behaviour Research and Therapy, 1*, 53–61.

Ayllon, T., & Azrin, N. H. (1964). Reinforcement and instructions with mental patients. *Journal of the Experimental Analysis of Behavior, 7*, 327–331.

Ayllon, T., & Azrin, N. H. (1965). The measurement and reinforcement of behavior of psychotics. *Journal of the Experimental Analysis of Behavior, 8*, 357–383.

Ayllon, T., & Azrin, N. (1968). *The token economy: A motivational system for therapy and rehabilitation*. New York: Appleton-Century-Crofts.

Ayllon, T., Kuhlman, C., & Warzak, W. (1982). Programming resource room generalization using lucky charms. *Child Behavior Therapy, 4*, 61–67.

Ayllon, T., Layman, D., & Kandel, H. J. (1975). A behavioral–educational alternative to drug control of hyperactive children. *Journal of Applied Behavior Analysis, 8*, 137–146.

Ayllon, T. D., & Michael, J. (1959). The psychiatric nurse as a behavioral engineer. *Journal of the Experimental Analysis of Behavior, 2*, 323–334.

Azrin, N. H., & Foxx, R. M. (1971). A rapid method of toilet training the institutionalized retarded. *Journal of Applied Behavior Analysis, 4*, 89–99.

Azrin, N. H., Hake, D., Holz, W., & Hutchinson, R. (1965). Motivational aspects of escape from punishment. *Journal of the Experimental Analysis of Behavior, 8*, 31–57.

Azrin, N. H., & Holz, W. (1966). Punishment. In W. K. Honig (Ed.), *Operant behavior: Areas of research and application* (pp. 380–447). New York: Appleton-Century-Crofts.

Azrin, N. H., Holz, W., Ulrich, R., & Goldiamond, I. (1973). The control of the content of conversation through reinforcement. *Journal of Applied Behavior Analysis, 6*, 186–192.

Azrin, N. H., Hutchinson, R. R., & Hake, D. F. (1963). Pain-induced fighting in the squirrel monkey. *Journal of the Experimental Analysis of Behavior, 6,* 620.

Azrin, N. H., Hutchinson, R. R., & Hake, D. F. (1966). Extinction produced aggression. *Journal of the Experimental Analysis of Behavior, 9,* 191–204.

Azrin, N. H., & Lindsley, O. R. (1956). The reinforcement of cooperation between children. *Journal of Abnormal and Social Psychology, 52,* 100–102.

Azrin, N. H., & Nunn, R. G. (1973). Habit reversal: A method of eliminating nervous habits and tics. *Behaviour Research and Therapy, 11,* 619–628.

Azrin, N. H., & Nunn, R. G. (1974). A rapid method of eliminating stuttering by a regulated breathing approach. *Behaviour Research and Therapy, 12,* 279–286.

Azrin, N. H., & Nunn, R. G. (1977). Habit control in a day. New York: Simon & Schuster.

Azrin, N. H., Nunn, R. G., & Frantz, S. E. (1979). Comparison of regulated breathing versus abbreviated desensitization on reported stuttering episodes. *Journal of Speech and Hearing Disorders, 44,* 331–339.

Azrin, N. H., Nunn, R. G., & Frantz, S. E. (1980a). Habit reversal versus negative practice treatment of nailbiting. *Behaviour Research and Therapy, 18,* 281–285.

Azrin, N. H., Nunn, R. G., & Frantz, S. E. (1980b). Habit reversal versus negative practice treatment of nervous tics. *Behavior Therapy, 11,* 169–178.

Azrin, N. H., Nunn, R. G., & Frantz-Renshaw, S. E. (1980). Habit reversal treatment of thumbsucking. *Behaviour Research and Therapy, 18,* 195–399.

Azrin, N. H., Nunn, R. G., & Frantz-Renshaw, S. E. (1982). Habit reversal versus negative practice treatment of destructive oral habits (biting, chewing or licking of the lips, cheeks, tongue or palate). *Journal of Behavior Therapy and Experimental Psychiatry, 13,* 49–54.

Azrin, N. H., & Peterson, A. L. (1989). Reduction of an eye tic by controlled blinking. *Behavior Therapy, 20,* 467–473.

Azrin, N. H., & Peterson, A. L. (1990). Treatment of Tourette syndrome by habit reversal: A waiting list control group comparison. *Behavior Therapy, 21,* 305–318.

Azrin, N. H., & Powell, J. (1968). Behavioral engineering: The reduction of smoking behavior by a conditioning apparatus and procedure. *Journal of Applied Behavior Analysis, 1,* 193–200.

Azrin, N. H., & Wesolowski, M. D. (1975). Theft reversal: An overcorrection procedure for eliminating stealing by retarded persons. *Journal of Applied Behavior Analysis, 7,* 577–581.

Bachman, J., & Sluyter, D. (1988). Reducing inappropriate behavior of developmentally disabled adults using antecedent aerobic dance exercises. *Research in Developmental Disabilities, 9,* 73–83.

Baer, D. M. (1960). Escape and avoidance responses of preschool children to two schedules of reinforcement withdrawal. *Journal of the Experimental Analysis of Behavior, 3,* 155–159.

Baer, D. M., Peterson, R. F., & Sherman, J. A. (1967). The development of imitation by reinforcing behavioral similarity to a model. *Journal of the Experimental Analysis of Behavior, 10,* 405–416.

Baer, D. M., & Sherman, J. A. (1964). Reinforcement control of generalized imitation in young children. *Journal of Experimental Psychology, 1,* 37–49.

Baer, D. M., Wolf, M. M., & Risley, T. R. (1968). Some current dimensions of applied behavior analysis. *Journal of Applied Behavior Analysis, 1,* 91–97.

Baer, D. M., Wolf, M. M., & Risley, T. R. (1987). Some still-current dimensions of applied behavior analysis. *Journal of Applied Behavior Analysis, 20,* 313–327.

Bailey, J. S. (1977). *Handbook of research methods in applied behavior analysis.* Tallahassee, FL: Copy Grafix.

Bailey, J. S., & Burch, M. R. (2002). *Research methods in applied behavior analysis.* Thousand Oaks, CA: Sage.

Bailey, J., & Meyerson, L. (1969). Vibration as a reinforcer with a profoundly retarded child. *Journal of Applied Behavior Analysis, 2,* 135–137.

Bailey, J. S., & Pyles, D. A. (1989). Behavioral diagnostics. In E. Cipani (Ed.), *The treatment of severe behavior disorders: Behavior analysis approaches* (pp. 85–107). Washington, DC: American Association on Mental Retardation.

Bakke, B. L., Kvale, S., Burns, T., McCarten, J. R., Wilson, L., Maddox, M., & Cleary, J. (1994). Multicomponent intervention for agitated behavior in a person with Alzheimer's disease. *Journal of Applied Behavior Analysis, 27,* 175–176.

Bakken, J., Miltenberger, R., & Schauss, S. (1993). Teaching mentally retarded parents: Knowledge versus skills. *American Journal on Mental Retardation, 97,* 405–417.

Bandura, A. (1969). *Principles of behavior modification.* New York: Holt, Rinehart, & Winston.

Bandura, A. (1977). *Social learning theory.* Upper Saddle River, NJ: Prentice Hall.

Bandura, A., Ross, D., & Ross, S. (1963). Imitation of film mediated aggressive models. *Journal of Abnormal and Social Psychology, 66,* 601–607.

Barlow, D. H., & Hersen, M. (1984). *Single case experimental designs: Strategies for studying behavior change* (2nd ed.). New York: Pergamon.

Barnard, J. D., Christophersen, E. R., & Wolf, M. M. (1977). Teaching children appropriate shopping behavior through parent training in the supermarket setting. *Journal of Applied Behavior Analysis, 10,* 49–59.

Barrett, R. P. (Ed.). (1986). *Severe behavior disorders in the mentally retarded: Nondrug approaches to treatment.* New York: Plenum.

Barrios, B. A., & O'Dell, S. L. (1989). Fears and anxieties. In E. J. Mash & R. A. Barkley (Eds.), *Treatment of childhood disorders* (pp. 167–221). New York: Guilford.

Barrish, H. H., Saunders, M., & Wolf, M. M. (1969). Good behavior game: Effects of individual contingencies for group consequences on the disruptive behavior in a classroom. *Journal of Applied Behavior Analysis, 2,* 119–124.

Barton, L. E., Brulle, A. R., & Repp, A. C. (1986). Maintenance of therapeutic change by momentary DRO. *Journal of Applied Behavior Analysis, 19,* 277–282.

Beck, A. T. (1972). *Depression: Causes and treatment.* Philadelphia: University of Pennsylvania Press.

Beck, A. T. (1976). *Cognitive therapy and the emotional disorders.* New York: International Universities Press.

Beck, A. T., & Freeman, A. (1989). *Cognitive therapy of personality disorders.* New York: Guilford.

Beck, A. T., Rush, A. J., Shaw, B. F., & Emery, G. (1979). *Cognitive therapy of depression.* New York: Guilford.

Becker, W. C., & Carnine, D. C. (1981). Direct instruction: A behavior theory model for comprehensive educational intervention with the disadvantaged. In S. W. Bijou & R. Ruiz (Eds.), *Behavior modification: Contributions to education* (pp. 145–210). Mahwah, NJ: Erlbaum.

Belcher, T. L. (1994). Movement to the community: Reduction of behavioral difficulties. *Mental Retardation, 32,* 89–90.

Bellamy, G. T., Horner, R. H., & Inman, D. P. (1979). *Vocational habilitation of severely retarded adults.* Austin, TX: Pro-Ed.

Benson, H. (1975). *The relaxation response.* New York: William Morrow.

Berkowitz, S., Sherry, P. J., & Davis, B. A. (1971). Teaching self-feeding skills to profound retardates using reinforcement and fading procedures. *Behavior Therapy, 2,* 62–67.

Bernstein, D. A., & Borkovec, T. D. (1973). *Progressive relaxation training: A manual for the helping professions.* Champaign, IL: Research Press.

Berry, T. D., & Geller, E. S. (1991). A single subject approach to evaluating vehicle safety belt reminders: Back to basics. *Journal of Applied Behavior Analysis, 24,* 13–22.

Bijou, S. W. (1957). Patterns of reinforcement and resistance to extinction in young children. *Child Development, 28,* 47–54.

Bijou, S. W. (1958). Operant extinction after fixed interval schedules with young children. *Journal of the Experimental Analysis of Behavior, 1,* 25–29.

Bijou, S. W. (1976). *Child development: The basic stages of early childhood.* Englewood Cliffs, NJ: Prentice Hall.

Bijou, S. W., Peterson, R. F., & Ault, M. H. (1968). A method to integrate descriptive and experimental field studies at the level of data and empirical concepts. *Journal of Applied Behavior Analysis, 1,* 175–191.

Bijou, S. W., & Ruiz, R. (Eds.). (1981). *Behavior modification: Contributions to education.* Mahwah, NJ: Erlbaum.

Billingsley, F. F., & Romer, L. T. (1983). Response prompting and transfer of stimulus control: Methods, research, and a conceptual framework. *Journal of the Association for Persons with Severe Handicaps, 8,* 3–12.

Blount, R. L., Drabman, R. S., Wilson, N., & Stewart, D. (1982). Reducing severe diurnal bruxism in two profoundly retarded females. *Journal of Applied Behavior Analysis, 15,* 565–571.

Blumenthal, J. A., & McKee, D. C. (Eds.). (1987). *Applications in behavioral medicine and health psychology: A clinician's source book.* Sarasota, FL: Professional Resource Exchange.

Bostow, D. E., & Bailey, J. (1969). Modification of severe disruptive and aggressive behavior using brief timeout and reinforcement procedures. *Journal of Applied Behavior Analysis, 2,* 31–37.

Boudjouk, P., Woods, D., Miltenberger, R., & Long, E. (2000). Negative peer evaluation in adolescents: Effects of tic disorders and trichotillomania. *Child and Family Behavior Therapy* 22(1), 17–28.

Bowman, L. G., Piazza, C. C., Fisher, W. W., Hagopian, L. P., & Kogan, J. S. (1997). Assessment of preference for varied versus constant reinforcers. *Journal of Applied Behavior Analysis, 30,* 451–458.

Brigham, T. A. (1989). *Managing everyday problems.* New York: Guilford.

Bristol, M. M., & Sloane, H. N. (1974). Effects of contingency contracting on study rate and test performance. *Journal of Applied Behavior Analysis, 7,* 271–285.

Brobst, B., & Ward, P. (2002). Effects of public posting, goal setting, and oral feedback on the skills of female soccer players. *Journal of Applied Behavior Analysis, 35,* 247–257

Brothers, K. J., Krantz, P. J., & McClannahan, L. E. (1994). Office paper recycling: A function of container proximity. *Journal of Applied Behavior Analysis, 27,* 153–160.

Bryant, L. E., & Budd, K. S. (1982). Self-instructional training to increase independent work performance in preschool children. *Journal of Applied Behavior Analysis, 15,* 259–271.

Bucher, B., Reykdal, B., & Albin, J. (1976). Brief physical restraint to control pica in retarded children. *Journal of Behavior Therapy and Experimental Psychiatry, 7,* 137–140.

Burns, D. D. (1980). *Feeling good: The new mood therapy.* New York: Morrow.

Carns, A. W., & Carns, M. R. (1994). Making behavioral contracts successful. *School Counselor, 42,* 155–160.

Carr, E. G. (1988). Functional equivalence as a means of response generalization. In R. H. Horner, G. Dunlap, & R. L. Koegel (Eds.), *Generalization and maintenance: Lifestyle changes in applied settings* (pp. 221–241). Baltimore: Paul Brookes.

Carr, E. G., & Carlson, J. I. (1993). Reduction of severe behavior problems in the community using a multicomponent treatment approach. *Journal of Applied Behavior Analysis, 26,* 157–172.

Carr, E. G., & Durand, V. M. (1985). Reducing behavior problems through functional communication training. *Journal of Applied Behavior Analysis, 18,* 111–126.

Carr, E. G., Levin, L., McConnachie, G., Carlson, J. I., Kemp, D. C., & Smith, C. E. (1994). *Communication-*

based intervention for problem behavior: A user's guide for producing positive change. Baltimore: Paul Brookes.

Carr, E. G., McConnachie, G., Levin, L., & Kemp, D. C. (1993). Communication based treatment of severe behavior problems. In R. Van Houten & S. Axelrod (Eds.), *Behavior analysis and treatment* (pp. 231–267). New York: Plenum.

Carr, E. G., Newsom, C. D., & Binkoff, J. A. (1980). Escape as a factor in the aggressive behavior of two retarded children. *Journal of Applied Behavior Analysis, 13,* 101–117.

Carr, J. E. (1995). Competing responses for the treatment of Tourette syndrome and tic disorders. *Behaviour Research and Therapy, 33,* 455–456.

Carr, J., & Austin, J. (Eds.). (2001). *Handbook of applied behavior analysis.* Reno, NV: Context Press.

Carroll, L. A., Miltenberger, R. G., & O'Neill, H. K. (1992). A review and critique of research evaluating child sexual abuse prevention programs. *Education & Treatment of Children, 15,* 335–354.

Carroll-Rowan, L., & Miltenberger, R. G. (1994). A comparison of procedures for teaching abduction prevention to preschoolers. *Education and Treatment of Children, 17,* 113–128.

Carstensen, L. L., & Erickson, R. J. (1986). Enhancing the environments of elderly nursing home residents: Are high rates of interaction enough? *Journal of Applied Behavior Analysis, 19,* 349–355.

Carton, J. S., & Schweitzer, J. B. (1996). Use of a token economy to increase compliance during hemodialysis. *Journal of Applied Behavior Analysis, 29,* 111–113.

Catania, A. C. (Ed.). (1968). *Contemporary research in operant behavior.* Glenview, IL: Scott Foresman.

Cautela, J. (1977). *Behavior analysis forms for clinical intervention.* Champaign, IL: Research Press.

Cavalier, A. R., Ferretti, R. P., & Hodges, A. E. (1997). Self-management within a token economy for students with learning disabilities. *Research in Developmental Disabilities, 18,* 167–178.

Chadwick, B. A., & Day, R. C. (1971). Systematic reinforcement: Academic performance of underachieving students. *Journal of Applied Behavior Analysis, 4,* 311–319.

Chance, P. (1988). *Learning and behavior* (2nd ed.). Belmont, CA: Wadsworth.

Charlop, M. H., Burgio, L. D., Iwata, B. A., & Ivancic, M. T. (1988). Stimulus variation as a means of enhancing punishment effects. *Journal of Applied Behavior Analysis, 21,* 89–95.

Clark, H., Rowbury, T., Baer, A., & Baer, D. (1973). Time out as a punishing stimulus in continuous and intermittent schedules. *Journal of Applied Behavior Analysis, 6,* 443–455.

Coleman, C. L., & Holmes, P. A. (1998). The use of noncontingent escape to reduce disruptive behaviors in children with speech delays. *Journal of Applied Behavior Analysis, 31,* 687–690.

Cooper, J. O., Heron, T. E., & Heward, W. L. (1987). *Applied behavior analysis.* Columbus, OH: Merrill.

Cope, J. G., & Allred, L. J. (1991). Community intervention to deter illegal parking in spaces reserved for the physically disabled. *Journal of Applied Behavior Analysis, 24,* 687–693.

Corte, H., Wolf, M., & Locke, B. (1971). A comparison of procedures for eliminating self-injurious behavior of retarded adolescents. *Journal of Applied Behavior Analysis, 4,* 201–213.

Cowdery, G. E., Iwata, B. A., & Pace, G. M. (1990). Effects and side-effects of DRO as treatment for self-injurious behavior. *Journal of Applied Behavior Analysis, 23,* 497–506.

Croghan, L. M., & Musante, G. J. (1975). The elimination of a boy's high building phobia by in vivo desensitization and game playing. *Journal of Behavior Therapy and Experimental Psychiatry, 6,* 87–88.

Cuvo, A. J., Davis, P. K., O'Reilly, M. F., Mooney, B. M., & Crowley, R. (1992). Promoting stimulus control with textual prompts and performance feedback for persons with mild disabilities. *Journal of Applied Behavior Analysis, 25,* 477–489.

Cuvo, A. J., & Klatt, K. P. (1992). Effects of community based, videotape, and flashcard instruction of community-referenced sight words on students with mental retardation. *Journal of Applied Behavior Analysis, 25,* 499–512.

Cuvo, A. J., Leaf, R. B., & Borakove, L. S. (1978). Teaching janitorial skills to the mentally retarded: Acquisition, generalization, and maintenance. *Journal of Applied Behavior Analysis, 11,* 345–355.

Dancer, D. D., Braukmann, C. J., Schumaker, J. B., Kirigin, K. A., Willner, A. G., & Wolf, M. M. (1978). The training and validation of behavior observation and description skills. *Behavior Modification, 2,* 113–134.

Davis, C. A., Brady, M. P., Williams, R. E., & Hamilton, R. (1992). Effects of high probability requests on the acquisition and generalization of responses to requests in young children with behavior disorders. *Journal of Applied Behavior Analysis, 25,* 905–916.

Davis, M., Eshelman, E. R., & McKay, M. (1988). *The relaxation and stress reduction workbook.* Oakland, CA: New Harbinger Publications.

Davis, P., & Chittum, R. (1994). A group oriented contingency to increase leisure activities in adults with traumatic brain injury. *Journal of Applied Behavior Analysis, 27,* 553–554.

Day, H. M., Horner, R. H., & O'Neill, R. E. (1994). Multiple functions of problem behaviors: Assessment and intervention. *Journal of Applied Behavior Analysis, 27,* 279–289.

Deaver, C., Miltenberger, R., & Stricker, J. (2001). Functional analysis and treatment of hair twirling in a young child. *Journal of Applied Behavior Analysis, 34,* 535–538.

Deitz, S. M. (1977). An analysis of programming DRL schedules in educational settings. *Behaviour Research and Therapy, 15,* 103–111.

Deitz, S. M., & Malone, L. W. (1985). Stimulus control terminology. *The Behavior Analyst, 8*, 259–264.

Deitz, S. M., & Repp, A. C. (1973). Decreasing classroom misbehavior through the use of DRL schedules of reinforcement. *Journal of Applied Behavior Analysis, 6*, 457–463.

Deitz, S. M., & Repp, A. C. (1974). Differentially reinforcing low rates of misbehavior with normal elementary school children. *Journal of Applied Behavior Analysis, 7*, 622.

DeLuca, R., & Holborn, S. (1992). Effects of a variable ratio reinforcement schedule with changing criteria on exercise in obese and nonobese boys. *Journal of Applied Behavior Analysis, 25*, 671–679.

Demchak, M. (1990). Response prompting and fading methods: A review. *American Journal on Mental Retardation, 94*, 603–615.

DeVries, J. E., Burnette, M. M., & Redmon, W. K. (1991). AIDS prevention: Improving nurses' compliance with glove wearing through performance feedback. *Journal of Applied Behavior Analysis, 24*, 705–711.

Dickinson, A. M. (1989). The detrimental effects of extrinsic reinforcement on "intrinsic motivation." *The Behavior Analyst, 12*, 1–15.

Dixon, L. S. (1981). A functional analysis of photo–object matching skills of severely retarded adolescents. *Journal of Applied Behavior Analysis, 14*, 465–478.

Doerner, M., Miltenberger, R., & Bakken, J. (1989). Effects of staff self-management on positive social interactions in a group home setting. *Behavioral Residential Treatment, 4*, 313–330.

Doke, L. A., Wolery, M., & Sumberg, C. (1983). Treating chronic aggression: Effects and side effects of response-contingent ammonia spirits. *Behavior Modification, 7*, 531–556.

Doleys, D. M., Wells, K. C., Hobbs, S. A., Roberts, M. W., & Cartelli, L. M. (1976). The effects of social punishment on noncompliance: A comparison with time out and positive practice. *Journal of Applied Behavior Analysis, 9*, 471–482.

Dorsey, M. F., Iwata, B. A., Ong, P., & McSween, T. E. (1980). Treatment of self-injurious behavior using a water mist: Initial response suppression and generalization. *Journal of Applied Behavior Analysis, 13*, 343–353.

Doty, D. W., McInnis, T., & Paul, G. (1974). Remediation of negative side effects of an ongoing response cost system with chronic mental patients. *Journal of Applied Behavior Analysis, 7*, 191–198.

Drasgow, E., Yell, M. L., Bradley, R., & Shiner, J. G. (1999). The IDEA amendments of 1997: A school-wide model for conducting functional behavioral assessments and developing behavior intervention plans. *Education & Treatment of Children*, 22(3), 244–266.

Ducharme, J. M., & Van Houten, R. (1994). Operant extinction in the treatment of severe maladaptive behavior: Adapting research to practice. *Behavior Modification, 18*, 139–170.

Dunlap, G. (1993). Promoting generalization: Current status and functional considerations. In R. Van Houten & S. Axelrod (Eds.), *Behavior analysis and treatment* (pp. 269–296). New York: Plenum.

Dunlap, G., Kern-Dunlap, L., Clarke, S., & Robbins, F. (1991). Functional assessment, curricular revision, and severe behavior problems. *Journal of Applied Behavior Analysis, 24*, 387–397.

Durand, V. M. (1990). *Severe behavior problems: A functional communication training approach*. New York: Guilford.

Durand, V. M., Berotti, D., & Weiner, J. (1993). Functional communication training: Factors affecting effectiveness, generalization, and maintenance. In J. Reichle & D. P. Wacker (Eds.), *Communicative alternatives to challenging behavior: Integrating functional assessment and intervention strategies* (pp. 317–340). Baltimore: Paul Brookes.

Durand, V. M., & Carr, E. G. (1987). Social influences on "self-stimulatory" behavior: Analysis and treatment application. *Journal of Applied Behavior Analysis, 20*, 119–132.

Durand, V. M., & Carr, E. G. (1991). Functional communication training to reduce challenging behavior: Maintenance and application in new settings. *Journal of Applied Behavior Analysis, 24*, 251–264.

Durand, V. M., & Carr, E. G. (1992). An analysis of maintenance following functional communication training. *Journal of Applied Behavior Analysis, 25*, 777–794.

Durand, V. M., & Crimmins, D. B. (1988). Identifying the variables maintaining self-injurious behavior. *Journal of Autism and Developmental Disorders, 18*, 99–117.

Durand, V. M., & Crimmins, D. B. (1991). Teaching functionally equivalent responses as an intervention for challenging behavior. In R. Remington (Ed.), *The challenge of severe mental handicap: A behavior analytic approach* (pp. 71–95). New York: Wiley.

Durand, V. M., Crimmins, D. B., Caufield, M., & Taylor, J. (1989). Reinforcer assessment I: Using problem behavior to select reinforcers. *Journal of the Association for Persons with Severe Handicaps, 14*, 113–126.

Durand, V. M., & Mindell, J. A. (1990). Behavioral treatment of multiple childhood sleep disorders: Effects on child and family. *Behavior Modification, 14*, 37–49.

Dyer, K., Dunlap, G., & Winterling, V. (1990). Effects of choice making on the serious problem behaviors of students with severe handicaps. *Journal of Applied Behavior Analysis, 23*, 515–524.

D'Zurilla, T. J. (1986). *Problem solving therapy: A social competence approach to clinical intervention*. New York: Springer.

D'Zurilla, T. J., & Goldfried, M. R. (1971). Problem solving and behavior modification. *Journal of Abnormal Psychology, 78*, 107–126.

Edelstein, B. A. (1989). Generalization: Terminological, methodological, and conceptual issues. *Behavior Therapy, 20*, 311–324.

Elder, J. P., Edelstein, B. A., & Narick, M. M. (1979). Adolescent psychiatric patients: Modifying aggressive behavior with social skills training. *Behavior Modification, 3*, 161–178.

Elder, S. T., Ruiz, Z. R., Deabler, H. L., & Dillenhofer, R. L. (1973). Instrumental conditioning of diastolic blood pressure in essential hypertensive patients. *Journal of Applied Behavior Analysis, 6*, 377–382.

Ellingson, S., Miltenberger, R., Stricker, J., Galensky, T., & Garlinghouse, M. (2000). Functional assessment and treatment of challenging behavior in the classroom setting. *Journal of Positive Behavioral Intervention, 2*, 85–97.

Ellingson, S., Miltenberger, R., Stricker, J., Garlinghouse, M., Roberts, J., Galensky, T., & Rapp, J. (2000). Functional analysis and treatment of finger sucking. *Journal of Applied Behavior Analysis, 33*, 41–51.

Elliott, A., Miltenberger, R., Bundgaard, J., & Lumley, V. (1996). A national survey of assessment and treatment techniques used by behavior therapists. *Cognitive and Behavioral Practice, 3*, 107–125.

Elliott, A., Miltenberger, R., Rapp, J., Long, E., & McDonald, R. (1998). Brief application of simplified habit reversal to stuttering in children. *Journal of Behavior Therapy and Experimental Psychiatry, 29*, 289–302.

Ellis, A., & Bernard, M. E. (1985). *Clinical applications of rational–emotive therapy*. New York: Plenum.

Ellis, A., & Dryden, W. (1987). *The practice of rational emotive therapy*. New York: Springer.

Ellis, J., & Magee, S. K. (1999). Determination of environmental correlates of disruptive classroom behavior: Integration of functional analysis into public school assessment process. *Education & Treatment of Children, 22*(3), 291–316.

Epstein, R. (1996). *Self help without hype*. Tucker, GA: Performance Management Publications.

Erfanian, N., & Miltenberger, R. G. (1990). Contact desensitization in the treatment of dog phobias in persons who have mental retardation. *Behavioral Residential Treatment, 5*, 55–60.

Etzel, B. C., & LeBlanc, J. M. (1979). The simplest treatment alternative: The law of parsimony applied to choosing appropriate instructional control and errorless learning procedures for the difficult-to-teach child. *Journal of Autism and Developmental Disabilities, 9*, 361–382.

Etzel, B. C., LeBlanc, J. M., Schilmoeller, K. J., & Stella, M. E. (1981). Stimulus control procedures in the education of young children. In S. W. Bijou & R. Ruiz (Eds.), *Behavior modification contributions to education* (pp. 3–37). Mahwah, NJ: Erlbaum.

Evans, B. (1976). A case of trichotillomania in a child treated in a home token program. *Journal of Behavior Therapy and Experimental Psychiatry, 7*, 197–198.

Everett, P. B., Hayward, S. C., & Meyers, A. W. (1974). The effects of a token reinforcement procedure on bus ridership. *Journal of Applied Behavior Analysis, 7*, 1–9.

Evers, R. A. F., & Van De Wetering, B. J. M. (1994). A treatment model for motor tics based on a specific tension reduction technique. *Journal of Behavior Therapy and Experimental Psychiatry, 25*, 255–260.

Favell, J. E., & McGimsey, J. F. (1993). Defining an acceptable treatment environment. In R. Van Houten & S. Axelrod (Eds.), *Behavior analysis and treatment* (pp. 25–45). New York: Plenum.

Favell, J. E., McGimsey, J. F., & Jones, M. L. (1978). The use of physical restraint in the treatment of self-injury and as positive reinforcement. *Journal of Applied Behavior Analysis, 11*, 225–241.

Fawcett, S. B., & Fletcher, R. K. (1977). Community applications of instructional technology: Training writers of instructional packages. *Journal of Applied Behavior Analysis, 10*, 739–746.

Ferster, C. B. (1961). Positive reinforcement and behavioral deficits in autistic children. *Child Development, 32*, 347–356.

Ferster, C. B., & DeMeyer, M. K. (1962). A method for the experimental analysis of the behavior of autistic children. *American Journal of Orthopsychiatry, 32*, 89–98.

Ferster, C. B., & Skinner, B. F. (1957). *Schedules of reinforcement*. Upper Saddle River, NJ: Prentice Hall.

Finney, J. W., Rapoff, M. A., Hall, C. L., & Christopherson, E. R. (1983). Replication and social validation of habit reversal treatment for tics. *Behavior Therapy, 14*, 116–126.

Fisher, J., & Neys, R. (1978). Use of a commonly available chore to reduce a boy's rate of swearing. *Journal of Behavior Therapy and Experimental Psychiatry, 9*, 81–83.

Fisher, W., Iwata, B., & Mazaleski, J. (1997). Noncontingent delivery of arbitrary reinforcers as treatment for self-injurious behavior. *Journal of Applied Behavior Analysis, 30*, 239–249.

Fisher, W., Piazza, C. C., Bowman, L. G., Hagopian, L. P., Owens, J. C., & Slevin, I. (1992). A comparison of two approaches for identifying reinforcers for persons with severe and profound disabilities. *Journal of Applied Behavior Analysis, 25*, 491–498.

Fisher, W., Piazza, C., Bowman, L., Kurtz, P., Sherer, M., & Lachman, S. (1994). A preliminary evaluation of empirically derived consequences for the treatment of pica. *Journal of Applied Behavior Analysis, 27*, 447–457.

Fleece, L., Gross, A., O'Brien, T., Kistner, J., Rothblum, E., & Drabman, R. (1981). Elevation of voice volume in young developmentally delayed children via an operant shaping procedure. *Journal of Applied Behavior Analysis, 14*, 351–355.

Forehand, R., Sturgis, E. T., McMahon, R. J., Aguar, D., Green, K., Wells, K. C., & Breiner, J. (1979). Parent behavioral training to modify child noncompliance: Treatment generalization across time and from home to school. *Behavior Modification, 3*, 3–25.

Foster, S. L., Bell-Dolan, D. J., & Burge, D. A. (1988). Behavioral observation. In A. S. Bellack & M. Hersen (Eds.), *Behavioral assessment: A practical handbook* (3rd ed., pp. 119–160). New York: Pergamon.

Fox, D. K., Hopkins, B. L., & Anger, W. K. (1987). The long-term effects of a token economy on safety performance in open pit mining. *Journal of Applied Behavior Analysis, 20,* 215–224.

Foxx, R. M. (1998). A comprehensive treatment program for inpatient adolescents. *Behavioral Interventions, 13,* 67–77.

Foxx, R. M., & Azrin, N. H. (1972). Restitution: A method of eliminating aggressive–disruptive behavior of retarded and brain damaged patients. *Behaviour Research and Therapy, 10,* 15–27.

Foxx, R. M., & Azrin, N. H. (1973). The elimination of autistic self-stimulatory behavior by overcorrection. *Journal of Applied Behavior Analysis, 6,* 1–14.

Foxx, R. M., & Bechtel, D. R. (1983). Overcorrection: A review and analysis. In S. Axelrod & J. Apsche (Eds.), *The effects of punishment on human behavior* (pp. 133–220). New York: Academic Press.

Foxx, R. M., McMorrow, M. J., Bittle, R. G., & Bechtel, D. R. (1986). The successful treatment of a dually diagnosed deaf man's aggression with a program that included contingent electric shock. *Behavior Therapy, 17,* 170–186.

Foxx, R. M., & Rubinoff, A. (1979). Behavioral treatment of caffeinism: Reducing excessive coffee drinking. *Journal of Applied Behavior Analysis, 12,* 335–344.

Foxx, R. M., & Shapiro, S. T. (1978). The timeout ribbon: A nonexclusionary timeout procedure. *Journal of Applied Behavior Analysis, 11,* 125–136.

France, K. G., & Hudson, S. M. (1990). Behavior management of infant sleep disturbance. *Journal of Applied Behavior Analysis, 23,* 91–98.

Franco, D. P., Christoff, K. A., Crimmins, D. B., & Kelly, J. A. (1983). Social skills training for an extremely shy young adolescent: An empirical case study. *Behavior Therapy, 14,* 568–575.

Frederickson, L. W. (Ed.). (1982). *Handbook of organizational behavior management.* New York: Wiley.

Freeman, A., Simon, K. M., Beutler, L. E., & Arkowitz, H. (Eds.). (1989). *Comprehensive handbook of cognitive therapy.* New York: Plenum.

Friedrich, W., Morgan, S. B., & Devine, C. (1996). Children's attitudes and behavioral intentions toward a peer with Tourette's syndrome. *Journal of Pediatric Psychology, 21,* 307–319.

Friman, P. C., Finney, J. W., & Christopherson, E. R. (1984). Behavioral treatment of trichotillomania: An evaluative review. *Behavior Therapy, 15,* 249–265.

Friman, P. C., & Hove, G. (1987). Apparent covariation between child habit disorders: Effects of successful treatment for thumbsucking on untargeted chronic hairpulling. *Journal of Applied Behavior Analysis, 20,* 421–425.

Friman, P. C., McPherson, K. M., Warzak, W. J., & Evans, J. (1993). Influence of thumb sucking on peer social acceptance in first grade children. *Pediatrics, 91,* 784–786.

Friman, P. C., & Poling, A. (1995). Making life easier with effort: Basic findings and applied research on response effort. *Journal of Applied Behavior Analysis, 28,* 583–590.

Fuller, P. R. (1949). Operant conditioning of a vegetative organism. *American Journal of Psychology, 62,* 587–590.

Galensky, T. L., Miltenberger, R. C., Stricker, J. M., & Garlinghouse, M. A. (2001). Functional assessment and treatment of mealtime problem behaviors. *Journal of Positive Behavioral Interventions, 3,* 211–224.

Gambrill, E. D. (1977). *Behavior modification: Handbook of assessment, intervention, and evaluation.* San Francisco: Jossey-Bass.

Garcia, J., Kimeldorf, D. J., & Koelling, R. A. (1955). A conditioned aversion toward saccharin resulting from exposure to gamma radiation. *Science, 122,* 157–158.

Geller, E. S., & Hahn, H. A. (1984). Promoting safety belt use at industrial sites: An effective program for blue collar employees. *Professional Psychology: Research and Practice, 15,* 553–564.

Gentry, W. D. (Ed.). (1984). *Handbook of behavioral medicine.* New York: Guilford.

Gershoff, E. T. (2002). Corporal punishment by parents and associated child behaviors and experiences: A metaanalytic and theoretical review. *Psychological Bulletin, 128,* 539–579.

Glynn, S. M. (1990). Token economy approaches for psychiatric patients: Progress and pitfalls over 25 years. *Behavior Modification, 14,* 383–407.

Goetz, E., & Baer, D. (1973). Social control of form diversity and the emergence of new forms in children's blockbuilding. *Journal of Applied Behavior Analysis, 6,* 209–217.

Goh, H., & Iwata, B. A. (1994). Behavioral persistence and variability during extinction of self injury maintained by escape. *Journal of Applied Behavior Analysis, 27,* 173–174.

Goldfried, M. R. (1988). Application of rational restructuring to anxiety disorders. *The Counseling Psychologist, 16,* 50–68.

Goldfried, M. R., Decenteceo, E. T., & Weinberg, L. (1974). Systematic rational restructuring as a self-control technique. *Behavior Therapy, 5,* 247–254.

Goldiamond, I. (1965). Self-control procedures in personal behavior problems. *Psychological Reports, 17,* 851–868.

Goldiamond, I. (1974). Toward a constructional approach to social problems: Ethical and constitutional issues raised by applied behavior analysis. *Behaviorism, 2,* 1–85.

Gray, J. J. (1979). Positive reinforcement and punishment in the treatment of childhood trichotillomania. *Journal of Behavior Therapy and Experimental Psychiatry, 10,* 125–129.

Green, C. W., Reid, D. H., Canipe, V. S., & Gardner, S. M. (1991). A comprehensive evaluation of reinforcer identification processes for persons with profound multiple handicaps. *Journal of Applied Behavior Analysis, 24,* 537, 552.

Green, C. W., Reid, D. H., White, L. K., Halford, R. C., Brittain, D. P., & Gardner, S. M. (1988). Identifying reinforcers for persons with profound handicaps: Staff opinion versus systematic assessment of preferences. *Journal of Applied Behavior Analysis, 21,* 31–43.

Green, R. B., Hardison, W. L., & Greene, B. F. (1984). Turning the table on advice programs for parents: Using placemats to enhance family interactions at restaurants. *Journal of Applied Behavior Analysis, 17,* 497–508.

Greenwood, C. R., Delquadri, J., & Carta, J. J. (1988). *Classwide peer tutoring (CWPT).* Delray Beach, FL: Education Achievement Systems.

Guevremont, D. C., Osnes, P. G., & Stokes, T. F. (1988). The functional role of verbalizations in the generalization of self-instructional training with children. *Journal of Applied Behavior Analysis, 21,* 45–55.

Guttman, N., & Kalish, H. I. (1956). Discriminability and stimulus generalization. *Journal of Experimental Psychology, 51,* 79–88.

Hagopian, L. P., Fisher, W. W., & Legacy, S. M. (1994). Schedule effects of noncontingent reinforcement on attention-maintained destructive behavior in identical quadruplets. *Journal of Applied Behavior Analysis, 27,* 317–325.

Hall, C., Sheldon-Wildgen, J., & Sherman, J. A. (1980). Teaching job interview skills to retarded clients. *Journal of Applied Behavior Analysis, 13,* 433–442.

Hall, R. V., Lund, D., & Jackson, D. (1968). Effects of teacher attention on study behavior. *Journal of Applied Behavior Analysis, 1,* 1–12.

Halle, J. W. (1989). Identifying stimuli in the natural environment that control verbal responses. *Journal of Speech and Hearing Disorders, 54,* 500–504.

Halle, J. W., & Holt, B. (1991). Assessing stimulus control in natural settings: An analysis of stimuli that acquire control during training. *Journal of Applied Behavior Analysis, 24,* 579–589.

Halvorson, J. A. (1971). The effects on stuttering frequency of pairing punishment (response cost) with reinforcement. *Journal of Speech and Hearing Research, 14,* 356–364.

Handen, B. L., Parrish, J. M., McClung, T. J., Kerwin, M. E., & Evans, L. D. (1992). Using guided compliance versus time-out to promote child compliance: A preliminary comparative analysis in an analogue context. *Research in Developmental Disabilities, 13,* 157–170.

Handen, B. L., & Zane, T. (1987). Delayed prompting: A review of procedural variations and results. *Research in Developmental Disabilities, 8,* 307–330.

Hanley, G. P., Piazza, C. C., & Fisher, W. W. (1997). Noncontingent presentation of attention and alternative stimuli in the treatment of attention-maintained destructive behavior. *Journal of Applied Behavior Analysis, 30,* 229–237.

Hansen, D. J., Tishelman, A. C., Hawkins, R. P., & Doepke, K. (1990). Habits with potential as disorders: Prevalence, severity, and other characteristics among college students. *Behavior Modification, 14,* 66–88.

Haring, T. G., & Kennedy, C. H. (1990). Contextual control of problem behaviors in students with severe disabilities. *Journal of Applied Behavior Analysis, 23,* 235–243.

Hartmann, D. P., & Wood, D. D. (1990). Observational methods. In A. S. Bellack, M. Herson, & A. E. Kazdin (Eds.), *International handbook of behavior modification and therapy* (2nd ed., pp. 107–138). New York: Plenum.

Hasazi, J. E., & Hasazi, S. E. (1972). Effects of teacher attention on digit reversal behavior in an elementary school child. *Journal of Applied Behavior Analysis, 5,* 157–162.

Haseltine, B., & Miltenberger, R. (1990). Teaching self-protection skills to persons with mental retardation. *American Journal on Mental Retardation, 95,* 188–197.

Hayes, S. C. (1994). Content, context, and types of psychological acceptance. In S. C. Hayes, N. S. Jacobsen, V. M. Follette, & M. J. Dougher (Eds.), *Acceptance and change: Content and context in psychotherapy* (pp. 13–32). Reno, NV: Context Press.

Hayes, S. C. (1995). *Acceptance and commitment therapy: A working manual for the treatment of emotional avoidance disorders.* Reno, NV: Context Press.

Hayes, S. C., Barlow, D. H., & Nelson-Gray, R. O. (Eds.). (1999). *The scientist practitioner: Research and accountability in the age of managed care* (2nd ed.). Boston: Allyn & Bacon.

Hayes, S. C., Strosahl, K. D., & Wilson, K. G. (1999). *Acceptance and commitment therapy: An experiential approach to behavior change.* New York: Guilford.

Hayes, S. C., & Wilson, K. (1994). Acceptance and commitment therapy: Altering the verbal support for experiential avoidance. *Behavior Analyst, 17,* 289–304.

Hermann, J. A., Montes, A. I., Dominguez, B., Montes, F., & Hopkins, B. L. (1973). Effects of bonuses for punctuality on the tardiness of industrial workers. *Journal of Applied Behavior Analysis, 6,* 563–570.

Hersen, M., & Bellack, A. S. (Eds.). (1985). *Handbook of clinical behavior therapy with adults.* New York: Plenum.

Hersen, M., & Van Hasselt, V. B. (Eds.). (1987). *Behavior therapy with children and adolescents: A clinical approach.* New York: Wiley.

Higbee, T. S., Carr, J. E., & Patel, M. R. (2002). The effects of interpolated reinforcement on resistance to extinction in children diagnosed with autism: A preliminary investigation. *Research in Developmental Disabilities, 23,* 61–78.

Himle, M. B., & Miltenberger, R. G. (in press). Preventing unintentional firearm injury in children: The need for behavioral skills training. *Education & Treatment of Children.*

Hobbs, S. A., Forehand, R., & Murray, R. G. (1978). Effects of various durations of time-out on noncompliant behavior of children. *Behavior Therapy, 9,* 652–656.

Hobbs, T. R., & Holt, M. M. (1976). The effects of token reinforcement on the behavior of delinquents in cottage settings. *Journal of Applied Behavior Analysis, 9,* 189–198.

Holland, J. G., & Skinner, B. F. (1961). *The analysis of behavior: A program for self-instruction*. New York: McGraw-Hill.

Hollon, S. D., & Jacobson, V. (1985). Cognitive approaches. In M. Hersen & A. S. Bellack (Eds.), *Handbook of clinical behavior therapy with adults* (pp. 169–197). New York: Plenum.

Holz, W. C., Azrin, N. H., & Ayllon, T. (1963). Elimination of the behavior of mental patients with response-produced extinction. *Journal of the Experimental Analysis of Behavior, 6*, 407–412.

Homme, L., Csany, A. P., Gonzales, M. A., & Rechs, J. R. (1970). *How to use contingency contracting in the classroom*. Champaign, IL: Research Press.

Honig, W. K. (Ed.). (1966). *Operant behavior: Areas of research and application*. New York: Appleton-Century-Crofts.

Horner, R. D. (1971). Establishing use of crutches by a mentally retarded spina bifida child. *Journal of Applied Behavior Analysis, 4*, 183–189.

Horner, R. H., & Carr, E. G. (1997). Behavioral support for students with severe disabilities: Functional assessment and comprehensive intervention. *Journal of Special Education, 31*, 84–104.

Horner, R. H., & Day, H. M. (1991). The effects of response efficiency on functionally equivalent competing behaviors. *Journal of Applied Behavior Analysis, 24*, 719–732.

Horner, R. H., Day, H. M., Sprague, J. R., O'Brien, M., & Heathfield, L. T. (1991). Interspersed requests: A nonaversive procedure for reducing aggression and self-injury during instruction. *Journal of Applied Behavior Analysis, 24*, 265–278.

Horner, R. H., Dunlap, G., & Koegel, R. L. (Eds.). (1988). *Generalization and maintenance: Lifestyle changes in applied settings*. Baltimore: Paul Brookes.

Horner, R. H., & Keilitz, I. (1978). Training mentally retarded adolescents to brush their teeth. *Journal of Applied Behavior Analysis, 8*, 301–309.

Horner, R. H., Sprague, J. R., O'Brien, M., & Heathfield, L. T. (1990). The role of response efficiency in the reduction of problem behaviors through functional equivalence training: A case study. *Journal of the Association for Persons with Severe Handicaps, 15*, 91–97.

Horner, R. H., Sprague, T., & Wilcox, B. (1982). General case programming for community activities. In B. Wilcox & G. T. Bellamy (Eds.), *Design of high school programs for severely handicapped students* (pp. 61–98). Baltimore: Paul Brookes.

Houlihan, D., Schwartz, C., Miltenberger, R., & Heuton, D. (1994). Rapid treatment of a young man's balloon (noise) phobia using in vivo flooding. *Journal of Behavior Therapy and Experimental Psychiatry, 24*, 233–240.

Howie, P. M., & Woods, C. L. (1982). Token reinforcement during the instatement and shaping of fluency in the treatment of stuttering. *Journal of Applied Behavior Analysis, 15*, 55–64.

Hughes, H., Hughes, A., & Dial, H. (1979). Home-based treatment of thumbsucking: Omission training with edible reinforcers and a behavioral seal. *Behavior Modification, 3*, 179–186.

Hume, K. M., & Crossman, J. (1992). Musical reinforcement of practice behaviors among competitive swimmers. *Journal of Applied Behavior Analysis, 25*, 665–670.

Hupp, S. D., & Reitman, D. (1999). Improving sports skills and sportsmanship in children diagnosed with attention deficit/hyperactivity disorder. *Child and Family Behavior Therapy, 21*(3), 35–51.

Hussian, R. A. (1981). *Geriatric psychology: A behavioral perspective*. New York: Van Nostrand Reinhold.

Hussian, R. A., & Davis, R. L. (1985). *Responsive care: Behavioral interventions with elderly persons*. Champaign, IL: Research Press.

Ingham, R. J., & Andrews, G. (1973). An analysis of a token economy in stuttering therapy. *Journal of Applied Behavior Analysis, 6*, 219–229.

Isaacs, W., Thomas, J., & Goldiamond, I. (1960). Application of operant conditioning to reinstate verbal behavior in psychotics. *Journal of Speech and Hearing Disorders, 25*, 8–12.

Iwata, B. A., Bailey, J. S., Neef, N. A., Wacker, D. P., Repp, A. C., & Shook, C. L. (Eds.). (1997). *Behavior analysis in developmental disabilities 1968–1995: Reprint series* (Vol. 3). Lawrence, KS: Society for the Experimental Analysis of Behavior.

Iwata, B. A., Dorsey, M. F., Slifer, K. J., Bauman, K. E., & Richman, G. S. (1982). Toward a functional analysis of self-injury. *Analysis and Intervention in Developmental Disabilities, 2*, 3–20.

Iwata, B. A., Pace, G. M., Cowdery, G. E., & Miltenberger, R. G. (1994). What makes extinction work: Analysis of procedural form and function. *Journal of Applied Behavior Analysis, 27*, 131–144.

Iwata, B. A., Pace, G. M., Kalsher, M. J., Cowdery, G. E., & Cataldo, M. F. (1990). Experimental analysis and extinction of self-injurious escape behavior. *Journal of Applied Behavior Analysis, 23*, 11–127.

Iwata, B. A., Vollmer, T. R., & Zarcone, J. R. (1990). The experimental (functional) analysis of behavior disorders: Methodology, applications, and limitations. In A. C. Repp & N. N. Singh (Eds.), *Perspectives on the use of nonaversive and aversive interventions for persons with developmental disabilities* (pp. 301–330). Sycamore, IL: Sycamore.

Iwata, B. A., Vollmer, T. R., Zarcone, J. R., & Rodgers, T. A. (1993). Treatment classification and selection based on behavioral function. In R. Van Houten & S. Axelrod (Eds.), *Behavior analysis and treatment* (pp. 101–125). New York: Plenum.

Iwata, B. A., Wong, S. E., Riordan, M. M., Dorsey, M. F., & Lau, M. M. (1982). Assessment and training of clinical interviewing skills: Analogue analysis and field replication. *Journal of Applied Behavior Analysis, 15*, 191–204.

Jackson, D. A., & Wallace, R. F. (1974). The modification and generalization of voice loudness in a fifteen year old retarded girl. *Journal of Applied Behavior Analysis, 7*, 461–471.

Jacobson, E. (1938). *Progressive relaxation*. Chicago: University of Chicago Press.

Jacobson, N. S., & Margolin, G. (1979). *Marital therapy: Strategies based on social learning and behavior exchange principles*. New York: Brunner Mazel.

James, J. E. (1981). Behavioral self-control of stuttering using time-out from speaking. *Journal of Applied Behavior Analysis, 14*, 25–37.

Jeffery, R. W., Bjornson-Benson, W. M., Rosenthal, B. S., Kurth, C. L., & Dunn, M. M. (1984). Effectiveness of monetary contracts with two repayment schedules on weight reduction in men and women from self-referred and population samples. *Behavior Therapy, 15*, 273–279.

Johnston, J. M., & Pennypacker, H. S. (1981). *Strategies and tactics of human behavioral research*. Mahwah, NJ: Erlbaum.

Johnston, J. M., & Shook, J. (1987). Developing behavior analysis at the state level. *The Behavior Analyst, 10*, 199–233.

Jones, F. H., & Miller, W. H. (1974). The effective use of negative attention for reducing group disruption in special elementary school classrooms. *Psychological Record, 24*, 435–448.

Jones, R. T., & Kazdin, A. E. (1980). Teaching children how and when to make emergency telephone calls. *Behavior Therapy, 11*, 509–521.

Jones, R. T., Kazdin, A. E., & Haney, J. L. (1981). Social validation and training of emergency fire safety skills for potential injury prevention and life saving. *Journal of Applied Behavior Analysis, 14*, 249–260.

Kahng, S., & Iwata, B. A. (1998). Computerized systems for collecting real-time observational data. *Journal of Applied Behavior Analysis, 31*, 253–261.

Kahng, S., Iwata, B. A., Fischer, S. M., Page, T. J., Treadwell, K. R. H., Williams, D. E., & Smith, R. G. (1998). Temporal distributions of problem behavior based on scatter plot analysis. *Journal of Applied Behavior Analysis, 31*, 593–604.

Kale, R. J., Kaye, J. H., Whelan, P. A., & Hopkins, B. L. (1968). The effects of reinforcement on the modification, maintenance, and generalization of social responses of mental patients. *Journal of Applied Behavior Analysis, 1*, 307–314.

Kamps, D. M., Barbetta, P. M., Leonard, B. R., & Delquadri, J. (1994). Classwide peer tutoring: An integration strategy to improve reading skills and promote peer interactions among students with autism and general education peers. *Journal of Applied Behavior Analysis, 27*, 49–61.

Kanfer, F., & Gaelick-Buys, L. (1991). Self-management methods. In F. H. Kanfer & A. P. Goldstein (Eds.), *Helping people change: A textbook of methods* (4th ed., pp. 161–201). New York: Pergamon.

Karoly, P., & Kanfer, F. (1982). *Self-management and behavior change: From theory to practice*. New York: Pergamon.

Kazdin, A. E. (1977). *The token economy: A review and evaluation*. New York: Plenum.

Kazdin, A. E. (1980). Acceptability of alternative treatments for deviant child behavior. *Journal of Applied Behavior Analysis, 13*, 259–273.

Kazdin, A. E. (1982). The token economy: A decade later. *Journal of Applied Behavior Analysis, 15*, 431–445.

Kazdin, A. E. (1994). *Behavior modification in applied settings* (4th ed.). Pacific Grove, CA: Brooks/Cole.

Kazdin, A. E., & Bootzin, R. R. (1972). The token economy: An evaluative review. *Journal of Applied Behavior Analysis, 5*, 343–372.

Kazdin, A. E., & Klock, J. (1973). The effect of nonverbal approval on student attentive behavior. *Journal of Applied Behavior Analysis, 6*, 643–654.

Kazdin, A. E., & Polster, R. (1973). Intermittent token reinforcement and response maintenance in extinction. *Behavior Therapy, 4*, 386–391.

Kearney, C., & Silverman, W. (1990). A preliminary analysis of a functional model of assessment and treatment for school refusal behavior. *Behavior Modification, 14*, 340–366.

Keller, F. S., & Schoenfeld, W. N. (1950). *Principles of psychology: A systematic text in the science of behavior*. New York: Appleton-Century-Crofts.

Kelley, M. L., & Stokes, T. F. (1982). Contingency contracting with disadvantaged youths: Improving classroom performance. *Journal of Applied Behavior Analysis, 15*, 447–454.

Kelley, M. L., & Stokes, T. F. (1984). Student–teacher contracting with goal setting for maintenance. *Behavior Modification, 8*, 223–244.

Kemp, D. C., & Carr, E. G. (1995). Reduction of severe problem behavior in community employment using an hypothesis-driven multicomponent intervention approach. *Journal of the Association for Persons with Severe Handicaps, 20*, 229–247.

Kendall, G., Hrycaiko, D., Martin, G. L., & Kendall, T. (1990). The effects of an imagery rehearsal, relaxation, and self-talk package on basketball game performance. *Journal of Sport and Exercise Psychology, 12*, 157–166.

Kendall, P. C. (1989). The generalization and maintenance of behavior change: Comments, considerations, and the "no-cure" criticism. *Behavior Therapy, 20*, 357–364.

Kendall, P. C., & Braswell, L. (1985). *Cognitive behavioral therapy for impulsive children*. New York: Guilford.

Kennedy, C. H. (1994). Manipulating antecedent conditions to alter the stimulus control of problem behavior. *Journal of Applied Behavior Analysis, 27*, 161–170.

Kern, L., Childs, K., Dunlap, G., Clarke, S., & Falk, G. (1994). Using assessment-based curricular interventions to improve the classroom behavior of a student with behavioral challenges. *Journal of Applied Behavior Analysis, 27*, 7–19.

Kirschenbaum, D. S., & Flanery, R. C. (1983). *Behavioral contracting: Outcomes and elements*. In M. Hersen, R. M. Eisler, & P. M. Miller (Eds.), Progress in behavior modification (pp. 217–275). New York: Academic Press.

Kirschenbaum, D. S., & Flanery, R. C. (1984). Toward a psychology of behavioral contracting. *Clinical Psychology Review, 4,* 597–618.

Klesges, R. C., Malott, J. M., & Ugland, M. (1984). The effects of graded exposure and parental modeling on the dental phobias of a four-year-old girl and her mother. *Journal of Behavior Therapy and Experimental Psychiatry, 15,* 161–164.

Knight, M. F., & McKenzie, H. S. (1974). Elimination of bedtime thumbsucking in home settings through contingent reading. *Journal of Applied Behavior Analysis, 7,* 33–38.

Kohlenberg, R. J., & Tsai, M. (1991). *Functional analytic psychotherapy: Creating intense and curative therapeutic relationships.* New York: Plenum.

Kramer, F. M., Jeffery, R. W., Snell, M. K., & Forster, J. L. (1986). Maintenance of successful weight loss over 1 year: Effects of financial contracts for weight maintenance or participation in skills training. *Behavior Therapy, 17,* 295–301.

Ladoucher, R. (1979). Habit reversal treatment: Learning an incompatible response or increasing the subject's awareness? *Behaviour Research and Therapy, 17,* 313–316.

Ladoucher, R., & Martineau, G. (1982). Evaluation of regulated breathing method with and without parental assistance in the treatment of child stutterers. *Journal of Behavior Therapy and Experimental Psychiatry, 13,* 301–306.

Lahey, B. B., McNees, M. P., & McNees, M. C. (1973). Control of an obscene "verbal tic" through timeout in an elementary school classroom. *Journal of Applied Behavior Analysis, 6,* 101–104.

Lalli, J. S., Browder, D. M., Mace, F. C., & Brown, D. K. (1993). Teacher use of descriptive analysis data to implement interventions to decrease students' problem behaviors. *Journal of Applied Behavior Analysis, 26,* 227–238.

Lalli, J. S., Casey, S. D., & Cates, K. (1997). Noncontingent reinforcement as treatment for severe problem behavior: Some procedural variations. *Journal of Applied Behavior Analysis, 30,* 127–137.

Lalli, J. S., Zanolli, K., & Wohn, T. (1994). Using extinction to promote response variability in toy play. *Journal of Applied Behavior Analysis, 27,* 735–736.

Lane, K. L., Umbreit, J., & Beebe-Frankenberger, M. E. (1999).Functional assessment research on students with or at risk for EBD: 1990–present. *Journal of Positive Behavioral Interventions, 1,* 101–111.

Larson, P. J., & Maag, J. W. (1999). Applying functional assessment in general education classrooms: Issues and recommendations. *Remedial and Special Education, 19,* 338–349.

LaVigna, G. W., & Donnellan, A. M. (1986). *Alternatives to punishment: Solving behavior problems with nonaversive strategies.* New York: Irvington.

Latner, J. D., & Wilson, G. T. (2002). Self monitoring and the assessment of binge eating. *Behavior Therapy, 33,* 465–477.

Leal, J., & Galanter, M. (1995). The use of contingency contracting to improve outcome in methadone maintenance. *Substance Abuse, 16*(3), 155–167.

Leckman, J., & Cohen, D. (1999). Evolving models of pathogenesis. In J. Leckman & D. Cohen (Eds.). *Tourette's Syndrome: Ticks, Obsessions, and Compulsions* (pp. 155–176). New York: Wiley.

Lee, M., & Miltenberger, R. (1996). School refusal behavior: Classification, assessment, and treatment issues. *Education and Treatment of Children, 19,* 474–486.

Leitenberg, H., Burchard, J. D., Burchard, S. N., Fuller, E. J., & Lysaght, T. V. (1977). Using positive reinforcement to suppress behavior: Some experimental comparisons with sibling conflict. *Behavior Therapy, 8,* 168–182.

Lennox, D. B., & Miltenberger, R. G. (1989). Conducting a functional assessment of problem behavior in applied settings. *Journal of the Association for Persons with Severe Handicaps, 14,* 304–311.

Lennox, D. B., Miltenberger, R. G., & Donnelly, D. (1987). Response interruption and DRL for the reduction of rapid eating. *Journal of Applied Behavior Analysis, 20,* 279–284.

Lerman, D. C., & Iwata, B. A. (1993). Descriptive and experimental analyses of variables maintaining self-injurious behavior. *Journal of Applied Behavior Analysis, 26,* 293–319.

Lerman, D. C., & Iwata, B. A. (1995). Prevalence of the extinction burst and its attenuation during treatment. *Journal of Applied Behavior Analysis, 28,* 93–94.

Lerman, D. C. & Iwata, B. A. (1996a). A methodology distinguishing between extinction and punishment effects associated with response blocking. *Journal of Applied Behavior Analysis, 29,* 231–233.

Lerman, D. C., & Iwata, B. A. (1996b). Developing a technology for the use of operant extinction in clinical settings: An examination of basic and applied research. *Journal of Applied Behavior Analysis, 29,* 345–382.

Lerman, D. C., Iwata, B. A., Shore, B. A., & Kahng, S. (1996). Responding maintained by intermittent reinforcement: Implications for the use of extinction with problem behavior in clinical settings. *Journal of Applied Behavior Analysis, 29,* 153–171.

Lerman, D. C., Iwata, B. A., & Wallace, M. D. (1999). Side effects of extinction: Prevalence of bursting and aggression during the treatment of self-injurious behavior. *Journal of Applied Behavior Analysis, 32,* 1–8.

Lerman, D. C., Iwata, B. A., Zarcone, J. R., & Ringdahl, J. (1994). Assessment of stereotypic and self-injurious behavior as adjunctive responses. *Journal of Applied Behavior Analysis, 27,* 715–728.

Levy, R. L. (1987). Compliance and clinical practice. In J. A. Blumenthal & D. C. McKee (Eds.), *Applications in behavioral medicine and health psychology: A clinician's source book* (pp. 567–587). Sarasota, FL: Professional Resource Exchange.

Lewis, T. J., Scott, T. M., & Siugai, G. M. (1994). The problem behavior questionnaire: A teacher-based instrument to develop functional hypotheses of problem behavior in general education classrooms. *Diagnostique, 19,* 103–115.

Liberman, R. P., Teigen, J., Patterson, R., & Baker, V. (1973). Reducing delusional speech in chronic paranoid schizophrenics. *Journal of Applied Behavior Analysis, 6,* 57–64.

Lindsley, O. R. (1968). A reliable wrist counter for recording behavior rates. *Journal of Applied Behavior Analysis, 1,* 77–78.

Linscheid, T., Iwata, B. A., Ricketts, R., Williams, D., & Griffin, J. (1990). Clinical evaluation of the self-injurious behavior inhibiting system (SIBIS). *Journal of Applied Behavior Analysis, 23,* 53–78.

Little, L. M., & Kelley, M. L. (1989). The efficacy of response cost procedures for reducing children's noncompliance to parental instructions. *Behavior Therapy, 20,* 525–534.

Long, E., Miltenberger, R., Ellingson, S., & Ott, S. (1999). Augmenting simplified habit reversal in the treatment of oral–digital habits exhibited by individuals with mental retardation. *Journal of Applied Behavior Analysis, 32,* 353–365.

Long, E., Miltenberger, R., & Rapp, J. (1999). Simplified habit reversal plus adjunct contingencies in the treatment of thumb sucking and hair pulling in a young girl. *Child and Family Behavior Therapy, 21*(4), 45–58.

Long, E., Woods, D., Miltenberger, R., Fuqua, R. W., & Boudjouk, P. (1999). Examining the social effects of habit behaviors exhibited by individuals with mental retardation. *Journal of Developmental and Physical Disabilities, 11,* 295–312.

Lovaas, O. I., Berberich, J. P., Perdoff, B. F., & Schaeffer, B. (1966). Acquisition of imitative speech by schizophrenic children. *Science, 151,* 705–706.

Lovaas, O. I., Newsom, C., & Hickman, C. (1987). Self-stimulatory behavior and perceptual reinforcement. *Journal of Applied Behavior Analysis, 20,* 45–68.

Lovaas, O. I., & Simmons, J. Q. (1969). Manipulation of self-destruction in three retarded children. *Journal of Applied Behavior Analysis, 2,* 143–157.

Luce, S., Delquadri, J., & Hall, R. V. (1980). Contingent exercise: A mild but powerful procedure for suppressing inappropriate verbal and aggressive behavior. *Journal of Applied Behavior Analysis, 13,* 583–594.

Luce, S. C., & Hall, R. V. (1981). Contingent exercise: A procedure used with differential reinforcement to reduce bizarre verbal behavior. *Education & Treatment of Children, 4,* 109–327.

Ludwig, T. D., & Geller, E. S. (1991). Improving the driving practices of pizza deliverers: Response generalization and modeling effects of driving history. *Journal of Applied Behavior Analysis, 24,* 31–44.

Lumley, V., Miltenberger, R., Long, E., Rapp, J., & Roberts, J. (1998). Evaluation of a sexual abuse prevention program for adults with mental retardation. *Journal of Applied Behavior Analysis, 31,* 91–101.

Luthans, F., & Kreitner, R. (1985). *Organizational behavior modification and beyond: An operant and social learning approach.* Glenview, IL: Scott Foresman.

Lutzker, J., & Martin, J. (1981). *Behavior change.* Pacific Grove, CA: Brooks/Cole.

Maag, J. W. (1999). *Behavior management: From theoretical implications to practical applications.* San Diego: Singular Publishing Group.

Mace, F. C., Hock, M. L., Lalli, J. S., West, B. J., Belfiore, P., Pinter, E., & Brown, D. F. (1988). Behavioral momentum in the treatment of noncompliance. *Journal of Applied Behavior Analysis, 21,* 123–141.

Mace, F. C., & Lalli, J. S. (1991). Linking descriptive and experimental analyses in the treatment of bizarre speech. *Journal of Applied Behavior Analysis, 24,* 553–562.

Mace, F. C., Lalli, J. S., Lalli, E. P., & Shea, M. C. (1993). Functional analysis and treatment of aberrant behavior. In R. Van Houten & S. Axelrod (Eds.), *Behavior analysis and treatment* (pp. 75–99). New York: Plenum.

Mace, F. C., Page, T. J., Ivancic, M. T., & O'Brien, S. (1986). Effectiveness of brief time-out with and without contingent delay: A comparative analysis. *Journal of Applied Behavior Analysis, 19,* 79–86.

Mace, F. C., & Roberts, M. L. (1993). Factors affecting selection of behavioral interventions. In J. Reichle & D. P. Wacker (Eds.), *Communicative alternatives to challenging behavior: Integrating functional assessment and intervention strategies* (pp. 113–133). Baltimore: Paul Brookes.

Madsen, C. H., Becker, W. C., & Thomas, D. R. (1968). Rules, praise, and ignoring: Elements of elementary classroom control. *Journal of Applied Behavior Analysis, 1,* 139–150.

Magrab, P. R., & Papadopoulou, Z. L. (1977). The effect of a token economy on dietary compliance for children on hemodialysis. *Journal of Applied Behavior Analysis, 10,* 573–578.

Malott, R. W. (1986). Self management, rule-governed behavior, and everyday life. In H. W. Reese & L. J. Parrott (Eds.), *Behavioral science: Philosophical, methodological, and empirical advances* (pp. 207–228). Mahwah, NJ: Erlbaum.

Malott, R. W. (1989). The achievement of evasive goals: Control by rules describing contingencies that are not direct acting. In S. C. Hayes (Ed.), *Rule-governed behavior: Cognition, contingencies, and instructional control* (pp. 269–322). New York: Pergamon.

Malott, R. W., Malott, M. E., & Trojan, E. A. (2000). *Elementary principles of behavior* (4th ed.). Upper Saddle River, NJ: Prentice Hall.

Malott, R. W., Whaley, D. L., & Malott, M. E. (1993). *Elementary principles of behavior* (2nd ed.). Upper Saddle River, NJ: Prentice Hall.

Mann, R. A. (1972). The behavior-therapeutic use of contingency contracting to control an adult behavior problem: Weight control. *Journal of Applied Behavior Analysis, 5,* 99–109.

Marcus, B. A., & Vollmer, T. R. (1995). Effects of differential negative reinforcement on disruption and compliance. *Journal of Applied Behavior Analysis, 28,* 229–230.

Marholin, D., & Gray, D. (1976). Effects of group response cost procedures on cash shortages in a small business. *Journal of Applied Behavior Analysis, 9*, 25–30.

Marholin, D., & Steinman, W. (1977). Stimulus control in the classroom as a function of the behavior reinforced. *Journal of Applied Behavior Analysis, 10*, 465–478.

Martin, G., & Pear, J. (1992). *Behavior modification: What it is and how to do it* (4th ed.). Upper Saddle River, NJ: Prentice Hall.

Martin, G., & Pear, J. (1999). *Behavior modification: What it is and how to do it* (6th ed.). Upper Saddle River, NJ: Prentice Hall.

Martin, G. L., & Hrycaiko, D. (1983). *Behavior modification and coaching: Principles, procedures, and research.* Springfield, IL: Charles C. Thomas.

Mason, S. A., McGee, G. G., Farmer-Dougan, V., & Risley, T. R. (1989). A practical strategy for ongoing reinforcer assessment. *Journal of Applied Behavior Analysis, 22*, 171–179.

Mastellone, M. (1974). Aversion therapy: A new use for the old rubber band. *Journal of Behavior Therapy and Experimental Psychiatry, 5*, 311–312.

Masters, J., Burish, T., Hollon, S., & Rimm, D. (Eds.). (1987). *Behavior therapy: Techniques and empirical findings* (3rd ed.). New York: Harcourt, Brace, Jovanovich.

Mathews, J. R., Friman, P. C., Barone, V. J., Ross, L. V., & Christophersen, E. R. (1987). Decreasing dangerous infant behavior through parent instruction. *Journal of Applied Behavior Analysis, 20*, 165–169.

Matson, J. L., Sevin, J. A., Fridley, D., & Love, S. R. (1990). Increasing spontaneous language in three autistic children. *Journal of Applied Behavior Analysis, 23*, 227–233.

Matson, J. L., & Stephens, R. M. (1978). Increasing appropriate behavior of explosive chronic psychiatric patients with a social skills training package. *Behavior Modification, 2*, 61–76.

Mayo Clinic Foundation. (1989). *Relaxed breathing.* Rochester, MN: Mayo Clinic Foundation.

Mazaleski, J. L., Iwata, B. A., Vollmer, T. R., Zarcone, J. R., & Smith, R. C. (1993). Analysis of the reinforcement and extinction components in DRO contingencies with self-injury. *Journal of Applied Behavior Analysis, 26*, 143–156.

McClannahan, L. E., & Risley, T. R. (1975). Design of living environments for nursing home residents: Increasing participation in recreation activities. *Journal of Applied Behavior Analysis, 8*, 261–268.

McGimsey, J. F., Greene, B. F., & Lutzker, J. R. (1995). Competence in aspects of behavioral treatment and consultation: Implications for service delivery and graduate training. *Journal of Applied Behavior Analysis, 28*, 301–315.

McGinnis, J. C., Friman, P. C., & Carlyon, W. D. (1999). The effects of token reward on "intrinsic" motivation for doing math. *Journal of Applied Behavior Analysis, 32*, 375–379.

McLaughlin, T. F., & Malaby, J. (1972). Intrinsic reinforcers in a classroom token economy. *Journal of Applied Behavior Analysis, 5*, 263–270.

McNeil, C. B., Clemens-Mowrer, L., Gurwitch, R. H., & Funderburk, B. W. (1994). Assessment of a new procedure to prevent timeout escape in preschoolers. *Child and Family Behavior Therapy, 16*(3), 27–35.

McSweeny, A. J. (1978). Effects of response cost on the behavior of a million persons: Charging for directory assistance in Cincinnati. *Journal of Applied Behavior Analysis, 11*, 47–51.

Meichenbaum, D. (1977). *Cognitive behavior modification: An integrative approach.* New York: Plenum.

Meichenbaum, D. (1985). *Stress inoculation training.* Elmsford, NY: Pergamon.

Meichenbaum, D., & Cameron, R. (1973). Training schizophrenics to talk to themselves: A means of developing attentional controls. *Behavior Therapy, 4*, 515–534.

Meichenbaum, D., & Goodman, J. (1971). Training impulsive children to talk to themselves: A means of developing self control. *Journal of Abnormal Psychology, 77*, 115–126.

Melamed, B. G. (1979). Behavioral approaches to fear in dental settings. In M. Hersen, R. M. Eisler, & R. M. Miller (Eds.), *Progress in behavior modification* (Vol. 7, pp. 172–205). New York: Academic Press.

Melamed, B. G., & Siegel, L. J. (1975). Reduction of anxiety in children facing hospitalization and surgery by use of filmed modeling. *Journal of Consulting and Clinical Psychology, 43*, 511–521.

Melin, L., & Gotestam, K. G. (1981). The effects of rearranging ward routines on communication and eating behaviors of psychogeriatric patients. *Journal of Applied Behavior Analysis, 14*, 47–51.

Meyer, L. H., & Evans, I. M. (1989). *Nonaversive interventions for behavior problems: A manual for home and community.* Baltimore: Paul Brookes.

Meyers, A., Mercatoris, M., & Sirota, A. (1976). Use of overt self-instruction for the elimination of psychotic speech. *Journal of Consulting and Clinical Psychology, 44*, 480–483.

Michael, J. (1982). Distinguishing between discriminative and motivational functions of stimuli. *Journal of the Experimental Analysis of Behavior, 37*, 149–155.

Michael, J. L. (1991). A behavioral perspective on college teaching. *The Behavior Analyst, 14*, 229–239.

Michael, J. L. (1993a). *Concepts and principles of behavior analysis.* Kalamazoo, MI: Society for the Advancement of Behavior Analysis.

Michael, J. L. (1993b). Establishing operations. *The Behavior Analyst, 16*, 191–206.

Milan, M. A., & McKee, J. M. (1976). The cellblock token economy: Token reinforcement procedures in a maximum security correctional institution for adult male felons. *Journal of Applied Behavior Analysis, 9*, 253–275.

Miller, D. L., & Kelley, M. L. (1994). The use of goal setting and contingency contracting for improving children's homework. *Journal of Applied Behavior Analysis, 27,* 73–84.

Miller, L. K. (1981). *Principles of everyday behavior analysis* (2nd ed.). Pacific Grove, CA: Brooks/Cole.

Miller, L. K., & Miller, O. L. (1970). Reinforcing self-help group activities of welfare recipients. *Journal of Applied Behavior Analysis, 3,* 57–64.

Miller, W. H. (1975). *Systematic parent training: Procedures, cases, and issues.* Champaign, IL: Research Press.

Miltenberger, R. G. (1998). Methods for assessing antecedent influences on problem behaviors. In J. Luiselli & J. Cameron (Eds.), *Antecedent control procedures for the behavioral support of persons with developmental disabilities* (pp. 47–65). Baltimore: Paul Brookes.

Miltenberger, R. G. (1999). Understanding problem behaviors through functional assessment. In N. Wieseler & R. Hanson (Eds.), *Challenging behavior in persons with mental health disorders and developmental disabilities* (pp. 215–235). Washington, DC: AAMR.

Miltenberger, R. G., & Fuqua, R. W. (1981). Overcorrection: Review and critical analysis. *The Behavior Analyst, 4,* 123–141.

Miltenberger, R. G., & Fuqua, R. W. (1985a). A comparison of three treatment procedures for nervous habits. *Journal of Behavior Therapy and Experimental Psychiatry, 16,* 196–200.

Miltenberger, R. G., & Fuqua, R. W. (1985b). Evaluation of a training manual for the acquisition of behavioral assessment interviewing skills. *Journal of Applied Behavior Analysis, 18,* 323–328.

Miltenberger, R. G., Fuqua, R. W., & McKinley, T. (1985). Habit reversal with muscle tics: Replication and component analysis. *Behavior Therapy, 16,* 39–50.

Miltenberger, R. G., Fuqua, R. W., & Woods, D. W. (1998). Applying behavior analysis with clinical problems: Review and analysis of habit reversal. *Journal of Applied Behavior Analysis, 31,* 447–469.

Miltenberger, R. G., Handen, B., & Capriotti, R. (1987). Physical restraint, visual screening, and DRI in the treatment of stereotypy. *Scandinavian Journal of Behavior Therapy, 16,* 51–58.

Miltenberger, R. G., Lennox, D. B., & Erfanian, N. (1989). Acceptability of alternative treatments for persons with mental retardation: Ratings from institutional and community based staff. *American Journal on Mental Retardation, 93,* 388–395.

Miltenberger, R. G., Long, E., Rapp, J., Lumley, V., & Elliott, A. (1998). Evaluating the function of hair pulling: A preliminary investigation. *Behavior Therapy, 29,* 211–219.

Miltenberger, R. G., Rapp, J., & Long, E. (1999). A low tech method for conducting real time recording. *Journal of Applied Behavior Analysis, 32,* 119–120.

Miltenberger, R., Roberts, J., Ellingson, S., Galensky, T., Rapp, J., Long, E., & Lumley, V. (1999). Training and generalization of sexual abuse prevention skills for women with mental retardation. *Journal of Applied Behavior Analysis, 32,* 385–388.

Miltenberger, R. G., & Thiesse-Duffy, E. (1988). Evaluation of home-based programs for teaching personal safety skills to children. *Journal of Applied Behavior Analysis, 21,* 81–87.

Miltenberger, R. G., Thiesse-Duffy, E., Suda, K. T., Kozak, C., & Bruellman, J. (1990). Teaching prevention skills to children: The use of multiple measures to evaluate parent versus expert instruction. *Child and Family Behavior Therapy, 12,* 65–87.

Miltenberger, R. G., Wagaman, J. R., & Arndorfer, R. E. (1996). Simplified treatment and long-term follow-up for stuttering in adults: A study of two cases. *Journal of Behavior Therapy and Experimental Psychiatry, 27,* 181–188.

Miltenberger, R. G., & Woods, D. W. (1998). Disfluencies. In S. Watson & F. Gresham (Eds.), *Handbook of child behavior therapy* (pp. 127–142). New York: Plenum.

Miltenberger, R. G., Wright, K. M., & Fuqua, R. W. (1986). Graduated in vivo exposure with a severe spider phobic. *Scandinavian Journal of Behavior Therapy, 15,* 71–76.

Mitchell, W. S., & Stoffelmayr, B. E. (1973). Application of the Premack principle to the behavioral control of extremely inactive schizophrenics. *Journal of Applied Behavior Analysis, 6,* 419–423.

Montesinos, L., Frisch, L. E., Greene, B. F., & Hamilton, M. (1990). An analysis of and intervention in the sexual transmission of disease. *Journal of Applied Behavior Analysis, 23,* 275–284.

Morris, R. J. (1991). Fear reduction methods. In F. H. Kanfer & A. P. Goldstein (Eds.), *Helping people change: A textbook of methods* (4th ed., pp. 161–201). New York: Pergamon.

Munk, D. D., & Repp, A. C. (1994). The relationship between instructional variables and problem behavior: A review. *Exceptional Children, 60,* 390–401.

Neef, N. A. (Ed.). (1994). Functional analysis approaches to behavioral assessment and treatment [Special Issue]. *Journal of Applied Behavior Analysis, 27.*

Neef, N. A., Lensbower, J., Hockersmith, I., DePalma, V., & Gray, K. (1990). In vivo versus simulation training: An interactional analysis of range and type of training exemplars. *Journal of Applied Behavior Analysis, 23,* 447–458.

Neef, N. A., Mace, F. C., & Shade, D. (1993). Impulsivity in students with serious emotional disturbances: The interactive effects of reinforcer rate, delay, and quality. *Journal of Applied Behavior Analysis, 26,* 37–52.

Neef, N. A., Mace, F. C., Shea, M. C., & Shade, D. (1992). Effects of reinforcer rate and reinforcer quality on time allocation: Extensions of the matching theory to educational settings. *Journal of Applied Behavior Analysis, 25,* 691–699.

Neef, N. A., Shade, D., & Miller, M. S. (1994). Assessing influential dimensions of reinforcers on choice in students with serious emotional disturbance. *Journal of Applied Behavior Analysis, 27,* 575–583.

Neisworth, J. T., Hunt, F. M., Gallop, H. R., & Madle, R. A. (1985). Reinforcer displacement. A preliminary study of the clinical application of the CRF/EXT effect. *Behavior Modification, 9,* 103–115.

Neisworth, J. T., & Moore, F. (1972). Operant treatment of asthmatic responding with the parent as therapist. *Behavior Therapy, 3,* 95–99.

Nelson, G. L., & Cone, J. D. (1979). Multiple baseline analysis of a token economy for psychiatric inpatients. *Journal of Applied Behavior Analysis, 12,* 255–271.

Nezu, A. M., Nezu, C. M., & Perri, M. G. (1989). *Problem solving therapy for depression: Theory, research, and clinical guidelines.* New York: Wiley.

Noell, G. H., Witt, J. C., LaFleur, L. H., Mortenson, B. P., Ranier, D. D., & LeVelle, J. (2000). Increasing intervention implementation in general education following consultation: A comparison of two follow up strategies. *Journal of Applied Behavior Analysis, 33,* 271–284.

Novaco, R. (1977). Stress inoculation: A cognitive therapy for anger and its application to a case of depression. *Journal of Consulting and Clinical Psychology, 45,* 600–608.

Nunn, R. G., & Azrin, N. H. (1976). Eliminating nailbiting by the habit reversal procedure. *Behaviour Research and Therapy, 14,* 65–67.

O'Banion, D. R., & Whaley, D. L. (1981). *Behavioral contracting: Arranging contingencies of reinforcement.* New York: Springer.

Ollendick, T. H. (1981). Self-monitoring and self administered overcorrection: The modification of nervous tics in children. *Behavior Modification, 5,* 75–84.

Olsen-Woods, L., Miltenberger, R., & Forman, G. (1998). The effects of correspondence training in an abduction prevention training program. *Child and Family Behavior Therapy, 20,* 15–34.

O'Neill, G. W., Blanck, L. S., & Joyner, M. A. (1980). The use of stimulus control over littering in a natural setting. *Journal of Applied Behavior Analysis, 13,* 370–381.

O'Neill, G. W., & Gardner, R. (1983). *Behavioral principles in medical rehabilitation: A practical guide.* Springfield, IL: Charles C. Thomas.

O'Neill, R. E., Horner, R. H., Albin, R. W., Sprague, J. R., Storey, K., & Newton, J. S. (1997). *Functional assessment and program development for problem behavior: A practical handbook.* Pacific Grove, CA: Brooks/Cole.

O'Neill, R. E., Horner, R. H., Albin, R. W., Storey, K., & Sprague, J. R. (1990). *Functional analysis of problem behavior: A practical guide.* Sycamore, IL: Sycamore.

Pace, G. M., Ivancic, M. T., Edwards, G. L., Iwata, B. A., & Page, T. J. (1985). Assessment of stimulus preference and reinforcer value with profoundly retarded individuals. *Journal of Applied Behavior Analysis, 18,* 249–255.

Pace, G. M., Iwata, B. A., Cowdery, G. E., Andree, P. J., & McIntyre, T. (1993). Stimulus (instructional) fading during extinction of self-injurious escape behavior. *Journal of Applied Behavior Analysis, 26,* 205–212.

Pace, G. M., Iwata, B. A., Edwards, G. L., & McCosh, K. C. (1986). Stimulus fading and transfer in the treatment of self-restraint and self-injurious behavior. *Journal of Applied Behavior Analysis, 19,* 381–389.

Page, T. J., Iwata, B. A., & Neef, N. A. (1976). Teaching pedestrian skills to retarded persons: Generalization from the classroom to the natural environment. *Journal of Applied Behavior Analysis, 9,* 433–444.

Parrish, J. M., Cataldo, M. F., Kolko, D. J., Neef, N. A., & Egel, A. L. (1986). Experimental analysis of response covariation among compliant and inappropriate behaviors. *Journal of Applied Behavior Analysis, 19,* 241–254.

Patterson, G. R. (1975). *Families: Applications of social learning to family life.* Champaign, IL: Research Press.

Paul, G. L., & Lentz, R. J. (1977). *Psychological treatment for chronic mental patients: Milieu versus social learning programs.* Cambridge, MA: Harvard University Press.

Paul, R. H., Marx, B. P., & Orsillo, S. M. (1999). Acceptance-based psychotherapy in the treatment of an adjudicated exhibitionist: A case example. *Behavior Therapy, 30,* 149–162.

Pavlov, I. P. (1927). *Conditioned reflexes* (G. V. Anrep, Trans.). London: Oxford University Press.

Phillips, E. L. (1968). Achievement place: Token reinforcement procedures in a home-based style rehabilitation setting for "pre-delinquent" boys. *Journal of Applied Behavior Analysis, 1,* 213–223.

Phillips, E. L., Phillips, E. A., Fixsen, D. L., & Wolf, M. M. (1971). Achievement place: Modification of the behaviors of predelinquent boys within a token economy. *Journal of Applied Behavior Analysis, 4,* 45–59.

Piazza, C. C., & Fisher, W. (1991). A faded bedtime with response cost protocol for treatment of multiple sleep problems in children. *Journal of Applied Behavior Analysis, 24,* 129–140.

Pierce, W. D., & Epling, W. F. (1995). *Behavior analysis and learning.* Upper Saddle River, NJ: Prentice Hall.

Pinkston, E. M., Reese, N. M., LeBlanc, J. M., & Baer, D. M. (1973). Independent control of a preschool child's aggression and peer interaction by contingent teacher attention. *Journal of Applied Behavior Analysis, 6,* 115–124.

Plummer, S. Baer, D. M., & LeBlanc, J. M. (1977). Functional considerations in the use of procedural time-out and an effective alternative. *Journal of Applied Behavior Analysis, 10,* 689–705.

Poche, C., Brouwer, R., & Swearengin, M. (1981). Teaching self-protection to young children. *Journal of Applied Behavior Analysis, 14,* 169–176.

Poche, C., Yoder, P., & Miltenberger, R. (1988). Teaching self-protection skills to children using television techniques. *Journal of Applied Behavior Analysis, 21,* 253–261.

Polenchar, B. E., Romano, A. G., Steinmetz, J. E., & Patterson, M. M. (1984). Effects of US parameters on classical conditioning of cat hindlimb flexion. *Animal Learning and Behavior, 12*, 69–72.

Poling, A., & Grossett, D. (1986). Basic research designs in applied behavior analysis. In A. Poling & R. W. Fuqua (Eds.), *Research methods in applied behavior analysis: Issues and advances* (pp. 7–27). New York: Plenum.

Poling, A., & Ryan, C. (1982). Differential reinforcement of other behavior schedules. *Behavior Modification, 6*, 3–21.

Poppen, R. (1988). *Behavioral relaxation training and assessment*. New York: Pergamon.

Porterfield, J. K., Herbert-Jackson, E., & Risley, T. R. (1976). Contingent observation: An effective and acceptable procedure for reducing disruptive behavior of young children in a group setting. *Journal of Applied Behavior Analysis, 9*, 55–64.

Premack, D. (1959). Toward empirical behavior laws I: Positive reinforcement. *Psychological Review, 66*, 219–233.

Pryor, K. (1985). *Don't shoot the dog: The new art of teaching and training*. New York: Bantam.

Rachlin, H. (1976). *Behavior and learning*. San Francisco: W.H. Freeman.

Rapp, J., Carr, J., Miltenberger, R., Dozier, C., & Kellum, K. (2001). Using real-time recording to enhance the analysis of within session functional analysis data. *Behavior Modification, 25*, 70–93.

Rapp, J., Miltenberger, R., Galensky, T., Ellingson, S., & Long, E. (1999). A functional analysis of hair pulling. *Journal of Applied Behavior Analysis, 32*, 329–337.

Rapp, J., Miltenberger, R., Galensky, T., Ellingson, S., Long, E., Stricker, J., & Garlinghouse, M. (2000). Treatment of hair pulling maintained by digital–tactile stimulation. *Behavior Therapy*.

Rapp, J., Miltenberger, R., Galensky, T., Roberts, J., & Ellingson, S. (1999). Brief functional analysis and simplified habit reversal treatment for thumb sucking in fraternal twin brothers. *Child and Family Behavior Therapy, 21*(2), 1–17.

Rapp, J., Miltenberger, R., Long, E. (1998). Augmenting simplified habit reversal with an awareness enhancement device: Preliminary findings. *Journal of Applied Behavior Analysis, 31*, 665–668.

Rapp, J., Miltenberger, R., Long, E., Elliott, A., & Lumley, V. (1998). Simplified habit reversal for hair pulling in three adolescents: A clinical replication with direct observation. *Journal of Applied Behavior Analysis, 31*, 299–302.

Rapport, M. D., Murphy, H. A., & Bailey, J. S. (1982). Ritalin vs. response cost in the control of hyperactive children: A within subject comparison. *Journal of Applied Behavior Analysis, 15*, 205–216.

Rasey, H. W., & Iverson, I. H. (1993). An experimental acquisition of maladaptive behavior by shaping. *Journal of Behavior Therapy & Experimental Psychiatry, 24*, 37–43.

Reichle, J., & Wacker, D. P. (Eds.). (1993). *Communicative alternatives to challenging behavior: Integrating functional assessment and intervention strategies*. Baltimore: Paul Brookes.

Reid, D., Parsons, M., & Green, C. (1989). *Staff management in human services: Behavioral research and application*. Springfield, IL: Charles C. Thomas.

Reid, D. H., Parsons, M. B., Phillips, J. F., & Green, C. W. (1993). Reduction of self-injurious hand mouthing using response blocking. *Journal of Applied Behavior Analysis, 26*, 139–140.

Rekers, G. A., & Lovaas, O. I. (1974). Behavioral treatment of deviant sex-role behaviors in a male child. *Journal of Applied Behavior Analysis, 7*, 173–190.

Repp, A. C. (1983). *Teaching the mentally retarded*. Upper Saddle River, NJ: Prentice Hall.

Repp, A. C., Barton, L. E., & Brulle, A. R. (1983). A comparison of two procedures for programming the differential reinforcement of other behaviors. *Journal of Applied Behavior Analysis, 16*, 435–445.

Repp, A. C., & Deitz, S. M. (1974). Reducing aggressive and self-injurious behavior of institutionalized retarded children through reinforcement of other behaviors. *Journal of Applied Behavior Analysis, 7*, 313–325.

Repp, A. C., & Horner, R. H. (1999). Functional analysis of problem behavior: From effective analysis to effective support. Belmont, CA: Wadsworth.

Repp, A. C., & Karsh, K. G. (1994). Hypothesis-based interventions for tantrum behaviors of persons with developmental disabilities in school settings. *Journal of Applied Behavior Analysis, 27*, 21–31.

Repp, A. C., & Singh, N. N. (Eds.). (1990). *Perspectives on the use of nonaversive and aversive interventions for persons with developmental disabilities*. Sycamore, IL: Sycamore.

Rescorla, R. A., & Wagner, A. R. (1972). A theory of Pavlovian conditioning: Variations in the effectiveness of reinforcement and nonreinforcement. In A. H. Black & W. F. Prokasy (Eds.), *Classical conditioning II*. New York: Appleton-Century-Crofts.

Reynolds, G. S. (1961). Behavioral contrast. *Journal of the Experimental Analysis of Behavior, 4*, 57–71.

Reynolds, G. S. (1968). *A primer of operant conditioning*. Glenview, IL: Scott Foresman.

Richman, G. S., Reiss, M. L., Bauman, K. E., & Bailey, J. S. (1984). Training menstrual care to mentally retarded women: Acquisition, generalization, and maintenance. *Journal of Applied Behavior Analysis, 17*, 441–451.

Rincover, A. (1978). Sensory extinction: A procedure for eliminating self-stimulatory behavior in psychotic children. *Journal of Abnormal Child Psychology, 6*, 299–310.

Rincover, A., Cook, R., Peoples, A., & Packard, D. (1979). Sensory extinction and sensory reinforcement principles for programming multiple adaptive behavior change. *Journal of Applied Behavior Analysis, 12*, 221–233.

Ritter, B. (1968). The group desensitization of children's snake phobias using vicarious and contact desensitization procedures. *Behaviour Research and Therapy, 6,* 1–6.

Ritter, B. (1969). Treatment of acrophobia with contact desensitization. *Behaviour Research and Therapy, 7,* 41–45.

Roberts, M. C., & Peterson, L. (Eds.). (1984). *Prevention of problems in childhood: Psychological research and applications.* New York: Wiley.

Roberts, M. L., Mace, F. C., & Daggett, J. A. (1995). Preliminary comparison of two negative reinforcement schedules to reduce self-injury. *Journal of Applied Behavior Analysis, 28,* 579–580.

Roberts, M. W., & Powers, S. W. (1990). Adjusting chair timeout procedures for oppositional children. *Behavior Therapy, 21,* 257–271.

Robinson, P. W., Newby, T. J., & Ganzell, S. L. (1981). A token system for a class of underachieving hyperactive children. *Journal of Applied Behavior Analysis, 14,* 307–315.

Rogers, R. W., Rogers, J. S., Bailey, J. S., Runkle, W., & Moore, B. (1988). Promoting safety belt use among state employees: The effects of a prompting and stimulus control intervention. *Journal of Applied Behavior Analysis, 21,* 263–269.

Rogers-Warren, A. R., Warren, S. F., & Baer, D. M. (1977). A component analysis: Modeling, self-reporting, and reinforcement of self-reporting in the development of sharing. *Behavior Modification, 1,* 307–322.

Rolider, A., & Van Houten, R. (1985). Movement suppression time-out for undesirable behavior in psychotic and severely developmentally delayed children. *Journal of Applied Behavior Analysis, 18,* 275–288.

Rortvedt, A. K., & Miltenberger, R. G. (1994). Analysis of a high probability instructional sequence and time-out in the treatment of child noncompliance. *Journal of Applied Behavior Analysis, 27,* 327–330.

Romaniuk, C., & Miltenberger, R. (2001). The influence of preference and choice of activity on problem behavior. *Journal of Positive Behavioral Interventions, 3,* 152–159.

Romaniuk, C., Miltenberger, R., Conyers, C., Jenner, N., Jurgens, M., & Ringenberg, C. (2002). The influence of activity choice on problem behaviors maintained by escape versus attention. *Journal of Applied Behavior Analysis, 35,* 349–362.

Rosenbaum, M. S., & Ayllon, T. (1981a). The habit reversal technique in treating trichotillomania. *Behavior Therapy, 12,* 473–481.

Rosenbaum, M. S., & Ayllon, T. (1981b). Treating bruxism with the habit reversal technique. *Behaviour Research and Therapy, 19,* 87–96.

Rosenthal, T., & Steffek, B. (1991). Modeling methods. In F. Kanfer & A. Goldstein (Eds.), *Helping people change: A textbook of methods* (4th ed., pp. 70–121). Elmsford, NY: Pergamon.

Rusch, F. R., Rose, T., & Greenwood, C. R. (1988). *Introduction to behavior analysis in special education.* Upper Saddle River, NJ: Prentice Hall.

Russo, D. C., Cataldo, M. F., & Cushing, P. J. (1981). Compliance training and behavioral covariation in the treatment of multiple behavior problems. *Journal of Applied Behavior Analysis, 14,* 209–222.

Ruth, W. J. (1996). Goal setting and behavior contracting for students with emotional and behavioral difficulties: Analysis of daily, weekly, and total goal attainment. *Psychology in the Schools, 33,* 153–158.

Sajwaj, T., Libet, J., & Agras, S. (1974). Lemon juice therapy: The control of life threatening rumination in a six month old infant. *Journal of Applied Behavior Analysis, 7,* 557–563.

Salend, S. J., Ellis, L. L., & Reynolds, C. J. (1989). Using self-instructions to teach vocational skills to individuals who are severely retarded. *Education and Training in Mental Retardation, 24,* 248–254.

Sasso, G. M., Reimers, T. M., Cooper, L. J., Wacker, D., Berg, W., Steege, M., Kelly, L., & Allaire, A. (1992). Use of descriptive and experimental analyses to identify the functional properties of aberrant behavior in school settings. *Journal of Applied Behavior Analysis, 25,* 809–821.

Schaefer, H. H. (1970). Self-injurious behavior: Shaping "head banging" in monkeys. *Journal of Applied Behavior Analysis, 3,* 111–116.

Schaeffer, C. E., & Millman, H. L. (1981). *How to help children with common problems.* New York: Van Nostrand Reinhold.

Schleien, S. J., Wehman, P., & Kiernan, J. (1981). Teaching leisure skills to severely handicapped adults: An age-appropriate darts game. *Journal of Applied Behavior Analysis, 14,* 513–519.

Schlinger, H. D. (1993). Separating discriminative and function-altering effects of verbal stimuli. *The Behavior Analyst, 16,* 9–23.

Schreibman, L. (1975). Effects of within-stimulus and extra-stimulus prompting on discrimination learning in autistic children. *Journal of Applied Behavior Analysis, 8,* 91–112.

Schwartz, B. (1989). *Psychology of learning and behavior* (3rd ed.). New York: W.W. Norton.

Scotti, J. R., McMorrow, M. J., & Trawitzki, A. L. (1993). Behavioral treatment of chronic psychiatric disorders: Publication trends and future directions. *Behavior Therapy, 24,* 527–550.

Shapiro, A. K., Shapiro, E., Bruun, R. D., & Sweet, R. D. (1978). *Gilles de la Tourette syndrome.* New York: Raven.

Shapiro, E. S., Barrett, R. P., & Ollendick, T. H. (1980). A comparison of physical restraint and positive practice overcorrection in treating stereotypic behavior. *Behavior Therapy, 11,* 227–233.

Sharenow, E. L., Fuqua, R. W., & Miltenberger, R. G. (1989). The treatment of muscle tics with dissimilar competing response practice. *Journal of Applied Behavior Analysis, 22,* 35–42.

Siegal, G. M., Lenske, J., & Broen, P. (1969). Suppression of normal speech disfluencies through response cost. *Journal of Applied Behavior Analysis, 2,* 265–276.

Singh, N. N., Dawson, M. J., & Manning, P. (1981). Effects of spaced responding DRL on the stereotyped behavior of profoundly retarded persons. *Journal of Applied Behavior Analysis, 14,* 521–526.

Singh, N. N., Watson, J. E., & Winton, A. S. (1986). Treating self-injury: Water mist spray versus facial screening or forced arm exercise. *Journal of Applied Behavior Analysis, 19,* 403–410.

Skinner, B. F. (1938). *The behavior of organisms: An experimental analysis.* New York: Appleton-Century-Crofts.

Skinner, B. F. (1948). *Walden two.* New York: Macmillan.

Skinner, B. F. (1951). How to teach animals. *Scientific American, 185,* 26–29.

Skinner, B. F. (1953a). *Science and human behavior.* New York: Free Press.

Skinner, B. F. (1953b). Some contributions of an experimental analysis of behavior to psychology as a whole. *American Psychologist, 8,* 69–78.

Skinner, B. F. (1956). A case history in scientific method. *American Psychologist, 11,* 221–233.

Skinner, B. F. (1957). *Verbal behavior.* New York: Appleton-Century-Crofts.

Skinner, B. F. (1958). Reinforcement today. *American Psychologist, 13,* 94–99.

Skinner, B. F. (1966). What is the experimental analysis of behavior? *Journal of the Experimental Analysis of Behavior, 9,* 213–218.

Skinner, B. F. (1968). *The technology of teaching.* Upper Saddle River, NJ: Prentice Hall.

Skinner, B. F. (1969). *Contingencies of reinforcement: A theoretical analysis.* New York: Appleton-Century-Crofts.

Skinner, B. F. (1971). *Beyond freedom and dignity.* New York: Knopf.

Skinner, B. F. (1974). *About behaviorism.* New York: Knopf.

Skinner, B. F. (1977). Why I am not a cognitive psychologist. *Behaviorism, 5,* 1–10.

Smith, R. G., & Iwata, B. A. (1997). Antecedent influences on behavior disorders. *Journal of Applied Behavior Analysis, 30,* 343–375.

Smith, R. G., Iwata, B. A., Goh, H., & Shore, B. A. (1995). Analysis of establishing operations for self-injury maintained by escape. *Journal of Applied Behavior Analysis, 28,* 515–535.

Smith, R. G., Iwata, B. A., Vollmer, T. R., & Zarcone, J. R. (1993). Experimental analysis and treatment of multiply controlled self-injury. *Journal of Applied Behavior Analysis, 26,* 183–196.

Snell, M. E., & Gast, D. L. (1981). Applying the time delay procedure to the instruction of the severely handicapped. *Journal of the Association for the Severely Handicapped, 6,* 3–14.

Solnick, J. V., Rincover, A., & Peterson, C. R. (1977). Some determinants of the reinforcing and punishing effects of time-out. *Journal of Applied Behavior Analysis, 10,* 415–424.

Spiegler, M., & Guevremont, D. (1993). *Contemporary behavior therapy* (2nd ed.). Pacific Grove, CA: Brooks/Cole.

Spiegler, M., & Guevremont, D. (1998). *Contemporary behavior therapy* (3rd ed). Pacific Grove, CA: Brooks/Cole.

Spiegler, M., & Guevremont, D. (2003). *Contemporary behavior therapy* (4th ed). Belmont, CA: Wadsworth.

Sprague, J. R., & Horner, R. H. (1984). The effects of single instance, multiple instance, and general case training on generalized vending machine use by moderately and severely handicapped students. *Journal of Applied Behavior Analysis, 17,* 273–278.

Sprague, J. R., & Horner, R. H. (1995). Functional assessment and intervention in community settings. *Mental Retardation and Developmental Disabilities Research Reviews, 1,* 89–93.

Stabler, B., & Warren, A. B. (1974). Behavioral contracting in treating trichotillomania: A case note. *Psychological Reports, 34,* 293–301.

Stajkovic, A. D., & Luthans, F. (1997). A meta-analysis of the effects of organizational behavior modification on task performance, 1975–95. *Academy of Management Journal, 40,* 1122–1149.

Starke, M. (1987). Enhancing social skills and self-perceptions of physically disabled young adults: Assertiveness training versus discussion groups. *Behavior Modification, 11,* 3–16.

Steege, M. W., Wacker, D. P., Cigrand, K. C., Berg, W. K., Novak, C. G., Reimers, T. M., Sasso, G. M., & DeRaad, A. (1990). Use of negative reinforcement in the treatment of self-injurious behavior. *Journal of Applied Behavior Analysis, 23,* 459–467.

Steinman, W. M. (1970). The social control of generalized imitation. *Journal of Applied Behavior Analysis, 3,* 159–167.

Stickney, M., & Miltenberger, R. (1999). Evaluation of procedures for the functional assessment of binge eating. *International Journal of Eating Disorders, 26,* 196–204.

Stickney, M., Miltenberger, R., & Wolff, G. (1999). A descriptive analysis of factors contributing to binge eating. *Journal of Behavior Therapy and Experimental Psychiatry, 30,* 177–189.

Stock, L. Z., & Milan, M. A. (1993). Improving dietary practices of elderly individuals: The power of prompting, feedback, and social reinforcement. *Journal of Applied Behavior Analysis, 26,* 379–387.

Stokes, T. F., & Baer, D. M. (1977). An implicit technology of generalization. *Journal of Applied Behavior Analysis, 10,* 349–367.

Stokes, T. F., Baer, D. M., & Jackson, R. L. (1974). Programming the generalization of a greeting response in four retarded children. *Journal of Applied Behavior Analysis, 7,* 599–610.

Stokes, T. F., & Kennedy, S. H. (1980). Reducing child uncooperative behavior during dental treatment through modeling and reinforcement. *Journal of Applied Behavior Analysis, 13,* 41–49.

Stokes, T. F., & Osnes, P. G. (1989). An operant pursuit of generalization. *Behavior Therapy, 20,* 337–355.

Stokes, T. F., Osnes, P. G., & DaVerne, K. C. (1993). Communicative correspondence and mediated generalization. In

J. Reichle & D. P. Wacker (Eds.), *Communicative alternatives to challenging behavior: Integrating functional assessment and intervention strategies* (pp. 299–315). Baltimore: Paul Brookes.

Stricker, J., Miltenberger, R., Garlinghouse, M., Deaver, C., & Anderson, C. (2001). Evaluation of an awareness enhancement device for the treatment of digit sucking in children. *Journal of Applied Behavior Analysis, 34,* 77–80.

Stricker, J., Miltenberger, R., Garlinghouse, M., & Tulloch, H. (2003). Augmenting stimulus intensity with an Awareness Enhancement Device in the treatment of finger sucking. *Education and Treatment of Children, 26,* 22–29.

Striefel, S., Bryan, K. S., & Aikens, D. A. (1974). Transfer of stimulus control from motor to verbal stimuli. *Journal of Applied Behavior Analysis, 7,* 123–135.

Stuart, R. B. (1977). *Behavioral self-management: Strategies, techniques, and outcomes.* New York: Brunner Mazel.

Stuart, R. B. (1980). *Helping couples change: A social learning approach to marital therapy.* New York: Guilford.

Suda, K., & Miltenberger, R. (1993). Evaluation of staff management strategies to increase positive interactions in a vocational setting. *Behavioral Residential Treatment, 8,* 69–88.

Sulzer-Azaroff, B., Drabman, R., Greer, R. D., Hall, R. V., Iwata, B. A., & O'Leary, S. (Eds.). (1988). *Behavior analysis in education 1967–1987: Reprint series* (Vol. 3). Lawrence, KS: Society for the Experimental Analysis of Behavior.

Sulzer-Azaroff, B., & Mayer, G. R. (1991). *Behavior analysis for lasting change.* Fort Worth, TX: Holt, Rinehart, & Winston.

Sundel, S. S., & Sundel, M. (1993). *Behavior modification in the human services* (3rd ed.). Newbury Park, CA: Sage.

Swain, J. C., & McLaughlin, T. F. (1998). The effects of bonus contingencies in a classwide token program on math accuracy with middle school students with behavioral disorders. *Behavioral Interventions, 13,* 11–19.

Swan, G. E., & MacDonald, M. L. (1978). Behavior therapy in practice: A national survey of behavior therapists. *Behavior Therapy, 9,* 799–807.

Swiezy, N. B., Matson, J. L., & Box, P. (1992). The good behavior game: A token reinforcement system for preschoolers. *Child and Family Behavior Therapy, 14*(3), 21–32.

Tanner, B. A., & Zeiler, M. (1975). Punishment of self-injurious behavior using aromatic ammonia as the aversive stimulus. *Journal of Applied Behavior Analysis, 8,* 53–57.

Teng, E. J., Woods, D. W., Twohig, M. P., & Marcks, B. A. (2002). Body-focused repetitive behavior problems: Prevalence in a nonreferred population and differences in perceived somatic activity. *Behavior Modification, 26,* 340–360.

Terrace, H. S. (1963a). Discrimination learning with and without "errors." *Journal of Experimental Analysis of Behavior, 6,* 1–27.

Terrace, H. S. (1963b). Errorless transfer of a discrimination across two continua. *Journal of the Experimental Analysis of Behavior, 6,* 223–232.

The Association for Persons with Severe Handicaps (1987, May). Resolution on the cessation of intrusive interventions. *TASH Newsletter, 5,* 3.

Thomas, D. R., Becker, W. C., & Armstrong, M. (1968). Production and elimination of disruptive classroom behavior by systematically varying teacher attention. *Journal of Applied Behavior Analysis, 1,* 35–45.

Thoreson, C. E., & Mahoney, M. J. (1974). *Behavioral self-control.* New York: Holt, Rinehart, & Winston.

Thorndike, E. L. (1911). *Animal intelligence: Experimental studies.* New York: Macmillan.

Touchette, P. E., MacDonald, R. F., & Langer, S. N. (1985). A scatter plot for identifying stimulus control of problem behavior. *Journal of Applied Behavior Analysis, 18,* 343–351.

Tryon, W. W. (1998). Behavioral observation. In A. S. Bellack & M. Hersen (Eds.), *Behavioral assessment: A practical handbook* (4th ed., pp. 79–103). Boston: Allyn & Bacon.

Tucker, M., Sigafoos, J., & Bushell, H. (1998). Use of noncontingent reinforcement in the treatment of challenging behavior: A review and clinical guide. *Behavior Modification, 22,* 529–547.

Turner, S. M., Calhoun, K. S., & Adams, H. E. (Eds.). (1981). *Handbook of clinical behavior therapy.* New York: Wiley.

Twohig, M. P., & Woods, D. W. (2001). Habit reversal as a treatment for chronic skin picking in typically developing adult male siblings. *Journal of Applied Behavior Analysis, 34,* 217–220.

Ullmann, L. P., & Krasner, L. (Eds.). (1965). *Case studies in behavior modification.* New York: Holt, Rinehart, & Winston.

Ulrich, R., Stachnik, T., & Mabry, J. (Eds.). (1966). *Control of human behavior: Expanding the behavioral laboratory.* Glenview, IL: Scott Foresman.

Van Houten, R., & Axelrod, S. (Eds.). (1993). *Behavior analysis and treatment.* New York: Plenum.

Van Houten, R., & Nau, P. A. (1981). A comparison of the effects of posted feedback and increased police surveillance on highway speeding. *Journal of Applied Behavior Analysis, 14,* 261–271.

Van Houten, R., Nau, P., MacKenzie-Keating, S., Sameoto, D., & Colavecchia, B. (1982). An analysis of some variables influencing the effectiveness of reprimands. *Journal of Applied Behavior Analysis, 15,* 65–83.

Van Houten, R., & Rolider, A. (1984). The use of response prevention to eliminate nocturnal thumbsucking. *Journal of Applied Behavior Analysis, 17,* 509–520.

Veltum, L. G., & Miltenberger, R. G. (1989). Evaluation of a self-instructional package for training initial assessment interviewing skills. *Behavioral Assessment, 11,* 165–177.

Verplanck, W. S. (1955). The control of the content of conversation: Reinforcement of statements of opinion.

Journal of Abnormal and Social Psychology, 55, 668–676.

Vollmer, T. R., Bouvero, J. C., Wright, C. S., Van Camp, C., & Lalli, J. S. (2001). Identifying possible contingencies during descriptive analyses of severe behavior disorders. *Journal of Applied Behavior Analysis, 34,* 269–287.

Vollmer, T. R., & Iwata, B. A. (1991). Establishing operations and reinforcement effects. *Journal of Applied Behavior Analysis, 24,* 279–291.

Vollmer, T. R., & Iwata, B. A. (1992). Differential reinforcement as treatment for severe behavior disorders: Procedural and functional variations. *Research in Developmental Disabilities, 13,* 393–417.

Vollmer, T. R., Iwata, B. A., Cuvo, A. J., Heward, W. L., Miltenberger, R. G., & Neef, N. A. (Eds.). (2000). *Behavior analysis: Applications and extensions 1968–1999: Reprint series* (Vol. 5). Lawrence, KS: Society for the Experimental Analysis of Behavior.

Vollmer, T. R., Iwata, B. A., Zarcone, J. R., Smith, R. G., & Mazaleski, J. L. (1993). The role of attention in the treatment of attention-maintained self-injurious behavior: Noncontingent reinforcement and differential reinforcement of other behavior. *Journal of Applied Behavior Analysis, 26,* 9–22.

Vollmer, T. R., Marcus, B. A., & Ringdahl, J. E. (1995). Noncontingent escape as treatment for self-injurious behavior maintained by negative reinforcement. *Journal of Applied Behavior Analysis, 28,* 15–26.

Vollmer, T. R., Progar, P. R., Lalli, J. S., Van Camp, C. M., Sierp, B. J., Wright, C. S., Nastasi, J., & Eisenschink, K. J. (1998). Fixed-time schedules attenuate extinction-induced phenomena in the treatment of severe aberrant behavior. *Journal of Applied Behavior Analysis, 31,* 529–542.

Vollmer, T. R., Ringdahl, J. E., Roane, H. S., & Marcus, B. A. (1997). Negative side effects of noncontingent reinforcement. *Journal of Applied Behavior Analysis, 30,* 161–164.

Vollmer, T. R., Roane, H. S., Ringdahl, J. E., & Marcus, B. A. (1999). Evaluating treatment challenges with differential reinforcement of alternative behavior. *Journal of Applied Behavior Analysis, 32,* 9–23.

Wacker, D. P., & Berg, W. K. (1983). Effects of picture prompts on the acquisition of complex vocational tasks by mentally retarded adolescents. *Journal of Applied Behavior Analysis, 16,* 417–433.

Wacker, D. P., Berg, W. K., Berrie, P., & Swatta, P. (1985). Generalization and maintenance of complex skills by severely handicapped adolescents following picture prompt training. *Journal of Applied Behavior Analysis, 18,* 329–336.

Wacker, D. P., Berg, W. K., Wiggins, B., Muldoon, M., & Cavanaugh, J. (1985). Evaluation of reinforcer preferences for profoundly handicapped students. *Journal of Applied Behavior Analysis, 18,* 173–178.

Wacker, D. P., Steege, M. W., Northup, J., Sasso, G., Berg, W., Reimers, T., Cooper, L., Cigrand, K., & Donn, L. (1990). A component analysis of functional communication training across three topographies of severe behavior problems. *Journal of Applied Behavior Analysis, 23,* 417–429.

Wagaman, J., Miltenberger, R., & Arndorfer, R. (1993). Analysis of a simplified treatment for stuttering in children. *Journal of Applied Behavior Analysis, 26,* 53–61.

Wagaman, J., Miltenberger, R., & Williams, D. (1995). Treatment of a vocal tic by differential reinforcement. *Journal of Behavior Therapy and Experimental Psychiatry, 26,* 35–39.

Wagaman, J., Miltenberger, R., & Woods, D. W. (1995). Long-term follow-up of a behavioral treatment for stuttering in children. *Journal of Applied Behavior Analysis, 28,* 233–234.

Walker, C. E., Hedberg, A. G., Clement, P. W., & Wright, L. (1981). *Clinical procedures for behavior therapy.* Upper Saddle River, NJ: Prentice Hall.

Warzak, W. J., Kewman, D. G., Stefans, V., & Johnson, E. (1987). Behavioral rehabilitation of functional alexia. *Journal of Behavior Therapy and Experimental Psychiatry, 18,* 171–177.

Warzak, W. J., & Page, T. J. (1990). Teaching refusal skills to sexually active adolescents. *Journal of Behavior Therapy and Experimental Psychiatry, 21,* 133–139.

Waterloo, K. K., & Gotestam, K. G. (1988). The regulated breathing method for stuttering: An experimental evaluation. *Journal of Behavior Therapy and Experimental Psychiatry, 19,* 11–19.

Watson, D. L., & Tharp, R. G. (1993). *Self-directed behavior: Self modification for personal adjustment* (6th ed.). Pacific Grove, CA: Brooks/Cole.

Watson, J. B. (1913). Psychology as the behaviorist views it. *Psychological Review, 20,* 158–177.

Watson, J. B. (1924). *Behaviorism.* New York: W.W. Norton.

Watson, J. B., & Rayner, R. (1920). Conditioned emotional reactions. *Journal of Experimental Psychology, 3,* 1–4.

Watson, T. S., & Allen, K. D. (1993). Elimination of thumb-sucking as a treatment for severe trichotillomania. *Journal of the American Academy of Child and Adolescent Psychiatry, 32,* 830–834.

Watson, T. S., & Gresham, F. (Eds.). (1998). *Handbook of child behavior therapy.* New York: Plenum.

Wells, K. C., Forehand, R., Hickey, K., & Green, K. D. (1977). Effects of a procedure derived from the overcorrection principle on manipulated and nonmanipulated behaviors. *Journal of Applied Behavior Analysis, 10,* 679–687.

Wesolowski, M. D., Zencius, A. H., & Rodriguez, I. M. (1999). Mini-breaks: The use of escape on a fixed time schedule to reduce unauthorized breaks from vocational training sites for individuals with brain injury. *Behavioral Interventions, 14,* 163–170.

Whitman, T. L., Mercurio, J. R., & Caponigri, V. (1970). Development of social responses in two severely retarded children. *Journal of Applied Behavior Analysis, 3,* 133–138.

Whitman, T. L., Scibak, J. W., & Reid, D. H. (1983). *Behavior modification with the severely and profoundly retarded: Research and application*. New York: Academic Press.

Whitman, T. L., Spence, B. H., & Maxwell, S. (1987). A comparison of external and self-instructional teaching formats with mentally retarded adults in a vocational training setting. *Research in Developmental Disabilities, 8*, 371–388.

Wilder, D. A., & Carr, J. E. (1998). Recent advances in the modification of establishing operations to reduce aberrant behavior. *Behavioral Interventions, 13*, 43–59.

Williams, C. D. (1959). The elimination of tantrum behavior by extinction procedures. *Journal of Abnormal and Social Psychology, 59*, 269.

Williams, G. E., & Cuvo, A. J. (1986). Training apartment upkeep skills to rehabilitation clients: A comparison of task analysis strategies. *Journal of Applied Behavior Analysis, 19*, 39–51.

Williams, J. L. (1973). *Operant learning: Procedures for changing behavior*. Pacific Grove, CA: Brooks/Cole.

Winett, R. A., Neale, M. S., & Grier, H. C. (1979). Effects of self-monitoring and feedback on residential electricity consumption. *Journal of Applied Behavior Analysis, 12*, 173–184.

Winton, A. S., & Singh, N. N. (1983). Suppression of pica using brief physical restraint. *Journal of Mental Deficiency Research, 27*, 93–103.

Wolf, M. M., Risley, T. R., & Mees, H. L. (1964). Application of operant conditioning procedures to the behavior problems of an autistic child. *Behaviour Research and Therapy, 1*, 305–312.

Wolko, K. L., Hrycaiko, D. W., & Martin, G. L. (1993). A comparison of two self-management packages to standard coaching for improving practice performance of gymnasts. *Behavior Modification, 17*, 209–223.

Wolpe, J. (1958). *Psychotherapy by reciprocal inhibition*. Stanford, CA: Stanford University Press.

Wolpe, J. (1961). The systematic desensitization treatment of neurosis. *Journal of Nervous and Mental Disease, 112*, 189–203.

Wolpe, J. (1990). *The practice of behavior therapy* (4th ed.). New York: Pergamon.

Woods, D., & Miltenberger, R. (1995). Habit reversal: A review of applications and variations. *Journal of Behavior Therapy and Experimental Psychiatry, 26*, 123–131.

Woods, D., & Miltenberger, R. (1996a). A review of habit reversal with childhood habit disorders. *Education and Treatment of Children, 19*, 197–214.

Woods, D., & Miltenberger, R. (1996b). Are persons with nervous habits nervous? A preliminary examination of habit function in a nonreferred population. *Journal of Applied Behavior Analysis, 29*, 123–125.

Woods, D., Miltenberger, R., & Flach, A. (1996). Habits, tics, and stuttering: Prevalence and relation to anxiety and somatic awareness. *Behavior Modification, 20*, 216–225.

Woods, D., Miltenberger, R., & Lumley, V. (1996a). Sequential application of major habit reversal components to treat motor tics in children. *Journal of Applied Behavior Analysis, 29*, 483–493.

Woods, D., Miltenberger, R., & Lumley, V. (1996b). A simplified habit reversal treatment for pica-related chewing. *Journal of Behavior Therapy and Experimental Psychiatry, 27*, 257–262.

Woods, D., Murray, L., Fuqua, R., Seif, T., Boyer, L., & Siah, A. (1999). Comparing the effectiveness of similar and dissimilar competing responses in evaluating the habit reversal treatment for oral-digital habits in children. *Journal of Behavior Therapy and Experimental Psychiatry, 30*, 289–300.

Woods, D. W., & Twohig, M. P. (2002). Using habit reversal to treat chronic vocal tic disorder in children. *Behavioral Interventions, 17*, 159–168.

Woods, D. W., Twohig, M. P., Fuqua, R. W., & Hanley, J. M. (2000). Treatment of stuttering with regulated breathing: Strengths, limitations, and future directions. *Behavior Therapy, 31*, 547–568.

Wright, D. G., Brown, R. A., & Andrews, M. E. (1978). Remission of chronic ruminative vomiting through a reversal of social contingencies. *Behaviour Research and Therapy, 16*, 134–136.

Wright, K. M., & Miltenberger, R. G. (1987). Awareness training in the treatment of head and facial tics. *Journal of Behavior Therapy and Experimental Psychiatry, 18*, 269–274.

Wurtele, S. K., Marrs, S. R., & Miller-Perrin, C. L. (1987). Practice makes perfect? The role of participant modeling in sexual abuse prevention programs. *Journal of Consulting and Clinical Psychology, 55*, 599–602.

Wurtele, S. K., Saslawsky, D. A., Miller, C. L., Marrs, S. R., & Britcher, J. C. (1986). Teaching personal safety skills for potential prevention of sexual abuse: A comparison of treatments. *Journal of Consulting and Clinical Psychology, 54*, 688–692.

Wysocki, T., Hall, G., Iwata, B., & Riordan, M. (1979). Behavioral management of exercise: Contracting for aerobic points. *Journal of Applied Behavior Analysis, 12*, 55–64.

Yates, B. T. (1986). *Applications in self-management*. Belmont, CA: Wadsworth.

Zarcone, J. R., Iwata, B. A., Hughes, C. E., & Vollmer, T. R. (1993). Momentum versus extinction effects in the treatment of self-injurious escape behavior. *Journal of Applied Behavior Analysis, 26*, 135–136.

Zeigler, S. G. (1994). The effects of attentional shift training on the execution of soccer skills: A preliminary investigation. *Journal of Applied Behavior Analysis, 27*, 545–552.

Zeiler, M. D. (1971). Eliminating behavior with reinforcement. *Journal of the Experimental Analysis of Behavior, 16*, 401–405.

Zlutnick, S., Mayville, W. J., & Moffat, S. (1975). Modification of seizure disorders: The interruption of behavioral chains. *Journal of Applied Behavior Analysis, 8*, 1–12.

CREDITS

This page constitutes an extension of the copyright page. We have made every effort to trace the ownership of all copyrighted material and to secure permission from copyright holders. In the event of any question arising as to the use of any material, we will be pleased to make the necessary corrections in future printings. Thanks are due to the following authors, publishers, and agents for permission to use the material indicated.

3: From Durand, V. M., and Carr, E. G. (1992). An analysis of maintenance following functional communication training. *Journal of Applied Behavior Analysis, 25,* 777–794. Copyright © 1992 University of Kansas Press. Reprinted by permission of the author and publisher. **53:** From Carr, E. G., Newsom, C. D., & Binkoff, J. A. (1980). Escape as a factor in the aggressive behavior of two retarded children. *Journal of Applied Behavior Analysis, 13,* 101–117. Copyright © 1980 University of Kansas Press. Reprinted by permission of the author and the publisher. **55:** From DeVries, J. E., Burnette, M. M, & Redmon, W. K. (1991). AIDS prevention: Improving nurses' compliance with glove wearing through performance feedback. *Journal of Applied Behavior Analysis, 24,* 705–711. Copyright © 1991 University of Kansas Press. Reprinted by permission of the author and the publisher. **56:** From Franco, D. P., Christoff, K. A., Crimmins, D. B., & Kelly, J. A. (1983). Social skills training for an extremely shy young adolescent: An empirical case study. *Behavior Therapy, 14,* 568–575. Copyright © 1983. Reprinted by permission of Jeffrey Kelly. **59:** Foxx, R. M., & Rubinoff, A. (1979). Behavioral treatment of caffeinism: Reducing excessive coffee drinking. *Journal of Applied Behavior Analysis, 12,* 335–344. Copyright © 1979 University of Kansas Press. Reprinted by permission of Richard Foxx and the publisher. **73:** From Liberman, R. P., Teigen, J., Patterson, R., & Baker, V. (1973). Reducing delusional speech in chronic paranoid schizophrenics. *Journal of Applied Behavior Analysis, 6,* 57–64. Copyright © 1973 University of Kansas Press. Reprinted by permission of Robert P. Liberman, James R. Teigen, and the publisher. **74:** From Kazdin, A. E., & Klock, J. (1973). The effect of nonverbal approval on student attentive behavior. *Journal of Applied Behavior Analysis, 6,* 643–654. Copyright © 1973 University of Kansas Press. Reprinted by permission of Alan Kazdin and the publisher. **97:** From Hasazi, J. E., & Hasazi, S. E. (1972). Effects of teacher attention on digit reversal behavior in an elementary school child. *Journal of Applied Behavior Analysis, 5,* 157–162. Copyright © 1972 University of Kansas Press. Reprinted by permission of Joseph E. Hasazi and the publisher. **116:** From Luce, S., Delquadri, J., & Hall, R. V. (1980). Contingent exercise: A mild but powerful procedure for suppressing inappropriate verbal and aggressive behavior. *Journal of Applied Behavior Analysis, 13,* 583–594. Copyright © 1980 University of Kansas Press. Reprinted by permission of the publisher. **117:** From Clark, H., Rowbury, T., Baer, A., & Baer, D. (1973). Time out as a punishing stimulus in continuous and intermittent schedules. *Journal of Applied Behavior Analysis, 6,* 443–455. Reprinted by permission of the author. **141:** From Guttman, N., & Kalish, H. I. (1956). Discriminability and stimulus generalization. *Journal of Experimental Psychology, 51,* 79–88. Reprinted by permission of the author's heir. **145:** Reprinted with Special Permission of King Features Syndicate. **157:** From W. D. Pierce and W. F. Epling, *Behavior analysis and learning,* 1995, p. 65. Copyright © 1995 Prentice-Hall, Inc. Reprinted by permission of the author. **178:** From O'Neill, G. W., & Gardner, R. (1983). *Behavioral principles in medical rehabilitation: A practical guide,* p. 49. Springfield, IL: Charles C. Thomas. Reprinted by permission of the author. **180:** From Fleece, L., Gross, A., O'Brien, T., Kistner, J., Rothblum, E., & Drabman, R. (1981). Elevation of voice volume in young developmentally delayed children via an operant shaping procedure. *Journmal of Applied Behavior Analysis, 14,* 351–355. Reprinted by permission of the author. **181:** From Horner, R. D. (1971). Establishing use of crutches by a mentally retarded spina bifida child. *Journal of Applied Behavior Analysis, 4,* 183–189. Copyright © 1971 Journal of Applied Behavior Analysis. Reprinted by permission of the author. **205:** From Matson, J. L., Sevin, J. A., Fridley, D., & Love, S. R. (1990). Increasing spontaneous language in three autistic children. *Journal of Applied Behavior Analysis, 23,* 227–233. Copyright © 1990 University of Kansas Press. Reprinted by permission of the publisher. **219:** From Bellamy, G. T., Horner, R. H., & Inman, D. P. (1979). *Vocational habilitation of severely retarded adults.* Austin, TX: Pro-Ed Journals. Reprinted by permission of the author. **227:** From Horner, R. H., & Keilitz, I. (1978). Training mentally retarded adolescents to brush their teeth. *Journal of Applied Behavior Analysis, 8,* 301–309. Reprinted by permission of the author. **239:** From Poche, C., Brouwer, R., & Swearengin, M. (1981). Teaching self-protection to young children. Journal of Applied Behavior Analysis, 14, 169–176. Reprinted by permission. **247:** From Jones, R. T., Kazdin, A. E., & Haney, J. L. (1981). Social validation and training of emergency fire safety skills for potential injury prevention and life saving. *Journal of Applied Behavior Analysis, 14,* 249–260. Copyright © 1981 University of Kansas Press. Reprinted by permission of the publisher. **267:** From Touchette, P. E., MacDonald, R. F., & Langer, S. N. (1985). A scatter plot for identifying stimulus control of problem behavior. *Journal of Applied Behavior Analysis, 18,* 343–351. Copyright © 1985 University of Kansas Press. Reprinted by permission of the publisher. **271:** From "Toward a Functional Analysis of Self-injury," by B. A. Iwata, M. F. Dorsey, K. J. Slifer, K. E. Bauman, G. S. Richman, 1994, *Journal of Applied Behavior Analysis,* 27, p. 205. Copyright 1994 by Society for the Experimental Analysis of Behavior. Reprinted by permission. **273:** From Arndorfer, R. E., Miltenberger, R. G., Woster, S. H., Rortvedt, A. K., & Gaffaney, T. (1994). Home-based descriptive and experimental analysis of problem behaviors in children. *Topics in Early Childhood Special Education, 14,* 64–87. Reprinted by permission of the author. **274:** From Durand, V. M.,

& Carr, E. G. (1987). Social influence of "self-stimulatory" behavior: Analysis and treatment application. *Journal of Applied Behavior Analysis, 20*, 119–132. Copyright © 1987 University of Kansas Press. Reprinted by permission of the publisher. **298:** From Kazdin, A. E., and Polster, R. (1973). Intermittent token reinforcement and response maintenance in extinction. *Behavior Therapy*, Vol. 4, 386–391. Copyright © 1973 Academic Press. Reprinted by permission of the publisher. All rights reserved. **326:** From Bostow, D. E., & Bailey, J. (1969). Modification of severe disruptive and aggressive behavior using brief timeout and reinforcement procedures. *Journal of Applied Behavior Analysis, 2*, 31–3. Copyright © 1969 University of Kansas Press. Reprinted by permission of the author. **332:** From Singh, N. N., Dawson, M. J., & Manning, P. (1981). Effects of spaced responding DRL on the stereotyped behavior of profoundly retarded persons. *Journal of Applied Behavior Analysis, 14*, 521–526. Copyright © 1981 University of Kansas Press. Reprinted by permission of the author and the publisher. **352:** From Melin, L., & Gotestam, K. G. (1981). The effects of rearranging ward routines on communication and eating behaviors of psychogeriatric patients. *Journal of Applied Behavior Analysis, 14*, 47–51. Copyright © 1981 University of Kansas Press. Reprinted by permission of the author. **353:** From Rogers, R. W., Rogers, J. S., Bailey, J. S., Runkle, W., & Moore, B. (1988) Promoting safety belt use among state employees: The effects of a prompting and stimulus control intervention. *Journal of Applied Behavior Analysis, 21*, 263–269. Copyright © 1988 University of Kansas Press. Reprinted by permission of the author. **355:** From Brothers, K. J., Krantz, P. J., & McClannahan, L. E. (1994). Office paper recycling: A function of container proximity. *Journal of Applied Behavior Analysis, 27*, 153–160. Copyright © 1994 University of Kansas Press. Reprinted by permission of the author. **357:** From Vollmer, T. R., Iwata, B. A., Zarcone, J. R., Smith, R. G., & Mazaleski, J. L. (1993). The role of attention in the treatment of attention-maintained self-injurious behavior: Noncontingent reinforcement and differential reinforcement of other behavior. *Journal of Applied Behavior Analysis, 26*, 9–22. Copyright © 1993 University of Kansas Press. Reprinted by permission of the author. **377:** From Mathews, J. R., Friman, P. C., Barone, V. J., Ross, L. V., & Christopherson, E. R. (1987). Decreasing dangerous infant behavior through parent instruction. *Journal of Applied Behavior Analysis, 20*, 165–169. Copyright © 1987 University of Kansas Press. Reprinted by permission of the author. **395:** From Foxx, R. M., & Azrin, N. H. (1973). The elimination of autistic self-stimulatory behavior by overcorrection. *Journal of Applied Behavior Analysis, 6*, 1–14. Copyright © 1973 University of Kansas Press. Reprinted by permission of the author. **418:** From Davis, C. A., Brady, M. P., Williams, R. E., & Hamilton, R. (1992). Effects of high probability requests on the acquisition and generalization of responses to requests in young children with behavior disorders. *Journal of Applied Behavior Analysis, 25*, 905–916. Copyright © 1992 University of Kansas Press. Reprinted by permission of the author. **421:** From Ayllon, T., Kuhlman, C., & Warzak, W. (1982). Programming resource room generalization using lucky charms. *Child Behavior Therapy, 4*, 61–67. Reprinted by permission of the author. **461:** From Wagaman, J., Miltenberger, R., & Arndorfer, R. (1993). Analysis of a simplified treatment for stuttering in children. *Journal of Applied Behavior Analysis, 26*, 53–61. Copyright © 1993 University of Kansas Press. Reprinted by permission of the author. **481:** From Milan, M. A., & McKee, J. M. (1976). The cellblock token economy: Token reinforcement procedures in a maximum security correctional institution for adult male felons. *Journal of Applied Behavior Analysis, 9*, 253–275. Copyright © 1976 University of Kansas Press. Reprinted by permission of the author. **482:** From McLaughlin, T. F., & Malaby, J. (1972). Intrinsic reinforcers in a classroom token economy. *Journal of Applied Behavior Analysis, 5*, 263–270. Copyright © 1972 University of Kansas Press. Reprinted by permission of the author. **483:** From McLaughlin, T. F., & Malaby, J. (1972). Intrinsic reinforcers in a classroom token economy. *Journal of Applied Behavior Analysis, 5*, 263–270. Copyright © 1972 University of Kansas Press. Reprinted by permission of the author. **484:** From Hobbs, T. R., & Holt, M. M. (1976). The effects of token reinforcement on the behavior of delinquents in cottage settings. *Journal of Applied Behavior Analysis, 9*, 189–198. Copyright © 1976 University of Kansas Press. Reprinted by permission of the author. **485:** From Nelson, G. L., & Cone, J. D. (1979). Multiple baseline analysis of a token economy for psychiatric inpatients. *Journal of Applied Behavior Analysis, 12*, 255–271. Copyright © 1979 University of Kansas Press. Reprinted by permission of the author. **503:** From Miller, D. L., & Kelley, M. L. (1994). The use of goal setting and contingency contracting for improving children's homework. *Journal of Applied Behavior Analysis, 27*, 73–84. Copyright © 1994 University of Kansas Press. Reprinted by permission of the author. **504:** From Miller, D. L., & Kelley, M. L. (1994). The use of goal setting and contingency contracting for improving children's homework. *Journal of Applied Behavior Analysis, 27*, 73–84. Copyright © 1994 University of Kansas Press. Reprinted by permission of the author. **519:** From Masters, J., Burish, T., Hollon, S., & Rimm, D. (Eds.). (1987). *Behavior therapy: Techniques and empirical findings*, 3rd. edition, Copyright © 1987 Harcourt Brace Jovanovich. Reprinted by permission of Academic Press. **522:** From Poppen, R. (1988). *Behavioral relaxation training and assessment*, pp.30–34. Copyright © 1988 Pergamon Press. Reprinted by permission of the author. **525:** From Morris, R. J. (1991). Fear reduction methods. In F. H. Kanfer and A. P. Goldstein (Eds.), *Helping people change: A textbook of methods*, 4th Edition, pp. 161–201. Reprinted with permission of Elsevier. **528:** From Erfanian, N., & Miltenberger, R. (1990). Contact desensitization in the treatment of dog phobias in persons who have mental retardation. *Behavioral Residential Treatment, 5*, 55–60. Reprinted by permission of the author.

NAME INDEX

SUBJECT INDEX